To possess The Eonian Books
is to be like Noah having kno...   ...d

Dear Reader,

Welcome to *The Eonian Books: Matthew to Revelation*, the 2016 PROTOTYPE edition.

This book is a PROTOTYPE of the 2017 edition which is titled *The Eonian Life Bible New Testament*, and has a different cover and some stylistic changes.

In the new 2017 edition, the word "Satan" has been changed to "adversary" or "enemy". "Devil" has generally been changed more accurately to "slanderer". At 1 Corinthians 10\20-21 "demons" has been changed to "idols". Throughout Revelation 2 and 3 "angels" has been changed to "messengers". The appendix on pages 285-293 has, for the sake of space, been omitted. Also the type has been set slightly larger.

Also in the new 2017 edition, the words "identify", "identification", and "making identifications" have been changed to, respectively, "baptise", "baptism", and "baptising". Although those words in this 2016 PROTOTYPE edition perhaps better represent the meanings of the Greek words behind them, the "baptism" related words are readily recognised and better advertise the different forms of baptism: in water, in undergoing suffering, in spirit, into Moses, into Jesus.

Also in the new 2017 edition, the words "holy" and "holiness" have generally been changed to "separate" and "separateness", which much better represent the meanings of the Greek words behind them.

In this PROTOTYPE edition you will find a few typographical corrections, made by means of glued inserts. You will find these on pages 37, 108, 247, 248, 250, 266, 300. Typographical errors on pages 222 and 249 have been corrected in ink.

I give you my word that I have been labouring for twenty years with the aim of producing for you the most accurate Bible translation in the English language, daily pressing on and on to retrieve the true teachings of the Lord Jesus and his apostles.

For the new 2017 edition – and for the Old Testament translation – see www.eonianlifebible.com.

With the peace and joy of the Lord Jesus,
Christopher Sparkes, Pulborough, November 2017

Published by Filament Publishing Ltd
16, Croydon Road, Waddon,
Croydon, Surrey CR0 4PA
info@filamentpublishing.com
Telephone: +44 (0) 208 688 2598
www.filamentpublishing.com

The Eonian Books: Matthew to Revelation

ISBN 978-1-910819-16-6

The right of Christopher Sparkes to be identified as the author of this work has been asserted by him in accordance with the Designs and Copyright Act of 1988.

© Christopher Sparkes 2016

Printed by Ingram Spark

Typeset in Garamond

eonian books: a gate to eonian life

Detail from *The Holy Yowl, Western Meadowlark* 2013
an oil painting by the translator

BY THE SAME AUTHOR

Poetry
Kissing Through Glass (Mighty Conqueror Productions, 1986)
One Word of Truth (Sons of Camus, 2011)
Counter Intelligence (www.secretpoetry.co.uk, 2015)
Academic
So You Want to Be a Writer? (with Ray Sparkes, Packard Publishing, 2004)
Grammar Without Groans (with Ray Sparkes, Packard Publishing, 2004)

Contents

---

1. *the world*: John's Gospel is universal. See, for example, John 2\6, 2\13, 3\25, 4\5-42, 5\1, 6\4.

[God] at *the* end of these days spoke to us by means of *His* Son whom He appointed heir of all things, through whom also He designed the Eons. ~ Hebrews 1\2

By faith we understand the Eons to have been framed by an oracle of God, for the things being seen not to have come about out of things being visible. ~ Hebrews 11\3

And what more could I say? For time would fail in narrating about Gideon, Barak and Samson and Jephthah, and David and Samuel and the prophets, [33] who through faith overcame kingdoms, practised righteousness, obtained promises, stopped mouths of lions, [34] snuffed out *the* power of fire, escaped edges of a sword, out of weakness acquired strength, grew mighty in war, made the armies of foreigners fall back. [35] Women received back their dead out of resurrection, and others were tortured, not having accepted deliverance so that they might attain to a better resurrection. [36] And others received a trial of mockings and floggings, yes, in addition, of shackles and jail. [37] They were stoned; they were sawn up; they were put to the test; they died by murder of a sword; they wandered about in sheepskins, in goatskins, being destitute, oppressed, ill-treated [38] – of whom the world was not worthy, wandering around in deserts, and in mountains, and in caves, and in holes in the ground. [39] And all these, being well proven through faith, did not receive the promise, [40] God having foreseen something better involving us, so that they should not be complete without us. ~ Hebrews 11\32-40

οὕτως	γὰρ	ἠγάπησεν	ὁ θεὸς	τὸν κόσμον	ὥστε	τὸν	υἱὸν	αὐτοῦ
so much	for	loved	God	the world	that	the	son	of Him

τὸν μονογενῆ	ἔδωκεν	ἵνα	πᾶς	ὁ	πιστεύων	εἰς	αὐτὸν
the only	He gave	in order that	everyone	the	believing	in	him

μὴ	ἀπόληται	ἀλλ᾽	ἔχῃ	ζωὴν	αἰώνιον
not	might suffer destruction	but	might have	life	Eonian ~ John 3\16

καὶ	πᾶς	ὁ	ζῶν	καὶ	πιστεύων	εἰς	ἐμέ	οὐ μὴ
and	everyone	the	living	and	believing	in	me	most certainly not

ἀποθάνῃ	εἰς	τὸν	αἰῶνα	πιστεύεις	τοῦτο
will die	throughout	the	Eon	do you believe	this ~ John 11\26

Preface: English translations

Nothing that we can ever experience in this flesh is so brilliantly and magnificently transforming as bringing ourselves, as it were, face-to-face with the pure word of God that was delivered by angels. When Moses came down from the mountain with the two tablets in his hand his face so shone that the Israelites were afraid to go near him. Yet now with the spirit of Jesus, all believers in Jesus, with faces uncovered, have a radiance far surpassing that of Moses: 'For if that being done away with was with radiance, then how much more *will* that remaining *be* in radiance?' (2 Corinthians 3\11). The Sons and Daughters of God are 'reflecting the radiance of *the* Lord', and 'are being transformed into the same image, from radiance to radiance'. God has shone in their hearts, 'for *the* brightness of the knowledge of the radiance of God in *the* face of Jesus Christ' (2 Corinthians 3\18, 4\6). And 'even if our outward man is being brought to decay, still day by day the inward *man* is being renewed' (2 Corinthians 4\16). With the book in your hand, you have now the word of God translated into English for the first time in every pearl of purity and truth.

The translation of the Books of God into English – now the most powerful language in the world – has been long and slow. Its pages are engraved in blood and fire and gold. The Anglo-Saxons were the first to take it upon themselves to make translations of the God-authorized writings into the Anglo tongue. Around 1380 John Wycliffe, declaring the word of God to be above the so-called 'sacraments' of the religious system, completed the first full translation of the Bible, but was able to work only from the faulty Latin *Vulgate*, making a translation of a translation: 'helle' (Hell) from Latin 'inferno', instead of 'grave' from Greek ᾅδης (= *hades*) (Acts 2\27); 'weren maad' (were made) from Latin 'facta sunt', instead of 'arose' from Greek ἐγένετο (= *egeneto*) (John 1\3); 'euerlastynge' (everlasting) from Latin 'aeternam', instead of 'Eonian' from Greek αἰώνιος (= *aionios*) (John 3\16); 'that is fro the bigynnyng' from Latin 'qui ab initio est', instead of 'from the beginning' from Greek ἀπ' ἀρχῆς (1 John 2\13, 2\14); and so on. Wycliffe died on 31 December 1384. In 1401 a law was passed ordering that heretics should be burned at the stake, and Archbishop Arundel declared it illegal to read the English Bible. In 1428 Wycliffe's corpse was dug up by the church and burned, under the reign of Henry VI.

All that had been available to those translators was the undependable *Vulgate* (of c. 390 AD). However, in the year 1522, the Dutch humanist scholar, Desiderius Erasmus, compiled a Greek New Testament. This enabled the divine genius William Tyndale[1] (? – 1536) to translate, for the first time ever, the New Testament into English directly from the original, underlying Greek. Tyndale also made translations into English of some of the Hebrew of the Old Testament. He found that Greek is better suited to English translation than it is to the less flexible Latin, and that the Hebrew finds agreement with English 'a thousand times more'. However, before Tyndale could complete his work, he was strangled and burned in Vilvorde by the religious sheriffs of this world, under the reign of Henry VIII. (Of the perpetual violence and vicious persecution of the righteous, Tyndale had asked, simply, 'Why?') But another fire was raging, an unquenchable one, in William Tyndale's heart: that he might make available the Books of God to everybody, and in a language and style which was clear and comprehensible. His every intention was pure and noble. The work was imperfect, but he had to work alone; with little for reference; against the law; in a rush; hunted by the religious authorities; then he was cut short. His style has an extraordinary clarity that rings even now, and, as David Daniell demonstrates, is unequalled in English translations.

An enemy of Tyndale's, George Joye, altered some of Tyndale's translation, deliberately omitting at John 5, for example, the word 'resurrection' because Joye preferred the ancient myth of eternal and undying man that Tyndale knew to be a cruel hoax.

These were the days when you were still burned alive for having English translations. In 1519 in Coventry six Christian men and a Christian widow were burned alive for having the ten

---

1. For a deep appreciation of Tyndale's work see David Daniell's superb introductions to his modern-spelling editions.

commandments and the Lord's Prayer in English and teaching them to their children. The fire was a slow death. The children were threatened with death for repeating what they'd learned. In 1530 it was made illegal to own or buy any copy of the Bible. The official 'Bible' was the Latin *Vulgate*. For the Establishment held that the Latin translation was the only true Bible.

However, soon after the assassination of Tyndale, his Bibles were being distributed throughout England. Tyndale's translation became the inspiration and base for further translations, as the fire for translating spread across the land (despite Cuthbert Tunstall, Bishop of London, burning all he could of Tyndale's books, once in a large bonfire outside St Paul's). In 1535 Miles Coverdale (in frequent exile; possibly ally to Tyndale in Antwerp) issued the first complete *printed* Bible. In 1537 and 1549 John Rogers published a complete English Bible – and he was burned in 1555, under the reign of Queen Mary. Rogers went to his death 'as if he had been led to a wedding' and died 'washing his hands in the flame as he was in burning' (John Foxe).

In order to halt the public's access to the Books of God, Rome reacted and issued a statement in its Council of Trent (1545-1563) concerning the Latin *Vulgate* that 'no one is to dare or presume to reject it under any pretext whatever'. But, feeling the force and pressure of change, in 1582 Rome issued its own English translation of the New Testament, the *Douai-Rheims New Testament*, and in 1609 its own translation of the Old Testament. This *Douai-Rheims* was – purposely – almost unreadable in places. For example, its Ephesians 3\6-12 read: 'The Gentils to be coheires and concorporat and comparticipant of his promis in Christ Jesus by the Gospel.' And: 'Let the charity of the fraternity abide in you' (Hebrews 13\1). As if to say, you see, we told you the Bible is not for ploughboys.

In 1611 the famous *King James Version* (KJV) was published, taking 80 per cent, it is said, from Tyndale, but the *Vulgate* a major influence and the *Douai-Rheims* and its notes also being a minor influence. The KJV's fifty or more men ensured a restoration of wholly inappropriate Latinity where they could drive it in: its style was painted with textures of Latinity and complexity in order to keep the Bible at a safe distance from the public and locked in the hands of the clergy. For example: 'fidelity' for Tyndale's 'faithfulness' (Titus 2\10); 'he made for the altar a brasen gate of network under the compass thereof beneath unto the midst of it' (Exodus 34\8); and 'Sufficient unto the day is the evil thereof' (Matthew 6\34). Accordingly, its title page reads 'APPOINTED TO BE READ IN CHURCHES'; in other words, not at home; not for the hands of 'the boy that driveth the plough' after all.

Tyndale, by contrast, had wanted the purest sense and clarity so that everybody could understand. He famously said to a bickering scholar, 'If God spare my life, ere many years I will cause a boy that driveth the plough shall know more of the Scripture than thou dost.' And he wrote of it that it is 'to open our eyes' to God and should be 'plainly laid before their eyes in their mother tongue, that they might see the ... meaning of the text', away from 'juggling with the text'. And: 'For ... whoever read it or hear it reasoned ... it will begin immediately to make him every day better and better.' And of himself: 'my part be not in Christ, if mine heart be not to follow and live ... as I teach.'

Since the KJV there has been a contest of English versions (around 150) and manuscripts (the multiple Byzantine type Greek texts against a few mutilated Alexandrian), each new version promoting itself with some new gimmick, all of them stale with regurgitated cliché. Of course language constantly changes, but this in no way excuses the multitudinous blunders, inherited and new. And truly, I say to you this day, as belief has given way to considerations of profit and increasing levels of paraphrase and colloquialism (over-reactions to ancient Latinity?), the versions have become worse. (Who, since Tyndale, *are* the translators? What did they believe?)

Once the Latin language and then a Latinate style kept the distance between bishop and ploughboy. Now though, scores of versions are available to anybody, a different sort of confusion. Yet the scandal is, not one of all these versions reflects the whole truth of the prophets and apostles and the true Eonian gospel promise of Jesus Christ which is so urgent for this desperate generation. After all these centuries, after all these versions, there has not been a pure and true translation. None of them would translate back into the same Hebrew and Greek of the prophets and apostles.

This means that for any reader or teacher of the Bible the information they are receiving might be unreliable – and unsafe doctrines surge on and on, unchecked. Still shining through are the themes of God's creation of the universe, Jesus' birth and death and resurrection, the forgiveness of violations, the prophecies of Jesus' return to the Earth and of the eventual new Earth. But the untold constant faults in the translations have upheld the long traditions of the natural religion of man so that the whole truth has been concealed.

The root of this scandal is that around the time of the third and fourth and fifth centuries 'a furious storm of wind arose'. Men concocted brews of ancient Babylonian polytheistic religious forms, mixing them up with the writings of the prophets and apostles. They produced creeds and arguments and allegories and twisted translations (*Septuagint* and *Vulgate*). Ever since, there have followed further writings, creeds, confessions, statements, articles, upholding one way or another echoes of the ancient religious mystical forms. All the versions have been overshadowed and haunted by those dark forces of traditions of Babylonian myths, handed down via creeds and the *Vulgate*. These have ensured that the truth has remained safely wrapped up in mythical polytheistic Babylonian idolatry, priestcraft, ritual performance, echoes of designating men to impossible regions of gods and devils, gods in men's bellies, and every form of tradition. They have, in a borrowed phrase from Tyndale at 2 Samuel 7\14, quenched the sparkle of the prophets and apostles.

Every translation I have looked at, whatever the language, rages with the same perpetuated errors, with translators apparently under the same intoxicating influences. In all these haunted versions the chief means of upholding ancient tradition has been by mistranslations of words and phrases and cunning falsifications of grammar. But the Star of Bethlehem did not trail across the sky to old Babylon, but to a new birth. Babylon, back then, to God's people, signified wickedness and captivity. Yet even today the world is still charmed with its mythology and is in captivity to its deceitful heritage.

The Eonian Books has disregarded all tradition's error and corrected everything. Some of these are discussed over the next few pages; some in the appendices; some are highlighted in the subject headings of *The Eonian Books* translation; many others are explained in detail in the companion volume *The Earth-Shaking Truth*; and more still in my other forthcoming books. The most abundant mistranslations have been over the Hebrew word עוֹלָם (= *olam*), 'Eon' (438 occurrences) – 181 occurrences of which are the phrase לְעוֹלָם (= *le olam*), 'throughout the Eon'; the Greek words αἰών (= *aion*), 'Eon' (126 occurrences); and αἰώνιος (= *aionios*), 'Eonian' (enduring for, relating to, an Eon) (71 occurrences); and the Greek phrase εἰς τὸν αἰῶνα (= *eis ton aiona*), 'throughout the Eon' (27 times). That, allowing for some idiomatic uses, accounts for well over 600 errors with just these parts alone.[2]

It's not difficult: αἰών (= *aion*) means 'Eon' and it is where our word 'Eon' comes from. And αἰώνιος (= *aionios*) means 'Eonian'. There's no difficulty with these. An 'Eon' is a long age, and 'Eonian' means enduring for or relating to an Eon. And עוֹלָם (= *olam*) means 'Eon', the same as αἰών (= *aion*). These words 'Eon' and 'Eonian' ought to be on every believer's lips, because it concerns his or her gospel promise from Jesus: life throughout the coming Eon. The translators, though, rejecting the prophets' visions of the Eons, often, perversely, want the word αἰών as 'world'. (The Greek for 'world' is κόσμος (= *kosmos*), not αἰών.) Then, entirely inconsistently, they have its adjective form, αἰώνιος, as 'eternal', as in their (errant) phrase 'eternal life'. Very well then, if they want αἰών as 'world', to be consistent they ought to have its adjective form, αἰώνιος (= *aionios*), as 'worldly', and they should be proclaiming a message of 'worldly life'.

The constant mistranslation of those Hebrew and Greek words and phrases has meant the concealing of the coming Messianic Eon, and therefore also of the true gospel promise of 'Eonian life', which is life throughout the Messianic Eon. Gesenius suggests that the Hebrew word עוֹלָם (= *olam*) is properly 'what is hidden; specially *hidden time*' (p. 612). How appropriate and what irony that the Eons and the gospel promise of 'Eonian life' have been so concealed by mistranslations

---

2. Every occurrence of these words and phrases (and others too) is tabulated in my forthcoming book *The Eon*.

of that very Hebrew word. The mistranslations of the abstract noun αἰών (= *aion*), 'Eon', by the KJV and others as a concrete noun 'world', as an adjective 'eternal', and as an adverb 'ever', have held the world back. The full gospel promise has been withheld; the pronouncement of the coming Eon has been delayed.

In contrast, the correct translation of these two frequently occurring words, עוֹלָם (= *olam*) and αἰών (= *aion*), uncovers the earth-shaking discovery of the prophets' and apostles' visions of the Eons past, of the Eons coming, of the imminent Messianic Eon – and of the gospel promise of 'Eonian life', which means having an indestructible and incorruptible body and mind in the coming Eons. For whoever believes in Jesus 'will most certainly not die throughout the Eon' (John 11\26). For, after the resurrection, 'they do not have the capacity to die any more, for they are equal to the angels' (Luke 20\35-36). Jesus promised this: 'in the Eon which is coming, Eonian life' (Mark 10\30, Luke 18\30).

For there is 'one God, the Father ... and one Lord, Jesus Christ' (1 Corinthians 8\6); 'one Lord' and 'one God and Father' (Ephesians 4\5-6). And Jesus was 'raised from *the* dead by the magnificent power of the Father' (Romans 6\4). This resurrection of Jesus was through the agency of the Angel of God who is the Holy Spirit: 'a mighty earthquake broke out, for *the* Angel of *the* Lord, descended from Heaven, came *and* rolled back the stone, away from the door, and he was sitting on it. His appearance was like lightning, and his garment as white as snow' (Matthew 28\2-3); and 'Having been put to death in flesh, [Jesus] was, though, made alive by *the* Spirit' (1 Peter 3\18). And the prophets and apostles have declared that a Messianic Eon is coming on the Earth, 'the Sovereign Rulership of God' (Daniel 9\24-7, Matthew 3\2): first an Eon of 490 years; then Jesus comes to the Earth; then another Eon of 1,000 years. And in Jerusalem the prophets and apostles will be raised from the dust of the ground (Luke 13\33-34, Matthew 23\37). And there will be a resurrection of the righteous from the dust of the ground (Genesis 3\19, Ezekiel 37, 1 Corinthians 15). And those in the graves will hear the voice of Jesus and, like Lazarus, they will come out (John 5\25), in an indestructible body, for we 'trust in God Who raises the dead' (2 Corinthians 1\9). And all these righteous people will live throughout the coming Eons, until the destruction of this Earth and the appearance of the new Earth, then they will live in the Holy City with God and Jesus (Revelation 21 & 22, Ephesians 2\6, 2\21-22, 2 Corinthians 6\16). For, Jesus said, 'where I am, there will my servant also be' (John 12\26). And 'The heavens, *yes* the heavens, *belong* to Yahweh, but the Earth He has given to the sons of Adam' (Psalm 115\16); and 'Exalted *are* the submissive, for they will inherit the land [or Earth]' (Matthew 5\5). Until his return at the end of the 490 year Eon, Jesus must remain in Heaven (Acts 3\21).

The Eonian Books translation is grammatically pure and internally harmonious. It presents how the writers of Matthew to Revelation – Matthew, Mark, Luke, John, Paul, Jacob (James), Peter and Jude – would like their writings to be translated and understood, that is, fully free from 'juggling with the text'.

So frozen and degenerate has become the heart of the world in 'this Eon of darkness' and 'evil' (Galatians 1\4, Ephesians 6\12) that nothing could be more welcome than the restoration of the pure and bold proclamations of the prophets and apostles.

The holy Scrolls of God are 'given by inspiration of God ... in order that the man of God can be complete' (2 Timothy 3\16-17). *The Eonian Books* translation is the first English translation to be free of every stranglehold of ancient religious tradition, and the first to bring out the full light of Jesus and the prophets and apostles. The golden keys to at last unlock the whole truth are grammar and internal harmony. Grammatical purity means, where possible, word for word, phrase by phrase translation from the Greek, and each word true to its form and meaning, not bent to fit orthodoxy or translators' hasty or vain ideas. The honest method of grammatical purity ensures, indeed, guarantees, that the Greek is reproduced accurately, and the whole truth is unlocked. This has never been done before. This is the hour for correction. This is a declaration of the original truth and light of the prophets and apostles. This is a declaration of the approaching new Eon and the gospel of Eonian life. The old voices of the prophets and apostles of God are back.

cjs, December 2015

✱

Conventions

Italics and asterisks in the text of the translation

Italicized words or phrases in the translation are words or phrases which have been supplied in the translation to make good English from the original Greek. For the sake of appearances, the words 'There' and 'My' at the starts of Romans 8\1 and 1 John 4\1, although supplied, are not italicized. I have kept such supplied words to the barest reasonable minimum. Subject headings are also italicized.

* A small superscripted asterisk in the text indicates a comment in the Companion Notes, of which there are at present over 12,000. They describe translations and themes from Genesis to Revelation. They will in time be published (then the small asterisks will be enlarged).

Greek textual basis

The Eonian Books Translation: Matthew to Revelation is based (with written permission) on the Greek of the Robinson-Pierpont Byzantine Textform 2005, compiled by Maurice A Robinson and William G Pierpont. My renderings should be checked against the Robinson-Pierpont Greek text, not the Textus Receptus. My use of the Robinson-Pierpont text (RP) means slight variations to the Textus Receptus (TR) text which underlies the New Testament of the 1611 *King James Version* (KJV). The differences, although quite numerous, are minor and affect no themes or narratives, but do enhance some passages.

The Robinson-Pierpont Textform is a major and welcome advancement in textual authority. It has the most impressive early support and agreement from other early versions and other writers over a large geographical area and over a long period of time.

Robinson and Pierpont say of the Textus Receptus: 'Certainly the *Textus Receptus* had its problems, not the least of which was its failure to reflect the Byzantine Textform in an accurate manner' (Robinson and Pierpont, p. 533); and: 'The overall text of those early printed editions [of TR] differs from the Byzantine Textform in over 1800 instances, generally due to the inclusion of weakly supported non-Byzantine readings' (ibid, p. i).

The variations sometimes mean (in translation) no more than 'a' or 'the'; sometimes 'Christ Jesus' instead of 'Jesus Christ' (eg 1 Timothy 1\2, making it consistent with Paul's style at 2 Timothy 1\2; Hebrews 3\1); sometimes different words; sometimes the absences of words which the TR has; sometimes the inclusion of words which the TR does not have. Some differences (in translation) are:–

The sentence 'So they went their way' closes Matthew 20\4 in the TR text, but opens Matthew 20\5 in the RP text. The RP's Matthew 23\13 and 14 are the TR's Matthew 23\14 and 13. At Matthew 26\26 the TR text has 'having exalted', but the RP text has 'having given thanks', in agreement with the next verse, 26\27. Mark 12\32 does not have θεός (= *theos*), which the TR text does have. Mark 15\34 in the RP text is 'Eloi, Eloi, lima sabachthani', whereas in the TR text it's 'Eloi, Eloi, lamma sabachthani'. Where at Luke 1\35 the RP has 'that Holy One who will be born', the TR has 'that Holy One who will be born out of you' (adding ἐκ σοῦ, 'out of you'). Where at Luke 20\19 the RP has 'afraid', the TR has 'afraid of the people' (adding τὸν λαόν, 'the people'). Where at Acts 13\23 the RP text has 'brought salvation', the TR text has 'raised a Saviour'. Also at Acts 13\23 the RP text does not have the word 'Jesus' at the end which the TR does have. At Acts 21\11 the RP text has 'feet and hands' instead of the TR's 'hands and feet'. The RP's Romans 14\24-26 is found in the TR at Romans 16\25-27. The RP's 2 Corinthians 1\6-7 is slightly different to the TR's, both in text arrangement and verse division (the clause 'and our gladly-held expectation for you *is* certain' is in verse 6 in the RP text, but it opens verse 7 in the TR text). So also is the RP's 2 Corinthians 12\21 slightly different, the RP text giving the assurance of 'will not humble' (ταπεινώσει, future indicative), but the TR having the more tentative 'may not humble' (ταπεινώσῃ, subjunctive). At Ephesians 5\21 the RP text has 'in reverence of Christ', whereas the TR text has 'in reverence of God'. At the end of Hebrews 2\7 the TR text has the clause 'and You set him over the works of Your hands', but the RP text does not have this. At Jude 24 the TR text has 'Now to Him Who is able to care for you', whereas the

RP text has 'Now to Him being able to care for them'. At Revelation 9\16 the RP text has 'a hundred million [or, myriad of myriads]' instead of the TR's 'two hundred million [or, two myriads of myriads]'. At Revelation 21\16 the RP text has '12,012' instead of the TR's '12,000'. Revelation 21\24 has minor differences, the RP text not including (surely rightly) the TR text's addition 'of those saved', and the RP text adds 'for him', and there are other minute differences in the verse. The most numerous differences between the two texts are in Revelation.

The larger variations are some omissions. The RP text does not have (in translation):– 'and fire' at Matthew 3\11; the TR's Luke 17\36; the TR's Acts 8\37; the TR's sentence at the end of Acts 9\5, 'it is hard for you to kick against the goads'; the TR's first two parts of Acts 9\6; the TR's Acts 15\34; the TR's latter part of Acts 24\6; the TR's Acts 24\7; the TR's first part of Acts 24\8. The RP happily omits 'the foul comma' at 1 John 5\7-8, an apostasy which should never have been smuggled in.

Often the RP text has more logic to it than does the TR reading, and often the RP text has a more genuine ring to it than the TR text. For example (in translation): at James 5\11 the TR text has 'of Job, you have seen [εἴδετε, indicative], then, the outcome', whereas the RP text, more logically, has 'of Job. Understand [ἴδετε, imperative], then, the outcome', the imperative being in agreement with the imperatives surrounding it. At Revelation 1\5 the RP text has the joyful 'him loving us', present participle, whereas the TR text has the far less happy 'him having loved us', past. At Revelation 1\6 the TR text has 'made us kings', but the RP text has 'made us a kingdom'. At Revelation 22\19 the TR text has the curious 'God shall take away his part from the book of life', whereas the RP text has the exceedingly more logical 'may God take away his share from the Tree of Life'. No Greek manuscript has 'book of life' there: the TR is at fault in adopting it, as is the KJV in following it.

The fact is, there is no single Greek manuscript of the New Testament which can be claimed to represent exactly the prophets' and apostles' original manuscripts. Who could say which it is? Also, of all the 5,000 known manuscripts there are no two manuscripts which are identical. However, Robinson and Pierpont have been able to show, as they say, that: 'The Byzantine Textform preserves with a great consistency the type of New Testament text that dominated the Greek-speaking world' (p. v); and: 'Byzantine-priority presents as canonical the Greek New Testament text as it has been attested, preserved, and maintained by scribes throughout the centuries' (p. vii); and: 'Manuscripts and readings must be evaluated in regard to their antiquity, diversity, and continuity within transmissional [written from copies] history. Individual scribes must be characterized in regard to their degree of care when copying from their exemplars. A proper implementation of each of these factors results in a well-established representation of the traditionally disseminated Byzantine Textform. This Textform dominated textual transmission in the primary Greek-speaking regions for more than a thousand years, and it is this Textform that holds the strongest transmissional claim to represent the canonical autographs' (p. xv).

The claim that the Byzantine Textform was neither dominant nor in the majority until the ninth century Robinson and Pierpont refute, by saying: 'it simply does not accord with the known facts. Sufficient manuscript and patristic evidence exists from the mid-fourth century onward ... patristic writers beyond the fourth century rarely reflect any text resembling a predominantly *non*-Byzantine document' (pp. 582-83).

After 27 years of their 'intense collaboration (1976-2003)' (p. xxiii), Robinson and Pierpont were able to conclude that their text, in its present edition, 'sets forth a text that – within the framework of its underlying theory – is considered to reflect the canonical autographs in a highly accurate manner' (p. xvi); and: 'the editors here present the newly edited Byzantine Textform as the strongest representative of the canonical autographs of the Greek New Testament text. It has been toward the fulfillment of this most noble and sacred goal that the editors have labored and now present the completion of their task' (p. xxiii).

1 Timothy 3\16

At 1 Timothy 3\16 it is vital to depart from both the TR text and from the RP text on which my translation is based. These texts have the word θεός (= *theos*), 'God', so that the KJV, for example, reads: 'God was manifest in the flesh' (the word 'the' in that clause is a saucy and unattractive addition, there being no article in the Greek). There are also, though, ancient Greek manuscripts which read ὅς ('who', or 'which', or 'he who', or 'he'). *The Eonian Books* translation follows that latter textual reading, and has 'He was brought to light in flesh'.

The manuscript scholar John Burgon, in his *Revision Revised*, 1883, complains of the texts which have ὅς that the neuter noun μυστήριον (= *musteerion*), 'mystery', is followed by a masculine pronoun ὅς (= *hos*) (*Revision Revised*, p. 426). First though, the masculine pronoun does not have to agree with what Burgon saw as its antecedent, μυστήριον. The masculine pronoun acts as the subject of the verb δικαιόω (= *dikaioo*), meaning 'was declared righteous', which follows the pronoun and points to Jesus. As antecedent, it can be either an understood reference to Jesus or a remote reference to him. There is such a remote antecedent in 1 John 3\5: 'you know that he was brought to light in order that he might take away our violations' – that 'he' we know is Jesus; it is just understood.

Second, Paul in Colossians 1\27 has the same construction which Burgon objected to at 1 Timothy 3\16, μυστήριον (neuter) followed by ὅς (masculine). Paul writes: 'this mystery [μυστήριον] among the nations, which [ὅς] is Christ among you'. That is, a neuter noun followed by a masculine pronoun, just as in 1 Timothy 3\16. Notice that 'to make known ... the mystery among the nations ... expectation of magnificence' at Colossians 1\27 is a quiet echo of 1 Timothy 3\16. Notice too that the mystery relates to 'Christ', not God. At Colossians 4\3 also, Paul speaks of 'the mystery of Christ'. So too is the *post-resurrection* Christ the subject of 'the mystery' at 1 Timothy 3\16.

My 1895 edition of Westcott's and Hort's *Revised Version* (NT originally 1881) has in the margin at 1 Timothy 3\16: 'The word *God* [θεός], in place of *He who* [ὅς], rests on no sufficient ancient evidence'. That was a lie, and they must have known it. (Westcott and Hort's rendering of 1 Timothy 3\16 is an ungrammatical horror.) Burgon was able to cite 289 manuscripts having θεός. However, Burgon also described 6 manuscripts having ὅς. It is true that there are far more texts having θεός than there are texts having ὅς, but this is a war of truth, not a simple matter of painting by numbers.

Burgon suggested that ΘC, which is a contracted, uncial form of θεός (contracted as 'a sacred name', *nomina sacra*, as some shy men might write G-d for God), got altered to OC, the contracted form of ὅς (eg, Burgon, pp. 442-43). This would be done, Burgon suggests, by the removal of the line in the theta, Θ, either blurred in time or erased deliberately, creating the appearance of an omicron, O: that would then come to be a reading in favour of ὅς. However, if any changing was done, much more likely is it that a line was later *added* to the O, omicron, of OC, to make it into a theta, Θ, done either accidentally, or pulled off deliberately by post-Nicene scribes who saw their chance. The addition of a line would be easier to pull off than the removal of a line.

There has long been contention over whether or not there is a line in the omicron in Manuscript A. People see what they want to see. Dr. Henry Alford, another great Victorian scholar, and who wrote the lovely song *Come, Ye Thankful People, Come*, speaks of the advantage of microscopic evidence settling the dispute. Writing some two decades before Burgon, Alford had this to say of Manuscript A (his italics): 'ος ... *'is now [a] matter of certainty*. The black line at present visible in the o, is a modern retouching of an older but not original fainter one, due apparently to the darkening of the stroke of an ϵ seen through from the other side. I have examined the page, and find that a portion of the virgula of the ϵ, seen through, and now corroded through, extends nearly through the Θ, not however quite in, but somewhat above, its centre, as Sir Frederick Madden has observed to me. It was to complete this that Junius made a dot ... Besides which, the mark of abbreviation above the line is modern, not corresponding with those in the MSS. Sir Frederick Madden now informs me that a very powerful microscope has been applied by Professor Maskelyne, at his request, to the passage in the MS, and the result has been that *no trace of either virgula in the o, or mark of contraction over it, can be discovered*. It is to be hoped, therefore, that A will never again be cited on the side of [the Received Text]' (Alford, *The Greek Testament*, Vol. III, p. 332).

Alford wrote of the satisfaction of establishing the ὅς reading at 1 Timothy 3\16: 'There is hardly a passage in the N.T., in which I feel more deep personal thankfulness for the restoration of the true and wonderful connexion of the original text' (ibid, p. 333).

Textual and grammatical debates aside, the matter is easily decided on internal criteria. On purely internal evidence, the KJV's 'God ... in ... flesh' cannot be correct. It's all out of joint: there is nothing from Genesis to Revelation to support any notion that God ever appeared in flesh. God, that is, the Father, has not ever appeared in flesh. Jesus said 'God *is* spirit' (John 4\24). God is not flesh; God is spirit.

John says: 'every spirit who professes Jesus Christ to have come in flesh is from God' (1 John 4\2-3, 2 John 7). It was not the Father who 'came in flesh'. It would make no sense for John to say that the Son came in flesh, but then for Paul to have said that God came in flesh. God is 'the God and Father of our Lord Jesus Christ' (Ephesians 1\3). The Son cannot be the Father of the Son. The Son was born in flesh, and even after his resurrection he denied being a spirit, saying, 'a spirit does not have flesh and bones as you see me having' (Luke 24\39), although having a spiritual body not subject to death (1 Corinthians 15\44-46). God is spirit and always was spirit, and never was flesh, and never will be flesh. No sluicegate of polytheistic spin-doctoring could ever overpower this ecstatic truth.

John Burgon, otherwise a great scholar, has much to say about his textual preference for θεός at 1 Timothy 3\16 and about the phrase 'the mystery of godliness' (*Revision Revised*, pp. 497-98). He has little to say, though, about what follows in 1 Timothy 3\16, that it is all so obviously about the resurrected Son, and that it is quite irrelevant to the Father: 'he was declared righteous in spirit; he was seen by angels; he was proclaimed among nations; he was believed in *the* world; he was taken up in magnificence.' Who, then, was 'in flesh' but the Son, 'the Son of the Father' (2 John 3)? Does God need to be 'declared righteous'? Who could declare Him so? Who was 'seen by angels' but the Son? The angels had been seeing God ever since the day He created them. Who was 'proclaimed among nations' but the Son? Who was 'taken up', to be magnified in Heaven by God, but the Son? Just as we 'will live with him by *the* power of God', so is it also written that 'Christ ... lives by *the* power of God' (2 Corinthians 13\4), and 'the fountainhead of Christ *is* God' (1 Corinthians 11\3).

It might be said in accusation that I've made my doctrine ('God is spirit') then I've picked my text (ὅς). However, it would be reasonable to reply, you've picked your text (θεός), then you've made your doctrine. First, though, my doctrine is internal, and is entirely consistent internally, and it fits the context, whereas the other reading fits only an imported, external doctrine. And second, all argument is demolished without any further need of discussion by those simple words spoken by Jesus, 'God *is* spirit'. It is honouring to God and Christ to represent them in truth. Recall how God spoke to Job's friend Eliphaz: 'Yahweh said to Eliphaz the Temanite, "My anger glows hot against you and against your two friends, for you have not spoken of Me *what is* right" ' (Job 42\7).

Now this internal solution to 1 Timothy 3\16 has been brought to light, it is time to be gladly shaking the dust of our feet on the troublesome θεός reading.

And there is yet more. Burgon wanted θεός because, dissatisfied that 'God is one' (Romans 3\30 et cetera), he took it that the KJV reading of 'God was manifest in the flesh' is some mystical statement about a divine incarnation and birth. However, 1 Timothy 3\16 certainly has nothing at all to do with any sort of incarnation and birth. The statement that Jesus 'was brought to light in flesh' signifies his post-resurrection appearances to his disciples. The six astounding statements which describe the 'mystery of godliness' – all indicated by passive verbs – are a summary of the magnificent events concerning Jesus after his resurrection, nothing at all to do with anybody's birth:

He was brought to light in flesh;	~ Mark 16\12, 16\14, John 21\14, 1 John 1\2
he was declared righteous in spirit;	~ John 20\17, 1 Corinthians 15\42-46, Hebrews 9\14
he was seen by angels;	~ Matthew 28\2, John 20\12, Acts 1\10
he was proclaimed among nations;	~ Romans 14\25, Colossians 1\27-28
he was believed in *the* world;	~ Acts 2\41, Romans 1\8
he was taken up in magnificence.	~ Mark 16\19, Luke 24\51, Acts 1\9-11

The Greek for 'he was brought to light' is ἐφανερώθη (= *ephanerothee*). This word ἐφανερώθη has nothing to do with any incarnation of anybody. The word in that exact form occurs in relation to Jesus' post-resurrection appearances:[3] 'After these things, he was brought to light [ἐφανερώθη] in a different form' (Mark 16\12); 'Later, in their sitting together eating, he was brought to light [ἐφανερώθη] to the eleven' (Mark 16\14); 'This *is* the third time now that Jesus was brought to light [ἐφανερώθη] to the disciples' (John 21\14); and, 'for the life also was brought to light [ἐφανερώθη] – and *that which* we have seen and given witness to, and proclaim to you, the Eonian life which was in relation to the Father, and was brought to light [ἐφανερώθη] to us' (1 John 1\2). (In the gospels the KJV wrongly has those as active verbs, such as 'he appeared', so that the positive link to 1 Timothy 3\16 is less likely to be noticed.) The same verb is used in the active form at John 21\1: 'After these things, Jesus again brought himself to light [ἐφανέρωσεν] to the disciples on the Sea of Tiberias'. Luke says Jesus gave directions to the apostles 'to whom with much indubitable evidence he presented himself alive after his suffering, being seen by them throughout forty days, and speaking of the things concerning the Sovereign Rulership of God' (Luke 1\2-3). These are passages we should have in mind in relation to Jesus 'being brought to light' in 1 Timothy 3\16.

These post-resurrection appearances of Jesus are exactly what Paul is referring to at 1 Timothy 3\16 in his saying Jesus 'was brought to light [ἐφανερώθη] in flesh'. The phrase 'in flesh' is set in apposition to the phrase, 'in spirit'. So the resurrection body is flesh, but it is incapable of violation. Jesus was born flesh, resurrected flesh and bones (Luke 24\39, Ezekiel 37\4-13), and received the resurrection 'spiritual body' (1 Corinthians 15\42-46). The 'spiritual *was* not first, but the natural. The spiritual *came* afterwards'.

So centuries of debates about some mystical incarnation were an irrelevance.

Revelation 21\6
There is one other word where I find it needful to depart from the RP text. At Revelation 21\6 it has the word γέγονα (= *gegona*), making God say 'I have become the Alpha and the Omega'. If Jesus had been the speaker, that would be harmonious with his being newly titled by God on his entry into Heaven (Philippians 2\9). But verse 21\7 ('I will be God to him') shows that this is God speaking as God and Father to his sons, not Jesus who is 'Lord' (Matthew 7\21) and 'brother' (Romans 8\29). And consequently, God's being the speaker here makes the RP text's verb form γέγονα disharmonious with the unchangeable nature of God in its suggestion that God became titled. (Who could title *Him*!) The TR and related texts, though, have γέγονε (= *gegone*), 'it has come / come to pass / come into existence / happened' (that is, the culmination of God's redemption plan), and this is all harmonious with the context. Those other texts then agreeably have ἐγώ εἰμι (= *ego eimi*), 'I am', so that God is saying 'I am the Alpha and the Omega'. The RP text, though, omits ἐγώ εἰμι, leaving the title 'Alpha and Omega' vulnerable to the disagreeable verb γέγονα. In further support of my argument for γέγονε, Revelation 16\17 sees an angel saying 'It has come!' and the verb form in both texts is the agreeable γέγονε. Consequently, I am bound to follow the TR text at Revelation 21\6.

The order of the gospels and the letters
My one other departure from the Robinson-Pierpont text is in the order of the apostles' letters. I have retained – with some hesitation – the usual order, rather than the RP text's order. (Eonian Document 4 discusses this further, p. 283.) Although Robinson and Pierpont discovered in their labours that there was a favoured order in the early days (Robinson and Pierpont, p. iii), this was a popular (and sensible) practice, rather than a stipulated internal foundation (as there is a stipulated order with the Hebrew Books). There is no internal passage to lay down the order of the Greek Books of Matthew to Revelation. For this reason, the usual order of the Greek Books cannot be said to count as erroneous, and is therefore acceptable, and I have decided, at least for

---

3. The full list of occurrences of this passive verb form ἐφανερώθη is: Mark 16\12, 16\14, John 21\14, Colossians 1\26, 1 Timothy 3\16, 1 John 1\2 (twice), 3\2, 3\5, 3\8, 4\9.

now, not to disturb it.

John 3\13

There is one other textual contention I want to discuss here, and that is the clause ὁ ὢν ἐν τῷ οὐρανῷ (= *ho hon en to ourano*) appearing at the end of John 3\13. The KJV and many other versions have Jesus referring to himself as 'the Son of Man who is in Heaven' – and that while Jesus was standing in Jerusalem talking to a priest, yet at the same time saying he was in Heaven! Clearly there is a problem. There might be as many versions which include those words as there are versions which do not have them. Some versions fiddle with the Greek and make a false representation of it.

The truth is, either the translation 'who is in Heaven' is wrong, or the Greek text on which that is based is wrong. The Greek phrase ὁ ὢν ἐν τῷ οὐρανῷ (= *ho hon en to ourano*), which the KJV's 'who is in Heaven' pretends to represent, is in the RP and TR texts, but it is not found in all manuscripts. Some refer to it as an ancient gloss, an editor's fancy addition. Despite this, most commentators seem in favour of its retention, and that is for varied reasons. Some comments are comical, suggesting it proves Jesus was not in Jerusalem but in Heaven; others saying that he was in both Jerusalem and Heaven at the same time! For example, Origen: 'Non dixit qui fuit, sed qui est in caelo' (He did not say he was here, but he is in Heaven); and Augustine: 'Ecce, hic erat et in caelo erat' (Behold, he was here, and he was in Heaven).

Unlike 1 Timothy 3\16, this passage cannot be settled internally. It can only be settled externally. The best evidence – all of which he cites in detail – comes from Burgon who lays down the facts and tells us that, along with his other manifold data, the clause is 'more ancient (by 200 years) than the evidence for omitting [it]' (*Revision Revised*, p. 134).

It is neither sensible nor possible to contest here Burgon's mass of evidence of its antiquity. And it is, therefore, not the clause which has to be omitted but the translation which has to be corrected. This is no difficulty: the phrase ὁ ὢν ἐν τῷ οὐρανῷ occurs elsewhere, so there is also internal harmony (unlike with the TR reading of 1 Timothy 3\16). At Luke 15\18 and 15\21 and John 3\27 οὐρανός (= *ouranos*), normally 'Heaven', 'sky', stands metonymically (that is, by association) for God as 'the Exalted One' or 'the Heavenly One'. And so is it with οὐρανός at John 3\13. The sensible translation of the phrase ὁ ὢν ἐν τῷ οὐρανῷ is 'who is in the Exalted One', or 'who is in the Heavenly One'. That aligns harmoniously with John 14\10, 'I *am* in the Father'.

I have compiled much fuller commentary on this passage in the Companion Notes.

Pneuma hagion & 'holy spirit'

The Greek phrase πνεῦμα ἅγιον (= *pneuma hagion*) occurs 92 times. 42 of the 92 occurrences are in the Book of Acts. It could not be more obvious that this phrase πνεῦμα ἅγιον does not always refer to the same thing. In Acts 11 there is an easily discerned distinction between 'the Spirit' who is the Holy Spirit, who is the Angel of God, and the spirit which has filled believers: the Holy Spirit, referred to by Peter as 'the Spirit' and 'the Angel' (in verses 12 and 13) speaks to Peter, and then 'the divine spirit' falls on Peter's audience in verses 15 and 16.

I have categorized πνεῦμα ἅγιον in its 92 occurrences as being used for three different meanings:

1) There are <u>42 occurrences</u> of miracle-operating power, such as the divine spirit and power which empowered the miracle of the creation of Jesus in the virgin Maria, and by means of which the apostles performed signs and wonders. These 42 are: Matthew 1\18, 1\20, 3\11, Mark 1\8, Luke 1\15, 1\35, 1\41, 1\67, 3\16, 4\1, 11\13, John 1\33, 7\39, 20\22 (compare Luke 24\49), Acts 1\5, 2\4, 2\33, 2\38, 4\8, 4\31, 6\3, 6\5, 7\55, 8\15, 8\17, 8\18, 8\19, 9\17, 10\44, 10\45, 10\47, 11\15, 11\16, 11\24, 13\9, 13\52, 15\8, 19\2 (twice), 19\6, 1 Corinthians 12\3, Hebrews 2\4.

2) There are <u>16 occurrences</u> of the divine spirit which is the new and sanctified nature, the spirit and nature of God and Christ, the renewed mind, which is in the regenerated believer today. This is not quite the same thing as the miracle-operating power. These 16 occurrences are in the letters

of the apostle Paul, plus one in Jude: Romans 5\5, 9\1, 14\17, 15\13, 15\16, 1 Corinthians 2\13, 6\19, 2 Corinthians 6\6, Ephesians 1\13, 4\30, 1 Thessalonians 1\5, 1\6, 4\8, 2 Timothy 1\14, Titus 3\5, Jude 20.

3) There are 34 occurrences of the personality of the Holy Spirit, which is one of the many titles of the Angel of God. These 34 are: Matthew 12\32, 28\19, Mark 3\29, 12\36, 13\11, Luke 2\25, 2\26, 3\22, 12\10, 12\12, John 14\26, Acts 1\2, 1\8, 1\16, 5\3, 5\32, 7\51, 9\31, 10\38, 13\2, 13\4, 15\28, 16\6, 20\23, 20\28, 21\11, 28\25, 2 Corinthians 13\14, Hebrews 3\7, 6\4, 9\8, 10\15, 1 Peter 1\12, 2 Peter 1\21. These are easily identified as the personality, as distinct from the spirit which is power or that which is new nature, by such phrases as the Holy Spirit speaking, and signifying, and being seen, and witnessing (Acts 1\16, 8\29, et cetera especially in Acts). I generally refer to him by my own preferred title 'the Angel of God' (Acts 10\3, Galatians 4\14).

The Angel of God is God's most eminent and powerful angel, with over 40 titles from Genesis to Revelation, even being involved with God in creation (Genesis 1\26, Psalm 104\30, Job 26\13), and in the Flood (Genesis 6\3). He patrolled the Earth to guard it from Satan (Genesis 1\2). He was there at the burning bush (Exodus 3\2). He was the cloud and fire guiding the Israelites out of Egypt (Exodus 14\19), and he would protect and bring the Israelites into the promised land (Exodus 33\2). He was involved in counselling King David (Psalm 51\11, 139\7); delivering Israel from 185,000 hostile Assyrians (2 Kings 19\35); giving the proclamations to the prophets (1 Peter 1\11-12, 2 Peter 1\21). He appeared at Jesus' identification in water and he anointed and empowered him (Isaiah 61\1, Matthew 3\16, Mark 1\8, 1\10). He was involved in Jesus' resurrection (Matthew 28\2, 1 Peter 3\18). He took Jesus, after his resurrection, down to Tartarus, the underworld of imprisoned angels (1 Peter 3\19, 2 Peter 2\4, Jude 6 et cetera). He empowered the twelve (Acts 1\8), and there was his presence at the appearance of fire when he came to the twelve (Acts 2\1-4); and he counselled and guided the apostles during the Acts period (Acts 1\2, 5\19 et cetera); he got rid of Herod (Acts 12\23); and he gave prophecy to Paul (1 Timothy 4\1).

In order to make the absolutely vital distinctions between these three meanings of πνεῦμα ἅγιον – and so that nobody is led into the delusion that this angel, the Holy Spirit, lives inside people – I render the first two meanings of πνεῦμα ἅγιον as 'divine spirit' and the third meaning, the Angel of God, as 'the Holy Spirit', capitalized. The 34 listed occurrences of him are only those by his title of 'Holy Spirit'. This Angel of God, the Holy Spirit, is honoured with many titles, and, in order to distinguish him from other angels, and for consistency and clarity, I capitalize all of them, including his description as 'a man' (Acts 10\30), but not at Mark 16\5 as 'a young man'. His full list of titles in the Greek Books is: the Spirit, the Counsellor, the Angel, the Spirit of the Lord, the Spirit of Truth, His Angel, the Angel of the Lord, the Spirit of God, the Spirit of Holiness, the Spirit of your Father, My Spirit, the Angel of God, a Holy Angel, the Eonian Spirit, the Spirit of Christ, My Angel, a man. In all his titles, including πνεῦμα ἅγιον, this angel is referred to 116 times (in my current understanding and assessment) in the God-authorized Greek Books. He is also referred to (with at least 24 titles) 183 times (again, in my current understanding and assessment) in the God-authorized Hebrew Books. That is a total of 299 direct mentions of the Angel of God who is the Holy Spirit.

That these titles are all of the one and the same Angel of God is proven by the following Transcendent Logic of interchangeability of his titles, an interchangeability which can be easily checked by anybody who is prepared to devote the time. My Eonian Documents 9 and 10 (respectively, *Classifications of Spirit, The Three Meanings of* πνεῦμα ἅγιον), and my booklet *Who Is the Counsellor and the Holy Spirit?* explain all these things in exquisite detail, but here is a summary: anybody who looks into these things will find them to be so:–

'the Spirit of the Lord' (Luke 4\18, Isaiah 61\1, Acts 10\38) = 'the Spirit of Adonai Yahweh' (Isaiah 61\1) = 'My Spirit' (Matthew 12\18, Isaiah 42\1) = 'the Spirit of God' (Matthew 3\16, with Luke 4\18) = 'the Spirit' (Mark 1\10, John 1\32-33, with Luke 4\18) = 'the Holy Spirit' (Luke 3\22, with Luke 4\18) = 'the Spirit of Yahweh' (1 Samuel 10\6, Judges 13\25 with 13\3, 13\6, 13\9, 13\18, 14\6) = 'the Spirit of Elohim' (Genesis 1\2, 1 Samuel 10\10, with 1 Samuel 10\6) = 'the Angel of His Presence' (Exodus 33\14-15, Isaiah 63\10 with 63\14) = 'the Angel of Yahweh' (Judges 13\3 with 13\6, 13\25) = 'the Angel of Elohim' and 'a Man of Elohim' (Judges 13\6, 13\9, 13\18, 13\21, with 13\3, 13\25) = 'the Holy Spirit' whose name is secret (Judges 13\18, Matthew 28\19) = 'the Holy Spirit' and 'the Counsellor' and 'the Spirit of Truth' (John 14\16, 14\17, 14\26, 15\26, 16\7, 16\13) = 'the Holy Spirit' and 'the Spirit of Christ' (1 Peter 1\11 with 1\12) = 'the Angel of the Lord' (Acts 8\26, Matthew 1\20) = 'the Angel of God' (Acts 10\3, Galatians 4\14, with Judges 13\6) = 'the Holy Spirit'.

The Holy Spirit angel's title as 'the Angel of His Presence' (Isaiah 63\9) is a perfect description for him. David had his presence and he asked God that he might not be taken away from him (Psalm 51\11, 139\7, Matthew 22\43). He led Jesus into the wilderness (Luke 4\1). During the Acts period the believers had his presence (Mark 13\11). So too will Jesus' disciples have the Counsellor's presence again in the coming Eon, for Jesus told his disciples that 'the Holy Spirit' will be 'with' them and 'alongside' them and 'among' them 'throughout the Eon' (Matthew 28\20, Mark 13\11, John 14\16, 14\26, 15\26).

The name of the Holy Spirit who is the Angel of God is secret (Judges 13\18). His name will be made known to believers in the coming Eon ('the name ... of the Holy Spirit'; Matthew 28\19). Whoever might dare to speak falsely against the Angel of God does not have forgiveness throughout the Eon, but is liable to Eonian condemnatory sentence (Mark 3\29).

Paul commands, 'Let nobody defraud you of the prize by means of a voluntary humility and worship of angels' (Colossians 2\18). This Holy Spirit angel is he whom John was about to worship, but the Angel told him, 'See not *to do that*. I am a fellow servant of you, and of your brothers the prophets, and of those who keep the oracles of this Scroll. Worship God' (Revelation 22\9, 19\10).

Scroll

There are certain Greek words which are usually translated as 'book' and 'scripture'. I prefer these as 'Scroll' (sometimes literal, and sometimes put by metonymy for the writing in them) and sometimes 'Writing' (John 10\35, 5\47). These words are: βίβλος (= *biblos*); βιβλίον (= *biblion*); βιβλαρίδιον (= *biblaridion*, derived from βίβλος) which is 'little Scroll'; and γραφή (= *graphee*). These I render variously, according to context, as, for example: 'Scroll' or 'Scrolls' (Matthew 21\42, Mark 12\24), or 'passage' (Mark 12\10, Luke 4\21, John 13\18, Acts 8\32, 8\35) or 'text' (John 20\9, Acts 1\16) or 'Writings' (2 Peter 3\16, John 10\35). The word 'Scroll' is historically accurate, and imagery which appeals to me. Luke 4\17 and 4\20 set the imagery: 'a Scroll [βιβλίον] of the prophet Isaiah ... unrolling the Scroll ... he rolled up the Scroll'; and at Revelation 6\14, 'the sky was parted, being rolled up like a scroll [βιβλίον] rolling itself up'.

The Translation

The Eonian Books: Matthew to Revelation is a translation, from Greek, of the oracles of God and Christ as revealed to the prophets and apostles, their salvation-bringing message for all mankind of the one true God Who is 'the God and Father of the Lord Jesus Christ'. Matthew to Revelation provides the full canon of God-authorized Greek books, issued as God-authorized, and received as God-authorized. No other fancy-sounding early documents are admitted.

The Eonian Books translation brings to light the Earth-shaking truth of God, and the radiance and energizing light of Jesus – all that was revealed by the Angel of God to the prophets and apostles, and by Jesus himself, and the oracles which the prophets and apostles at other times spoke from their own authority (Romans 13\1, Titus 3\1, Hebrews 13\17).

Perfection in translation and any notion of literal translation are not attainable. Translation loses grammatical idiosyncracies, idioms, and connotations, and it might gain connotations it should not. Genesis 1\1 sets the pattern. Should we write (rendering the Hebrew literally) 'In beginning created God ...', or (turning that into English grammar) 'In *the* beginning God created'? Obviously the latter, making readable English. It's the same with the Greek: it has a different grammar to English. Literal translation is not a possible concept. However, a translation can be untrue and impure, sending deceiving messages: 'was' instead of 'is to rise'; 'end of the world' instead of 'end of the Eon'; 'world that was' instead of 'world to come'; 'before the world began' instead of 'in advance of Eonian times', putting the future into the past; support of dogma hostile to the mind of the messenger prophet. A translation, on the other hand, can be true and pure, transmitting the words and spirit of the messenger.

In every word of this translation, I have laboured – and continue to labour – to make the closest equivalent of the Greek, as much as that is possible, following grammatical rules, in order to get an imitation of the original writer's style. For a mild example, at Matthew 16\15 I have 'But whom do you pronounce me to be?' (Also at 16\13, Mark 8\27, 8\29, Luke 9\18, 9\20, Acts 13\25.) The verb at the end of that is εἶναι (= *einai*), an infinitive, 'to be'. The KJV version of that is 'But whom say ye that I am?', putting the infinitive εἶναι = *einai* as 'I am', a first person indicative, and so needing to add 'that' (which the Greek does not have), so making the rendering loose; it does not translate back into the same Greek. *The Eonian Books* corresponds to the Greek, being lexically parallel. The KJV's rendering gives the impression that the underlying Greek has ἐγώ εἰμι (= *ego eimi*), 'I am', as in the 'I am' statements of Jesus, but the Greek is the infinitive εἶναι, 'to be'. This deceiving impression not only hamstrings word search, but also opens the tent door for many a stinking camel in respect of the most important matters. Other than in interlinears, I have yet to find an English version which has this infinitive correctly here. For another example, a frequent expression of Paul's (14 times; first at Romans 3\4) is the exclamation μὴ γένοιτο (= *mee genoito*). This means, quite simply, 'may it not be'. The KJV, however, puts that as 'God forbid', neither word matching the Greek, a name in vain, and a paraphrastic failure to represent Paul's Greek, and hence unreliable.

When the two ladies went to Jesus' tomb, the Angel of God told them, ἠγέρθη (Matthew 28\6 et cetera). Whereas the KJV wrongly has that as 'He is risen' or 'He has risen', *The Eonian Books* has it as 'He has been raised' – a phenomenal difference – because the verb is passive, not active. Even a child was able to describe to me the implications. The most wonderful and significant event in history is that the Son of God was murdered but was raised from death by the Father, yet in the KJV we are given God's Angel's report of it in a corrupted form, blighted with Mysticism. The correct form, 'He has been raised', harmonizes with Paul's expression that 'Christ was raised from *the* dead by the magnificent power of the Father' (Romans 6\4). And so *The Eonian Books* translation can be trusted to give a reliable imitation of the Greek.

Effective translating is a resolution of the tension between, on the one hand, craving for integrity in reproducing as closely as possible the syntaxes and semantics of the foreign language and, on the other hand, the similar degree of craving for an ornate literary quality of beauty in the translator's native language. Integrity for accuracy and quest for style enhance each other.

If you want to assess a translation's reliability, look first at its verbs, the tenses, voices and moods. Matthew 3\15 opens ἀποκριθεὶς δὲ ὁ Ἰησοῦς εἶπεν πρὸς αὐτόν – which is, 'But answering, Jesus said to him'. Of a few English versions I have in front of me, one is exact in its rendering of that; one is close; others are way off, with just two words. If we are not getting a close representation of the original, it leaves us wondering what else the translator felt like cutting out. Some versions are not only made from a mutilated Greek manuscript, but are deplete in translation as well, buried in paraphrase. A paraphrase version could be made from another version, without even looking at the Greek and Hebrew. The fad for paraphrasing God's Scrolls is destructive. It is to put the language structures and literary forms of God's angels, prophets, Messiah and apostles into one's own forms. So paraphrasing gives only some remote idea of the original. It puts God's message yet another mountain away from the gold-carrying river. For copyright reasons I will not cite contemporary examples, so I'll make one up – Original version: 'The old wind-bag Polonius not without irony told Claudius that "Brevity is the soul of wit".' Paraphrase version: 'The talkative old man Polonius was a hypocrite when he said to the king he'd keep his words short.' The paraphrase version would not translate exactly back into the original, and is inferior.

This is not to suggest that in translating the holy Scrolls there has to be an identical representation of every item, a demand not possible (all those Greek participles, for one thing): structures have to be suited to English, and with all considerations for pleasing literary quality.

It is not the same with fictional works where loose paraphrasing can actually be enhancing.[4] But a loose paraphrasing of sacred legal works is wholly inappropriate: it loses sight of deliberate structures and expressions. And it loses deep meanings. It gives a false reflection of the original. Thinking to bring it to life, they put it to death. It is a dishonour with the holy Scrolls because it is a protest that the original is inadequate, or not to the writer's taste. It makes steps back from the original literary forms, diluting, weakening them, so distancing readers at yet another remove from the most important and greatest literary forms in the world. In deep contrast, imitation of the original literary forms draws you closer to the truth and beauty of the divine oracles, the tongues of prophets and angels. Paraphrasing them is like Renaissance paintings of Biblical scenes set in a phoney foreground.

This translation is titled *The Eonian Books* because this title draws attention to the true gospel promise of 'Eonian life', as proclaimed by the prophet Daniel (Daniel 12\2), and by Jesus (the phrase appears 25 times in the gospels) and by the apostles (19 times in the letters). Jesus and Paul spoke of 'the Eon which is coming', and David and Jesus proclaimed life 'throughout the Eon'. Only in the God-authorized Hebrew and Greek Writings of the prophets and apostles have the Eons been revealed (Hebrews 1\2, 11\3). No book of man has such a scope or vision or detail of the past and future. The Books of God alone give the vision and scope of all the Eons, from the creation of the Earth and of man, described by Moses in Genesis 1 and 2, up to the appearance of the New Earth and the Holy City, prophesied by the apostle and prophet John in Revelation 21 and 22.

Ever since Eden, God – He is the true God – has communicated with mankind in five ways. First, He spoke directly to Adam and Eve. Second, after Adam and Eve, and until the apostles, He spoke to the prophets and apostles and to Jesus' mother Maria through angels. Third, God has spoken through His Son Jesus (Hebrews 1\2). Fourth, after Jesus' ascension, God spoke to Paul and John by means of Jesus making appearances (uniquely) to them. Fifth, during this Eon He speaks only through what is written in the God-authorized Hebrew and Greek Books: those Books must therefore be translated in purity and truth and interpreted in purity and truth. No other generation until this post-apostolic Eon has had the complete writings of the messages of angels and the prophets and of the Messiah and the apostles, and nobody, therefore, until the generations of this Eon has had the complete vision of the Eons which God has designed.

As God gave Adam and Eve food from every herb-bearing seed of the ground and the fruit of every tree yielding seed, the purest raw energy food, so does *The Eonian Books* translation give you raw energy spiritual food, pure in its forms.

The Eonian Books announces the gospel of the coming Eon which is the vision of the men of the single spirit. Those who believe Jesus' words in their true representation will, after their resurrection – or they might be already alive when the Eon commences – have life throughout the Eon which is coming, and they will have minds that are not subject to violation and bodies that are indestructible, no longer subject to death.

They will be like Jesus. John says: '*My* richly loved, we are now Sons of God, and it is not yet brought to light what we will be. We do know, however, that when [Jesus] is brought to light we will be like him, for we will see him as he is' (1 John 3\2). They are 'Sons of God' (John 1\12 et cetera), 'Sons of the living God' (Romans 9\26), 'Sons of the Most High' (Luke 6\35), 'Sons and Daughters of the Lord Almighty' (2 Corinthians 6\18), 'members of the resurrection' (Luke 20\36), and they will live throughout the coming 490 year Eon, and then throughout the 1,000 year Eon, and then they will be seated with God and Jesus in the New Jerusalem, the Holy City (Galatians 4\26, Ephesians 1\3, 2\6-22, Hebrews 12\23, Revelation 21\2). This is mankind attaining his most exalted state. And this is the true God, and Eonian life.

cjs, May 2015

✱

---

4. Matthew Arnold said of translating Homer: 'the translator must without scruple sacrifice, where it is necessary, verbal fidelity to his original'. One translator of Homer describes omitting some of Homer's adjectives because they lose force in English, and the translation is enhanced without them.

† The Gospel Accounts of Jesus Christ*

†

Matthew*

Jesus' ancestry (Luke 3\23-38)

1\1

scroll* of *the* ancestry* of Jesus Christ,* son* of David, son of Abraham.

² Abraham fathered* Isaac, and Isaac fathered Jacob, and Jacob fathered Judah and his brothers, ³ and Judah fathered Pharez and Zarah out of Thamar, and Pharez fathered Hezrom, and Hezrom fathered Ram, ⁴ and Ram fathered Amminadab, and Amminadab fathered Nahshon, and Nahshon fathered Salma, ⁵ and Salma fathered Boaz out of Rahab, and Boaz fathered Obed out of Ruth, and Obed fathered Jesse, ⁶ and Jesse fathered David the king.

And David the king fathered Solomon out of her *who had been the wife* of Uriah, ⁷ and Solomon fathered Rehoboam, and Rehoboam fathered Abijam, and Abijam fathered Asa, ⁸ and Asa fathered Jehoshaphat, and Jehoshaphat fathered Jehoram, and Jehoram fathered Uzziah, ⁹ and Uzziah fathered Jotham, and Jotham fathered Ahaz, and Ahaz fathered Hezekiah, ¹⁰ and Hezekiah fathered Manasseh, and Manasseh fathered Amon, and Amon fathered Josiah, ¹¹ and Josiah fathered Jeconiah and his brothers at the time of the Babylonian deportation.

¹² And after the Babylonian deportation Jeconiah* fathered Shealtiel, and Shealtiel fathered Zorobabel, ¹³ and Zorobabel fathered Abiud, and Abiud fathered Eliakim, and Eliakim fathered Azor, ¹⁴ and Azor fathered Zadok, and Zadok fathered Achim, and Achim fathered Eliud, ¹⁵ and Eliud fathered Eleazar, and Eleazar fathered Matthan, and Matthan fathered Jacob.

¹⁶ And Jacob fathered Joseph, the husband of Maria,* out of whom was born Jesus, the one called Christ.

¹⁷ So all the generations* from Abraham until David *were* 14 generations, and from David until the Babylonian deportation *there were* 14 generations, and from the Babylonian deportation until the Christ *there were* 14 generations.

Creation account of Jesus in the virgin Maria, through divine power (Heb. 3\2), & proclamation to Joseph by the Angel of God

¹⁸ The generating of Jesus Christ,* though, came about in the following manner. Now when his mother Maria was engaged to Joseph before they came together,* she was found *to be* with a child* through the agency of *the* divine spirit.* ¹⁹ Then her husband Joseph, being righteous,* and not wanting to expose her to public shame, made up his mind to divorce her secretly.

²⁰ However, while he reflected on* these things, surprisingly* *the* Angel of *the* Lord* was seen* by him in a dream,* saying, 'Joseph, son of David,* do not be afraid to take Maria as your wife, for that which is generated* in her is through the agency of *the* divine spirit.* ²¹ And she will give birth to a son, and you shall call* his name Jesus,* for he himself will save his people from their violations.'

²² Now all of this came about in order that what was spoken* by* the Lord through the agency of* the prophet* might be fulfilled,* where he says, ²³ 'Mark this: the virgin* will be with a child,* and she will give birth to a son, and they will call his name Emmanuel,'* which, being translated, is 'God with us'.*

²⁴ Then Joseph, having been roused from sleep, did as the Angel of *the* Lord* had commanded him, and he took *Maria* to himself as his wife, ²⁵ and he did not know her until she had given birth to her firstborn* son, and he called his name Jesus.*

Jesus born into an Israel long divorced from God (Jer. 3\8, Hos. 1\9). *The wise men. Herod. Flight to Egypt*

2\1 Now *after* Jesus' having been born in Bethlehem of Judea in *the* days of Herod the king, it so happened that* magi from *the* East arrived in Jerusalem, ² saying, 'Where is he who has been born King of the Jews? For we have seen his star* in the East, and we have come* to pay honour to* him.'

³ But Herod the king, on hearing *these things,* was disturbed, and all Jerusalem with him.

⁴ And having gathered together all the senior priests* and scribes of the people, he kept

enquiring of them where the Christ would be born.

⁵   And they said to him, 'In Bethlehem of Judea,* for this has been written through the agency of the prophet:

⁶   "And you, Bethlehem of Judah,
    are by no means the least
    among the governmental towns* of Judah,
    for out of you will come a ruler
    who will shepherd My people Israel." '* *

⁷   Then Herod secretly called the wise men,* *and* he enquired of them in detail* the time of the shining of the star. ⁸ Then he sent* them into Bethlehem, *and* he said, 'As you go,* search out* exactly* about the young child, and when you have found *him* report back to me, so that I too can go *and* pay honour to* him.'

⁹   And when they had heard the king, they departed.

    And* the star which they had seen in the East kept going ahead of them until it came *and* fixed itself over where the young child was. ¹⁰ And on seeing the star, they rejoiced exceedingly with immense exuberance.

¹¹   And *when* they went into the house,* they saw the young child with his mother Maria, and they bowed down then knelt before* him, and they opened their treasure cases *and* presented to him gifts, gold and frankincense and myrrh.*

¹²   And they were divinely warned* in a dream not to return to* Herod, *so* they returned to their own country by another route.

¹³   But on having made their departure, surprisingly* *the* Angel of *the* Lord* was seen* by Joseph in a dream, saying, 'Rise up, and take the young child and his mother, and flee into Egypt,* and stay there until I bring you word, for Herod is on the point of* searching for the young child in order to destroy him.'

¹⁴   And he rose up, *and* he took the young child and his mother by night, and he withdrew into Egypt, ¹⁵ and he stayed there until the death of Herod, so that what was spoken by* the Lord through the agency of* the prophet might be fulfilled, saying, 'Out of Egypt* I called My son.'*

¹⁶   Then when Herod saw that he had been outwitted by the magi, he was exceedingly enraged, and, having dispatched* *some men*, he massacred all the boys* from two years old* and under in Bethlehem and in all its vicinity,* in keeping with the time which he had enquired in detail* from the magi.*

¹⁷   Then that which was spoken through the agency of the prophet Jeremiah was fulfilled, where he says:

¹⁸   'A voice was heard in Ramah,
    lamentation and weeping
    and severe mourning,
    Rachel weeping for her children,*
    and not willing* to be comforted,*
    because they are no more.'*

¹⁹   But *when* Herod died, *the* Angel of the Lord* was surprisingly seen* by Joseph in a dream in Egypt, ²⁰ saying, 'Rise up, and take the young child and his mother, and go into *the* land of Israel, for those who were looking for the child's life have died.'

²¹   And he rose up, *and* he took the young child and his mother, and he arrived in *the* land of Israel. ²² But hearing that Archelaus was ruling over Judea in place of his father Herod, he was frightened to set off back there. But having been divinely warned in a dream, he turned aside into the regions of Galilee, ²³ and he came and settled in a town called Nazareth, so that what was spoken* through the agency of the prophets might be fulfilled, *saying*, 'He will be called a Nazarene.'*

*The submissive of Israel are identified
with God & the coming Christ by John the Identifier
by means of the expression of a public water ritual
received by John from God (Mat. 21\25,
Mark 11\30, Luke 20\4)
in order 'to make ready a people' (Luke 1\17).
Proclamation by John that Jesus will identify them
with the anointing of the divine spirit (Acts 1\5,
2\33, 1 Cor. 12\13, Gal. 3\27, Col. 2\12);*
& which is a washing from violations (Acts 22\16)

3\1   **A**nd in those days John the Identifier* appeared on the scene,* making a proclamation in the desert of Judea, ² and saying, 'Submit,* for the Sovereign Rulership* of the heavens* has drawn near.'*

³   For this is the one who was spoken of through the agency of the prophet Isaiah, saying:

    'The voice of one calling out
    in the wilderness,
    "Prepare the way of the Lord;
    make straight His paths." '*

⁴ And this same John had a garment of camel hairs, and a belt of leather around his waist, and his food was locusts and wild honey. ⁵ Then Jerusalem and all Judea went out to him, and all the region around the Jordan, ⁶ and they were identified* by him in the Jordan, pouring out their violations.

⁷ But seeing many of the Pharisees and Sadducees coming to his identification, he said to them, 'Progeny of snakes!* Who warned* you to flee away from the coming indignation?* ⁸ In that case, produce fruit in keeping with submission. ⁹ And do not think to say among yourselves, "We have Abraham as father," for I say to you that out of* these stones God is able to raise up sons for Abraham. ¹⁰ But the axe has already been laid at the root of the trees. Every tree, therefore, not producing good fruit gets cut down and is thrown into fire.*

¹¹ 'It is true that I identify you in water towards submission. But the one coming after me is mightier than me, whose sandals I am not worthy to carry. He will identify you in *the* divine spirit.** ¹² His winnowing-shovel *is* in his hand, and he will thoroughly purge his threshing-floor,* and gather together his wheat into the barn. The chaff,* though, he will burn up with inextinguishable fire.'

Jesus insists on being identified with the submissive of Israel. He sees the Angel of God*

¹³ Then Jesus came away from Galilee to the Jordan to John, to be identified by him. ¹⁴ John, though, tried to deter him, saying, 'I need to be identified by you, yet you come to me!' ¹⁵ But answering, Jesus said to him, 'Let *it* be so now, for in this way it is proper for us to fulfil all righteousness.'

Then he allowed him. ¹⁶ And after being identified Jesus came up immediately out of the water, and then the skies were opened to him, and he saw the Spirit of God* descending in the manner of a dove* and alighting* over him. ¹⁷ And a voice came* out of the skies saying, 'This is My Son,* the Richly Loved One,* in whom I have found delight.'*

Jesus led by the Angel of God into the wilderness. Testing by the Devil

4\1 Then Jesus was led up by the Spirit* into the wilderness to be put to the test* by the Devil.

² And after fasting forty days and forty nights, he became hungry, ³ and the Tempter* approached him* and said, 'If you are the Son of God,* speak so that these stones might become loaves of bread.'

⁴ But in answer, he said, 'It has been written: "Man shall not live by means of bread only, but by every utterance proceeding through the mouth of God." '*

⁵ Then the Devil took him along to the Holy City, and he set him on the pinnacle of the Temple buildings, ⁶ and he said to him, 'If you are the Son of God, throw yourself down, for it has been written:

"He will give His angels charge over you,*
and they will lift you up on *their* hands,
in case at any time you should strike
your foot against a stone." '*

⁷ Jesus said to him, 'Additionally,* it has been written: "You shall not put the Lord God to the test." '**

⁸ The Devil also* took him along to an exceedingly high mountain, and he showed him all the kingdoms* of the world order* and their magnificence.*

⁹ And he said to him, 'All these things I will give you if you fall down *and* worship* me.'*

¹⁰ Then Jesus said to him, 'Get behind me, Satan,* for it has been written: "You shall worship *the* Lord your God, and you shall serve Him only." '*

¹¹ At that the Devil left him, and so then* angels came and attended to* him.

Proclamation of the kingdom & Sovereign Rulership of the heavens. Disciples called*

¹² Now *when* he heard that John had been handed over,* Jesus withdrew into Galilee. ¹³ And he left Nazareth, *and* he came *and* settled in Capernaum, on the sea-coast in the regions of Zabulon and Nephthali, ¹⁴ so that what was spoken through the agency of the prophet Isaiah might be fulfilled, saying:

¹⁵ 'Land of Zabulon,
     and land of Nephthali,
     road of *the* sea,
     across the Jordan,
     Galilee of the nations,*
¹⁶ the people who were sitting in darkness
     have seen a splendid light,

and for those who were sitting in a region
and dark shadow of death
a light has arisen for them.'*

[17] From that time Jesus began to make a proclamation, and to say,* 'Submit, for the Sovereign Rulership* of the heavens* has drawn near.'*
[18] And as he was walking by the Sea of Galilee, he saw two brothers, Simon, who was known as Peter, with his brother Andrew, casting a large net into the sea, for they were fishermen.
[19] And he said to them, 'Follow me, and I will make you fishers of men.'
[20] And at once leaving the nets, they followed him. [21] And going on from there, he saw two other brothers, Jacob, *son* of Zebedee, and his brother John in the boat with their father Zebedee, setting their nets in order, so he called them, [22] and they at once left the boat and their father and followed him.

Teaching & healing. Crowds follow Jesus*
[23] And Jesus went about all Galilee teaching in their synagogues and making a proclamation of the gospel of the Sovereign Rulership,** and healing every sickness and every debility among the people. [24] And the report about him went out to all Syria, and they brought to him all who were sick, people with various diseases and oppressed by torments,* and those who were under the power of demons,* and lunatics, and paralytics, and he cured them. [25] And a vast mass of people from Galilee, and Decapolis, and Jerusalem, and Judea, and beyond the Jordan followed him.

Teaching on the mountain *
5\1 And on seeing the crowds, he went up into the mountain. And when he was seated his disciples came to him, [2] and opening his mouth he taught them, saying:

[3] 'Exalted* *are* the poor in spirit,
for theirs is the Sovereign Rulership*
of the heavens.*
[4] Exalted *are* the mourners,
for they will be comforted.
[5] Exalted *are* the submissive,
for they will inherit the land.**
[6] Exalted *are* those who hunger and thirst
after righteousness, for they will be filled.
[7] Exalted *are* the compassionate,

for they will find compassion.
[8] Exalted *are* the pure in heart,
for they will see God.
[9] Exalted *are* the peacemakers,
for they will be called Sons* of God.*
[10] Exalted *are* those who have been persecuted
on account of righteousness,
for theirs is the Sovereign Rulership
of the heavens.
[11] Exalted *are* you whenever
they reproach you
and persecute you
and speak all kinds of offensive words,
lying about you on account of me.
[12] Rejoice, and be exceedingly glad,
for manifold *is* your reward
in the heavens,**
because in the same way
they persecuted the prophets
who *were* before you.

True disciples represent salt & light *
[13] 'You represent* the salt of the land,* but if the salt becomes tasteless,* by what can* it be salted? Then it no longer has potency for anything but to be thrown out and trodden underfoot by men.
[14] 'You represent* the light of the world. A city set on a high mountain cannot be hidden.
[15] Nor do they light a lamp* and put it underneath the grain measure, but on a candlestick,* and it shines for all those in the house. [16] Let your light shine like this before men so that they might see your noble works and magnify* your Father in the heavens.*

Sovereign Rulership & law
[17] 'Think not that I have come to disintegrate* the law or the prophets.* I have come not to disintegrate,* but to fulfil *them.* [18] For truly* I say to you, until Heaven and the Earth pass away* not one iota* nor one merest ornament* will in any way pass from the law until it might all come into being.*
[19] 'Whoever, therefore, might subvert one of the shortest of these commandments, and teaches men the same, will be called the least in the Sovereign Rulership of the heavens. But whoever carries *them* out and teaches *them*, he will be called eminent in the Sovereign Rulership of the heavens. [20] For I say to you that, unless your righteousness abounds above *that* of the scribes and Pharisees, you will certainly not enter into the Sovereign Rulership

of the heavens.

Law. murder. Liability to the fire
of Jerusalem's rubbish dump
in the Valley of Hinnom (γέεννα, *gehenna*),
(Mat. 23\15, Joshua 15\8 etc.)
²¹ 'You have heard that it was said to the ancients, "You shall not murder,* and whoever murders will be liable to judgement." ²² But I say to you, everybody who becomes angry with his brother without a cause will be liable to judgement. And whoever says to his brother, "Empty head!"* will be in danger of the Sanhedrin. But whoever says, "Fool!" will be liable to the fire of the Valley of Hinnom.*
²³ 'If, therefore, you offer up your gift to the altar and remember there that your brother has something against you, ²⁴ leave your gift there before the altar, and go your way. First be reconciled to your brother, and then come *and* offer your gift.
²⁵ 'Be quickly well-minded towards your opponent while you are on the road with him, in case *the* opponent might hand you over to the judge, and the judge hands you over to the officer, and you are thrown into jail. ²⁶ Truly I say to you, you will certainly not come out of there until you have paid the last kodrantes.*

The law. adultery *
²⁷ 'You have heard that it has been said, "You shall not commit adultery."* ²⁸ But I say to you, everybody looking at a married woman in order to lust after her has already committed adultery with her in his heart.
²⁹ 'And if your right eye causes you to stumble, pluck it out and throw *it* away from you, for it is more profitable for you that one part of your body should suffer destruction than *that* your whole body should be thrown into the Valley of Hinnom. ³⁰ And if your right hand causes you to stumble, cut it off and throw *it* from you, for it is more profitable for you that one part of your body should suffer destruction than *that* your whole body should be thrown into the Valley of Hinnom.*

The law. divorce *
³¹ 'And it was said that "Whoever puts away his wife, let him give her a certificate of divorce."*
³² 'But I say to you, whoever puts away his wife, except on account of fornication, causes her to commit adultery, and whoever marries

her who has been put away commits adultery.

The law. perjury
³³ 'Additionally,* you have heard that it was said to the ancients, "You shall not swear falsely, but you shall carry out your oaths to the Lord."*
³⁴ 'But I say to you, do not swear at all; neither by Heaven, for it is *the* governmental seat of God; ³⁵ nor by the Earth, for it is *the* footstool of His feet; nor by Jerusalem, for it is *the* city of the Majestic King. ³⁶ Nor shall you swear by your head, because you are not able to make one hair white or black. ³⁷ But let your word be "Yes yes, no no," whereas the excess of these is out of something* bad-natured.*

The law. retaliation
³⁸ 'You have heard that it was said, "An eye in exchange for an eye, and a tooth in exchange for a tooth."* ³⁹ But I say to you, do not resist the malicious person, but whoever strikes you on *the* right cheek, turn the other to him as well.* ⁴⁰ And to him who wishes to go to law with you and take away your outer jacket, let him have the long robe as well. ⁴¹ And whoever compels you to go one mile, go two with him. ⁴² Give to him who asks you, and do not turn away from him who wants to borrow from you.

The law. love
⁴³ 'You have heard that it was said, "You shall love* your neighbour,"* and "Hate your enemy". ⁴⁴ But I say to you, love your enemies; speak good words* to those who curse you; do good to those who hate you; and pray for those who treat you maliciously and persecute you, ⁴⁵ so that you might become Sons* of your Father in the heavens.* For He causes His Sun* to rise on an evil man and on a good man, and He sends rain on a righteous man as well as on an unrighteous man. ⁴⁶ For if you love those who love you, what reward do you have? Do not even* the tax collectors do the same? ⁴⁷ And if you greet only your friends,* what exceptional thing do you do? Do not even* the tax collectors do that?
⁴⁸ 'You must, therefore, be* perfect, just as your Father in the heavens* is perfect.

True disciples excel religious traditions

6\1 'Be vigilant not to carry out your acts of compassion* in front of men* with the purpose

of being seen by them. Otherwise you have no reward in the presence˙ of your Father in the heavens.˙ ² When, therefore, you carry out *your* acts of compassion, do not send a trumpet-blast ahead of you, in the way the hypocrites˙ do in the synagogues and in the streets, so that they might be honoured˙ by men. Truly I say to you, they receive their reward. ³ But *when* you carry out your acts of compassion, do not let your left *hand* come to know what your right *hand* is doing, ⁴ so that your acts of compassion might be in secret, and your Father Who observes in secret will Himself reward you in the open.
⁵ 'And when you pray, you must not be like the hypocrites, for they are fond of standing to pray in the synagogues and at the corners of the open places, so that they might be observed by men. Truly I say to you, they receive their reward. ⁶ But you, when you pray, go into your private room, and shut your door, pray to your Father Who is hidden, and your Father Who observes in secret will reward you in the open.
⁷ 'But when you pray, do not use vain repetitions like the other nations, for they think that they will be heard in their vast speaking. ⁸ So do not be like them, for your Father knows what things you need before you ask Him.˙

Prayer for the disciples ˙
⁹ 'Pray, therefore, in this way:

'Our Father, in the heavens,˙
may Your name be sanctified;˙
¹⁰ may Your Sovereign Rulership appear;˙
may Your will be brought to pass,˙
as in Heaven, so also˙ on˙ the Earth.˙
¹¹ Give us this day˙ our sufficient˙ bread,
¹² and forgive our offences,˙
as we ourselves in turn˙
forgive˙ our debtors.˙
¹³ And bring us not into adversity,˙
but deliver us˙ from˙ the Evil One,˙
for Yours is the Sovereign Rulership,˙˙
and the might, and the magnificence,
throughout the Eons.˙˙ Amen.˙

Forgiveness under law (contrast with the forgiveness later under Paul's gospel. Rom. 2\16, Eph. 1\7, Col. 1\14)˙
¹⁴ 'For if you forgive men their transgressions, your heavenly˙ Father will forgive you as well. ¹⁵ But if you do not forgive men their transgressions, neither will your Father forgive your transgressions.˙

Fasting
¹⁶ 'In addition, when you fast, do not become like the hypocrites, sombre in countenance, for they disfigure their faces so that they might be seen by men *to be* in a fast. Truly I say to you, they have their reward. ¹⁷ But you, in fasting, anoint your head, and wash your face, ¹⁸ so that you should not be noticed by men as *being* in a fast, but only to your Father Who is hidden,˙ and your Father Who observes in secret will reward you.

Treasure with God
¹⁹ 'Do not store up for yourselves treasures on the Earth, where moth and rust cause perishing, and where thieves break through and steal. ²⁰ But store up for yourselves treasures in Heaven,˙ where neither moth nor rust cause perishing, and where thieves do not break through or steal. ²¹ For where your treasure is, there will your heart also be.

The eye the lamp of the body
²² 'The eye is the lamp of the body. If, therefore, your eye is clear-sighted,˙ your whole body will be full of light. ²³ But if your eye is evil,˙ your whole body will be dark. If, therefore, the light in you is darkness, how extreme *is* that darkness!

God & mammon
²⁴ 'Nobody is able to serve two masters, for either he will not care for the one and he will love the other, or he will cling to one and despise the other. You are not able to serve God and mammon.˙ ²⁵ On account of this, I say to you, do not be over-anxious about your life, what you will eat, or what you will drink, nor even about your body, what you will put on. Is life not more than food, and the body than clothing? ²⁶ Observe the birds of the sky,˙˙ for they do not sow, nor do they reap, nor do they gather into barns, yet your heavenly˙ Father feeds them. Are you not of far more worth than these?˙

Relief from anxiety
²⁷ 'But who among you, by being anxious, is able to prolong one forearm's length˙ to his stature? ²⁸ And why are you anxious about clothing? Consider the lilies of the field, how they grow. They neither toil nor spin, ²⁹ and yet I say to you that not even Solomon in all his glory was arrayed like one of these. ³⁰ But if

God so enrobes the herbage of the field, which is there today and tomorrow is thrown into the oven, *will He* not much more *enrobe* you, you of little faith? [31] Do not, therefore, be anxious, saying, "What shall we eat?" or, "What shall we drink?" or, "What shall we be clothed with?" [32] For the nations run after all these things. For your heavenly Father knows that you need all these things. [33] But search first for the Sovereign Rulership* of God, and His righteousness, and all these things will be added to you. [34] Take no thought, therefore, about tomorrow, for tomorrow is sure to* take thought for its own things. The present day *has* evil enough of its own.*

The measure of judgement

7\1 'Do not judge, in order that you might not be judged. [2] For with whatever judgement* you judge, you will be judged. And by whatever measure you measure out, it will be measured out to you.

A log in the eye

[3] 'Why, though, do you look at the chip in the eye of your brother, but you do not perceive the log in your own eye? [4] Or how can you say to your brother, "Allow me to pull the chip from your eye"? But look,* the log *is* in your own eye! [5] You hypocrite! First pull the log out of your own eye, and then you will see clearly to pull the chip out of your brother's eye.

Pearls to pigs

[6] 'Do not give holy things to the dogs, nor throw your pearls in front of the pigs,* in case they trample them with their feet, and, having turned, they will tear you up.

Ask & search & knock

[7] 'Ask, and it will be given to you. Search, and you will find. Knock, and it will be opened to you. [8] For everybody who asks receives, and he who searches finds, and to him who knocks it will be opened. [9] Or what man is there among you who, if his son should ask for bread, will give him a stone, [10] and, if he should ask for a fish, will give him a snake? [11] If you, then, being grudging, know to give good gifts to your sons, how much more will your Father in the heavens give good things to those who ask Him?

Summary of the law

[12] 'Therefore all things, whatever you wish that men should do to you, you also do the same to them,* for this represents* the law and the prophets.

The narrow gate & the wide gate
– life or destruction (John 3\16)

[13] 'Enter in through the narrow gate, for wide *is* the gate and broad the road leading off into* destruction,* and those entering in* through* it* are many.* [14] How narrow, *though, is* the gate and constricted* the road leading into* life,* and those* finding* it are few.

Pseudo prophets. Good & bad trees *

[15] 'But turn your attention from the pseudo prophets* who come to you in clothing of sheep,* but inwardly are ferocious* wolves.* [16] You will recognize them fully from* their fruits. Do they gather a bunch of grapes* from thorn bushes, or figs from* thistles? [17] Consequently, every good tree produces good fruits, but the corrupt tree produces noxious fruits. [18] A good tree is not able to produce bad fruits, nor a corrupt tree to produce good fruits. [19] Every tree not producing good fruits is cut down and thrown into fire. [20] Then you will surely recognize them from their fruits.*

Entrance into the Sovereign Rulership of the heavens *

[21] 'Not everybody who says to me, "Lord, Lord," will enter into the Sovereign Rulership* of the heavens, but, rather, he who does the will of My Father in the heavens. [22] Many will say to me in that day,* "Lord, Lord, did we not act as spokesmen* through your name, and through your name drive out demons, and through your name perform many works of power?" [23] And then I will profess to them, "I never* came to know you. Depart away from me, you working lawlessness."*

A house built on the 'rock'* of Jesus
(πέτρα, petra; 16\18, 1 Cor. 10\4)

[24] 'Therefore, every one who hears these oracles of mine and puts them into practice, I will liken him to a wise man who built his house on a rock,* [25] and down came the rain, and the torrents came, and the winds blew and crashed against that house, but it did not fall down, for it had been founded on a rock.* [26] And everybody who hears these oracles of mine and does not put them into practice will

be likened to a foolish man who built his house on sand, [27] and down came the rain, and the torrents came, and the winds blew and lightly struck that house, and down it fell, and violent was its fall.'

[28] And it transpired,* when Jesus had finished these oracles, *that* the crowds were struck with astonishment* at his teaching, [29] for he was continually teaching them as *one* having authority, and not like the scribes.

Healing of a leper *

8\1 **A**nd when he had come down from the mountain, a vast mass of people followed him. [2] And it so happened that* a leper approached, and he knelt before him,* saying, 'Lord, if you are willing, you are able to cleanse me.'
[3] And stretching out *his* hand, Jesus touched him, saying, 'I am willing. Be cleansed.'
And instantly he was cleansed of his leprosy.
[4] And Jesus said to him, 'See you tell nobody, but go your way, show yourself to the priest, and, for a testimony* to them, offer the gift that Moses commanded.'*

Healing of a centurion's servant *

[5] And on his having gone into Capernaum, a centurion came to him, appealing to him, [6] and saying, 'Lord, my servant* is laid up at home, paralyzed, and terribly tormented.'
[7] And Jesus said to him, 'I will come *and* heal him.'
[8] And in answer, the centurion said, 'Lord, I am not worthy that you should enter underneath my roof, but speak only by a word and my servant* will be healed. [9] For I myself,* also a man, am under a system of authority,* having soldiers under myself, and I say to this one, "Go!" and he goes, and to another, "Come!" and he comes, and to my servant, "Do this!" and he does *it.*'
[10] When he heard *that,* Jesus was amazed, and he said to those following, 'Truly I say to you, not even in Israel have I found such strong faith. [11] But I say to you, many will come from the East and West, and they will sit down* with Abraham and Isaac and Jacob in the Sovereign Rulership of the heavens.* [12] But the offspring of the kingdom* will be thrown out into the outer darkness. There will be weeping and gnashing* of teeth.'*
[13] And Jesus said to the centurion, 'Go your

way, and, to the extent you have believed, may it be it done to you.'
And his servant was healed in that same hour.

Healing of Peter's mother-in-law. *
Many healed
[14] And *when* he had come into the house of Peter, Jesus saw his wife's mother laid up,* and sick with a fever. [15] And he touched her hand, and the fever left her, and she was lifted up* and she waited on him.
[16] And it having turned evening, they brought to him many who were under the power of demons, and he drove out the spirits by a word, and healed all who were sick, [17] so that what was spoken through the agency of the prophet Isaiah might be fulfilled, saying:

'He took our infirmities,
and he took away our sicknesses.'*

A scribe who might follow him *
[18] Then seeing a vast mass of people around him, Jesus gave an order to depart to the other side.
[19] And one certain scribe approaching said, 'Teacher, I will follow you wherever you might go.'
[20] And Jesus said to him, 'The foxes have holes, and the birds of the sky* *have* roosts, but the Son of Man* has nowhere he might lay his head.'
[21] And another of his disciples said to him, 'Lord, allow me first to go and bury my father.'
[22] But Jesus said to him, 'Follow me, and leave the dead to bury their own dead.'*

He calms the storm *
[23] And on his stepping into the boat, his disciples followed him. [24] And suddenly a furious shaking* came up on the sea, so that the boat was getting covered over by the waves.
He, though, was sleeping, [25] and the disciples came *and* roused him, saying, 'Lord, save us! We're perishing!'
[26] And he said to them, 'Why are you fearful, you of little faith?'
Then having risen up, he rebuked the winds and the sea, and a mighty calm descended.*
[27] And the men were astounded, saying, 'Who is this, that even the winds and the sea obey him?'

Healing of two men under the power of demons *

²⁸ And when he had come to the other side, into the country of the Gergesenes, two men under the power of demons came out of the tombs to meet him, so exceedingly violent* that nobody was able to pass by that way.
²⁹ And then they called out, saying, 'What have we to do with you, Jesus, Son of God? Have you come here to torment* us before *the* time?'
³⁰ Now a good distance off from them, a herd of many pigs was feeding, ³¹ and the demons pleaded with him, saying, 'If you drive us out, allow us to go off into the herd of pigs.'
³² So he said to them, 'Go!'

And *when* they came out, they went into the herd of pigs, and just then the whole herd of pigs rushed headlong down the steep place into the sea, and they died in the waters.
³³ And those who kept *them* fled and went their ways into the city, *and* they related it all, as well as about the men under the power of demons.
³⁴ And then the whole city went out for an encounter with Jesus, and at their seeing him they pleaded that he might depart from their vicinities.

Healing of a man sick with palsy.
Forgiveness of violations *

9\1 And he boarded the boat, *and* he ferried across *the sea*, and he came into his own town.
² And it came about that* they brought to him a paralytic lying on a bed, and Jesus, on seeing their faith, said to the paralytic, 'Son, be of good courage. Your violations stand disregarded for you.'
³ And at this some of the scribes came and said among themselves, 'This *man* blasphemes.'
⁴ And Jesus, who had perceived their thoughts, said, 'Why do you think up evil in your hearts?
⁵ For which is easier to say, "Your violations stand disregarded," or to say, "Rise up and walk"? ⁶ But so that you might perceive that the Son of Man has authority on the Earth to forgive violations ...'
Then he said to the paralytic man, 'Rise, gather up your bed, and go to your home.'
⁷ And he rose up *and* departed to his home.
⁸ And *when* the crowds saw they marvelled, and they magnified God Who had given such authority to men.*

The calling of Matthew. Eating
with violators at Matthew's feast *

⁹ And on passing along from there, Jesus saw a man named Matthew sitting at the tax office, and he said to him, 'Follow me.'
And he rose up *and* followed him.
¹⁰ And it so happened,* as he was sitting eating in the house, that there were many tax collectors and violators having turned up *and* they were eating together with Jesus and his disciples.
¹¹ And on seeing *this* the Pharisees said to his disciples, 'Why does your Teacher eat with tax collectors and violators?'
¹² But *when* he heard that, Jesus said to them, 'Those who are strong do not have need of a physician, but those having a sickness. ¹³ But go *and* learn what *this* means:* "I desire compassion, and not sacrifice."* For I have come to call not *the* righteous, but violators to submission.'

Friends of the bridegroom.
Parables of wineskins & garments *

¹⁴ Then the disciples of John came to him, saying, 'Why do we and the Pharisees fast often, but your disciples do not fast?'
¹⁵ And Jesus said to them, 'Can the sons of the bridegroom mourn as long as the bridegroom is with them? But days will come when the bridegroom will have been taken away from them, and then they will fast.
¹⁶ 'But nobody puts a patch of new flannel over an old garment, for its patch pulls away from the garment, and a worse tear comes.
¹⁷ 'Nor do they put freshly made wine into old wineskins.* Otherwise the wineskins burst, and the wine runs out, and the wineskins are ruined. But new wine they put into new wineskins, and both are preserved together.'

Healing of a lady with a flow of blood.
Raising of the daughter of Jair **

¹⁸ While he was speaking these things to them, it so happened that* a civil ruler came, and he was kneeling before* him, saying, 'My daughter died just now, but come *and* lay your hand on her, and she will revive.'
¹⁹ And Jesus rose up *and* followed him, and so *did* his disciples.
²⁰ And just then a lady* having had a hemorrhage for twelve years approached from behind *and* she touched the hem of his garment, ²¹ for she kept saying within herself, 'If I only touch his garment, I will be cured.'
²² But Jesus turned around and saw her, *and*

said, 'Daughter, be of good courage. Your faith has healed you.'

And the lady was healed from that hour. [23] Then Jesus came into the house of the ruler, and, seeing the flute players and the crowd wailing loudly, [24] he said to them, 'Go out of the room,* for the young girl is not dead, but sleeping.'

And they laughed at him. [25] But when the crowd were put out, he went in *and* took her by the hand, and the young girl was lifted up. [26] And this report went out into all that region.

Healing of two blind men *

[27] And as Jesus passed on from there, two blind men followed him, calling out, and saying, 'Have compassion on us, Son of David!'*

[28] And *when* he arrived at the house, the blind men approached him, and Jesus said to them, 'Do you believe that I am able to do this?'

They said to him, 'Yes, Lord.'

[29] Then he touched their eyes, saying, 'May it be done for you according to your faith.'

[30] And their eyes were opened, and Jesus strictly ordered them, saying, 'See to it *that* nobody must know.'

[31] But they went off *and* made him known in all that region.

Healing of a dumb man
under power of a demon

[32] But as they were leaving, it so happened that* they brought to him a dumb man under the power of a demon.

[33] And when the demon had been driven out, the dumb man spoke, and the crowds were amazed, saying, 'Never has it been seen like this in Israel.'

[34] But the Pharisees said, 'He drives out demons through the agency of the prince of the demons.'*

Proclaiming the gospel
& healing the crowds *

[35] And Jesus went around all the towns and the villages teaching in their synagogues, and heralding the gospel concerning the Sovereign Rulership, and healing every disease and every bodily weakness among the people. [36] But *when* he saw the crowds, he was moved with compassion for them, because they were distressed* and scattered about, like sheep not having a shepherd.*

[37] Then he said to his disciples, 'The harvest *is* truly plentiful, but the labourers few. [38] Ask, therefore, the Lord of the harvest that He will send out labourers into His harvest.'

The authorization of the 12.* Shaking the dust.
The Angel of God speaks for them (10\20)

10\1 **A**nd when he had called his twelve disciples,* he gave them authority over unclean spirits, to drive them out, and to heal every disease and every bodily weakness.

[2] Now the names of the twelve apostles are these: first, Simon who is known as Peter, and his brother Andrew; Jacob, the *son* of Zebedee, and his brother John; [3] Philip and Bartholomew; Thomas, and Matthew the tax collector; Jacob, the *son* of Alphaeus, and Lebbaeus, whose surname is Thaddaeus; [4] Simon the Canaanite;* and Judas Iscariot, the one who for his part* betrayed him.

[5] Jesus authorized these twelve, instructing them, saying, 'Do not go out into a road of other nations, and do not enter into a town of Samaritans. [6] But go rather to the lost sheep of *the* house of Israel.

[7] 'And as you go, make a proclamation, saying, "The Sovereign Rulership of the heavens* has drawn near."* [8] Heal the sick; cleanse the lepers;* drive out demons. Freely you have received; freely give.

[9] 'Take along neither gold, nor silver, nor copper* in your belts, [10] nor travel sack* for the road, nor two garments, nor sandals, nor staffs, for the workman is worthy of his livelihood.'*

[11] 'And in whatever town or village you enter, enquire who in it is worthy, and remain there until you depart. [12] But on entering into any household, greet it,* [13] and if the house is worthy, let your peace come over it, but if it is not worthy let your peace return to you. [14] And as for whoever does not receive you or hear your words, on your departing out of that house or town shake the dust off your feet.* [15] Truly I say to you, it will be more bearable on *the* day of judgement* for *the* land of Sodom and Gomorrha than for that town.

[16] 'Listen now. I authorize you as sheep in the thick of wolves.* Become, therefore, as cunning as snakes, and as guileless as doves. [17] But beware of men, for they will give you into the hands of the Sanhedrins, and they will scourge you in their synagogues. [18] And you will be brought before presidents and kings on account of me, for a testimony to them and to the

nations. [19] But when they hand you over, do not be anxious over how or what you should speak, for it will be given to you in that hour what you should speak. [20] For it is not you who speak, but the Spirit of your Father* speaking among* you.* [21] 'But brother will hand over brother to death, and a father a child, and children will rebel against parents and have them put to death. [22] And you will be hated by everybody on account of my name, but the one enduring until *the* end* will be preserved.* [23] But when they persecute you in this city, flee into the next, for, truly I say to you, you will certainly not have finished going around* the cities of Israel until the Son of Man comes.* [24] 'A pupil is not above the teacher, nor a servant above his master. [25] It is sufficient for the disciple that he becomes like his teacher, and the servant like his lord. If they have called the master of the house Beelzebub, how much more those of his household? [26] You should not, therefore, fear them, for nothing is concealed which will not be revealed, nor hidden which will not be made known. [27] 'What I tell you in the darkness, speak in the daylight; and what you hear in your ear, proclaim across the housetops. [28] 'And you should not fear those who condemn the body to death, but are not able to condemn *your* life to death.* But you should, rather, revere Him Who is able to destroy both life* and body in the Valley of Hinnom.* [29] Are two sparrows not sold for an assarion?* Not even one from among them will fall on the ground but by the will* of your Father. [30] But even the hairs of your head are all numbered. [31] You should not, therefore, fear. You are of far more worth than many sparrows.* [32] 'Everybody, therefore, who will make a profession concerning me before men, I in turn* will make a profession* concerning* him before my Father in *the* heavens. [33] But whoever denies me before men, I in turn* will deny him before my Father in *the* heavens.

*Families divided over Jesus**

[34] 'Do not think that I came to bring peace over the Earth. I came not to bring peace, but a sword. [35] For I have come to set a man at variance against his father:

"and a daughter against her mother,
and a daughter-in-law
against her mother-in-law,

[36] and the adversaries of the man
will be his own household.'"*

Taking up the 'stake' (σταυρός, stauros)

[37] 'He who loves his father or mother above me is not worthy of me. And he who loves son or daughter above me is not worthy of me. [38] And he who does not take up his stake* and follow after me is not worthy of me. [39] 'He who finds his life will lose it, and he who loses his life on account of me will find it.* [40] 'He who receives you receives me, and he who receives me receives Him Who authorized me. [41] He who receives a prophet in *the* name of a prophet will receive a reward of a prophet,* and he who receives a righteous man in *the* name of a righteous man will receive a reward of a righteous man. [42] And whoever gives just a cup of cold water to drink to one of the lowly* in *the* name of a disciple, truly I say to you, he certainly will not lose his reward.'

*His testimony concerning John**

11\1 **A**nd it came about,* when Jesus had finished giving instructions to* his twelve disciples, *that* he departed from there to teach and to make a proclamation in their cities. [2] But when John in jail heard about the works of the Christ, he sent two of his disciples, [3] *who* said to him, 'Are you the Coming One,* or are we to expect another?' [4] And in answer, Jesus said to them, 'Go *and* relate to John what you hear and see. [5] *The* blind receive sight, and *the* lame walk; lepers are cleansed, and *the* deaf hear;* *the* dead are raised,* and the poor have the gospel proclaimed to them.* [6] And exalted is he who finds nothing to stumble over on account of me.' [7] But when these had gone, Jesus began to say to the crowds concerning John, 'What did you go out into the wilderness to gaze on? A reed swayed by the wind? [8] If not,* what did you go out to see? A man clothed in soft garments? Look, those who wear soft clothing are in the royal houses. [9] If not,* what did you go out to see? A prophet? Yes, I say to you, and surpassing a prophet. [10] For this is about whom it has been written:

"See now, I authorize
My messenger before your face,
who will prepare your way ahead of you."'*

[11] 'Truly I say to you, among those born of women there has not been raised* anybody more eminent than John the Identifier. However, the most lowly* in the Sovereign Rulership of the heavens is more eminent than he *is*.* [12] But from the days of John the Identifier until now the Sovereign Rulership of the heavens forces itself on men's attention,* and *the* forceful are taking hold of it.* [13] For all the prophets and the law prophesied until John.* [14] And, if you are willing to receive *it*, he represents* Elijah who is to come.* [15] He who has ears to hear, let him hear.

[16] 'To what, though, shall I liken this generation? It is like children sitting in marketplaces, and calling to their friends,* [17] and saying:

"We played the flute to you
and you did not dance;
we played a lament to you
and you did not lament."*

[18] 'For John came neither eating nor drinking, and they say, "He has a demon." [19] The Son of Man came eating and drinking, and they say, "Look, a gluttonous man, and an excessive wine drinker, a friend of tax collectors and violators." But wisdom is vindicated* by its children.'

Day of judgement

[20] Then he began to rebuke the cities* in which the majority of his works of power had taken place, because they did not submit: [21] 'Woe to you, Chorazin! Woe to you, Bethsaida! For if the works of power happening among you had taken place in Tyre and Sidon, they would have submitted long ago* in sackcloth and ashes. [22] 'But I say to you, it will be more tolerable for Tyre and Sidon in the day of judgement* than for you. [23] And you, Capernaum, who were exalted up to the sky, will be brought down to *the* grave,* for if the works of power happening among you had taken place in Sodom, it would have remained until this day. [24] But I say to you that it will be more tolerable for *the* land of Sodom in the day of judgement* than for you.'

Praising the Father's will.
Jesus' first statement of his authority (28\18).
Rest for the weary

[25] At that time, in answer Jesus said, 'I thank You, Father, Lord of Heaven and Earth, because You hid these things from *the* sophisticated and cunning, and You have unveiled them to infants. [26] Yes,* Father, for this became well pleasing in Your sight. [27] 'Everything has been handed over to me by* my Father.* And nobody fully knows* the Son except the Father, nor does anybody fully know* the Father except the Son, and he to whomever the Son purposes to reveal *Him*. [28] 'Come to me, all those* growing exhausted* and being heavily laden,* and I will give you rest. [29] Take my yoke on* you, and learn from* me, for I am meek and lowly in heart, and you will find rest for your lives.* [30] For my yoke is easy, and my burden *is* light.'

He rebukes Pharisees
concerning the Sabbath:
the Sabbath was made for man *

12\1 **A**t that time Jesus went on the Sabbath day through the grain fields, and his disciples were hungry, and they began to pluck and eat ears of corn.

[2] But the Pharisees watching said to him, 'Look, your disciples are doing what is not lawful to do on a Sabbath.'

[3] But he said to them, 'Have you not read what David did when he was hungry, and those who were with him, [4] how he went into the House of God and ate the loaves of presentation which were not lawful for him or those with him to eat, except only for the priests? [5] Or have you not read in the law that on the Sabbaths the priests in the Temple profane the Sabbath and are without guilt?*

[6] 'But I say to you that something more splendid than* the Temple is here. [7] But if you were aware of what this means* – "I desire mercy, and not sacrifice"* – you would not have condemned the guiltless. [8] For the Son of Man is Lord of the Sabbath."*

Healing of a withered hand.*
Pharisees conspire against him

[9] And he departed from there *and* went into their synagogue, [10] and it so happened that* there was a man whose hand was withered.

And in order that they might accuse him, they questioned him, saying, 'Is it lawful to heal on the Sabbaths?'

[11] But he said to them, 'What man will there be from among you who will have one sheep, and if it falls into a pit on a Sabbath he will not take hold of it and lift *it* out? [12] Of how much

more worth, then, is a man than a sheep?* Therefore it is lawful to do good on the Sabbaths.'
¹³ Then he said to the man, 'Stretch out your hand.'

And he stretched *it* out, and it was restored, as sound as the other.
¹⁴ But the Pharisees went out *and* held a council against him, as to how they might do away with him. ¹⁵ But Jesus, being aware, withdrew from there, and a vast mass of people followed him, and he healed them all, ¹⁶ and he strictly charged them that they should not make him publicly known, ¹⁷ so that what was spoken through the agency of the prophet Isaiah might be fulfilled, saying:

¹⁸ 'Behold My servant whom I have chosen,
My Richly Loved One*
in whom I Myself* have found delight;
I will put My Spirit* over him
and he will declare judgement to the nations.
¹⁹ He will not contend, nor make an outcry,
nor will anyone in the streets hear his voice.*
²⁰ He will not break a bruised reed
and he will not quench a smouldering flax
until he brings the judgement to a victory,
²¹ and *the* nations will set their hope
in his name.'*

Healing of a blind & dumb man.
Defamation of the Angel of God.
Abundance of the heart.
First mention of the coming Eon (12\32)
²² Then a man under the power of a demon, blind and dumb, was brought to him, and he healed him, so that the blind and dumb man both spoke and saw.
²³ And all the crowds were amazed, and said, 'Is this not the Son of David?'
²⁴ But the Pharisees heard, *and* they said, 'This *man* does not drive out demons except by Beelzebub, ruler of the demons.'
²⁵ But being aware of their thoughts, Jesus said to them, 'Every kingdom divided against itself is reduced* to desolation, and every city or house divided against itself will not stand. ²⁶ And if Satan drives out Satan, he is divided against himself. How, then, will his kingdom stand?
²⁷ 'And if I drive out demons by* Beelzebub, by* whom do your sons drive *them* out? On account of this, they will be your judges.* ²⁸ But if I drive out demons by* the Spirit of God,* it

follows that the Sovereign Rulership of God has been previewed for you.*
²⁹ 'Or otherwise, how is anybody able to enter into the house of the strong man and plunder his belongings, unless he first binds the strong man so that* he can* then plunder his house? ³⁰ He who is not with me is against me, and he who does not gather with me scatters. ³¹ On account of this I say to you, men will be forgiven for every violation and injurious speaking, but for injurious speaking* concerning the Spirit* men will not be forgiven.*
³² 'And whoever speaks a word against the Son of Man it will be forgiven him, but whoever speaks against the Holy Spirit** it will not be forgiven him, neither in this present Eon,* nor in the *Eon* coming.*
³³ 'Either make the tree good and its fruit good, or else make the tree corrupt and its fruit rotten, for the tree becomes known from *the* fruit.
³⁴ 'Progeny of snakes!* How are you, being evil, able to speak good things? For out of the overflow of the heart the mouth speaks. ³⁵ The good man, out of the good treasury of the heart, brings out good things,* and an evil man, out of the evil treasury, brings out evil things.
³⁶ 'But I say to you that, whatever careless word men might speak, they will give an account of it in *the* day of judgement.* ³⁷ For from your words you will be justified, and from your words you will be condemned.'

The sign of Jonah. *Jesus will be buried*
for 3 days & 3 nights, 72 hours.
Scribes & Pharisees condemned.
Result of collaboration with unclean spirits
³⁸ Then some of the scribes and the Pharisees answered, saying, 'Teacher, we want to see a sign from you.'
³⁹ But in answer, he said to them, 'An evil and adulterous generation searches after a sign, and no sign will be given to it except the sign of the prophet Jonah.* ⁴⁰ For just as Jonah was three days and three nights in the belly of the whale,* so will the Son of Man be three days and three nights in the heart of the ground.'* ⁴¹ Ninevite men will stand up in the judgement* with this generation, and they will condemn it, because they submitted at the proclamation of Jonah, and, as you are seeing,* one more important than* Jonah *is* here. ⁴² *The* Queen of *the* South will be raised up in the judgement* with this

generation, and she will condemn it, for she came from the ends of the Earth to hear the wisdom of Solomon, and, as you are seeing, one more important than* Solomon *is* here.

[43] 'But when an unclean spirit has gone from the man, it roams through waterless places, searching for rest, and does not find *it*. [44] Then it says, "I will return to my house where I came out from," and on going back it finds *it* unoccupied, swept clean, and arranged in order.* [45] Then it goes and takes with itself seven other spirits more evil than itself, and they enter in *and* live there, and the final condition of that man becomes worse than the first. It will be like this for this evil generation as well."**

True brothers *

[46]   But while he was still speaking to the crowds, it so happened that* his mother and brothers were standing outside, looking to speak to him.
[47]   Then somebody said to him, 'Look, your mother and your brothers are standing outside, looking to speak to you.'
[48]   But in answer, he said to him who had spoken to him, 'Who is my mother? And who are my brothers?'
[49]   And pointing his hand towards his disciples, he said, 'Here are my mother and my brothers! [50] For whoever does the will of my Father in *the* heavens, he is my brother, and sister, and mother.'

Eight parables of the kingdom, concerning Israel *

13\1 **A**nd on that day, having gone out from the house, Jesus was sitting down beside the sea. [2] And a vast mass of people gathered around him, so he boarded a boat and sat down, and the whole crowd was standing on the shore.

1st parable – the sower *

[3]   And he spoke many things to them in parables, saying, 'Listen.* The sower went out to sow, [4] and in his sowing some *seeds* fell beside the road, and the birds came and devoured them up. [5] And some fell on the rocky places where they did not have much soil, and they immediately sprung up through having no depth of soil, [6] and *when the* Sun rose it was scorched, and through having no root they withered away. [7] And some fell on the thorn bushes, and the thorn bushes sprung up and

choked them. [8] But some fell on the good soil, and yielded fruit, one a hundred-fold, one sixty-fold, one thirty-fold. [9] He who has ears to hear, let him hear.'

Mysteries of the Sovereign Rulership of the heavens.* Judgement on Israel's unbelief, foretold by Isaiah *

[10]   And the disciples came and said to him, 'Why do you speak to them in parables?'
[11]   And in answer, he said to them, 'Because it has been given to you to know the mysteries of the Sovereign Rulership of the heavens, but to them it has not been given. [12] For whoever has, it will be given to him, and he will be made to abound. But whoever does not have, even what he has will be taken from him.[13] Because of this I speak to them in parables, because in seeing they do not see; and in hearing they do not hear; nor do they understand. [14] And against them the prophecy of Isaiah is fulfilled, which says:

"In hearing you will hear
yet in no way will you understand,
and in seeing you will see
yet in no way will you perceive.
[15] For the heart of this people
has grown callous,*
and with the ears they hardly hear
and they have closed their eyes,
in case at any time they should see
with the eyes
and they should hear with the ears
and should understand with the heart
and they would turn
and I would heal them."*

Disciples exalted for believing

[16] 'But exalted* *are* your eyes because they see, and your ears because they hear. [17] For truly I say to you that many prophets and righteous *men* have longed to get a sight of what you are seeing yet they never saw, and to hear what you hear yet they never heard.

Explanation of 1st parable – a sower *

[18]   'You listen, now, to the parable of the sower. [19] When anybody hears the oracle of the Sovereign Rulership* and does not understand *it*, the Evil One* comes along and catches away what was sown in his heart. This represents* him who was sown beside the road. [20] And he who was sown on the rocky places, this

represents* him who hears the oracle and immediately receives *it* and accepts it with gladness, [21] but he has no root in himself, but is unstable,* and on tribulation or persecution arising on account of the oracle he immediately stumbles. [22] And he who was sown among the thorn bushes, this represents* him who hears the oracle, but the anxiety of this Eon* and the deceitfulness of riches choke the oracle, and it becomes unfruitful. [23] But he who was sown on the good soil, this represents* him who hears the oracle and understands, who really bears fruit, and makes yields, one even a hundred-fold, and one sixty-fold, and one thirty-fold.'

2nd parable – wheat & tares
[24] He put another parable to them, saying, 'The Sovereign Rulership* of the heavens is comparable to* a man sowing good seeds in his field. [25] But while the men were sleeping, his enemy* came and sowed tares* between* the wheat,* and he went his way. [26] But when the blade had sprung up and produced fruit, then the tares were seen* as well. [27] The servants of the master of the house came *and* said to him, "Sir, did you not sow good seeds in your field? From where, then, is it infested with* tares?" [28] And he said to them, "A hostile* man did this." And the servants said to him, "Do you wish, then, that we should go and collect them up?" [29] But he said, "No, in case, in collecting together the tares you might root up the wheat with them as well. [30] Let both grow together until the harvest, and at *the* time of the harvest I will say to the reapers, 'First collect up the tares, and fasten them in bundles in order to burn them up. But the wheat bring into my barn.' " '

3rd parable – a mustard seed *
[31] He put another parable to them, saying, 'The Sovereign Rulership* of the heavens is comparable to* a grain of mustard* which a man took *and* sowed in his field, [32] which is smaller than all the seeds,* but when it is grown it is larger than the vegetables,* and it becomes a tree so that the birds of the sky* come and roost in its branches.'

4th parable – leaven *
[33] He spoke another parable to them: 'The Sovereign Rulership of the heavens is comparable to* leaven* which a woman took *and* hid in three measures of meal, until the whole

of it was leavened.'

[34] Jesus spoke all these things to the crowds in parables, and he was not speaking to them without a parable, [35] so that what was spoken through the agency of the prophet might be fulfilled, saying:

'I will open my mouth in parables;
I will speak out things
which have been kept secret
since* *the* foundation* of *the* world order.'**

Explanation of 2nd parable – the tares. *
sons of the kingdom & sons of the Devil
(23\35, John 8\44, 1 John 3\12)
[36] Then Jesus dismissed the crowd *and* went into the house, and his disciples came to him saying, 'Explain* to us the parable of the tares of the field.'
[37] And in answer, he said to them, 'He who sows the good seeds represents* the Son of Man, [38] and the field represents* the world,* and the good seeds represent* the sons of the kingdom.* But the tares represent* the sons of the Evil One,** [39] and the enemy who sowed them represents the Devil, and *the* harvest represents* *the* completion of the Eon,** and the reapers represent* the angels.
[40] 'Just as, therefore, the tares are pulled up and consumed in fire, so will it be at the completion of this Eon.** [41] The Son of Man will authorize his angels, and they will collect up out of his kingdom* all the stumbling blocks and those committing lawlessness, [42] and they will throw them into the furnace of fire.* In that place there will be weeping and gnashing of teeth. [43] Then the righteous* will shine like the Sun in the kingdom of their Father. He who has ears to hear, let him hear.

5th parable – hidden treasure
[44] 'Additionally,* the Sovereign Rulership* of the heavens is comparable to* treasure lying hidden in the field, which a man, having found, hides, and out of the gladness of it he goes and sells everything, as much as he has,* and he buys that field.

6th parable – a pearl
[45] 'Additionally,* the Sovereign Rulership of the heavens is comparable to* a merchant man searching for beautiful pearls, [46] who, having found a single extremely expensive pearl, went

and sold everything, as much as he had, and he bought it.

7th parable – the dragnet (cp. Luke 13\28)
47 'Additionally,* the Sovereign Rulership* of the heavens is comparable to* a dragnet thrown into the sea, and it caught every kind,* 48 which, when it was full, they pulled up onto the shore, and sat down *and* collected up the good *fish* into containers, but the useless *fish* they threw out. 49 So will it be at the completion of the Eon.** The angels will go out and separate the evil from among the righteous, 50 and throw them into the furnace of the fire. There will be weeping and gnashing of teeth.'

8th parable – a householder
51 Jesus said to them, 'Have you understood all these things?'

They said to him, 'Yes, Lord.'
52   Then he said to them, 'Because of this, every scribe discipled into the Sovereign Rulership of the heavens is comparable to* a man *who is* a master of a house, who brings out of his treasure *things* new and old.'

53 And it came about,* when Jesus had finished these parables, *that* he withdrew from there.
54 And *when* he had come into his fatherland, he was teaching them in their synagogue, *causing them* to be so much* struck with astonishment* as to even say,* 'From where *is* this man *getting* this wisdom and the works of power? 55 Is this not the son of the carpenter?* *Is* his mother not called Maria, and his brothers Jacob, and Joses, and Simon, and Judas? 56 And his sisters, are they not all among* us? Where, then, *is* this man *getting* all these things from?'
57 And they took offence at him.

A prophet not without honour *
   But Jesus said to them, 'A prophet is not without honour, except in his fatherland and in his own house.'
58 And he did not do many works of power there because of their unbelief.

Life of John ends in assassination *
14\1 **A**t that time Herod the tetrarch heard of the report concerning Jesus, 2 and he said to his courtiers, 'This is John the Identifier. He has been raised from* the dead, and for that reason the works of power display their force* in him.'

3 For Herod had arrested John, shackled him, and had *him* put in jail on account of* Herodias, the wife of his brother Philip. 4 For John kept saying to him, 'It's not lawful for you to have her.' 5 And he wanted to put him to death, *but* he feared the crowd because they held him as a prophet. 6 But *when* a birth-feast of Herod was being held, the daughter of Herodias danced in their presence and pleased Herod *so much* 7 that he promised with an oath to give her whatever she might ask for.
8   And being previously instigated by her mother, she said, 'Give me here the head of John the Identifier on a dish.'
9 And the king was grieved. Nevertheless, on account of* the oaths and those who sat eating with him, he ordered *it* to be given *to her.* 10 And he sent word* *and* had John beheaded* in the jail. 11 And his head was brought in on a dish, and it was presented to the girl, and she brought *it* to her mother. 12 And his disciples came *and* took the body, and they buried it and went and told Jesus.

The 5,000 *
13 And on hearing *of this*, Jesus withdrew from there in a boat to a deserted place on his own.

   And the crowds having heard him followed him on foot from* the cities. 14 And *when* he went out, Jesus saw a large crowd, and he was moved with compassion towards them, and he healed their infirm.
15   And it having turned to evening, his disciples came to him saying, 'This is a deserted place, and the hour is already late. Send the crowd away so that they might go into the villages *and* buy food for themselves.'
16   But Jesus said to them, 'They do not need to go away. You give them *something* to eat.'
17 But they said to him, 'We have nothing here but five loaves and two fish.'
18 He said, 'Bring them here to me.'
19 He directed the crowds to sit down on the grass, and, taking the five loaves and the two fish *and* looking up into the sky, he exalted* *God*, and after breaking the loaves he gave *them* to the disciples, and the disciples *gave them* to the crowd. 20 And all ate and were satisfied, and they took up the fragments of what was left, twelve hand baskets full. 21 And those who had eaten were about five thousand* men, besides women and children.

He walks over the sea *

²² And at once Jesus compelled the disciples to board the boat and to go ahead of him to the other side, while he sent the crowds away.

²³ And he dismissed* the crowds *and* went up into the mountain on his own to pray,* and *as* evening was approaching he was alone there.

²⁴ But the boat by now was in *the* middle of the sea, buffeted by the waves, for the wind was hostile. ²⁵ And in *the* fourth watch of the night Jesus came to them, walking over the sea.

²⁶ And at seeing him walking over the sea, the disciples were troubled, saying, 'It's an apparition,' and they called out from fear.

²⁷ But at once Jesus spoke to them, saying, 'Be of good courage. I Am.* Do not be afraid.'

²⁸ And in answering him, Peter said, 'Lord, if it is you, command me to come to you over the water.'

²⁹ And he said, 'Come.'

And Peter came down from the boat, *and* he walked over the waters to go to Jesus. ³⁰ But on seeing the boisterous wind, he was frightened, and, beginning to be overwhelmed by the sea, he called out, saying, 'Lord, save me!'

³¹ And straightaway Jesus stretched out *his* hand *and* held onto him, and he said to him, 'You of little faith! Why did you hesitate?'

³² And *as* they went up into the boat, the wind stopped.

³³ Then those in the boat came *and* knelt before* him, saying, 'Truly you are the Son of God.'

Further healings *

³⁴ And they ferried across *the sea, and* they came into the land of Gennesaret. ³⁵ And *when* they recognized him, the men of that place sent an order into all that neighbourhood, and they brought to him all who were diseased, ³⁶ and they asked him that they might only touch the fringe of his garment, and as many who touched *it* were completely cured.

He rebukes traditions of scribes
& Pharisees as contradicting the Scrolls. *
Defiling of a man is internal

15\1 Then the scribes and Pharisees from Jerusalem came to Jesus saying, ² 'Why do your disciples transgress the tradition of the elders? For they do not wash their hands when they eat bread.'

³ But in answer, he said to them, 'Why do you for your part* transgress the commandment of God on account of your tradition? ⁴ For God commanded, saying,* "Honour your father and mother," and, "The one speaking ill of a father or mother, let him be put to death."* ⁵ You, though, say, 'Whoever says to the father or mother, 'Whatever you might be profited from me *is* a gift *dedicated to God*.' " ⁶ And *so* he does not honour his father or his mother at all. So you make void* the commandment of God by your tradition. ⁷ Hypocrites! Well did Isaiah prophesy concerning you, saying:

⁸ "This people approach Me
with their voice
and honour Me with *their* lips,
but their heart keeps
a far distance from Me,
⁹ but they worship Me in vain,
teaching *as* doctrines
the injunctions of men." "*

¹⁰ And he called the crowd, *and* said to them, 'Listen, and understand. ¹¹ What goes into the mouth does not defile the man, but what comes out of the mouth, this defiles a man.'

Parable of the blind leading the blind *

¹² Then his disciples came to him and they said, 'Do you know that the Pharisees were offended at hearing that oracle?'*

¹³ But in answer, he said, 'Every plant which my heavenly* Father did not plant will be rooted up.* ¹⁴ Leave them. They are blind leaders of *the* blind.* And if a blind *man* should lead a blind *man*, both will fall into a ditch.'

¹⁵ And in answer, Peter said to him, 'Explain* this parable to us.'

¹⁶ But Jesus said, 'Are you also still without understanding? ¹⁷ Do you not yet perceive that everything which enters into the mouth goes into the belly, and is expelled into a waste-bowl? ¹⁸ But those things which proceed out of the mouth come out from the heart, and these defile the man.

¹⁹ 'For out of the heart proceed evil reasonings, murders, adulteries, fornications, thefts, false witnessings, blasphemies. ²⁰ These are the things defiling the man, but eating with unwashed hands does not defile the man.'

Healing of a Canaanite woman's daughter *

²¹ And going out from there, Jesus withdrew into the regions of Tyre and Sidon.

[22] And it so happened that a Canaanite woman came out from those regions, *and* she called out to him, saying, 'Have pity on me, Lord, Son of David! My daughter is miserably tormented with a demon.'
[23] But he answered her not a word.

And his disciples came *and* asked him, saying, 'Dismiss her, for she's shouting out after us.'
[24] But in answer, he said, 'I was not authorized except to the lost sheep of *the* house of Israel.'
[25] All the same, she came *and* threw herself at his feet* saying, 'Lord, help me.'
[26] But in answer, he said, 'It's not fair to take the bread of the children and to throw *it* to the little dogs.'
[27] But she said, 'Indeed, Lord, for even the little dogs eat from the scraps which fall from the table of their masters.'
[28] Then answering, Jesus said to her, 'Oh* woman, your faith *is* mighty! Let it be for you just as you wish.'

And her daughter was made whole from that hour.

Many more healed*

[29] And departing from there, Jesus came alongside the Sea of Galilee, and he ascended into the mountain. He was sitting down there, [30] and large crowds came to him, having with them *the* lame, blind, dumb, crippled, and many others, and they laid them down beside the feet of Jesus and he healed them [31] so that the crowds were amazed, seeing *the* dumb speaking, *the* crippled made sound, *the* lame walking, and *the* blind seeing. And they magnified the God of Israel.

The 4,000*

[32] Then Jesus called his disciples, *and* he said, 'I'm filled with compassion for the crowd, because they have continued with me for three days already, and they do not have anything they can eat, and I do not want to send them away hungry, in case they collapse on the road.'
[33] And his disciples said to him, 'Where *could we get* so many loaves from in a remote place, to satisfy so large a crowd?'
[34] And Jesus said to them, 'How many loaves do you have?'

And they said, 'Seven, and a few small fish.'
[35] And he ordered the crowd to sit down on the ground. [36] And he took the seven loaves and the fish, gave thanks, broke *them* up, and gave

them to his disciples, and the disciples *distributed them* to the crowd. [37] And all ate and were satisfied, and of the fragments which were left over they took up seven large lunch baskets full. [38] And those who ate were four thousand* men, besides women and children. [39] And he sent the crowd away, boarded the boat, and he went into the vicinity of Magdala.

Jews demand a sign*

16\1 Then the Pharisees and the Sadducees came testing *him, and* asked him to show them a sign out of Heaven.
[2] And in answer, he said to them, 'When it's evening,* you say, "Fair weather, for the sky is fiery red,"* [3] and in *the* morning, "Today a storm, for the sky is fiery red* *and* sullen." Hypocrites! You certainly know how to discern the face of the sky, but are you not able *to discern* the signs of the times?* [4] An evil and adulterous generation searches after a sign, and a sign will not be given to it except the sign of the prophet Jonah.'

And he left them, *and* departed.

Leaven of Pharisees & Sadducees*

[5] And *when* his disciples came to the far side, they had forgotten to bring loaves.
[6] Then Jesus said to them, 'Be vigilant and guard yourselves from the leaven of the Pharisees and Sadducees.'
[7] And they reasoned among themselves, saying, '*This is* because we took no loaves.'
[8] Perceiving *this*, Jesus said to them, 'Why do you reason among yourselves, you of little faith, that you took no loaves? [9] Do you not yet understand, nor remember the five loaves of the five thousand and how many hand baskets you took up, [10] nor the seven loaves of the four thousand* and how many lunch baskets you took up? [11] How do you not perceive that not concerning bread did I say to you to turn attention away from the leaven of the Pharisees and Sadducees?'
[12] Then they understood that he said to turn away not from the leaven* of bread, but from the teaching of the Pharisees and Sadducees.

Peter's declaration of Jesus as the Son of God.
Peter a 'stone' (πέτρος, petros; John 1\42), Jesus the 'rock' (πέτρα, petra; 1 Cor. 10\4, Rom. 9\33, 1 Peter 2\8, Mat. 7\24-25, Luke 6\48, Isaiah 8\14, 28\16).

The new Christ-authorized Ekklesia (then of Israel only; Ex. 18\25-26, Num. 11\16-17, Psalm 22\22-25 etc.), built on himself as the Messiah

13　And on coming into the regions of Caesarea Philippi, Jesus questioned his disciples, saying, 'Whom do men pronounce me, the Son of Man, to be?'**

14　And they said, 'Some *say* John the Identifier, and others Elijah, and others Jeremiah, or one of the prophets.'

15　He said to them, 'But whom do you pronounce me to be?'**

16　And in answer, Simon Peter said,* 'You are the Christ, the Son of the living God.'

17　And in answer, Jesus said to him, 'Exalted are you, Simon Barjonah, for flesh and blood* has not revealed *it* to you, but my Father in the heavens.

18　And I also say to you that you are a stone,* and on this rock** I will build my* Ekklesia,* and gates of *the* grave** will not overpower it.* 19 And I will give you* the keys of the Sovereign Rulership of the heavens, and whatever you might fasten on the Earth *so* will it be, having been fastened* in the heavens; and whatever you might release on the Earth *so* will it be, having been released* in the heavens.'*

20　Then he ordered his disciples that they should tell nobody that he was Jesus, the Christ.

Jesus to suffer. He again predicts*
his death & resurrection. Rebuke of Peter**

21　From that time on, Jesus began to show his disciples that it was needful for him to depart into Jerusalem, and to suffer many things at the hands of the elders and senior priests and scribes, and to be condemned to death, and to be raised *on* the third day.

22　Then taking him aside, Peter began to rebuke him, saying, '*May God be* merciful to you, Lord!* This will certainly not be for you.'

23　But he turned *and* said to Peter, 'Get behind me, adversary!* You're a snare to me, for you are not directing your mind on the things of God, but *on* the things of men.'

True discipleship. No death*
*for some until the signs of the Acts period**

24　Then Jesus said to his disciples, 'If anybody is willing to come after me, let him deny himself and take up his stake,* and let him follow me.

25　'For whoever might desire to save his life will lose it, and whoever might lose his life* on account of me will find it.*

26　'For what is a man profited if he should gain the whole world but lose his life? Or what will a man give in exchange for his life?* 27 For the Son of Man is going to come in the magnificence of his Father* with his angels, and then he will give reward to each in keeping with his works.

28　'Truly I say to you, there are some standing here who will most certainly not taste death until* they see the Son of Man having appeared in his Sovereign Rulership.'*

His radiance shown
in the transformation.
*Voice out of a cloud**

17\1 And after six days, Jesus took alongside *him* Peter and Jacob and his brother John, and he brought them alone up into a high mountain. 2 And he was transformed before them, and his face shone like the Sun, and his clothing became as white as the light. 3 And to their amazement* Moses and Elijah were seen* by them, talking together with him.

4　And in reaction, Peter said to Jesus, 'Lord, it's good for us to be here.* If you would like, let us make three booths here, one for you, and one for Moses, and one for Elijah.'

5　While he was still speaking, surprisingly a radiant cloud overshadowed them, and at that moment a voice out of the cloud said, 'This is My Son, the Richly Loved One,* in whom I have found delight. Listen to him.'

6　And on hearing *that*, the disciples fell face-down, and they were extremely terrified.

7　And Jesus approached, *and* touched them, and said, 'Rise up, and do not be terrified.'

8　And on lifting their eyes they saw nobody, except Jesus alone.

*His sufferings explained. Elijah comes first**

9　And as they were coming down from the mountain, Jesus instructed them, saying, 'Tell the vision to nobody, until the Son of Man has risen from among* the dead.'

10　And his disciples asked him, saying, 'Why, then, do the scribes say that Elijah must come first?'

11　And in answer, Jesus said to them, 'Elijah does indeed come first, and he will restore* all things. 12 However, I say to you, Elijah has already come, and they did not recognize him, but they did in his case* whatever they pleased.

In the same way, the Son of Man also is about to suffer by them.'
[13] Then the disciples understood that he spoke to them concerning John the Identifier.

Healing of a lunatic son *
[14] And *when* they had drawn near the crowd, a man approached him, kneeling down to him, and saying, [15] 'Lord, have pity on my son, for he's an epileptic* and suffers severely, for he frequently falls into the fire, and frequently into the water, [16] and I brought him to your disciples, and they were unable to cure him.'
[17] And in answer, Jesus said, 'Oh* unbelieving and perverse generation! How long will I be with you? How long can I* put up with you? Bring him here to me.'
[18] And Jesus rebuked it, and the demon departed away from* him, and the boy was cured from that hour.
[19] Then the disciples came to Jesus alone, *and* they said, 'Why were we not able to drive it out?'
[20] And Jesus said to them, 'On account of your unbelief. For truly I say to you, if you have faith like a grain of mustard seed *and* say to this mountain, "Move from here to there," even that will move, and nothing will be impossible for you. [21] However, this kind does not go out except by prayer and fasting.'

He again predicts his death & resurrection *
[22] And while they were staying in Galilee, Jesus said to them, 'The Son of Man is about to be given into *the* hands of men, [23] and they will murder him, and on the third day he will be raised up.'
And they were exceedingly filled with grief.

Taxes from a fish's mouth
[24] And *when* they had come to Capernaum, those *who* take the double-drachma* came to Peter, and they said, 'Does your Teacher not pay the double-drachma?'
[25] He said, 'Yes.'
And when he went into the house, Jesus anticipated him, saying, 'What do you think, Simon? From whom do the kings of the Earth receive tax or tribute,* from their own sons, or from the outsiders?'*
[26] Peter said to him, 'From the outsiders.'*
Jesus said to him, 'Consequently,* the sons are freemen.* [27] Nevertheless, so that we should not give them offence, go to the sea, cast out a hook, and take the fish coming up first, and on your opening its mouth you will find a silver coin.* Take that to give to them for me and for yourself.'

Receiving the Sovereign Rulership of the heavens like children. *Offences against children* *
18\1 In that hour the disciples came to Jesus, saying, 'Who, then, is the more eminent in the Sovereign Rulership of the heavens?'
[2] And Jesus called a little child *and* set him at the focus of their attention,* [3] and he said, 'Truly I say to you, unless you turn and become like little children, you will by no means enter into the Sovereign Rulership of the heavens.
[4] Whoever, therefore, abases himself like this little child is more eminent in the Sovereign Rulership* of the heavens. [5] And whoever will receive such a child in my name receives me.
[6] But as for whoever might cause offence to one of these little ones* who believe in me, it would be more profitable for him that a millstone turned by a donkey should be hung around his neck, and he were drowned in the depth of the sea.
[7] Woe to the world because of offences! For it must be that offences come. Yet woe to that man* by means of whom the offence comes!
[8] And if your hand or your foot keeps on causing you to offend, cut them off and throw *them* away from you. It's better for you to enter into life maimed or crippled, rather than having two hands or two feet *and* to be thrown into the Eonian* fire. [9] And if your eye keeps on causing you to offend, pluck it out and throw *it* from you, for it's better for you to enter into life one-eyed, rather than having two eyes to be thrown into the fire of the Valley of Hinnom.*
[10] Take care you do not despise one of these little ones, for I say to you that their angels in *the* heavens continually behold the face of my Father in the heavens. [11] For the Son of Man has come to save that which was lost.

Parable of a lost sheep *
[12] What do you think? If a man should have a hundred sheep and one of them has gone astray, does he not leave the ninety-nine on the mountains *and* go looking for the one which has gone astray? [13] And if it should be that he finds it, truly I say to you that he rejoices more over it than over the ninety-nine which have not gone astray. [14] Likewise, it is not *the* desire

of your Father in *the* heavens that one of these little ones should suffer destruction.

Rebuke & reconciliation under the authority
of the Mosaic-instituted legislative assembly
for Israel (Ex. 18\25-26),
represented in Jesus' day
by the Christ-authorized apostles
¹⁵ 'In addition, if your brother commits a violation* against you, go and rebuke* him between yourself and him alone. If he will hear you, you have won your brother over. ¹⁶ But if he will not hear *you*, take one or two more with you, so that by the mouth of two or three witnesses every word might stand.* ¹⁷ If, though, he fails to listen to them, tell the legislative assembly,* but if he fails to listen to the legislative assembly* as well, let him be to you like the foreigner and the tax collector.
¹⁸ 'Truly I say to you, whatever you might fasten on the Earth *so* will it be, having been fastened* in Heaven; and whatever you might release on the Earth *so* will it be, having been released* in Heaven.
¹⁹ 'Again, truly I say to you, that if two of you might agree on the Earth concerning any matter, whatever they might ask, it will be done for them by my Father in *the* heavens. ²⁰ For where two or three are gathered together in my name,* there am I in their company.'**

Peter's question. Forgiveness
in the future 70 times 7 (490) years
in Daniel 9\24-27 which is the coming Eon
& the kingdom of God
²¹ Then Peter came up to him, *and* he said, 'Lord, how often shall my brother commit a violation against me and I should forgive him? Up to seven times?'
²² Jesus said to him, 'I say to you, not up to seven times, but up to seventy times seven.*

Parable of the king's accounts.
Forgiveness under law (see 6\14)
²³ 'On account of this, the Sovereign Rulership* of the heavens was likened to a man, a king, who wanted to settle up an account with his servants. ²⁴ And *when* he had begun to make settlement, a debtor of ten thousand talents* was brought to him. ²⁵ But having nothing to make payment *with*, his master ordered him* to be sold, with his wife and children and everything, as much as he had, and repayment to be made. ²⁶ So the servant fell down *and*

bowed his knee to him, saying, "*My* lord, have patience with me, and I will repay you everything."
²⁷ 'And moved with compassion, the master of that servant released him, and forgave him the debt.
²⁸ 'But the same servant went out *and* found one of his fellow servants who was owing him a hundred denarions,* and he seized him and began throttling *him*, demanding, "Pay me what you owe!" ²⁹ And his fellow servant fell down at his feet, imploring him, saying, "Have patience with me, and I will repay you everything." ³⁰ But he refused, and he went off *and* threw him into jail until he would pay what was owing. ³¹ But seeing what things had taken place, his fellow servants were exceedingly grieved, and they went *and* narrated to their master everything that had happened. ³² Then his master called him, *and* he said to him, "You wicked servant! I forgave you all that debt because you begged me. ³³ Was it not binding on you also to have had mercy on your fellow servant, just as I also had mercy on you?" ³⁴ And in anger, his master give him into the hands of the torturers* until he would pay everything which was owing to him.
³⁵ 'So will my heavenly* Father* likewise do to you, if every one of you does not from your hearts forgive* his brother his trespasses.'

In Judea, more crowds healed *

19\1 ＡＮＤ it came about, when Jesus had finished these oracles, *that* he withdrew from Galilee and came into the regions of Judea beyond the Jordan. ² And vast masses of peoples followed him, and he healed them there.

Dispute with Pharisees
concerning marriage
& divorce under law *
³ Then the Pharisees came to him, testing him, and saying to him, 'Is it lawful for a man to put away his wife on account of any cause?'*
⁴ But in answer, he said to them, 'Have you not read that He *Who* created *them* from the beginning* created* them a male and a female, ⁵ and He said, "For this reason,* a man will leave *his* father and mother, and he will be joined to* his wife, and the two will become* one flesh,"* ⁶ so that no longer are they two, but one flesh? That, therefore, which God has

paired together, let man not break apart.'

⁷ They said to him, 'Why, then, did Moses command to give a scroll* of divorce, and to put her away?'*

⁸ He said to them, 'Moses, in view of your hardness of heart, permitted you to put away your wives, but from *the* beginning* it was not like this. ⁹ But I say to you, whoever might put away his wife, except for fornication, and might marry another, commits adultery,* and whoever might marry her *who is* put away commits adultery.'

¹⁰ His disciples said to him, 'If this is the case of the man with the wife, it is not advantageous to marry.'

¹¹ But he said to them, 'Not all make room for this oracle, except those to whom it has been given. ¹² For there are eunuchs who were born that way from *their* mother's womb, and there are eunuchs who were made eunuchs by men, and there are eunuchs who made themselves eunuchs* because of* the Sovereign Rulership of the heavens.* The one able to accept *this*, let him accept *it*.'

Receiving little children in his name *

¹³ Then young children were brought to him, so that he might lay hands on them and pray,* but the disciples reprimanded them.

¹⁴ But Jesus said, 'Leave the little children,* and do not forbid them to come to me, for the Sovereign Rulership of the heavens is of this kind.'

¹⁵ And after laying hands on them, he moved on* from there.

A rich young ruler. *
First mention of 'Eonian life'
in Matthew (Dan. 12\2, Psalm 133\3)

¹⁶ And then it came about that somebody approached him, *and* he said, 'Good Teacher, what good thing should I do so that I might have Eonian* life?'

¹⁷ And he said to him, 'Why do you call me good? Nobody *is* good except one, God. But if you want to enter into *Eonian* life, keep the commandments.'

¹⁸ He said to him, 'Which ones?'

And Jesus said, 'You shall not commit murder. You shall not commit adultery. You shall not steal. You shall not bear false testimony. ¹⁹ Honour *your* father and mother. And you shall love your neighbour as yourself.'*

²⁰ The young man said to him, 'All these have I kept since my youth. What do I still fall short in?'

²¹ Jesus said to him, 'If you are wishing to be* perfect, go *and* sell your property, and give to *the* poor, and you will have treasure in Heaven.* Then come *and* follow me.'

²² But *when* he heard that saying, the young man went away grieving, for he had many possessions.

The eye of a needle *

²³ Then Jesus said to his disciples, 'Truly I say to you that with difficulty a rich man will* enter into the Sovereign Rulership of the heavens. ²⁴ And additionally* I say to you, it's easier *for* a camel* to pass through an eye of a needle than for a rich man to enter into the Sovereign Rulership of God.'*

²⁵ And *when* they heard, his disciples were exceedingly struck with astonishment, saying, 'Who, then, can be saved?'

²⁶ But looking straight at *them*, Jesus said to them, 'With men this is impossible, but with God all these things *are* possible.'

Disciples' future seats of government
in 'New Jerusalem' (Rev. 21\5, 21\12-14).
Receiving a hundred-fold & Eonian life *

²⁷ Then in answer, Peter said to him, 'Look, we have abandoned* everything and followed you. What, then, will we have?'

²⁸ And Jesus said to them, 'Truly I say to you that you who have followed me will also, in the making new of all things* at the time *when* the Son of Man will have taken his seat on the throne of his magnificence, sit down on twelve thrones,* ruling over* the twelve tribes of Israel.* ²⁹ And everybody who has forsaken houses, or brothers, or sisters, or father, or mother, or wife, or children, or lands on account of my name will receive a hundred-fold, and they will inherit Eonian* life.

Parable of a vineyard

³⁰ 'But many first will be last, and *the* last first.*

20\1 **F**or the Sovereign Rulership of the heavens is comparable to a man, a master of a house, who went out at dawn to hire labourers for his vineyard. ² And having agreed with the labourers a denarion* for a day, he ordered them into his vineyard. ³ And he went out at about *the* third hour, *and* he saw others standing idle in the marketplace, ⁴ and he said to them,

"You go into the vineyard as well, and I will pay you whatever is right." ⁵ So* they went their way.**

'He went out again at about *the* sixth and *the* ninth hour, *and* he did the same. ⁶ And about the eleventh hour he went out *and* found other *men* standing idle, and he said to them, "Why have you been standing around here idle all day long?" ⁷ They said to him, "Because nobody has hired us." He said to them, "You also go into the vineyard, and whatever is due you will receive."

⁸ 'But when evening came, the lord of the vineyard said to his foreman, "Call the labourers and pay them the wage, beginning from *the* last to the first." ⁹ And *when* those who *were hired* at about the eleventh hour came, they received a denarion each. ¹⁰ And *when* the first came, they were reckoning that they would receive more, but they themselves also received a denarion each. ¹¹ And *when* they had received *it*, they kept murmuring against the master of the house, ¹² saying, "These last have worked one hour, and you have made them equal to us who have borne the burden and the scorching heat of the day."

¹³ 'But in answer, he said to one of them, "Friend, I do you no injustice. Did you not agree with me for a denarion? ¹⁴ Take up yours, and go your way. But I want to give to this last one in turn* the same that *I gave* you. ¹⁵ Or is it not lawful for me to do what I want in what *are* my own affairs? Is your eye grudging because I am generous?"

¹⁶ 'Likewise, the last will be first, and the first last, for many are designated, but few chosen.'*

He again predicts his death & resurrection *

¹⁷ And Jesus, going up to Jerusalem, took the twelve disciples on their own on the road, and he said to them, ¹⁸ 'Look, we are going up to Jerusalem, and the Son of Man will be given into the hands of the senior priests and scribes, and they will condemn him to death, ¹⁹ and they will give him into the hands of the nations to mock and to scourge *him*, and to hang *him* on a stake,* and on the third day he will be raised.'*

Answer to the mother of the sons
of Zebedee: an overwhelming into death *

²⁰ Then the mother of the sons of Zebedee came to him with her sons, kneeling,* and asking something from him.

²¹ And he said to her, 'What do you want?'

She said to him, 'Say that these two sons of mine might sit, the one at your right hand, and the other at the left hand, in your Sovereign Rulership.'

²² But in answer, Jesus said, 'You have no idea what you are asking for. Are you able to drink from the cup which I am about to drink, and to be flooded with the overwhelming which I am about to be flooded with?'

They said to him, 'We are able.'

²³ And he said to them, 'You can* drink my cup, and you will be flooded *with* the overwhelming which I am about to be flooded* *with*,* but to sit at my right hand and at my left hand is not for me to give, but *is* for whom it has been prepared by my Father.'

²⁴ And *when* the ten heard, they were annoyed with the two brothers.

²⁵ But Jesus called them, *and* he said, 'You know that the rulers of the other nations lord it over them, and the high-ranking* stamp down their authority on them. ²⁶ It will not, however, be like that among you. Rather, whoever wants to become* eminent among you will be your servant.* ²⁷ And whoever wants to be* first among you must be* your servant, ²⁸ just as the Son of Man came not to be served, but to serve, and to give his life* *as* a redemption price in the place of many.'

Healing of two blind men *

²⁹ And as they were departing from Jericho a large crowd followed him. ³⁰ And it came about that *when* two blind *men* sitting at the roadside heard that Jesus was walking by they called out, saying, 'Have pity on us, Lord, Son of David!'

³¹ But the crowd told them to be quiet, but they kept calling out all the more, saying, 'Have pity on us, Lord, Son of David!'

³² And Jesus stopped *and* called them, and he said, 'What do you want *me* to do for you?'

³³ They said to him, 'Lord, that our eyes might be opened.'

³⁴ So Jesus, moved with compassion, touched their eyes, and instantly their eyes regained sight, and they followed him.

His first entry into Jerusalem *

21\1 **A**nd then when they drew near Jerusalem and arrived in Bethsphage, at the Mount of Olives, Jesus sent off two disciples, ² saying to them, 'Go ahead into the village facing you, and you will at once find a donkey tied, and a colt˚ with her. Untie *them and* bring *them* to me, ³ and if anybody says anything to you say, "The Lord has need of them," and he will send˚ them right away."

⁴   But all this arose so that what was spoken through the agency of the prophet might be fulfilled, saying:

⁵   'Say to the daughter of Zion,
"See, your King comes to you,
meek and mounted on a donkey and a colt,
the foal of a yoked donkey." ˚

⁶ And the disciples went and did as Jesus ordered them, ⁷ *and* they led the donkey and the colt, and put their garments on them, and he took his seat on them. ⁸ And a vast crowd˚ spread their outer garments on the road, and others were cutting down branches from the trees and spreading *them* out on the road.
⁹ And the crowds who were going ahead and those following were calling out, saying:

'Hosanna to the Son of David!
Exalted˚ *is* the Coming One˚
in *the* name of *the* Lord!
Hosanna in the highest *realms*!"˚˚

¹⁰   And as he went into Jerusalem, the whole city was stirred, saying, 'Who is this?'
¹¹   And the crowd kept saying,˚ 'This is Jesus, the Prophet,˚ the one from Nazareth of Galilee.'

Cleansing the Temple ˚
¹²   And Jesus went into the Temple of God, and he threw out all those selling and buying in the Temple, and he overthrew the tables of the money changers and the benches of those selling doves.
¹³   And he said to them, 'It has been written:

"My House will be called
the House of Prayer;
you, though, have made it
a cave˚ of bandits." "˚˚

¹⁴ And *the* lame and blind came to him in the Temple, and he healed them.
¹⁵ And *when* the senior priests and scribes saw the wonders which he performed, and the children calling out in the Temple and saying, 'Hosanna to the Son of David!', they were incensed, ¹⁶ and they said to him, 'Do you hear

what these are saying?'
And Jesus said to them, 'Yes. Have you never˚ read:

"Out of the mouth of babies˚ and sucklings
You have established praise"?"˚

¹⁷   And he left them, *and* went outside the town into Bethany, and he passed the night there.

Cursing a fig tree ˚
¹⁸   Now early in the morning, on his coming back into the town, he was hungry.
¹⁹   And on seeing a particular fig tree on the road, he came up to it and found nothing on it except just leaves, and he said to it, 'May there no longer be fruit from you throughout the Eon.'"˚
    And the fig tree instantly dried up.
²⁰   And at seeing *that*, the disciples were amazed, saying, 'How instantly the fig tree has dried up!'˚
²¹   And in answer, Jesus said to them, 'Truly I say to you, if you have faith and do not doubt, you will not only perform that thing of the fig tree, but if you say even to this mountain, "Be removed, and be hurled into the sea!", it will happen,²² and all things, whatever you might ask in prayer believing, you will receive.'˚

Teaching in the Temple. Confrontation
over his authority & John's identifying the people ˚
²³   And when he went into the Temple, the senior priests and the elders of the people came to him *as he was* teaching, saying, 'By what kind of authority do you do these things, and who gave you this authority?'
²⁴   And in answer, Jesus said to them, 'I in turn˚ will ask you one question, for which, if you answer me, I in turn˚ will tell you by what authority I do these things. ²⁵ The identification of John, where was it from – from Heaven,˚ or from˚ men?'
    And they reasoned with themselves, saying, 'If we should say, "From˚ Heaven,"' he will say to us, "Why, then, did you not believe him?" ²⁶ But if we should say, "From men," we fear the multitude, for all consider John as a prophet.'
²⁷   And in answering Jesus, they said, 'We do not know.'
    And he in turn˚ said to them, 'Nor do I tell you by what authority I do these things.
²⁸   'But what do you think? A man had two

children, and he came to the first, *and* said, "Son, go and work today in my vineyard," [29] and in answer, he said, "I choose not *to go*," but he regretted* *it* afterwards *and* he went. [30] And coming to the second, he said the same. And in answer, he said, "I go, sir," but did not go. [31] Which out of the two did the will of *his* father?'

They said to him, 'The first.'*

Jesus said to them, 'Truly I say to you that the tax collectors and the prostitutes go into the Sovereign Rulership of God ahead of you. [32] For John came to you in *the* way of righteousness, and you did not believe him, but the tax collectors and the prostitutes believed him.* But you, having seen, did not afterwards submit to believe him.

Parable of vine dressers *

[33] 'Hear another parable. A certain man was a landlord who planted a vineyard, and he erected a fence round it, and dug a winepress in it, and he built a tower, and rented it out to farmers, and took a journey abroad.* [34] And when the season of the fruits drew near, he assigned his servants to the farmers to gather up his fruits. [35] 'And the farmers seized his servants, *and* one they flogged, and one they murdered, and one they stoned. [36] Again, he assigned more servants, more numerous than the first, and they did the same to them. [37] But later he assigned his own son to them, saying, "They will stand in awe of my son." [38] But the farmers, seeing the son, said among themselves, "This is the heir. Come, let's murder him and take possession of his inheritance." [39] And they caught hold of him, and threw *him* outside the vineyard, and they murdered *him*.* [40] So when the lord of the vineyard comes, what will he do to those farmers?'

[41] They said to him, 'He will bring *those* evil men to a wretched end, and let *his* vineyard out to other farmers of such character that they will give him the fruits in their seasons.'

[42] Jesus said to them, 'Did you never read in the Scrolls:*

"*The* stone which the builders rejected
this came to be for *the* head of *the* corner;
this came about* from *the* Lord
and it is a wonder in our eyes."?'*

[43] 'Because of this, I say to you, the kingdom of God will be taken away from you, and it will be given to people* producing its fruits. [44] And whoever falls on this stone* will be shattered. But on whomever it falls, it will crush him into powder.'*

[45] And the senior priests and Pharisees, hearing his parables, came to know that he was speaking about them. [46] But in looking to arrest him, they feared the crowds, because they were taking him for a prophet.

Parable of a wedding feast of the son of a king *

22\1 And in answer, Jesus spoke to them again in parables, and he said, [2] 'The Sovereign Rulership of the heavens is like a man *who was* a king, who arranged a wedding feast for his son, [3] and he ordered his servants to call those who had been invited to the wedding feast, but they would not come.

[4] 'Again, he sent more servants, saying, "Say to those who had been invited, 'Look, I have prepared my dinner. My oxen and fattened animals *are* slaughtered, and everything *is* ready. Come to the wedding feast.'" [5] But not making much of it, they went their ways, one to his own field, another to his commerce, [6] and the rest seized his servants *and* treated *them* insolently and murdered *them*. [7] But *when* the king heard *of it* he was enraged, and he sent out his armies *and* destroyed those murderers, and he burned up their city. [8] Then he said to his servants, "The wedding feast is ready, but those who were invited were not worthy. [9] So go out on the thoroughfares of the public roads, and invite to the wedding feast as many whom you find."

[10] 'So those servants went out into the highways, *and* gathered everybody together, as many whom they found, both evil and good, and the wedding feast became filled with guests.

[11] 'And *when* the king came in to gaze on the guests, he saw a man there not clothed with a garment for a wedding feast, [12] and he said to him, "Friend, how did you come in here not wearing a wedding garment?" And he was speechless. [13] Then the king said to the servants, "Bind his feet and hands, *and* take him away and throw *him* into the outer darkness. In that place there will be weeping and gnashing of teeth."

[14] 'For many are designated, but few chosen.'*

Confrontation concerning census tax *

[15] Then the Pharisees went *and* laid plans for

how they might trap him in a discourse.
[16] And they sent their own followers to him with the Herodians, saying, 'Teacher, we know that you are truthful, and you teach the way of God in truth, and it does not concern you about anybody, for you disregard the status* of men.
[17] 'Tell us, therefore, what is your opinion? Is it lawful to give tribute* to Caesar, or not?'
[18] But perceiving their evil, Jesus said, 'Why do you test me, hypocrites? [19] Show me the coin of the census tax.'

And they brought a denarion to him.
[20] And he said to them, 'Whose image and inscription *is* this?'
[21] They said to him, 'Caesar's.'

Then he said to them, 'Render, therefore, to Caesar the things of Caesar,* and to God the things of God.'
[22] And *when* they heard *this* they were astounded, and they left him *and* went their way.

Confrontation with Sadducees
concerning events in the day of resurrection *
[23] On that same day, the Sadducees, those alleging there not to be* a resurrection, came to him and questioned him, [24] saying, 'Teacher, Moses said, "If anybody should die having no children, his brother shall marry his wife as the next of kin,* and he shall raise up seed for his brother."* [25] Now, there were seven brothers with us, and the first, having married, died, and, having no seed, left his wife to his brother [26] – in the same way the second also, and the third, to the seventh, [27] and at last the woman also died. [28] So in the resurrection, whose wife will she be of the seven? For they all had her.'
[29] But in answer, Jesus said to them, 'You are in error, not knowing the Scrolls, nor the power of God.* [30] For in the resurrection they neither marry, nor are given in marriage, but are like the angels of God in Heaven.*
[31] 'But concerning the resurrection of the dead, did you not read what was spoken to you by God, saying, [32] "I am* the God of Abraham, and the God of Isaac, and the God of Jacob?*" God is not the God of *the* dead, but of *the* living." *
[33] And *when* they heard, the crowds were struck with astonishment at his teaching.

Testing by a lawyer:
the most important commandment in the law *
[34] But when the Pharisees heard that he had put the Sadducees to silence, they gathered themselves together, [35] and one of them, a scholar in the law,* asked, putting him to the test, saying, [36] 'Teacher, what kind of commandment *is* the most important in the law?*'
[37] And Jesus said to him, 'You shall love *the* Lord your God in all your heart, and in all your being, and in all your mind.* [38] This is *the* first and most important commandment. [39] And *the* second *is* like it: You shall love your neighbour as yourself.* [40] On these two commandments hang the whole law and the prophets.'

Testing the Pharisees
concerning the line of David *
[41] But when the Pharisees were assembled together, Jesus questioned them, [42] saying, 'What do you think concerning the Christ? Whose son is he?'

They said to him, 'David's.'
[43] He said to them, 'How then does David, *speaking* by means of *the* Spirit,* call him Lord, saying:

[44] "The Lord said to my Lord,
'Sit at* My right hand*
until I make your enemies
a footstool for your feet' "?*

[45] 'If, then, David calls him "Lord", how is he his son?'
[46] And nobody was able to answer him a word, nor did anybody from that day on dare to question him any longer.

Rebuking crowds & disciples that they observe
& 'put into practice' (ποιεῖτε, poyeite, indicative)
falsehoods taught by the imposter rulers
who stole the seat of Moses (Joshua 15\63 etc.);
Jesus commanding 'do not put into practice'
(ποιεῖτε, poyeite, imperative) their things,
reflected in 'keep away from the leaven of the Pharisees
and Sadducees' (Mat. 16\6, Mark 8\15,
Acts 5\28, 5\42). Eight woes against imposters.
Their liability to destruction in the fire
of 'the Valley of Hinnom' (γέεννα, gehenna),
equivalent of Hebrew גיא הנם (ge hinnom),
(Josh. 15\8, 2 Kings 23\10, Jer. 7\31-32, 32\35,
Psalm 106\37-38, 2 Chron. 33\1-9 etc.)

23\1 Then Jesus spoke to the crowds and to his disciples, [2] saying, 'The scribes and the Pharisees have taken their place on the seat of Moses, [3] so everything which they command you to observe you do observe* and you do put into practice.* But do not put into practice* in line with their works, for they speak but they do not put into practice.* [4] For they tie up burdens, heavy and difficult to bear, and they lay *them* on men's shoulders, but they do not choose to touch them with a finger of their own. [5] But they do all their works for the purpose of being gazed at* by men. And they make their phylacteries broad, and enlarge the fringes of their garments, [6] and they like the prime seats* in the feasts, and the prime seats in the synagogues, [7] and the formal greetings in the marketplaces, and to be called by men "Rabbi, Rabbi".

One Teacher – the Messiah,
one Father – God in the heavens

[8]　'But do not be called "Rabbi", for one is your guide, the Christ. And you are all brothers. [9] And do not call *anyone* on the Earth your father, for one is your Father, the one in the heavens. [10] Neither be called guides, for one is your guide, the Christ. [11] But the most eminent among you will be your servant. [12] And whoever exalts himself will be abased, and whoever abases himself will be exalted.

[13]　'But woe to you, scribes and Pharisees, hypocrites! For you devour the houses of widows, and for a pretence you pray at enormous length. On account of this, you will receive a stronger judgement.*

[14]　'Woe to you, scribes and Pharisees, hypocrites! For you shut up the Sovereign Rulership of the heavens in men's faces, for you neither go in, nor do you allow those entering to go in.*

[15]　'Woe to you, scribes and Pharisees, hypocrites! For you go around sea and dry *land* to make one proselyte,* and when it's done you make him twice as much a son of the Valley of Hinnom* as yourselves.

[16]　'Woe to you, blind guides saying, "Whoever swears by the Sanctuary, it's nothing, but whoever swears by the gold of the Sanctuary is bound!" [17] You fools and blind *men*! For which is more important, the gold, or the Sanctuary which sanctifies the gold?

[18]　'And *you say*, "Whoever swears by the altar, it's nothing, but whoever swears by the gift which is on it, he's guilty." [19] Fools and blind men! For which *is* more important, the gift, or the altar which sanctifies the gift? [20] Whoever, therefore, swears by the altar, swears by it and by all things on it. [21] And he who swears by the Sanctuary swears by it and by Him Who inhabits it. [22] And he who swears by Heaven swears by the throne of God, and by Him Who sits on it.

[23]　'Woe to you, scribes and Pharisees! Hypocrites! For you tithe mint and dill and cummin, and you have left aside the weightier things of the law – judgement, mercy, and faith. It is right to carry out these, and not be leaving aside those other things.

[24]　'Blind guides, filtering out the gnat, but gulping down the camel!

[25]　'Woe to you, scribes and Pharisees, hypocrites! For you ceremonially cleanse the outside of the cup and the dish, but inside they are full of plunder and injustice. [26] Blind Pharisee! First cleanse the inside* of the cup and dish, so that the outside of them might become clean as well.

[27]　'Woe to you, scribes and Pharisees, hypocrites! For you are like whitened tombs* which appear outwardly beautiful, but inside are full of bones of *the* dead and all uncleanness. [28] So do you also appear outwardly righteous to men, but inside you are full of hypocrisy and lawlessness.

[29]　'Woe to you, scribes and Pharisees, hypocrites! For you found the tombs of the prophets and decorate the monuments of the righteous, [30] and you say, "If we had been around in the days of our fathers, we would not have been partakers with them in the blood of the prophets," [31] so that you give witness against yourselves that you are sons of those who murdered the prophets. [32] Fill up,* then, the measure of your fathers!* [33] Snakes! Progeny of vipers!* How can you escape from the judgement* of the Valley of Hinnom?*

[34]　'On account of this, you understand,* I authorize for you prophets and sophisticated men and scribes, and some of them you will murder and hang on a stake,* and some of them you will scourge in your synagogues and persecute from town to town, [35] so that against you might come all righteous blood poured out on the Earth, from the blood of the righteous Abel to the blood of Zechariah,* son of Berechiah, whom you murdered* between the Sanctuary and the altar.

[36]　'Truly I say to you, all these things will come against this generation.*

His prophecy of the destruction of Jerusalem

37 'Jerusalem, Jerusalem, murdering the prophets and stoning those who have been sent to her! How often would I have gathered together your children, in the way that a bird gathers together her chicks under the wings,* but you have not been willing!

38 'See now, your house is being left to you desolate. 39 For I say to you, you will by no means see me from now until you will say:

"Exalted* *is* the Coming One,*
in *the* name of *the* Lord." '*

Prophecy of destruction of the Temple.
Answering the disciples' three questions
concerning the last days & the mighty tribulation,
the pseudo Christ, & Jesus' return
& 'magisterial presence' (παρουσία, *parousia*)
as the true Christ in power & radiance

24\1 ▊nd Jesus went out *and* departed from the Temple, and his disciples came to point out to him the buildings of the Temple.

2 But Jesus said to them, 'Do you not see all these things? Truly I say to you, there will not be left here stone on stone* which is not going to be demolished.'*

3 And as he was sitting on the Mount of Olives, the disciples came to him alone, saying, 'Tell us, when will these things be, and what *will be* the sign of your magisterial presence,* of, that is,* the completion of the Eon?'**

Answer to the first question:
'when will these things be?' (Mark 13\5)

4 And in answer, Jesus said to them, 'Watch *that* nobody should lead you adrift. 5 For many will come trading on* my name, saying, "I am the Christ,"** and they will deceive many. 6 But you will be about to hear of battles and rumours of battles.* Be vigilant *and* do not be terrified, for these things have to come to pass,* but the end is not yet.

Answer to the second question: 'what will be
the sign of your magisterial presence?' (Mark 13\8)

7 'For nation will be roused against nation, and kingdom against kingdom,* and there are going to be famines, and pestilences, and earthquakes in various places. 8 But these *are* a beginning of birth-pangs.

9 'Then they will hand you over into tribulation, and they will murder you,* and you will be hated by all the nations on account of my name.

10 'And then many will be made to stumble,** and they will hand each other over, and they will hate each other. 11 And many pseudo prophets* will be raised up, and they will deceive many. 12 And because of lawlessness being multiplied, the love of many* will grow cold. 13 But the one having endured until *the* end will be preserved. 14 And this gospel of the Sovereign Rulership will be proclaimed in all the inhabited world* with a view to a testimony to all the nations. And then the end will come.

15 'When, therefore, you see the Abomination of Desolation,* which was spoken of through the agency of the prophet Daniel, standing in *the* holy place – he who reads, let him observe attentively – 16 then those in Judea should flee into the mountains.* 17 The one on the rooftop should not come down to take his things out of his house, 18 and the one in the field should not turn behind to collect his clothes.* 19 But woe to those who are pregnant, and to those breastfeeding in those days!* 20 But pray that your flight might not occur in the winter, nor on a Sabbath day.

21 'For then there will be a mighty tribulation, the like of which has not arisen from *the* beginning of *the* world* until this time, no, and nor will it by any means arise *again*. 22 And if those days were not shortened, no flesh would be preserved. For the sake of the elect, though, those days will be cut short.*

23 'Then if anybody will say to you, "Look,* here *is* the Christ!" or "There!", do not believe *it*. 24 For pseudo christs* and pseudo prophets* will be raised up, and they will perform impressive signs and wonders, in order, if possible, to deceive even the elect.*

25 See,* I have told you ahead of time. 26 So if they say to you, "Look, he's in the desert," do not go out, *or* "Look* in the private rooms," do not believe *it*. 27 For just as the lightning comes from *the* East, and flashes as far as *the* West, so also will be the magisterial presence* of the Son of Man.* 28 For wherever there might be a carcass, there the eagles will be gathered together.

Answer to the third question:
'completion of the Eon'

29 'But immediately after the tribulation of those days, the Sun will be darkened,* and the Moon will not give its lustre,* and the stars* will

fall from the sky,* and the powers of the skies will be shaken.*

30 'And then the sign of the Son of Man* will blaze in the sky,* and then all the tribes of the land will mourn, and they will see the Son of Man coming on the clouds* of Heaven* with power and immense magnificence.* 31 And he will authorize his angels with a loud-sounding trumpet,* and they will gather together his chosen out of* the four winds, from one end of *the* skies* to *the other* end of them.**

Parable of a fig tree *

32 'Now learn the parable from the fig tree. When its branch has already become supple* and it puts out leaves, you come to know that the summer *is* near. 33 So you, in the same way, when you see all these things, you must understand that it is near, at *the* doors.

34 'Truly I say to you, this generated oracle* will by no means pass away until* all the things such as these arise. 35 Heaven* and the Earth will pass away,* but my oracles will certainly not pass away.

Rebellion as in the days of Noah.*
Return &*'magisterial presence'* (παρουσία, *parousia*) of Jesus with clouds of angels.
The righteous to be with Jesus (John 14\3)

36 'But concerning that day and hour, nobody has any intuitive knowledge – not even the angels of the heavens** – except My Father* alone.

37 'But just as the days of Noah, so also will be the magisterial presence* of the Son of Man.* 38 For just as in the days before the flood, they were eating and drinking, marrying and giving in marriage, until the day Noah went into the ark, 39 and they did not come to know until the flood came and wiped everybody out,* so also will be the magisterial presence* of the Son of Man.

40 'Then two will be in the field; the one will be taken, and the other will be left. 41 Two *women will be* grinding in the mill; one will be taken, and the other will be left.*

42 'Be watchful,* therefore, for you do not have any intuitive knowledge of what time your Lord comes. 43 But know this: that if the master of the house had intuitively known in which watch the thief was coming, he would have been on guard and not allowed his house to be broken into.

44 'On account of this, you also must become ready, for the Son of Man comes in an hour which you do not expect.

Parable of a faithful servant

45 'Who, then, is the faithful and wise servant whom his master has made ruler at the head of his household, to give them food in due season? 46 'Exalted *is* that servant whom his master, in his coming, will find doing this. 47 Truly I say to you, he will make him ruler in charge of all his property. 48 But if that evil servant should say in his heart, "My master delays to come," 49 and should begin to beat the fellow servants, and to eat and drink with the drunkards, 50 the master of that servant will come in a day in which he does not expect, and in a hour he is not aware of, 51 and he will cut him in two, and assign his portion with the hypocrites. In that place there will be weeping and gnashing of teeth.

Parable of 10 virgins * in a time
of darkness * before the return of Jesus

25\1 'At that point, the Sovereign Rulership of the heavens will be likened to ten virgins who, having taken their torches,* went out to meet the bridegroom. 2 But five of them were prudent, and five foolish. 3 Those being foolish, having taken their torches, took no oil with them, 4 but the wise took oil in their containers with their torches.

5 'But the bridegroom lingered, *and* they all became drowsy and went to sleep. 6 But in *the* middle of the night an uproar* arose: "Look,* the bridegroom's coming! Come out to meet him." 7 Then all those virgins were woken and they trimmed their torches. 8 But the foolish ones said to the wise ones, "Give us some of your oil, because our torches are being snuffed out."

9 'The wise *virgins,* though, answered, saying, "In case there is not enough for us and for you, you rather, though, go for yourselves to those who sell and buy." 10 But as they went their way to make the purchase the bridegroom came, and those ready went in with him to the wedding feast, and the door was shut.

11 'Afterwards the other virgins came as well, saying, "Lord, lord, open for us." 12 But in answer, he said, "Truly I say to you, I do not know you." 13 Watch therefore, for you know neither the day nor the hour in which the Son of Man comes.

Parable of the talents *

[14] 'For *this is* as if a man travelling on a journey abroad* called his own servants and handed over his property to them. [15] And to one he gave five talents,* and to another two, and to another one, to each according to his own ability, and he at once took a journey abroad.*

[16] 'Then the one receiving the five talents went *and* traded with them, and he made five additional talents. [17] And similarly, the one *receiving* the two also gained two more. [18] But the *servant* receiving the one went off and dug in the ground, and hid his master's money.

[19] 'And after a long time the master of those servants came and compared accounts with them. [20] And so the one receiving the five talents came *and* brought five additional talents, saying, "Master, you handed me five talents. Look, I have gained five more talents in addition to those." [21] And his master said to him, "Well done, good and faithful servant! You have been faithful over a few things. I will appoint you over many things. Enter into the joyfulness* of your master."

[22] 'And the one receiving the two talents also came *and* said, "Master, you handed me two talents. Look, I have gained another two talents in addition to those." [23] His master said to him, "Well done, good and faithful servant! You have been faithful over a few things. I will set you ruler over many things. Enter into the joyfulness of your master."

[24] 'The one receiving the one talent also came *and* said, "Master, I came to know you, that you are a hard man, reaping where you did not sow, and gathering where you did not scatter, [25] and, being afraid, I went off *and* hid your talent in the ground. Look, have *what is* your own." [26] In answer, his master said to him, "Evil and slothful servant! You knew that I reap where I did not sow, and gather where I did not scatter. [27] You ought, in that case, to have put my money with the bankers so that* on my return I should have received back my own with interest. [28] So take the talent away from him, and give *it* to him who has the ten talents. [29] For to everybody who has it will be given, and he will be in abundance. But from him who does not have, even what he does have will be taken away from him. [30] Then throw the unprofitable servant into the outer darkness. In that place there will be weeping and gnashing of teeth."

At the end of the 490 year Eon:
judgement of other nationalities in Israel,
according to how they treated Jesus' brothers
(12\49-50, 28\10,
Rom. 8\29, Heb. 2\11, 2\17) *

[31] 'But when the Son of Man comes in his magnificence, and all the holy angels with him,* then he will sit on a governmental seat of his magnificence,* [32] and all the nations* will be assembled* before him, and he will separate them off from one another, as the shepherd separates the sheep off from the goats. [33] And he will set the sheep on his right, but the goats* on* *the* left. [34] Then the king will say to those on his right, "Come, those having been favoured,* *and* belonging to my Father, inherit the kingdom* prepared for you from* *the* foundation* of *the* world order.* [35] For I was hungry and you gave me food. I was thirsty and you gave me drink. I was a stranger and you took me in. [36] I had little clothing* and you clothed me. I was sick and you visited me. I was in jail and you came to me."

[37] 'Then the righteous will answer him, saying, "Lord, when did we see you hungry and feed *you*, or thirsting and give *you* drink? [38] When did we see you a stranger and take *you* in, or having little clothing and we clothed *you*? [39] Or when did we see you sick, or in jail and visit you?"

[40] 'And in answer, the king will say to them, "Truly I say to you, as much as you have done for even one of the least of these brothers of mine,* you have done for me."

[41] 'Then he will say in turn* to those from *the* left hand side, "Depart from me, you under a curse,* into the Eonian* fire* which has been prepared for the Devil and his angels.* [42] For I was hungry and you gave me nothing to eat. I was thirsty and you gave me nothing to drink. [43] I was a stranger and you did not take me in, having little clothing but you did not clothe me, sick and in jail but you did not visit me."

[44] 'Then they too will answer, saying, "Lord, when did we see you hungry, or thirsty, or a stranger, or having little clothing, or sick, or in jail, and we did not provide for you?" [45] Then he will answer them, saying, "Truly I say to you, as much as you did not do for one of the least of these, neither did you do *it* for me." [46] And these will go away into Eonian punishment,* but the righteous* into Eonian* life.'*

Conspiracy against Jesus by priests, scribes, & elders *

26\1 𝔄nd it came about, when Jesus had finished all these oracles, *that* he said to his disciples, ² 'You know that after two days comes the Passover, and the Son of Man will be handed over* to be hanged on a stake.'*

³ Then the senior priests and the scribes and the elders of the people assembled together in the hall of the high priest, who was called Caiaphas, ⁴ and they consulted together so that they might seize Jesus by trickery and murder *him.* ⁵ But they said, 'Not during the Festival, so that there might not be any uproar among the people.'

Second anointing
with precious ointment at Bethany *

⁶ Now on Jesus being in Bethany, in Simon the leper's house, ⁷ a woman came to him holding an alabaster flask of precious ointment, and on his having sat down she poured *it* over his head. ⁸ But *when* his disciples saw they became indignant, saying, 'Why this waste? ⁹ For this ointment could have been sold for a large sum of money and given to *the* poor.' ¹⁰ But perceiving *this,* Jesus said to them, 'Why do you cause trouble for this woman? For she has performed an excellent deed for me. ¹¹ For you always have the poor with you, but you do not always have me. ¹² For in pouring this ointment on my body, she did *it* for my embalming. ¹³ Truly I say to you, wherever this gospel will be proclaimed in all the world, this also which she has done will be recounted in memory of her.'*

Conspiracy by Judas *

¹⁴ Then one of the twelve, who was called Judas Iscariot, went to the senior priests, ¹⁵ *and* he said, 'What are you willing to give me, so that I will give him into your hands?'

And they weighed out* for him thirty pieces of silver. ¹⁶ And from that time he was looking for an opportunity to give him into their hands.

Jesus' final Passover. The betrayer condemned *

¹⁷ Now on the first *day* of the Unleavened Bread, the disciples came to Jesus, saying to him, 'Where would you like us to prepare for you to eat the Passover?'*

¹⁸ And he said, 'Go into the city to our good friend,* and say to him, "The Teacher says, 'My time is at hand. I will celebrate the Passover at

your house with my disciples.' " '

¹⁹ And the disciples did as Jesus directed them, and they prepared the Passover.

²⁰ And when evening came, he sat down with the twelve. ²¹ And as they ate, he said, 'Truly I say to you, one of you will betray me.'

²² And being exceedingly sorrowful, each of them began to say to him, 'Lord, am I *the one?*'

²³ But in answer, he said, 'He who dipped *his* hand with me in the dish will betray me. ²⁴ The Son of Man goes as it has been written concerning him, but woe to that man by means of whom the Son of Man is betrayed! It would have been better for that man if he had not been born.'

²⁵ Then in answer, Judas, who was going to be betraying him, said, 'I am not *the one, am I,* Rabbi?'

He said to him, 'You yourself said *it.*'*

Jesus announces the new covenant for the houses
of Israel & Judah (Jer. 31\31),
the broken bread & the cup representing
his body & blood, broken & poured out
for many, fulfilling the Passover lamb,
& he looks forward to the Eon
& the new Passover feast (Lev. 23\5) *

²⁶ And as they were eating, Jesus took bread, *and* having given thanks* he broke *it* up and gave *it* to the disciples, and he said, 'Take *and* eat. This represents* my body.'*

²⁷ And he took the cup and having given thanks* he gave *it* to them, saying, 'Drink out of it, all of you. ²⁸ For this represents* my blood of the new covenant, which is poured out for many for forgiveness of violations. ²⁹ But I say to you, I will by no means drink from this fruit of the vine from this time until that day when I drink a new kind of it with you in the kingdom of my Father.'

³⁰ And *when* they had sung a psalm, they went off into the Mount of Olives.

He predicts the disciples' flight & Peter's denial *

³¹ Then Jesus said to them, 'All of you will stumble because of me during this night. For it has been written:

"I will strike the shepherd,
and the sheep of the flock
will be scattered."'*

³² 'But after my being raised,* I will go ahead of you* into Galilee.'

³³ But in answer, Peter said to him, 'If all will stumble because of you, I will never stumble.'

³⁴ Jesus said to him, 'Truly I say to you, in this night, before a rooster crows, you will deny me three times.'

³⁵ Peter said to him, 'Even if it were needful for me to die together with you, I will certainly not deny you.'

And all the disciples in turn* said the same.

Agony in Gethsemane *

³⁶ Then Jesus arrived with them at a locality called Gethsemane, and he said to the disciples, 'Sit here, while I go over there *and* pray.'*

³⁷ And he took along with him Peter and the two sons of Zebedee, *and* he began to be full of anguish and to be distressed.

³⁸ Then Jesus said to them, 'My inner being* is crushed with anguish, even to the point of death. Remain here, and be watchful with me.'

³⁹ And he went on a little further *and* fell on his face, praying, and saying, 'My Father, if it is possible, let this cup pass away from me. Nevertheless, not as I will, but as You *will.*'

⁴⁰ And he came to the disciples and found them composed for sleeping, and he said to Peter, 'So did you not have the strength to watch with me *for* one hour? ⁴¹ Watch and pray so that you do not enter into temptation.* The spirit *is* willing, but the flesh *is* weak.'

⁴² He went away again the second time, *and* he prayed,* saying, 'My Father, if it is not possible for this cup to pass from me unless I drink it, may Your will be done.'

⁴³ And he came *and* again found them composed for sleeping, for their eyes were heavy. ⁴⁴ And he left them, *and* went away again, and he prayed a third time,* saying the same words.

⁴⁵ Then he came to his disciples, and said to them, 'Are you still* sleeping and taking your rest?* Look, the hour has drawn near,* and the Son of Man will be betrayed into *the* hands of violators. ⁴⁶ Rise up, *and* let us be going. Look, he who is going to betray me has made his way here.'*

Arrest of Jesus.* He heals Malchus

⁴⁷ And while he was still speaking, along came* Judas, one of the twelve, and with him a large mob with swords and clubs, from the senior priests and elders of the people.

⁴⁸ Now he who betrayed him had arranged a signal with them, saying, 'He whom I embrace is the one. Seize him.' ⁴⁹ And he at once went to Jesus, and said, 'Greetings, Rabbi!', and he ostentatiously kissed* him.

⁵⁰ And Jesus said to him, 'Friend,* *do* what you have come for.'

Then they came *and* took hold of Jesus, and seized him. ⁵¹ And then one of those with Jesus drew back *his* hand *and* unsheathed* his sword, and he struck the servant of the high priest *and* took off his earlobe.

⁵² Then Jesus said to him, 'Return your sword to its place, for all who take up *the* sword will die by *the* sword. ⁵³ Or do you think that I am not even now able to call on my Father and He will instantly send me more than twelve legions of angels? ⁵⁴ How, then, will the Scrolls be fulfilled that it has to come about in this way?'

⁵⁵ In that same hour Jesus said to the crowds, 'Have you come out as if against a bandit* with swords and clubs to take me? I used to sit among you daily teaching in the Temple, and you did not seize me. ⁵⁶ But all this has arisen so that the Scrolls of the prophets might be fulfilled.'

Then all the disciples forsook him and fled.

His examination & mocking
before the high priest Caiaphas *

⁵⁷ And those who had seized Jesus led *him* away to Caiaphas, the high priest, where the scribes and the elders had assembled together. ⁵⁸ But Peter followed him from a distance, as far as the hall of the high priest, and he went in *and* sat with the officers to see out the end.

⁵⁹ Now the senior priests and elders and the whole Sanhedrin were looking for false evidence against Jesus, so that they might put him to death, ⁶⁰ but they found none. And even though many false witnesses came forward, they did not find *any evidence.*

However, at last two false witnesses came forward, ⁶¹ and they declared, 'This *man* said, "I can demolish the Sanctuary of God,* and rebuild it within three days." '

⁶² And the high priest stood up, *and* said to him, 'Do you not give any answer? What do these testify against you?'

⁶³ But Jesus continued maintaining his peace.

And in response, the high priest said to him, 'I put you on your oath by the living God that you tell us if you are the Christ, the Son of God.'

⁶⁴ Jesus said to him, 'You yourself said *it.* However, I say to you, in the future[*] you will see the Son of Man sitting at[*] *the* right hand[*] of power,^{**} and coming among the clouds[*] of the heavens.'[*]
⁶⁵ Then the high priest tore his robe apart, saying, 'He has spoken blasphemy! What further need do we have of witnesses? Look, now we have heard his blasphemy. ⁶⁶ What do you think?'

And in answer, they said, 'He's deserving of death.'[*]
⁶⁷ Then they spat in his face, and struck him with their fists, and others slapped *him* with the palms of their hands, ⁶⁸ saying, 'Prophesy to us, Christ! Who is it who is striking you?'

Peter's denial[*]
⁶⁹ Now Peter was sitting outside in the courtyard, and a servant girl came to him, saying, 'You also were with Jesus the Galilean.'
⁷⁰ But he made a denial in the presence of everybody, saying, 'I do not know what you are saying.'
⁷¹ And *when* he had gone out into the porch another *girl* saw him, and she said to those who were there, 'This *man* also was with Jesus the Nazarene.'[*]
⁷² And he again made a denial with an oath, *saying,* 'I do not know the man.'
⁷³ And after a short while those who were standing around came forward *and* said to Peter, 'Surely you are from them as well, for even your dialect[*] gives you away.'
⁷⁴ Then he began to curse and to swear, 'I do not know the man.'

And immediately a rooster crowed, ⁷⁵ and Peter remembered the words of Jesus who had said to him, 'Before a rooster crows you will deny me three times.'

And he went outside *and* wept bitterly.

Delivered into the hands of Pilate

27\1 And when morning came, all the senior priests and elders of the people took counsel together against Jesus about *how* they might murder him. ² And they bound him, *and* led *him* away, and gave him into the hands of Pontius Pilate, the governor.

Judas' remorse but not submission to God
³ Then Judas, who had betrayed him, having seen that *Jesus* was condemned, *and* being seized with remorse, returned the thirty pieces of silver to the senior priests and elders, ⁴ saying, 'I have violated, having betrayed innocent blood.'

But they said, 'What *is that* to us? See to *that* yourself.'
⁵ And having tossed[*] the pieces of silver in the Sanctuary, he withdrew, and went off *and* hanged himself.'^{**}
⁶ And the senior priests took the silver pieces, *and* said, 'It's not lawful to put them into the treasury, since they are *the* price of blood.'
⁷ And having taken counsel, they bought[*] with them the Potter's Field as a burial ground for foreigners. ⁸ So to this day that field is called the Field of Blood.[*] ⁹ Then that which was spoken by the prophet Jeremiah[*] was fulfilled, saying, 'And I took the thirty pieces of silver, the price of him on whom a value had been fixed, *he* on whom those from *the* sons of Israel had fixed a value, ¹⁰ and they gave them for the Potter's Field, in keeping with what *the* Lord appointed me.'[*]

Examination before Pilate.[*]
Crowd prefers Barabbas.
Pilate admonished by his wife.
Pilate washes his hands & releases Barabbas
& delivers Jesus to be assassinated
¹¹ But Jesus stood in front of the governor, and the governor questioned him, saying, 'Are you the King of the Jews?'

And Jesus said to him, 'You yourself said *it.*'
¹² And while he was being accused by the senior priests and the elders, he answered nothing.
¹³ Then Pilate said to him, 'Do you not hear how many things they testify against you?'
¹⁴ And he did not answer him so much as one word, so as to extremely astound the governor.
¹⁵ Now at a[*] Festival, the governor was accustomed to release one prisoner to the crowd, whomever they wanted.
¹⁶ And they had at that time a notorious prisoner called Barabbas, ¹⁷ so when they were gathered together, Pilate said to them, 'Whom do you choose I should release to you, Barabbas, or Jesus, called Christ?'
¹⁸ *He said this* because he was aware that they had handed him over on account of malice.
¹⁹ But as he was sitting on the judgement seat, his wife sent a message to him saying, 'Have nothing to do with[*] that righteous man, for I

suffered many things today in a dream because of him.'

20 Nevertheless, the senior priests and elders persuaded the crowds that they should ask for Barabbas, and they should put Jesus to death.

21 And in answer, the governor said to them, 'Which of the two do you want me to release to you?'

And they said, 'Barabbas.'

22 Pilate said to them, 'What shall I do, then, with Jesus, they call Christ?'

They all said to him, 'Let him be hanged on a stake!'*

23 And the governor said, 'Why? What evil did he commit?'

But they kept calling out all the more, saying, 'Let *him* be hanged on a stake!'*

24 And *when* Pilate saw he was getting nowhere, but, rather, an uproar was rising, he took water *and* washed *his* hands in front of the crowd, saying, 'I am guiltless from the blood of this righteous man. You see *to it.*'

25 And in answer, all the people said, '*Let* his blood *be* on us, and on our offspring.'*

26 Then he released Barabbas to them, but having scourged Jesus he handed *him* over so that he might be hanged on a stake.*

Crown of thorns.* Death

27 Then the soldiers of the governor took Jesus into the Judgement Hall,* *and* gathered the whole cohort against him. 28 And they stripped him, *and* put a scarlet robe on him. 29 And they wove a crown of thorns *and* put *it* on his head, and *they put* a reed in his right *hand*, and bowing down before him they mocked him, saying, 'Hail, King of the Jews!', 30 and they spat at him, *and* took the reed and kept beating at his head.

31 And after they had mocked him, they took the robe off him, and put his garments on him, and led him away in order to hang *him* on a stake.*

32 And they went out *and* came across* a man of Cyrene, Simon by name, *and* they compelled this *man* to carry his stake.*

33 And they came to a place called Golgotha, which is called Place of a Skull, 34 *and* they gave him vinegar to drink mingled with gall, and *when* he had tasted from *it* he would not drink *it.*

35 And they began hanging him on a stake,* *and* they shared out his garments, throwing lots.*

36 And they sat down *and* kept guard over him there, 37 and they put up over his head his written accusation: 'This is Jesus, the King of the Jews'.*

38 Then two bandits* were hanged on stakes* together with him, one on the right, and another on *the* left.*

39 And those who passed by blasphemed him, wagging their heads, 40 and saying, 'You demolishing the Temple, and rebuilding *it* in three days, save yourself! If you are the Son of God, come down off the stake.'*

41 And in the same way the senior priests, also mocking together with the scribes and elders and Pharisees, said, 42 'He saved others. He's not able to save himself. If he is the King of Israel, let him come down off the stake* now, and we will believe him. 43 He trusted in God – let Him rescue him now, if He wants* him, seeing that he said, "I am *the* Son of God." '

44 And the bandits* as well, who were hanged on stakes with* him, kept reproaching him.*

45 Now from *the* sixth hour, there was darkness over all the land until *the* ninth hour.

46 And at about the ninth hour Jesus shouted out with a loud voice, saying, 'Eli, Eli, lama sabachthani?'* – which is to say, 'My God, my God, why have You forsaken me?'*

47 And some of those who were standing there, *when* they heard, said, 'He's calling for Elijah.'

48 And one of them at once ran up and took a sponge, and soaked *it* with vinegar and put *it* on a reed, and he was going to offer* *it* to him to drink, 49 but the rest said, 'Leave *him* alone. Let's see whether Elijah is coming to save him.'

Graves of dead holy people opened
(*John 5\25*). Declaration of centurion *

50 And shouting out again with a loud voice,* Jesus yielded up *his* spirit.* 51 And at that moment* the veil of the Sanctuary was torn into two from top to bottom, and the land suffered an earthquake,* and rocks were split, 52 and tombs were opened, and many bodies of the holy people fallen asleep were raised,* 53 and they came out of the tombs after his resurrection, *and* they went into *the* Holy City and they were seen by many.

54 And *when* the centurion and those with him who kept guard over Jesus saw the earthquake and the things that had happened, they were tremendously frightened, saying, 'Truly this was the Son of God.'

55 And there were many women there, watching from a distance, who had followed

Jesus from Galilee providing for him, [56] among whom was Maria Magdalene, and Maria the mother of Jacob and Joses, as well as the mother of the sons of Zebedee.

His burial by Joseph of Arimathea *
[57] And when evening came, a wealthy man from Arimathea named Joseph, who was himself also discipled to Jesus, [58] went to Pilate *and* asked for the body of Jesus. Then Pilate ordered for the body to be handed over, [59] and Joseph, having taken the body, wrapped it in a clean linen cloth, [60] and laid it in his own new monument* which he had cut out in the rock, and he rolled a big stone to the entrance of the tomb, *and* he went his way.
[61] And Maria Magdalene was there, and the other Maria, sitting opposite the burial place.

[62] Now the next day, which is after the Preparation,* the senior priests and Pharisees came together to Pilate, [63] saying, 'Your Excellency,* we have been reminded that while he was still alive that deceiver* said, "After three days I am raised."* [64] So order the burial place to be made secure until the third day, in case his disciples, coming by night, might steal him away and say to the people, "He has been raised* from the dead," and the last deception* will be worse than the first."*
[65] Then Pilate said to them, 'You can have a guard. Go and make *it* as secure as you know how.'
[66] So they went along and made the burial place secure, sealing the stone in the presence of the guard.

His resurrection declared to the two Marias by the Angel of God. Jesus appears to them*

28\1 Now at the end* of the Sabbaths,* in the dawning into *the* First of Weeks,* Maria Magdalene and the other Maria came to gaze at the burial place. [2] And a mighty earthquake broke out,* for *the* Angel of *the* Lord,* descended from* Heaven, came *and* rolled back the stone, away from the door, and he was sitting on it. [3] His appearance was like lightning, and his garment as white as snow. [4] And those keeping guard shook for fear of him, and they became as if dead.
[5] But the Angel* answered and said to the women, 'Do not fear, for I know that you are looking for Jesus who has been hanged on a stake.* [6] He is not here, for he has been raised,* just as he said. Come *and* see the place where the Lord lay. [7] And go quickly *and* say to his disciples that he has been raised* from the dead, and, as you will see, he will go ahead of you* into Galilee. You will see him there. See,* I have told you.'
[8] And going off in a hurry from the tomb with fear and immense exuberance, they ran to bring word to his disciples.
[9] However, as they were going to tell his disciples, it came about that Jesus met* them, saying, 'Greetings!'*
And they went up to him *and* seized hold of his feet, and they were kneeling before* him.
[10] Then Jesus said to them, 'Do not be afraid. Go *and* announce to my brothers* that they can go into Galilee and they will see me there.'

Priests' & elders' bribing of the soldiers
[11] And as they were going, some of the guard then went off into the city *and* told the senior priests all the things that had happened.
[12] And they assembled together with the elders, and held counsel, *and* gave a sufficient sum of silver to the soldiers, [13] telling them, 'Say that his disciples came by night *and* stole him away, ourselves being asleep.[14] And if this comes to the ears of the governor, we will satisfy him and keep you out of trouble.'
[15] So taking the money, they did as they had been instructed, and this account has been widely circulated by the Jews up to the present day.

All authority conferred on Jesus (11\27).
Authorization of the 11 to travel the world
in the future Eon & disciple entire nations
to come under the government of God & Christ
(Isaiah 11\10, Mat. 12\21, Rom. 15\12).
The new names of the Father
& of Jesus (Phil. 2\9, Rev. 3\12, 19\12)
& of the Angel of God (Judges 13\18)
to be revealed in that time
[16] The eleven disciples, however, made their way into Galilee to the mountain where Jesus had appointed* them. [17] And on seeing him, they knelt before* him, although some hesitated.
[18] And Jesus approached them, *and* spoke to them, saying, 'All authority in Heaven and on Earth has been given to me. [19] In going out,* disciple all the nations, relating* them into the name of* the Father,* and of the Son,* and of

the Holy Spirit,** [20] teaching them to observe all
things which I have commanded you. And, as
you will see, I am with you all the days,* until
the completion of the Eon.*** Amen."

~ ◆◆ ~

† The Gospel Accounts of Jesus Christ †

Mark

The 'beginning of the gospel' (Luke 1\2, John 1\1).
Proclamation of John the Identifier: two types
of identification with God, water & spirit

1\1

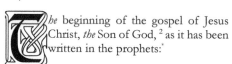

he beginning of the gospel of Jesus Christ, *the* Son of God, [2] as it has been written in the prophets:

'See, I am authorizing My messenger
before your face
who will prepare your way ahead of you,
[3] a voice of one calling out in the wilderness,
"Prepare the way of *the* Lord;
make straight His paths." '

[4] John arose, making identifications in the desert, and proclaiming an identification of submission for *the* forgiveness of violations. [5] And the whole province of Judea and those of Jerusalem kept going out to him, and they were all identified by him in the River Jordan, pouring out their violations.
[6] Now John was clothed in camel hair and with a leather belt round his waist, and he fed on locusts and wild honey.
[7] And he would make a proclamation, saying, 'He who comes after me *is* mightier than me, the buckle of whose sandals I am not worthy to stoop down to unfasten. [8] It is true that I identified you in water, but he will identify you in *the* divine spirit.'

Identification of Jesus with the submissive
in the water ritual John received from God
& the appearance of the Angel of God. Fasting.
Testing of Jesus in wilderness by the Devil
[9] And it arose in those days *that* Jesus came from Nazareth of Galilee, and he was identified by John in the Jordan.
[10] And immediately on going up from the water, he saw the skies being split open, and the Spirit coming like a dove down over him, [11] and a voice came out of the skies: 'You are My Son, the Richly Loved One, in whom I have found delight.'
[12] And immediately the Spirit sent him out into the wilderness. [13] And he was there in the

wilderness *for* forty days, being tested by Satan, and he was with the wild animals, and angels attended to him.

John arrested. Proclamation by Jesus
of the Sovereign Rulership of God
[14] Now after John had been arrested, Jesus came into Galilee proclaiming the gospel of the Sovereign Rulership of God, [15] and saying, 'The time has been fulfilled, and the Sovereign Rulership of God has drawn near. Submit, and believe in the gospel.'

Disciples called
– Andrew, Simon and Jacob
[16] Then as he was walking beside the Sea of Galilee, he saw Simon and Andrew, the brother of Simon, casting a small net in the sea, for they were fishermen.
[17] And Jesus said to them, 'Come after me, and I will appoint you to become fishers of men.'
[18] And they at once forsook their nets, *and* followed him.
[19] And *when* he had moved on a little from there, he saw Jacob, the *son* of Zebedee, and his brother John, as they were in a boat mending the nets. [20] And he straightaway called them, and they left their father Zebedee in the boat with the hired servants, *and* they went away following him.

The teaching of Jesus is with authority.
Healing of a man with an unclean spirit
[21] Then they came to Capernaum, and at once on the Sabbath, having entered the synagogue, he began teaching. [22] And they were struck with astonishment at his teaching, for he taught them as one having authority, and not like the scribes.
[23] Now in their synagogue there was a man with an unclean spirit, and he called out, [24] saying, 'Leave *us* alone! What is our business with you, Jesus, Nazarene? Have you come to destroy us? I know you, who you are – the Holy One of God.'
[25] And Jesus rebuked it, saying, 'Be quiet, and come out of him.'
[26] And when the unclean spirit had thrown him into convulsions and yelled with a shriek, it came out of him.
[27] And they were all astounded, so much as to question among themselves, saying, 'What does this mean? What new teaching *is* this where he

commands with authority even* the unclean spirits and they obey him?'
²⁸ And immediately the report of him spread throughout all the region around Galilee.

Healing of Peter's mother-in-law *
²⁹ And as soon as they had come out of the synagogue, they went in the house of Simon and Andrew with Jacob and John.
³⁰ But the mother-in-law of Simon was laid up sick with a fever, and they straightaway told him about her, ³¹ and he went to *her and* took her hand *and* helped her up, and the fever instantly left her, and she began waiting on them.

Many healings.
His proclamation throughout Galilee *
³² And when evening came *and* the Sun went down, they kept bringing to him all who were diseased, including those under the power of demons. ³³ And all the town was congregated at the door, ³⁴ and he healed many who were badly sick with various diseases, and he drove out many demons, and he would not allow the demons to speak because they had knowledge of him.
³⁵ And rising quite early at night, he went out and departed into a deserted place, and he was praying there. *
³⁶ And Simon and those with him followed after him, ³⁷ and *when* they found him they said to him, 'Everybody is looking for you.'
³⁸ And he said to them, 'Let's go into the neighbouring towns, so that I might make a proclamation there as well, because for this I have come.'
³⁹ And he was making a proclamation in their synagogues throughout all Galilee, as well as driving out demons.

Healing of a leper *
⁴⁰ And a leper came to him, begging him and kneeling down to him, and saying to him, 'If you are willing, you are able to cleanse me.'
⁴¹ And Jesus, being moved with compassion, reached out his hand, touched him, and said to him, 'I am willing. Be cleansed.'
⁴² And at his having spoken, the leprosy instantly departed from him, and he was cleansed.
⁴³ And he warned him strongly, *and* immediately sent him away, ⁴⁴ and he said to

him, 'See to it that you do not speak anything to anybody, but go and show yourself to the priest, and for your cleansing offer for a testimony to them those things which Moses commanded.'
⁴⁵ But he went off *and* began to publicize *it* with many words* and to spread the matter, *and* as a result *Jesus* was no longer able to openly enter* into any town, but was outside in deserted places, and they kept coming to him from every quarter.

Healing of a paralytic
& forgiveness of violations *
2\1 Then some days later he went again into Capernaum, and it was reported that he was in a house. ² And at once many gathered together, for *them* to no longer have* room, not even through the door, and he was declaring the oracle to them. ³ And they came to him, bringing along a paralyzed man being carried by four *men*. ⁴ And *when* they were not able to approach him because of the crowd, they uncovered the roof where he was, and *when* they had broken the roof up they lowered the stretcher which the paralyzed man was lying on.
⁵ And Jesus, seeing their faith, said to the paralytic, 'Son, you have been forgiven for your violations.'
⁶ But some of the scribes were sitting there and reasoning in their hearts: ⁷ 'Why does this *man* speak blasphemies? Who is able to forgive violations except one – God?'
⁸ And instantly perceiving in his spirit* that they were disputing inwardly like this, he said to them, 'Why do you dispute these things in your hearts? ⁹ Which is easier, to say to a paralyzed man, "You have been forgiven your violations," or to say, "Rise up, and gather your stretcher, and walk around"? ¹⁰ But so that you might see that the Son of Man has authority on the Earth to forgive violations ...'
Then he said to the paralyzed man, ¹¹ 'I say to you, rise up, and gather your stretcher, and go your way to your home.'
¹² And once he was lifted up, and, gathering the stretcher, he went out in the presence of them all, so that they were all astounded, and they magnified God, saying, 'We have never seen anything like this.'

Calling of Matthew. Eating
with violators at Matthew's feast*

¹³ And he went out once again beside the sea, and all the crowd kept coming to him, and he was teaching them.

¹⁴ And *as* he passed by, he saw Levi, the *son* of Alphaeus, sitting in charge of* the tax office, and he said to him, 'Follow me.'

And he rose up *and* followed him.

¹⁵ And it came about that when Jesus was sitting eating in his house, many tax collectors and violators were sitting together with Jesus and his disciples, for there were many, and they followed him.

¹⁶ And *when* the scribes and Pharisees saw him eating with tax collectors and violators, they kept saying to his disciples, 'Why *is it* that he eats and drinks with tax collectors and violators?'

¹⁷ Jesus heard, *and* he said to them, 'Not those who are strong have need of a physician, but those having a sickness. I came to call not the righteous, but violators into submission.'

Friends of the bridegroom.
Parables of wineskins & garments*

¹⁸ And the disciples of John and *those* of the Pharisees were fasting, and they came and said to him, 'Why do the disciples of John and those of the Pharisees fast, but your disciples do not fast?'

¹⁹ And Jesus said to them, 'Can the sons of the bridegroom fast while the bridegroom is with them? As long as they have the bridegroom with them, they are not able to fast. ²⁰ But the days will come when the bridegroom will be taken away from them, and then in those days they will fast.

²¹ 'And nobody sows a piece of new cloth over an old garment, otherwise its patch pulls away from the old, and a worse tear comes. ²² And nobody puts new wine into old wineskins. Otherwise the freshly made wine bursts the wineskins, and the wine leaks out, and the wineskins will be ruined. But new wine must be put into new wineskins.'

He rebukes the Pharisees:
the Sabbath made for man*

²³ And he happened* to be going along through grain fields during the Sabbaths, and his disciples began to make their way, picking the ears of corn.

²⁴ And the Pharisees said to him, 'Look! Why are they doing that which is unlawful during the Sabbaths?'

²⁵ And he said to them, 'Did you never read what David did when he was in need and was hungry, he, and those with him, ²⁶ how he went into the House of God in *the days* of Abiathar, a* high priest, and ate the loaves of the presentation, which is not lawful to eat, except by the priests, and he gave *some* to those who were with him as well?'

²⁷ In addition, he said to them, 'The Sabbath came into being* on account of man, not man on account of the Sabbath. ²⁸ So then, the Son of Man is Lord also of the Sabbath.'

Healing of a withered hand:
Pharisees' conspiracy

3\1 And he entered the synagogue again, and a man was there *who* had a withered hand. ² And they were watching him, whether he might heal* him on the Sabbath, in order that they might accuse him.

³ And he said to the man having the withered hand, 'Rise up into the centre.'

⁴ And he said to them, 'Is it more lawful to do good on the Sabbath or to do evil, to save life or to murder?'

But they were silent.

⁵ Then he looked around at them with indignation, deeply grieved at the stubbornness of their hearts, *and* he said to the man, 'Stretch out your hand.'

And he stretched *it* out, and his hand was completely restored like the other one.

⁶ And the Pharisees went out *and* at once took counsel with the Herodians against him concerning how they might kill him.

Many healed: unclean spirits recognize who Jesus is*

⁷ And Jesus withdrew himself with his disciples to the sea, and a large crowd from Galilee followed him, and from Judea, ⁸ and from Jerusalem, and Idumea, and beyond the Jordan, and those around Tyre and Sidon.

When a large crowd had heard what impressive things he was doing, they came to him. ⁹ And he said to his disciples that a small boat should remain at hand for him on account of the crowd, so that they would not press him. ¹⁰ For he had healed many, so that those who had afflictions were converging on him so that they might touch him.

[11] And whenever the unclean spirits saw him, they fell down before him and called out, saying, 'You are the Son of God!'
[12] And he warned them strongly with many words* that they should not make him known.

The 12 chosen *

[13] And he went up into the mountains, and called *those* whom he himself wanted, and they went to him. [14] And he appointed twelve who should be with him, and whom he should authorize to make proclamation, [15] and to have authority to heal diseases, and to drive out demons.
[16] And to Simon he added *the* name Peter. [17] And for Jacob, the *son* of Zebedee, and John, the brother of Jacob, he added to them *the* name Boanerges, which is 'sons of thunder'. [18] And *there were also* Andrew; and Philip and Bartholomew; and Matthew and Thomas; and Jacob, the *son* of Alphaeus, and Thaddaeus, and Simon the Canaanite; [19] and Judas Iscariot, who for his part betrayed him.

Defamation of the Angel of God *

And they went into a house, [20] and a crowd came together again so that they found themselves unable even to eat bread. [21] And *when* those with him heard, they set out to seize hold of him, for they were saying that he was out of his mind.
[22] And the scribes who came down from Jerusalem said, 'He has Beelzebub, and he drives out the demons through the agency of the prince of the demons.'
[23] And he called them *and* began speaking to them in parables: 'How can Satan drive out Satan? [24] And if a kingdom is divided against itself, that kingdom is not able to stand. [25] And if a house is divided against itself, that house is not able to stand.
[26] 'And if Satan has risen up against himself, and is divided, he is not able to stand, but has come to an end.
[27] 'Nobody having gone into a strong man's house is in any way able to take any plunder unless he first binds the strong man, and then he will plunder his house.
[28] 'Truly I say to you, the sons of men will be forgiven for all violations, and for whatever blasphemies they might blaspheme. [29] But whoever speaks injuriously against the Holy Spirit* does not have forgiveness throughout the Eon,*** but is liable to Eonian* condemnatory sentence.'**
[30] *He said this* because they said, 'He has an unclean spirit.'

True brothers *

[31] Then his brothers and mother came to him, and they stood outside, *and* sent word to him, calling him.
[32] Meanwhile a crowd was sitting around him, and they said to him, 'Look, your mother and your brothers are outside looking for you.'
[33] And he answered them, saying, 'Who is* my mother, or my brothers?'
[34] And he took a glance around at those who were sitting around him, *and* he said, 'See, here are my mother and my brothers. [35] For whoever does the will of God is my brother, and my sister, and mother.'

Parables of the kingdom, concerning Israel *

4\1 And he began again to give teaching beside the sea, and a vast mass of people gathered to him, so that he went on board a boat on the sea to sit down, and the whole crowd was on the land close to the sea.

Parable of a sower *

[2] And he was teaching them many things in parables, and he said to them in his teaching, [3] 'Listen, a sower went out to sow seeds. [4] And it came about* in his sowing *that* some fell by the road, and the birds* came and devoured it up.
[5] 'But some *seed* fell on rocky ground, where it did not have much soil, and it sprang up at once because of its having no depth of soil, [6] but *when* the Sun rose it was scorched, and on account of its having no root it dried up.
[7] 'And some *seed* fell into the thorn bushes, and the thorn bushes grew up and choked it, and it yielded no fruit.
[8] 'And some *seed* fell into the good soil, and it yielded fruit, springing up and increasing, and some yielded thirty-fold, and some sixty-fold, and some a hundred-fold.'
[9] And he said,* 'He who has ears to hear, let him hear.'

Mystery of the Sovereign Rulership of God.*
Judgement on Israel's unbelief foretold by Isaiah *

[10] And when he came to be alone, those around him in company with the twelve asked him about the parable.

¹¹ And he said to them, 'It has been given to you to know the mystery of the Sovereign Rulership of God, but to those who are outside everything comes in parables, ¹² so that:

"In seeing they might see
yet they will not perceive,
and hearing they might hear
yet they will not understand;
otherwise they might turn
and *their* violations
would be forgiven them."*

Explanation of the parable of a sower *
¹³ And he said to them, 'Have you no intuitive knowledge of this parable? And how then will you know all the parables?
¹⁴ 'The sower* sows the oracle. ¹⁵ And one group are those along the road where the oracle is sown, but, when they have heard, Satan* comes straightaway and he takes away the oracle which was sown in their hearts.
¹⁶ 'And another group are those who, in the same way, are sown on the rocky ground, who, when they have heard the oracle, receive it at once with gladness, ¹⁷ but they have no root in themselves, but are inconstant, then when tribulation or persecution arises on account of the oracle, they immediately take offence.
¹⁸ 'And another group are those who are sown among the thorn bushes. These are those who hear the oracle, ¹⁹ but the anxieties of this Eon,* and the deceitfulness of riches, and the desires concerning other things coming in choke the oracle, and it becomes unfruitful.
²⁰ 'And another group are those who are sown on the good soil, who hear the oracle and receive *it*, and produce fruit, some thirty-fold, and some sixty-fold, and some a hundred-fold.'

Parable of a lamp *
²¹ And he said to them, 'Does a lamp shine so that it might be placed underneath the grain measure or underneath the bed? *Is it* not so that it might be set on the candlestick?'* ²² For nothing is hidden but that it will be brought to light.* Nor does any secret thing become covered up but that it should come into the light. ²³ If anybody has ears to hear, let him hear.'

²⁴ And he said to them, 'Take heed what you hear. With whatever measure you measure out, it will be measured back to you. And to you who hear, it will be added. ²⁵ For he who has, to him it will be given. And he who does not have, even what he does have will be taken away from him.'

Parable of stages of the Sovereign Rulership of God
²⁶ And he said, 'The Sovereign Rulership of God is like this.* *It is* as if a man should scatter seed onto the soil, ²⁷ and he should sleep and rise night and day, and the seed should sprout and grow long, yet he has no intuitive knowledge how. ²⁸ For the soil yields fruit spontaneously, first a blade, then an ear, then a full corn in the ear.* ²⁹ But when the fruit yields itself, he at once authorizes* the sickle because the harvest has come.'

Parable of a mustard seed *
³⁰ And he said, 'To what shall we liken the Sovereign Rulership of God? Or with* what parable can we compare it?* ³¹ *It is* comparable to a grain of mustard seed which, when it has been sown in the soil, is smaller than all the seeds in the soil. ³² But when it has been sown, it grows up and becomes larger than all *the* vegetables and it shoots out large branches, so that the birds of the sky* are able to roost underneath its shade.'
³³ And with many such parables he was speaking the oracle to them, as they were able to hear. ³⁴ And not without a parable did he speak to them, but alone he explained all these things to his disciples.

He calms a 'furious storm of wind' *
³⁵ And on that day, when evening came, he said to them, 'Let's pass over to the other side.'
³⁶ And when they had dismissed the crowd, they took him along with *them* since he was in the boat (and there were other small boats with it), ³⁷ and a furious storm of wind arose, and the waves were beating into the boat, so that it was already filling up.
³⁸ And he was on the stern sleeping on the headrest, and they woke him and said to him, 'Teacher, is it of no concern to you that we are in danger?'
³⁹ And having been woken up, he rebuked the wind, and said to the sea, 'Quiet! Be still!'
And the wind dropped, and there was* a mighty calm.
⁴⁰ And he said to them, 'So why are you

fearful? How you do not have faith?'
[41] And they were extremely frightened, and they said to one another, 'Who is this, then, that even the wind and the sea obey him?'

Healing of a man under
the power of the demon Legion *

5\1 And they came over to the other side of the sea, into the district of the Gadarenes.
[2] And when he disembarked from the boat, at once a man in an unclean spirit confronted him out of the tombs. [3] He had *his* home* among the tombs, and nobody was able to bind him, not even with chains, [4] for he had often been bound with foot chains and manacles, and the manacles had been broken apart by him, and the foot chains shattered in pieces, and nobody had the strength to restrain him. [5] And continually, night and day, in the mountains and in the tombs, he was calling out and lacerating himself with stones.
[6] But seeing Jesus from a distance, he ran and fell on his knees* in front of him, [7] and, calling out with a loud voice, he said, 'What is my business with you,* Jesus, Son of the Most High God? I adjure you by God that you do not torment me with interrogation!'*
[8] For he was saying to him, 'Come out of the man, unclean spirit!', [9] and he asked him, 'What *is* your name?'
And he answered, saying, 'My name *is* Legion, for we are many.'
[10] And he begged him with many words* that he would not drive them out of the district.*
[11] Now just there, near the mountain,* a large herd of pigs was feeding, [12] and all the demons asked him, saying, 'Send us into the pigs, so that we can go into them.'*
[13] And Jesus at once gave them permission. And the unclean spirits came out *and* went into the pigs, and the herd rushed impetuously down the cliff into the sea, and there were about two thousand, and they choked in the sea.
[14] And those who tended the pigs rushed off and made *it* known in the city and in the fields. And they went out to see what had happened, [15] and they came to Jesus and gazed at the man under the power of the demons, having had Legion, sitting, and provided with clothes, and of a sound mind, and they were astounded. [16] And those who had seen what happened to the man under the power of the demons described

it to them, and *about* the pigs, [17] and they began to beg him* to depart from their borders.
[18] And when he boarded the boat, the man *who had been* under the power of the demons asked him if he could be with him, [19] but Jesus did not allow him, but said to him, 'Go to your home, to your own *people*, and tell them what mighty things the Lord has done for you, and *that* he has had compassion on you.'
[20] And he departed, and he began to report in Decapolis what mighty things Jesus had done for him, and everybody was astounded.

Healing of a lady with a flow of blood.
Raising of the daughter of Jair *
[21] And when Jesus ferried across in the boat back to the other side, a vast crowd gathered to him, and he was by the sea.
[22] And then it so happened that* one of the rulers of the synagogue came, Jair* by name, and *when* he saw him he fell at his feet [23] and pleaded with him with many words,* saying, 'My little daughter lies at the point of death.* I *beg you* that you might come and lay hands on her so that she can be healed and she will live.'
[24] And *Jesus* went with him, and a large crowd was following him and pressing him.
[25] And a certain lady, having been with an issue of blood *for* twelve years, [26] and suffering many treatments at the hands of many physicians, and having spent everything she had and having benefitted nothing, but, rather, she deteriorated, [27] having heard about Jesus, came among the crowd *and* touched his garment from behind, [28] for she had said, 'If I can just touch his clothes, I will be cured.' [29] And instantly the issue* of her blood dried up, and she knew in *her* body that she had been healed from the infirmity.
[30] And Jesus, perceiving at once in himself that power had gone out of him, turned to the crowd *and* said, 'Who touched my clothes?'
[31] And his disciples kept saying to him, 'You see the crowd pressing you, yet you say, "Who touched me?" '
[32] And he was looking around to see her who had done this thing. [33] But the lady, being frightened, and trembling, perceiving what had happened to her, came and fell down before him, and told him all the truth.
[34] And he said to her, 'Daughter, your faith has cured you. Go in peace, and be cured from your infirmity.'

[35] While he was still speaking, *men* from the ruler of the synagogue came, saying, 'Your daughter has died. Why do you trouble the Teacher any further?'
[36] But as soon as Jesus heard the report being spoken, he said to the ruler of the synagogue, 'Don't be afraid. Only, go on believing.'
[37] And he allowed nobody to accompany him, except Peter, and Jacob, and John, the brother of Jacob. [38] And he came to the house of the ruler of the synagogue, and he saw a commotion, and weeping, and severe wailing.
[39] And *when* he had gone in he said to them, 'Why do you make a commotion and weep? The child has not died, but is sleeping.'
[40] And they began laughing at him. But *when* he had put them all out, he took along the father and the mother of the girl and those with him, and he went in where the girl was lying, [41] and he took the girl by the hand, *and* said to her, 'Talitha cumi,'* which, being translated, means 'Girl, I say to you, rise up.'
[42] And the girl at once stood up and began walking. Now she was twelve years *old*, and they were astounded with a tremendous ecstasy.* [43] And he charged them with many words* that nobody should come to know this, and he said *something* should be given to her to eat.

Astonishment at him.
A prophet not without honour *

6\1 **A**nd he departed from there and came into his fatherland, and his disciples followed him.
[2] And when the Sabbath came he began to teach in the synagogue, and many hearing were struck with astonishment, saying, 'Where is this *man getting* these things from, and what *is* this wisdom which has been given to him so that such works of power are performed through the agency of his hands? [3] Is this not the carpenter,* the son of Maria, the brother of Jacob, and Joses, and of Judas and Simon? And are his sisters not here, among* us?'

And they were offended by him.
[4] But Jesus said to them, 'A prophet is not without honour, except in his fatherland, and among relatives, and in his *own* house.'
[5] And he was not able to do any work of power there, except he laid hands on *and* healed a few infirm people. [6] And he was amazed at their unbelief. And he went around the villages in a circuit, teaching.

Authorization of the 12 *

[7] And he called the twelve and began to authorize them in pairs, and he gave them authority over unclean spirits, [8] and charged them that they should take up nothing for the road, except just a staff; not travel sack,* nor bread, nor copper in the belt, [9] but being shod with sandals, and they should not put on two garments.*
[10] And he said to them, 'Wherever you go into a house, remain there until you depart from there.
[11] 'And as for whoever does not receive you or hear you, depart from there, *and* shake off the dust underneath your feet for a testimony against them. Truly I say to you, it will be more tolerable for Sodom and Gomorrha in *the* day of judgement* than for that city.'
[12] And they went out *and* proclaimed that men should submit. [13] And they drove out many demons, and anointed with oil and healed many infirm.

Life of John ends in assassination *

[14] And Herod the king heard, for his name became* public, and he said that John the Identifier had been raised from *the* dead, and on account of this the works of power were displaying their force* in him.
[15] Others were saying, 'It's Elijah,' and others were saying, 'He's a prophet, or like one of the prophets.'
[16] But *when* Herod heard, he said, 'It's John, whom I beheaded.* He has been raised from the dead.'
[17] For Herod himself had given an order *and* seized John, and shackled him in the jail on account of Herodias, his brother Philip's wife, because he had married her. [18] For John had been saying to Herod, 'It's not lawful for you to have the wife of your brother.' [19] But Herodias kept holding onto a grudge against him, and was wanting to murder him, but was not able to, [20] because Herod feared John, knowing him a righteous and holy man, and he kept him safe, and *when* he heard him *John* would do many things, and *Herod* took pleasure in listening to him.
[21] And when a suitable day came, Herod on his birthday made a banquet for his high officials and military commanders, and the chief *men* of Galilee, [22] and the daughter of Herodias herself came in, and she danced and

pleased Herod and those who sat with *him*.

And the king said to the girl, 'Ask of me whatever you want, and I will give *it* to you.' ²³ And he swore to her, 'Whatever you ask of me, I will give *it* to you, up to half my kingdom.'

²⁴ And she went out *and* said to her mother, 'What shall I ask for?'

And she said, 'The head of John the Identifier.'

²⁵ And she at once hurried in to the king, *and* asked *him*, saying, 'I wish that you will give me right now the head of John the Identifier on a dish.'

²⁶ And having become exceedingly sorrowful, the king, on account of his oath and those who were eating with *him*, was unwilling to reject her. ²⁷ And the king immediately sent an executioner and ordered his head to be brought, and he went *and* beheaded* him in the jail, ²⁸ and he brought his head on a dish, and gave it to the girl, and the girl gave it to her mother.

²⁹ And *when* his disciples heard, they came and took up his corpse and laid it in a tomb.

The 5,000 *

³⁰ And the apostles gathered themselves together to Jesus, and they related everything to him, both what they had done and what they had taught.

³¹ And he said to them, 'Take yourselves alone into a deserted place, and rest for a while.'

For there were many coming and going, and they had no opportunity even to eat. ³² And they departed alone into a deserted place by boat.

³³ And *people* saw them departing, and many recognized him and ran together on foot there from all the cities, and they outran them, and they came together to him.

³⁴ And *when* Jesus went out he saw a large crowd, and he was moved with compassion towards them, because they were like sheep not having a shepherd, and he began to teach them many things.

³⁵ And *it* already being a late hour, his disciples came to him and said, 'This place is desolate, and already *it is* a late hour. ³⁶ Send them off so that they can go into the surrounding countryside and into the villages *and* buy bread for themselves, for they have nothing to eat.'

³⁷ But in answer, he said to them, 'You give them *something* to eat.'

And they said to him, 'Shall we go *and* buy two hundred denarions'' worth of bread and give them *something* to eat?'

³⁸ He said to them, 'How many loaves do you have? Go and see.'

And *when* they found out, they said, 'Five, and two fish.'

³⁹ And he ordered them to make everybody sit down, group by group,' on the green grass, ⁴⁰ and they sat down row by row,' by hundreds and by fifties.

⁴¹ And he took the five loaves and the two fish *and*, looking up to the sky, he exalted' *God* and broke up the loaves, and gave *them* to his disciples so that they might set *it* before them, and he divided the two fish among them all. ⁴² And they all ate, and were satisfied. ⁴³ And they took up twelve hand baskets full of fragments and *pieces* of the fish. ⁴⁴ And those who ate from the loaves were five thousand men.

Jesus walks over the sea *

⁴⁵ And he at once made his disciples get into the boat, and to go ahead to the other side to Bethsaida, while he sent the people away. ⁴⁶ And he departed from them, *and* went away into a mountain to pray.'

⁴⁷ And when evening came, the boat was in the middle of the sea, and he *was* alone on the land. ⁴⁸ Then *when* he saw them straining at the oars because the wind was against them, at about *the* fourth watch of the night he came to them, walking over the sea, and he intended to pass them by, ⁴⁹ but *when* they saw him walking over the sea, they supposed *him* to be a phantom, and they called out, ⁵⁰ for they all saw him and were troubled.

And he straightaway spoke with them, and said to them, 'Be of good courage. I Am.' Do not be afraid.'

⁵¹ And he went up to them in the boat, and the wind dropped, and they were exceedingly astonished, beyond measure, and they marvelled among themselves, ⁵² for they did not understand about the loaves, for their heart was hardened.

Many healed in Gennesaret *

⁵³ And when they had crossed over, they came to the land of Gennesaret, and anchored nearby.

⁵⁴ And on their coming out of the boat,

people* at once recognized him, [55] *and* they ran through that whole surrounding region, *and* they began to bring on stretchers those who were sick to where they were hearing that he was. [56] And wherever he went, into villages, or cities, or country places, they placed those who were sick in the marketplaces, and they begged him that they might only touch the fringe of his cloak, and as many who touched him were made whole.

Jesus rebukes the traditions as contradicting the Scrolls *

7\1 Then the Pharisees gathered together and went to him, as *did* some of the scribes *who* had come from Jerusalem. [2] And *when* they saw some of his disciples eating bread with defiled hands, that is,* with unwashed *hands*, they were critical. [3] For the Pharisees and all the Jews, unless they have diligently washed their hands with a fist* clenched, do not eat, holding fast to the tradition of the elders. [4] And if *returning* from *the* market, they do not eat unless they wash themselves. And there are many other things which they have received to hold to: washings of cups, and pots, copper utensils, and of beds.*

[5] Then the Pharisees and scribes asked him, 'Why do your disciples not walk in keeping with the tradition of the elders, but eat bread with unwashed hands?'

[6] But in answer, he said to them, 'Isaiah has prophesied excellently concerning you hypocrites.* As it has been written:

"This people honour Me with *their* lips,
but their heart is far from Me.
[7] But in vain they worship Me,
teaching *for* doctrines
the injunctions of men."*

[8] 'For, having forsaken the commandment of God, you hold the tradition of men, washings of pots and cups, and you do many other similar things.'

[9] And he said to them, 'You fully set aside the commandment of God, in order that you might observe your own tradition. [10] For Moses said,* "Honour your father and your mother", and, "The one speaking evil of *his* father or mother must certainly die."* [11] But you are approving when a man says to his father or mother, "By whatever you might have profited from me is

corban, which is a gift *dedicated to God*." [12] And you no longer allow him to do anything for his father or his mother, [13] making void* the oracle of God through your tradition which you have handed down, and you do many similar things.'

[14] And he called all the crowd, *and* he said to them, 'Listen to me, everyone, and understand. [15] There is nothing from outside a man *which*, by going into him, is able to defile him. But the *things* coming out from him, those are the things defiling man. [16] If anybody has ears to hear, let him hear.'

[17] And when he had gone into the house, away from the crowd, his disciples began asking him about the parable.

[18] And he said to them, 'So are even you undiscerning as well? Do you not perceive that nothing which enters into the man from outside is able to defile him, [19] because it goes not into his heart, but into the belly, then it goes out into the waste-bowl, purging all the food?'

[20] And he said, 'The thing issuing out of the man, that defiles the man. [21] For from inside, out of the heart of men, proceed ill-natured disputes, adulteries, fornications, murders, [22] thefts, frauds,* iniquities, guile, licentiousness, an evil eye, evil speaking, haughtiness, foolishness. [23] All these evil things issue from inside and defile the man.'

Healing of a Canaanite woman's daughter *

[24] And he rose up from there *and* went away into the borders of Tyre and Sidon, and he went into a house *and* wanted nobody to know, but he could not escape notice.* [25] For a woman, whose little daughter had an unclean spirit, had heard of him, *and* she came *and* fell down at his feet. [26] Now the woman was a Greek, a Syro-Phoenician by race, and she asked him if he would drive the demon out of her daughter.

[27] But Jesus said to her, 'Let the children be filled first, for it's not right to take the children's bread and to throw *it* to the little dogs.'

[28] But she answered and said to him, 'Yes Lord, for even the little dogs underneath the table eat from the children's crumbs.'

[29] And he said to her, 'On account of that remark, go your way. The demon has gone out of your daughter.'

[30] And *when* she went into her house she found

the demon gone, and her daughter had been thrown forcibly onto the bed.

Healing of a deaf & mute man
³¹ And he again departed out of the borders of Tyre and Sidon, *and* he came to the Sea of Galilee, through *the* centre of the districts of Decapolis. ³² And they brought to him a deaf man who had an impediment in his speech, and they pleaded with him to lay a hand on him.
³³ And he took him on his own, away from the crowd, *and* he put his fingers into his ears, and he spat, *and* touched his tongue, ³⁴ and he looked up into the sky, *and* with a deep sigh he said to him, 'Ephphatha,'* which means, 'Be opened.'
³⁵ And instantly his ears were opened, and the impediment of his tongue was released, and he spoke correctly. ³⁶ And he charged them that they should tell nobody, but the more he charged them all the more did they keep proclaiming *it,* ³⁷ and they were struck with astonishment beyond measure, saying, 'He has done all things well. He makes both the deaf hear and the dumb speak.'

The 4,000 *

8\1 **I**n those days *the* crowd was vast and had nothing to eat, *so* Jesus called his disciples, and said to them, ² 'I am moved with compassion for the crowd, because they have already been with me *for* three days, and they have nothing to eat, ³ and if I send them away hungry into their own houses they will faint on the road, for some of them have come from a long way.'
⁴ And his disciples answered him, 'From where could anybody be able to satisfy these *people* with loaves here in a deserted region?'
⁵ And he asked them, 'How many loaves do you have?'
And they said, 'Seven.'
⁶ And he instructed the crowd to sit down on the ground and, taking the seven loaves and giving thanks, he broke *them* up and gave *some* to his disciples so that they might set *them* in front of *them.* And they set *them* in front of the crowd, ⁷ and they had a few small fish, and he exalted* God, *then* requested for *these* to be set in front of *them* as well.
⁸ So they ate, and were filled, and they took up over seven lunch baskets of fragments. ⁹ And those who had eaten were about four

thousand.
And he sent them away, ¹⁰ and he at once boarded the boat in company with his disciples.

*Pharisees want a sign.**
Leaven of Pharisees & Herod
He came into the regions of Dalmanutha, ¹¹ and the Pharisees came out and began to dispute with him, seeking from him a sign from the heavens, in order to test him.
¹² And he groaned in his spirit, *and* said, 'Why does this generation repeatedly search after a sign? Truly I say to you, a sign will not be given to this generation.'*
¹³ And *when* he had departed from them, he went into the boat again *and* ferried across to the other side.
¹⁴ Now *the disciples* had forgotten to take loaves, and they had no more than one loaf with them in the boat.
¹⁵ And he instructed them, saying, 'Watch! Turn your attention away from the leaven of the Pharisees and the leaven of Herod.'
¹⁶ And they were reasoning with each other, saying, '*This is* because we have no loaves.'
¹⁷ And being conscious of *it,* Jesus said to them, 'Why do you reason because you have no loaves? Do you not yet perceive, nor understand? Have you still hardened your heart? ¹⁸ Having eyes, do you not see? And having ears, do you not hear?* And do you not remember? ¹⁹ When I broke up the five loaves for the five thousand, how many hand baskets full of fragments did you take up?'
They said to him, 'Twelve.'
²⁰ 'And when *I broke up* the seven for the four thousand, how many lunch basket fillings of fragments did you take up?'
And they said, 'Seven.'
²¹ And he said to them, 'How do you not understand?'

Healing of a blind man
²² And he came into Bethsaida, and they brought a blind man to him and asked him that he might touch him. ²³ And he took hold of the blind *man* by the hand *and* led him out of the village, and he spat into his eyes *and* laid *his* hands on him, *and* he was asking him, 'Can you see anything?'
²⁴ And looking up, he said, 'I see the men walking around like trees.'
²⁵ Then he again laid *his* hands on his eyes and

made him look up, and he was restored, and saw everybody distinctly.

²⁶ And he sent him away to his house, saying, 'Neither go into the village, nor tell *it* to anybody in the village.'

Peter's declaration of Jesus as the Christ *

²⁷ And Jesus and his disciples went into the villages of Caesarea Philippi, and on the road he was questioning his disciples, saying to them, 'Whom do men pronounce me to be?'**

²⁸ And they answered, 'John the Identifier, and others Elijah, but others one of the prophets.'

²⁹ Then he said to them, 'But you, whom do you pronounce me to be?'**

And in answer, Peter said to him, 'You are the Christ.'

³⁰ And he warned them that they should not tell anybody about himself.

He foretells his death
& resurrection.* Rebuke of Peter *

³¹ And he began to teach them that it was necessary for the Son of Man to suffer many things, and to be rejected by the elders and by the senior priests and the scribes, and to be murdered, and after three days to rise.

³² And he spoke the oracle openly, and Peter took hold of him and began to remonstrate with him.

³³ But he turned round and looked at his disciples, *and* he rebuked Peter, saying, 'Get behind me, adversary!* For you are directing your mind not on the things of God, but the things of men.'

True discipleship *

³⁴ And having called the crowd in company with his disciples, he said to them, 'Whoever is willing to come after me, let him deny himself, and take up his stake,* and let him follow me. ³⁵ For whoever might wish to save his life will lose it. But whoever might lose his own life,* on account of me and of the gospel, he will save it.

³⁶ 'For in what way will it profit a man if he gains the whole world, but loses* his own life?*

³⁷ Or what can a man give *in* exchange for his life?* ³⁸ For whoever in this adulterous and violating generation might have been ashamed of me and of my oracles, the Son of Man will also be ashamed of him when he comes in the magnificence of his Father with the holy angels.'

No death for some
until the signs of the Acts period *

9\1 **A**nd he said to them, 'Assuredly I say to you, there are some of these standing here who will most certainly not taste death* until they see the Sovereign Rulership of God appear in power.'

His radiance shown in
the transformation. Voice out of a cloud *

² And six days afterwards Jesus took Peter, and Jacob, and John, and he led them up into a high mountain alone by themselves. And he was transformed* in front of them, ³ and his garments became shining, gleaming* white like snow, such as no launderer on the Earth is able to make white.

⁴ And Elijah was seen together with Moses,* and they were speaking with Jesus.

⁵ And in reaction, Peter said to Jesus, 'Rabbi, it's good for us to be here, so let us make three booths, one for you, and one for Moses, and one for Elijah.'

⁶ For he did not know what to say, as they were so afraid.

⁷ Then a cloud came, overshadowing them, and a voice came out of the cloud: 'This is My Son, the Richly Loved One.* Listen to him.'

⁸ Yet the moment they looked round, they no longer saw anybody, except Jesus only, in company with them.

His sufferings explained. Elijah comes first *

⁹ And as they were coming down from the mountain, he charged them that they should relate to nobody what things they had seen until the Son of Man would rise out from among *the* dead. ¹⁰ And they kept hold of that remark to themselves, questioning in company what it might mean* to rise from among* *the* dead.

¹¹ And they asked him, saying, 'The scribes say that Elijah must come first.'

¹² And in answer, he told them, 'Elijah does indeed come first and he restores* all things. And how has it been written about the Son of Man that he should suffer many things and be esteemed as nothing? ¹³ But I say to you, Elijah has indeed come, and they have done to him whatever they pleased, as it has been written about* him.'

Healing of a lunatic son *

¹⁴ And on approaching the disciples, he saw a

large crowd around them, and the scribes in discussion with them. [15] And straightaway, when all the crowd saw him, they were much amazed, and they ran *and* greeted him.

[16] And he asked the scribes, 'What are you arguing against them?'

[17] And somebody answering from among the crowd said, 'Teacher, I have brought to you my son *who* has a dumb spirit. [18] And wherever it seizes him, it dashes him down, and he foams and gnashes* his teeth, and he withers with dehydration, and I told your disciples so that they might drive it out, but they did not have the power.'

[19] And in answer, he said, 'Oh* generation without faith! How long must I be among you? How long shall I bear with you? Bring him to me.'

[20] And they brought him to him, and on seeing him the spirit immediately threw *the boy* into convulsions, and falling on the ground he was rolled about, foaming.

[21] And *Jesus* asked his father, 'How long a time is it that this has been happening to him?'

And he said, 'Since childhood. [22] And often it has thrown him into both fire and water, in order that it might destroy him. But if you could do anything, being moved with pity for us, help us.'

[23] And Jesus said* to him, 'If you can believe, all things *are* possible for him who believes.'

[24] And at once the father of the child called out *and* said with tears, 'Lord, I believe. Help my unbelief.'

[25] But Jesus, seeing that a crowd was running along together, rebuked the unclean spirit, saying to it, 'Dumb and deaf spirit, I command you, come out of him, and go into him no longer.'

[26] And it shrieked, and threw him into many convulsions, *and* it came out,* and he became as if dead, so that many said that he had died. [27] But Jesus took him by the hand, *and* lifted him, and he stood up.

[28] And when he went into a house, his disciples asked him privately, 'Why were we not able to drive it out?'

[29] And he replied to them, 'This kind can come out by nothing but prayer and fasting.'

He predicts his death & resurrection *

[30] And they departed from there, *and* they were passing through Galilee, and he did not

wish that anybody should know, [31] for he kept on teaching his disciples, and saying to them, 'The Son of Man will be given into *the* hands of men, and they will murder him, and, after having been murdered, he will be raised on the third day.'

[32] But they did not understand the statement, and they were afraid to ask him.

Being servants in the Sovereign Rulership of God

[33] And he came into Capernaum, and *when* he was in the house he asked them, 'What were you discussing among yourselves on the road?'

[34] But they held their peace with each other, for they had been discussing with each other on the road who was most eminent.

[35] And taking a seat, he addressed the twelve, and said to them, 'If anybody has the desire to be* first he will be last of all, and the servant of all.'

Receiving little children in his name *

[36] And he took a child *and* set him in front of them, and he took him up in *his* arms *and* said to them, [37] 'Whoever receives one of such children in my name receives me, and whoever receives me receives not me but Him Who authorized me.'

[38] And John answered him, saying, 'Teacher, we saw somebody who does not follow us driving out demons in your name, and we prohibited him because he does not follow us.'

[39] But Jesus said, 'Do not prevent him, for there is nobody who will do a work of power in my name and he will be readily able to speak evil of me. [40] For he who is not against you is for you.* [41] For whoever might give you a cup of water to drink in my name because you are Christ's, truly I say to you, he will certainly not lose his reward.

Offences against children *

[42] 'And whoever shall have caused one of these little ones* who believes in me to stumble, it would be better for him that a millstone be hung around his neck and he were hurled into the sea.

A choice between entering Eonian life
and the Sovereign Rulership of God,
or being thrown into the fire of the Valley of Hinnom.
Prophetic hyperbole concerning that fire
(Isaiah 66\24, Rev. 14\11)

[43] 'And if your hand should cause you to stumble, cut it off. It would be better for you to enter into life maimed than having two hands to go into the Valley of Hinnom,* into the inextinguishable fire, [44] where:

"Their worm does not die,
and the fire is not extinguished."*

[45] 'And if your foot should cause you to stumble, cut it off. It would be better for you to enter into life lame than having two feet to be thrown into the Valley of Hinnom, into the inextinguishable fire, [46] where:

"Their worm does not die,
and the fire is not extinguished."*

[47] 'And if your eye should cause you to stumble, pluck it out. It would be better for you to enter into the Sovereign Rulership of God with one eye than having two eyes to be thrown into the fire of the Valley of Hinnom,* [48] where:

"Their worm does not die,
and the fire is not extinguished."*

[49] 'For everybody will be salted with fire,* and every sacrifice will be salted with salt. [50] Salt *is* good, but if the salt has become saltless with what will you restore it? Have salt within yourselves, and be at peace among each other.'

Dispute with Pharisees concerning divorce *

10\1 **A**nd after rising from there, he came into the districts of Judea by the other side of the Jordan, and crowds came to him again, and, as he usually did, he once again began teaching them.
[2] And approaching in order to test him, *some* Pharisees asked him if it is lawful for a man to put away a wife.
[3] But in answer, he said to them, 'What did Moses command you?'
[4] And they said, 'Moses gave permission to write a scroll* of divorce, and to put *her* away.'*
[5] And in answer, Jesus said to them, 'In view of the hardness of your heart he wrote this mandate for you. [6] But from *the* beginning of creation God created them a male and a female.
[7] On account of this,* a man will leave his father and mother, and he will be joined to* his wife, [8] and the two will become* one flesh,* so

then no longer are they two, but one flesh. [9] That which, therefore, God has paired together, let man not break apart.'
[10] And in the house, his disciples asked him again about the same thing.
[11] And he said to them, 'Whoever puts away his wife and marries another commits adultery against her. [12] And if a woman puts away her husband and becomes married to another, she commits adultery.'

Receiving the Sovereign Rulership of God like little children *
[13] And they were carrying young children to him so that he might touch them, but the disciples were reprimanding those who brought *them.*
[14] But Jesus saw *and* was indignant, and he said to them, 'Allow the little children to come to me, and do not hinder them, for the Sovereign Rulership of God is of this kind. [15] Truly I say to you, whoever does not receive the Sovereign Rulership of God like a little child most certainly cannot enter into it.'
[16] And he was taking them up in his arms, *and* he put *his* hands on them, *and* kept speaking good words* to them.

The rich young ruler. *Treasure in Heaven*
[17] And as he went out into a road, somebody came running up, and, kneeling down to him, he asked him, 'Good Teacher, what shall I do so that I might inherit Eonian* life?'
[18] But Jesus said to him, 'Why do you call me good? Nobody *is* good but one – God.
[19] 'You know the commandments: Do not commit adultery. Do not murder. Do not steal. Do not bring false testimony. Do not defraud. Honour your father and mother."*
[20] And in answer, he said to him, 'Teacher, I have been on my guard against all these ever since my youth.'
[21] Then Jesus, looking intently at him, felt brotherly love for him, and he said to him, 'One thing is still falling short for you. Go your way, *and,* as much as you have, sell and give to the poor, and you will have treasure in Heaven.* And come, take up the stake,* *and* follow me.'
[22] But being sombre at that saying, he went away grieved, for he had many possessions.

Eye of a needle *
[23] And Jesus looked around *and* said to his

disciples, 'With what difficulty will those who are relying on riches enter into the Sovereign Rulership of God!'
[24] And the disciples were astounded at his oracles.

But answering again, Jesus said to them, 'Sons,* how difficult it is *for* those who are relying on riches to enter into the Sovereign Rulership of God! [25] It's easier *for* a camel to pass through the eye of the needle than *for* a rich man to enter into the Sovereign Rulership of God.'
[26] And they were exceedingly struck with astonishment, saying to themselves, 'Who, then, can be saved?'
[27] But Jesus, looking at them, said, 'With men *this is* impossible, but not with God. For with God all things are possible.'

Disciples' future thrones in Israel.
Receiving a hundred-fold in the coming Eon
(Luke 18\30, 1 Tim. 6\19) & Eonian life
[28] Peter began to say to him, 'Look, we have left everything and followed you.'
[29] In answer, Jesus said, 'Truly I say to you, there is nobody who has left behind a house, or brothers, or sisters, or father, or mother, or wife, or children, or lands, for the sake of me and the gospel, [30] but he will receive a hundred-fold now, in this time, houses, and brothers, and sisters, and mothers, and children, and lands, in association with persecutions, and, in the Eon* which is coming, Eonian* life.**
[31] 'But many first will be last, and the last first.'

He again predicts his death & resurrection
[32] And they were on the road ascending into Jerusalem, and Jesus was going on in front of them, and they were amazed, and *as* they followed they were afraid.

And he again took aside the twelve, *and* he began to relate to them what things were about to happen to him, [33] *saying*, 'Look now, we are going up into Jerusalem, and the Son of Man will be given into the hands of the senior priests and scribes, and they will condemn him to death and give him into the hands of the nations. [34] And they will mock him, and scourge him, and spit on him, and they will murder him, and on the third day he will be raised.'

Answer to the mother of the sons
of Zebedee: an overwhelming into death *
[35] And Jacob and John, the sons of Zebedee, came to him, saying, 'Teacher, we would like you to do for us whatever we might ask.'
[36] And he said to them, 'What would you like me to do for you?'
[37] And they said to him, 'Grant us that we might sit, one at your right hand, and the other at your left hand, in your magnificence.'
[38] But Jesus said to them, 'You do not know what you ask. Are you able to drink the cup which I drink, and be flooded with the overwhelming which I am about to be flooded with?'
[39] And they said to him, 'We are able.'

But Jesus said to them, 'You will indeed drink the cup which I drink, and you will be flooded with the overwhelming which I am about to be flooded* with. [40] But to sit at my right hand and at *my* left hand is not mine to give, but *is* for whom it has been prepared.'
[41] And the ten on hearing *that* began to be resentful about Jacob and John, [42] but Jesus called them over *and* said to them, 'You know that those who are regarded as rulers over the nations exercise lordship over them, and their high officials exercise authority over them. [43] However, it shall not be so among you. But whoever wishes to become* eminent among you shall be your servant, [44] and whoever of you wishes to become* first shall be servant of all.
[45] For even the Son of Man came not to be served, but to serve, and to give his life* *as* a redemption price on behalf of many.'

Healing of blind Bartimaeus *
[46] And they came into Jericho. Then on his having gone out from Jericho, he and his disciples and a large crowd, a son of Timaeus, Bartimaeus, who *was* blind, was sitting beside the road begging.
[47] And on hearing that it was Jesus the Nazarene,* he began to call out, and to say, 'Son of David, Jesus, have pity on me!'
[48] And many were reprimanding him that he should hold his tongue, but all the more did he keep calling out, 'Son of David, have pity on me!'
[49] And Jesus stopped *and* asked for him to be called over, and they called the blind man over *and* said to him, 'Take courage. Rise up. He's

calling you.'

50 And he threw off his coat *and* rose up and went to Jesus.

51 And in answer, Jesus said to him, 'What do you want that I should do for you?'

And the blind man said to him, 'Rabbouni,* that I might regain sight.'

52 And Jesus said to him, 'Go your way. Your faith has saved you.'

And he recovered his sight instantly, and he followed Jesus on the road.

His triumphal entry into Jerusalem *

11\1 And when they drew near to Jerusalem, to Bethsphage and Bethany, at the Mount of Olives, he sent off two of his disciples, 2 and he said to them, 'Go into the village facing you, and as soon as you have gone into it, you will find a colt tied, which nobody* among men has sat on. Untie it, and lead *it* away, 3 and if anybody says to you, "Why are you doing this?", say that the Lord needs it, then he will send *it* here right away.*

4 And they went their way, and found the colt tied at a doorway outside, near the crossroads, and they untied it.

5 And some of those who were standing there said to them, 'What are you doing, untying the colt?'

6 And they spoke to them just as Jesus had commanded, and they allowed them.

7 And they led the colt to Jesus, and they threw their garments over it, and he sat on it. 8 And many spread out their garments on the road, and others were chopping down foliage from the trees and spreading *it* on the road.

9 And those going ahead and those following were calling out, saying:

'Hosanna! Exalted* *is* the Coming One*
in *the* name of *the* Lord.*
10 Exalted* *is* the Sovereign Rulership
of our father David
which is coming
in *the* name of *the* Lord.*
Hosanna in the highest *realms*!'*

11 And Jesus went into Jerusalem and into the Temple, and after his looking around at everything the hour was already late, *and* he went out to Bethany in company with the twelve.

Cursing a fig tree *

12 And the next morning, *when* they had departed from Bethany, he was hungry, 13 and, seeing at a long way off a fig tree having leaves, he went over *to see* if he might find anything at all on it, and he came up to it *and* found nothing but leaves, for it was not *the* fig season.

14 And in reaction, Jesus said to it, 'Let nobody any more eat fruit from you throughout the Eon.'***

And his disciples heard him.

Cleansing the Temple *

15 And they came into Jerusalem, and Jesus went into the Temple, *and* he began to drive out those selling and buying in the Temple, and he overthrew the tables of the money changers, and the seats of those selling doves, 16 and he would not allow that anybody may carry a container through the Temple.

17 Then he did some teaching, saying to them, 'Has it not been written that:

"My House will be called
a House of Prayer
for* all the nations,
but you have made it
a cave of bandits."?'***

18 And the scribes and senior priests heard, and they began to find a way to destroy him, for they feared him because all the crowd was struck with astonishment at his teaching.

19 And when evening came, he went out of the city.

Faith to move mountains *

20 And in the morning, as they went along, they saw the fig tree dried up from *the* roots.

21 And Peter, calling *it* to mind, said to him, 'Rabbi, look, the fig tree which you cursed has dried up.'

22 And in answer, Jesus said to them, 'Have faith in God. 23 For truly I say to you, whoever says to this mountain, "Be removed, and be hurled into the sea!", and does not doubt in his heart, but believes that those things which he says will come to pass, *so* will it be for him, whatever he says. 24 On account of this, I say to you, whatever things you ask *in* praying, believe that you receive *them*, and they will come to pass.*

*Forgiveness under law (contrast with
the forgiveness later under Paul's gospel.
Rom. 2\16, Eph. 1\7, Col. 1\14)*
²⁵ 'Likewise, when you stand praying, be forgiving if you have anything against anybody, so that your Father in the heavens might also forgive you for your fallings aside. ²⁶ But if you do not forgive, neither will your Father in the heavens forgive your offences.'

*Teaching in the Temple.
Confrontation over his authority
& the identifying of John*
²⁷ And they came again into Jerusalem, and as he was walking in the Temple the senior priests and the scribes and the elders came to him, ²⁸ and they said to him, 'By what kind of authority do you do these things, and who gave you this particular authority that you should do these things?'
²⁹ And in answer, Jesus said to them, 'I in turn will ask you one question, and you answer me, and I will tell you by what authority I do these things. ³⁰ The identification of John, was *it* from Heaven, or from men? Answer me.'
³¹ So they reasoned among themselves, saying, 'If we say, "From Heaven," he will say, "Why, then, did you not believe him?" ³² Should, though, we say, "From men"?'
They feared the people, for everybody reckoned that John truly was a prophet, ³³ and in answer, they said to Jesus, 'We do not know.'
And in answer, Jesus said to them, 'Neither do I tell you by what authority I do these things.'

Parable of the vine dressers

12\1 And he began to speak to them in parables.
'A man planted a vineyard, and he placed a fence around *it*, and dug the wine vat, and built a watch house, and let it out to vine dressers, then he took a journey abroad. ² And in due course, he assigned a servant to the farmers, so that he might receive some of the fruit of the vineyard from the vine dressers. ³ But they caught hold of him, *and* beat him, and sent *him* away empty handed.
⁴ 'And again he assigned to them another servant, and they stoned him and struck *him* on the head, *and* they sent *him* away *and* insulted *him*. ⁵ And again he sent another, but they murdered him and many others, scourging

some, and murdering others.
⁶ 'So then, still having one son, his own richly loved one, he last of all assigned him to them as well, saying, "They will have respect for my son." ⁷ But those farmers said among themselves, "This is the heir. Come, let's murder him, and the inheritance will be ours." ⁸ And they took him, *and* murdered *him*, and left *him* outside the vineyard. ⁹ What, therefore, will the lord of the vineyard do? He will come and destroy the farmers, and he will give the vineyard to others. ¹⁰ 'And have you not even read this passage? –

"*The* stone which the builders rejected
is what has become *the* head of *the* corner.
¹¹ This came about from *the* Lord
and it is a wonder in our eyes." '

¹² And they looked for a way to seize him, but they feared the people because they knew that he had levelled the parable against them, and they left him *and* went their way.

Confrontation concerning census tax
¹³ And they sent some of the Pharisees and the Herodians to him, so that they might catch him out in a word.
¹⁴ And they came *and* said to him, 'Teacher, we know that you are full of integrity, and it does not concern you about anybody, for you disregard the status of men, but you teach the way of God with truth. Is it lawful to give census tax to Caesar, or not? ¹⁵ Should we give, or should we not give?'
But knowing their hypocrisy, he said to them, 'Why do you test me? Bring me a denarion, so that I can see *it*.'
¹⁶ And they brought *it*, and he said to them, 'Whose image and superscription *is* this?'
They said to him, 'Caesar's.'
¹⁷ And in answer, Jesus said to them, 'Render to Caesar the things of Caesar, and to God the things of God.'
And they were astounded at him.

*Confrontation with the Sadducees
concerning events in the day of resurrection*
¹⁸ Then Sadducees, of such nature that they allege there not to be a resurrection, came to him and they questioned him, saying, ¹⁹ 'Teacher, Moses wrote for us that if anybody's brother dies, and he leaves behind a wife and

leaves remaining no children, his brother should take his wife and be raising up seed for his brother.*

²⁰ 'There were seven brothers, and the first took a wife, and in dying left no seed. ²¹ And the second took her and died, and neither did he leave any seed. And the same *with* the third. ²² And the seven had her, and left no seed. Last of all, the woman died as well. ²³ In the resurrection, when they will rise, *to* which of them will she be wife? For the seven had her as a wife.'

²⁴ And in answer, Jesus said to them, 'Are you not, on account of this, in error, not knowing the Scrolls nor the power of God?* ²⁵ For when they will rise from *the* dead, neither do they marry, nor are they given in marriage, but they are like the angels in the heavens. ²⁶ 'But concerning the dead, that they are raised, have you not read in the Scroll* of Moses* when God spoke to him in the bush, saying, "I *am* the God of Abraham, and the God of Isaac, and the God of Jacob"?* ²⁷ He is not the God of *the* dead, but God of *the* living. You, therefore, are in dreadful error.'

Testing by a scholar of the law.
the most important commandment *
to love God Who 'is one' (Deut. 6\4 etc.)
²⁸ And one of the scribes came forward, having heard them reasoning together, *and* perceiving that he had answered them judiciously, questioned him, 'Of what nature is *the* first of all the commandments?'

²⁹ And Jesus answered him, '*The* first of all the commandments *is*: "Hear, Israel, *the* Lord our God is one Lord. ³⁰ And you shall love *the* Lord your God out of all your heart, and out of all your being, and out of all your mind, and out of all your strength."* This *is the* first commandment.

³¹ 'And *the* second *is* similar to this: You shall love your neighbour as yourself.* There is no other commandment more important than these.'

³² And the scribe said to him, 'Right, Teacher, you have spoken in line with truth that He* is one,* and there is no other besides Him. ³³ And to love Him out of all your heart, and out of all your intelligence, and out of all the being, and out of all the strength, and to love *one's* neighbour as oneself is more important than all the whole burnt offerings and sacrifices.'

³⁴ And seeing that he answered intelligently, Jesus said to him, 'You are not far away from the Sovereign Rulership of God.'

And nobody dared to question him any more.

His testing Pharisees concerning the line of David *
³⁵ And in reaction, Jesus said, *while* he was teaching in the Temple, 'How do the scribes say that the Christ is *the* Son of David? ³⁶ For David himself said* by the agency of* *the* Holy Spirit:*

"The Lord said to my Lord,
'Sit at* My right hand*
until I have set your enemies
as a footstool for your feet.' "*

³⁷ 'David himself, therefore, called* him Lord, so how then is he his son?'

And the vast crowd listened to him with delight.

Beware of the scribes *
³⁸ And he said to them in his teaching, 'Turn your attention away from the scribes wanting to walk about in robes, and *to receive* greetings in the marketplaces, ³⁹ and the most important seats in the synagogues, and the prime places at the feasts, ⁴⁰ who devour widows' houses, and for exhibition pray at immense length. These will receive a heavier judgement.'*

A generous widow *
⁴¹ And Jesus sat down opposite the treasury, *and* observed how the people were throwing copper coins into the treasury, and many of the rich were putting much in. ⁴² And one poor widow coming along put in two leptons,* which is a kodrantes.*

⁴³ And he called his disciples, *and* he said to them, 'Truly I say to you, this widow, and she a poor one, has put *in* more than all those putting *money* into the treasury. ⁴⁴ For they put in everything out of what was abounding to them, but she, out of her destitution, put in everything, as much as she had, her entire livelihood.'

His prophecy of the destruction of the Temple.
Teaching on the Mount of Olives
answering the disciples' two questions
concerning the last days
& the mighty tribulation,

the pseudo Christ, & Jesus' return
*as the true Christ in power & radiance**

13\1 **A**nd as he was going out of the Temple, one of his disciples said to him, 'Teacher, look, what stones and what buildings!' [2] And in answer, Jesus said to him, 'You see these impressive buildings? There will certainly be no stone left on stone,* nor will they escape being reduced to rubble."

[3] And as he was sitting on the Mount of Olives facing the Temple, Peter and Jacob and John and Andrew asked him privately, [4] 'Tell us, when will these things be? And what *will be* the sign when all these things will be accomplished?'

Answer to the question:
'when will these things be?' (Mat. 24\4)
[5] And in answering them, Jesus went on to say, 'Take heed in case anybody deceives you. [6] For many will come trading on* my name, saying, "I Am!"* and they will deceive many.

[7] 'And when you will hear of battles and rumours of battles,* do not be disturbed, for it has to come to pass, but the end *is* not yet.

The sign of his magisterial presence (Mat. 24\7)
[8] 'For nation will be roused against nation, and kingdom against kingdom,* and there are going to be earthquakes in different places, and there are going to be famines and troubles. These *are* a beginning of birth-pangs.

[9] 'You, though, be vigilant for yourselves, for they will hand you over to sanhedrins and you will be beaten in synagogues, and you will stand before rulers and kings on account of me, for a testimony to them. [10] And the gospel must first be proclaimed to all the nations.

[11] 'But whenever they might be leading *you* away, handing you over, do not get anxious beforehand what you should say, nor premeditate, but whatever will be given to you in that hour, speak that, for you are not the one speaking, but the Holy Spirit.*

[12] 'Now brother will betray brother to death, and a father a child, and children will rise up against parents* and they will put them to death. [13] And you will be hated by everybody on account of my name, but he who endures to *the* end will be preserved.

[14] 'But when you see the Abomination of Desolation,* which was spoken of by the prophet Daniel, standing where it ought not –

he who reads, let him observe attentively – then let those in Judea flee into the mountains. [15] And let him who is on the housetop not go down into the house, nor go in to take anything out of his house. [16] And let him who is in the field not turn back again to collect his coat.

[17] 'But woe to those who are pregnant, and to those breastfeeding in those days! [18] And pray that your flight might not occur in winter. [19] For those days will be a tribulation the like of which has not arisen from *the* beginning of creation which God created until this time,* nor will it by any means arise *again.* [20] And unless *the* Lord were not to shorten the days, no flesh would have been preserved. But on account of the elect whom He has chosen out, He has shortened the days.

[21] 'Then if anybody says to you, "Look, here's the Christ!", or, "Look,* there!", do not believe *it.* [22] For pseudo christs and pseudo prophets* will be raised up,* and they will give signs and wonders* to seduce, if possible, even* the elect. [23] So look out. See,* I have told you these things in advance.

[24] 'But in those days, after that tribulation, the Sun will be darkened, and the Moon will not give its light, [25] and the stars of the sky will be falling, and the powers in the skies will be shaken.*

[26] 'And then they will see the Son of Man coming among clouds* with mighty power and magnificence. [27] And then he will authorize his angels, and they will gather together his chosen *people* out of the four winds, from *the* extremity of *the* Earth to *the* extremity of the sky.

*Parable of a fig tree**
[28] 'But learn the parable from the fig tree. When its branch has already become tender and it puts out its leaves, you come to know that summer is near. [29] So you also, when you see these things coming to pass, recognize that it's near, at *the* doors.

[30] 'Truly I say to you, this generated oracle* will certainly not have passed away until all these things will have taken place. [31] Heaven and the Earth will pass away, but my oracles will by no means pass away.

[32] 'But concerning that day and the hour, nobody knows – not even the angels in Heaven, nor the Son – except the Father.* [33] Take heed, be vigilant, and pray, for you do not know when the crisis* is. [34] *It is* comparable to a man

going out of the country, leaving his house, and giving the authority to his servants and his work to each, and he instructed the doorkeeper that he ought to keep watch. [35] 'Watch, therefore, for you do not know when the lord of the house is coming, in the evening, or at midnight, or at *the* crowing of the rooster, or in *the* morning, [36] in case coming suddenly he should find you composing yourselves for sleep. [37] And what I say to you, I say to all – watch.'

Priests' conspiracy to murder Jesus *

14\1 Now after two days it was the Passover and the *Festival of* Unleavened *Bread*, and the senior priests and the scribes were looking how they might arrest him by guile *and* murder *him*. [2] But they said, 'Not during the Festival, in case there might be an uproar of the people.'

Anointing with precious ointment at Bethany *

[3] And *when* he was in Bethany in the house of Simon the leper, as he was sitting a woman came in holding an alabaster flask of ointment of pure spikenard of large price, and she broke the flask *and* poured *it* on his head. [4] And some were indignant within themselves, and they were saying, 'Why has this waste of the ointment come about?'** [5] For this perfumed ointment could have been sold for more than three hundred denarions* and given to the poor.'

And they were incensed with her. [6] But Jesus said, 'Leave her alone. Why do you cause trouble for her? She has performed a beautiful deed for me. [7] For you always have the poor in company with you, and you can do good *for* them whenever you want, but you do not always have me. [8] She did what she had *in her power to do.* * She has had the anticipation to anoint my body for the embalming. [9] Truly I say to you, wherever this gospel will be proclaimed throughout the whole world, what this *woman* has done will also be spoken of in memory of her.'*

Conspiracy by Judas *

[10] And Judas Iscariot, one of the twelve, went off to the senior priests so that he might hand him over to them. [11] And *when* they heard *it* they were delighted, and they promised to give him money, so he kept searching out how he might conveniently betray him.

Jesus' final Passover. He predicts his betrayal *

[12] And on the first day of Unleavened *Bread* when they killed the Passover, his disciples said to him, 'Where do you want us to go *and* make preparations, so that you can eat the Passover?' [13] And he sent two of his disciples, and said to them, 'Go into the city, and a man there carrying a pitcher of water will meet you. Follow him, [14] and wherever he goes in, say to the house owner, "The Teacher says, 'Where is the guest room* where I can eat the Passover in company with my disciples?' " [15] And he himself will show you a large upper room spread out *and* ready. Make preparations for us there.'

[16] And his disciples went away and came into the city, and they found *it* just as he had said to them, and they prepared the Passover.

[17] And when evening arose, he arrived with the twelve.

[18] And as they were sitting together and eating bread, Jesus said, 'Truly I say to you, one from among you who is eating in company with me will betray me.'

[19] And one by one they began to be grieved and to say to him, 'Is it I?', and another, 'Is it I?'

[20] But in answer, he said to them, 'It is one of the twelve, he who is dipping into the dish with me. [21] The Son of Man goes as it has been written concerning him. But woe to that man by means of whom the Son of Man is betrayed! It would have been better for that man if he had not been born.'*

Jesus announces the new covenant
& looks forward to the Eon
& the new Passover feast *

[22] And as they were eating Jesus took bread, and he exalted* *God, and* he broke *the bread* up and gave *it* to them, and said, 'Take *and* eat. This represents* my body.'

[23] And he took the cup, *and when* he had given thanks he gave *it* to them, and they all drank from it.

[24] And he said to them, 'This represents my blood of the new covenant which is being poured out on behalf of many. [25] Truly I say to you, I will not drink any more from the fruit of the vine until that day when I drink it of a new kind in the Sovereign Rulership of God.'

He predicts the disciples' flight
& Peter's betrayal *

²⁶ And *when* they had sung a song, they went out into the Mount of Olives.

²⁷ And Jesus said to them, 'All of you will stumble on account of me during this night, for it has been written:

"I will strike the shepherd
and the sheep will be scattered."'*

²⁸ 'But after my being raised,* I will go ahead of you into Galilee.'

²⁹ But Peter said to him, 'Even if all will be offended, I, however, *will* not.'

³⁰ And Jesus said to him, 'Truly I say to you today,* that in this night, before a rooster crows twice, you will deny me three times.'

³¹ But he kept saying the more vehemently,* 'If it were needful for me to die with you, I will not deny you in any way.'

And they all said the same as well.

Agony in Gethsemane *

³² And they came into a place whose name *is* Gethsemane, and he said to his disciples, 'Sit here while I pray.'*

³³ And he took Peter and Jacob and John with him, and he began to be struck with amazement and deeply oppressed, ³⁴ and he said to them, 'My inner being is exceedingly sorrowful, even to the point of death. Remain here, and keep awake.'

³⁵ And he went forward a little *and* fell on the ground, and he was praying that, if it were possible, the hour might pass away from him.

³⁶ And he said, 'Abba, Father, all things *are* possible for you. Take this cup away from me. Nevertheless, not what I will, but what you *will*.'

³⁷ And he came and found them having composed themselves for sleeping, and he said to Peter, 'Simon, are you composed for sleeping?* Did you not have the strength to watch *for* one hour? ³⁸ Watch and pray, so that you might not enter into temptation.* The spirit *is* willing, but the flesh is weak.'

³⁹ And again he went away *and* prayed,* saying the same thing. ⁴⁰ And *when* he returned, he again found them composed for sleeping,* for their eyes were heavy, and they did not know how they should answer him.

⁴¹ And he came the third time, and said to them, 'Are you still* sleeping and taking your rest?* That is sufficient.* The hour has come. See now, the Son of Man is being betrayed into the hands of violators. ⁴² Rise up, and let us be going. Look, he who is betraying me has drawn near.'*

Betrayal by Judas & arrest *

⁴³ And just then, while he was still speaking, Judas, being one of the twelve, arrived, and with him a large crowd with swords and clubs, from the senior priests and the scribes and the elders.

⁴⁴ Now he who was betraying him had given them an arranged signal, saying, 'Whomever I embrace is the one. Seize him, and lead *him* away, safely secured.'

⁴⁵ And as soon as he arrived, he walked straight up to him, and said to him, 'Rabbi, Rabbi,' and he ostentatiously kissed him.*

⁴⁶ And they thrust their hands on him and seized him. ⁴⁷ But somebody among those standing nearby drew a sword, *and* he struck the servant of the high priest and cut off his ear.

⁴⁸ And in response, Jesus said to them, 'Have you come out as if against a bandit* with swords and clubs to take me? ⁴⁹ I was among you daily in the Temple teaching, and you did not seize me. But *this is* so that the Scrolls must be fulfilled.'*

⁵⁰ And they all forsook him, and fled. ⁵¹ And one particular young man followed him, having thrown a linen cloth round *his* unclothed *body*, and the young men seized him, ⁵² but, leaving the linen cloth behind, he fled from them, without clothing.

Examination & mocking before Caiaphas *

⁵³ And they led Jesus away to the high priest, and all the senior priests and the elders and the scribes were assembled before him.

⁵⁴ And Peter followed him from a long way off, as far as into the courtyard of the high priest, and he was sitting with the officers and warming himself at the fire.

⁵⁵ And the senior priests and the whole Sanhedrin were searching for a testimony against Jesus as a case for murdering him, but they were unable to find *one*, ⁵⁶ for many were bringing a false testimony against him, but their testimonies were not the same.*

⁵⁷ And some rising up brought false evidence against him, saying, ⁵⁸ 'We heard him say, "I will destroy this Temple which is made with hands,*

and within three days I will build another one, not made with hands." '

⁵⁹ And so neither in this was their testimony identical.

⁶⁰ And the high priest, taking a stand in the centre, questioned Jesus further, saying, 'Do you answer nothing? What are these testifying against you?'

⁶¹ But he held his peace, and answered nothing.

Again the high priest was questioning him, and he said to him, 'Are you the Christ, the Son of the Exalted One?'*

⁶² And Jesus said, 'I Am.* And you will see the Son of Man sitting at* *the* right hand* of power, and coming with the clouds* of the heavens.'

⁶³ Then the high priest tore his clothes, *and* he said, 'What need do we have of any further witnesses? ⁶⁴ You have heard the blasphemy. What do you think?'

And they all condemned him to be deserving of death.

⁶⁵ And some began to spit on him, and to blindfold his face and hit him, and say to him, 'Prophesy!' and the officers were striking him with slaps in the face.*

Denial by Peter *

⁶⁶ And while Peter was in the court below, one of the servant girls of the high priest came forward, ⁶⁷ and seeing Peter warming himself she looked at him *and* said, 'You were with Jesus the Nazarene as well.'

⁶⁸ But he made a denial, saying, 'I do not know or even understand what you are saying.'

And he went out into the porch, and a rooster crowed.

⁶⁹ And the servant girl, seeing him again, began to say to those standing nearby, 'This one is from among them.'

⁷⁰ And he once again denied it.

And after a little while, those standing nearby said to Peter, 'Surely you are from among them, for you are a Galilean, and your dialect gives *you* away.'

⁷¹ But he began cursing and swearing, 'I do not know this man whom you speak about.'

⁷² And a rooster crowed the second time. And Peter called to mind the remark which Jesus had spoken to him, 'Before a rooster crows twice, you will have denied me three times.' And having cogitated about it, he wept.

Examination before Pilate *

15\1 **A**nd first thing in the morning the senior priests formed a council in association with the elders and scribes and the whole Sanhedrin, and they bound Jesus* *and* led *him* away, and they handed *him* over to Pilate.

² And Pilate questioned him, 'Are you the King of the Jews?'

And in answer, he said to him, 'You yourself say *it*.'*

³ And the senior priests kept vehemently accusing him.

⁴ And Pilate questioned him again, saying, 'Do you not answer anything? You see how many things they are testifying against you.'

⁵ But Jesus no longer answered anything, so that Pilate was amazed.

Barabbas released *

⁶ Now at a* Festival *Pilate* used to release to them one prisoner, whomever they asked for.

⁷ And there was one named Barabbas, kept bound with fellow insurrectionists, who had committed a murder in the insurrection. ⁸ And the crowd, calling out, began to beg *him to do* for them as he customarily* did.

⁹ But Pilate answered them, saying, 'Are you willing that I should release to you the King of the Jews?'

¹⁰ For he knew that the senior priests had handed him over because of envy. ¹¹ The senior priests, though, vehemently stirred up the crowd so that he might instead release Barabbas to them.

¹² And Pilate, answering again, said to them, 'What, then, are you wanting I should do *to him* whom you call the King of the Jews?'

¹³ And they called out again, 'Hang him on a stake!'*

¹⁴ Then Pilate said to them, 'Why? What evil did he do?'

And they called out all the more, 'Hang him on a stake!'*

¹⁵ And Pilate, determining to carry out whatever *would be* satisfactory for the crowd, released Barabbas to them, and *when* he had had *him* scourged he handed Jesus over, so that he might be hanged on a stake.*

Crown of thorns *

¹⁶ And the soldiers led him away into the court, which is *the* Judgement Hall, and they called together the whole cohort. ¹⁷ And they

clothed him with purple, and they wove a crown of thorns *and* placed it on him, [18] and they began to make greetings to him, saying, 'Hail, King of the Jews!' [19] And they kept striking his head with a reed, and spitting on him, and bending *their* knees in honour of him. [20] And when they had done with mocking him, they took the purple clothing off him and put his own clothes on him, and they led him out so that they might hang him on a stake.*

Death.* His Aramaic call of 'Eloi, Eloi, lima sabachthani?'

[21] And they compelled somebody passing by, Simon, a Cyrenian, coming away from a field, the father of Alexander and Rufus, that he should carry his stake.*
[22] And they led* him to Golgotha, a place which, being translated, is Place of a Skull. [23] And they were offering him wine mingled with myrrh to drink, but he did not accept *it*.
[24] And after having hanged him on a stake,* they divided his garments among themselves, throwing lots over them for what each should take.*
[25] And it was *the* third hour when they hanged him on a stake.* [26] And the inscription of his accusation was written down: 'The King of the Jews'.*
[27] And together with him they hanged on a stake* two bandits,* one on his right, and one on his left. [28] And the passage was fulfilled which says, 'And he was numbered with transgressors.'*
[29] And those passing by were blaspheming him, shaking their heads, and saying, 'Aha! You razing the Temple and building *it* in three days, [30] save yourself and come down off the stake.'*
[31] In the same way the senior priests, similarly mocking, kept saying to one another, together with the scribes, 'He saved others. He is not able to save himself. [32] The Christ, the King of Israel! Let him come down off the stake,* so that we might see and believe.'
And those who were hanged on stakes along with* him heaped insults on him.
[33] And when *the* sixth hour came, darkness came* over the whole land until *the* ninth hour. [34] Then at the ninth hour, Jesus called out with a loud voice, saying, 'Eloi, Eloi, lima sabachthani?',* which, being translated, is 'My God, my God, why have You forsaken me?'*

[35] And some of those standing nearby, hearing, said, 'Look,* he's calling for Elijah.'
[36] And somebody ran up and soaked a sponge full of vinegar, and put *it* on a reed, and he was giving *it* to him to drink, saying, 'Let *him* be. Let's see if Elijah comes to take him down.'

Belief of the centurion *

[37] And Jesus uttered a loud cry, *and* he breathed out his last.* [38] And the veil of the Temple was torn into two, from top to bottom. [39] And the centurion who stood opposite him, seeing that he had called out like this, and had breathed out his last,* said, 'Truly this man was *the* Son of God.'*
[40] And there were women as well looking on from a long way off, among whom also was Maria Magdalene; and Maria, the mother of Jacob the Junior and of Joses; and Salome, [41] she who, when he was in Galilee, had followed him and provided for him, in company with* many other women who came up with him into Jerusalem.

Burial by Joseph of Arimathea *

[42] And evening being already come, because it was *the* Preparation, which is the day before the Sabbath, [43] Joseph of Arimathea, an honourable counsellor,* who himself also was waiting for the Sovereign Rulership of God, came and took courage *and* went to Pilate and asked for the body of Jesus. [44] And Pilate was surprised that he was already dead, and he called the centurion *and* asked him if he had been dead a long time.* [45] And *when* he came to know *it* from the centurion, he granted the body to Joseph. [46] And *Joseph* bought a fine linen cloth *and* he took him down *and* wrapped *him* in the linen cloth, and laid him in a memorial tomb which had been cut out of a rock, and he rolled a stone across the door of the tomb. [47] And Maria Magdalene, and Maria, *the mother* of Joses, were looking on attentively at where he had been lain.

Maria Magdalene & the other Maria buy spices on a work day after the high day Sabbath

16\1 And *when* the Sabbath* had passed,* Maria Magdalene, and Maria, *the mother* of Jacob, and Salome, bought* aromatics so that they might go *there and* anoint him.

His resurrection
declared to the women
by the Angel of God (Mat 28\2)

[2] And really early on the First of Weeks,* they* went to the tomb, the Sun having risen, [3] and they said to themselves, 'Who is going to roll away the stone from the door of the tomb for us?'

[4] And *when* they looked up, they saw that the stone had been rolled away – for it was extremely large – [5] and they went into the tomb, *and* they saw a young man* sitting at the right, clothed in a white robe, and they were absolutely astounded.

[6] But he said to them, 'Do not be afraid. You are looking for Jesus the Nazarene who has been hanged on a stake.* He has been raised.* He is not here. Look at the place where they laid him.

[7] 'But you go your way. Say to his disciples – and to Peter – that he goes ahead of you into Galilee. You will see him there, just as he said to you.'

[8] And they went out *and* fled from the tomb, and trembling and ecstasy* took hold of them, and they spoke nothing to anybody, for they were frightened.

Post-resurrection appearances to the disciples *

[9] Now, having risen early *on the* first *day* of *the* week,* he was brought to view first to Maria Magdalene from whom he had driven out seven demons.

[10] She went off *and* told those who had been in company with him, grieving and mourning, [11] and *when* they heard that he was alive and had been seen by her they did not believe *her*.

[12] After these things, he was brought to light* in a different form* to two of them *as* they walked along, going into a field, [13] and they went off *and* told *it* to the rest, *and* they did not believe them either.

Immediate authorization of the 11
to proclaim the gospel, performed during
the Acts period and after (compare Mat. 28\18-20
*authorization for the future time of the Eon).**
Those believing & identifying with God
& Jesus will be saved. Signs followed

[14] Later, in their sitting together eating, he was brought to light* to the eleven, and he reproached them for their unbelief and hardness of heart, because they did not believe those who had seen him *after* his having been raised.*

[15] And he said to them, 'In going out* into all the world,* proclaim the gospel to every creation.* [16] The one believing and being identified* will be saved,* but the one disbelieving will be condemned.* [17] And these signs will follow those who believe: through my name they will drive out demons; they will speak with new languages; [18] they will pick up snakes; and if they drink anything deadly it will not in any way hurt them;* they will lay hands on *the* sick and they will recover.'

Jesus taken up into Heaven *

[19] Then after speaking to them, the Lord was taken up into Heaven,* and he sat at* *the* right hand* of God.

Disciples fulfill their immediate authorization

[20] And they went out *and* made proclamations everywhere, the Lord working with *them*, and confirming the oracle by means of the signs following *it*. Amen.

~ ◆◆ ~

† The Gospel Accounts of Jesus Christ †

Luke

The physician Luke (Col. 4\14)
shows his integrity
in his prologue to Theophilus.
The beginning of the oracle (Mark 1\1, John 1\1)

1\1

eeing that many have undertaken* to draw up* a narrative* concerning the matters* which have been fully accomplished* among us ² – just as those who, from *the* beginning,* having become eye witnesses and servants of the oracle,* handed *those things* on to us – ³ so did it seem right to me, having accurately* followed all things from the first, to write to you in methodical order, most excellent Theophilus, ⁴ in order that you might gain full knowledge of the certainty of the words about which you have been instructed.

Proclamation to Zacharias
by the angel Gabriel
of the birth of John the Identifier
⁵ In the days of Herod, the king of Judea, there was a certain priest, Zacharias by name, out of the division of Abijah, and his wife *was* out of the daughters of Aaron, and her name *was* Elizabeth, ⁶ and they were both righteous in the sight of God, walking without blame in all the commandments and legal requirements of the Lord.
⁷ Now there had been no child for them because Elizabeth was barren, and they were both advanced in their days. ⁸ And it came about that, in executing his priestly office in the order of his division before God, ⁹ in keeping with the custom of the priestly service, it fell to him by lot to burn incense *when* he went into the Sanctuary of the Lord. ¹⁰ And the whole assembly of the people were praying outside at the hour of incense.
¹¹ And an angel of *the* Lord* was seen by him, standing at *the* right side of the altar of incense, ¹² and *when* Zacharias saw him, he was troubled, and fear fell on him.
¹³ But the angel said to him, 'Do not fear, Zacharias, because your prayer was heard, and your wife Elizabeth will give birth to* a son for

you,* and you shall call his name John. ¹⁴ And he will be an exuberance and an extreme joy to you, and many will rejoice at his birth. ¹⁵ For he will be eminent in the sight of the Lord, and he will drink neither any wine nor strong liquor, and he will be filled with *the* divine spirit, even from* his mother's womb. ¹⁶ And he will turn many of the sons of Israel towards *the* Lord their God.
¹⁷ 'And he will go out ahead of Him in *the* spirit* and power* of Elijah, in order to turn hearts of fathers towards *their* children,* and *the* disobedient in wisdom of *the* righteous, to make ready a people having been prepared for *the* Lord.'
¹⁸ And Zacharias said to the angel, 'By what *means* will I know this, for I am an old man, and my wife *is* advanced in her days?'
¹⁹ And in answer, the angel said to him, 'I am Gabriel, who stands in the presence of God, and I was authorized to speak to you and to announce to you the good news of these things. ²⁰ And you will see that you will be dumb, and not able to speak until the day in which these things might come to pass, because you did not believe my words which will be fulfilled in their own time.'
²¹ And the people were expecting Zacharias, and they wondered about his delaying so long in the Sanctuary. ²² And *when* he came out he was not able to speak to them, and they perceived clearly that he had seen a vision in the Sanctuary, and he kept making signs to them and remained speechless.
²³ And it came about,* as soon as the week of his officiating service was completed, *that* he departed to his own home.
²⁴ Now after those days his wife Elizabeth conceived, and she secluded herself *for* five months saying, ²⁵ 'The Lord has done this for me in *the* days in which He condescended to take away my disgrace among men.'**

Creation account of Jesus in Maria,
through divine power (Heb. 3\2),
& proclamation to Maria by the angel Gabriel
²⁶ And in the sixth month, the angel Gabriel was authorized from God *to go* into a town of Galilee whose name *was* Nazareth, ²⁷ to a virgin betrothed to a man whose name *was* Joseph, out of *the* house of David, and the name of the virgin *was* Maria.
²⁸ And on making his entrance, the angel said to her,* 'Greetings, you who have been shown

merciful goodwill! The Lord *is* with you. Favoured* *are* you among women.'

²⁹ But at seeing *him,* she was disturbed over his oracle, and she was reasoning what kind of greeting this might be.

³⁰ And the angel said to her, 'Do not fear, Maria, for you have found favour* from God. ³¹ And, as you will see, you will conceive in *your* womb, and you will give birth to a son, and you shall call his name Jesus.

³² 'He will be eminent, and he will be called the Son of the Most High.* And the Lord God will give to him the governmental seat of his father David. ³³ And he will reign over the house of Jacob throughout the Eons,** and there will be no end of his Sovereign Rulership.*

³⁴ Then Maria said to the angel, 'How will this be, since I do not know a man?'

³⁵ And in answer, the angel said to her, '*The* divine spirit* will come to fall on you, and the power of *the* Most High will overshadow you.* Therefore that Holy One who will be born* will be called the Son of God.* ³⁶ And look, your relative Elizabeth has herself also conceived a son in her old age, and this is *the* sixth month for her known as barren. ³⁷ For no word with God is impossible.'

³⁸ And Maria said, 'Here I am, the maid servant* of *the* Lord! Let it be to me in keeping with your oracles.'

And the angel departed from her.

Maria's visit to Elizabeth

³⁹ And Maria rose up in those days *and* went with haste into the hill country, into a town of Judah, ⁴⁰ and she went into the house of Zacharias and greeted Elizabeth.

⁴¹ And it so happened* *that* when Elizabeth heard the greeting of Maria, the baby leaped in her womb, and Elizabeth was filled with *the* divine spirit.

⁴² And she spoke out with a loud voice, and said, 'Favoured *are* you among women, and favoured* *is* the fruit of your womb. ⁴³ And where *does* this *come* from for me, that the mother of my Lord should come to me? ⁴⁴ For, indeed,* as soon as the voice of your greeting came into my ears, the baby leaped in joy in my womb. ⁴⁵ And exalted *is* she who believed, for there will be a fulfillment of those things spoken to her from *the* Lord.'

⁴⁶ And Maria said:

'My inner being* magnifies* the Lord,
⁴⁷ and my spirit has exulted
in God my Saviour.
⁴⁸ For He has looked on the lowly state
of His maid servant,*
for it will be seen* that from now on
all generations will declare me favoured.*
⁴⁹ For the Mighty One has done
excellent things for me,
and holy *is* His name,
⁵⁰ and His mercy to those revering Him
endures from generation to generation.
⁵¹ He acted in strength with His arm;
He has scattered the haughty
in *the* imagination of their hearts.
⁵² He has pulled down potentates*
from thrones, and lifted up *the* lowly.
⁵³ The hungry He has filled with good things
and *the* rich He has sent away empty.
⁵⁴ He has taken His servant Israel by the hand*
in order to remember *His* mercy
⁵⁵ – as He spoke to our fathers,
to Abraham and to his seed –
throughout the Eon.'**

⁵⁶ And Maria stayed together with her *for* about three months, then she went back to her home.

Birth of John the Identifier

⁵⁷ Now the time was fulfilled* for Elizabeth to deliver her child,* and she gave birth to* a son.

⁵⁸ And her neighbours and her relatives heard that *the* Lord was magnifying His mercy with her, and they rejoiced with her.

⁵⁹ And it was on the eighth day *that* they came to circumcise the child, and they were for calling him Zacharias, after the name of his father.

⁶⁰ And in answer, his mother said, 'No, rather, he shall be called John.'

⁶¹ And they said to her, 'There is nobody among your relatives who is called by this name.'

⁶² And they were making signs to his father *as to* what he might want him to be called.

⁶³ And he asked for a writing tablet, *and* wrote, saying, 'His name is John.'

And they were all amazed. ⁶⁴ And his mouth was opened instantly, as was his tongue, and he began to speak, exalting* God.

⁶⁵ And fear came over those who lived around them, and all these things were being spoken about in the whole hill country of Judea.

66 And all who heard laid *them* up in their hearts, saying, 'What, then, will this child become?'

And *the* hand of *the* Lord was with him.
67 And his father Zacharias was filled with *the* divine spirit, and he prophesied, saying:

68 'Exalted* *be** the Lord, the God of Israel,
  for He has looked on*
  and worked redemption
  for His people,*
69 and He has raised up for us
  a horn of salvation
  in the house of His servant David,
70 as He spoke through the agency
  of *the* mouth
  of His holy prophets from of old,*
71 salvation from our enemies
  and from the hand of all who hate us,
72 to fulfill mercy with our fathers
  and to remember His holy covenant,
73 *the* oath which He swore
  to our father Abraham,
  to grant us *that*,
74 being delivered out of *the* hand
  of our enemies,
  we should serve Him without fear,
75 in holiness and righteousness before Him
  all the days of our life.
76 And you, child, will be called
  the prophet of *the* Most High,*
  for you will go ahead of *the* face of *the* Lord
  to prepare His ways,
77 to give knowledge of salvation to His people
  in forgiveness of their violations,
78 on account of *the* tender compassion
  of our God,
  by which *the* Dayspring* from on high
  has looked on us,*
79 to intervene favourably*
  for those sitting in darkness
  and a shadow of death,
  to direct our feet onto *the* road of peace.'

80 And the child grew, and was strengthened in spirit, and he was in the deserts until *the* day of his manifestation to Israel.

Birth of Jesus *

2\1 **A**nd it came about in those days *that* a decree went out from Caesar Augustus *for* all the inhabited world to be registered. 2 This registration was first made when Cyrenius was governor of Syria. 3 And everybody went to be registered, each to his own town. 4 And Joseph also went up from Galilee, out of *the* town of Nazareth, into Judea, into a town of David, which is called Bethlehem, on account of his being out of *the* house and paternal lineage of David, 5 to be registered together with Maria who was engaged to him *to become his* wife, she being expectant with a child.
6 And it came about, in their being there, *that* the days of her giving birth became due. 7 And she gave birth to her son,* the firstborn,** and she wrapped him in strips of cloth, and laid him in the feeding trough,* because there was not a place for them in the guest room.*

The shepherds
8 And in the same region there were shepherds resting in the fields, keeping watch over their flock at night. 9 And then *the* Angel of *the* Lord* stood by them, and *the* radiance of *the* Lord shone around them, and they trembled with extreme fear.
10 And the Angel* said to them, 'Do not be afraid. For mark this:* I announce to you good news* of immense exuberance, which will be for all the people,* 11 that in a town of David a Saviour was born for you* today, who is Christ *the* Lord.* 12 And this *will* be a sign for you: You will find a baby wrapped in strips of cloth, lying in a feeding trough.'**
13 Then suddenly a crowd of a heavenly host with the Angel appeared*, praising God, and saying:

14 'Magnificence* to God
  in *the* highest *realms*,
  and peace on Earth;
  goodwill among men.'*

15 And it came about, as the angels departed from them into the sky, that the shepherd men said to one another, 'Come now, let us at once go into Bethlehem, and see this episode which has come about, which the Lord has made known to us.'
16 And they went with haste, and they discovered Maria and Joseph, and the baby lying in the feeding trough.* 17 And *after* seeing *him*, they publicly related the account which had been told to them concerning this child. 18 And all who heard were astounded at the things which had been spoken to them by the shepherds.

¹⁹ But Maria guarded all these words, pondering *them* in her heart.
²⁰ And the shepherds returned, magnifying and praising God for everything which they had heard and seen, as it had been spoken to them.

The child & the law of Moses fulfilled
²¹ And when eight days were fulfilled for the circumcising of him, he was given the name Jesus, which he had been named by the angel before he was conceived in the womb.
²² And when the days of their purification in keeping with the law of Moses were fulfilled, they brought him up to Jerusalem to present *him* to the Lord, ²³ as it has been written in *the* law of *the* Lord: 'Every male who opens the womb will be called holy to the Lord,' ²⁴ and to offer a sacrifice in keeping with what has been said in *the* law of *the* Lord: 'A pair of turtle-doves, or two young pigeons.'

Simeon spoken to by the Angel of God
²⁵ And then it came about that there was a man in Jerusalem whose name *was* Simeon, and this man *was* just and devout, eagerly expecting *the* Consolation of Israel, and *the* Holy Spirit was over him, ²⁶ and it was divinely communicated to him by the Holy Spirit that he would not see death before he had seen the Christ of *the* Lord.
²⁷ And he went under the impulse of the Spirit into the Temple, and, on the parents bringing in the child Jesus to carry out the custom of the law concerning him, ²⁸ he in turn took him up in his arms, and he exalted God, and said:

²⁹ 'Let Your servant now depart in peace,
Lord, in keeping with Your oracle,
³⁰ for my eyes have seen Your salvation,
³¹ which You have prepared
before all the peoples,
³² a light for a revelation of the nations
and *the* preeminence of Your people Israel.'

³³ And Joseph and the mother *of Jesus* were marvelling at those things being spoken concerning him.
³⁴ And Simeon invoked favour on them, and he said to *Jesus'* mother Maria, 'Mark this: this *child* is destined for a falling and rising up of many in Israel, and for a sign spoken against. ³⁵ And as for you, a sword will pierce through your own being as well, so that reasonings of many hearts might be unveiled.'

Anna, the prophetess
³⁶ And Anna, daughter of Phanuel, out of *the* tribe of Asher, was a prophetess. She was advanced in years, *and* had lived with a husband *for* seven years after her marriage.
³⁷ And she *was* an eighty-four year-old widow, who did not depart from the Temple, serving with fastings and prayers, night and day. ³⁸ And standing nearby at the same hour, she gave thanks to the Lord, and she spoke about Him to all those waiting for redemption in Jerusalem.

Jesus grows in strength & wisdom
³⁹ And when they had ended all things in keeping with the law of *the* Lord, they returned into Galilee, to their town Nazareth. ⁴⁰ And the child grew, and he was strengthened in spirit, being filled with wisdom, and *the* favour of God was on him.

In childhood, among rabbis
⁴¹ Now his parents went to Jerusalem every year at the Festival of the Passover. ⁴² And when he was twelve years, they went up to Jerusalem in keeping with the custom of the Festival.
⁴³ And having completed the days, on their returning the child Jesus remained behind in Jerusalem, and Joseph and his mother did not know. ⁴⁴ But supposing him to be among the group of travellers, they went a day's journey and searched up and down for him among their relatives and among acquaintances. ⁴⁵ And *when* they did not find him, they turned back to Jerusalem, searching up and down for him.
⁴⁶ And it came about after three days *that* they found him in the Temple, sitting in *the* presence of the teachers, both listening to them and asking them questions. ⁴⁷ And all those listening to him were astounded at his understanding and answers.
⁴⁸ And on seeing him they were struck with astonishment, and his mother said to him, 'Child, why have you acted in this way towards us? You can see that your father and I have been distressed in searching up and down for you.'
⁴⁹ And he said to them, 'Why *is it* that you were looking for me? Do you not know that I must be occupied in the things of my Father?'
⁵⁰ And they did not understand the word which he spoke to them. ⁵¹ And he went down

with them and they came into Nazareth, and he was subject to them, but his mother kept all these sayings in her heart.

⁵²   And Jesus progressed in wisdom and stature, and in favour before God and men.

Proclamation of John the Identifier.
*His testimony, & imprisonment *

3\1   Now in *the* fifteenth year of the government of Tiberius Caesar, in the governing of Pontius Pilate of Judea, and Herod ruling as tetrarch of Galilee, and his brother Philip ruling as tetrarch of Iturea and of *the* region of Trachonitis, and Lysanias ruling as tetrarch of Abilene, ² and Annas and Caiaphas were in *the* high priesthood, an oracle of God came to John,* the son of Zacharias, in the wilderness.

³   And he went into all the country around the Jordan, proclaiming an identification of submission for the forgiveness of violations, ⁴ as it has been written in the Scroll* of oracles of the prophet Isaiah, saying:

'A voice of one calling out in the wilderness,
"Prepare the way of *the* Lord;
make straight His beaten tracks.
⁵ Every valley will be filled,
and every mountain and hill
will be made level,
and the crooked *places* will be made
into a straight *path*
and the rough *tracks* into smooth roads,
⁶ and all flesh will see the salvation of God." '

⁷   So he said to the crowds who were coming out to be identified by him,* 'Progeny of snakes!' Who warned you to flee away from the coming indignation? ⁸ In that case, produce fruits worthy of submission, and do not begin to say among yourselves, "We have Abraham as father," for I say to you that out of these stones God is able to raise up sons for Abraham. ⁹ And now the axe also lies at the root of the trees. Every tree, therefore, not producing good fruit is cut down and gets thrown into fire.'

¹⁰   And the crowds asked him, saying, 'What should we do, then?'

¹¹   And in answer, he said to them, 'He who has two coats, let him impart to him who does not have *one*; and he who has food, let him do the same.'

¹²   Then tax collectors also came to be identified, and they said to him, 'Teacher, what shall we do?'

¹³   And he said to them, 'Exact nothing more beyond what you have been authorized.'

¹⁴   Then some men on military service also questioned him, saying, 'And what shall we do?'

And he said to them, 'Oppress nobody,* nor make false accusation, and be content with your pay.'*

John prophesies about Jesus.
Three types of identification: water & spirit
& burning by fire (3\16; 3\17 & Acts 2\3;
3\16-17 & 1 Cor. 3\15);
cp. also trial of fire (Mat. 20\22-23,
Mark 10\38-39, Luke 12\50, 1 Peter 1\7)

¹⁵   And as the people were in expectation, and everybody was reasoning in their hearts concerning John, whether or not he might be the Christ, ¹⁶ John answered, saying to everyone, 'I identify you with water, but he who is coming is mightier than me, the latchet of whose sandals I am not worthy to unfasten. He will identify you with *the* divine spirit and with fire.'* ¹⁷ His winnowing-fan *is* in his hand, and he will thoroughly purge his threshing-floor, and he will gather the wheat into his granary, but he will burn up the chaff with an inextinguishable fire.'

¹⁸   Then in many other respects he comforted and brought good news to the people.

¹⁹   But Herod the tetrarch, being rebuked* by him concerning Herodias, his brother Philip's wife, and for all *the* evil things which Herod had done, ²⁰ added this as well: on top of everything, he also shut John up in jail.

Identification of Jesus with the submissive
in the public water ritual John received from God.
*The appearance of the Angel of God *

²¹   Now, in all the people being identified,* and Jesus being identified, and in his praying,* it came about for the sky to be opened.*

²²   And the Holy Spirit,* in a bodily form,* descended over him in the manner of a dove, with* a voice to come* out of the sky, saying, 'You are My Son, the Richly Loved One.* In you I have found delight.'*

Age & genealogy of Jesus (Mat. 1\1-17)

²³   And Jesus himself was about 30 years in beginning *his proclamation*, being *the* son, as was reckoned by law,* of Joseph, *the son* of Heli, ²⁴ *the son* of Matthath, *the son* of Levi, *the son* of

Melchi, *the son* of Janna, *the son* of Joseph, ²⁵ *the son* of Mattathiah, *the son* of Amos, *the son* of Nahum, *the son* of Esli, *the son* of Nagge, ²⁶ *the son* of Maath, *the son* of Mattathiah, *the son* of Semei, *the son* of Joseph, *the son* of Judah, ²⁷ *the son* of Johanan, *the son* of Rhesa, *the son* of Zorobabel, *the son* of Salathiel, *the son* of Neri, ²⁸ *the son* of Melchi, *the son* of Addi, *the son* of Cosam, *the son* of Elmodam, *the son* of Er, ²⁹ *the son* of Jose, *the son* of Eliezer, *the son* of Jorim, *the son* of Matthat, *the son* of Levi, ³⁰ *the son* of Simeon, *the son* of Judah, *the son* of Joseph, *the son* of Jonan, *the son* of Eliakim, ³¹ *the son* of Melea, *the son* of Menan, *the son* of Mattatha, *the son* of Nathan, *the son* of David,˙ ³² *the son* of Jesse, *the son* of Obed, *the son* of Boaz, *the son* of Salmon, *the son* of Nahshon, ³³ *the son* of Amminadab, *the son* of Ram, *the son* of Hezron, *the son* of Pharez, *the son* of Judah,˙ ³⁴ *the son* of Jacob, *the son* of Isaac, *the son* of Abraham, *the son* of Terah, *the son* of Nahor, ³⁵ *the son* of Serug, *the son* of Reu, *the son* of Peleg, *the son* of Eber, *the son* of Salah, ³⁶ *the son* of Arphaxad,˙ *the son* of Shem, *the son* of Noah, *the son* of Lamech, ³⁷ *the son* of Methusalah, *the son* of Enoch, *the son* of Jared, *the son* of Mahalaleel, *the son* of Cainan, ³⁸ *the son* of Enos, *the son* of Seth, *the son* of Adam, *the Son* of God.˙˙

The Angel of God leads Jesus into the wilderness.
Jesus tested by the Devil˙

4\1 **A**nd Jesus, being full of divine spirit,˙ returned from the Jordan, and he was led by˙ the Spirit˙ into the wilderness, ² being tested by the Devil˙ *for* forty days. And he did not eat anything during those days, and on their being ended he was hungry afterwards.˙

³ And the Devil said to him, 'If you are the Son of God, speak to this stone so that it might become˙ bread.'

⁴ And Jesus made an answer to him, saying, 'It has been written that "Man shall not live on bread alone, but on every utterance of God." '˙

⁵ And the Devil˙ led him up into a high mountain, *and* in a moment of time he showed him all the kingdoms of the inhabited world.˙

⁶ And the Devil said to him, 'I will give you all this authority, and all their splendour, for it has been handed over to me and to whomever I wish to give it. ⁷ If, therefore, you will worship before me, all this will be yours.'˙

⁸ And in answer, Jesus said to him, 'Get behind me, Satan.˙ It has been written: "You shall worship *the* Lord your God, and you shall serve Him only." '˙

⁹ And he led him into Jerusalem, and set him on the pinnacle of the Temple, and he said to him, 'If you are *the* Son of God, throw yourself down from here. ¹⁰ For it has been written that:

> "He will give His angels charge concerning you,
> to thoroughly protect you,˙
> ¹¹ and they will lift you up on *their* hands,
> in case at any time
> you should strike your foot
> against a stone." '˙

¹² And in answer, Jesus said to him, 'It has been spoken that "You shall not put *the* Lord your God to the test." '˙˙

¹³ And having ended every testing,˙ the Devil departed from him until a *convenient* time.

¹⁴ And Jesus returned in the power of the Spirit˙ into Galilee, and a report concerning him went out throughout the entire surrounding region. ¹⁵ And he himself was teaching in their synagogues, *and* he was praised˙ by everybody.

At Nazareth a proclamation of himself from the Scroll of Isaiah.˙
Attempt to assassinate him

¹⁶ And he came into Nazareth where he had been brought up, and in keeping with his custom he went into the synagogue on the Sabbath day and he stood up to read aloud.

¹⁷ And a Scroll of the prophet Isaiah was handed over to him, and, unrolling the Scroll,˙ he found the place where this was written:

> ¹⁸ 'The Spirit of the Lord˙ *is* over me,˙
> on account of which He has anointed me
> to proclaim the gospel to *the* poor;
> He has authorized me to heal
> the broken-hearted,
> to proclaim deliverance to the captives
> and recovery of sight to *the* blind,
> to send off in deliverance
> those having been crushed,
> ¹⁹ to proclaim *the* welcome year of *the* Lord.'˙

²⁰ And he rolled up the Scroll˙ *and* gave *it* back to the attendant, *and* he sat down. And the eyes of everybody in the synagogue stayed fixed on him.

²¹ And he began to say to them, 'Today this

passage is fulfilled in your ears.'

²² And all spoke well of him, and they marvelled at the oracles of merciful goodwill which proceeded out of his mouth.

And they said, 'Is this not the son of Joseph?'

²³ And he said to them, 'You will doubtless speak this parable to me: Physician, heal yourself.* Whatever we have heard being done in Capernaum, do here also in your fatherland.'

²⁴ And he said, 'Truly, I say to you, no prophet is accepted in his fatherland.* ²⁵ But in truth I tell you, many *were* widows in Israel in the days of Elijah, at the time the sky was shut up for three years and six months, when a severe famine arose over all the land. ²⁶ And Elijah was sent to none of them except to Sarepta, a *town* of Sidon, to a woman *who was* a widow. ²⁷ And there were many lepers in Israel in the time of the prophet Elijah, and none of them was cleansed except Naaman the Syrian.'

²⁸ And everybody in the synagogue, *when they* heard these things, was filled with boiling fury,* ²⁹ and they rose up and threw him out of *the* town, and led him to an overhanging brow of the mountain which their town had been built on, to throw him down headlong, ³⁰ but, passing right through them, he went his way.

He teaches at Capernaum.
Healing of a man with an unclean spirit *

³¹ And he came down into Capernaum, a town of Galilee, and he was teaching them on the Sabbaths, ³² and they were struck with astonishment at his teaching, for his speech was with authority.

³³ And in the synagogue there was a man who had the spirit of an unclean demon, and it called out with a loud voice, ³⁴ saying, 'Hey, what do we *have* to do with you, Jesus, Nazarene? Have you come to destroy us? I know you, who you are – the Holy One of God.'

³⁵ And Jesus rebuked it, saying, 'Be muzzled, and come out of him!'

And throwing him in front of them, the demon came out of him, nothing having injured him.

³⁶ And astonishment arose over everybody, and they spoke to one another, saying, 'What kind of oracle *is* this that he gives orders to the unclean spirits with authority and power, and they come out?'

³⁷ And a ringing in the ears* concerning him went out into every place of the surrounding country.

Healing of Peter's mother-in-law *

³⁸ And he rose up out of the synagogue, *and* he went into the house of Simon. And the mother-in-law of Simon was being gripped with a high fever, and they appealed to him concerning her. ³⁹ And he stood over her *and* rebuked the fever, and it left her, and she rose up at once *and* served them.

⁴⁰ And at the sinking of the Sun, all, as many who had sick ones with various diseases, brought them to him, and he laid his hands on each one of them *and* healed them.

Demons know who he is *

⁴¹ And demons also came out from many, screaming and saying, 'You are the Christ, the Son of God!'

And he rebuked *them, and* did not allow them to speak because they knew him to be* the Christ.

⁴² And day being come, he departed *and* went into a deserted place, and the crowds were looking for him, and they came to him and were detaining him not to depart from them.*

⁴³ But he said to them, 'I must also proclaim the gospel, the Sovereign Rulership of God,* to different cities, because for this I have been authorized.'

⁴⁴ And he was making proclamation in the synagogues of Galilee.

Disciples chosen *

5\1 **A**nd it came about, while the crowds were pressing on him to hear the oracle of God, that he was standing beside the Lake of Gennesaret, ² and he saw two boats moored beside the lake, but the fishermen had gone from them *and* had washed out their nets. ³ And he went into one of the boats, which was Simon's, *and* he asked him to push out a little away from the land. And he sat down *and* was teaching the crowds from the boat.

⁴ Now when he had finished speaking, he said to Simon, 'Launch out into the deep, and let down your nets for a catch.'

⁵ And in answer, Simon said to him, 'Master, in toiling all through the night we have taken nothing. Nevertheless, at your word I will let the net down.'

⁶ And on doing this they netted a large shoal

of fish, and their net was being torn, [7] and they signalled to their companions, those in the other boat, that they should come to help them. And they came and filled both the boats, so that they were beginning to sink.

[8] And Simon Peter saw it *and* fell at the knees of Jesus, saying, 'Depart from me, for I am a violating man, Lord.'

[9] For astonishment seized hold of him and all those gathered with him at the haul of the fish that they had taken, [10] and likewise Jacob, and John, sons of Zebedee, who were companions of Simon.

And Jesus said to Simon, 'Do not fear. From now on you will be catching* men.'

[11] And having brought their boats to land, they left behind everything and followed him.

Healing of a leper.*
Withdrawals into the wilderness
[12] And it so happened, in his being in one of the towns, that at that moment* a man covered in leprosy saw Jesus, and he fell on *his* face, *and Jesus* was implored by him, saying, 'Lord, if you are willing, you are able to cleanse me.'

[13] And he stretched out *his* hand *and* touched him, saying, 'I am willing. Be made clean.'

And the leprosy instantly departed from him.

[14] And he charged him to tell nobody, but he said, 'Go *and* show yourself to the priest, and make an offering concerning your cleansing, as Moses commanded, with a view to a testimony to them.'

[15] But still more the report about him spread, and vast crowds of people kept coming together to listen, and to be healed by him from their infirmities.

[16] *Jesus*, though, would withdraw himself into the wilderness and pray.*

Healing of a paralytic,
& forgiveness of violations*
[17] And it came about, in one of the days in which he was teaching, that there were Pharisees and teachers of the law sitting by, who had come out of every village of Galilee, and Judea, and Jerusalem, and the power of *the* Lord was *present* to heal them.

[18] And then it so happened that men were carrying on a bed a man who was paralyzed, and they were trying to bring him in and to lay *him* in front of him. [19] And on not finding any way by which they might bring him in because

of the crowd, they went up on the rooftop *and* let him down with the bed through the tiles, right in front of Jesus.

[20] And seeing their faith, he said to him, 'Man, you have been forgiven for your violations.'

[21] And the scribes and the Pharisees began to reason, saying, 'Who is this who speaks blasphemies? Who is able to forgive violations except God alone?'

[22] But Jesus, knowing full well their reasonings, said in answer to them, 'Why do you reason in your hearts? [23] Which is easier, to say, "You have been forgiven for your violations," or to say, "Rise up and walk"? [24] But so that you might know that the Son of Man has authority on Earth to forgive violations ...'

Then he said to the paralytic, 'I say to you, rise up, and take your bed, *and* go to your home.'

[25] And at once rising up before them, he took up what he had been lying on, *and* he departed to his home, magnifying God.

[26] And amazement* seized hold of everybody, and they magnified God, and they were filled with reverence, saying, 'We have seen strange things today.'

Choosing of Levi (Matthew)
& eating with violators at his feast*
[27] And after these things he went out and looked attentively at a tax collector, Levi by name, sitting at the tax office, and he said to him, 'Follow me.'

[28] And he left behind everything, rose up, *and* followed him.

[29] And Levi put on a large banquet for him in his own house, and there was a large company of tax collectors and others who were sitting down in company with them.

[30] And their scribes and the Pharisees murmured against his disciples, saying, 'Why do you eat and drink with the tax collectors and violators?'

[31] And in answer, Jesus said to them, 'Those who are in good health have no need of a physician, but those who are sick. [32] I have come to call not the righteous, but violators into submission.'

Friends of the bridegroom.
Parable of wineskins & garments*
[33] And they said to him, 'Why do the disciples of John fast often and make petitions, and those of the Pharisees *do* as well, but yours eat and

drink?'
³⁴ And he said to them, 'Are you able to compel the sons of the bridegroom to fast in the time when the bridegroom is in company with them? ³⁵ But the days will also come when the bridegroom will be taken away from them, *and* then they will fast in those days.'
³⁶ And he spoke a parable to them as well: 'Nobody puts a piece of new garment on an old garment. Otherwise the new one will also tear, and *the* piece from the new one will not line up with the old.
³⁷ 'And nobody pours freshly made wine into old wineskins. Otherwise the new wine will burst the wineskins, and it will be spilled out, and the wineskins will perish. ³⁸ But new wine must be poured into new wineskins, then both are preserved. ³⁹ And nobody having drunk *the* old immediately wants *the* new *wine*, for he says, "The old is more tasteful." '

He rebukes the Pharisees
concerning the Sabbath *

6\1 **A**nd it came about during a Sabbath, *the* second after the first,* *that* he was passing through the grain fields, and his disciples were plucking the ears of corn and rubbing *them* with *their* hands.
² But some of the Pharisees said to them, 'Why do you do what is not lawful to do on the Sabbaths?'
³ And answering them, Jesus said to them, 'Have you not read this, what David did when he was hungry, himself, and those who were in company with him, ⁴ how he went into the House of God and took the loaves of the presentation, and gave *some* also to those who were with him, which is not lawful to eat, except only by the priests?'
⁵ And he said to them, 'The Son of Man is Lord also of the Sabbath.'

Healing of a withered hand. *
Pharisees' conspiracy
⁶ And it also came about on another Sabbath *that* he went into the synagogue and was teaching. And there was a man *there*, and his right hand was withered. ⁷ And the scribes and Pharisees kept watching if he would heal on the Sabbath day, so that they could find an accusation against him.
⁸ But he knew their reasonings, and he said to the man having the withered hand, 'Rise up,

and stand out in the centre.'
And he rose up *and* was standing.
⁹ Then Jesus said to them, 'I will ask you something: Is it lawful on the Sabbaths to do good or to do evil, to save or to kill?'*
¹⁰ And looking around at them all, he said to the man, 'Stretch out your hand.'
And he did so, and his hand was restored, as whole as the other. ¹¹ But they were filled up with senseless rage, and they talked to one another about what they might do to Jesus.

The 12 chosen *
¹² And it came about in those days *that* he went out into the mountain to pray, and he was spending the night in prayer to God.*
¹³ And when it became day he called his disciples, and he chose out twelve from them, whom he also named apostles: ¹⁴ Simon, whom he also named Peter,* and his brother Andrew; Jacob and John; Philip and Bartholomew; ¹⁵ Matthew and Thomas; Jacob, the *son* of Alphaeus; and Simon, called the Zealot; ¹⁶ and Judas,* *the brother* of Jacob; and Judas Iscariot who for his part became a traitor.

Crowds healed *
¹⁷ And on coming down in company with them, he stopped on a level place, and *there was* a crowd of his disciples, as well as a large crowd of the people from all Judea and Jerusalem and the sea-coast of Tyre and Sidon who had come to hear him and to be healed from their diseases, ¹⁸ and those who were troubled by unclean spirits, and they were healed. ¹⁹ And the whole crowd were looking to touch him, for power was going out from him and he healed everyone.

Teaching on the plain (6\17). *
Exaltation & woe
²⁰ And he lifted up his eyes towards his disciples, and he said:

'Exalted *are* the poor,
for yours is the Sovereign Rulership of God.
²¹ Exalted *are* those hungering now,
for you will be filled.
Exalted *are* those weeping now,
for you will laugh.
²² Exalted are you when men will hate you,
and when they cut you off
and reproach *you*

and reject your name as evil
on account of the Son of Man.
23 Rejoice in that day, and leap for joyfulness,
for you will see that your reward
in Heaven* *is* manifold,
for their fathers acted along
those same lines
towards the prophets.
24 'But woe to you wealthy,
because you have your due consolation.
25 Woe to you who have been filled,
for you will be hungry.
Woe to you who laugh now,
for you will mourn and weep.
26 Woe *to you* when all men speak well of you,
for their fathers did all those things
to the pseudo prophets.*

*True discipleship: concerning enemies
& retaliation. Sons of the Most High
like Jesus (1\32, 6\35, 8\28, John 1\12,
Rom. 8\16, 2 Cor. 6\18, Gal. 3\26, 1 John 3\1)*
27 'But to you who hear I say: Love your
enemies. Do good to those who hate you. 28
Speak good words to* those who curse you.
Pray for those who use you spitefully.
29 'And to him who hits you on the jaw, offer
the other *side* as well.* And to one taking away
your long robe, do not keep back the outer
jacket as well.
30 'And to everyone asking you, give; and do
not ask back from anyone taking away your
things.
31 'And as you would wish that men should do
to you, you in turn do to them in the same
way.*
32 'And if you love those who love you, what
kind of advantage is that to you? For even
violators love those who love them. 33 And if
you do good to those who do good to you,
what kind of advantage is that to you? For
even* violators do the same.
34 'And if you make a loan *to anyone* from one
whom you hope to receive back, what kind of
advantage is that to you? For even violators
lend to violators in order that they might
receive the same things back.
35 'But love your enemies, and do good, and
lend, hoping for nothing back, and manifold
will be your reward, and you will be the Sons of
the Most High,* for He is kind to the ungrateful
as well as *to the* evil.* 36 Become compassionate,
therefore, in the same way your Father also is
compassionate.

37 'And do not judge, and you will not in any
way be judged. Do not condemn, and you will
not in any way be condemned. Forgive, and you
will be forgiven.
38 'Give, and it will be given to you. A good
measure, pressed down, and shaken together,
and running over will the professional
measurers give into your garment-fold.* For
with the same measure which you measure out,
it will be measured back to you.'

Parable of the blind leading the blind *
39 And he spoke a parable to them: 'Is a blind
man able to lead a blind man?* Will they not
both fall into a ditch? 40 The disciple is not
above his teacher, but everybody instructed will
be like his teacher.
41 'And why do you regard the chip in your
brother's eye, but you do not consider the log
in your own eye? 42 Or how are you able to say
to your brother, "Brother, let me pull out the
chip in your eye," yet you yourself do not see
the log in your own eye? You hypocrite! First
pluck the log out of your own eye, and then
you will see clearly to pull out the chip in the
eye of your brother.

*Good & bad trees.
Abundance of the heart* *
43 'For there is not a good tree producing
corrupt fruit, nor a corrupt tree producing good
fruit. 44 For each tree is known by its own fruit.
For men do not gather figs from thorn bushes,
nor do they gather a bunch of grapes from a
bramble bush.
45 'The good man out of the good treasure of
his heart produces what *is* good,* whereas the
evil man out of the evil treasure of his heart
produces what *is* evil, for his mouth speaks out
of the abundance of the heart.

A house built on the 'rock' of Jesus
(πέτρα, petra; Mat.16\18, 1 Cor. 10\4)*
46 'And why do you call me "Lord, Lord", but
do not do what I say? 47 Anybody who comes to
me, and hears my oracles and carries them out,
I will explain to you what he is like. 48 He is like
a man building a house, who dug down, then
went deep, and laid a foundation on the rock,*
and *when* a flood rose up the torrent beat against
that house, but it did not have the force to
shake it, for it had been founded on the rock.*
49 But he who hears and does not act is like a
man *who* built a house on the ground without a

foundation, *and* the torrent beat against it, and straightaway it collapsed, and violent was the destruction of that house.'

Healing of a centurion's servant *

7\1 **N**ow when he had completed all his oracles in the ears of the people, he went into Capernaum.
2 And a certain centurion's servant, having a sickness, was about to die. He was highly valued by him, 3 and on hearing about Jesus he sent the elders of the Jews to him, begging him that he might come *and* cure his servant.
4 And on coming to Jesus, they begged him with urgency, saying that the one for whom he should do this is* worthy, 5 *and saying*, 'For he loves our nation, and he himself built the synagogue for us.'
6 Then Jesus was going in company with them, but, being already not far from the house, the centurion sent friends* to him, saying to him, 'Lord, do not trouble yourself, for I am not worthy that you should come underneath my own roof, 7 so neither do I count myself worthy to come to you. You speak a word, though, and my servant will be healed. 8 For I myself* also am a man having been appointed* under authority, having soldiers under me, and I say to this one, "Go!" and he goes, and to another, "Come!" and he comes, and to my servant, "Do this!" and he does *it.*'
9 And *when* Jesus heard these things, he was astonished at him, and, turning around to the people who followed him, he said, 'I say to you, not even in Israel have I found such strong faith.'
10 And those *who* had been sent returned to the house *and* found the sick servant in good health.

The only son of a widow is raised
by the power of Jesus' word

11 And it came about soon afterwards *that* he went into a town called Nain, and many of his disciples and a large crowd went with him.
12 Now when he drew near the gate of the town, it so happened that *a man* having died was being carried out, an only* son of his mother, and she *was* a widow, and a considerable crowd of the town *was* with her.
13 And *when* the Lord saw her, he was moved with compassion for her, and he said to her, 'Do not weep.'

14 And coming forward he touched the coffin, and those carrying *him* stood still.
And he said, 'Young man, I say to you, rise up.'
15 And the dead *man* sat up, and he began to speak. And he presented him to his mother.
16 And fear gripped everybody, and they magnified God, saying, 'An eminent prophet has been raised* among us,' and 'God has visited His people.'
17 And this report about him went out in all Judea, and in all the surrounding region.

His testimony concerning John the Identifier *

18 And the disciples of John brought word back to him about all these things.
19 And John, calling a certain couple of his disciples, sent *them* to Jesus, saying, 'Are you the Coming One, or are we to look for another?'
20 And the men came to him, and they said, 'John the Identifier has sent us to you, saying, "Are you the Coming One, or should we look for another?" '
21 And in that hour he healed many from diseases and plagues, and of evil spirits, and he enabled many blind to see.
22 Then in answer, Jesus said to them, 'Go your way, *and* report back to John what you have seen and heard, how *the* blind are seeing again, *the* lame walk, lepers are cleansed, *the* deaf hear, *the* dead are being raised, the gospel is proclaimed to *the* poor. 23 And exalted is he whoever might not be made to stumble in me.'
24 And *when* the messengers of John had departed, he began to speak to the crowds about John: 'What have you gone out into the wilderness to look at? A reed shaken by *the* wind? 25 But what have you gone out to see? A man clothed in soft garments? Look, those in exotic clothing are living it out in luxury in royal palaces. 26 But what did you go out to see? A prophet? Yes, I say to you, and one more eminent than a prophet. 27 This is *he* concerning whom it has been written:

"Mark this: I authorized My messenger before your face,
  who will prepare your way ahead of you."*

28 'For I say to you, among those born of a woman* nobody is a more eminent prophet than John the Identifier. However, he who *is* least in the Sovereign Rulership of God is more eminent than he is.'*

²⁹ And all the people hearing, including the tax collectors identified into the identification of John, declared God as just. ³⁰ But the Pharisees and the scholars did away with the counsel of God for themselves, not having been identified by him.

³¹ *And Jesus said,* 'To what, then, shall I liken the men of this generation, and what are they like? ³² They are like little children sitting in a marketplace, and calling to one another, and saying:

"We played the flute to you
and you did not dance;
we played a lament to you
and you did not weep."'*

³³ 'For John the Identifier came neither eating bread nor drinking wine, and you say, "He has a demon." ³⁴ The Son of Man has come eating and drinking, and you say, "Look, a glutton and a wine drinker, a friend of tax collectors and violators!" ³⁵ And yet wisdom is justified by all her children.'

Anointing at a Pharisee's house.
Forgiveness of violations

³⁶ And one of the Pharisees asked him that he might eat in company with him. And he went into the Pharisee's house, *and* he was sitting down. ³⁷ And then it came about that a woman in the town who was a violator, coming to know that *Jesus* was sitting to eat in the house of the Pharisee, brought an alabaster flask of ointment, ³⁸ and she stationed herself behind *him* at his feet, weeping, *and* she began to wet his feet with tears, and she was wiping *them* with the hairs of her head, and she was kissing his feet and anointing *them* with the ointment.

³⁹ Now seeing *this*, the Pharisee who had invited him spoke within himself, saying, 'This man, if he were a prophet, would have known who and what manner of woman *this is* who touched him, that she is a violator.'

⁴⁰ And in response, Jesus said to him, 'Simon, I have something to say to you.'

And he said, 'Teacher, say it.'

⁴¹ 'There were two debtors to a certain creditor. One owed five hundred denarions,* and the other *owed* fifty ⁴² but had nothing to make payment *with, and* he freely forgave both. Say, therefore, which of them will love him more?'

⁴³ And in answer, Simon said, 'I take it* that *it*

is he for whom he freely forgave the more.'

And he said to him, 'You have judged rightly.'

⁴⁴ And he turned towards the woman, *and* he said to Simon, 'Do you mark this woman? I went into your house *and* you gave me no water on my feet, but she has washed my feet with tears and wiped *them* with the hairs of her head. ⁴⁵ You gave me no kiss, but she, from the *time* I came in, has not ceased kissing my feet. ⁴⁶ You did not anoint my head with oil, but she has anointed my feet with ointment, ⁴⁷ for which reason, I say to you, her many violations have been forgiven, for the reason that she had strong love. But he for whom little has been forgiven loves little.'

⁴⁸ And he said to her, 'Your violations have been forgiven.'

⁴⁹ And those eating together with *him* began to say among themselves, 'Who is this who even* forgives violations?'

⁵⁰ But he said to the woman, 'Your faith has saved you. Go in peace.'

Gospel of the Sovereign Rulership of God
proclaimed to every town & village.
Support of substance
from certain women & many others

8\1 **A**nd it came about* afterwards that he travelled around through every town and village announcing and proclaiming the gospel, the Sovereign Rulership of God,* and the twelve together with him, ² as well as certain women who had been cured from evil spirits and infirmities; Maria who is called Magdalene, from whom seven demons had gone out; ³ and Joanna, wife of Chuza (a manager of Herod); and Susanna; and many others, who were providing for them from their own resources.

Parables of the kingdom, concerning Israel.
Parable of a sower *

⁴ And *when* a large crowd was assembling together, and those from town to town* kept coming to him, he spoke by means of a parable: ⁵ 'A sower went out to sow his seed, and in his sowing some fell at the roadside, and it was trampled on and the birds of the sky* devoured it up. ⁶ And some *seed* fell on the rock, and on sprouting it dried up, on account of its lacking moisture. ⁷ And some *seed* fell in *the* middle of the thorn bushes, and the thorn bushes sprang up together *and* stifled it. ⁸ And other *seed* fell on

the good soil, and sprang up *and* produced fruit, a hundred-fold.'

And having declared these things, he called out, 'He who has ears to hear, let him hear.'

Mysteries of the Sovereign Rulership of God.
Judgement on Israel's unbelief foretold by Isaiah
⁹ And his disciples questioned him, saying, 'What might this parable signify?'
¹⁰ And he said, 'To you it has been given to know the mysteries of the Sovereign Rulership of God, but to the rest in parables, so that:

"In seeing they might not see,
and in hearing they might not understand."'

Explanation of the parable of a sower
¹¹ 'Now the parable signifies this: The seed represents the oracle of God. ¹² And those by the roadside represent those who hear, *but* then the Devil comes and snatches the oracle away from their heart, so that, having believed, they cannot be saved. ¹³ And those on the rock *represent* those who, when they hear, receive the oracle with gladness, but they have no root, *and* who believe for a season, but in a time of trial they fall away.
¹⁴ 'And that which fell among the thorn bushes, these represent those who have heard and gone on their way, *but* they become stifled under *the* cares and riches and pleasures of living, and they bring no fruit to maturity. ¹⁵ But that *seed* in the good soil represents those who with a noble and good heart have heard the oracle *and* keep it secure, and produce fruit in patient endurance.

Parable of a lamp
¹⁶ 'But nobody, having lit a lamp, covers it with a bowl, or puts it underneath a bed, but he sets *it* on a candlestick, so that those who enter might see the light. ¹⁷ For nothing is hidden which will not become brought to light, nor kept secret which will not become known and brought to light. ¹⁸ So consider how you listen. For whoever has, to him it will be given. And whoever does not have, even what he thinks he has will be taken from him.'

True brothers (Rom. 8\29, Heb. 2\11 etc.)
¹⁹ Then his mother and brothers came to him, and they were not able to meet him because of the crowd.
²⁰ And it was reported to him, saying, 'Your mother and your brothers are standing outside, wanting to see you.'
²¹ And in answer, he said to them, 'My mother and my brothers are those who hear the oracle of God and are carrying it out.'

He calms the storm
²² Now it came about one day that he and his disciples went into a boat, and he said to them, 'Let us go over to the other side of the lake.'

And they put out to sea, ²³ but as they were sailing he fell off into a sleep, and a stormy wind came down onto the lake, and they were being swamped, and were in danger.
²⁴ And they came to him *and* woke him, saying, 'Master, Master, we're perishing!'

Then, being roused, he rebuked the wind and the roughness of the waters, and they ceased, and it became calm.
²⁵ And he said to them, 'Where is your faith?'

And being afraid, they marvelled, saying to each other, 'Who is this, then, that he commands even the winds and water, and they obey him?'

Healing of a man under
the power of the demon Legion
²⁶ And they sailed down into the country of the Gadarenes, which is on the opposite side to Galilee. ²⁷ And on his disembarking onto the land, a certain man from the town met him, having had demons for a long time, and he was wearing no outer garment, nor did he live in any house, but in the tombs.
²⁸ And seeing Jesus he called out, and he fell down before him, and with a loud voice said, 'What do I have to do with you, Jesus, Son of the Most High God? I implore you, do not torment me with interrogation.' ²⁹ For he had commanded the unclean spirit to come out of the man, for many times it had held him in its grip, and he was being kept under guard, shackled with manacles and in foot chains, but he would break the shackles *and* be driven by the demon into uninhabited places.
³⁰ And Jesus asked him, saying, 'What is your name?'

And because many demons had gone into him, he said, 'Legion.'
³¹ And he begged him that he would not command them to go out into the abyss.
³² Now there was a considerable herd of pigs feeding there on the mountain, and they asked him if he would allow them to go into them,

and he allowed them. [33] Then the demons came out of the man *and* went into the pigs, and the herd rushed violently down the cliff *and* into the lake and were choked.

[34] When those who fed *them* saw what had happened, they fled and related *it* in the town and in the fields. [35] Then they went out to see what had been happening, and they came to Jesus and found the man from whom the demons had departed seated at the feet of Jesus, clothed, and of sound mind, and they were afraid. [36] And those who had seen *it* also related to them how the man under the power of the demon was saved. [37] However, the whole populace of the surrounding area of the Gadarenes asked him to depart from them, because they were gripped by an extreme fear, so he embarked on a boat *and* went back.

[38] But the man out of whom the demons had departed begged to be* with him, but Jesus sent him away, saying, [39] 'Return to your home, and relate what mighty things God has done for you.'

And he went his way, proclaiming throughout the whole town what mighty things Jesus had done for him.

*Healing of a lady with a flow of blood.**
*Raising of the daughter of Jair**

[40] And it came about, on Jesus' returning, *that* the crowd gladly received him, for they were all waiting for him.

[41] And then it happened that a man named Jair* came, and he *was* a president of the synagogue, and he fell down at the feet of Jesus *and* asked him to come into his house, [42] because he had an only* daughter, about twelve years old, and she was dying.

But as he went on, the people were pressing him, [43] and a lady who had been with an issue of blood for twelve years, who had spent all *her* living on physicians, but could not be cured by anybody, [44] came behind *and* touched the hem of his garment, and instantly her issue of blood stopped.

[45] And Jesus said, 'Who was touching me?'

And when everybody made denial, Peter and those with him said, 'Master, the crowd throngs and presses, yet you ask, "Who was touching me?" '

[46] And Jesus said, 'Somebody has touched me, for I perceived *that* power emanated from me.'

[47] And *when* the lady saw that she was not hidden she came trembling, and, falling down

before him, she declared to him in front of all the people for what reason she had touched him, and how she was healed instantly.

[48] And he said to her, 'Be of good courage, daughter. Your faith has saved you. Go in peace.'

[49] While he was still speaking, somebody from the *entourage* of the president of the synagogue came, saying to him, 'Your daughter has died. Do not trouble the Teacher.'

[50] But *when* he heard, Jesus answered him, saying, 'Do not fear. Only believe, and she will be restored.'

[51] And on *his* coming into the house, he would not allow anybody to go in except Peter, and John, and Jacob, and the father and mother of the girl.

[52] And everybody was sobbing and mourning *over* her, but he said, 'Do not weep. She is not dead, but sleeping.'

[53] And they were ridiculing him, knowing that she had died.

[54] And he put everybody outside, and took hold of her by the hand, *and* he called out, saying, 'Young girl, rise up.'

[55] And her spirit returned, and she rose up straightaway, and he directed *that something should be given to her* to eat. [56] And her parents were astounded, but he charged them to tell nobody what had happened.

*Authorization of the 12**

9\1 Then he called the twelve together *and* gave them power and authority over all demons and to cure diseases. [2] And he authorized them to proclaim the Sovereign Rulership of God, and to heal the sick.

[3] And he said to them, 'Take nothing for the road, neither staffs, nor travel sack,* nor bread, nor money, nor have two coats each.*

[4] 'And whatever house you might go into, stay there, and depart from there. [5] And *for* whoever might not receive you, on your going out from that town shake off even* the dust from your feet as a testimony against them.'*

[6] And they departed, *and* passed through the villages, proclaiming the gospel, and healing everywhere.

*Life of John ends in assassination**

[7] Now Herod the tetrarch heard of all the things being done by him, and he was

bewildered because it was said by some that John had been raised from *the* dead, [8] and by some that Elijah had been brought to view, and by others that one of the prophets of the ancients had risen.

[9] And Herod said, 'John I have beheaded,* but who is this concerning whom I hear such things?'

And he investigated seeing him.

The 5,000 *

[10] And on their returning, the apostles related to *Jesus* what they had done. And he took them *and* retired privately into an area of a deserted town called Bethsaida. [11] But the crowds came to know *and* followed him. All the same, he received them *and* spoke to them concerning the Sovereign Rulership of God, and he cured those *who* had need of healing.

[12] And the day began to wear away, and the twelve came *and* said to him, 'Send the crowd away, so that they might go into the surrounding villages and fields *and* lodge and find food supplies, for we are in a deserted place here.'

[13] But he said to them, 'You give them *something* to eat.'

But they said, 'There are no more than five loaves and two fish for us, unless we go and buy food for all this people.'

[14] For there were about five thousand men.

But he said to his disciples, 'Make them sit down in groups of fifty.'

[15] And they did that, and made them all sit down.

[16] Then he took the five loaves and the two fish *and*, looking up towards the sky, he exalted* God and broke them up, and gave *them* to the disciples to place before the crowd. [17] And they ate and all were filled, and twelve hand baskets of fragments were picked up.

Peter's declaration of Jesus as the Christ of God *

[18] Subsequently it came about, in his being alone praying, *that* the disciples were with him, and he asked them, saying, 'Whom do the crowds pronounce me to be?'**

[19] And in answer, they said, 'John the Identifier. But others *say* Elijah, and others that one of the prophets of the ancients has risen.'

[20] But he said to them, 'But you, whom do you pronounce me to be?'**

And in answer, Peter said, 'The Christ of God.'*

He predicts his death & resurrection *

[21] And making strict warning, he ordered *them* to tell this to nobody, [22] saying, 'It is necessary for the Son of Man to suffer many things, and to be rejected by the elders and senior priests and scribes, and to be murdered, and to rise* *on* the third day.'

True discipleship.* No death for some until the signs of the Acts period *

[23] And he said to everybody, 'If anybody wants to come after me, let him deny himself, and he must take up his stake* and follow me.* [24] For whoever wants to save his life will lose it, but whoever might lose his life* on account of me will save it. [25] For how is a man profited *if* he gains the whole world, but has destroyed or suffered the loss of himself?'**

[26] 'For whoever might have been ashamed of me and of my oracles, the Son of Man will be ashamed of him when he will come in the magnificence of himself and of the Father and of the holy angels.

[27] 'But truly I say to you, there are some of these standing here who will most certainly not taste death* until they see the Sovereign Rulership of God.'

His radiance shown in the transformation. Voice out of a cloud *

[28] And it came about, around eight days after these oracles, that he took Peter and John and Jacob, *and* he went up into the mountain to pray.*

[29] And in his praying the appearance* of his face became different, and his clothing flashed like lightning.* [30] Then two men were talking with him, who were Moses* and Elijah, [31] who, being seen in radiance, were speaking of his death* which he was about to accomplish in Jerusalem. [32] But Peter and those with him were weighed down with sleep, and on fully waking they saw his radiance and the two men who stood with him.

[33] And it came about* in their departing* from him *that* Peter, not knowing what he was saying, said to Jesus, 'Master, it's good for us to be* here, so let us make three tents, one for you, and one for Moses, and one for Elijah.'

[34] But while he was speaking these things, a cloud materialized and it overshadowed them,

and they were afraid as they went into the cloud.

[35] And a voice came out of the cloud, saying, 'This is My Son, the Richly Loved One.* Listen to him.'

[36] And in the coming to pass* of the voice, Jesus was found alone. And they kept silent, and in those days they reported to nobody any of these things which they had seen.

Healing of a lunatic son *

[37] And the next day it came about, on their coming down from the mountain, that a large crowd met him.

[38] And then it so happened that a man of the crowd called out, saying, 'Teacher, I implore you, have a look at my son, for he is my only* *son.* [39] And, as you will see, a spirit takes him, and it suddenly calls out, and it throws him into convulsions with foaming, and, making a complete wreck of him, it hardly departs from him, [40] and I asked your disciples if they could drive it out, but they were not able.'

[41] And in answer, Jesus said, 'Oh* unbelieving and perverse generation! How long shall I be among you and bear with you? Bring your son here.'

[42] But as he was still approaching, the demon dashed him down and violently convulsed him, so Jesus rebuked the unclean spirit and healed the child, and he gave him back to his father.

[43] And they were all struck with wonder at the majesty of God.

He again predicts his death & resurrection *

But *as* they all were wondering at everything that Jesus did, he said to his disciples, [44] 'Let these oracles sink down into your ears, for the Son of Man is about to be betrayed into the hands of men.'

[45] But they did not understand this remark, and it was veiled from them so that they did not perceive it, and they were afraid to ask him about this remark.

Receiving little children in his name *

[46] Then a discussion arose among them about who of them might be the most eminent.

[47] And Jesus perceived the disputing of their heart, *and* he took a child *and* set him beside himself, [48] and he said to them, 'Whoever receives this child in my name receives me, and whoever receives me receives Him Who authorized me, for the one subsisting as lowliest* among you all, this one will be eminent.'

[49] And in answer, John said, 'Master, we saw somebody driving out demons in your name, and we stopped him, because he does not follow in company with us.'

[50] And Jesus said to him, 'Do not forbid *him,* for whoever is not against us is for us.'

Rejection at a Samaritan village

[51] And it came about, in the fulfilling of the days for his being taken up, that* he resolutely set his face to go to Jerusalem, [52] and he authorized messengers ahead of him.

And they went off *and* came into a village of the Samaritans, so as to make preparations for him, [53] but they did not receive him, because his face was heading for Jerusalem.

[54] And *when* his disciples Jacob and John saw, they said, 'Lord, do you wish that we should call fire down from the sky and consume them, just as Elijah also did?'

[55] But he turned *and* rebuked them, and he said, 'You do not know what manner of spirit you are. [56] For the Son of Man has come not to destroy men's lives,* but to save.'

And they went off into a different village.

A scribe who might follow him *

[57] And it so happened, as they were going along the road, that somebody said to him, 'Lord, I will follow you wherever you go.'

[58] And Jesus said to him, 'The foxes have holes, and the birds of the sky* *have* nests, but the Son of Man has nowhere he might lay his head.'

[59] And he said to another, 'Follow me.'

But he said, 'Lord, allow me first to go *and* bury my father.'

[60] But Jesus said to him, 'Leave the dead to bury their own dead,* but you go your way *and* proclaim the Sovereign Rulership of God.'

[61] And another also said, 'Lord, I will follow you, but allow me first to go *and* say goodbye to those in my house.'

[62] But to him Jesus said, 'Nobody who lays his hand on a plow, while gazing to the things behind, is fit for the Sovereign Rulership of God.'

Authorization of the 70 *

10\1 **N**ow after these things, the Lord appointed seventy* others as well, and he authorized *them* in twos *to go* ahead of him into every town and habitation, wherever he himself was about to go.

2 So he said to them, 'The harvest *is* vast, but the labourers few. Pray, therefore, to the Lord of the harvest, that He might send out labourers into His harvest.

3 'Go your ways. Mark this: that I authorize you as lambs* in *the* thick of wolves.* 4 Carry no purse, nor travel sack,* nor sandals, and greet nobody on the road.*

5 'And whatever house you might go into, first say, "Peace to this house." 6 And if there is a son of peace there, your peace will rest over it. But if not, it will return to you. 7 And remain in the same house, eating and drinking things alongside them, for the labourer is worthy of his hire.* Do not go moving from house to house.

8 'And *in* whatever town you might enter and they receive you, eat the things laid before you. 9 'And heal the sick in it, and say to them, "The Sovereign Rulership of God has drawn near* to you." 10 But whatever town you go into and they do not receive you, go out into its streets *and* say, 11 "Even the dust out of your town which has clung to us we are wiping off against you. Yet come to know this – that the Sovereign Rulership of God has drawn near* to you."

12 '*But* I say to you, it will be more tolerable in that day for Sodom than for that town. 13 Woe to you, Chorazin! Woe to you, Bethsaida! For if the works of power which have been taking place in you had taken place in Tyre and Sidon, they would have submitted long ago,* sitting in sackcloth and ashes. 14 But it will be more tolerable for Tyre and Sidon in the judgement than for you. 15 And you, Capernaum, which has been elevated to the sky, you will be brought down to the grave.*

16 'He who hears you hears me. And he who rejects you rejects me. And he who rejects me rejects Him Who authorized me.'

Jesus saw the dramatic approach
of Satan (Mat. 3\13, Luke 4\2, 4\13).
Status in Jesus 'among the exalted' (Eph. 1\3)
17 And the seventy returned with exuberance, saying, 'Lord, even the demons are subject to us through your name.'

18 And he said to them, 'I watched Satan, falling out of the sky like lightning.* 19 See now, I have given you the authority to tread on snakes and scorpions,* and on all the power of the enemy, and nothing will in any way harm you. 20 Yet rejoice not at this, in that the spirits are subject to you, but rejoice that your names are written among the exalted.'*

21 In the same hour, Jesus rejoiced in *his* spirit, and he said, 'I praise You, Father, Lord of Heaven and Earth,* that You hid these things from *the* sophisticated and cunning,* and You revealed them to infants. Yes, Father, for this was well pleasing in Your sight.'

22 And he turned to the disciples, *and* he said,* 'All things were delivered to me by my Father, and nobody knows* who the Son is except the Father, and Who the Father is except the Son and to whomever the Son wishes to reveal *Him*.'

23 And turning to the disciples, he said privately, 'Exalted *are* the eyes which see the things you see. 24 For I say to you, many prophets and kings have desired to see what you see and they have not seen, and to hear what you hear and they have not heard.'

Testing by a scholar of the law.
the most important commandment.
Parable of a good Samaritan
25 Then it so happened that a certain scholar in the law stood up, putting him to the test,* and he said, 'Teacher, what must I do to inherit Eonian* life?'

26 But he said to him, 'What has been written in the law? How do you read *it*?'

27 And in answer, he said, 'You shall love *the* Lord your God with all your heart, and out of all your being, and out of all your strength, and out of all your mind, and your neighbour as yourself.'*

28 And he said to him, 'You have answered correctly. Do this, and you will live.'*

29 But wanting to justify himself, he said to Jesus, 'And who is my neighbour?'

30 And taking that up,* Jesus said, 'A certain man was going down from Jerusalem into Jericho, and he fell among bandits* who, both stripping and inflicting wounds on him, went off, leaving *him*, as his fate would have it,* half dead.

31 'Now, by chance, a certain priest was going down by that road, and *when* he saw him he passed by on the opposite side. 32 And in the same way, a Levite also being at the place came and saw *him* and he passed by on the opposite side. 33 But a certain Samaritan on a journey

came down to him, and *when* he saw him he was moved with compassion, [34] and he went *and* bound up his wounds, pouring oil and wine, and he set him on his own animal, *and* brought him to an inn and took care of him. [35] And on departing the next day, he took out two denarions* *and* gave *them* to the inn keeper, and he said to him, "Take care of him, and, whatever more you expend, on my return I myself will repay you."

[36] Which, therefore, of these three, do you consider to have emerged as a neighbour to him who fell among the bandits?"*

[37] And he said, 'He who showed compassion towards him.'

Then Jesus said to him, 'You go *and* do likewise.'

Maria & Martha

[38] Now it so happened, as they proceeded on their way, that he went into a certain village, and a certain woman named Martha received him into her house. [39] And she had a sister called Maria, who also was seating herself at Jesus's feet *and* she was listening to his discourse.

[40] Martha, though, was distracted over repeatedly serving, and she came to him, and she said, 'Lord, is it of no concern to you that my sister has left me to serve alone? So tell her that she ought to help me.'

[41] And in answer, Jesus said to her, 'Martha, Martha, you are anxious and agitated about many things. [42] But there is need of one thing, and Maria chooses* that good portion which will not be taken away from her.'

Prayer for the disciples*

11\1 ▉nd it came about, in his being in a certain place praying, *that* when he had brought *it* to a close, one of his disciples said to him, 'Lord, teach us to pray, as John also taught his disciples.'

[2] And he said to them, 'When you pray, say:

'Our Father in the heavens,*
may Your name be sanctified;*
may Your Sovereign Rulership appear;*
may Your will be brought to pass,*
as in Heaven, *so* also on the Earth.
[3] Give us our sufficient* bread,
according to the day,*
[4] and forgive us our violations,*

for we ourselves in turn* forgive
everybody indebted to us.
And bring us not into adversity,*
but deliver* us from* the Evil One.'*

The persistent friend.
The divine spirit given to those who ask

[5] And he said to them, 'Who among you shall have a friend, and he will go to him in the middle of the night and say to him, "Friend, lend me three loaves, [6] since a friend has come to me from a journey, and I have nothing which I can set in front of him", [7] and he will answer from inside and say, "Do not cause me trouble. Already the door has been shut, and my children are with me in bed. I am not able to rise and give *it* to you."? [8] I say to you, even if he will not give him *anything*, yet, rising up to be* his friend, because of his shameless insisting on him being roused, he will give him as much as he needs.

[9] 'And I say to you, ask, and it will be given to you. Search, and you will find. Knock, and it will be opened to you. [10] For everybody who asks receives, and he who looks finds, and to him who knocks it will be opened.

[11] 'And *if* a son were to ask for bread from any of you who *is* a father, would he give him a stone? Or if *he asks for* a fish, would he give him a snake instead of a fish?

[12] 'And if he were also to ask for an egg, would he give him a scorpion? [13] If you, then, being evil, know how to give good gifts to your children, how much more will the Father from Heaven give *the* divine spirit* to those who ask Him?'

Healing of a mute man. Demons to be judges*

[14] And he was driving out a demon, and it was dumb, and it came about,* *when* the demon had gone out, *that* the dumb man spoke, and the crowds were amazed.

[15] But some of them said, 'He drives out demons through the agency of Beelzebub, ruler of the demons.'

[16] And others, putting *him* to the test, were looking for a sign from him out of Heaven.

[17] But knowing their purposes, he said to them, 'Every kingdom divided against itself is brought to ruin, and a house *divided* against a house falls. [18] If Satan is divided against even himself, how will his kingdom stand, seeing that you say I drive out demons through the agency of Beelzebub? [19] And if I drive out demons

through the agency of Beelzebub, by whom do your sons drive *them* out? By this logic, they themselves will be judges over you.
²⁰ 'But if I drive out demons by a finger of God, then the Sovereign Rulership of God has come to you. ²¹ As long as a strong man, being fully armed, guards his own estate, his possessions are in peace. ²² But as soon as somebody stronger than himself comes at him *and* overpowers him, he takes away from him his weaponry in which he trusted, and he will divide his spoils.
²³ 'He who is not with me is against me, and he who does not gather with me scatters.
²⁴ 'When the unclean spirit has gone out *and* away from the man, it roams through waterless places, looking for rest, and, not finding any, it says, "I will return to my house from where I came out." ²⁵ And when it comes it finds *it* swept and adorned, ²⁶ then it goes and brings seven different spirits more wicked than itself, and they go *and* settle down there, and the latter *state* of that man becomes worse than the first.'

Exalted for obedience to the written oracle
²⁷ And it so happened,* in his speaking these things, *that* a certain lady, lifting up her voice out of the crowd, said to him, 'Exalted *is* the womb which gave birth to you, and *the* breasts which you suckled.'
²⁸ But he said, 'Rather, exalted *are* those who hear the oracle of God and keep it.'

Rebuke of those looking for signs,
except the sign of Jonah *
²⁹ And as the crowds were thickly gathered together, he began to say, 'This is an evil generation. It looks for a sign, and no sign will be given to it except the sign of the prophet Jonah. ³⁰ For as Jonah became a sign to the Ninevites, so will the Son of Man also be to this generation.
³¹ 'The Queen of *the* South will be raised up in the judgement with the men of this generation, and she will condemn them, for she came from the ends of the Earth to hear the wisdom of Solomon, and, see now, one more important than* Solomon *is* here.
³² 'Men of Nineveh will stand up as witnesses in the judgement with this generation, and they will condemn it because they submitted at the proclamation of Jonah, and, see now, one more important than* Jonah *is* here.

The eye the lamp of the body *
³³ 'But nobody having lit a lamp puts *it* in a cellar, nor underneath the grain measure, but on the candlestick, so that those who come in can see *its* glow.
³⁴ 'The lamp of the body is the eye. Therefore, when the eye is clear-sighted, all your body is full of light, but when it is evil your body *is* also darkness. ³⁵ See to it, therefore, that the light in you is not darkness. ³⁶ If your whole body, therefore, *is* illuminated, not having any part darkness, everything will be full of light, as when the lamp gives you light with its shining.'

Woes on Pharisees.
Their conspiracy against Jesus *
³⁷ Now in his speaking, a certain Pharisee asked him if he would have dinner with him, and he went in *and* was reclining. ³⁸ But *when* the Pharisee noticed, he was surprised that he had not first performed washings before the dinner.
³⁹ The Lord, however, said to him, 'Look now, you Pharisees ceremonially clean the outside of the cup and the dish, but the inside of you is full of robbery and evil. ⁴⁰ You fools! Did he who made the outside not also make the inside?
⁴¹ 'But rather, give donations to the poor *from* the things *which are* internal, and then all things become clean to you.
⁴² 'But woe to you, Pharisees! For you pay tithes of mint and rue, and every kind of herb, and you pass over the justice and the love of God. It would have been good to do these things, while not leaving aside the others.
⁴³ 'Woe to you, Pharisees! For you love the privileged seats in the synagogues and greetings in the marketplaces.
⁴⁴ 'Woe to you, scribes and Pharisees! Hypocrites! For you are like unmarked tombs, and the men walking above do not realize.'
⁴⁵ Then in answer, one of the scholars of the law said to him, 'Teacher, in saying these things, you insult us as well.'
⁴⁶ And he said, 'Woe to you also, scholars of the law! For you load men up* with burdens heavy to bear, and you yourselves will not touch the burdens with one of your fingers.
⁴⁷ 'Woe to you! For you found the monuments of the prophets, and your fathers murdered them. ⁴⁸ Consequently, you testify and you consent to the deeds of your fathers, for they murdered them and you found their monuments.
⁴⁹ 'And because of this, the wisdom of God

said, "I will assign prophets and apostles to them, but some of them they will murder and drive out," [50] so that the blood of all the prophets poured out since* *the* foundation* of *the* world order* will be required from this generation, [51] from the blood of Abel to the blood of Zechariah who perished between the altar and the House. Truly I say to you, it will be required from this generation.

[52] 'Woe to you, scholars of the law! For you have taken away the key of knowledge. You do not enter in yourselves, and you hold back those who are entering in.'

[53] And while he was saying these things to them, the scribes and the Pharisees began to be extremely angry, and to draw him out concerning many things, [54] lying in wait for him, looking to catch something out of his mouth so that they could accuse him.

Beware the leaven of the Pharisees *

12\1 In the meantime, with myriads* of the crowd being gathered together so that they trampled one another down, he began to say to his disciples first of all, 'Be vigilant for yourselves from the leaven* of the Pharisees, which is hypocrisy. [2] For there is nothing concealed which will not become revealed, nor hidden which will not become known. [3] Instead of which, whatever you have spoken in the darkness will be heard in the light, and whatever you have spoken to the ear in the closed rooms will be proclaimed on the housetops.

[4] 'But I say to you, my friends, you should not be in fear of those who kill the body, and after those things they are not able to do anything more. [5] But I will warn you Whom you should fear: fear Him Who, after putting to death, has authority to throw *your corpse* into the Valley of Hinnom.* Yes, I say to you, fear Him.

[6] 'Are five sparrows not sold for two assarion?* Yet not one of them is forgotten before God. [7] But even the hairs of your head have all been numbered. Do not, therefore, fear. You are of far more worth than many sparrows.*

[8] 'But I say to you, whoever might acknowledge me in the presence of men, the Son of Man will also acknowledge him in the presence of the angels of God. [9] But he who has disowned me in the presence of men will be utterly disowned in the presence of the angels of God.

Defamation of the Angel of God *

[10] 'And for everybody who will speak a word against the Son of Man, it will be forgiven him. But for him who speaks injuriously against the Holy Spirit,* it will not be forgiven.

[11] 'And when they bring you before the synagogues and the rulers and the authorities, do not be anxious how or what you reply in defence, or what you should say. [12] For the Holy Spirit* will teach you in that same hour what you should say.'

Parable of a rich man. Treasure in Heaven

[13] And somebody out of the crowd said to him, 'Teacher, tell my brother to share the inheritance with me.'

[14] But he said to him, 'Man, who appointed me a judge or a divider between you?'

[15] And he said to them, 'Beware, and keep yourselves from covetousness, because his life for anybody does not consist* in the abundance of his possessions.'

[16] And he spoke a parable to them, saying, 'The estate of a certain rich man produced abundant yields, [17] and he was reasoning within himself, saying, "What shall I do, because I do not have anywhere I can gather together my fruit?"

[18] 'And he said, "I will do this: I will tear down my granaries and build bigger ones, and gather up there all my produce and my good things. [19] And I will say to myself,* 'Man,* you have many good things gathered together for many years. Take your ease, eat, drink, *and* be merry.' " [20] But God said to him, "Fool! This night they demand your life* from you. Then whose will those things be which you have prepared?" [21] This is how *it will be* with him who hoards up for himself and is not bountiful towards God.'

[22] Then he said to his disciples, 'On this account, I say to you, take no thought for your life, what you should eat, nor what you should put on the body. [23] Your life* is more than food, and the body *is more* than clothing.

[24] 'Consider the ravens, for they neither sow nor reap, *and* for whom there is neither storehouse nor granary, yet God feeds them. Of how much far more worth are you than the birds!*

[25] 'And who of you, in being anxious, is able to add one forearm's length* to his height? [26] If you, then, are not able *to do* even *the* least thing, why are you anxious about the remaining things?

²⁷ 'Consider the lilies, how they grow. They neither labour, nor do they spin, and yet I tell you, not even Solomon in all his glory was arrayed like one of these. ²⁸ But if God so clothes the herbage which today is in the field and tomorrow is thrown into the furnace, how much more you, you of little faith?
²⁹ 'And do not strive for what you eat, or what you drink, and do not be in anxiety.
³⁰ 'For all the nations of the world run after these things, and your Father knows that you have need of these things. ³¹ But look instead for the kingdom of God, and all these things will be added to you.
³² 'Do not fear, little flock, for your Father took delight in giving you the kingdom.
³³ 'Sell your possessions, and give donations to the poor. Make never deteriorating money-bags for yourselves, an unfailing treasure in the heavens where a thief cannot approach, or a moth cannot corrupt. ³⁴ For where your treasure is, there will your heart also be.

Parable of bridegroom's friends.
Preparation for his return to Jerusalem *
³⁵ 'Let your waist be belted, and the lamps burning, ³⁶ and yourselves like men waiting for their master, whenever he might return from the wedding feast, so that at his coming and knocking they can open to him at once. ³⁷ Exalted *are* those servants whom the master at his coming will find watching. Truly I say to you, he will tighten his belt around himself and make them sit down to eat, and he will come *and* serve them. ³⁸ And if he comes in the second watch, or comes in the third watch, and finds *them* like this, exalted are those servants.
³⁹ 'But know this, that if the master of the house had known at what hour the thief was coming, he would have watched, and not allowed his house to be dug through.
⁴⁰ 'And you yourselves, therefore, be ready, for the Son of Man comes in the hour you do not expect.'

Parable of two house managers
⁴¹ Then Peter said to him, 'Lord, do you speak this parable to us, or to everybody as well?'
⁴² And the Lord said, 'Who, then, is that faithful and prudent house manager whom the master will set over his household to issue a ration of wheat in due time? ⁴³ Exalted *is* that servant whom the master at his coming will find acting this way. ⁴⁴ Truly I say to you, he

will make him ruler over all his possessions.
⁴⁵ 'But if that servant might say in his heart, "My master hesitates to come," and he might begin to beat the men servants and servant girls, and to eat and drink, and to become drunk, ⁴⁶ the master of that servant will come in a day when he does not expect, and in an hour of which he is not aware, and he will he cut him in two, and he will appoint his portion with the unbelieving. ⁴⁷ But that servant who knew his master's will and did not make preparation, nor act in line with his will, will be beaten with many *lashes*. ⁴⁸ But he who did not know, and committed things deserving of *beatings*, will be beaten with few *lashes*.
'And everybody to whom much is given, much will be required from him. And to whom much was committed, they will ask the more of him.

Judgement of fire on the Earth.
Jesus' overwhelming into death.
Families divided over Jesus *
⁴⁹ 'I came to hurl* fire into the Earth. And what do I have in mind if it has already been set alight? ⁵⁰ But I have an overwhelming I am about to be flooded* with. And how I am being pressed until it's completed! ⁵¹ Do you suppose that I came to give peace in the Earth? I tell you, no, but rather division.
⁵² 'For from now on, there will be five in one house divided three against two, and two against three.

⁵³ 'Father will be divided against son
    and son against father,
    mother against daughter
    and daughter against mother,
    mother-in-law against her daughter-in-law
    and daughter-in-law
    against her mother-in-law.'*

Discernment of this present time.
Just judgement *
⁵⁴ And he said to the crowds as well, 'When you see the cloud rising up from *the* West, you say at once, "A rain-storm is coming," and it happens. ⁵⁵ And when a South wind *is* blowing, you say, "There will be scorching heat," and it happens. ⁵⁶ Hypocrites! You know to discern the face* of the Earth and the sky, but how do you not discern this time?
⁵⁷ 'And why do you not even judge from yourselves what is right? ⁵⁸ For when you go

with your adversary to a magistrate, make efforts on the road* to be set free from him, in case he might drag you off* to the judge, and the judge should hand you over to the officer of justice, and that officer should throw you into jail. [59] I tell you, you will in no way come out from there until you will have paid even the last lepton."*

Two tragedies. Warning of submission

13\1 **A**nd at the same time some were telling him about the Galileans whose blood Pilate mixed with their sacrifices.

[2] And in answer, Jesus said to them, 'Do you suppose that these Galileans happened to be violators* above all the Galileans because they have suffered such things? [3] I say to you, no. But if you do not submit, you will all likewise suffer destruction.

[4] 'Or those eighteen on whom the tower in Siloam fell and killed them, do you think that these were debtors beyond all men who lived in Jerusalem?* [5] I tell you, no. But if you do not submit, you will all likewise suffer destruction.'

Parable of a fig tree *

[6] Then he related this parable: 'A certain *man* planted a fig tree in his vineyard, and he came looking for fruit on it, but did not find any.

[7] 'Then he said to the dresser of his vineyard, "That's three years I've been coming looking for fruit on this fig tree and not finding *any*. Cut it down. Why does it even waste the ground?"

[8] 'But he said in answer to him, "Sir, let it alone this year as well, until I dig around it and throw manure on, [9] and, indeed, if it should produce fruit, *good*, but if not, cut it down in the coming year." '

Healing in a synagogue of a lady with a spirit of infirmity.
Objection by president of the synagogue

[10] And he was teaching in one of the synagogues on the Sabbath. [11] And it came about that a lady was there *who* for eighteen years had a spirit causing* infirmity, and she was bent double, and completely unable to straighten up properly.

[12] And *when* Jesus saw her, he called and said to her, 'Lady, you have been set free from your infirmity.'

[13] And he laid hands on her, and at once she was made upright again, and she magnified God.

[14] But the president of the synagogue, answering with resentment because Jesus had healed on the Sabbath day, said to the crowd, 'There are six days in which it is right to work. In these, therefore, come *and* be healed, and not on the Sabbath day.'

[15] So the Lord answered him, and said, 'Hypocrites! Does each one of you on the Sabbath not loose his ox or donkey from the stall, and lead *it* out to give *it* a drink? [16] And this *lady*, being a daughter of Abraham whom Satan has gone and bound eighteen years,* ought she not to be released from this bondage on the Sabbath day?'

[17] And by his saying these things, all who were opposed to him were put to shame, and all the crowd were rejoicing at all the magnificent things which were being done by him.

Parables of the kingdom, concerning Israel. *
Parable of a mustard seed.* Parable of leaven *

[18] Then he said, 'What is the Sovereign Rulership of God like, and to what shall I compare it?* [19] It is comparable to a grain of mustard seed which a man took *and* threw into his grove, and it grew and flourished into a large tree, and the birds of the sky* roosted in its branches.'

[20] He further* said, 'To what shall I liken the Sovereign Rulership of God?* [21] It is comparable to leaven which a woman took *and* hid in three measures of meal, until the whole was leavened.'*

Entrance into the Sovereign Rulership of God.*
Reality of the dragnet (13\28 with Mat. 13\47-50)

[22] And he travelled throughout the towns and villages teaching, and he had made progress into Jerusalem.

[23] Then somebody said to him, 'Lord, those being saved, are they few?'

But he said to them, [24] 'Strive to enter through the narrow gate, for, I tell you, many will search to enter in, and they will not be able. [25] 'From the time the master of the house has been roused and shuts the door, and you begin to stand outside and to knock at the door saying, "Lord, Lord, open to us," then in answer he will say to you, "I do not know where you are from," [26] then you will begin to say, "We have eaten and drunk before you, and you taught in our streets," [27] but he will say, "I tell you, I do not know where you are from.

Depart from me, all you workers of iniquity."
[28] 'There will be weeping and the gnashing of teeth when you see Abraham, and Isaac, and Jacob, and all the prophets in the kingdom of God, but yourselves being thrown out. [29] And they will come from East and West, and North and South, and sit down to eat in the kingdom of God. [30] And, indeed, there are some last who will be first, and there are some first who will be last.'

Jesus warned about Herod. Judgement
on Herod & Jerusalem for rejecting Jesus
[31] On the same day, certain Pharisees came to him saying, 'Go out, and depart from here, for Herod means to have you murdered.'*
[32] And he said to them, 'Go *and* tell that fox,* "Look, I drive out demons, and I carry out cures today and tomorrow, and the third *day* I come to an end."* [33] Nevertheless, I must proceed today and tomorrow and the *day* following, for it is not accepted *for* a prophet to perish outside Jerusalem.*

His commiseration & prophecy
of the destruction of Jerusalem *
[34] 'Jerusalem, Jerusalem, murdering the prophets and stoning those who have been sent to her! How often I wanted to gather your children together, in the way a hen *gathers* her brood underneath *her* wings, but you did not want it!
[35] 'See now, your house is being left to you desolate, and I say to you, you will by no means see me until it will come to it when you say:

"Exalted* *is* the Coming One,*
in *the* name of *the* Lord." *

Healing on a Sabbath of a man with dropsy
14\1 And it came about,* at his going into the house of one of the senior members of the Pharisees to eat bread on a certain Sabbath, that they were engaged in watching him intently.
[2] And it so happened* that in front of him there was a certain man with dropsy.
[3] And in reaction, Jesus addressed the scholars of the law and Pharisees, saying, 'Is it lawful to heal on the Sabbath?'
[4] But they kept quiet.
And taking hold of *the man*, he healed him and let *him* go.
[5] And making an answer to them, he said,

'Whose son or ox might fall into a pit* and you would not on the Sabbath immediately draw him up?'
[6] And they had no acumen* to make any answer back to these things.

Parable of a marriage feast *
[7] And he related a parable to those who were invited, noticing how they were picking out the prime couches, *and* saying to them, [8] 'When you are invited by anybody to a wedding feast, do not take a seat in the prime couches, in case a man more distinguished than yourself might have been invited by him, [9] and he who invited you will come *and* say to you, "Give this *man* a place," and you with shame will move on to occupy the last place. [10] But when you are invited, go *and* take a seat in the lowest place so that when he who invited you might come and say to you, "Friend, come up higher," then there will be honour for you in the presence of those who sit down to eat with you. [11] For everybody who exalts himself will be abased, and he who abases himself will be exalted.'
[12] Then he said as well to him who invited him, 'When you give a dinner or a feast, invite not your friends, or your brothers, or your relatives, or rich neighbours, in case they also should invite you in return, and it might become a recompense to you; [13] but when you give a banquet invite *the* poor, *the* crippled, *the* lame, *the* blind, [14] and you will be exalted, since they have nothing to recompense you, for you will be recompensed in the resurrection of the righteous.'*

Parable of a large banquet *
[15] And *when* one of those sitting down to eat with him heard these things, he said to *Jesus*, 'Exalted *is* he who will eat *the* banquet* in the kingdom of God.'
[16] But he said to him, 'A certain man made a large banquet, and invited many, [17] and he sent his servant at the hour of the banquet to say to those who had been invited, "Come, for everything is already prepared." [18] And they all began in unison to make an excuse. The first said to him, "I have bought a field, and I need to go out and see to it. I ask you to accept my apologies." [19] And another said, "I have bought five yoke of oxen, and I am going to test them. I ask you to accept my apologies." [20] And another said, "I have married a wife, and because of this I am not able to come." [21] And

that servant came *and* reported these things to his master. Then the master of the house, being angry, said to his servant, "Go out quickly into the streets and lanes of the town, and bring in here the poor, and crippled, and lame, and blind." ²² In due course* the servant said, "Sir, it has been done as you ordered, and still there is room." ²³ And the master said to the servant, "Go out into the highways and hedges, and compel *them* to come in so that my house might be full." ²⁴ For I say to you, not one of those men who had been invited will get a taste of my banquet. For many are called, but few *are* chosen.'

True discipleship. *Parables of a tower & salt*
²⁵ Now large crowds were going along with him, and turning he said to them, ²⁶ 'If anybody comes to me and does not love less* his father, and mother, and wife, and sons, and brothers, and sisters, and yes, even his own life* as well, he is not able to be* my disciple.*
²⁷ 'And whoever does not carry his stake* and come after me is not able to be my disciple.
²⁸ 'For who among you, wanting to build a tower, does not, having first sat down, calculate the expense, whether he has the things for completion, ²⁹ so that, in case of his having laid its foundation, and not having strength to finish off, everybody seeing should begin to mock him, ³⁰ saying, "This man began to build, but he lacked the strength to finish off"?'
³¹ 'Or what king, proceeding to engage in war against another king, does not first sit down *and* consider whether he is able with ten thousand to meet him who comes against him with twenty thousand? ³² If not, while the other is still a long way off, he sends a delegation and asks for the terms for peace.
³³ 'So likewise,* everybody among you who does not separate himself from everything which he possesses is not able to be* my disciple.
³⁴ 'Salt *is* good, but if the salt becomes insipid, with what shall it be seasoned? ³⁵ It is fit neither for the land, nor for manure. They throw it out. He who has ears to hear, let him hear.'

Parable of a lost sheep *

15\1 When all the tax collectors and violators approached him to hear him.
² But the Pharisees and scribes muttered, saying, 'This *man* receives violators, and he eats

with them.'
³ And he spoke this parable to them, saying, ⁴ 'What man among you who has a hundred sheep, and loses one of them, does not leave the ninety-nine in the wilderness and go after that one which has been lost until he finds it? ⁵ And *when* he finds *it*, he lays *it* on his own shoulders, rejoicing. ⁶ And arriving at the house, he calls together the friends and the neighbours, saying to them, "Rejoice with me, for I have found my sheep which was lost."
⁷ 'I say to you, there will be such joyfulness in Heaven over one violator submitting, more than over ninety-nine righteous who have no need of submission.

Parable of a lost coin
⁸ 'Or what woman having ten drachmas,* if she should lose one drachma, does not light a lamp, and sweep the house, and search diligently until she finds *it*? ⁹ And on making the find, she calls together friends and neighbours, saying, "Rejoice with me, for I have found the drachma which I lost."
¹⁰ 'In the same way, I say to you, there is joyfulness in the sight of the angels of God over one violator submitting.'

Parable of a prodigal son
¹¹ And he said, 'A certain man had two sons. ¹² And the younger of them said to *his* father, "Father, give me that portion of the property falling *to me*." And he divided the estate among them. ¹³ And after not many days the younger son gathered everything together, *and* he took a journey abroad* into a distant country,* and he wasted his substance there, living in debauchery.* ¹⁴ But *when* he had spent everything, a severe famine arose throughout that land, and he began to be in want. ¹⁵ And *he* went and attached himself to one of the citizens* of that country, and he sent him into his fields to feed pigs. ¹⁶ And he was longing to fill his stomach from the carob tree pods which the pigs were feeding on, but nobody gave him *any.*
¹⁷ 'When, though, he came to his senses, he said, "How many hired servants of my father abound in food, and I am perishing from famine! ¹⁸ I *will* rise up *and* go to my father, and I will say to him, "Father, I have violated against the Heavenly One,* and before you, ¹⁹ and I no longer deserve to be called your son. Make me like one of your hired servants.""

²⁰ 'And *he* rose up *and* went to his father. But *when* he was still a long way off, his father saw him and was moved with compassion, *and* he ran and fell on his neck and fervently kissed him. ²¹ And the son said to him, "Father, I have committed a violation against the Heavenly One,* and before you, and I am no longer worthy to be called your son." ²² But the father said to his servants, "Bring out the best robe and clothe him, and give *him* a ring for his hand, and sandals for *his* feet, ²³ and bring the fattened calf *and* sacrifice *it* and *let us* eat *and* be merry. ²⁴ For this son of mine was dead and is alive again, and was lost and is found." And they began to celebrate.

²⁵ 'And his oldest son was in a field, and when *he* came *and* drew near the house he heard music and dancing. ²⁶ And he called over one of the servants *and* began asking what these things might mean.* ²⁷ And he said to him, "Your brother has arrived, and your father has killed the fattened calf, because he has received him back safe and well." ²⁸ But he was angry, and he was not willing to go in, so his father went out *and* tried to console him.

²⁹ 'But in answer, he said to *his* father, "Look, for so many years I have been serving you, and I have never transgressed your order, and *yet* you never gave me a young goat, so that I could celebrate with my friends. ³⁰ But as soon as this son of yours comes along, who has eaten up your wealth with prostitutes, you have killed the fattened calf for him."

³¹ 'But he said to him, "Son, you are always* with me, and everything which is mine is yours. ³² It was right to celebrate and to be glad, for this brother of yours was dead and is alive again, and was lost and is found." '

Parable of an unjust manager

16\1 And he further said to his disciples, 'There was a certain rich man who had a house manager, and this man was accused by him that he was squandering his possessions. ² And *he* called him, *and* said to him, "What *is* this I hear about you? Discharge the account of your office of house manager, for you can no longer be house manager." ³ Then the house manager said in himself, "What shall I do? For my master is taking away the management from me. I do not have the strength to dig. I am ashamed to beg. ⁴ I am resolved what I can do,* so that when I will have been removed from

the office of house manager, they might receive me into their own homes." ⁵ So *he* called each one of his master's debtors, *and* he said to the first, "How much do you owe my master?" ⁶ And he said, "A hundred baths of oil." And he said to him, "Take your statement, and sit down quickly and write fifty." ⁷ Then to another he said, "And how much do you owe?" And he said, "A hundred measures of wheat." And he said to him, "Take your statement and write eighty." ⁸ And his master commended the dishonest house manager, because he had acted shrewdly. For the sons of this Eon* are more shrewd towards their own stock than *are* the sons of light.

⁹ 'And do I say to you,* make friends for yourselves out of the mammon* of unrighteousness,* so that when you fail they might receive you into permanent* habitations? ¹⁰ 'He who *is* faithful in *the* least is faithful in much as well, and he who *is* unrighteous in *the* least *is* also unrighteous in much. ¹¹ If, therefore, you have not been faithful in the dishonest mammon,* who will entrust the true *riches* to you? ¹² And if you have not been faithful in that which *is* a foreigner's, who will give you that which *is* your own?

¹³ 'No servant is able to serve two masters, for either he will hate one and love the other, or else he will cling to the one and despise the other. You cannot serve God and mammon.'*

Derision of covetous Pharisees.
God knows the heart
¹⁴ And the Pharisees, being money lovers, also heard all these things, and they were turning their noses up* at him.

¹⁵ And he said to them, 'You are those who justify yourselves in the sight of men, but God knows your hearts. For what is highly esteemed among men is an abomination in the sight of God. ¹⁶ Until John there were the law and the prophets.* Since that time, the Sovereign Rulership of God is proclaimed, and everybody is pressing to get into it.* ¹⁷ But it is easier *for* Heaven and Earth to pass away* than for one merest ornament* of the law to fail.

Rebuke of Pharisees' beliefs
concerning divorce & remarriage *
¹⁸ 'Everybody who puts away his wife and marries another commits adultery, and everybody who marries her who was put away from a husband commits adultery.

The rich man & Lazarus:
Jesus' satirical narrative rebuking
impossible mystical beliefs about death *

[19] 'Now there was a certain rich man, and he was habitually clothed in a purple robe and fine linen, and he revelled in luxury every day. [20] And there was a certain poor man named Lazarus, who had been laid beside his porch, being full of sores, [21] and he was longing to be fed from the crumbs which fell from the rich man's table, and even the dogs came *and* licked at his sores.

[22] 'And it came to pass *that* the poor man died, and he was carried by the angels into the garment-fold* of Abraham.* And the rich man also died, and was buried. [23] And in Hades** he lifted up his eyes, being there in torments,* *and* he saw* Abraham from afar, and Lazarus in his garment-folds.*

[24] 'And calling out, he said, "Father Abraham, have mercy on me, and send Lazarus so that he might dip* the tip of his finger in water and cool my tongue, for I am in anguish in this flame."

[25] 'But Abraham said, "Son, remember that in your lifetime you had all your good things, and in the same way Lazarus *had* worthless things. But now this man is comforted, and you are in distress. [26] And beside all these things, a vast chasm has been fixed between us and you, so that those who want to pass from here to you are not able to, nor can they cross from your side to us." [27] Then he said, "In that case, I entreat you, father, that you would send him to the house of my father [28] – for I have five brothers – so that he might solemnly give testimony* to them that they also might not come into this place of torment."*

[29] 'Abraham said to him, "They have Moses and the prophets. Let them hear those."

[30] 'And he said, "No, father Abraham, but if one from *the* dead should go to them, they will submit." [31] And he said to him, "If they do not hear Moses and the prophets, not even if somebody should rise from among *the* dead will they be persuaded." '

Judgement on deceivers *

17\1 Then he said to the disciples, 'It's inevitable but that snares* should come, but woe *to him* through whom they come! [2] It would be better for him if a millstone turned by a donkey were hanged around his neck and he should be thrown into the sea, rather than that he should be a cause of stumbling to one of these lowly *people.**

Being forgiving

[3] 'Be vigilant over yourselves. If your brother should commit a violation against you, rebuke him. Then if he should submit, forgive him. [4] And if he should commit a violation against you seven times in the day, and seven times in the day he should turn back,* saying, "I yield," you should forgive him.'

Apostles' request for faith

[5] And the apostles said to the Lord, 'Give us more faith.'

[6] And the Lord said, 'If you had faith like a grain of mustard seed, you might say to this mulberry tree, "Be uprooted, and be planted in the sea," and it would obey you.

[7] 'But who among you has a servant who is plowing or looking after sheep *and* who has come from the field, *and* you have said to him, "Come at once* and sit back"?

[8] 'Rather, will he not say to him, "Prepare something I can eat, and dress yourself* *and* serve me while I eat and drink, and after these things you may eat and drink"? [9] Is he thankful to that servant because he did the things commanded? I think not.

[10] 'So you, as well, when you have done all those things commanded of you, say, "We are unworthy* servants. We have done what we had to do." '

Healing of 10 lepers

[11] And it came about, in his going up into Jerusalem, that he passed through *the* centre of Samaria and Galilee. [12] And on his being about to go into a certain village, ten leprous men who were standing at a distance met him. [13] And they raised *their* voices, and said, 'Jesus, Master, have compassion on us.'

[14] And *when he* saw *them* he said to them, 'Go *and* show yourselves to the priests.'

And it came about *that*, in going off on their way, they were cleansed. [15] And one from among them, seeing that he was healed, turned back *and* magnified God with a loud voice, [16] and he fell down on *his* face at the feet of *Jesus*, giving thanks to him – and he was a Samaritan. [17] And in response, Jesus said, 'Were there not ten cured? But where *are* the nine? [18] Were there not any found *who* returned to give the

preeminence to God, except this foreigner?'*
¹⁹   And he said to him, 'Rise up *and* go your way. Your faith has cured you.'

Days of the Son of Man
like the days of Noah *
²⁰   And *when* he was asked by the Pharisees when the Sovereign Rulership* of God was coming, he answered them and said, 'The Sovereign Rulership of God does not come with an outward show.* ²¹ Nor will they say, "Look here!" or, "Look there!" For, see now,* the Sovereign Rulership* of God is in your presence.'*
²²   And he said to the disciples, 'The days will come when you will long to see one of the days of the Son of Man, but you will not see *it.* ²³ And they will say to you, "Look here," or, "Look* there." Do not go after *them*, or follow *them.*
²⁴   'For just as the flashing lightning gives illumination from one part under *the* sky to another part under *the* sky, so will the Son of Man be in his day. ²⁵ But first he must undergo much suffering and be rejected by this generation.
²⁶   'And as it came to pass in the days of Noah, so will it be also in the days of the Son of Man.*
²⁷ They were eating, they were drinking, they were marrying wives, they were being given in marriage, until the day when Noah went into* the ark and the flood came and destroyed them all.
²⁸   'In the same way did it also come to pass in the days of Lot. They were eating, they were drinking, they were buying, they were selling, they were planting, they were building, ²⁹ but the day when Lot went out from Sodom fire and brimstone rained from *the* sky and destroyed everything.
³⁰   'It will be like this in the day the Son of Man is revealed. ³¹ In that day, whoever will be on the housetop, with his belongings in the house, let him not come down to take them away. And in the same manner, let him in the field not turn back for the things behind.
³²   'Remember Lot's wife. ³³ Whoever searches to save his life* will lose it, and whoever will lose it will preserve it.
³⁴   'I tell you, in that night there will be two on a bed; one will be taken, and the other will be left. ³⁵ Two *women* will be grinding together; one will be taken, and the other will be left.*
³⁶   [*no verse 36 in RP Greek text*]*

³⁷   And in answer, they said to him, 'Where, Lord?'
And he said to them, 'Wherever the body* *is*, there the eagles will be gathered together.'

Parable of a persistent widow
18\1 **A**nd he also spoke a parable to them to show that it is always good to pray,* and not to lose heart, ² saying, 'There was a certain judge in a town, not revering God, and not respecting any man. ³ And there was a widow in that town, and she was repeatedly coming to him, saying, "Grant me justice from my adversary." ⁴ And for a long time he did not want to, but eventually he said in himself, "Even though I do not revere God, nor do I respect any man, ⁵ yet because this widow keeps bothering me I will give her justice, so that she does not endlessly come and grind me down." '
⁶   And the Lord said, 'Hear what the dishonest judge says. ⁷ And will God not execute the avenging of His own chosen *people* who call out to Him day and night, although He delays long over them? ⁸ I tell you, He will carry out the avenging of them speedily. All the same, will the Son of Man in his coming find faith on the Earth?'*

Parable of a Pharisee & tax collector
⁹   And he spoke this parable to some who also trusted in themselves that they were righteous and made nothing of the rest: ¹⁰ 'Two men went up into the Temple to pray, the one a Pharisee, and the other a tax collector. ¹¹ The Pharisee took his stand *and* began to pray these things to* himself: "God, I thank You that I am not like the rest of men, *the* grasping, unjust, adulterers, nor like this tax collector. ¹² I fast twice in the week. I give tithes of everything from all that I earn."
¹³   'And the tax collector, standing far off, would not even lift up eyes to Heaven, but was striking on his breast, saying, "God, be reconciled to me, a violator."
¹⁴   'I say to you, this *man* went down to his house justified rather than that other *man*. For everybody who exalts himself will be abased, and he who abases himself will be exalted.'

Receiving the Sovereign Rulership
of God like little children *
¹⁵   And they brought infants to him as well so that he might touch them, but *when* the disciples

saw they rebuked them.
¹⁶ But Jesus called them *and* said, 'Allow the little children to come to me, and do not forbid them, for the Sovereign Rulership of God is of this kind. ¹⁷ Truly I say to you, whoever will not receive the Sovereign Rulership of God like a little child will certainly not enter into it.'

A rich young ruler. Treasure in Heaven*
¹⁸ And a certain ruler questioned him, saying, 'Good Teacher, what must I do to inherit Eonian* life?'
¹⁹ But Jesus said to him, 'Why do you call me good? Nobody is good except one – God.
²⁰ 'You know the commandments: Do not commit adultery. Do not murder. Do not steal. Do not bring false witness. Honour your father and your mother.'*
²¹ And he said, 'All these have I kept since my boyhood.'
²² But *when* Jesus heard these things, he said to him, 'Still one thing is lacking to you. Sell everything, as much as you have, and distribute to *the* poor, and you will have treasure in Heaven,* then come *and* follow me.'
²³ But hearing these things he became grieved, for he was tremendously rich.
²⁴ But seeing him becoming grieved, Jesus said, 'With what difficulty do those having riches enter into the Sovereign Rulership of God!
²⁵ 'For it is easier for a camel* to pass through an eye of a needle than *for* a rich man to enter into the Sovereign Rulership of God.'
²⁶ And those listening said, 'Who, then, is able to be saved?'
²⁷ But he said, 'The things impossible with men are possible with God.'

*Receiving many times more
& Eonian life in the coming Eon
(Mark 10\30) for forsaking everything* *
²⁸ Then Peter said, 'In our case, we have left everything and followed you.'
²⁹ And he said to them, 'Truly I say to you, there is nobody who has left a house, or parents, or brothers, or wife, or children, on account of the Sovereign Rulership of God, ³⁰ who will not receive manifold more in this present time, and, in the Eon* which is coming, Eonian* life.'*

He again predicts his death & resurrection *
³¹ And *he* took the twelve aside, and he said to

them, 'Now, we are going up to Jerusalem, in order that all things which have been written through the prophets will be accomplished by the Son of Man. ³² For he will be given into the hands of the nations, and he will be mocked, and insulted, and spat on. ³³ And *when* they have scourged *him*, they will murder him, and on the third day he will be raised.'
³⁴ And they understood nothing of these things, and this declaration was hidden from them, and they did not discern the things which were being spoken.

Healing of a blind man *
³⁵ And it came about, in his drawing near to Jericho, *that* a certain blind man was sitting at the roadside begging. ³⁶ And on hearing a crowd pass along, he kept asking what this might mean. ³⁷ And they told him that Jesus the Nazarene* was passing by.
³⁸ And he called out, saying, 'Jesus, Son of David, have pity on me!'
³⁹ And those going in front rebuked him that he should hold his peace, but he continued all the more, calling out, 'Son of David, have pity on me!'
⁴⁰ And Jesus stopped *and* commanded him to be brought to him, and on his drawing near he questioned him, ⁴¹ saying, 'What do you wish that I should do for you?'
And he said, 'Lord, that I may receive my sight.'
⁴² And Jesus said to him, 'Receive your sight. Your faith has healed you.'
⁴³ And instantly he received his sight, and he followed him, magnifying God. And all the people saw and gave praise to God.

At Jericho. Salvation of Zacchaeus

19\1 And he entered Jericho, *and* was passing through *it*, ² and *there was* a man there named Zacchaeus, and he was a chief tax collector, and he was rich. ³ And he was searching to see Jesus, who he might be, but he was unable to because of the crowd, since he was short in stature. ⁴ So he ran ahead, *and* climbed up onto a sycamore tree so that he might see him, for he was about to cross through that *road.*
⁵ And when he came up to the place, Jesus looked up *and* saw him, and he said to him, 'Zacchaeus, hurry *and* come down, for today I have to stay* in your house.'

⁶ And *he* hurried *and* came down, and received him, rejoicing.

⁷ And everybody seeing began to murmur, saying, 'He went in to be a guest with a violating man.'

⁸ But taking his stand, Zacchaeus said to the Lord, 'Look now, Lord, half my possessions I give to the poor, and if I have extorted anything from anybody by false accusation I will make restoration four times over.'

⁹ And Jesus said to him, 'Today salvation has come to this house, since he also is a son of Abraham. ¹⁰ For the Son of Man came to search and to save that which was lost.'

Parable of talents.* Regional responsibilities for the diligent

¹¹ And as they were hearing these things, he went on to speak a parable, on account of his being near Jerusalem, and because they thought that the kingdom of God was about to be brought to light at that moment.

¹² So he said, 'A certain nobleman* went into a distant country to receive a kingdom for himself, then to return. ¹³ And he called ten of his servants *and* gave them ten minas,* and he said to them, "Engage yourselves in business until I come back." ¹⁴ But his citizens* hated him, and they sent a delegation after him, saying, "We are unwilling *for* this *man* to reign over us." ¹⁵ 'And it came about, on his coming back again, that he received the kingdom, *and* he directed to be called to him those servants to whom he had given the money, so that he might come to know how much each had gained by trading.

¹⁶ 'Then the first came up, saying, "Master, your mina has made another ten minas." ¹⁷ And he said to him, "Well done, good servant. Because you have been faithful in the smallest thing, take authority over ten cities."*

¹⁸ 'And the second came up, saying, "Master, your mina has made another five minas." ¹⁹ And he likewise said to him, "And you be over five cities."

²⁰ 'And another came up, saying, "Master, look now, *here is* your mina which I was keeping stored up in a sweat cloth. ²¹ For I feared you, because you are a harsh man. You take up what you did not lay down, and reap what you did not sow."

²² 'So he said to him, "I will condemn you out of your own mouth, wicked servant! You had known that I am a hard man, taking up what I did not lay down, and reaping what I did not sow. ²³ Why, then, did you not invest my money at a money changer's table, so that at my return I might have collected it with interest?" ²⁴ And he said to those standing by, "Take the mina away from him, and give *it* to him who has ten minas."

²⁵ 'But they said to him, "Lord, he has ten minas." ²⁶ For I say to you, to everybody who has it will be given; and from him who does not have, even what he does have will be taken away from* him. ²⁷ But as for those enemies of mine who were unwilling *for* me to rule over them, bring *them* here and execute *them* in front of me.'*

His triumphal entry into Jerusalem.* Commiseration over Jerusalem*

²⁸ And having spoken these things, he went on ahead, going up into Jerusalem.

²⁹ And it came about, as he drew near to Bethsphage and Bethany, towards the Mount known as Olives, *that* he sent two of his disciples, ³⁰ saying, 'Withdraw into the village opposite, where, on your entering, you will find a tethered foal which nobody among men has ever* sat on. Untie it, and bring *it*. ³¹ And if anybody might ask you, "Why are you untying *it?*", say this to him: "Because the Lord has need of it." '*

³² And those who had been sent went their way, *and* they found *it* just as he had said to them.

³³ And as they were untying the foal, its owners said to them, 'Why are you untying the foal?'

³⁴ And they said, 'The Lord needs it.'

³⁵ So they led it to Jesus, and threw their own garments on the foal, *and* they set Jesus on it.

³⁶ And as he was making his way, they were spreading down their garments in the road. ³⁷ And as he was already drawing near the descent of the Mount of Olives, all the multitude of the disciples began to rejoice *and* to praise God with a loud voice for all *the* works of power which they had seen, ³⁸ saying:

'Exalted* *is* the King,
the Coming One,
in *the* name of *the* Lord!*
Peace in Heaven,
and magnificence in *the* highest *realms!*'

³⁹ And some of the Pharisees from the crowd

said to him, 'Teacher, rebuke your disciples.'
[40] And in answer, he said to them, 'I tell you, if these should be silent, look, the stones will call out.'
[41] And as he drew near and looked over the city, he lamented over it, [42] saying, 'If only you yourselves had known, and especially in this day of yours, the things for your peace! But now they are hidden away from your eyes. [43] For *the* days will come against you when your enemies will construct a rampart around you, and they will close around you, and hem you in on every side, [44] and they will dash you to the ground, *you* and your children among* you, and they will not leave stone on stone* among you.* The reason for these things *is that* you do not know the season of your visitation.'*

Cleansing the Temple *
[45] And he entered the Temple, *and* he went on to throw out those selling and buying in it, [46] saying to them, 'It has been written:

"My House is the House of Prayer;
you, though, have made it
a cave of bandits." '**

[47] And he was giving teaching day by day in the Temple. But the senior priests and the scribes and the chief of the people were looking for a way to murder him, [48] yet they could not find how they could do *it*, as all the people were completely enraptured in listening to him.

Teaching in the Temple. Confrontation
over his authority & John's identification *

20\1 **A**nd it came about, on one of those days while he was teaching the people in the Temple and proclaiming the gospel, *that* the priests and the scribes came forward with the elders, [2] and they spoke to him, saying, 'Tell us, by what kind of authority do you do these things, or who is it who gave you this authority?'
[3] And he answered and said to them, 'I in turn will ask you one matter, and you make an answer to me. [4] The identification of John, was it from Heaven, or from men?'
[5] And they reasoned among themselves, saying, 'If we should say, "From Heaven",* he will say, "Why did you not believe him?" [6] But if we should say, "From men", all the people will stone us, for it is held *among them for* John to

be* a prophet.'*
[7] And they answered *that* they did not know where *it was* from.
[8] And Jesus said to them, 'Neither will I tell you by what authority I do these things.'

Parable of vine dressers *
[9] Then he began to speak this parable to the people: 'A man planted a vineyard and let it out to vine dressers, and he took a journey abroad* for a long* time.* [10] And in due course he assigned a servant to the farmers so that they should give him something from* the fruit of the vineyard, but the farmers flogged him, and sent *him* away empty handed. [11] And he sent a different servant, but *when* they had beaten him as well and treated *him* shamefully, they sent *him* away empty handed. [12] And he sent a third, and *when* they had wounded him as well they threw *him* out. [13] Then the master of the vineyard said, "What shall I do? I will send my richly loved son. Surely *when* they see him they will respect *him*." [14] But *when* they saw *him* the farmers reasoned among themselves, saying, "This is the heir. Come on, let's murder him, so that the inheritance can become ours." [15] So *after* throwing him outside the vineyard, they murdered *him*. What, therefore, will the master of the vineyard do to them?'
[16] *Some of the audience answered,* 'He will come and destroy these farmers, and give the vineyard to others.'
And on hearing they said, 'May it not be!'
[17] But looking fixedly at them, he said, 'What, then, is this which has been written:

"*The* stone which the builders rejected,
this has become *the* head of *the* corner"?*

[18] 'Everybody who falls on that stone will be broken into pieces, but on whomever it will fall it will grind him into powder.'*
[19] And the senior priests and the scribes looked for a way to seize him at that same time, but they were afraid* because they knew that he had spoken this parable against them.

Confrontation concerning census tax *
[20] And they watched *him and* sent out secret agents* feigning themselves to be* righteous in order that they might seize on his remarks, with a view to informing on him to the administration and the authority of the president.

²¹ And they questioned him, saying, 'Teacher, we know that you speak and teach rightly, and you have no regard for character,* but you teach the way of God with truth. ²² Is it lawful for us to give census tax to Caesar, or not?'
²³ But discerning their duplicity, he said to them, 'Why are you testing me? ²⁴ Show me a denarion.* Whose image and inscription does it have?'

And in answer, they said, 'Caesar's.'
²⁵ And he said to them, 'Then give to Caesar the things of Caesar, and to God the things of God.'
²⁶ And they did not have the acumen* to seize on his speech in front of the people, so having marvelled at his answer they were silent.

Confrontation with Sadducees
concerning the resurrection of the dead
²⁷ Then some of the Sadducees, those contradicting* there is to be* a resurrection, came to him *and* questioned him, ²⁸ saying, 'Teacher, Moses wrote for us, "If anybody's brother should die having a wife, and he should die childless, then his brother should take his wife and raise up seed for his brother."*
²⁹ 'Now suppose* there were seven brothers, and the first took a wife *and* died childless, ³⁰ then the second took her *as his* wife and he died childless, ³¹ and the third likewise took her, and similarly the seven also left no children and died, ³² and last of all the woman died as well. ³³ So, in the resurrection, whose wife does she become? For the seven had her as a wife.'
³⁴ And in answer Jesus said to them, 'The sons of this Eon* marry, and are given in marriage. ³⁵ But those who will be counted worthy to attain to that Eon** and to the resurrection from among *the* dead neither marry nor are they given in marriage. ³⁶ For they do not have the capacity to die any more,* for they are equal to the angels and are Sons of God, being members of the resurrection.*
³⁷ 'But that the dead are raised, even Moses pointed *this* out at the bush when he called *the* Lord the God of Abraham, and the God of Isaac, and the God of Jacob.* ³⁸ But He is God* not of *the* dead, but of *the* living, for all live by means of Him."*
³⁹ Then some of the scribes, in answering, said, 'Teacher, you have spoken well.'
⁴⁰ And after that, they no longer dared to ask him anything.

His testing of the Pharisees
concerning the line of David
⁴¹ And he said to them, 'How do they proclaim the Christ to be* *the* Son of David, ⁴² seeing that David himself says in *the* Scroll* of Psalms:

"The Lord said to my Lord,
'Sit at* My right hand'
⁴³ until I make your enemies
a footstool for your feet' "?*

⁴⁴ 'David, therefore, calls him "Lord". And how is he his son?'

Stronger condemnation for the scribes*
⁴⁵ Then as all the people were listening, he said to his disciples, ⁴⁶ 'Turn your attention away from the scribes, those wanting to walk about in robes and liking salutations in the marketplaces, and prime seats in the synagogues, and prime couches at banquets, ⁴⁷ who swallow up widows' houses, and for exhibition pray at vast length. These will receive a stronger judgement.'*

The generous widow*
21\1 And he looked up *and* saw *the* rich men dropping their gifts into the treasury.
² And he saw also a needy widow, putting two leptons* in it, ³ and he said, 'Truly I say to you, this poor widow has put in more than everyone. ⁴ For all these, out of what was abounding to them have put *money* into the offerings of God, but she out of her lack has put in all the livelihood which she had.'

His prophecy of destruction of the Temple
(Rev. 11\2). *Answering two questions concerning the tribulation, & Jesus' return as the true Christ in power & radiance*
⁵ And as some were remarking about the Temple Court, how it was adorned with beautiful stones and devoted gifts,* he said, ⁶ '*As for* these things which you are gazing at, days will come when stone will not be left on stone, *and* which will not be thrown down.'
⁷ And they* asked him, saying, 'So Teacher, when will these things be, and what *is* the sign when these things might be about to take place?'*
⁸ And he said, 'Take heed that you are not misled, for many will come trading on* my name, saying, "I Am,"* and "The season has

drawn near.'" Do not, therefore, go after them. ⁹ But when you hear of wars and revolutions, do not be fearful, for these things have to come to pass* first, but the end *is* not straightaway.'

¹⁰ Then he was saying to them, 'Nation will be roused against nation, and kingdom against kingdom,* ¹¹ and there will be violent earthquakes in many places, and famines, and plagues, and there will be fearful sights and mighty signs from *the* sky.

Before the beginning of sorrows,
'the days of vengeance'

¹² 'But before all these things, they will grip their hands on you and persecute *you*, handing you over to synagogues and jails as you are brought in front of kings and rulers on account of my name. ¹³ But it will turn out for you as a testimony.

¹⁴ 'Settle *it*, therefore, in your hearts, not to premeditate *what* to speak in defence. ¹⁵ For I will give you a mouth and wisdom which all those opposing you will not be able to make a reply to, or to resist.

¹⁶ 'And you will be betrayed even by parents, and relatives, and brothers, and friends, and *some* from among you they will condemn to death.* ¹⁷ And you will be hated by everybody on account of* my name. ¹⁸ But not a hair of your head will in any way perish.* ¹⁹ In your patient endurance keep a hold on* your lives.*

²⁰ 'But when you see Jerusalem being encircled by military camps, then come to know that her desolation has drawn near.* ²¹ Then let those in Judea flee into the mountains, and let those in her region depart, and do not let those in the country area enter into her.

²² 'For these are the days of vengeance,* so that all things having been written might be accomplished.

²³ 'But woe to those who have *a child* in *the* womb, and to those breastfeeding in those days! For there will be severe distress over the land, and indignation among this people. ²⁴ And they will fall by *the* blade of *the* sword, and be led away captive into all the nations.

Jerusalem trampled (Rev. 11\2).
The mighty tribulation & Jesus' return

'And Jerusalem will be trampled down* by *the* nations, until the times of *the* nations* are fulfilled.*

²⁵ 'And there will be signs in *the* Sun and Moon and stars, and on the Earth a distress of nations in perplexity, a resounding of sea and a rolling surge of waves, ²⁶ men fainting from fear and an expectation of what is befalling the inhabited world, for the powers of the skies will be shaken,* ²⁷ and then they will see the Son of Man coming in a cloud,* with power and immense magnificence.

²⁸ 'But *when* these things begin to arise,* be elated,* and lift up your heads, because your deliverance draws near.'

Parable of a fig tree *

²⁹ And he spoke a parable to them: 'See the fig tree, and all the trees. ³⁰ When they are already sprouting shoots, on your looking you yourselves know from *experience* that summer is already near. ³¹ So you also, when you see these things coming to pass, know that the Sovereign Rulership of God is near.

³² 'Truly I say to you, this generated *oracle* will by no means have passed away until all these things might have taken place. ³³ Heaven and Earth will pass away,* but my utterances will by no means pass away.

³⁴ 'But be vigilant for yourselves in case at any time your hearts are loaded down with surfeiting,* and drinking, and anxieties of life, and that day* should come suddenly against you. ³⁵ For it will come like a snare* against all those sitting on the face of the whole Earth.* ³⁶ Be watchful, therefore, praying on every occasion,* so that you might be counted worthy to escape all the things which are about to arise,* and to stand in the presence of the Son of Man.'

³⁷ And by day he would teach in the Temple, and at night he would go out *and* stay in the mountain called Olives. ³⁸ And all the people would come to him early in the morning in the Temple to hear him.

Senior priests & scribes conspire
to murder him. *Satan takes over Judas*

22\1 Now the Festival of Unleavened *Bread*, called Passover, was drawing near. ² And the senior priests and the scribes were searching how they might murder him, for they were fearful of the people.

³ Meanwhile Satan went into Judas, the one surnamed Iscariot,* being out of the number of the twelve. ⁴ And he went his way *and* spoke with the senior priests and the chief magistrates

concerning in what way he might hand him over to them. ⁵ And they were delighted, and agreed to give him money, ⁶ and he fully consented, and looked for an opportunity to hand him over to them in the absence of the crowd.

The Passover *

⁷ Then the day of Unleavened *Bread* approached, in which the Passover must be killed, ⁸ and he sent Peter and John, saying, 'Go *and* prepare the Passover for us, so that we can eat *it*.'
⁹ And they said to him, 'Where do you have in mind we should make preparations?'
¹⁰ And he said to them, 'Mark this: on your going into the city a man carrying a jar of water will meet you. Follow him to the house that he goes in, ¹¹ and say to the master of the house, "The Teacher says to you, 'Where is the guest room* where I can eat the Passover with my disciples?'" ¹² And that *man* will show you a large upper room, spread out. Make preparations there.'
¹³ And *they* went off *and* found *it* just as he had said to them, and they prepared the Passover.

Jesus announces the new covenant
& looks forward to the Eon
& the new Passover feast *

¹⁴ And when the hour had come, he and the twelve apostles with him were leaning back, ¹⁵ and he said to them, 'With longing* I have deeply yearned to eat this Passover with you before I suffer. ¹⁶ For I say to you, I will certainly not eat from it any more, until it might be fulfilled in the Sovereign Rulership of God.'
¹⁷ And *when* he had received *the* cup *and* given thanks, he said, 'Take this, and divide *it* among yourselves. ¹⁸ For I say to you, I certainly will not drink from the produce of the vine until the Sovereign Rulership of God might appear.'
¹⁹ And he took a loaf *and* gave thanks, and broke *it* up, and gave *some* to them, saying, 'This represents my body which is being given on your behalf. Do this for a memorial of me.'
²⁰ In the same manner, he in turn took the cup after eating, saying, 'This cup *represents** the new covenant in my blood, which is poured out for you.*
²¹ 'But, look now, the hand of him *who* is betraying me *is* with me on the table. ²² And indeed, the Son of Man goes as it has been marked out,* but woe to that man by whom he

gets betrayed!'
²³ And they began to question this together among themselves, who of them it might be who was about to do this. ²⁴ And a rivalry also arose among them, *concerning* who among them was thought to be* the most eminent.
²⁵ And he said to them, 'The kings of the nations lord it over them, and those wielding authority over them are known as benefactors. ²⁶ But you *must* not *be* like that. Rather, let the most eminent among you be like the youngest, and he who leads like him who serves. ²⁷ For who *is* more eminent, he who sits to eat, or he who serves? *Is it* not he who sits to eat? But I am among you as one who serves. ²⁸ But you are those who have continued with me in my trials.* ²⁹ And I assign to you – just as my Father has assigned to me – a kingdom, ³⁰ so that you may eat and drink at my table, and you will sit on thrones judging the twelve tribes of Israel.*

He predicts Peter's denial *

³¹ And the Lord said, 'Simon, Simon! Look, Satan has made a claim on you all* for sifting *you* like wheat.* ³² But I have pleaded concerning you that your faith might not fail, and, once you have turned back, you might establish your brothers.'
³³ And he said to him, 'Lord, I am ready to go both into jail and to death with you.'
³⁴ And he said, 'I tell you, Peter, a rooster will certainly not crow today* before you have denied three times *that* you know me'.
³⁵ And he said to them, 'When I authorized you without money-bag, and travel sack, and sandals, did you suffer need in anything?'
And they said, 'Nothing.'
³⁶ So he said to them, 'But now he who has a money-bag, let him take *it*, and likewise a travel sack.* And the one not having anything, let him sell his garment and buy a sword.* ³⁷ For I say to you, this which has been written must still be fulfilled in me: "And he was reckoned with transgressors."* For concerning myself this also has completion.'
³⁸ And they said, 'Lord, look, here *are* two swords.'
And he said to them, 'That is enough.'*

Agony in Gethsemane *

³⁹ And he went outside, and, in keeping with his custom, he went to the Mount of Olives, and his disciples followed him as well.
⁴⁰ And on arriving at the place, he said to

them, 'Pray that you do not enter into temptation.'*

⁴¹ And he himself was parted about a stone's throw from them, and, falling on *his* knees, he prayed,* ⁴² saying, 'Father, if You are willing, remove this cup from me. Nevertheless, not my wish, but let Yours be done.'

⁴³ And an angel from Heaven was seen by him, strengthening him. ⁴⁴ And being in agony, he prayed more intensely, and his sweat became like large clots of blood falling to the ground.*

⁴⁵ And having risen from prayer, he came to the disciples. He found them sleeping from grief, ⁴⁶ and he said to them, 'Why are you sleeping? Rise up and pray that* you might not enter into temptation.'*

Betrayal by Judas. Healing of Malchus*

⁴⁷ And while he was still speaking, a crowd approached, and he who was called Judas, one of the twelve, was going in front of them, and he drew near to Jesus to embrace him.

⁴⁸ But Jesus said to him, 'Judas, are you betraying the Son of Man with a kiss?'

⁴⁹ And seeing what was about to happen, those around him said to him, 'Lord, should we strike *them* with a sword?'

⁵⁰ And someone among them struck the servant of the high priest, and took off his right ear.

⁵¹ But in reaction, Jesus said, 'Permit even this.'

And he touched his ear *and* he healed him.

⁵² Then Jesus said to those who had come against him, senior priests, and chief magistrates of the Temple, and elders, 'Have you come out with swords and clubs as if against a bandit?'* ⁵³ When I was with you daily in the Temple, you did not stretch out hands against me. But this is your hour, and of the power of darkness.'*

His arrest.* Peter's denial*

⁵⁴ Then *they* seized him *and* led *him away*, and brought him into the house of the high priest. And Peter was following at a distance. ⁵⁵ And they lit a fire in the middle of the courtyard and sat down together, *and* Peter sat down among them.

⁵⁶ But a certain servant girl saw him as he sat by the firelight, and, looking at him intently, she said, 'This *man* was with him as well.'

⁵⁷ But he contradicted him, saying, 'Woman, I do not know him.'

⁵⁸ And after a little while, a different *person* seeing him said, 'You are from among them as well.'

And Peter said, 'Man, I am not.'

⁵⁹ And *after* about an hour had elapsed, somebody else made positive assertions, saying, 'Truly, this *man* was with him as well, and he is definitely a Galilean.'

⁶⁰ And Peter said, 'Man, I do not know what you are talking about.'

And at once, while he was still speaking, *the* rooster crowed. ⁶¹ And the Lord turned round *and* looked straight at Peter. And Peter remembered the oracles of the Lord when he had said to him, 'Before a rooster crows, you will deny me three times.' ⁶² And Peter went outside *and* wept bitterly.

His examination & mocking
before elders & priests & scribes
& the Sanhedrin.* His assertion of 'I Am'

⁶³ And the men who were holding Jesus were mocking and flogging him.

⁶⁴ And they blindfolded him, *and* they were striking his face, and they kept questioning him, saying, 'Prophesy! Who is it who struck you?'

⁶⁵ And they kept speaking many other blasphemous things against him.

⁶⁶ And as soon as it became day, the council of the elders of the people, senior priests and scribes were gathered together, and they led him to their Sanhedrin, saying, ⁶⁷ 'If you are the Christ, tell us.'

And he said to them, 'If I told you, you would certainly not believe *it*. ⁶⁸ But if I should ask *you* also, you would not answer me or let *me* go. ⁶⁹ From this time the Son of Man will be seated at* *the* right* hand of the Power of God.'*

⁷⁰ Then they all said, 'So you are the Son of God, then?'

And he said to them, 'You say that I am.'*

⁷¹ And they said, 'Why do we still have need of any further witness, for we ourselves have heard out of his mouth?'

His examination before Pilate.*
Witnesses lie about Jesus

23\1 **A**nd the whole number of them rose up *and* led him to Pilate.

² And they began to accuse him, saying, 'We found this *man* subverting the nation, and forbidding to give census tax to Caesar, *and* proclaiming himself to be* Christ, a King.'

³ And Pilate questioned him, saying, 'Are you

the King of the Jews?'

And in answer to him, he said '*As* you say.'
⁴ Then Pilate said to the senior priests and the crowds, 'I find nothing reprehensible in this man.'
⁵ But they kept insisting, saying, 'He stirs up the people, teaching throughout all of Judea, beginning from Galilee *and* as far as here.'
⁶ But *when* Pilate heard 'Galilee', he asked if the man was a Galilean. ⁷ And as soon as he came to know that he was under Herod's jurisdiction, he sent him to Herod, he also being in Jerusalem in those days.

Examination before Herod
⁸ And Herod, seeing Jesus, was exceedingly glad, for he had been wanting to see him for some time, on account of his hearing many things about him, and he was hoping to see some sign accomplished by him. ⁹ Then he questioned him by many words, but he answered him nothing.
¹⁰ And the senior priests and the scribes stood by, vigorously accusing him.
¹¹ And Herod with his troops treated him with contempt, and mocked *him*, and dressed him in luxurious clothes, *and* he sent him back to Pilate. ¹² And in that same day Pilate and Herod became friends with each other,* whereas they had previously been at enmity with each other.

Pilate releases Barabbas *
¹³ And Pilate called together the senior priests and the rulers and the people, ¹⁴ *and* he said to them, 'You have brought me this man who is supposedly turning away the allegiance of the people, whereas I have examined *him* in your presence and I have found nothing reprehensible in this man concerning which you bring accusation against him. ¹⁵ Nor, indeed, *does* Herod, for I sent you to him, and the result is that nothing worthy of death has been done by him. ¹⁶ Having chastized him, I will then let *him* go.'
¹⁷ For by custom he must release somebody to them at each Festival.
¹⁸ And they called out in a mass, saying, 'Away with this *man*! But release Barabbas to us!' ¹⁹ *It was he* who, on account of a certain insurrection *which* had taken place in the city, as well as for a murder, had been thrown into jail.
²⁰ So Pilate, wanting to release Jesus, addressed *them* again.
²¹ But they kept calling out, saying, 'Hang *him*

on a stake! Hang him on a stake!'*
²² Then a third *time* he spoke to them, 'Why, what evil has this *man* committed? I have found no grounds in him for the death penalty. So I will scourge him *and* let *him* go.'
²³ And they were pressing with loud voices, demanding for him to be hanged on a stake.* And their voices and those of the senior priests had the strength to prevail. ²⁴ And Pilate pronounced sentence for their request to be carried out,* ²⁵ and he released him *who* had been put in jail on account of sedition and murder, the one they had asked for. But Jesus he handed over to their will.

He predicts the days of tribulation.*
Rulers & soldiers mock him
²⁶ And as they led him away, they seized hold of Simon, a certain Cyrenian, coming from a field, *and* they put the stake* on him, to carry *it* behind Jesus. ²⁷ And a large crowd of the people were following him, as well as women who were also beating their breasts and lamenting for him.
²⁸ But Jesus turned to them *and* said, 'Daughters of Jerusalem, do not weep over me, but weep for yourselves and for your children. ²⁹ For be aware of this: the days are coming in which they will say, "Exalted *are* the barren, and *the* wombs which did not give birth,* and the breasts which did not breastfeed." ³⁰ Then they will go on to say to the mountains, "Fall on us," and to the hills, "Cover us."* ³¹ For if they do these things in the case of the moist wood,** what must happen in the case of the dry *wood*?'
³² And two others, criminals,* were also led with him to be put to death. ³³ And when they came to the place called the Skull, they hanged him and the criminals on a stake* there, one on *his* right, and the other on *his* left.
³⁴ Then Jesus said, 'Father, forgive them, for they do not know what they are doing.'
And they parted his garments, *and* they threw lots.*
³⁵ And the people stood looking on.
And the rulers with them were also mocking, saying, 'He saved others – let him save himself, if he is the Christ, the chosen one of God.'
³⁶ And the soldiers also mocked him, coming up close to him and offering him vinegar, ³⁷ and saying, 'If you are the King of the Jews, save yourself.'
³⁸ And an inscription was also written over him in letters of Greek, and Latin, and Hebrew:

'This is the King of the Jews.'*

Jesus uses Moses' phrase of assertion,
'Truly, I say to you this day'
(Deut. 4\26, 4\39, 4\40, 5\1, etc.),
to tell the man who makes a dying confession
that he will be in the Paradise
which is the New Jerusalem in the new Earth
(Rev. 2\7 with 22\2, 22\14)

³⁹ And one of the criminals hanged on stakes kept railing at him, saying, 'If you are the Christ, save yourself, as well as us.'

⁴⁰ But in answer, the other rebuked him, saying, 'Do you not revere even God, seeing you are under* the same sentence, ⁴¹ and we justly so? For we are receiving a due recompense for what we did, but this man has done nothing wrong.'

⁴² And he said to Jesus, 'Lord, remember me when you appear in your Sovereign Rulership.'*

⁴³ And Jesus said to him, 'Truly, I say to you this day,* you will be with me in the Paradise.'*

Death *

⁴⁴ And it was about *the* sixth hour, and darkness arose over the whole land until *the* ninth hour. ⁴⁵ And the Sun was darkened, and the veil of the Sanctuary was torn *down the* middle.

⁴⁶ And calling out with a loud voice, Jesus said, 'Father, into Your hands I entrust my spirit.'

And having said that, he breathed his last.**

Declaration of a centurion *

⁴⁷ Now seeing what had happened, the centurion magnified God, saying, 'Certainly this was a righteous man.'

⁴⁸ And all the crowds who had converged on this spectacle, seeing the things taking place, beat their breasts, *and* they turned back.

⁴⁹ But all those who knew him, and the women who followed with him from Galilee, continued standing far off, gazing on these things.

His burial by Joseph of Arimathea *

⁵⁰ And there was a man by the name of Joseph, *who* was a counsellor,* a good and righteous man, ⁵¹ who had not voted with their counsel and action, from Arimathea, a town of the Jews, and who himself also was waiting for the Sovereign Rulership of God. ⁵² This *man* went to Pilate *and* requested the body of Jesus.

⁵³ And he took it down *and* wrapped it in a linen cloth, and he laid it in a tomb cut out of stone, in which nobody had been lain before.

⁵⁴ And it was *the* Preparation Day, *and* the Sabbath was drawing near. ⁵⁵ And *the* women also, who had come with him from Galilee, followed *and* they saw the tomb, and how his body was lain. ⁵⁶ And they went back *and* prepared aromatics and ointments,* and they rested *on the* Sabbath,** in keeping with the commandment.*

His resurrection *

24\1 Then, on the First of Weeks,* while still early in the morning, they came to the tomb, carrying *the* aromatics which they had prepared, and some *others with* them. ² And they found the stone rolled away from the tomb, ³ and they went in, *but* they did not find the body of the Lord Jesus. ⁴ And it so happened, in their being perplexed about this, that suddenly two men in shining clothing came into their view.

⁵ And at their becoming filled with fear and bending *their* faces to the ground, *the angels* said to them, 'Why do you search for the living with the dead? ⁶ He is not here, but he has been raised.* Bring to your mind how he spoke to you *when* he was still in Galilee, ⁷ saying, "The Son of Man has to be handed over into the hands of violating men, and to be hanged on a stake,* and the third day to rise." '

⁸ And they remembered his oracles, ⁹ and on their returning from the tomb they told all these things to the eleven, and to all the others.

¹⁰ Now it was Maria Magdalene, and Joanna, and Maria *the mother* of Jacob, and the rest with them, who told these things to the apostles, ¹¹ and their words seemed in their sight like idle tales, and they did not believe them.

¹² Then Peter rose up *and* ran to the tomb, and, stooping down to look, he saw the linens laid out on their own, and he went away wondering to himself what had happened.

Appearance to Cleopas
& another on the Emmaus road*

¹³ Now as it happened, two of them were going on in that same day into a village called Emmaus, sixty stadium lengths* distance from Jerusalem. ¹⁴ And they were talking to each other concerning all these things which had taken place, ¹⁵ and it came about, in their conversing and reasoning together, that Jesus

himself drew near *and* he was walking along with them. [16] But their eyes were restrained, *so that they* were not able to recognize him.

[17] And he said to them, 'What *are* these words which you are exchanging with each other as you walk along and are downcast in countenance?'

[18] And one of them, whose name *was* Cleopas, said in answer to him, 'Are you a visitor alone *in* Jerusalem, and have not come to know the things having taken place in these days?'

[19] And he said to them, 'What kind of things?'

And they said to him, 'The things concerning Jesus the Nazarene,* who was a man *who was* a prophet mighty in deed and oracle before God and all the people, [20] and how the senior priests and our rulers delivered him to *the* sentence of death, and hanged him on a stake.* [21] But we were hoping that he was the one who would redeem Israel, but then, besides* all these things, today brings the third day from the time when all this* took place. [22] But also, certain women among us went early to the tomb *and* they astounded us, [23] and, on their not finding his body, they came back saying as well that they had seen a vision of angels who say he is living. [24] And some of those with us went to the tomb, and they found *it* just as the women had also spoken, but they did not see him.'

[25] And he said to them, 'Oh dullards, and slow of heart to believe in everything which the prophets have spoken! [26] Ought the Christ not to have suffered these things, and to enter into his magnificence?'

[27] And beginning from Moses and from all the prophets, he gave them an exposition of all the things in the Scrolls concerning himself.

[28] And they drew near to the village where they were heading, and he made out as if to be going further, [29] but they constrained him, saying, 'Stay with us, for it's approaching evening, and the day has worn away.'

So he went in to stay with them. [30] And it came about, in his sitting down with them, *that* he took the bread, *and* he exalted* *God*, and broke *the bread* up, *and* handed *some* to them. [31] And their eyes were opened, and they recognized him, and he became invisible to them.

[32] And they said to each other, 'Was our heart not burning in us while he was talking with us on the road, and while he was opening up the Scrolls to us?'

Final appearance. *Opening understanding for the Scrolls.*
Immediate authorization to continue his work *

[33] And rising up at the same hour, they went back to Jerusalem, and found the eleven gathered together, and those with them, [34] saying, 'The Lord really has been raised,* and he was seen by Simon.'

[35] And on the road they related the things in detail, and how he became recognized to them at the breaking of the bread.

[36] And as they were narrating these things, Jesus himself stood in their presence, and he said to them, 'Peace be to you.'

[37] But being terrified and filled with fear, they supposed that they were seeing a spirit.

[38] And he said to them, 'Why are you disturbed, and why do doubts arise in your hearts? [39] See my hands and my feet, that I myself am he.* Touch me, and see, for a spirit does not have flesh and bones* as you see me having.'

[40] And having said this, he showed them *his* hands and feet.

[41] And while they still did not believe out of *their* exuberance and marvelling, he said to them, 'Do you have anything edible here?'

[42] And they gave him a piece of a grilled fish and some honeycomb, [43] and he took *it and* ate *it* in their presence.

[44] And he said to them, 'These *are* the oracles which I spoke to you while I was with you, that all things must be fulfilled which have been written in the Law of Moses, and the Prophets, and the Psalms* concerning me.'

[45] Then he opened their mind to understand the Scrolls, [46] and he said to them, 'So has it been written, and so must the Christ suffer in this way and rise out from *the* dead on the third day, [47] and submission and forgiveness of violations be proclaimed in his name to all the nations, beginning from Jerusalem. [48] And you are witnesses of these things.

[49] 'And see now, I authorize over you the promise of my Father*. But remain in the city of Jerusalem until you are clothed with power from on high.'

Jesus carried up into Heaven *

[50] And he led them out as far as Bethany, and lifting up his hands he invoked favour on* them. [51] And it came about, in his invoking favour on* them, *that* he stood apart from them, and he was carried up into Heaven.*

[52] And having eulogized[*] him, they went back into Jerusalem with immense exuberance, [53] and they were continually in the Temple, praising and eulogizing[*] God. Amen.

~ ◆◆ ~

† The Gospel Accounts of Jesus Christ †

John

Prologue
John speaks of 'the beginning of the gospel'
(as Mark 1\1, Luke 1\2, Phil. 4\15,
1 John 1\1, 2\7, 2\13, 2\14, 3\11, etc.),
which is 'the oracle of the truth of the gospel'
& 'the oracle of life ... in relation to the Father'
(1 John 1\1-2, Col. 1\5, 1 Thes. 2\13).
This oracular pronouncement (ὁ λόγος, ho logos)
was 'pointing to', 'in relation to' (πρός, pros),
God, & the source of the oracle was God

1\1

In the beginning* was the oracle,* and the oracle* was pointing to* God,* and the oracle source* was* God.* ² This *oracle* was pointing to* God* in *the* beginning.

Everything arose (ἐγένετο, egeneto)
through the proclamation of 'the oracle
of the truth of the gospel' of God (Col. 1\5)
³ Everything* arose* through* it, and apart from it* there arose* not even one thing which has arisen.* ⁴ In it* was life, and the life was the light of men. ⁵ And the light shines in the darkness, and the darkness did not overpower it.

Proclamation of John the Identifier *
⁶ There was a man authorized from* God, his name John.* ⁷ This same one came for a witness, in order that he might bring witness concerning the light, so that through him,* *Christ*, all might believe.* ⁸ That one, *John*, was not the light, but *he came* so that he might witness about the light.

The world has now 'come to be' (ἐγένετο,
egeneto) under the domain of the Son of God
since his entry & exaltation in Heaven (Acts 2\33,
Rom. 9\5, Phil. 2\9-11, Col. 1\14-20 etc.).
Sons of God (Luke 6\35, Rom. 8\16, 1 John 3\1)
⁹ *That light* was the true light* who enlightens* every man coming into the world. ¹⁰ He was in the world,* and the world has come to be* through him,* yet the world did not know him. ¹¹ He came to his own,* yet *his* own* did not receive him. ¹² But to as many who received

him, he gave them authority to become Sons of God,* to those who are believing in his name, ¹³ who were born not out of bloodlines, nor out of the will of the flesh, nor out of the will of a man, but out of God.

The oracle of God spoken by Gabriel
created Jesus (Luke 1\26-38, Heb. 3\2).
Riddle of John that Jesus, born & coming
after John, is ahead of him in honour. *
Law superceded by merciful goodwill
¹⁴ And the oracle* became* flesh,* and he lived among us, and we discerned* his preeminence – a preeminence* exactly like* an only *son* * alongside* a father* – abounding in merciful goodwill and truth.
¹⁵ John gives testimony concerning him, and he called out, saying, 'This is* he of whom I said, "The one coming after* me has been* ahead of* me,* because he was* superior to* me." '*
¹⁶ And we have all received out of his fulness, and merciful goodwill for merciful goodwill. ¹⁷ For the law was given through Moses. Merciful goodwill and truth came through* Jesus Christ.

Nobody has seen God (Ex. 33\20-23).
The authority of John
¹⁸ Nobody* has seen* God at any time.** The only* Son,* he who is in the garment-fold* of the Father, he expounds* *Him.* *
¹⁹ And this is the testimony of John when the Jews sent priests and Levites out of Jerusalem so that they might ask him, 'Who are you?'
²⁰ And he professed, and did not make denial, and professed, 'I myself am not the Christ.'
²¹ And they asked him, 'What then, are you Elijah?'
And he said, 'I am not.'*
They asked, 'Are you the Prophet?'
And he answered, 'No.'
²² So they said to him, 'Who are you? *Tell us*, so that we might give an answer to those having sent us. What do you say about yourself?'
²³ He said:

'I am a voice calling out in the wilderness,
"Make straight the way of *the* Lord."'*

'– as the prophet Isaiah said.'
²⁴ And those who had been sent were from among the Pharisees, ²⁵ and they questioned

him, and said to him, 'Why do you make identifications then, if you are not the Christ, nor Elijah, nor the Prophet?'

²⁶ John answered them, saying, 'I identify with water, but among you stands one whom you do not know. ²⁷ This is the one who is coming after me, who has been* ahead of* me,* of whom I am not worthy that I should unfasten the strap of *his* sandal.'

²⁸ These things took place in Bethania* beyond the Jordan, where John was making identifications.

²⁹ The next day he saw Jesus coming to him, and he said, 'Behold the Lamb* of God who takes away the violation of the world. ³⁰ This is he concerning whom I said, "After me comes a man* who has been* ahead of* me, because he was superior to* me."* ³¹ And I did not know him other than that he should be brought to light* to Israel.* On account of this I came making identifications in the water.'

John the Identifier saw the Angel of God
& John affirms that Jesus is the Son of God *

³² And John gave testimony, saying, 'I saw the Spirit* descending out of *the* sky in the manner of a dove, and he remained over him. ³³ And I did not know him, except that he having authorized me to identify in water said to me, "On him whom you will see the Spirit* descending and remaining over him, that is he who identifies in *the* divine spirit."* ³⁴ And I have seen, and I have given testimony, that this one is the Son of God.'

John speaks of Jesus as the lamb sacrifice of God.
Disciples called. *Vision of the revealing*
of Jesus with angels (cp. Genesis 28\12)

³⁵ Again the next day John was standing with two of his disciples, ³⁶ and, fixing his gaze on Jesus *as* he was walking about, he said, 'Behold the Lamb* of God!'

³⁷ And the two disciples heard him speaking and they followed Jesus.

³⁸ Then Jesus turned and saw them following, *and* he said to them,* 'What are you looking for?'

And they said to him, 'Rabbi' – which means, being translated, Teacher – 'where are you staying?'

³⁹ He said to them, 'Come and see.'

They went and saw where he was staying,

and they remained with him that day. It was now about *the* tenth hour.

⁴⁰ One of the two who heard *this* from John and followed him was Andrew, the brother of Simon Peter.

⁴¹ He first found his own brother Simon, and said to him, 'We have found the Messiah,' which, being translated, is *the* Christ.

⁴² And he brought him to Jesus.

And looking at him, Jesus said, 'You are Simon, the son of Jonah. You shall be called Cephas', which, translated, *is* 'stone'.*

⁴³ The following day he wanted to set out for Galilee, and he found Philip and said to him, 'Follow me.'

⁴⁴ Now Philip was from Bethsaida, out of the town of Andrew and Peter.

⁴⁵ Philip found Nathanael, and he said to him, 'We have found *him* whom Moses wrote about in the law and the prophets, Jesus, the son of Joseph,* from Nazareth.'

⁴⁶ And Nathanael said to him, 'Is it possible *for* there to be* anything good out of Nazareth?'

Philip said to him, 'Come and see.'

⁴⁷ Jesus saw Nathanael coming to him, and he said of him, 'Look, truly an Israelite, in whom there is no guile!'

⁴⁸ Nathanael said to him, 'Where do you know me from?'

Jesus answered, and said to him, 'Before Philip called you, *when* you were underneath the fig tree, I saw you.'

⁴⁹ Nathanael answered, and said to him, 'Rabbi, you are the Son of God. You are the King of Israel.'

⁵⁰ Jesus answered, and said to him, 'Do you believe because I said to you, "I saw you underneath the fig tree"? You will see mightier *things* than these.'

⁵¹ Then he said to him, 'Truly, truly, I say to you *people*,* after this time you will see the sky opened, and the angels of God ascending and descending over the Son of Man.'*

Wedding at Cana

2\1 **A**nd on the third day a marriage feast took place in Cana of Galilee, and the mother of Jesus was there, ² and Jesus also was invited with his disciples to the marriage.

³ And on their running short of wine,* the mother of Jesus said to him, 'They have no more wine.'

⁴ Jesus said to her, 'What *is* that to me and you, woman? My hour has not yet come.'

⁵   His mother said to the attendants, 'Do whatever he might tell you.'*

⁶   And there were six stone waterjars there, standing in keeping with the purification of the Jews, each containing two or three measures.

⁷   Jesus said to them, 'Fill the waterjars with water.'

And they filled them to *the* brim.

⁸   Then he said to them, 'Now draw *some* off, and carry *it* to the superintendent of the dining hall.'

And they brought *it*, ⁹ but when the superintendent of the dining hall tasted the water turned to* wine – and he did not know where it was from, although the attendants who had drawn the water knew – the superintendent of the dining hall called the bridegroom, ¹⁰ and he said to him, 'Everybody at the beginning puts out the good wine, and then the inferior *wine* when they have drunk freely. You, *though*, have kept the good wine until now.'

¹¹ Jesus performed this beginning of the signs in Cana of Galilee, and brought to light* his preeminence, and his disciples put their faith in him.

First cleansing of the Temple.
*He predicts his death & resurrection**
of his body as a sanctuary (cp. Rom. 6\4)

¹² After this he went down to Capernaum, he, and his mother, and his brothers, and his disciples, and they remained there for a few days.

¹³   And the Jews' Passover was at hand, and Jesus went up to Jerusalem, ¹⁴ and he found sitting in the Temple those who sold oxen and sheep and doves, and the money changers. ¹⁵ And *when* he had made a whip out of small cords, he drove them all out of the Temple, as well as the sheep and the oxen, and he poured out the small coins of the money changers and overturned the tables.

¹⁶   And to those who sold doves he said, 'Get these things away from here! Do not turn my Father's House* into a house of merchandise.'

¹⁷   And his disciples remembered that it has been written: 'Zeal for Your House consumes me.'*

¹⁸   So the Jews answered, and said to him, 'What sign do you show us, seeing that you do these things?'

¹⁹   Jesus answered, and said to them, 'You destroy* this sanctuary, and in three days I will raise it up.'*

²⁰ So the Jews said, 'This Sanctuary was forty-six years in being built,* and will you raise it up* in three days?'

²¹   But he was speaking concerning the sanctuary of his body.* ²² So when he had been raised* from among *the* dead, his disciples remembered that he had said this, and they believed the Scroll, and the oracles which Jesus had spoken.

²³ Then when he was in Jerusalem at the Passover for the Festival, many seeing the signs which he was doing believed in his name. ²⁴ But Jesus himself* did not entrust himself to them in view of his having knowledge of everybody,* ²⁵ and he did not have any need that anybody should give testimony about man, for he knew what was in a man.*

Nicodemus & spiritual birth: born 'from above'
(ἄνωθεν, *anothen, also 3\3, 3\7, 3\31, 19\11*)

3\1 **N**ow there was a man of the Pharisees, his name Nicodemus, a ruler of the Jews.

²   This *man* came to him by night, and said to him, 'Rabbi, we perceive* that you are a teacher come from God, for nobody would be able to perform these signs which you perform if God were not with him.'

³   Jesus answered, and said to him, 'Truly, truly, I say to you, unless a person is born* from above,* he is not able to perceive* the Sovereign Rulership* of God.'

⁴   Nicodemus said to him, 'How is a man able to be born *when* he is old? Is he able to enter into* the womb of his mother a second time and be born?'*

Jesus compares blowing of the wind
*to resurrection by the agency of the spirit.**
Jesus is in the Father, 'the Heavenly One' (3\13,
10\30, 10\38, 14\10, 14\20, 17\21-23)

⁵   Jesus answered, 'Truly, truly, I say to you, unless a man is born* out of* water* and* out of spirit,* he is not able to enter into* the Sovereign Rulership* of God.* ⁶ That which is born out of flesh is flesh, and that which is born* out of* spirit is spirit.** ⁷ Do not marvel that I said to you, "It is needful* for you to be born* from above."* ⁸ The wind* blows* wherever* it pleases,* and you hear its* sound,* but you do not know where it comes from and

where it goes to. It is like this for everyone having been born* out of the spirit.*

9 Nicodemus replied, and said to him, 'How are these things able to arise?'*

10 Jesus answered, and said to him, 'Are you the teacher of Israel, and you have not come to know these things? 11 Truly, truly, I say to you, we speak what we know, and give testimony to what we have seen, but you do not receive our testimony. 12 If I have told you earthly things and you do not believe, how will you believe if I tell you the most exalted* things?

13 'And nobody has ascended* into* Heaven,* except the one come down from* Heaven,* the Son of Man, who is in the Heavenly One.'**

*Nicodemus hears the gospel
of Eonian life (ζωὴ αἰώνιος, zoe aionios)
or destruction (Mat. 7\13)*

14 'And* in the way that* Moses lifted up the snake in the wilderness,* so* does the Son of Man have to be lifted up, 15 in order that everyone believing in* him might not suffer destruction,* but might have Eonian* life.'**

16 'For God so much* loved the world* that He gave His only* Son, in order that everyone believing in him might not suffer destruction,* but might have* Eonian* life.'**

17 'For God authorized His Son into the world not so that he might judge the world, but so that through him the world might be saved. 18 The one believing in him is not judged, but the one not believing has already been judged, because he has not believed in the name of the only* Son of God.

19 'And this is the judgement: that the light has come into the world, and men loved the darkness rather than the light, because their works were actively evil. 20 For everybody who carries out evil hates the light and does not come to the light, so that his works might not be brought home* to him. 21 But he who exercises the truth comes to the light so that his works might be brought to light,* for they have been operated by God.'

*John the Identifier's testimony of Jesus
as the bridegroom.* Jesus' birth came
'from above' (ἄνωθεν, anothen, 3\31)*

22 After these things, Jesus and his disciples came into the region of Judea, and he stayed there with them, and he was making identifications. 23 And John was *there* also,

making identifications in Aenon* near to Salim, because there was a large amount of water there, and *people* were coming and being identified. 24 For John had not yet been thrown into jail.

25 An argument with a Jew* broke out* from some of John's disciples concerning purification.

26 And they came to John, and said to him, 'Rabbi, he who was with you on the other side of the Jordan, the one to whom you gave testimony, look, he's making identifications, and they're all coming to him.'

27 John answered, and said, 'A man is able to receive nothing unless it has been given to him from the Exalted One.* 28 You yourselves give testimony that I said I am not the Christ, but that I was authorized ahead of* him. 29 He who has the bride is *the* bridegroom, but the friend of the bridegroom who stands and hears him rejoices immensely because of the bridegroom's voice. So then, this exuberance of mine has been fulfilled.

30 'He must become more eminent, but I *must* become lesser. 31 The one having come from above* is above all. The one being out of the Earth is of the Earth and speaks of* the Earth. He who comes from Heaven* is above all. 32 And what he has seen and heard, this he attests, but nobody accepts his testimony.

33 'He who has accepted his testimony has fixed his seal that God is true. 34 For he whom God has authorized speaks the oracles of God, for God does not give the spirit** out of* a measuring-jar.*

35 'The Father loves the Son, and has given all things into* his hand. 36 The one believing in* the Son has Eonian* life; but the one not obeying the Son will not see life, but the indignation of God remains against* him.'

*Woman of Samaria at Jacob's Fountain.
God is spirit (4\24), not flesh*

4\1 When, therefore, the Lord came to know that the Pharisees had heard that Jesus was making and identifying more disciples than John 2 – although Jesus himself was not making identifications, but his disciples *were* – 3 he left Judea, and departed into Galilee.

4 And it was necessary for him to pass through Samaria, 5 so he came into a town of Samaria, called Sychar, near the area of ground which Jacob gave to his son Joseph.

⁶ Now Jacob's Fountain was there, so Jesus, being weary from the journey, was sitting down by the fountain.˙ It was about *the* sixth hour, ⁷ *and* a woman from Samaria came to draw water.

Jesus said to her, 'Give me *something* to drink.' ⁸ For his disciples had gone away into the town so that they might buy food.

⁹ Then the woman of Samaria said to him, 'How is it that you, being a Jew, ask for a drink from me, being a woman of Samaria?'

For Jews have no familiar associations with Samaritans.

¹⁰ Jesus answered, and said to her, 'If you had known the gift of God, and who it is who said to you, "Give me a drink," you would have asked him, and he would have given you living water.'

¹¹ The woman said to him, 'Sir, you have no bucket to draw with, and the well is deep. From where, then, do you get that living water? ¹² Surely you are not more eminent than our father Jacob who gave us the well˙ and drank out of it himself, and his sons, and his livestock?'

¹³ Jesus answered, and said to her, 'Everybody drinking˙ out of this water will be thirsty again. ¹⁴ But whoever drinks out of the water which I will give him will certainly not thirst throughout˙ the Eon,˙ but the water which I will give him will become in him a fountain˙ of water springing up into Eonian˙ life.'

¹⁵ The woman said to him, 'Sir, give me this water so that I will not thirst, nor come here to draw *water.*'

¹⁶ Jesus said to her, 'Go *and* call your husband, and come back here.'

¹⁷ The woman answered, and said, 'I do not have a husband.'

Jesus said to her, 'You say well "I have no husband,"˙ ¹⁸ for you have had five husbands, and the one whom you have now is not your husband. What you have spoken is true.'

¹⁹ The woman said to him, 'Sir, I see that you are a prophet. ²⁰ Our fathers worshipped in this mountain, and you say that the place where it is necessary to worship is in Jerusalem.'

²¹ Jesus said to her, 'Woman, believe me, an hour is coming when you will worship the Father neither in the mountain nor in Jerusalem.˙ ²² You do not know whom you worship. We know whom we worship, for salvation˙ is out of the Jews. ²³ But an hour is coming, and is now on its way, when the real worshippers will worship the Father in spirit and truth, for the Father also looks for such *people* to worship Him. ²⁴ God *is* spirit,˙ and those who worship Him must worship in spirit and truth.'

²⁵ The woman said to him, 'I know that *the* Messiah is coming, who is called Christ. When he comes, he is going to clarify all these things for us.'

²⁶ Jesus said to her, 'I Am˙ – the one˙ speaking˙ to you.'

²⁷ And his disciples arrived at this *point*, and they were amazed that he was speaking with a woman, yet nobody said, 'What are you looking for?' or, 'Why are you speaking with her?'

²⁸ Then the woman left her waterjar, and went her way into the town, and she said to the men, ²⁹ 'Come *and* see a man who has told me everything that I have done. Could this be the Christ?'

³⁰ They went out of the town, and they were coming to him.

³¹ In the meantime, though, his disciples urged him, saying, 'Rabbi, you ought to eat.'

³² But he said to them, 'I have food to eat which you do not know about.'

³³ So the disciples said to each other, 'Has nobody brought him anything to eat?'

³⁴ Jesus said to them, 'My food is that I should do the will of Him having authorized me, and finish His work. ³⁵ You say, do you not, that it is only four months and the harvest is coming? Look now, I say to you, lift up your eyes and see the fields, for already they are white, ready for the harvest. ³⁶ And he who reaps receives wages and gathers fruit towards Eonian˙ life, so that both he who sows and he who reaps might rejoice together. ³⁷ And in this is the true saying that it is one who sows and another who reaps. ³⁸ I sent you to reap what you did not toil over. Others have done the labour, and you have entered into their toils.'

³⁹ And many of the Samaritans of that town believed in him on account of the words of the woman giving testimony that 'He told me everything that I have done.'

⁴⁰ So when the Samaritans came to him, they asked him to stay with them, and he stayed there for two days. ⁴¹ And many more believed because of his oracles.

⁴² And they were saying to the woman, 'Now no longer do we believe through your word, for we have heard ourselves, and we know that this

truly is the Saviour of the world,* the Christ.'

Healing of a nobleman's son

43 Now after the two days he departed from there, and he went away into Galilee. 44 For Jesus himself gave testimony that a prophet has no honour in his fatherland.* 45 So when he came into Galilee, the Galileans received him, having seen all the things which he did in Jerusalem during the Festival, for they also went to the Festival.

46 So Jesus again went into Cana of Galilee, where he had made the water become* wine. And there was a certain royal official whose son was ill in Capernaum. 47 Having heard that Jesus had come from Judea into Galilee, he went to him and asked him if he would come down and heal his son, for he was about to die.

48 So Jesus said to him, 'If you *people** do not see signs and wonders, you will not in any way believe.'

49 The royal officer said to him, 'Sir, come down before my child dies.'

50 Jesus said to him, 'Go your way. Your son is alive.'

And the man believed the oracles which Jesus had spoken to him, and he went his way. 51 But as he was still going down, his servants met him and spoke, saying, 'Your boy is alive.' 52 So he enquired of them the hour in which he became better, and they said to him, 'Yesterday, *at the* seventh hour, the fever left him.'

53 So the father knew that *it was* at the same hour in which Jesus said to him, 'Your son is alive,' and he himself believed, as well as his whole household.

54 Jesus performed this second sign as he departed from Judea into Galilee.

Healing of a crippled man.
Objection that Jesus called God his Father

5\1 ▉fter these things it was the Festival of the Jews, and Jesus went up into Jerusalem.

2 Now in Jerusalem there is a pool at the sheep-gate, which in Hebrew *is* called Bethesda, having five covered colonnades. 3 Among these a large crowd of those who were sick were lying down – the blind, lame, withered – waiting for the moving of the water. 4 For from time to time an angel went down into the pool and agitated the water. Then he who stepped in first, after the agitation of the water, was made

well *from* whatever disease he was held by.

5 And a certain man was there, having been in infirmity *for* thirty-eight years. 6 On seeing him lying down, and knowing that he had already been *there* for a long time, Jesus said to him, 'Do you want to become* whole?'

7 The infirm man answered him, 'Sir, I have nobody who, when the water has been agitated, can put me into the pool, but just as I am going in somebody else steps down in front of me.'

8 Jesus said to him, 'Rise up, pick up your stretcher, and walk.'

9 And instantly the man was cured, and he picked up his stretcher and walked.

However, it was the Sabbath on that day, 10 so the Jews said to him who had been healed, 'It's a Sabbath. It's not legal for you to pick up a stretcher.'

11 He answered them, 'He who restored my health – that one there – said to me, "Pick up your stretcher and walk." '

12 So they asked him, 'Who is the man who said to you, "Pick up your stretcher and walk"?'

13 But he who had been healed did not know who it was, for Jesus had moved aside, there being a crowd in the place.

14 After these things, Jesus found him in the Temple, and he said to him, 'Look, you have become whole. Continue no longer in violation, so that something worse does not happen to you.'

15 The man departed, and he told the Jews that it was Jesus who had restored him. 16 And on account of this, the Jews kept troubling* Jesus, and they were looking to murder him because he did these things on a Sabbath.

17 But Jesus answered them, 'Up to now my Father has been working, and I also have been working.'

18 So because of this, the Jews tried all the harder to murder him, because not only was he breaking the Sabbath, but he even called God *his* own Father, making himself equal to God.**

19 So Jesus answered, and said to them, 'Truly, truly, I say to you, the Son is able to do nothing from himself, but only what he might see the Father doing. For whatever things He does, the Son also does these things in the same manner. 20 For the Father loves the Son, and shows him everything which He Himself does, and He will show him works mightier than these so that you might marvel. 21 For as the Father raises up and gives life to the dead, so the Son also gives

life to whomever he wishes. [22] For the Father judges nobody, but He has given all judgement to the Son,˙ [23] in order that all might honour the Son, just as they honour the Father. He not honouring the Son does not honour the Father Who authorized him.

[24] 'Truly, truly, I say to you that he who hears my oracle and believes in Him having authorized me has Eonian˙ life, and he will not come into judgement, he has passed from death into life.˙

Resurrections of life & judgement:
immediate resurrections 'now', without judgement
(11\43-44, Mat. 27\52-53)
[25] 'Truly, truly, I say to you that a time is coming, and is now, when the dead will hear the voice of the Son of God, and those having heard will live. [26] For just as the Father has life in Himself, so has He also given *it* to the Son to have life in himself, [27] and He has also given him authority to execute judgement,˙˙ because he is the Son of Man.

Eonian order of resurrections (Luke 14\14,
1 Cor. 15\22-23, Rev. 20\4, 20\11-15)
[28] 'Do not be amazed at this, for a time is coming in which all those in the graves will hear his voice,˙ [29] and they will come out, those who have worked good things into a resurrection of life,˙ and those who have worked evil things into a resurrection˙ of judgement.˙ [30] I am able to do nothing on my own. As I hear, I judge, and my judgement˙ is just,˙ because I search not my own will, but the will of the Father having authorized me.

Testimony of John
& of the Father concerning Jesus.
Jesus authorized by the Father (Mat. 3\17 etc.).
The gospel of Eonian life
[31] 'If I alone give testimony concerning myself, my testimony is not true. [32] There is another who gives testimony concerning me, and I know that the testimony which he testifies concerning me is true. [33] You have sent word to John, and he has given testimony to the truth. [34] 'But I do not receive testimony from man, but I declare these things so that you might be saved. [35] He was the burning and shining lamp, and you were pleased to rejoice in his light for a while.
[36] 'But I have the testimony weightier than

John's. For the works which the Father has given me that I should complete, those same works which I myself perform, they give testimony concerning me that the Father has authorized me.

[37] 'And the one having authorized me, the Father, has Himself given testimony concerning myself.˙ You have neither heard His voice at any time,˙ nor have you seen His appearance.˙ [38] And you do not have His oracle remaining in you, for you do not believe him whom He sent.

[39] 'Search˙ the Scrolls, for you suppose in them to have Eonian˙ life, and those are what are giving testimony concerning me. [40] But you are not willing to come to me so that you might have life.

[41] 'I do not receive approval from men. [42] But I know you, that you do not have the love of God in yourselves.

[43] 'I have come in the name of my Father, and you do not receive me. If another should come in his own name,˙ you will receive him.

Moses wrote about Jesus (Deut. 18\5, 18\18, etc.)
[44] 'How can you believe, you who receive approval from one another, and do not look for the approval from the only God?
[45] 'Do not think that I will accuse you to the Father. There is one accusing you – Moses, on whom you have set your hope. [46] For if you had believed Moses,˙ you would have believed me, for he wrote about me.˙ [47] But if you do not believe his Writings, how can you believe my oracles?'

The 5,000 ˙

6\1 After these things, Jesus sailed away across the Sea of Galilee, of Tiberias, [2] and a vast mass of people were following him because they saw his signs which he was performing on those who were diseased.
[3] Then Jesus went up into the mountain, and he was sitting there with his disciples.
[4] Now the Passover, a Festival of the Jews, was near,˙ [5] so Jesus raised *his* eyes, and, having seen that a vast mass of people were coming to him, he said to Philip, 'Where can we buy loaves from, so that these *people* can eat?'
[6] However˙ he said this testing him, for he himself knew what he was going to do.
[7] Philip answered him, 'Two hundred denarions'˙ worth of loaves would not be

sufficient for them, so that each of them could take a little.'

8 One of his disciples, Andrew, the brother of Simon Peter, said to him, 9 'There is a little boy here who has five barley loaves and two cooked fish, but what is that for so many?'

10 And Jesus said, 'Make the men sit down.'

Now there was plenty of grass in the place, so the men sat down, about five thousand in number. 11 And Jesus took the loaves and gave thanks, *and* he distributed *them* to the disciples, and the disciples *distributed them* to those seated, and the same with the cooked fish, as much as they wanted.

12 And when they were filled he said to his disciples, 'Gather up the remaining fragments, so that none of it might be wasted.'

13 So they gathered *everything* up and filled twelve hand baskets of fragments from the five barley loaves which were left over from those who had eaten.

14 So *when* the men saw what sign Jesus had performed, they said, 'This is truly the Prophet who was to come into the world."*

He walks over the sea
15 So Jesus, perceiving that they were about to come and seize him by force so that they might make him king, withdrew into the mountain alone *by* himself.

16 And when it grew late, his disciples went down to the sea, 17 and they boarded onto a boat, *and* they were ferrying over the sea towards Capernaum. Now darkness had risen, and Jesus had not come to them, 18 and the sea was being agitated by a strong wind blowing. 19 Then when they had rowed about twenty-five or thirty stadium lengths,* they saw Jesus walking across the sea and drawing near to the ship, and they were afraid.

20 But he said to them, 'I Am.* Do not be afraid.'

21 Then they were willing to receive him into the boat, and instantly the boat came to the place which they were heading for.

Jesus compares himself to the manna fallen from Heaven (Ex. 16\13-19)
22 The following day, the crowd standing on the other side of the sea saw* that there was no other small boat there, except the one which his disciples had boarded, and *that* Jesus had not gone with his disciples in the small boat, but his disciples had departed alone, 23 but other small boats came out from Tiberias near the place where they had eaten bread *after* the Lord had given thanks. 24 So when the crowd saw that Jesus was not there, nor his disciples, they themselves got into the boats and went into Capernaum, looking for Jesus.*

25 And *when* they found him *on* the other side of the sea, they said to him, 'Rabbi, when did you get here?'

26 Jesus answered them, and said, 'Truly, truly, I say to you, you look for me not because you saw signs, but because you ate the loaves and were satisfied. 27 Labour not for the food perishing, but for the food enduring into Eonian* life, which the Son of Man will give you, for this one the Father, God, has set a seal on.'*

28 So they said to him, 'What should we do, so that we might do the works of God?'

29 Jesus answered, and said to them, 'This is the work of God: that you should believe in him whom He has authorized.'

30 So they said to him, 'What sign will you carry out then, so that we might see and believe you? What will you perform? 31 Our fathers ate the manna in the wilderness. As it has been written: "He gave them bread from Heaven to eat." '*

32 Then Jesus said to them, 'Truly, truly, I say to you, Moses did not give you the bread from Heaven, but my Father gives you the true bread from Heaven. 33 For the bread of God is the one coming down from Heaven* and he gives life to the world.'

34 So they said to him, 'Lord, give us this bread always."*

35 And Jesus said to them, 'I am* the bread of life. He who comes to me will certainly not* hunger, and he who believes in me will certainly not* thirst at any time.* 36 But I said to you that, although you have seen me, you still do not believe. 37 All whom* the Father gives me will come to me, and he who comes to me I will certainly not drive outside.

38 'For I have come down from* Heaven* not that I should do my own will, but the will of Him having authorized me. 39 And this is the will of the Father *Who* authorized me: that I should not lose *anybody* out of whom He has given me, but that I should raise them* up in the last day.* 40 And this is the will of Him *Who* authorized me: that everybody who sees the

Son and believes in him should have Eonian˙ life, and I should raise him up in the last day.˙"

[41] So the Jews were murmuring about him, because he had said, 'I am˙ the bread come down from Heaven.'

[42] And they were saying, 'Is this not Jesus, the son of Joseph, whose father and mother we know? How is it, then, that he says, "I have come down from˙ Heaven"?˙"

[43] So Jesus answered, and said to them, 'Do not murmur among yourselves. [44] Nobody is able to come to me unless the Father, the one having authorized me, draws him,˙ and I will raise him up in the last day.˙ [45] It has been written in the prophets: "And they will all be taught by God."˙ Everybody, therefore, who hears from the Father, and has learned, comes to me.

He speaks of having seen the Father, & his living 'through the Father' (1 Cor. 11\3, 2 Cor. 13\4). To 'live throughout the Eon' (Psalm 133\3)

[46] 'Not that anybody has seen the Father, except the one being from God˙ – he has seen the Father. [47] Truly, truly, I say to you, he who believes in me˙ possesses Eonian˙ life.

[48] 'I am˙ the bread of life. [49] Your fathers ate manna in the wilderness and died. [50] This is the bread coming down from Heaven so that anybody can eat from it and not die. [51] I am˙ the living bread come down from Heaven.˙ If anybody eats from this bread, he will live throughout the Eon,˙ but the bread which I will give is my flesh, which I will give for the life of the world.'

[52] So the Jews were contending with each other, saying, 'How can this man give us flesh to eat?'

[53] So Jesus said to them, 'Truly, truly, I say to you, unless you eat the flesh of the Son of Man and drink his blood, you do not have life in you. [54] He who feeds on my flesh and drinks my blood has Eonian˙ life, and I will raise him up in the last day.˙ [55] For my flesh most truly is food, and my blood most truly is drink. [56] He who feeds on my flesh and drinks my blood remains in me, and I in him.

[57] 'As the living Father authorized me, and I live through the Father,˙ the one feeding on me will also live through˙ me. [58] This is that bread come down from Heaven, not comparable to how your fathers ate the manna and died. He who eats this bread will live throughout the

Eon."

Many desert him. Peter's declaration

[59] He said these things in a synagogue while teaching in Capernaum.

[60] Therefore many of his disciples, *when* they heard, said, 'This speech is hard. Who can listen to it?'

[61] But Jesus, knowing in himself that his disciples murmured about this, said to them, 'Does this cause you to stumble? [62] What, then, if you shall see the Son of Man ascending to where he was before? [63] It is the spirit which gives life. The flesh profits nothing. The oracles which I have spoken to you are spirit, and they are life. [64] But there are some among you who do not believe.'

For Jesus knew from *the* beginning˙ who those were who would not believe, and who it was who would betray him.

[65] And he said, 'For this reason I said to you that nobody is able to come to me unless it is given to him from my Father.˙"

[66] At this, many of his disciples went back and no longer walked about with him.

[67] So Jesus said to the twelve, 'Surely you as well are not wanting to go off?'

[68] So Simon Peter answered him, 'Lord, to whom could we go? You have the oracles of Eonian˙ life. [69] And we have believed and come to know that you are the Christ, the Son of the living God.'

Judas identified as a devil

[70] Jesus answered them, 'Did I not choose you, the twelve? Yet one of you is a devil.˙"

[71] Now he was speaking of Judas Iscariot, *the son* of Simon, for he was about to betray him, being one of the twelve.

His brothers go to the Festival of Booths

7\1 After these things, Jesus was walking around in Galilee, for he did not want to walk in Judea because the Jews were looking to murder him.˙

[2] Now the Jews' Festival of Booths was near, [3] so his brothers said to him, 'Move on from here and go into Judea, so that your disciples also might be spectators of the works which you do. [4] For nobody does anything in secret and himself seeks to be in public. If you are doing these things, show˙ yourself to the world.'

5 For not even his brothers believed in him.

6 So Jesus said to them, 'My time has not yet come, but your own time is always at hand. 7 The world cannot hate you, but it hates me because I give testimony about it that its works are evil. 8 You go up to this Festival. I am not going to this Festival just now,* for my time has not yet fully come.'

9 And *after* he had said these things to them, he stayed in Galilee. 10 But when his brothers had gone up, then he also went up to the Festival, not openly, but as if in secret.

11 So the Jews were looking for him in the Festival, and they said, 'Where is that *man?*'

12 And there was much murmuring among the crowds concerning him. Some were saying, 'He's good.' Others said, 'No, rather, he leads the crowd adrift.'

13 However, nobody spoke in public about him on account of fear of the Jews.*

His teaching in the Temple,
making himself known.
Objections & attempt to arrest him

14 Then when the Festival was already halfway through, Jesus went up into the Temple and he began to teach.

15 And the Jews were amazed, saying, 'How come this *man* knows literature,* without having received instruction?'

16 So Jesus answered them, and said, 'My teaching is not mine, but His Who authorized me. 17 If anybody wishes to do His will, he will come to know about the teaching, whether it is from God, or I speak on my own. 18 He who speaks from his own initiative searches for his own preeminence. But it is he who searches for the preeminence* of Him having authorized him: this one is true, and unrighteousness is not in him. 19 Did Moses not give you the law? Yet nobody among you keeps the law. Why do you look to murder me?'

20 The crowd answered, and said, 'You have a demon! Who is endeavouring to murder you?'

21 Jesus answered, and said to them, 'I performed one work, and you are all struck with astonishment. 22 For this reason, Moses gave you circumcision – not that it is from Moses, but from the fathers – and you circumcise a man on a Sabbath. 23 If a man receives circumcision on a Sabbath, so that the law of Moses should not be broken, are you angry with me because I made a man entirely sound on a Sabbath? 24 Judge not in relation to appearance, but judge a righteous judgement.'

25 Then some of those of Jerusalem said, 'Is this not he whom they are searching to murder? 26 And look now, he speaks publicly, yet they say nothing to him. The rulers really have not ascertained, *have they*, that this truly is the Christ?* 27 However, we know where this *man* is from. But when the Christ comes, nobody knows where he is from.'

28 So Jesus called out in the Temple *in his* teaching, saying, 'You know both me and you know where I am from, and yet I have not come from my own initiative. But He Who authorized me is true, He Whom you do not know. 29 I know Him, because I am from Him, and He authorized me.'

30 So they were looking to arrest him, yet nobody laid a hand on him because his hour had not yet come.

31 But many from the crowd believed in him, and they were saying, 'When the Christ comes, will he do more signs than these which this *man* has done?'

32 The Pharisees heard the crowd murmuring these things about him, and the Pharisees and the senior priests sent officers so that they might arrest him.

33 So Jesus said, 'I will only be with you a little while, and I will withdraw to Him Who authorized me. 34 You will look for me but you will not find *me*, and where I am you are not able to come.'*

35 So the Jews said among themselves, 'Where is he going to go that we will not find him? Is he about to go to the dispersed of the Greeks and then teach the Greeks? 36 What is this remark which he spoke, "You will look for me but you will not find *me*," and "Where I am you are not able to come"?'

Diverse opinions concerning Jesus

37 Now on the last day, the solemn* *day* of the Festival, Jesus stood up and called out,* saying, 'If anybody is thirsty, let him come to me and let him drink. 38 Whoever believes in me, just as the Scroll has said of me, "Out of his inside will flow rivers of living water."* 39 But he spoke this* referring to the spirit which* those believing in him were about to receive, because *the* divine spirit was not yet *given*, because Jesus had not yet been magnified.'

40 Then many out of the crowd, *when* they

heard this declaration, said, 'Truly, this is the Prophet.'

⁴¹ Some said, 'This is the Christ.'

Others said, 'No, for surely the Christ does not come out of Galilee. ⁴² Does the Scroll not say that the Christ comes out of the seed of David, and from the village of Bethlehem where David was?'*

⁴³ So a division arose among the crowd on account of him. ⁴⁴ But some of them wanted to arrest him, although nobody laid hands on him.
⁴⁵ Then the officers went to the senior priests and Pharisees, and they said to them, 'Why did you not bring him?'

⁴⁶ The officers answered, 'Never* did a man speak like this man.'

⁴⁷ Then the Pharisees answered them, 'Have you also been led adrift? ⁴⁸ Has anybody among the rulers believed in him, or among the Pharisees? ⁴⁹ But this crowd, who do not know the law, are laid under a curse.'*

⁵⁰ Nicodemus, who came to Jesus by night, being one of them, said to them, ⁵¹ 'Does our law judge a man unless it has heard from him first, and knows what he does?'

⁵² They answered, and said to him, 'Are you also out of Galilee? Search, and see that no prophet has been raised* out of Galilee.'

⁵³ And each *man* went off to his own house.

8\1 **B**ut Jesus went to the Mount of Olives.

The woman taken in adultery *

² And at dawn he again presented himself at the Temple, and all the people came, and he took a seat *and* taught them.

³ And the scribes and Pharisees brought to him a woman caught in adultery, and they set her in the centre, ⁴ *and* they said to him, testing *him*, 'Teacher, this woman was caught committing adultery, in the act. ⁵ Now Moses in the law made command to us for such women to be stoned.* You then, what do you say?'

⁶ But they said this testing him, so that they might have *something* to accuse him of. But Jesus stooped down *and* wrote with a finger,* without making a show of it.*

⁷ So when they persisted in asking him, he bent back up *and* said to them, 'Let him who is without violation among you throw a stone at her first.'*

⁸ And bending back down again, he wrote in the ground.* ⁹ But those having heard and being convicted* by conscience went out one by one,

beginning with the elders, and Jesus remained alone, with the woman being* at *the* centre.

¹⁰ And bending back up, and seeing nobody except the woman, Jesus said to her, 'Woman, where are those accusers of yours? Did not anybody condemn you?'

¹¹ And she said, 'Nobody, Sir.'

And Jesus said, 'Neither do I condemn you. Go and commit violation no more.'

Jesus declares himself as 'the light of the world'
& as 'I Am' (8\18, 8\24)

¹² So Jesus spoke to them again, saying, 'I am* the light of the world.* He who follows me will most certainly not walk in the darkness, but he will have the light of life.'

¹³ So the Pharisees said to him, 'You give testimony concerning yourself. Your testimony is not true.'

¹⁴ Jesus answered, and said to them, 'Even if I give testimony concerning myself, my testimony is true, because I know where I came from and where I am going, but you do not know where I come from and where I am going.

¹⁵ 'You judge in relation to the flesh. I judge nobody.* ¹⁶ And yet if I judge, my judgement is true, because I am not alone, but I and the Father having authorized me *judge.*

¹⁷ 'And it has been written in the law also, your own *law,* that the testimony of two men is true.* ¹⁸ I Am* – the one giving testimony concerning myself, and Him having authorized me, the Father, He gives testimony concerning me.'

¹⁹ So they said to him, 'Where is your Father?'

Jesus answered, 'You know neither me nor my Father. If you had known me, you would have known my Father as well.'

²⁰ Jesus spoke these oracles in the treasury, teaching in the Temple, yet nobody arrested him, for his hour had not yet come.

Dispute concerning lineage from Abraham

²¹ So Jesus again said to them, 'I withdraw myself, and you will look for me, and you will die in your violation. Where I am going you are not able to come.'*

²² So the Jews said, 'Surely he will not kill himself in that he says, "Where I am going you

are not able to come"?'

²³ And he said to them, 'You are from below. I am from above. You are out of this world; I am not out of this world. ²⁴ For that reason I said to you that you will die in your violations. For if you do not believe that I Am,* you will die in your violations.'

²⁵ So they said to him, 'Who are you?'

And Jesus said to them, 'What from the beginning** I have also* been telling you. ²⁶ I have many things to say and to judge concerning you, but He having authorized me is true, and I speak to the world those things which I have heard from Him.'

²⁷ They did not understand that he was speaking to them of the Father.

²⁸ So Jesus said to them, 'When you have lifted up the Son of Man, then you will know that I Am,* and I do nothing on my own, but I speak these things just as my Father taught me, ²⁹ and He having authorized me is with me. The Father has not left me alone, since I always do the things pleasing to Him.'

³⁰ As he spoke these things, many put their faith in him.

³¹ So to those Jews having given credence towards* him Jesus said, 'If you remain in my word, you truly are my disciples, ³² and you will know the truth, and the truth will set you free.'

³³ They answered him, 'We are Abraham's seed, and we have been in bondage to nobody at any time.* How can you say that* you will be made freemen?"*

³⁴ Jesus answered them, 'Truly, truly, I say to you, everybody who commits violation is a slave of violation. ³⁵ The servant, however, does not remain in the house throughout the Eon. The son remains throughout the Eon.* ³⁶ If the Son, therefore, should make you free, you really will be freemen.*

³⁷ 'I know that you are Abraham's seed, but you search to murder me because my oracle finds no entrance in you. ³⁸ I speak what I have perceived from my Father, and you, therefore, *speak* what you have perceived from your father.'

³⁹ They answered, and said to him, 'Our father is Abraham.'

Jesus said to them, 'If you were Abraham's sons, you would be doing the works of Abraham. ⁴⁰ But now you search to murder me, a man who has spoken to you the truth which I have heard from God. Abraham did not do

that. ⁴¹ You are carrying out the works of your father."

So they said to him, 'We have not been born out of fornication.* We have one Father, God.'

⁴² So Jesus said to them, 'If God were your Father you would have loved me, for from God I went out and am here. I have come not on my own initiative, but *from* the one Who authorized me. ⁴³ Why do you not come to know my speech? *It is* because you are not able to hear my oracles.

⁴⁴ 'You are out of *your* father the Devil, and you have a will to carry out the lusts of your father. He was a murderer from *the* beginning,* and he has not stood in the truth because there is no truth in him. When he speaks falsehood,* he speaks out of his own *character,* for he is a liar,* and the father of *lies.*

⁴⁵ 'But because I speak the truth, you do not believe me. ⁴⁶ Who among you convicts* me of violation? But if I speak the truth, why do you not believe me? ⁴⁷ He who is from God hears the declarations of God. Because of this you do not hear, since you are not from God.'

⁴⁸ So the Jews answered, and said to him, 'Were we not right in saying that you are a Samaritan, and you have a demon?'

⁴⁹ Jesus answered, 'I myself do not have a demon, but I honour my Father, whereas you dishonour me. ⁵⁰ But I do not search my own preeminence.* There is one Who searches and judges. ⁵¹ Truly, truly, I say to you, if anybody keeps my oracle, he will certainly not see death throughout the Eon."*

⁵² So the Jews said to him, 'Now we know that you have a demon. Abraham and the prophets died, but you say, "If anybody keeps my oracle he will certainly not taste death throughout the Eon."*** ⁵³ Are you more eminent than our father Abraham who died, and the prophets *who* died? Whom do you make yourself out *to be?*'

Abraham had vision of the coming
'day of Christ' (Phil. 1\10 etc.)

⁵⁴ Jesus answered, 'If I magnify myself, my magnificence is nothing. It is my Father Who magnifies me, He Whom you say that He is your God. ⁵⁵ Yet you have not known Him, but I know Him. And if I should say that I do not know Him I will be like you, a liar. But I do know Him, and I keep His oracle. ⁵⁶ Your father Abraham leaped for exuberance* in that he might perceive* my day, and he did

perceive˙ *it* and he rejoiced."

Jesus looks ahead to the resurrection
of Abraham who 'is to rise' (γενέσθαι, *genesthai*),
aorist infinitive, with strong future aspect;
as at 3\9, 5\6, 13\19, 14\29, Mat. 24\6,
Mark 1\17, 10\43, 13\7, Luke 21\9, 21\28,
23\24, Acts 26\28, Rev. 1\1, 4\1, 22\6, etc.
He again affirms his eminence as 'I Am'

⁵⁷ So the Jews said to him, 'You are not yet fifty years *old*, and have you seen Abraham?'
⁵⁸ Jesus said to them, 'Truly, truly, I say to you, before˙ Abraham is to rise,˙ I Am."
⁵⁹ Then they took up stones so that they might throw *them* at him, but Jesus was hidden, and he went out of the Temple, going through the thick of them, and so he passed right through *them*.

Obstinate attempts to deny
that Jesus cured a man born blind

9\1 **A**nd in passing on, Jesus saw a man blind from birth.
² And his disciples asked him, saying, 'Rabbi, who violated, this *man*, or his parents, that˙ he should be born blind?"
³ Jesus answered, 'Neither this *man* has violated, nor his parents, but *he was born blind* so that the works of God should be brought to light˙ in him. ⁴ While it is day I must perform the works of Him having authorized me. Night is coming, when nobody is able to work. ⁵ As long as I am in the world, I am˙ *the* light of the world.'
⁶ *When* he had said these things, he spat on *the* ground and made clay out of the spit, and he smeared the clay on the eyes of the blind man.
⁷ And he said to him, 'Go *and* wash in the pool of Siloam' (which, translated, is 'sent').
So he went his way and washed and came back seeing.
⁸ Then the neighbours and those who had previously seen that he was blind said, 'Is this not the one who sits and begs?' ⁹ Some said, 'It is him,' but others *said* that 'He is like him.'
He, though, said, 'I am *he*."
¹⁰ Then they said to him, 'How were your eyes opened?'
¹¹ He answered, and said, 'A man called Jesus made clay and anointed my eyes, and he said to me, "Go to the pool of Siloam and wash yourself," and *when* I went and washed I received my sight.'

¹² So they said to him, 'Where is he?'
He said, 'I do not know.'
¹³ They brought him who *was* previously blind to the Pharisees.
¹⁴ Now it was a Sabbath when Jesus made the clay and opened his eyes, ¹⁵ so again the Pharisees also asked him how he had received his sight.
And he said to them, 'He put clay on my eyes, and I washed, and I see.'
¹⁶ Then some of the Pharisees said, 'This man is not from God, since he does not keep the Sabbath.'
Others said, 'How is a violating man able to perform such signs?'
So there was division among them.
¹⁷ They said to the blind *man* again, 'What do you say about him – that he opened your eyes?'
So he said, 'He's a prophet.'
¹⁸ Then the Jews did not believe about him that he had been blind and had received sight until they called the parents of him who had received sight.
¹⁹ And they questioned them, saying, 'Is this your son, of whom you say that he was born blind? How, in that case, does he now see?'
²⁰ But his parents answered them, and said, 'We know that this is our son, and that he was born blind. ²¹ But how he now sees we do not know, or who has opened his eyes we do not know. He's of age. Ask him. He can speak for himself.'
²² His parents spoke these things because they feared the Jews, for the Jews had agreed together already that if anybody should confess him as the Christ, he should be put out of the synagogue. ²³ This is why his parents said, 'He's of age. Ask him.'
²⁴ So a second time they called the man who had been blind, and they said to him, 'Give magnificence to God. We know that this man is a violator.'
²⁵ So he answered, and said, 'Whether he is a violator I do not know. One thing I do know, that I was blind, *and* now I see.'
²⁶ And they said to him again, 'What did he do to you? How did he open your eyes?'
²⁷ He answered them, 'I told you already, but you did not listen. Why do you want to hear again? You do not want to become his disciples as well, do you?'
²⁸ They heaped abuse on him, and said, 'You are that man's disciple, but we are the disciples

of Moses. [29] We know that God spoke to Moses, but we do not know where this *man* is from.'

[30] The man answered, and said to them, 'Well, in this matter it is astounding that you do not know where he is from, yet he opened my eyes. [31] Now we know that God does not hear violators. But if anybody is a reverer of God, and does His will, He hears him. [32] Not since of old* has it been heard of that anybody opened the eyes of somebody born blind. [33] If this *man* were not of God, he would not be able to do anything.'

[34] They answered, and said to him, 'You were born wholly in violations, and are you lecturing us?'

And they threw him outside.

[35] Jesus heard that they had thrown him outside, and when he found him he said to him, 'Do you believe in the Son of God?'

[36] He answered, and said, 'So* who is he, Lord, so that I might believe in him?'

[37] And Jesus said to him, 'You also have seen him, and he who speaks with you is that one.'

[38] And he said, 'Lord, I believe.'

And he fell on his knees* before him.

[39] And Jesus said, 'For judgement I have come into this world,* in order that those not seeing might see, and those seeing might become blind.'

[40] And *some* of the Pharisees who were with him heard these things, and they said to him, 'Are we also blind?'

[41] Jesus said to them, 'If you were blind, you would have no violation. But since you say that "We see," then your violation remains.'

Parable of a good shepherd

10\1 'Truly, truly, I say to you, he who does not come into the sheepfold by means of the door, but climbs up some other way, that one is a thief* and a bandit.* [2] But he who enters in through the door is a shepherd of the sheep. [3] To him the doorkeeper opens, and the sheep hear his voice, and he calls his own sheep by their name, and he leads them out. [4] And when he brings out his own sheep he goes ahead of them, and the sheep follow him because they know his voice. [5] But in no way will they follow a stranger, but they will flee away from him, because they do not recognize the voice of strangers.'

[6] Jesus spoke this allegory to them, but they did not know what the things he spoke to them meant.

[7] So Jesus further said to them, 'Truly, truly, I say to you, I am* the door for the sheep. [8] All who have appeared on the scene* are thieves* and bandits,* but the sheep did not listen to them.

[9] 'I am* the door. If anybody enters in through* me he will be saved, and he will go in and out and he will find pasture. [10] The thief does not come except that he might steal, and murder, and destroy. I came in order that they might have life,* and have *it* abundantly.

[11] 'I am* the good Shepherd. The good Shepherd lays down his life on behalf of the sheep. [12] But the hired servant, not even being a shepherd – *and* the sheep are not his own – sees the wolf coming, and he leaves the sheep and flees, then the wolf* snatches them away and scatters the sheep. [13] Now the hired servant* flees because he is a hired man, and he is not concerned about the sheep.

[14] 'I am* the good Shepherd, and I know those *who are* my own, and I am known by those who *are* mine. [15] As the Father knows me, I also know the Father, and I lay down my life for the sheep. [16] And I have other sheep who are not out of this flock.** I must bring them as well, and they will hear my voice,* and there will become one flock, with one Shepherd.*

[17] 'On account of this the Father loves me: because I lay down my life* so that I might receive* it again. [18] Nobody takes it from me, but I lay it down from my own will. I have authority to lay it down, and I have authority to receive* it again. I received this order from my Father.'

Diverse opinions about who Jesus is

[19] So a division arose again among the Jews because of these oracles, [20] and many of them said, 'He has a demon and is raving mad.* Why do you listen to him?'

[21] Others said, 'These are not the declarations of one under the power of a demon. Is a demon able to open eyes of *the* blind?'

He proves by his works
that he is the Christ

[22] And the Festival of the Dedication was taking place in Jerusalem, and it was winter, [23] and Jesus was walking around in the Temple in the Porch of Solomon.

²⁴ Then the Jews encircled him, and said to him, 'How long will you draw out our minds? If you are the Christ, tell us plainly.'
²⁵ Jesus answered them, 'I told you, and you did not believe. The works which I do in my Father's name give testimony concerning me. ²⁶ But you do not believe because you are not my sheep, as I said to you. ²⁷ My sheep hear my voice,˙ and I know them, and they follow me. ²⁸ And I give them Eonian˙ life, and they will most certainly not˙ suffer destruction throughout the Eon,˙˙ and nobody will snatch them out of my hand.
²⁹ 'My Father, Who gave *them* to me, is mightier than all, and nobody is able to snatch *them* out of the hand of my Father.
³⁰ 'The Father and I are one.'

Jesus escapes stoning. False accusation
that the Son makes himself out to be God.
θεός (*theos*), *normally* 'God', *also used for rulers,*
a Hebraism from אלהים (*elohim*) *at Ps. 82\1-6*
³¹ So the Jews took up stones once again so that they might stone him.
³² Jesus answered them, 'I have shown you many good works from my Father. For which of those works do you stone me?'
³³ The Jews answered him, saying, 'Not for a good work do we stone you, but for blasphemy, and because you, being a man, make yourself out *to be* God.'˙
³⁴ Jesus answered them back, 'Is it not written in your law, "I have said, 'You are gods' "?'˙ ³⁵ If He called gods˙ those to whom the oracle of God came˙ – and the Writing˙ cannot be broken – ³⁶ do you say of him whom the Father has sanctified and authorized into the world, "You blaspheme," because I said, "I am˙ the Son of God"?
³⁷ 'If I do not perform the works of my Father, do not believe me. ³⁸ But if I do, even if you do not believe me, believe the works, so that you might perceive and believe that the Father *is* in me, and I in him.'
³⁹ So they looked again to arrest him, but he slipped away, out of their reach, ⁴⁰ and he departed again beyond the Jordan into the place where John was at first making identifications, and he remained there.˙
⁴¹ And many came to him, and they were saying, 'John performed no sign, but everything which John spoke of this *man* was true.'
⁴² And many there believed in him.

The raising of Lazarus

11\1 **N**ow a certain *man* was sick, Lazarus, from Bethany, out of the village of Maria and her sister Martha. ² It was Maria, who anointed the Lord with ointment and wiped his feet with her hair, whose brother Lazarus was sick.
³ So his sisters sent word to him, saying, 'Look, Lord, the one whom you love is weakening.'
⁴ But when Jesus heard that, he said, 'This illness is not leading to˙ death, but *is* for the purpose of the magnificence of God, so that through it the Son of God might be magnified.'
⁵ Now Jesus loved Martha and her sister and Lazarus, ⁶ so then when he heard that he was sick he stayed *for* two days in the place where he was.
⁷ Then after that he said to the disciples, 'Let us go to Judea again.'
⁸ The disciples said to him, 'Rabbi, just now the Jews were looking to stone you, yet are you going back there?'
⁹ Jesus answered, 'Are there not twelve hours in the day? If anybody goes around in the daytime he does not stumble, because he sees the light of this world. ¹⁰ But if anybody goes around in the night, he stumbles because the light is not in him.'
¹¹ He said these things, and after this he said to them, 'Our friend Lazarus has fallen asleep. But I am going so that I might wake him out of sleep.'
¹² So his disciples said, 'Lord, if he has fallen asleep, he will recover.'
¹³ However, Jesus was speaking about death, but they thought that he was speaking about taking the rest of sleep.˙
¹⁴ So then Jesus said to them plainly, 'Lazarus is dead. ¹⁵ And I rejoice on your account that I was not there, so that you might believe. Nevertheless, let us go to him.'
¹⁶ So Thomas, known as Twin,˙ said to his fellow disciples, 'Let us go as well, so that we might die with him.'
¹⁷ Then on his arrival Jesus found him having already been in the tomb for four days.

Martha hears the gospel of the reward of life
'throughout the Eon' (εἰς τὸν αἰῶνα,
eis ton aiona), (*11\26, 8\51, 1 John 2\17, etc.*)
¹⁸ Now Bethany was near Jerusalem, about fifteen stadium lengths˙ away, ¹⁹ and many from among the Jews had gone to the women

connected with Martha* and Maria so that they could speak consolation to them over their brother. [20] So when Martha heard that Jesus was coming she met him, but Maria was sitting in the house.

[21] Then Martha said to Jesus, 'Lord, if you had been here, my brother would not have died. [22] But even now I know that whatever you ask God for God will give you.'

[23] Jesus said to her, 'Your brother will be raised.'

[24] Martha said to him, 'I know that he will be raised in the resurrection in* the last day.'*

[25] Jesus said to her, 'I am* the resurrection and the life. The one believing in* me, even though he might die, he will live. [26] And everyone living and believing in* me will most certainly not* die throughout* the Eon.*** Do you believe this?'*

[27] She said to him, 'Yes, Lord, I believe that you are the Christ, the Son of God, the one coming into* the world.'

[28] And having said these things, she went her way and called her sister Maria, saying secretly, 'The Teacher is here and he's calling for you.'

[29] As soon as she heard, she rose up quickly and went to him.

[30] Now Jesus had not yet arrived in the village, but he was in the place where Martha met him. [31] Then the Jews who were with her in the house, and were speaking consolation to her, saw that Maria rose up quickly, and they went out *and* followed her, saying, 'She's going to the tomb so that she can weep there.'

[32] So when Maria got to where Jesus was, she saw him *and* fell down at his feet, saying to him, 'Lord, if you had been here, my brother would not have died.'

[33] So when Jesus saw her weeping and the Jews who assembled with her weeping, he was deeply moved in *his* spirit, and he stirred himself, [34] and he said, 'Where have you lain him?'

They said to him, 'Lord, come and see.'

[35] Jesus shed tears.*

[36] Then the Jews said, 'See how he loved him!'

[37] But some of them said, 'Could not he who opened the eyes of the blind *man* not have acted so that this man would not have died?'

[38] So Jesus, again deeply moved within himself, went into the tomb, but it was a cave and a stone was lying against it.

[39] Jesus said, 'Take the stone away.'

Martha, the sister of him who had died, said to him, 'Lord, by this time he will stink, for it's *the* fourth day.'

[40] Jesus said to her, 'Did I not say to you that if you believe you would see the magnificence of God?'

[41] Then they took the stone away *from* where the dead *man* was lying, and Jesus lifted *his* eyes upwards, and said, 'Father, I thank You that You heard me. [42] And I know that You always hear me. But I said *it* because of the crowd who stand by, so that they might believe that You have authorized me.'

[43] And having said these things, he called out with a loud voice, 'Lazarus, come out!'

[44] And he who had been dead came out, *his* hands and feet bound with sheets, and his face wrapped with a sweat cloth.

Jesus said to them, 'Unbind him, and let *him* go.'

Many Jews believe. Conspiracy against him by senior priests & Pharisees. Caiaphas's prophecy *

[45] Then many of the Jews who came to Maria, and had regarded with wonder the things which Jesus had done, believed in him.

[46] But some of them went their ways to the Pharisees, and informed them of the thing which Jesus had done.

[47] So the senior priests and the Pharisees gathered a Sanhedrin, and they said, 'What are we doing, seeing that this man is performing many signs? [48] If we let him go on like this, everybody will believe in him, and the Romans will come and take away from us both the place and the nation.'*

[49] But one of them, Caiaphas, being high priest of that year, said to them, 'You know nothing at all. [50] Nor do you consider that it is in our interest that one man should die for the people so that the whole nation should not perish.'

[51] But he spoke this not from himself, but being high priest of that year he prophesied that Jesus was about to die for that nation, [52] and not for that nation only, but also so that he should gather together into one the Sons of God* who had been scattered about.

[53] So from that day on they consulted together as to how they might murder him.

The Pharisees issue an order to track Jesus *

[54] So Jesus was no more moving about

publicly among the Jews, but he went away from there into the region near the desert, to a town called Ephraim, and he stayed there with his disciples.
⁵⁵ Now the Passover of the Jews was near at hand, and many went out of the region up to Jerusalem before the Passover so that they might sanctify themselves.
⁵⁶ Then they were looking for Jesus, and they were conversing with each other *as* they were standing in the Temple: 'What do you think, that he will definitely not come to the Festival?'
⁵⁷ Now both the senior priests and the Pharisees had issued an order that if anybody knew where he was he should disclose *it* so that they might arrest him.

Anointing with precious ointment
at Bethany & objection by Judas *

12\1 So six days before the Passover, Jesus went to Bethany where Lazarus was who had died, he whom he had raised from *the* dead. ² So they made him a supper there, and Martha was serving, and Lazarus was one of those feasting at the table with him.
³ Then Maria took a litra* of ointment of spikenard of large price, *and* she anointed the feet of Jesus and wiped his feet with her hair, and the house was filled with the odour of the ointment.
⁴ Then one of his disciples, Judas, *son of* Simon Iscariot, who was about to betray him, said, ⁵ 'Why was this ointment not sold for three hundred denarions* and given to *the* poor?'
⁶ He said this not because he was concerned for the poor, but because he was a thief and had the money bag, and carried around whatever was put in.
⁷ So Jesus said, 'Leave her be. She has kept this for the day of my embalming. ⁸ For you always have the poor with you, but you do not always have me.'

Conspiracy against Lazarus
⁹ Then a large number of the Jews came to know that he was there, and they came not only on account of Jesus, but so that they might also see Lazarus whom he had raised from *the* dead.
¹⁰ But the senior priests consulted as to how they might kill Lazarus as well, ¹¹ because on account of him many of the Jews were withdrawing and believing in Jesus.

His triumphal entry into Jerusalem *
¹² On the next day, a large crowd who had come to the Festival, having heard that Jesus was coming into Jerusalem, ¹³ took branches of palm trees, and went out to meet him, and they were calling out:

'Hosanna!
Exalted* *is* the Coming One,
in *the* name of *the* Lord,
King of Israel.'*

¹⁴ And Jesus found a small donkey, *and* he sat on it, as it has been written:

¹⁵ 'Do not fear, daughter of Zion;
look, your King comes,
sitting on the foal of a donkey.'*

¹⁶ But his disciples did not perceive these things at first, but when Jesus had been magnified they subsequently remembered that these things had been written about him, and they had done these things for him.
¹⁷ Then the crowd who were with him, at the time he called Lazarus out of his tomb and raised him from *the* dead, were giving testimony. ¹⁸ On account of this, the crowd went out to meet him as well, because they heard about his having performed this sign.
¹⁹ Then the Pharisees said to each other, 'Do you see how you are profiting nothing?* Look how the world has gone after him.'

Greeks desire to see Jesus. He predicts his hour
of being magnified, attested by the Father's voice *
²⁰ And there were some Greeks among those going up to worship at the Festival, ²¹ so they made an approach to Philip, who was from Bethsaida of Galilee, and they appealed to him, saying, 'Sir, we want to see Jesus.'
²² Philip came and told Andrew, and Andrew and Philip in turn told Jesus.
²³ But Jesus answered them, saying, 'The hour has come for the Son of Man to be magnified.
²⁴ Truly, truly, I say to you, unless the grain* of the wheat falling into the ground should die, it remains alone. But if it should die, it bears much fruit.
²⁵ 'He who loves his life will lose it, and he who hates* his life* in this world will preserve it into Eonian* life.
²⁶ 'If anybody serves me, let him follow me.

And where I am, there will my servant also be. And if anybody serves me, the Father will honour him.

²⁷ 'At this moment my mind˙ has been troubled,˙˙ and what shall I say? "Father, save me from this hour"? But on account of this, I came for this hour. ²⁸ Father, magnify Your name.'

Then a voice came out of Heaven: 'I have both magnified *it*, and I will magnify *it* again.'

²⁹ So the crowd who stood by and heard suggested thunder to have struck. Others said, 'An angel has spoken to him.'

³⁰ Jesus answered, and said, 'This voice has come not for my sake, but for your sakes. ³¹ Now is *the* judgement of this world.˙ Now the ruler of this world˙ will be thrown out.˙ ³² And as for me, when˙ I am lifted up from the Earth, I will draw all *peoples* to myself.'

³³ However he said this signifying by what kind of death he was about to die.

³⁴ The crowd answered him, 'We have heard out of the law that the Christ remains throughout the Eon,˙ so how can you say, "The Son of Man must be lifted up"?˙ Who is this Son of Man?'

³⁵ So Jesus said to them, 'The light is with you for just a little while yet. Walk while you have the light so that darkness might not overtake you. For he who walks in darkness does not know where he is going. ³⁶ While you have the light, believe in the light so that you might become sons of light.'˙

Jesus spoke these things, then he departed and was hidden from them.

Judgement of Isaiah on Israel's unbelief

³⁷ But although he had performed so many signs in their presence, they did not believe in him, ³⁸ so that the oracle of the prophet Isaiah might be fulfilled, which said:

'Lord, who has believed our report,
and to whom has the arm
of *the* Lord been revealed?'˙

³⁹ On account of this, they were unable to believe, because, additionally, Isaiah said:˙

⁴⁰ 'He has blinded their eyes
and hardened their heart,
so that they do not see with *their* eyes
or understand with *their* heart

and be converted
and I would heal them."˙

⁴¹ Isaiah said these things when he saw His magnificence and spoke about Him.˙

Some rulers believe, but without a public declaration for fear of the Jews

⁴² Although many even˙ among the chief rulers also believed in him, yet because of the Pharisees they did not make profession in case they might be expelled from the synagogue, ⁴³ for they loved the glory of men more than the magnificence of God.

⁴⁴ But Jesus called out and said, 'He who believes in me believes not in me but in Him having authorized me. ⁴⁵ And he who sees me sees Him having authorized me.

⁴⁶ 'I have come as a light into the world, so that nobody who believes in me should remain in darkness.

⁴⁷ 'And if anybody hears my declarations but does not believe, I do not judge him, for I came not so that I might judge the world, but so that I might save the world.˙ ⁴⁸ He who rejects me and does not receive my declarations has that which judges him: the oracle which I have spoken. That will judge him in˙ the last day.˙

⁴⁹ 'For I have spoken not on my own, but the Father having authorized me gave me what commandment I should say, and what I should speak. ⁵⁰ And I know that His commandment means Eonian˙ life. Therefore whatever I speak, just as the Father has spoken to me, so do I speak.'˙

Jesus washes his disciples' feet. Further statements of I Am (13\19)

13\1 Now before the Festival of the Passover, Jesus – knowing that his hour had come that he should depart out of this world to the Father, having had love for his own˙ in the world – loved them to *the* end.

² And *when* supper had finished, the Devil had already put *it* into the heart of Judas Iscariot, *son* of Simon, that he should betray him.˙

³ Jesus, knowing that the Father had given all things into *his* hands,˙ and that he had emanated from God and was going away to God, ⁴ rose up from the supper table and laid aside the garments, and he took a towel *and* wrapped it around himself. ⁵ Then he put water into a

washing basin, and began to wash the disciples' feet, and to wipe *them* with the towel which he was wrapped with.

⁶ So he went over to Simon Peter, and Peter said to him, 'Lord, ought you to wash my feet?' ⁷ Jesus answered, and said to him, 'You do not know just now what I am doing, but you will know after these things.'

⁸ Peter said to him, 'Not at all may you wash my feet throughout the Eon.'*

Jesus answered him, 'Unless I wash you, you do not have any part with me.'

⁹ Simon Peter said to him, 'Lord, not my feet only, but *my* hands and head as well.'

¹⁰ Jesus said to him, 'He who has been bathed does not need to wash anything other than the feet, but is thoroughly clean. And you are clean, though not all.' ¹¹ For he knew him who was going to betray him. This is why he said, 'Not all of you are clean.'

¹² So when he had washed their feet and taken up his garments, he leaned back again, *and* said to them, 'Do you know what I have done for you? ¹³ You address me as the Teacher and the Lord, and you speak correctly, for I am.* ¹⁴ So if I, the Lord and the Teacher, have washed your feet, then you ought to wash each other's feet. ¹⁵ For I have given you an example so that you also should do as I have done.

¹⁶ 'Truly, truly, I say to you, the servant is not more eminent than his master, nor a messenger* more eminent than him having authorized him. ¹⁷ If you know these things, you are exalted if you carry them out. ¹⁸ I do not speak concerning you all. I myself know those whom I have chosen, but *it is* so that the passage might be fulfilled, *saying*: "He who eats bread with me has lifted up his heel against me."'* ¹⁹ From this time I tell you, before it is to arise,* so that when it has come to pass you might believe that I Am.*

²⁰ 'Truly, truly, I say to you, the one receiving whomever I might authorize receives me, and the one receiving me receives Him authorizing me.'

He predicts Judas's betrayal *

²¹ On having said these things, Jesus was troubled in spirit, and he gave testimony, and said, 'Truly, truly, I say to you, one of you will betray me.'

²² So the disciples looked towards each other, being perplexed about whom he was speaking.

²³ But one of his disciples was leaning on the garment-fold* of Jesus, the one whom Jesus loved, ²⁴ so Simon Peter made a sign to him, to ask who it might be about whom he had spoken.

²⁵ Then he sank back hard* on Jesus's chest *and* said to him, 'Lord, who is it?'

²⁶ Jesus answered, 'It is he to whom I am going to give the piece *of bread*, *when* I have dipped *it*.'

And he dipped* the piece *and* gave *it* to Judas Iscariot, *son* of Simon. ²⁷ And after the piece *of bread*, Satan then went into him.*

So Jesus said to him, 'What you are doing, do quickly.'

²⁸ Now nobody of those at the table knew for what purpose he had spoken this to him, ²⁹ for some were thinking that *it was* because Judas had the money bag *that* Jesus said to him, 'Buy what we need for the Festival,' or that he should give something to the poor.

³⁰ *When* he had received the piece *of bread*, this *man* went out at once, and it was night.

A new commandment. Heaven
no place for the disciples
(7\34, 8\21, 13\33, 14\2),
& they will be with Jesus again
when he returns to Earth (14\3, 14\28)

³¹ When he had gone out, Jesus said, 'Now the Son of Man has been magnified, and God has been magnified in him. ³² If God has been magnified in him, God also will magnify him in Himself, and He will straightaway magnify him. ³³ 'Little children, I will be with you for a little longer. You will search for me, and, just as I said to the Jews, "Where I am going you are not able to come,"* so do I now also say to you. ³⁴ 'I give you a new commandment: that you should love each other as I have loved you, so that you also should love each other. ³⁵ By this, all will know that you are my disciples: if you have love among yourselves.'

Peter will follow Jesus into death (21\18-19).
Jesus predicts Peter's denial *

³⁶ Simon Peter said to him, 'Lord, where are you going?'

Jesus answered him, 'Where I am going you cannot now follow me, but you will follow me afterwards.'*

³⁷ Peter said to him, 'Lord, why can I not follow you now? I will lay down my life for

you.'
³⁸ Jesus answered him, 'Will you lay down your life for me? Truly, truly, I say to you, a rooster will certainly not crow until˙ you completely deny me three times.'

The disciples to be in the Father's House,
the Temple, when Jesus returns,
so having residence alongside Jesus.
He is the only way to Eonian life

14\1 "Do not let your heart be agitated.˙ Believe in God. Believe also˙ in˙ me.˙
² 'In my Father's House˙ there are many homes.˙ And if not,˙ I would have told you.

I go to make ready a place for you. ³ And if I go and make ready a place for you, I will come again,˙ and I will receive you to myself, so that where I am you also might be.˙ ⁴ And you know where I go, and you know the way.'
⁵ Thomas said to him, 'Lord, we do not know where you are going, so how can we know the way?'
⁶ Jesus said to him, 'I am˙ the way and˙ the truth˙ and the life. Nobody comes to the Father if not through˙ me. ⁷ If you had known me, you would also have known my Father. But from now on you do know Him, and you have seen Him.'
⁸ Philip said to him, 'Lord, show us the Father, and that will satisfy˙ us.'
⁹ Jesus said to him, 'Have I been with you so long, yet you do not know me, Philip? He who has seen me has seen the Father. So how can you say, "Show us the Father"? ¹⁰ Do you not believe that I *am*˙ in the Father, and the Father is in me? The declarations which I speak to you I do not speak from˙ myself. But the Father Who continues in me, He activates the works.
¹¹ Believe me that I *am*˙ in the Father, and the Father *is* in me, but if not believe me because of the works themselves.
¹² 'Truly, truly, I say to you, he who believes in me will also do the works which I do, and he will do mightier *works* than these, because I am going to my Father.˙ ¹³ And whatever you will ask in my name, I will do it, so that the Father might be magnified in the Son. ¹⁴ If you ask me anything in my name, I will do *it*.˙
¹⁵ 'If you love me, keep my commandments.

The Angel of God promised as Counsellor
to the disciples throughout the Eon
to teach them all these things and remind them

of these oracles (14\26)
¹⁶ 'And I will ask the Father, and He will give you another˙ Counsellor,˙ so that he might continue with you throughout the Eon˙ ¹⁷ – the Spirit of Truth,˙ whom the world is not able to˙ receive, because it does not see him, nor does it know him. But you know him, for he remains alongside˙ you, and he will be among˙ you.
¹⁸ 'I will not leave you as orphans.˙ I am coming to you.˙ ¹⁹ A little while yet and the world sees me no more, but you see me, because I live and you yourselves will live. ²⁰ In that day˙ you will know that I *am* in my Father,˙ and you in me, and I in you.˙
²¹ 'He who has my commandments and keeps them is he who loves me. And he who loves me will be loved by my Father, and I will love him, and I will reveal myself to him.'
²² Judas (not Iscariot) said to him, 'Lord, what has happened, then, in that you are about to reveal yourself to us but not to the world?'
²³ Jesus answered, and said to him, 'If anybody loves me he will keep my oracle, and my Father will love him, and we will come to him and we will make a˙ home˙ alongside˙ him.˙ ²⁴ He who does not love me does not keep my oracles. And the oracle which you hear is not mine, but that of the Father having authorized me.
²⁵ 'I have spoken these things to you when I was remaining˙ with you. ²⁶ But the Counsellor,˙ *who is* the Holy Spirit,˙ whom the Father will authorize in my name,˙ that one˙ will teach you all these things, and bring all these things to your remembrance,˙ whatever I have said to you.˙
²⁷ 'I leave you peace. I give you my peace. Not as the world gives do I give to you. Do not let your heart be troubled, nor let it show cowardice.˙
²⁸ 'You heard how I said to you I am going away, and I am coming back to you.˙ If you loved me, you would have rejoiced in that I said I am going to the Father, for my Father is mightier than I *am*. ²⁹ And now I have told you before it is to arise,˙ so that when it does come to pass you might believe.
³⁰ 'No longer will I speak many things˙ with you, for the ruler of the world˙ is coming, and he has nothing in me. ³¹ But so that the world might know that I love the Father – and just as˙ the Father charged˙ me – I am doing this. Rise up, *and* let us go from here.

The true vine

15\1 ⟨I⟩ am* the true vine, and my Father is the vinedresser.* ² Every branch in me not producing fruit He removes,* and every *branch* producing fruit He prunes it so that it might produce more fruit.

³ 'You are already clean on account of the oracle which I have spoken to you. ⁴ 'Remain in me, *as* I also *remain* in you. As the branch is not able to produce fruit from itself unless it remains in the vine, so neither *can* you unless you remain in me.

⁵ 'I am* the vine; you *are* the branches. He who remains in me, and I in him, produces much fruit, for without me you are able to do nothing. ⁶ 'Unless anybody remains in me, he is thrown out like a branch, and he dries up, and they gather *them* up and throw them in the fire and they are burned.

⁷ 'If you remain in me, and my oracles remain in you, you will ask for whatever you wish, and it will come about* for you. ⁸ In this my Father is magnified: that you should produce* much fruit and you might become my disciples.

'No greater love'

⁹ 'As the Father loved me, so have I loved you. Remain in my love. ¹⁰ If you keep my commandments you will remain in my love, just as I have kept my Father's commandments and remain in His love. ¹¹ I have spoken these things to you so that the exuberance which *is* mine might remain in you, and your exuberance might be completely filled up. ¹² This is my commandment: that you love each other, just as I have loved you.

¹³ 'No greater* love has anybody than this, that somebody should lay down his life on behalf of his friends.* ¹⁴ You are my friends if you carry out whatever I command you.

¹⁵ 'No longer do I call you servants, for the servant does not know what his master does. But I have called you friends, for all things which I have heard from beside my Father I have made known to you. ¹⁶ Not that you chose me, but I chose you, and appointed you to go* and produce fruit, and your fruit should remain so that whatever you might ask the Father in my name He might give you.

¹⁷ 'I charge you with this: that you love each other.

Hatred & rejection by the world

¹⁸ 'If the world hates you, keep in mind that it hated me before *it hated* you.

¹⁹ 'If you were out of the world, the world would love its own. You are not of the world, though, but I chose you out of the world. On account of this the world hates you.

²⁰ 'Remember the oracle which I spoke to you: "A servant is not more eminent than his master." If they persecuted me, they will persecute you as well. If they kept my oracle, they will keep yours as well.

²¹ 'But they will do all these things to you on account of my name, because they do not know Him having authorized me. ²² If I had not come and spoken to them, they would not have any violation, but now they have no excuse for their violation.

²³ 'He who hates me also hates my Father.

²⁴ 'If I had not done among them the works which nobody else has done, they would not have violation. But now they have both seen and hated both me and my Father. ²⁵ But *this is* so that the oracle might be fulfilled which has been written in their law: "They hated me without a cause."*

The Angel of God as Counsellor again promised
to the disciples. They will be witnesses

²⁶ 'But when the Counsellor* comes, whom I will authorize to you from beside the Father,* the Spirit of Truth,* who goes out* from beside the Father,* he will give testimony about me. ²⁷ And you also will give testimony, because you have been with me from *the* beginning.*

Warning about persecution.
Further promise to the disciples
of the Angel of God
& his work to magnify Jesus

16\1 ⟨I⟩ have made declaration of these things to you so that you should not be offended. ² They will expel you from the synagogues, but the hour is coming in which* everybody condemning you to death* will think that he is presenting a service to God. ³ And they will do these things because they do not know the Father or myself.

⁴ 'But I have declared these things to you so that, when the hour comes, you might remember that I told them to you. But I did not say these things to you from *the* beginning,* because I was with you.

⁵ 'Now, though, I am going away to Him having authorized me, yet none of you is asking me, "Where are you going?" ⁶ But because I have declared these things to you, sorrow has filled your heart.

⁷ 'But I speak the truth to you. It is to your advantage that I should go away, for if I do not go away the Counsellor* cannot come to you. But if I depart, I will authorize him to you.

⁸ 'And *when* he comes, he will make the facts known to* the world concerning violation, and concerning righteousness, and concerning judgement: ⁹ concerning violation, because they do not believe in me; ¹⁰ concerning righteousness, because I am going away to my Father and you will behold me no more; ¹¹ and concerning judgement, because the ruler of this world* has been condemned.

¹² 'I still have many things to say to you, but you are not able to bear them just now. ¹³ But when that one comes, the Spirit of Truth,* he will guide you into all the truth, for he will speak not from his own initiative, but whatever things he hears he will speak, and he will announce to you the things coming. ¹⁴ He* will magnify me, for he will receive from *what is* mine, and he will announce *it* to you.* ¹⁵ All things, whatever the Father possesses, are mine.* On account of this I said that he receives from *what is* mine, and he will announce *it* to you. ¹⁶ A little while and you do not see me, and another little while and you will see me, because I am going away* to the Father.'

He predicts his resurrection
& going to the Father.
Their sorrows followed by exuberance *

¹⁷ So some from his disciples said to each other, 'What is this that he says to us, "Just a little while and you will not see me," and again, "Just a little while and you will see me," and, "Because I go away to the Father"?'

¹⁸ So they said, 'What is this that he says, "A little while"? We do not know what he is saying.'

¹⁹ Now Jesus knew that they were wanting to ask him, and he said to them, 'Are you discussing with each other about what I said, "Just a little while and you will not see me," and again, "Just a little while and you will see me"? ²⁰ Truly, truly, I say to you, you will weep and lament, but the world will rejoice and you will be grieved, but your grief will be turned into*

exuberance.

²¹ 'A woman, when she gives birth, has pain because her hour has come, but as soon as she gives birth to* the child she no longer remembers the suffering on account of the gladness that a person* has been born into the world. ²² And you, therefore, now indeed have grief. But I will see you again and your heart will rejoice, and nobody will take away your exuberance from you. ²³ And in that day you will ask me nothing. Truly, truly, I say to you, whatever you will ask the Father in my name, He will give you.

²⁴ 'Until now you have asked nothing in my name. Ask, and you will receive, so that your exuberance might be filled up.

²⁵ 'These things I have spoken to you in allegories, but an hour is coming when I will no longer speak to you in allegories, but I will announce to you in plain speech about the Father. ²⁶ In that day you will ask in my name. But I do not say to you that I will pray to the Father on your behalf, ²⁷ for the Father Himself loves you because you have loved me, and you have believed that I came from God. ²⁸ I came from the Father, and I have come into the world. Again,* I am leaving the world, and I am going to the Father.'

²⁹ His disciples said to him, 'Right, now you speak with clarity, and you speak without any figure of speech. ³⁰ Now we know that you know all things, and you do not need that anybody should ask you. In this we believe that you came from God.'

³¹ Jesus answered them, 'Now do you believe? ³² Be aware that an hour is coming, and has now come, when you will be scattered to your own* *home*, and you will leave me alone. I also am not alone, because the Father is with me.

³³ 'I have spoken these things to you so that you might have peace in me. In the world you will have tribulation. But be of good courage – I have conquered the world.'

Jesus' request to the Father *
– 'the only true God' – to be magnified,
even in advance of what is to come
in the world 'to be' (εἶναι, *einai, infinitive*)

17\1 Jesus spoke these things, and he raised his eyes to the sky, and he said, 'Father, the hour has come. Magnify Your Son so that Your Son also might magnify You, ² just as You have given him authority in relation to all flesh, so that he should give Eonian* life to the whole of what You have given him.

3 'And this is Eonian* life: that they might know You, the only true God, and he whom You have authorized, Jesus Christ. 4 I have magnified You on the Earth. I have completed the work which You gave me to do. 5 And now, Father, magnify me Yourself,* in Your presence,* with the magnificence which I have had* with You in advance of* the world to come.**

Prayer of Jesus for his brothers
6 'I have brought to light* Your name to the men whom You gave me out of the world. They were Yours, and You gave them to me, and they have kept Your oracle. 7 Now they have come to know that all things, whatever You have given me, are from You. 8 For I have given them the oracles which You gave me, and they received *them*, and they knew in truth that I came from* You, and they believed that You authorized me.

9 'I make request concerning them. I do not make request concerning the world, but concerning those whom You have given me, for they are Yours. 10 And all my things are Yours, and Your things mine,* and I have been magnified among them.

11 'And I am no longer in the world, but these are in the world, and I am coming to You. Holy Father, keep in Your own name those whom* You have given me so that they might be one, like ourselves. 12 When I was with them in the world, I was keeping them in Your own name. Those whom* You gave to me I have guarded, and none out of them has perished except the son of destruction,** so that the Scroll might be fulfilled.

13 'And now I am coming to You, and I speak these things in the world so that they might have my exuberance fulfilled in themselves. 14 I have given them Your oracle and the world hated them because they are not from the world, just as I am not from the world. 15 I ask not that You should take them from the world, but that You should guard them from the Evil One.* 16 They are not from the world, just as I am not from the world.

17 'Make them holy in Your truth. Your oracle is truth. 18 Just as You sent me into the world, so did I send them into the world. 19 And on behalf of them I sanctify myself, so that they also might be sanctified through truth.

Jesus loved by God in advance
of the coming world order
in the new Eon (Rom. 8\29, Eph. 1\4)
20 'Not only do I pray for these, but also for those who believe in me through their word, 21 so that they all might be one in the way that You, Father, *are* in me, and I *am* in You, so that they also might be one in us, and then* the world might believe that You sent me.

22 'And the magnificence which You gave me I have given to them, so that they might be one, just as we are one, 23 I in them, and You in me, so that they might be perfected into one, and then* the world might know that You authorized me, and You loved them, just as You have loved me.

24 'Father, I wish that those also whom You have given me might be with me where I am, so that they might behold my magnificence which You have given me, for You have loved me in advance of* *the* foundation* of *the* world order.*

25 'Righteous Father, the world also did not know You, but I knew You, and these have known that You authorized me. 26 And I made Your name known to them, and I will make *it* known, so that the love with which You loved me might be in them, and I in them.'

Men fall at Jesus' declaration of himself as 'I Am'
18\1 **W**hen he had spoken these oracles, Jesus went out with his disciples beyond the winter torrent of Kedron where there was an olive grove* which he and his disciples went into. 2 And Judas, who betrayed him, also knew the place, for Jesus often gathered there with his disciples.

3 So Judas, taking along the cohort and officers from the senior priests and Pharisees, came there with torches and lamps and weapons.

4 Then Jesus, knowing all the things which were coming against him, stepped forward *and* said to them, 'Whom are you looking for?'

5 They answered him, 'Jesus the Nazarene.'*

Jesus said to them, 'I Am.'*

And Judas, who betrayed him, was also standing with them, 6 then as soon as he had said to them 'I Am,'* they went over backwards and fell to *the* ground.

7 So he questioned them again, 'Whom are

you looking for?'

And they said, 'Jesus the Nazarene.'*

[8] Jesus answered, 'I have told you that I Am.* If, therefore, you are looking for me, let these go their way.'

[9] *He said this* so that the oracle might be fulfilled which he spoke, 'Out of those whom You gave me I have not lost one.'

[10] At that, Simon Peter, having a sword, drew it and struck the servant of the high priest and cut off his right ear. And the name of the servant was Malchus.

[11] So Jesus said to Peter, 'Put your sword into the sheath. Should I not drink the cup which my Father has given me?'

Arrest *

[12] So the cohort and the military commander and officers of the Jews took hold of Jesus and shackled him, [13] and they led him away to Annas first, for he was father-in-law to Caiaphas, who was the high priest that same year.* [14] Now it was Caiaphas who gave counsel to the Jews that it was profitable that one man should perish on behalf of the people.

Peter's denial.* Examination of Jesus & mocking before the high priest Caiaphas *

[15] And Simon Peter was following Jesus, and another disciple. And that disciple was known to the high priest, and he went with Jesus into the palace court of the high priest. [16] But Peter was standing near the door outside. Then that other disciple who was known to the high priest went out and spoke to the doorkeeper woman, and he brought Peter in.

[17] Then the servant girl, the doorkeeper, said to Peter, 'Are you not also *one* of this man's disciples?'

He said, 'I am not.'

[18] And the servants and officers *who* were standing there made a fire of coals, as it was cold, and they were warming themselves, and Peter was standing with them warming himself as well.

[19] The high priest then asked Jesus concerning his disciples, and concerning his teaching.

[20] Jesus answered him, 'I spoke openly to the world. I always taught in a synagogue, and in the Temple where the Jews always* come together, and I said nothing in secret. [21] Why do you question me? Question those who heard me as to what I said to them. Look, they know

what I said.'

[22] But on his saying these things, one of the officers who stood by gave Jesus a slap, saying, 'Do you answer the high priest like that?'

[23] Jesus answered him, 'If I have spoken evil, give testimony of the evil, but if well why do you strike me?'

[24] Annas* sent* him shackled to Caiaphas, the high priest.

[25] And meanwhile Simon Peter was standing and warming himself, so they said to him, 'Are you not also one of his disciples?'

He made a denial, and said, 'I am not.'

[26] One of the servants of the high priest, being a relative of him whose ear Peter had cut off, said, 'Did I not see you in the olive grove with him?'

[27] So Peter again made a denial.

And immediately a rooster crowed.*

Examination before Pilate.
The bandit Barabbas released

[28] Then they led Jesus from Caiaphas to the Judgement Hall, and it was early, but they themselves did not go into the Judgement Hall so that they might not be defiled, but so that they might eat the Passover.

[29] Then Pilate went outside to them, and said, 'What accusation do you bring against this man?'

[30] They answered, and said to him, 'If he were not a wrongdoer, we would not have handed him over to you.'

[31] Then Pilate said to them, 'You take him yourselves, and you judge him by your law.'

So the Jews said to him, 'It's not lawful for us to put anybody to death.'*

[32] *This was* so that the oracle of Jesus might be fulfilled which he spoke, signifying what kind of death he was going to die.

[33] Then Pilate went into the Judgement Hall again, and he called for Jesus and said to him, 'Are you the King of the Jews?'

[34] Jesus answered him, 'Do you say this thing from yourself, or did others speak to you about me?'

[35] Pilate answered, 'I am not a Jew, am I? Your own people and the senior priests have handed you over to me. What have you done?'

[36] Jesus answered, 'My kingdom is not out of this world.* If my kingdom were out of* this world, then my servants would fight, so that I might not be handed over to the Jews, but now

my kingdom is not from here.'

³⁷ So Pilate said to him, 'Is it not, then, that you are a king?'

Jesus answered, 'You say that I am a king. For this I was born, and for this I came into the world, so that I might testify to the truth. Everybody who is of the truth hears my voice.'

³⁸ Pilate said to him, 'What is truth?'

And on having said this he went outside again to the Jews, and he said to them, 'I find not a single case against him. ³⁹ But it's a custom for you that I should release one person to you during the Passover. Do you wish, therefore, that I release to you the King of the Jews?'

⁴⁰ Then they all shouted out again, saying, 'Not this *man*, but Barabbas!'

Barabbas, incidentally, was a bandit.*

Crown of thorns. *Pilate's sentence* *

19\1 So then Pilate took Jesus and had *him* flogged.

² And the soldiers wove a crown out of thorns *and* put *it* on his head, and they put a purple robe on him, ³ and said, 'Hail, King of the Jews!', and they gave him slaps with the palms of their hands.

⁴ So Pilate went outside again and said to them, 'Look, I present* him to you outside, so that you might know that I find no case against him.'

⁵ Then Jesus went outside, wearing the crown of thorns and the purple robe, and *Pilate* said to them, 'Behold the man!'

⁶ So when the senior priests and officers saw him, they shouted out, saying, 'Hang *him* on a stake! Hang him on a stake!'

Pilate said to them, 'You take *him* and hang him on a stake* yourselves, for I find no case against him.'

⁷ The Jews answered him, 'We have a law, and according to our law he ought to die, because he has been making himself out *to be* the Son of God.'

⁸ So when Pilate heard this word, he was all *the* more afraid, ⁹ and he went again into the Judgement Hall, and he said to Jesus, 'Where are you from?'

But Jesus gave him no response.

¹⁰ Then Pilate said to him, 'Will you not speak to me? Do you not know that I have authority to hang you on a stake,* and I have authority to release you?'

¹¹ Jesus answered, 'You were holding no authority over me unless it were given to you from above. This is why he who betrayed me to you has a more extreme violation.'

¹² From then on Pilate was looking to release him, but the Jews were shouting out, saying, 'If you let this *man* go, you are no friend of Caesar. Everybody making himself a king speaks against* Caesar.'*

¹³ So hearing this word, Pilate brought Jesus outside, and he sat down on the judgement seat in a place which is called the Stone Pavement, and in Hebrew Gabbatha.

¹⁴ And it was *the* Preparation of the Passover and about *the* sixth hour, and he said to the Jews, 'Behold your king!'

¹⁵ But they shouted, 'Away *with him*! Away *with him*! Hang him on a stake!'

Pilate said to them, 'Am I to hang your king on a stake?'*

The senior priests answered, 'We have no king but Caesar.'*

¹⁶ So then he handed him over to them so that he might be hanged on a stake.* And they took Jesus, and led *him* away.

Death at Golgotha *

¹⁷ And carrying his stake,* he went out to *the* Place of a Skull, as it was called, which in Hebrew is called Golgotha, ¹⁸ where they hanged him on a stake,* and two others with him, one on either side, and Jesus in the middle.

¹⁹ In addition, Pilate wrote an inscription and put *it* on the stake.* And it read, 'Jesus the Nazarene,* the King of the Jews.'*

²⁰ Then many of the Jews read this inscription, because the place where Jesus was hanged on a stake* was near the city, and it was written in Hebrew, Greek, Latin. ²¹ So the senior priests of the Jews said to Pilate, 'Do not write "The King of the Jews", but that "This one said 'I am King of the Jews.'" '

²² Pilate answered, 'What I have written I have written.'

²³ Then when the soldiers had hanged Jesus on a stake,* they took his garments and made four sections, a section for each soldier, and also *his* garment. Now the garment was without any seam, woven from the top in one piece.

²⁴ So they said to each other, 'Let us not tear it, but throw lots for it, for whose it will be.'

They said this so that the passage might be

fulfilled which says:

> 'They shared out my garments
> among themselves,
> and for my clothing they threw lots.'*

Provision for his mother. His death
So the soldiers did these things. ²⁵ But standing beside the stake* were the mother of Jesus, and his mother's sister, Maria the *wife* of Clopas, and Maria Magdalene.
²⁶ So Jesus, seeing *his* mother and the disciple whom he loved standing there, said to his mother, 'Woman, behold your son!'
²⁷ Then he said to the disciple, 'Behold your mother!'

And from that hour that disciple took her into his own *home.*
²⁸ After this Jesus saw that all things had already been completed, and, in order that the Scroll might be fulfilled, he said, 'I am thirsty.'
²⁹ Now a jar full of vinegar was standing *nearby*, and they soaked a sponge with vinegar, put hyssop around *it, and* brought it to *his* mouth.
³⁰ So when Jesus received the vinegar, he said, 'It has been completed.'

And bowing down *his* head, he gave up the ghost.*

³¹ Then, so that the bodies should not remain on the stake* over the Sabbath, because it was *the* Preparation – for the day of that* Sabbath was a high* *Sabbath** – the Jews asked Pilate that their legs might be shattered,* and they might be taken away.
³² Then the soldiers came and broke the legs of the first *man*, as well as of the other *man* who was hanged on a stake along with* him. ³³ But when they came to Jesus, *and* they saw that he was already dead, they did not break his legs, ³⁴ but one of the soldiers pierced his side with a lance, and immediately blood and water came out.

This account by John is historical truth
³⁵ And he who saw *it* testified, and his testimony is genuine, and he knows that he speaks true to fact, so that you will believe.* ³⁶ For these things took place so that the passage might be fulfilled, *saying*, 'Not a bone of him will be broken.'* ³⁷ And additionally, another passage says, 'They will look at him whom they

pierced through.'*

Burial by Joseph of Arimathea & Nicodemus *
³⁸ After these things, Joseph from Arimathea, being a disciple of Jesus, though secretly because of fear of the Jews,* asked Pilate that he might remove the body of Jesus, and Pilate gave permission, so he came and removed the body of Jesus. ³⁹ And Nicodemus, who had previously gone to Jesus at night, came as well, bringing a mixture of myrrh and aloes, about one hundred litras.* ⁴⁰ Then they took the body of Jesus, and bound it in linen strips with the spices, as is the custom among the Jews to prepare for burial.
⁴¹ Now in the place where he was hanged on a stake* there was an olive grove, and in the olive grove a new tomb in which nobody had yet been lain. ⁴² So they laid Jesus there because of the Preparation of the Jews, for the tomb was nearby.

His resurrection.
Maria Magdelene goes early
to the tomb & Jesus meets her

20\1 But on the First of Weeks,* it still being dark, Maria Magdelene went early to the tomb, and she saw the stone had been taken away from the tomb.
² So she ran and went to Simon Peter and to the other disciple whom Jesus loved, and she said to them, 'They have taken the Lord out of the tomb, and we do not know where they have laid him.'
³ So Peter and that other disciple went along, and they came to the tomb, ⁴ and they were both running together, although the other disciple ran on ahead faster than Peter and arrived at the tomb first. ⁵ And stooping to look in, he saw the linens laid out, but he did not go in.
⁶ Then Simon Peter came following him, and he went into the tomb, and he gazed intently on the linens laid out, ⁷ and the sweat cloth, which had been over his head, laid out, not with the linens, but rolled up in one spot by itself. ⁸ Then that other disciple who came first to the tomb went in as well, and he saw, and he believed. ⁹ For they had not as yet come to know the text that he must rise from *the* dead.
¹⁰ Then the disciples went off, back to their respective *homes.*
¹¹ Maria, though, stood near the tomb,

weeping outside. Then while she wept she stooped down into the tomb [12] and she saw two angels in white sitting, one at the head, and the other at the feet, where the body of Jesus had lain.

[13] And they said to her, 'Woman, why are you weeping?'

She said to them, 'Because they have taken my Lord away, and I do not know where they have put him.'

[14] And on saying these things, she turned herself around and saw Jesus standing,* but she did not recognize that it was Jesus.

[15] Jesus said to her, 'Woman, why are you weeping? Whom are you looking for?'

Supposing that he was the gardener, she said to him, 'Sir, if you carried him from here, tell me where you have put him and I will remove him.'

[16] Jesus said to her, 'Maria!'

Turning herself around, she said to him, 'Rabbouni!',* which is to say, 'Teacher'.*

[17] Jesus said to her, 'Do not touch me, for I have not yet ascended to my Father.* But go to my brothers and say to them that I am ascending to my Father and your Father, and to my God* and your God.'*

[18] Maria Magdalene came bringing word to the disciples that she had seen the Lord, and he had spoken these things to her.

Jesus proves his resurrection

[19] Then, it being evening that same day, the First of Weeks,* and the doors having been shut where the disciples were assembled on account of fear of the Jews, Jesus appeared and stood among them, and he said to them, 'Peace to you.'

[20] And *after* he had said this, he showed them *his* hands and his side.

So the disciples rejoiced at seeing the Lord.

He breathes on the 11
to receive the divine spirit
& gives authorization
to continue the work.*
Thomas's incredulity & exclamation

[21] Then Jesus said to them again, 'Peace to you. As the Father has sent* me, I also will authorize you.'

[22] And when he had spoken this he breathed on *them*, and said to them, 'Receive *the* divine spirit.'* [23] Anybody whose violations you forgive,

they are forgiven for them. Anybody whose you might hold back, they are held back.'

[24] But Thomas, one of the twelve, the one known as Twin, was not with them when Jesus came, [25] so the other disciples said to him, 'We've seen the Lord!'

But he said to them, 'Unless I see the mark of the nails in his hands, and put my finger into the mark of the nails, and put my hand into his side, I will certainly not* believe.'

[26] And after eight days, his disciples were again inside, and Thomas *was* with them, *and* Jesus came, the doors having been shut, and he stood in *their* company, and said, 'Peace to you.'

[27] Then he said to Thomas, 'Bring your finger here, and see my hands,* and reach your hand here and put *it* into my side, and turn not unbelieving, but believing.'

[28] And Thomas answered, and said to him, 'My Lord and my God!'*

[29] Jesus said to him, 'Because you have seen me you have believed. Exalted *are* those who have not seen yet have believed.'

[30] So Jesus also did many other signs in *the* presence of his disciples, which are not written in this Scroll.* [31] But these things have been written so that you will believe* that Jesus is the Christ, the Son of God, and that by believing you might have life in his name.

Another resurrection appearance
& a catch of 153 fish

21 \ 1 After these things, Jesus again brought himself to light to the disciples on the Sea of Tiberias, and he brought *himself* to light* in this way:

[2] Simon Peter, and Thomas (known as Twin), and Nathanael from Cana in Galilee, and the *sons* of Zebedee, and two others of his disciples were together.*

[3] Simon Peter said to them, 'I'm going out to fish.'

They said to him, 'We'll come with you as well.'

They departed and at once boarded the boat, but during that night they caught nothing. [4] And with morning having already broken, Jesus stood on the shore, but the disciples did not know that it was Jesus.

[5] So Jesus said to them, 'Sons, do you not have any substantial* food?'

They answered him, 'No.'

[6] And he said to them, 'Cast the net to the

right hand side of the boat, and you will find *fish.*'

Then they cast out, and they no longer had the strength to haul it back up because of the large number of fish.

⁷ Then that disciple whom Jesus loved said to Peter, 'It's the Lord.'

So *when* Simon Peter heard that it was the Lord, he put on *his*˙ outer garment – for he was uncovered – and he threw himself into the sea.˙

⁸ And the other disciples boarded the boat – for they were not far from the land, only about two hundred forearm's lengths˙ – dragging the net of fish. ⁹ So as soon as they went up on the land, they saw a fire of coals laid out there, and fish laid out on *it*, and a loaf.

¹⁰ Jesus said to them, 'Bring some of˙ the fish which you just caught.'

¹¹ Simon Peter went on board and drew to the land the net full of a hundred and fifty-three fish, and *although*˙ numbering so many the net did not rip.

¹² Jesus said to them, 'Come *and* eat.'

And not one of the disciples dared to enquire of him, 'Who are you?', knowing that it was the Lord.

¹³ Then Jesus came and took the loaf and he gave *some* to them, and the boiled fish in the same way.

¹⁴ This *is* the third time now that Jesus was brought to light˙ to the disciples, after having been raised˙ from *the* dead.

Peter restored & authorized

¹⁵ So when they had eaten, Jesus said to Simon Peter, 'Simon, *son* of Jonah, do you truly love˙ me more than these?'

He said to him, 'Yes, Lord, you know that I love˙ you.'

He said to him, 'Feed my lambs.'˙

¹⁶ He said to him again, a second time, 'Simon, *son* of Jonah, do you truly love˙ me?'

He said to him, 'Yes, Lord, you know that I love˙ you.'

He said to him, 'Tend my sheep.'

¹⁷ He said to him the third time, 'Simon, son of Jonah, do you love˙ me?'

Peter was sorrowful that he said to him the third time, 'Do you love˙ me?', and he said to him, 'Lord, you know all things.˙ You know that I love˙ you.'

Jesus said to him, 'Feed my sheep.'

Futures of Peter & John

¹⁸ 'Truly, truly, I say to you, when you were young you used to dress yourself and go around where you wanted, but when you grow old you will stretch out your hands, and somebody else will dress and lead˙ you to a place you do not want.'˙

¹⁹ He spoke this, though, signifying by what kind of death he would magnify God.

And having said this, he said to him, 'Follow me.'

²⁰ Then Peter turned around *and* saw the disciple whom Jesus loved following, he who had also leaned on his chest at supper, and had said, 'Lord, who is he who is going to betray you?'

²¹ On seeing him, Peter said to Jesus, 'Lord, but what about him?'

²² Jesus said to him, 'If I might want him to remain until I come,˙ what *is that* to you? You follow me.'

²³ So this saying spread among the brothers that that disciple was not going to die.˙ Yet Jesus did not say to him that he would not die, but, 'If I wish that he remains until I come, what *is that* to you?'

Epilogue

²⁴ This is the disciple giving testimony concerning these things and writing these things, and we know that his testimony is true.

²⁵ And there are many other things as well which Jesus did, which, if each one were written down, I do not imagine the world itself to contain the written books.˙˙ Amen.

~ ◆◆ ~

† The Acts of the Apostles* †

The physician Luke (Col. 4\14)
shows his integrity in his prologue.
Jesus' incontestable proofs of resurrection

1\1

ow I made* the former* account, oh* Theophilus, concerning all *the* things which Jesus began both to do and to teach [2] until the day in which he was received up, having given directions, through *the* Holy Spirit,* to the apostles whom he chose out,* [3] to whom, with many certain signs, he presented himself alive after his suffering, being seen by them throughout forty days, and speaking of the things concerning the Sovereign Rulership* of God.

The promise of the Father
of power from on high (Luke 24\49)
for the apostles' immediate authorization
to be witnesses to Jesus *
[4] And being assembled together *with them,* he ordered them not to depart from Jerusalem, but to wait for the promise of the Father,* 'About which,' *he said,* 'you heard from me, [5] because John identified* with water, but you will be identified with *the* divine spirit* after not many days from these.'
[6] So when they came together, they were questioning him, saying, 'Lord, are you at this time setting up the kingdom* for Israel?'
[7] And he said to them, 'It is not for you to know times or seasons which the Father has placed in His own authority. [8] But you will receive power *when* the Holy Spirit* comes to you,* and you will be witnesses to me both in Jerusalem and in all Judea, as well as in Samaria, and as far as *the* uttermost part of the land.'**

Jesus taken up by a cloud of angels *
& will return in the same manner
[9] And *when* he had spoken these things, *while they* were watching he was lifted up,* and a cloud withdrew* him from their eyes.*
[10] And as they were gazing intensely into the sky while he was going up, it became apparent that* two men* stood by them in white clothing, [11] who for their part* said, 'Men, Galileans, why do you stand gazing up into the sky? This Jesus, taken up from you into the sky, will come in

the same manner as you watched him being carried into the sky.'
[12] Then they returned to Jerusalem from a mountain called Olives Grove, which is near Jerusalem, being a Sabbath's distance.

Praying as one
[13] And when they had gone inside, they went up into the upper room where both Peter and Jacob were staying, as well as John and Andrew; Philip and Thomas; Bartholomew and Matthew; Jacob, *son* of Alphaeus, and Simon the Zealot; and Judas, *the brother* of Jacob. [14] These were all steadfastly continuing with one mind in prayer and supplication,* together with *the* women, and Maria, the mother of Jesus, and with his brothers.

Matthias chosen to replace Judas Iscariot
[15] And in those days Peter rose up in *the* presence of the disciples – and *the* number of the gathering was about a hundred and twenty in all – *and* he said, [16] 'Men, brothers, it was needful for this text to have been fulfilled, which the Holy Spirit* spoke beforehand* through* *the* mouth of* David concerning Judas, who became guide to those who seized Jesus.* [17] For he was numbered with us, and he obtained a part of this work. [18] So this *man* purchased a field out of the reward of unrighteousness, and, becoming* swollen,* he burst open in the middle, and all his bowels gushed out.* [19] And it became known to all those living in Jerusalem, so that that field was called, in their own dialect, Aceldama, that is to say, Field of Blood.* [20] For it has been written in a Scroll* of Psalms:

'Let his place of residence*
become a wilderness,
and let him not be living in it,*
and let another receive his office.'*

[21] 'So it is necessary, from among those consorting with us men during all *the* time in which the Lord Jesus went in and out among us, [22] beginning from the identification of John, until that day in which he was taken up from us, *for* one of these to become a witness with us of his resurrection.'
[23] And they appointed two, Joseph known as Barsabas, who was surnamed Justus, and Matthias.
[24] And they prayed *and* said, 'Lord, knower of

the hearts of everybody, show plainly which one out of these two You have chosen [25] to receive the part of this work and apostleship, from which Judas transgressed to go into his own place."*

[26] And they handed in their lots, and the lot fell on Matthias, and he was numbered with the eleven apostles.

The Day of Pentecost.
The presence of the Holy Spirit (1\8, 2\4)
who is the Angel of God
causes a sound like a violent wind-blast.
The 12 are filled with power from on high
(1\4, Luke 24\49), & the Angel gives them
utterance to speak Mediterranean languages

2\1 **A**nd in the fulfilling of *the* Day of Pentecost,* they were all with one mind in the same place.

[2] And suddenly out of* the sky* a ringing in the ears* came like a rushing of a violent wind-blast, and it filled the whole house where they were sitting. [3] And divided tongues, as if of fire,* were seen by them, and they rested over each one of them. [4] And they were all filled with *the* divine spirit,* and began to speak with other languages as the Spirit* was giving them utterance.*

[5] Now living in Jerusalem were Jews, devoted men, from every nation of those under Heaven.*

[6] But on this volume arising, the crowd gathered together, and they were confused because they heard them speaking, each one in his own dialect. [7] And they were all dumbfounded and astonished, saying to each other, 'Look!* Are all these who are speaking not Galileans?* [8] And how do we each hear our own dialect in which we were born? [9] Parthians, and Medes, and Elamites, and those who inhabit Mesopotamia, and in Judea, and Cappadocia, in Pontus, and Asia, [10] both Phrygia, and Pamphylia, Egypt, and the regions of Libya around Cyrene, and the repatriated* Romans, both Jews and proselytes, [11] Cretans and Arabians – we hear them speak in our languages the magnificent things of God."*

[12] And they were all astounded, and they were in perplexity, saying to each other, 'Whatever do you resolve this to be?'*

[13] But others, ridiculing, said that they were full of new wine.

Peter cites Joel as an example of signs
*from God. He proclaims to Israelites**
the resurrection of Jesus, their rejected Messiah

[14] But Peter, standing up with the eleven,* raised his voice and spoke out to them, 'Men, Jews, and all you living in Jerusalem, let this be known to you, and receive my declarations into your ears, [15] for these *men* are not drunk as you suppose,* for it's the third hour of the day.* [16] But this* is what has been spoken through the agency of* the prophet Joel:

[17] "And it will arise in the last days,*
says God, *that* I will pour out a measure
of My spirit on all flesh,*
and your sons and your daughters
will prophesy,
and your young men will see visions,
and your old men will dream dreams.
[18] And also in those days
I will pour out My spirit*
on My servants and on My maid servants,*
and they will prophesy.
[19] And I will show wonders in the sky above
and signs in the Earth below,
blood and fire and vapour of smoke.
[20] The Sun will be changed into darkness
and the Moon into blood,
before the mighty and blazing*
day of *the* Lord* comes.
[21] And it will arise *that* everyone
who calls on the name of *the* Lord
will be preserved."*

[22] 'Men, Israelites,* hear these oracles. Jesus the Nazarene,* a man made known* to you by God through works of power and wonders and signs which God worked through* him in your presence, as you yourselves also know, [23] this one, delivered up by the marked-out* counsel and foreknowledge of God, you,* having taken by evil hands, having fastened *him* to *a tree,* put to death* [24] him whom God raised up, having released *him* from the pains of death, because it was not possible for him to be held by it. [25] For David speaks about* him:

"I saw the Lord before my face
through every *event,*
that He was at* my right hand*
so that I should not be shaken.
[26] My heart rejoiced on account of this,
and my tongue rejoiced exceedingly;
and my flesh also will tabernacle in hope,

[27] because You will not abandon
my dead body* in the grave,*
nor will you allow Your Holy One
to experience corruption.
[28] You made paths of life known to me;
You will fill me with exuberance
with Your countenance."**

David still in the tomb
to this day, but Jesus raised
[29] 'Men, brothers, it is permitted to speak with
plainness to you concerning the patriarch
David, that he both died and was buried, and
his tomb is among us until this day.
[30] 'Therefore, being a prophet, and knowing
that God had sworn to him with an oath that
out of a fruit of his loins, in relation to the
flesh, in order to raise up the Christ to sit on his
governmental seat,* [31] he, foreseeing this, spoke
of the resurrection of the Christ, so that:

"His dead body* was not left in the grave,*
nor did his flesh experience corruption."**

[32] 'This Jesus God raised up, of which all of us
are witnesses.* [33] Therefore, having been exalted
to the right hand* of God, and receiving the
promise of the divine spirit* from* the Father,*
he has poured out this* which you now see and
hear.
[34] 'For David did not ascend into the heavens,*
but he himself says:

"The Lord said to my Lord,
'Sit at* My right hand*
[35] until I bend down your enemies
as a footstool for your feet.' "*

[36] 'Assuredly,* therefore, let all *the* house of
Israel know that God has made this same Jesus,
whom you hanged on a stake,* Lord and Christ.'

3,000 submit & are identified
with God & Christ & receive the divine spirit
[37] And *when* they heard *this*, they were stabbed
to the heart, and they said to Peter and to the
other apostles, 'What shall we do, men,
brothers?'
[38] Then Peter said to them, 'Submit,* and be
identified,* each one of you, in the name of
Jesus Christ, for forgiveness of violations, and
you will receive the free gift of the divine
spirit.* [39] For the promise is to you, and to your
children, and to all at a distance,* as many

whom *the* Lord our God will call.'
[40] And by many other oracles he earnestly
attested and encouraged *them*, saying, 'Be saved
from this villainous* generation.'*
[41] So those who received his oracle gladly
were identified, and that same day about three
thousand people were added. [42] And they were
continuing resolutely in the apostles' teaching,
and in fellowship, and in breaking bread, and in
prayers.

Revering God,
all things held in common
[43] And fear broke out for every person,* and
many wonders and signs were done through the
apostles. [44] And all who believed were together,
and had all things in common, [45] and they sold
possessions and goods* and divided them to
everybody, as anybody had need. [46] And
resolutely continuing every day* of one mind in
the Temple, and breaking bread from house to
house,* they were sharing their food with
extreme joy, and simplicity of heart, [47] praising
God, and having favour in relation to all the
people.
And from day to day the Lord added to the
Ekklesia** those who were being saved.

Healing of a lame man
at the Beautiful Gate
3\1 Now Peter and John were going up
together into the Temple at the hour of prayer,
the ninth *hour*.* [2] And a certain man, lame from
his mother's womb, was being carried, *and* they
were laying him down daily at the gate of the
Temple called Beautiful, to ask for gifts from
those who were going into the Temple, [3] who,
seeing Peter and John about to go into the
Temple, asked for gifts.
[4] And Peter, with John, fastening his eyes on
him, said, 'Look at us.'
[5] And he gave them his attention, expecting to
receive something from them.
[6] Then Peter said, 'Silver and gold do not
belong to me, but what I do have, this I give to
you – in the name of Jesus Christ the
Nazarene,* rise up and walk.'
[7] And taking him by the right hand, he raised
him up, and instantly his feet and ankle bones
were strengthened. [8] And he leaped up, *and*
stood and walked, and went into the Temple
with them, walking and leaping* and praising
God.

⁹ And all the people saw him walking and praising God, ¹⁰ and they recognized that this was the one sitting for gifts at the Beautiful Gate of the Temple, and they were filled with wonder and ecstasy* at what had happened to him.

Peter's proclamation that the people condemned Jesus who inaugurated Eonian life

¹¹ And as the lame *man* who was healed was holding onto Peter and John, all the people ran together towards them at the porch called the Porch of Solomon, completely astounded.

¹² And seeing *this*, Peter answered the people, 'Men, Israelites, why do you marvel over this? Or why do you look so intently at us, as if through our own power or holiness we made him walk? ¹³ The God of Abraham, and of Isaac, and of Jacob, the God of our fathers, has magnified His servant Jesus, whom you handed over, and you denied him in the presence of Pilate, *who* had determined to release *him*. ¹⁴ But you denied the Holy and Righteous One, and requested a man *who is* a murderer to be released to you, ¹⁵ and you murdered the inaugurator of life* whom God raised from *the* dead, of which we are witnesses. ¹⁶ And on the faith of his name, his name has made strong this *man* whom you see and know, and the faith which is through him has given him this complete wholeness among the presence of you all.

¹⁷ 'And now, brothers, I know that you acted according to ignorance, as your rulers also *did*. ¹⁸ But those things which God had announced before through the agency of *the* mouth of all His prophets, *that* the Christ should suffer, He fulfilled in this way.

¹⁹ 'Submit, therefore, and be converted, with a view to* the* erasure* of your violations, in order that* seasons of refreshing may come from *the* face of the Lord, ²⁰ and He might authorize him* who was proclaimed for you beforehand, Jesus Christ, ²¹ whom Heaven must receive until *the* times of restoration of all things* which God spoke of through the agency of *the* mouth of all His holy prophets from of old.*

²² 'For Moses said to the fathers, "*The* Lord our God will raise up for you, from among your brothers, a prophet like myself. You shall hear him in all things, whatever he shall speak to you. ²³ And it will come to pass *that* every person* who will not hear that prophet will be utterly destroyed from among the people."*

²⁴ 'Yes, and all the prophets from Samuel, and those next in order, as many who have spoken, also announced these days. ²⁵ You are sons of the prophets and of the covenant which God covenanted to our fathers, saying to Abraham, "And in your seed all the progeny of the Earth will be benefitted."*

²⁶ 'To you first, God, having raised up his servant Jesus, authorized him, benefitting* you by turning each one of you away from your iniquities.'

Peter & John imprisoned & forbidden to proclaim Jesus

4\1 Now as they were speaking to the people, the priests and the head guard of the Temple and the Sadducees confronted them, ² and they were exasperated because they taught the people, even to proclaim in Jesus the resurrection of *the* dead. ³ And they seized them, and put *them* in custody until the next day, for it was already evening. ⁴ But many of those who heard the oracle believed, and the number of the men was about five thousand.

⁵ And it so happened on the next day *that* their rulers and leaders and scribes were gathered together in Jerusalem, ⁶ with Annas, the high priest, and Caiaphas, and John, and Alexander, and as many who were out of the high priestly division.

⁷ And having set them in the centre, they were asking, 'By the means of what kind of power, or by what kind of name, did you do this?'

⁸ Then Peter, filled with *the* divine spirit, said to them, 'You rulers of the people, and leaders of Israel, ⁹ if we, by whom this *man* has been cured, are this day examined about a good work on* an impotent man, ¹⁰ let it be known to you all, and to all the people of Israel, that in the name of Jesus Christ the Nazarene,* whom you hanged on a stake,* whom God raised from *the* dead, in him this *man* stands here in your presence whole.

¹¹ "This is the stone
which has been treated with contempt
by you, the builders,
which has turned into
the head of *the* corner."*

¹² 'And not in any other is there salvation, for neither is there any other name given among

men by which to be saved."

¹³ And seeing the outspokenness of Peter and John, and perceiving that they were unlettered* and unprofessional men,* they were astounded, and they recognized them, that they had been* with Jesus. ¹⁴ But in seeing the man who had been healed standing with them, they had nothing to contradict.

¹⁵ So they ordered them to go outside the Sanhedrin, *and* they conferred with each other, ¹⁶ saying, 'What shall we do to these men? For indeed, a remarkable sign has come about through them, brought to light to all those inhabiting Jerusalem, and we are not able to deny *it*. ¹⁷ But in order that it might not be rumoured about to the people, we will threaten them with a strong warning to speak* no longer in this name to any man.'

¹⁸ And they called them *and* ordered them not to speak* out at all, nor to teach in the name of Jesus.

¹⁹ But Peter and John, making answer to them, said, 'If it is right in the sight of God to listen to you rather than to God, you judge. ²⁰ For we cannot but speak what we saw and heard.'

²¹ So having further threatened them, they let them go, finding no further means of punishing them, on account of the people, because everybody was magnifying God for what had happened, ²² for the man on whom this sign of healing had happened was over forty years *old*.

Prayer for extra boldness
to proclaim Jesus. The room shakes
²³ And *when* they had been released, they went back to their own *company* and reported everything which the senior priests and the leaders had said to them.

²⁴ And on hearing *it*, they lifted up *their* voice to God in one mind,* and said, 'Sovereign Lord, You are the God Who created Heaven and Earth, and the sea, and everything which *is* in them, ²⁵ Who through* *the* mouth of Your servant David said:*

"Why do* the nations rage
and the peoples imagine foolish things?
²⁶ The kings of the Earth stood up,
and the rulers were gathered together
against the Lord,
and against His anointed."'**

²⁷ 'For it's the truth *that* both Herod and Pontius Pilate, with *the* nations and peoples of

Israel, were gathered together against Your holy servant* Jesus whom You anointed,* ²⁸ to do whatever Your hand and Your counsel marked out in advance* to come about.*

²⁹ 'And as for now Lord, look on their threats and appoint Your servants* to speak Your oracle with all boldness,* ³⁰ by stretching out Your hand for healing, and for signs and wonders to be carried out through the name of Your holy servant* Jesus.'

³¹ And *when* they had implored *God*, the place in which they were assembled together was shaken, and they were all filled with *the* divine spirit, and they spoke the oracle of God with boldness.

All things in common
³² And the whole company of the believers were of one heart and of one mind, and not even one claimed any of their possessions to be* their own, but all things were in common to them. ³³ And the apostles were giving out with mighty power the testimony of the resurrection of the Lord Jesus, and immense favour was over them all.* ³⁴ For nor was anybody among them in need, for as many who were owners of lands or houses sold *them and* brought the prices of the things which were sold, ³⁵ and they laid *them* down at the apostles' feet, and distribution was made to anybody as he had need.

³⁶ And Joses, who was surnamed Barnabas by the apostles – which, being translated, is 'Son of Consolation' – a Levite, a Cypriot by birth, ³⁷ owned a field *and* sold *it, and* brought the money and laid *it* at the apostles' feet.

Ananias & Sapphira die for their deceit

5\1 **B**ut a certain man, Ananias by name, with his wife Sapphira, sold a possession, ² and they kept back *part* from the proceeds, his wife also being conscious of *it*. Then, having brought along a certain part, he laid *it* at the apostles' feet.

³ But Peter said, 'Ananias, why did Satan fill your heart *for* you to deceive the Holy Spirit,* and to covertly keep back* *something* from the value of the estate? ⁴ *Is it* not *so* that *while it* was kept back it remained your own,* and, having been sold, was it not in your own control? Why was this action conceived in your heart? You have lied not to men, but to God.'

⁵ Now Ananias, hearing these words, fell down and expired, and extreme fear fell on everybody

who heard these things. ⁶ And the younger *men* came *and* wrapped him up, and they carried *him* out *and* buried *him*.

⁷ And about three hours' interval passed and his wife came in as well, not knowing what had happened.

⁸ And Peter asked her, 'Tell me if you sold the estate for this price.'

And she said, 'Yes, for that price.'

⁹ And Peter answered her, 'Why *is it* that you agreed together to test the Spirit of *the* Lord?' Look now, the feet of those who buried your husband *are* at the door, and they will carry you out.'

¹⁰ Then straightaway she fell down at his feet and expired. And the young men came in *and* found her dead, and they carried *her* out *and* buried *her* beside her husband.

¹¹ And extreme fear fell over the whole Ekklesia and over all those who heard about these things.

Healing of many through the apostles

¹² And many signs and wonders were being worked among the people through the hands of the apostles. And they were all of one mind in the Porch of Solomon. ¹³ As for the rest, nobody dared to join them, but the people esteemed them highly. ¹⁴And more believers were added to the Lord, crowds of both men and women, ¹⁵ so that they brought the sick out along the streets, and laid *them* on beds and mattresses so that even the shadow of Peter passing by might overshadow some of them.

¹⁶ And the crowd from the towns around Jerusalem assembled together as well, bringing *their* sick and those troubled by unclean spirits, who were all cured.

The apostles imprisoned & freed
by the Angel of God,
& they continue proclaiming Jesus

¹⁷ The high priest, however, rose up, and all those who were with him – which was a sect of the Sadducees – were filled with envy, ¹⁸ and they gripped their hands on the apostles, and put them in a public jail.

¹⁹ But during the night *the* Angel of *the* Lord' opened the doors of the jail and led them out, *and* said, ²⁰ 'Go and stand in the Temple, *and* speak all these declarations of life to the people.'

²¹ And hearing *that*, they went into the Temple at about daybreak, and they were teaching. But the high priest and those with him arrived *and* they called together the Sanhedrin, and all the senate' of the sons of Israel, and they sent an order to the jail to have them brought.

²² But on their arriving the under-officers found them not in the jail, and on their return they gave report, ²³ saying, 'We found the jail locked with every security, and the guards standing at the doors, but on opening up we found nobody inside.'

²⁴ Now when they heard these words, both the high priest and the head guard of the Temple and the senior priests were perplexed about them, at what might become of this.'

²⁵ Then somebody came *and* made report to them, 'Look, the men whom you put in the jail are standing in the Temple and teaching the people.'

The apostles before
the Sanhedrin & high priest

²⁶ Then the head guard went with the officers, *and* brought them – not violently, for they feared the people – so that they might not be stoned.

²⁷ And they brought them *and* set *them* among the Sanhedrin, and the high priest asked them, ²⁸ saying, 'Did we not strictly order you not to teach in this name? And you have gone and filled Jerusalem with your teaching, and you intend to bring the blood of this man on us.'

²⁹ But in answer, Peter and the apostles said, 'We ought to obey God rather than men.' ³⁰ The God of our fathers raised up Jesus, whom you murdered,' by hanging on a tree.' ³¹ This one God exalted to His right hand,' as Ruler and Saviour, to give submission to Israel and forgiveness of violations, ³² and we are his witnesses of these declarations, and so also *is* the Holy Spirit,' whom' God gave to those who obey him.'

The superior wisdom of Gamaliel.
The apostles beaten & forbidden to proclaim Jesus,
then, when freed, proclaim daily from house to house

³³ But on their hearing *that*, they were pierced' and they were resolving to kill them.

³⁴ Then somebody in the Sanhedrin, a Pharisee named Gamaliel, a teacher of the law, honoured by all the people, rose up and ordered the apostles to be put outside for a little while.

³⁵ And he said to them, 'Men, Israelites, watch yourselves in what you are about to do in the case of these men. ³⁶ For before these days

Theudas rose up, affirming himself to be˙ somebody, to whom a number of men were joined,˙ about four hundred, who was executed, and all, as many who were persuaded by him, were disbanded, and they came˙ to nothing. ³⁷ After this, Judas the Galilean rose up in the days of the registration, and caused many people to revolt after him. He also perished, and they all, as many who were persuaded by him, were scattered. ³⁸ And now, I say to you, withdraw from˙ these men and leave them, because if this counsel or this work might be of men it will be overthrown. ³⁹ But if it is from God, you are not able to overthrow it, in case you are found fighters even against God.'
⁴⁰ And they were persuaded by him,˙ and, having called the apostles and beaten *them*, they charged *them* not to speak in the name of Jesus, and they let them go.
⁴¹ So they departed from *the* presence of *the* Sanhedrin, rejoicing that they were counted worthy to be disgraced for the name of Jesus. ⁴² And every day in the Temple, and from house to house,˙ they did not cease to teach and proclaim the gospel of Jesus the Christ.

Seven men chosen to serve at tables
to free up the apostles' time

6\1 And in those days the disciples multiplied, *and* a murmuring of the Hellenists arose˙ against the Hebrews, because˙ their widows were being overlooked˙ in the daily provision.
² And the twelve called the company of the disciples, *and* said, 'It is not agreeable to us, leaving the oracle of God to attend tables. ³ Therefore, brothers, select seven men from among yourselves, of good reputation,˙ full of divine spirit˙ and wisdom, for us to appoint in this duty. ⁴ But we will give ourselves continually to prayer,˙ and to the provision of the oracle.'
⁵ And the suggestion was pleasing before the whole company, and they chose Stephen, a man full of faith and of *the* divine spirit, and Philip, and Prochorus, and Nicanor, and Timon, and Parmenas, and Nicolas, a proselyte of Antioch, ⁶ whom they set before the apostles, and they prayed *and* laid hands on them.
⁷ And the oracle of God increased, and the number of the disciples multiplied vastly in Jerusalem, and a large number of the priests were obedient to the faith.

Stephen falsely accused & arrested
⁸ And Stephen, full of faith and power, worked mighty signs and wonders among the people.
⁹ Then certain *men* arose out of the synagogue, known as the Libertines, and Cyrenians, and Alexandrians, and of those from Cilicia and of Asia, *and* they disputed with Stephen, ¹⁰ but they did not have the acumen˙ to resist the wisdom and the spirit by which he spoke.
¹¹ Then they secretly induced men, saying, 'We have heard him speak blasphemous words against Moses and God.'
¹² And together they stirred up the people, and the leaders, and the scribes, and they accosted *Stephen and* seized him violently and brought *him* to the Sanhedrin, ¹³ and they set up pseudo witnesses saying, 'This man does not cease speaking blasphemous declarations against the holy place and the law. ¹⁴ For we have heard him say that this Jesus the Nazarene˙ will destroy this place, and he will change the customs which Moses handed down to us.'
¹⁵ And fastening their eyes on him, all who sat in the Sanhedrin saw his face as if a face of an angel.

Stephen's account of the patriarchs.
Israel's history & her Messiah Jesus

7\1 Then the high priest said, 'Are these things so?'
² And *Stephen* said, 'Men, brothers, and fathers, listen. The magnificent˙ God was seen by our father Abraham *in the time* he was in Mesopotamia, before he settled in Haran, ³ and He said to him, "Go out from your country, and from among your relatives,˙ and go into *the* land which I will show you."˙ ⁴ Then he went out from *the* land of *the* Chaldeans, *and* he settled in Haran, and from there, after his father died, *God* moved him into this country in which you now live. ⁵ And He gave him no inheritance in it, not even a space for a foot, yet He promised to give it to him for a possession, and to his seed after him,˙ there not *as yet* being any child for him.˙
⁶ 'And in this way God spoke that his seed would be a foreigner in a foreign land, and that they would enslave them, and ill-treat *them for* four hundred years. ⁷ "And," God said, "I Myself will judge the nation to whom they will be in bondage, and after these things they will come out and worship Me in this place."˙ ⁸ And

He gave him a covenant of circumcision, and so he fathered* Isaac, and circumcised him *on* the eighth day, and Isaac *fathered* Jacob, and Jacob *fathered* the twelve patriarchs. [9] And the patriarchs, being jealous against Joseph, sold *him* into Egypt, and God was with him, [10] and He delivered him out of all his tribulations, and He gave him favour and wisdom before Pharaoh, king of Egypt, and he appointed him ruler over Egypt and all his house.

[11] 'But a famine broke out over the whole land of Egypt and Canaan, and severe affliction, and our fathers found no sustenance. [12] But having heard that there was corn in Egypt, Jacob sent out our fathers the first time. [13] And in the second *visit* Joseph was made known to his brothers, and Joseph's people became known to Pharaoh. [14] Then having sent word, Joseph called for his father Jacob, and all *his* family, seventy-five people.** [15] And Jacob went down into Egypt and came to his end, he, and our fathers, [16] and they were relocated into Shechem, and they were laid in the tomb which Abraham bought for a sum of money from the sons of Emmor, *the father* of Shechem.

[17] 'But as the time of the promise which God had sworn to Abraham drew near, the people grew and multiplied in Egypt [18] until another king arose who did not know Joseph. [19] This *man*, dealing slyly with our race, ill-treated our fathers, causing their babies to be thrown out* for them to not survive.** [20] During this time Moses was born, and he was extremely fine looking,* *and* he was nourished in *his* father's house *for* three months. [21] And when he had been put outside, the daughter of Pharaoh took *him* up and nourished him *as* a son for herself. [22] 'And Moses was educated in all *the* wisdom of *the* Egyptians, and he was mighty in words and deeds. [23] And when *the* time of forty years was fulfilled for him,* it came into his heart to visit his brothers, the sons of Israel. [24] And seeing a certain *man* being ill-treated, he defended *him* and took vengeance for the one being treated roughly, striking the Egyptian, [25] for he supposed his brothers would understand that God, by means of his hand, was giving them deliverance. However, they did not understand. [26] And on the following day he showed himself to those who were fighting, and he was urging them into peace, saying, "Men, you are brothers. Why do you ill-treat each other?" [27] But he who was ill-treating the neighbour pushed him aside, saying, "Who

appointed you a ruler and a judge over us? [28] Do you not want to kill me in the way you killed the Egyptian yesterday?"* [29] Then Moses fled at this remark, and he became an inhabitant in *the* land of Midian where he fathered* two sons.

[30] 'And when forty years were fulfilled in the wilderness of Mount Sinai, *the* Angel of *the* Lord* was seen by him in a flame of a burning bush. [31] And Moses, on seeing *it*, was amazed at the vision, and on his drawing near to inspect *it* the voice of *the* Lord came* to him, [32] *saying*, "I am the God of your fathers, the God of Abraham, and the God of Isaac, and the God of Jacob." Then he fell into trembling, *and* Moses did not dare to look. [33] And the Lord said to him, "Loosen the sandals of your feet, for the place in which you stand is holy ground. [34] I have clearly seen* the ill-treatment of My people in Egypt, and I have heard their groaning and I have come down to deliver them. So come now, *and* I will send you into Egypt."*

[35] 'This Moses, whom they disowned in their saying "Who appointed you a ruler and judge?",* *is* the one whom God authorized as a ruler and a redeemer through the agency of *the* hand of *the* Angel* seen by him in the bush. [36] This *Moses* led them out, having worked wonders and signs in *the* land of Egypt, and in *the* Red Sea and in the wilderness *for* forty years. [37] 'This is the Moses who said to the sons of Israel, "*The* Lord our God will raise up a Prophet like me for you from among your brothers."* [38] This is he who was among the legislative assembly* in the wilderness, with the Angel* speaking to him on Mount Sinai,* and *with* our fathers, *and* who received a living utterance to give us, [39] to whom our fathers did not wish to become* subject,* but they pushed *him* away and turned their hearts back to Egypt, [40] saying to Aaron, "Make us gods who will go before us, since, *as for* this Moses who brought us out of *the* land of Egypt, we do not know what has become of him."* [41] And they sculptured a calf in those days, and offered a sacrifice to the idol, and they were rejoicing in the works of their hands.

[42] 'But God turned away, and gave them over to worship the array of the sky, as it has been written in a Scroll* of the prophets:

"Did you offer Me
slain animals and sacrifices

for forty years in the wilderness,
oh house of Israel?
43 You even took up the tent of Moloch
and the star* of your god Remphan,*
the figures which you made
in order to worship them,
and in that case I will carry you away
beyond Babylon.'"*

44 'Our fathers had the Tent of Testimony in the wilderness, just as He Who spoke to Moses arranged for *him* to make it in keeping with the pattern which he had seen, 45 which our fathers received by succession, and they brought it with Joshua* into the possession of the nations whom God drove out from *the* face of our fathers, until the days of David, 46 who found favour in the eyes of God, and he asked if he could find a Tabernacle for the God of Jacob. 47 Solomon, though, built Him a House, 48 but the Most High does not live in handmade temples, as the prophet says:

49 "Heaven *is* My seat of government*
and the Earth a footstool for My feet.
'What kind of House will you build *for* Me?',
says *the* Lord, 'or what place of My rest?
50 Has My own hand
not made all these things?' "'

51 'Stiff-necked and uncircumcised in heart and ears! You always resist the Holy Spirit.* As your fathers *did*, you also *do*. 52 Whom among the prophets did your fathers not persecute? And they murdered those who proclaimed in advance about the coming of the Righteous One, of whom you have now become betrayers and homicides, 53 you who received the law through the agency of* an injunction* of angels,* but you did not guard *it*.'

Stephen, seeing a vision
of Jesus, is assassinated
54 And on hearing these things, they were cut to their hearts,* and they were gnashing *their* teeth at him.
55 But being full of *the* divine spirit, he looked up intently into the sky,* *and* he saw *the* magnificence of God, and Jesus standing at* *the* right hand* of God, 56 and he said, 'Look, I see the heavens opened, and the Son of Man standing* at* *the* right hand* of God.'
57 And yelling at the top of their voices, they held their ears tight, and ran towards him in one

headlong rush, 58 and they threw *him* outside the city, *and* they kept hurling stones at *him*, and the witnesses laid aside* their clothes at the feet of a young man named Saul.*
59 And *as* they stoned Stephen, he was invoking *God* and saying,* 'Lord Jesus, receive my spirit.'*
60 And he bowed down *his* knees *and* called out with a loud voice, 'Lord, do not lay out this violation against them.'
And having said this, he fell asleep.*

8\1 **A**nd Saul was approving of the homicide of him.

Persecution against the Ekklesia, especially by Saul
And in that day a violent persecution broke out against the Ekklesia in Jerusalem, and all except the apostles were scattered throughout the districts of Judea and Samaria.
2 And devoted men carried Stephen away,* and they made a solemn lamentation over him.*
3 Saul, however, was ravaging the Ekklesia. Going from house to house, and dragging off both men and women, he committed *them* to jail.

Philip & the apostles
in a town in Samaria
4 Now those who had been scattered went everywhere proclaiming the oracle. 5 Then Philip, going down into a town of Samaria, proclaimed the Christ to them. 6 And the crowds unanimously gave attention to the things spoken by Philip, in their hearing of them and in their seeing the signs which he was doing. 7 For unclean spirits, calling out with a loud voice, went out of many who had *them*, and many who had been paralyzed and lame were healed. 8 And there came to be immense exuberance in that town.

Simon the sorcerer
9 But a certain man, Simon* by name, was formerly practising magic arts* in the town and astounding* the nation of Samaria, proclaiming himself to be somebody eminent, 10 to whom *those*, from *the* low to *the* eminent, were giving attention, saying, 'This is the mighty power of God.'
11 And they were giving him their attention because for a long time he had been astounding* them with magic arts.* 12 But when they believed Philip's proclamation of the good

things concerning the Sovereign Rulership* of God and the name of Jesus Christ, they were identified, both men and women.

¹³ Then Simon himself also believed, and when he had been identified he was steadfastly continuing with Philip, and, seeing the works of power and signs being done, he was amazed.

¹⁴ Now the apostles in Jerusalem, having heard that Samaria had received the oracle of God, sent to them Peter and John, ¹⁵ who came down *and* prayed concerning them that they might receive *the* divine spirit.* ¹⁶ For as yet it had* not fallen on any of them, but they had been identified only into* the name of Christ Jesus. ¹⁷ Then they laid hands on them, and they received *the* divine spirit.

¹⁸ But Simon, seeing that through the laying on of the apostles' hands the divine spirit* was given, offered them money, ¹⁹ saying, 'Give me this authority* as well, so that whomever I lay hands on might receive *the* divine spirit.'*

²⁰ But Peter said to him, 'May your money be destined for destruction with you, because you thought the free gift of God* could be purchased through money! ²¹ There is no portion or inheritance for you in this cause,* for your heart is not right in the eyes of God. ²² Unburden yourself, therefore, from this evil of yours, and pray to God, if, perhaps, you might be forgiven the thought of your heart. ²³ For I perceive you as being in a bile of bitterness and bondage* of unrighteousness.'

²⁴ Then in answer, Simon said, 'May you *people* pray to the Lord on my behalf that not a thing of what you have spoken might come on me.'

²⁵ Then having most earnestly given testimony and spoken the oracle of the Lord, they returned into Jerusalem and proclaimed the gospel to many villages of the Samaritans.

*Philip in Gaza instructs & identifies
an Ethiopian into Jesus. Philip carried
by the Angel of God to Ashdod (Rev. 1\10)*

²⁶ Then *the* Angel of *the* Lord* spoke to Philip, saying, 'Rise up, and go along to *the* South, on the road which goes down from Jerusalem to Gaza, which is desert.'

²⁷ And he rose up and set off, and he came across an Ethiopian man, a eunuch, a potentate* of Candace, the queen of Ethiopians, who was in charge of all her treasure, and he had come to Jerusalem to worship, ²⁸ and he was travelling back, sitting on his chariot and reading the prophet Isaiah.

²⁹ And the Spirit* said to Philip, 'Go over and adjoin yourself to that chariot.'

³⁰ And Philip ran up *and* heard him reading Isaiah, and he said, 'Do you understand, then, what you are reading?'

³¹ And he said, 'How can* I, unless somebody guides me?'

And he asked Philip to come up to sit with him. ³² Now the context of the passage which he was reading was this:

'He was led like a sheep to the slaughter,
and like a lamb* dumb
before the one shearing it,
so he did not open his mouth.
³³ In his low estate,
his justice was taken away;*
and who will tell of his generated *oracle,*
for his life is taken from the Earth?'*

³⁴ And in answer, the eunuch said to Philip, 'I ask you, about whom does the prophet speak this, about himself, or about some other man?'

³⁵ But Philip opened his mouth, and, beginning from this passage, proclaimed Jesus to him.

³⁶ And as they were going along the road, they came to some water, and the eunuch said, 'Look,* some water. What is there to stop me being identified?'

³⁷ [*no verse 37 in RP Greek text*]* ³⁸ And he ordered the chariot to stand still, and they both went down into the water, both Philip and the eunuch, and he identified him.

³⁹ And when they came up out of the water, *the* Spirit of *the* Lord* caught Philip away,* and the eunuch saw him no longer, but he went his way rejoicing. ⁴⁰ Philip, though, was found in Ashdod,* and as he passed through he made proclamations to all the cities, until he came to Caesarea.

*Jesus appears to Saul (Paul)
on the road to Damascus* *

9\1 Now Saul, still breathing out threats and homicide towards the disciples of the Lord, came to the high priest ² *and* asked him for letters to Damascus for the synagogues, so that if he found any *who* were of the Way, both men and women, he might bring *them* shackled to Jerusalem.

³ But in his journeying it so happened he drew near Damascus, and suddenly a bright light

flashed around him from the sky, [4] and he fell on the ground, *and* he heard a voice saying to him, 'Saul, Saul, why do you persecute me?' [5] And he said, 'Who are you, Sir?'*

And the Lord said, 'I am Jesus, whom you persecute.'* [6] * But rise up, and go into the town, and you will be told what you have to do.'

[7] And the men who were travelling with him stood speechless, hearing a voice, but seeing nobody. [8] And Saul was lifted up from the ground, and although his eyes were opened he saw nobody, and they led him by the hand *and* brought *him* into Damascus. [9] And he was three days without sight, and he neither ate nor drank.

Ananias of Damascus receives
Saul (Paul), who meets other disciples *

[10] And there was a certain disciple in Damascus, Ananias by name, and the Lord said to him in a vision, 'Ananias.'

And he said, 'See, Lord, I *am here.*'

[11] And the Lord *said* to him, 'Rise up, *and* go into the lane which is known as The Straight, and look in *the* house of Judas for a Tarsean, Saul by name, for, you understand,* he was praying, [12] and he saw in a vision a man named Ananias coming in and putting a hand on him so that he might recover his sight.'

[13] Then Ananias answered, 'Lord, I have heard from many about this man, how many evil things he has done to your holy* people in Jerusalem, [14] and here he has authority from the senior priests to bind all who call on your* name.'

[15] But the Lord said to him, 'Go your way, for this *man* is a chosen instrument for me, in order to bring my* name to the presence of the nations, and kings, and sons of Israel. [16] For I myself will warn him what numerous things he must suffer on behalf of my name.'

[17] And Ananias went his way and entered the house, and, putting hands on him, he said, 'Saul, brother, the Lord has sent me, the one seen* by you on the road which you came on, so that you might recover your sight and be filled with *the* divine spirit.'*

[18] And straightaway something like scales fell away from his eyes, and he received sight, and he rose up *and* was identified. [19] And *when* he had received nourishment, he regained his strength. Then for a few days Saul was with the disciples in Damascus.

Saul proclaims Jesus in the synagogues.
Attempts to murder him

[20] And straightaway in the synagogues he was proclaiming the Christ, that this one* is the Son of God.

[21] But all who heard were struck with astonishment, and they said, 'Is this not the one who ravaged those who called on this name in Jerusalem, and he has come here for this purpose, so that he might bring them shackled to the senior priests?'

[22] But Saul increased all the more in power,* and he confounded the Jews who lived in Damascus, proving* that this one is the* Christ.

A plot by Jews & then by Greeks
to assassinate Saul (Paul) gets discovered

[23] Now when many days were fulfilled, the Jews plotted together to murder him, [24] but their plot became known to Saul. And they were watching the gates both day and night so that they might murder him. [25] But the disciples took him at night, *and* let *him* down alongside the wall, lowering *him* in a basket.

[26] And *when* he arrived in Jerusalem, Saul tried* to join himself to the disciples, but they were all afraid of him, not believing that he was a disciple.

[27] But Barnabas took hold of him *and* presented* *him* to the apostles, and related to them how he had seen the Lord on the road, and that he* had spoken to him, and how he spoke without reserve in Damascus in the name of Jesus.

[28] And he went with them into Jerusalem, [29] and he spoke and debated without reserve in the name of the Lord Jesus. And he spoke and disputed with the Greeks, but they took *it* in hand to murder him. [30] But having come to know about *it*, the brothers brought him down to Caesarea, and sent him away into Tarsus.

Apostle-authorized Ekklesia groups enjoy peace

[31] So the Ekklesia groups throughout all Judea and Galilee and Samaria had peace, being built up and walking in the reverence of the Lord, and by the counsel* of the Holy Spirit* they were increased.*

Peter in Lydda.
Healing of Aeneas from palsy

[32] Now it came about that Peter, passing through all *parts of the region*, also came down to the holy people who lived in Lydda. [33] And he

found a certain man there named Aeneas, who was paralyzed *and* had been lying on a bed for eight years.
³⁴ And Peter said to him, 'Aeneas, Jesus, the Christ, heals you. Rise up, and spread a bed for yourself.'

And instantly he rose up. ³⁵ And all those living in Lydda and the Sharon Plain saw him, and they turned to the Lord.

Peter in Joppa & the raising of Tabitha
³⁶ Now in Joppa there was a certain woman disciple[*] named Tabitha, which being interpreted is the name Dorcas. She was full of good works and acts of compassion[*] which she carried out.[*]
³⁷ And it arose[*] in those days that she fell sick *and* died, and they bathed *her and* laid *her* in an upper room. ³⁸ And since Lydda was near Joppa, the disciples heard that Peter was there, *and* they sent word to him, pleading with *him* not to delay to come across to them.
³⁹ Then Peter rose up *and* went along with them, whom, on his arrival, they brought into the upper room, and all the widows stood around him weeping and displaying coats and garments which Dorcas had made *while* she was with them.
⁴⁰ But *when* he had put them all outside, Peter knelt down *and* prayed, and he turned towards the body *and* said, 'Tabitha, rise up!'

And she opened her eyes, and, on seeing Peter, she sat up. ⁴¹ And he gave her a hand *and* helped her to rise up, and he called in the holy people and widows *and* presented her alive.
⁴² And it came to be known throughout the whole of Joppa, and many believed in the Lord.
⁴³ And it transpired *that* he stayed a considerable number of days in Joppa with a certain Simon, a tanner.[*]

Cornelius sends for Peter

10\1 **A**nd there was a certain man in Caesarea, Cornelius by name, a centurion of the cohort called the Italian, ² a devoted *man* and one revering[*] God, along with all his household, both carrying out many works of compassion for the people and praying to God through everything.^{**}
³ He saw clearly in a vision, at about the ninth hour[*] of the day, *the* Angel of God[*] coming to him and saying to him, 'Cornelius!'
⁴ But gazing at him, and becoming frightened,

he said, 'What is it, lord?'[*]

And he said to him, 'Your prayers and your acts of compassion have gone up in remembrance in the sight of God.[*] ⁵ And now send men to Joppa, and send for Simon, surnamed Peter. ⁶ This *man* lodges with a certain Simon, a tanner, whose house is at the side of *the* sea.'
⁷ So when the Angel[*] who spoke to Cornelius had departed, he called two of his household servants, and a dutiful soldier of those who continually waited on him, ⁸ and he related everything to them, *and* he sent them on to Joppa.

Peter's vision concerning the nations [*]
⁹ And the next morning, as these *men* were passing along the road, and drawing near to the town, Peter went up on the house to pray *at* about the sixth hour.[*] ¹⁰ And he became hungry and wanted to eat, but while they were making preparations an ecstasy[*] came over him, ¹¹ and he saw the sky opened and a certain object descending on him, like a large sheet tied by four corners, and being let down to the Earth, ¹² in which were all the four-footed animals of the Earth, and the wild animals, and the reptiles, and the birds of the sky.[*]
¹³ And a voice came to him *saying*, 'Rise up, Peter, *and* kill, and eat.'
¹⁴ But Peter said, 'Not at all, Lord, for never[*] did I eat anything common or unclean.'
¹⁵ And a voice *said* to him again a second time, 'Do not call common the things which God has made clean.'
¹⁶ And this happened a third time, and the object was taken back up into the sky.
¹⁷ Now just while Peter was perplexed in himself at what this vision which he had seen might symbolize,[*] it so happened that the men also who were authorized from Cornelius made diligent enquiry for the household of Simon, *and* they stood at the gate, ¹⁸ and they called out *and* enquired if Simon, surnamed Peter, lodged there.
¹⁹ But while Peter turned the vision over in his mind, the Spirit[*] said to him, 'Look, *some* men are searching for you. ²⁰ But rise up, *and* come down and go along with them, doubting nothing, because I have sent them.'[*]
²¹ Then *when* Peter had gone down to the men he said, 'See, I am the one whom you are looking for. For what purpose are you here?'
²² And they said, 'Cornelius, a centurion, a

righteous and God-revering man, and of good reputation˙ among the whole nation of the Jews, was divinely instructed by a Holy Angel˙ to send for you to his house, and to hear words from you.'

²³ So he called them in *and* gave *them* lodging. And the next day Peter went out with them, and some brothers from Joppa accompanied him.

Peter with Cornelius.˙
Peter proclaims Jesus
& the first non-Israelites
receive the divine spirit˙

²⁴ And the next day they came into Caesarea, and Cornelius was expecting them, having called together his relatives and close friends. ²⁵ And it so happened that as Peter went in Cornelius met him *and* he fell down at his feet and worshipped˙ *him.*

²⁶ But Peter lifted him up, saying, 'Rise up. I myself am also a man.'

²⁷ And conversing with him, he went in and found many gathered together.

²⁸ And he said to them, 'You know how it is unlawful for a Jewish man to unite himself with or make any approach to another race,˙ but God has shown me to call no man common or unclean. ²⁹ So without any contradicting, I came, having been sent for. I ask, therefore, for what word did you send for me?'

³⁰ And Cornelius said, 'Four days ago, I was fasting until this hour, and in the ninth hour I was praying in my house, and it transpired that˙ a man˙ was standing before me in shining clothing,˙ ³¹ and he said, "Cornelius, your prayer has been heard, and your acts of compassion have been remembered in the sight of God. ³² Send word, therefore, to Joppa, and call Simon here, who is surnamed Peter. He's lodging in *the* house of Simon, a tanner, by *the* sea, who will speak to you *when* he comes." ³³ So I sent for you at once, and you did well in coming. Now, therefore, we are all present before God to hear all the things which have been commanded of you by God.'

³⁴ And opening *his* mouth, Peter said, 'In truth, I perceive that God is not a respecter of persons. ³⁵ But in every nation he who reveres˙ Him and works righteousness is acceptable to Him. ³⁶ *You know* the oracle which He authorized to the sons of Israel, proclaiming peace by means of Jesus Christ – this one is Lord of all – ³⁷ *and* you know *the* declaration which was published throughout the whole of Judea, beginning from Galilee, after the identification which John proclaimed, ³⁸ Jesus from˙ Nazareth, how God anointed him by *the* Holy Spirit˙ and with power,˙ who went about doing good, and healing all who were being overpowered by the Devil, for God was with him, ³⁹ and we are witnesses of all the things which he did, both in the country of the Jews and in Jerusalem.

'He whom they murdered, hanging *him* on a tree,˙ ⁴⁰ this one God raised up *on* the third day, *and* caused him to become˙ openly exhibited, ⁴¹ not to all the people, but to witnesses who had been chosen by God beforehand,˙ to us who ate and drank with him after his rising˙ from *the* dead.

⁴² 'And he charged us to make proclamation to the people, and to give full testimony that this is the one who is marked out˙ by God as judge˙ of *the* living and *the* dead. ⁴³ All the prophets give testimony to him *that,* through his name, whoever believes in him receives forgiveness of violations.'

⁴⁴ Yet while Peter was still speaking these words, the divine spirit fell on all those hearing the oracle. ⁴⁵ And those of the circumcision were astounded, as many believers who came with Peter, because the gift of the divine spirit˙ was poured out on the other nations as well. ⁴⁶ For they heard them speaking with foreign languages and magnifying God.

Then Peter answered, ⁴⁷ 'Can anybody forbid water for these not to be identified, those who received the divine spirit, the same as ourselves?'

⁴⁸ And he ordered them to be identified in the name of the Lord. Then they begged him to remain for a few days.

Peter's defence for proclaiming to the nations˙

11\1 **N**ow the apostles and brothers who were throughout Judea got to hear that the other nations also received the oracle of God. ² And when Peter had come up to Jerusalem, those of *the* circumcision were contending against him, ³ saying, 'You went inside *with* uncircumcised men, and you ate with them.'

⁴ But Peter made an explanation to them in order, from the beginning, saying, ⁵ 'I was in *the* town of Joppa praying, and in an ecstasy˙ I saw a vision. A certain object was coming down like a large sheet, sent down by four corners out of

the sky, and it came down to me. [6] I gazed into it intently *and* fixed my eyes, and I saw four-footed animals of the Earth, and the wild animals, and the reptiles, and the birds of the sky. [7] And I heard a voice saying to me, "Rise up, Peter, *and* kill, and eat." [8] But I said, "Not at all, Lord, for never did anything common or unclean go into my mouth." [9] But a voice answered me the second time out of the sky: "Do not call common the things which God has made clean."

[10] 'And this happened a third time, and everything was drawn back into the sky. [11] And then at once, standing in front of the house which I was in, *were* three men sent to me by authority from Caesarea. [12] And the Spirit* told me to go with them, doubting nothing. In addition, these six brothers also came along with me, and we went into the man's house. [13] And he reported to us how he had seen the Angel* in his house, standing, and saying to him, "Send men into Joppa and call for Simon, surnamed Peter, [14] who will pronounce declarations to you by which you and all your house will be saved."

[15] 'And in my beginning to speak, the divine spirit* fell on them, just as on us also in *the* beginning.* [16] Then I remembered the oracle of *the* Lord, how he had said, "John made identifications by water, but you will be identified in *the* divine spirit."*' [17] If, then, God gave them the same gift as also to us in our believing in the Lord Jesus Christ, then who was I that I might be able to hinder God?'

[18] Now hearing these things, they held their peace and magnified God, saying, 'Then truly has God given submission resulting in* life to the other nations as well.'

The good character of Barnabas.
Persecution & the gospel is spread

[19] Then those who were dispersed from the persecution which broke out over Stephen travelled as far as Phoenicia, and Cyprus, and Antioch, proclaiming the oracle to nobody except the Jews only. [20] And some of them were men from Cyprus and Cyrene, who, on coming into Antioch, spoke to the Greeks, proclaiming the Lord Jesus. [21] And *the* hand of *the* Lord was with them, and a large number, believing, turned to the Lord.

Barnabas & Saul proclaim in Antioch
[22] Then the report concerning them was heard

in the ears of the Ekklesia group in Jerusalem, and they sent out Barnabas to go as far as Antioch, [23] who, when he came *and* saw the merciful goodwill of God, rejoiced, and he was exhorting them all with purpose of heart to continue with the Lord. [24] For he was a good man, and full of *the* divine spirit and faith, and a large multitude was added to the Lord.

[25] Then Barnabas departed to Tarsus to look up and down for Saul, [26] and when he found *him* he brought him to Antioch. And it transpired *that* they were gathered together for a whole year with the Ekklesia group, and they taught a considerable multitude.

And in Antioch the disciples were first called Christians.*

Prophecy of a famine
[27] And in these days prophets came down from Jerusalem to Antioch. [28] And one Agabus by name, on rising up from among them, signified through the Spirit* *that* there was about to be a severe famine* over the whole inhabited world,* which did indeed come to pass *in the days* of Claudius Caesar. [29] But as any of the disciples prospered in anything, each of them marked out* *something* to send for relief to the brothers living in Judea, [30] which they did as well, sending it on to the leaders through *the* hands of Barnabas and Saul.

Jacob assassinated by Herod.
Peter imprisoned by Herod *
but freed by the Angel of God

12\1 Now at about that time, Herod the king put his hands to it to maltreat some of those from the Ekklesia. [2] And he murdered Jacob, the brother of John, with a sword. [3] And on seeing it was pleasing to the Jews, he proceeded further to arrest Peter as well – now they were the days of Unleavened Bread – [4] whom, as well as seizing, he put into custody, *and* he assigned four sets of soldiers to guard him, intending to bring him out to the people after the Passover.* [5] Then Peter was kept securely in the jail, intense prayer to God, though, being made on behalf of him by the Ekklesia.*

[6] But when Herod was about to bring him out, Peter in that night was sleeping between two soldiers, shackled with two chains, and guards in front of the door were keeping the jail.

[7] And then *the* Angel of *the* Lord* stood over *him*, and a light shone in the cell, and he

prodded Peter's side *and* raised him up, saying, 'Rise up quickly!'

And his chains fell from *his* hands.

[8] And the Angel* said to him, 'Dress yourself, and tie your sandals on.'

And he did that.

Then he said to him, 'Wrap your garment round, and follow me.'

[9] And as he was going out he was following him, and he did not know that what was happening through the Angel* was real, but he was thinking he was seeing a vision.

[10] Now after they passed *the* first and second guard-posts, they came to the iron gate which leads* into the town *and* which was opened for them automatically, and they exited *and* passed on through one street, and the Angel* immediately departed from him.

[11] And Peter, on coming to himself, said, 'Now I know for sure that *the* Lord sent His Angel,* and he delivered me out of *the* hand of Herod and *from* all the eager anticipation of the people of the Jews.'

[12] And on realizing, he came to the house of Maria, the mother of John, surnamed Mark, where a considerable number were gathered together and praying. [13] And when Peter knocked on the door of the porch, a servant girl, Rhoda by name, came to answer, [14] and, recognizing the voice of Peter, out of gladness she did not open the porch, and she ran in *and* reported Peter to be standing in front of the porch.

[15] But they said to her, 'You're raving mad!'

But she kept strongly asserting that it was so.

Then they said, 'It's his angel.'*

[16] But Peter continued knocking, and on opening *the door* they saw him and were astounded. [17] But signalling to them with *his* hand to hold their peace, he related to them how the Lord brought him out of the jail.

And he said, 'Report these things to Jacob,* and to the brothers.'

And he departed, *and* went away to another place.

Herod struck dead
by the Angel of God

[18] And when day broke there was no small disturbance among the soldiers *over* what, as a result, had become of Peter. [19] And Herod searched up and down for him and did not find him, *and* he made examinations of the guards

and ordered *them* to be led away. And he went down from Judea to Caesarea, *and* he spent *time* there.

[20] And Herod was highly displeased with *the* Tyrians and Sidonians, but they presented themselves before him of one mind, and, having won over Blastus, who *was* in charge of the king's bedroom, they were asking for peace, because their country was nourished from the royal *supply*.

[21] And on an appointed day, Herod dressed in royal clothing and took his seat on the throne, *and* he was making an oration to them, [22] and the people were calling out, 'A voice of a god, and not of a man!'*

[23] And immediately *the* Angel of *the* Lord* struck him, because he did not give the preeminence* to God. And he was chewed by worms *and* expired.*

The oracle of God increases

[24] And the oracle of God increased and multiplied. [25] And Barnabas and Saul returned to Jerusalem *and* fulfilled the work, also taking along John, surnamed Mark.

The apostle-authorized Ekklesia in Antioch.
Paul & Barnabas separated for the nations.
In Cyprus. Elymas (Barjesus) the sorcerer

13\1 Now here and there in the Ekklesia group which was in Antioch there were certain prophets and teachers, both* Barnabas, and Simeon, who was known as Niger, and Lucius of Cyrene, and Manaen, a foster-brother* of Herod the tetrarch, and Saul.

[2] As they were serving the Lord and fasting, the Holy Spirit* said, 'Separate for me Barnabas and Saul for the work to which I have called them.'

[3] Then they fasted and prayed, and *when* they had laid hands on them, they let *them* go. [4] So being sent out by the Holy Spirit,* they went down to Seleucia, and from there they sailed off to Cyprus. [5] And when they came into Salamis, they proclaimed the oracle of God in the synagogues of the Jews. And they had John *as* an assistant as well.

[6] And they passed through the inland as far as Paphos, *and* found a certain sorcerer, a pseudo prophet,* a Jew, whose name *was* Barjesus, [7] who was with the proconsul, Sergius Paulus, an intelligent man, *and*, having called for Barnabas and Saul, he was diligently looking to hear the

oracle of God. [8] But Elymas the sorcerer* (for that is his name in translation) opposed them, intending to turn the proconsul away from the faith.

[9] But Saul (also Paul), filled with *the* divine spirit, set his eyes on him, [10] *and* said, 'Oh *you* full of every guile and all fraud!* Son of a devil!* Enemy of all righteousness! Will you not cease to pervert the straight ways of *the* Lord? [11] And now, understand, the hand of *the* Lord *is* against you, and you will be blind, not seeing the Sun for a time.'

And immediately a mist and darkness fell on him, and he went about looking for somebody to lead *him* by the hand. [12] Then the proconsul, seeing what happened, believed, being struck with astonishment at the teaching of the Lord.

Paul proclaims Jesus
in the synagogue in Antioch.
Interest of the nations in Jesus

[13] Now having loosed *anchor* from Paphos *together with* those around *him*, Paul came to Perga of Pamphylia, and John, having withdrawn from them, returned to Jerusalem. [14] But crossing from Perga, they came to Antioch of Pisidia, and they went into the synagogue on the day of the Sabbaths*, *and* they sat down. [15] And after the reading of the law and the prophets, the rulers of the synagogue sent word by authority to them, saying, 'Men, brothers, if there is any oracle of exhortation among you for the people, speak up.'

[16] And Paul rose up, and, signalling with *his* hand, said, 'Men, Israelites, and those revering God, listen. [17] The God of this people chose our fathers, and lifted up the people in *their* sojourning in *the* land of Egypt, and with a high arm He brought them out of it. [18] And about forty years *was the* time He put up with their conduct in the wilderness. [19] And having destroyed seven nations in *the* land of Canaan, He divided their land to them by lot. [20] And after these things,* He gave judges *for* about four hundred and fifty years, until the prophet Samuel. [21] And afterwards they asked for a king, and God gave them Saul, son of Cis, a man out of *the* tribe of Benjamin, *for* forty years.* [22] 'And He took him out of the way, *and* He raised up for them David for king, *and*, having given testimony to him, He also said, "I found David, the *son* of Jesse, a man after My own heart, who will carry out all My wishes."* [23]

From the seed of this *man* God brought about salvation* to Israel, in agreement with a promise,* [24] John having previously made a proclamation – in advance of *the* presence of his appearing – an identification of submission to Israel. [25] And as John was running *his* race, he said, "Whom do you suppose me to be?* I am not *he*. But, consider now, one is coming after me, the sandals of whose feet I am not worthy to loosen."*

[26] 'Men, brothers, sons of *the* race of Abraham, and those among you revering God, to you the oracle of this salvation was authorized.* [27] For those living in Jerusalem and their rulers were ignorant of this *man*, yet they fulfilled the voices of the prophets, which are read every Sabbath, when they sentenced *him*. [28] And on nobody finding a cause of death, they begged Pilate to do away with him. [29] And when they had finished everything having been written concerning him, they took him down from the tree* *and* laid *him* in a tomb. [30] 'But God raised up* from *the* dead him [31] who was seen over many days by those who came up with him from Galilee to Jerusalem, who are witnesses of him to the people. [32] And we declare to you good news, the promise which was made to the fathers, [33] that God has fulfilled this to their sons, for us, raising up* Jesus, as it has also been written in the second Psalm:

"You are My son;
this day I have generated* you."*

[34] 'But that He raised him up* from *the* dead, being no longer to return into decay, He spoke in this way:

"I will give you the assured
holy things of David."*

[35] 'So He says in another *Psalm* as well:

"You will not allow Your holy one
to see decay."*

[36] 'For David, having served his own generation through the will of God, fell asleep and was added to his fathers, and he saw decay. [37] But he whom God raised up* did not see decay.* [38] 'Let it be known to you, therefore, men, brothers, that through this *man* the forgiveness

of violations is proclaimed to you. [39] And from all things by which you were not able to be pronounced righteous in the law of Moses,* everybody believing in this one is pronounced righteous.*

[40] 'See to it, therefore, *that* that spoken* by means of the prophets might not come against yourselves:

[41] "Look, you despisers,
and marvel, and perish away,
for in your days I carry out a work
which you would certainly not believe
if anybody might declare it to you."*

Many Jews urge Paul
& Barnabas to continue

[42] But when the Jews had departed out of the synagogue, the other nations were pleading that the declarations might be spoken to them on the intervening Sabbath. [43] And *when* the synagogue meeting was broken up, many of the Jews and worshipping proselytes followed Paul and Barnabas, who were addressing *and* urging them to continue in the merciful goodwill of God.

The apostles turn to the other nations.
Jewish opposition

[44] And on the following Sabbath, almost the whole town was gathered together to hear the oracle of God. [45] But the Jews, on seeing the crowds, were filled with envy, and they contradicted* those things spoken by Paul, contradicting* and blaspheming.

[46] But Paul and Barnabas, speaking boldly, said, 'It was necessary *for* the oracle of God to be spoken to you first, but, since you reject it, and you judge yourselves not worthy of Eonian* life, see now, we turn to the other nations. [47] For the Lord has commanded this to us:

"I have appointed you
as a light to nations,
for you* to be* for salvation
as far as *the* ends of the Earth." *

[48] And the other nations* rejoiced on hearing *this*, and they magnified the oracle of the Lord, and as many having been assigned* to Eonian* life believed.

[49] And the oracle of the Lord was broadcast throughout all the region. [50] But the Jews stirred up the religious and honourable women and the eminent men of the town, and they instigated a persecution against Paul and Barnabas, and expelled them from their boundaries.

[51] But having shaken off the dust of their feet against them,* they came to Iconium, [52] and the disciples were filled with exuberance and with *the* divine spirit.

Paul & Barnabas, persecuted
in Iconium, flee to Lycaonia

14\1 And in Iconium it came about to fall on* them to enter* together into the synagogue of the Jews, and to speak* in such a way for* a large number of Jews and Greeks to believe.* [2] But the unbelieving Jews stirred up the nations and affected their minds* for malice* against the brothers.

[3] And they remained a considerable time, speaking boldly in line with the Lord, Who gave testimony to His oracle of His merciful goodwill, giving signs and wonders to take place through the agency of their hands. [4] But the multitude of the town was divided, and some held with the Jews, but others with the apostles.

[5] And when there was an assault, both of the nations and also of the Jews with their rulers, *intending* to ill-treat and stone them, [6] they came to know about *it and* they fled to Lystra and Derbe, cities of Lycaonia, and to the surrounding region. [7] And they were proclaiming the gospel there.

Healing of a crippled man at Lystra.
Objection by Jews. Paul stoned almost to death[8]

And a certain man sat in Lystra, impotent in *his* feet, being lame out of his mother's womb *and* who had never walked.

[9] This *man* heard Paul speaking, who, gazing at him, and, perceiving that he had faith to be saved, [10] said with a loud voice, 'Stand up straight on your feet.'

And he leaped and walked about.

[11] And the crowds, seeing what Paul had done, lifted up their voices, saying in the speech of Lycaonia, 'The gods have come down to us in the likeness of men.'

[12] And Barnabas they called Zeus, and Paul *they called* Hermes,* because he was the leader in speaking.

[13] Then the priest of Zeus who was *appointed* to their town brought* garlands and oxen to the

gates, and they were wanting to make a sacrifice together with the crowds.

[14] But the apostles Barnabas and Paul heard, *and* they tore their clothes, and they rushed in among the crowd, calling out, [15] and saying, 'Men! Why do you do these things? We also are men of similar passions to yourselves, proclaiming the gospel to you to turn over from these vain things to the living God, Who created Heaven and Earth and the sea, and all the things in them, [16] Who in past generations allowed all nations to walk in their own ways.*

[17] And yet He did not leave Himself without a witness, doing good things, and giving you rain from the sky,** and fruit-bearing seasons, satisfying our hearts with food and gladness.'

[18] And saying these things, they with difficulty restrained the crowds from making a sacrifice to them.

[19] But Jews came there from Antioch and Iconium, and, having persuaded the people, they stoned Paul *and* dragged *him* outside the town, reckoning him to have died. [20] But the disciples encircled him, *and* he rose up *and* went into the town, and the next day he departed with Barnabas to Derbe.

Paul & Barnabas strengthen many.
They return to the apostle-authorized
Ekklesia in Antioch

[21] And he proclaimed the gospel to that town and made a considerable number of disciples, *and* they returned to Lystra, and Iconium, and Antioch, [22] boosting the morale* of the disciples, making exhortations to continue in the faith, and that through many tribulations we must enter into the Sovereign Rulership* of God.

[23] And *when* they had designated for themselves leaders for the Ekklesia,* *and* they had prayed with fastings, they committed them to the Lord, in Whom they had believed.

[24] And they passed through Pisidia *and* came to Pamphylia. [25] And they spoke the oracle in Perga, *and* they went down into Attalia, [26] and sailed from there to Antioch, from where they had been committed to the merciful goodwill of God for the work which they fulfilled.

[27] And they arrived and gathered the Ekklesia group together, *and* they related everything that God had done with them and how He had opened a door of faith to the nations. [28] And they stayed there no brief time with the disciples.

Paul & Barnabas contradict
pseudo teachers concerning circumcision

15\1 And certain *men* came down from Judea *and* they were teaching the brothers that 'If you are not circumcised in the custom of Moses, you are not able to be saved.'

[2] Now no small disagreement and disputation arose against Paul and Barnabas, *and* concerning this question they appointed* Paul and Barnabas, and certain others from among* them who were to go up* into Jerusalem to the apostles and leaders.

[3] So being seen off on their way by the Ekklesia, they passed through Phoenicia and Samaria, fully relating the conversion of the nations, and they infused immense exuberance in all the brothers.

Barnabas & Paul return to the apostle-authorized
Ekklesia in Jerusalem. Peter & Jacob proclaim
to Pharisees in Jerusalem that God had now chosen
*for the nations to hear the gospel**

[4] On their arriving in Jerusalem, they were welcomed by the Ekklesia and by the apostles and leaders,* and they related all things which God had done with them.

[5] But some of those from the sect of the Pharisees who believed rose up saying, 'It's necessary to circumcise them, and to charge *them* to observe the law of Moses.'

[6] And the apostles and the leaders gathered together to look into this matter.

[7] And after much disputation had taken place, Peter rose up *and* said to them, 'Men, brothers, you know how from early days* God among us, through my mouth, chose *for* the nations to hear the oracle of the gospel and to believe.* [8] And the heart-knowing God gave them witness, giving them the divine spirit,* just as He *did* to us as well, [9] and He discriminated in nothing between both us and them, having cleansed their hearts through faith. [10] Now why, therefore, do you put God to the test, laying a yoke on the neck of the disciples which neither we nor our fathers had the strength to carry? [11] But we believe that, through the merciful goodwill of the Lord Jesus Christ, we will be saved in the same manner as they also *will be.*'

[12] And all the multitude kept silence and were listening to Barnabas and Paul, relating in detail what mighty signs and wonders God had

operated through them among the nations.
[13] And after they had held their peace, Jacob answered, saying, 'Men, brothers, listen to me. [14] Simon has related how God first visited the nations, to receive out of them a people for His name. [15] And with this the oracles of the prophets harmonize, as it has been written:

[16] "After these things I will return,
and I will build again the tent* of David*
which has fallen down,
and that which has been demolished
I will build up again,
and I will make it straight,
[17] so that the remainder of men,
including* all the nations
who are called by My name,
might search after the Lord,
says *the* Lord,
Who operates all these things."*

[18] 'All His creations have been known to God from of old.'* [19] Therefore, I judge not to trouble those from the nations who are turning to God, [20] but to write to them to abstain from the pollutions of idols, and fornication, and things strangled, and blood.* [21] For Moses, from ancient generations, city by city, has those proclaiming him in the synagogues, being read every Sabbath.'

[22] Then it seemed good to the apostles and to the leaders, with the whole Ekklesia group, to send into Antioch men chosen out from among themselves, along with Paul and Barnabas, Judas surnamed Barsabas, and Silas, leaders among the brothers, [23] having written this by their hand:

'The apostles and the leaders and the brothers, to those throughout Antioch and Syria and Cilicia, brothers from among *the* nations – greetings. [24] Since we heard that certain *men* having gone out from among us disturbed you with words, unsettling your minds,* directing to be circumcised and to keep the law,'' to those to whom we gave no command, [25] it seemed good to us, having become of one mind, to send you chosen men with our richly loved Barnabas and Paul, [26] men hazarding their lives on behalf of the name of our Lord Jesus Christ. [27] We have sent by authority, therefore, Judas and Silas with them, declaring the same things through an oracle. [28] For it seemed good to the

Holy Spirit* not to lay any heavier burden on us except these necessary things: [29] that you abstain from foods offered to idols, and from blood, and from things strangled, and from fornication.* In always keeping yourselves from such things you will do well. Be prospered.'*

[30] So being released into Antioch, they gathered the crowd together *and* delivered the letter, [31] and they read *it and* rejoiced over the encouragement. [32] And Judas and Silas, being themselves also prophets, exhorted the brothers with many words and they strengthened *them.* [33] And after continuing for some time, they were released with peace from the brothers to the apostles. [34] [*no verse 34 in RP Greek text*]* [35] But Paul and Barnabas remained in Antioch, teaching and proclaiming the oracle of the Lord, with many others as well.

Sharp dispute between Paul & Barnabas.
Paul strengthens the apostle-authorized
Ekklesia in Syria & Cilicia
[36] But after a few days, Paul said to Barnabas, 'Let us turn back and visit our brothers in every town in which we proclaimed the oracle of the Lord, *to see* how they are holding up.'
[37] And Barnabas purposed to take along John, known as Mark. [38] But Paul reckoned it right not to take him who had fallen away from them in Pamphylia, and he did not travel with them for the work. [39] Then a sharp feeling* arose,* so as to separate them from each other, Barnabas taking Mark to sail away to Cyprus, [40] but Paul chose Silas *and* departed, after being committed by the brothers to the merciful goodwill of God. [41] And he passed through Syria and Cilicia, strengthening the Ekklesia groups.

Timothy joins Paul & Silas in strengthening
the apostle-authorized Ekklesia groups
16\1 **A**nd he arrived in Derbe and Lystra, and there was a certain disciple there, Timothy by name,* son of a certain Jewish woman, a believer, but of a Greek father, [2] who was of good reputation* among the brothers who were in Lystra and Iconium. [3] Paul wanted him to go with him, and he took *him and* had him circumcised on account of the Jews who were in those places, for they all knew that his father was a Greek.
[4] And as they were going through the cities, they delivered to them the decrees to guard,

those things decided on by the apostles and the leaders in Jerusalem. ⁵ So the Ekklesia groups were strengthened in the faith, and they increased in number daily.

They go to Macedonia.
Lydia converted at Philippi
⁶ Having passed through the Phrygian and the Galatian country, *and*, having been not permitted by the Holy Spirit* to proclaim the oracle in Asia, ⁷ on coming down to Mysia they were attempting to go into Bithynia,* but the Spirit* would not permit them.
⁸ And after passing through Mysia, they came down into Troas, ⁹ and during the night a vision was seen by Paul: a certain man, a Macedonian, was standing praying, and saying, 'Come over into Macedonia and help us.'
¹⁰ And when he saw the vision, we immediately got ready to go into Macedonia, concluding* that the Lord had called us* to proclaim the gospel to them. ¹¹ So after sailing from Troas, we ran with a straight course to Samothracia, and the next day to Neapolis, ¹² and from there to Philippi, which is *the* principal of the district, a town of Macedonia, a *Roman* colony, and we stayed in the town itself for several days.
¹³ And on the Day of the *Festival of* Weeks,* we went outside the town beside a river, where it was customary for prayer to take place,* and we sat down *and* spoke to the gathering women. ¹⁴ And a certain woman named Lydia, a seller of purple, of *the* town of Thyatira, who worshipped God, heard, *and* the Lord opened her heart to be attentive to the things spoken by Paul.
¹⁵ And when she had been identified,* as well as her household, she made an invitation, saying, 'If you have judged me to be believing in the Lord, come to my house *and* stay.'
And she urged us.

Healing of a girl with a spirit of Python.*
Paul & Silas imprisoned
¹⁶ And it so happened, as we were going to prayer, *that* a certain servant girl who had a spirit of Python met us,* who brought her masters much gain by fortune telling. ¹⁷ She followed Paul and us around, *and* she called out, saying, 'These men are the servants of the Most High God, who proclaim to us a road of salvation.'
¹⁸ And she was doing this for many days, but

Paul, having become annoyed, turned and said to the spirit, 'I charge you in the name of Jesus Christ to come out of her.'
And it came out at that same moment.
¹⁹ And her masters, seeing that the hope of their income had gone, seized Paul and Silas, *and* dragged *them* into the marketplace to the authorities, ²⁰ and, bringing them to the magistrates, they said, 'These men, being Jews, severely disturb our town, ²¹ and proclaim customs which it is not lawful for us, being Romans, to receive or to practice.'
²² And the crowd rose up together against them, and the magistrates tore off their clothes *and* gave an order to have *them* beaten with rods. ²³ And *when* they had beaten them with many stripes they threw *them* into jail, charging the jailer to keep them securely, ²⁴ who, having received such a charge, threw them in the inner jail, and fastened their feet in stocks.

Paul & Silas praising God are freed
by an earthquake. Jailer converted
²⁵ And towards midnight, Paul and Silas were praying *and* singing songs* to God, and the prisoners were listening to them. ²⁶ And suddenly a violent earthquake came so that the foundations of the jail were shaken, and immediately all the doors were opened and everybody's shackles were loosened.* ²⁷ And the jailer, having become roused out of sleep, and seeing the doors of the jail opened, drew out his sword *and* was about to kill himself, supposing that the prisoners had escaped.
²⁸ But Paul called out with a loud voice, saying, 'Do no injury to yourself, for we are all here.'
²⁹ And he asked for lamps, *and* he rushed in and fell down in a tremble before Paul and Silas, ³⁰ and he brought them outside *and* said, 'Sirs, what is it necessary for me to do so that I might be saved?'
³¹ And they said, 'Believe in the Lord Jesus Christ, and you will be saved, you and your house.'
³² And they spoke to him the oracle of the Lord, and to all those in his house. ³³ And having taken them along at the same hour of the night, he washed off their wounds, and he was identified, he and all his household, straightaway. ³⁴ And he brought them into his house *and* placed a meal* before them, and he rejoiced, the whole household having believed God.*

³⁵ And on day having risen, the magistrates dispatched* the floggers* saying, 'Release those men.'
³⁶ And the jailer reported these words to Paul: 'The magistrates have authorized that you might be released. So now, go out and depart in peace.'
³⁷ But Paul said to them, 'After lashing us publicly, without investigation, *we* being Roman men, they threw *us* into jail. And now, are they going to secretly throw us out* themselves?* Certainly not! Rather, let them come themselves and lead us out.'
³⁸ And the floggers* reported these words to the magistrates, and they were alarmed, hearing that they were Romans. ³⁹ And *they* came and apologized to them, and on leading *them* out they asked *them* to get out of the town. ⁴⁰ And they came out of the jail *and* went to Lydia, and, seeing the brothers, they exhorted them and departed.

Paul & Silas proclaim Jesus in the synagogue at Thessalonica & many believe, including Greeks. Jewish objection

17\1 Now they passed through Amphipolis and Apollonia, *and* they came to Thessalonica where there was a synagogue of the Jews. ² And in keeping with what was customary with Paul, he went in among them, and for three Sabbaths he reasoned with them from the Scrolls, ³ explaining and bringing evidence that it was necessary for the Christ to have suffered and to have risen from *the* dead, and that 'This is the Christ – Jesus, whom I proclaim to you.'
⁴ And some from among them were convinced, and threw in their lot with Paul and Silas, as well as a large number of people of the worshipping Greeks, and not a few of the leading women. ⁵ But the unbelieving Jews took along certain market loungers, evil men, gathered up a mob, and roused the town into an uproar, and on coming to the house of Jason they were looking to bring them out to the people.
⁶ But on not finding them, they dragged Jason and certain brothers before the rulers of the town,* calling out, 'Those who have turned the habitable world upside down* *are* these present right* here, ⁷ whom Jason has received, and these practise* everything contrary to the decrees of Caesar, claiming there to be* another* king, Jesus.'

⁸ And they agitated the crowd and the rulers of the town* hearing these things. ⁹ And after taking bail security from Jason and from the rest, they released them.

They make proclamation in the synagogue at Berea. Noble-minded Bereans. Many believe, including Greek women & men. Jewish objection

¹⁰ And during the night the brothers immediately sent Paul and Silas away to Berea, who, on arriving, went into the synagogue of the Jews. ¹¹ And these were more noble-minded* than those in Thessalonica, who received the oracle with all readiness of mind, closely examining the Scrolls daily, whether these things held up that way. ¹² Then many from among them believed, as well as not a few of the honourable Greek women and men.
¹³ But when the Jews from Thessalonica came to know that the oracle of God was proclaimed by Paul in Berea as well, they came there too, shaking up the crowds. ¹⁴ And then immediately the brothers sent Paul away as if to go out towards the sea, but Silas and Timothy remained there.
¹⁵ But those conducting Paul brought him to Athens, and, having received an order for Silas and Timothy to come to him as quickly as possible, they left.

Paul proclaims Jesus in Athens
¹⁶ Now *while* Paul waited for them in Athens, his spirit was stirred in him on seeing the city full of idols. ¹⁷ So he was reasoning in the synagogue with the Jews and those who worshipped, and in the marketplace daily among those chancing to be there.
¹⁸ And also some philosophers of the Epicureans and of the Stoics engaged him in conversation, and some said, 'What might this babbler* want to say?', and others, 'He seems to be a proclaimer of foreign* demons.'
They said these things because he proclaimed the gospel of Jesus and the resurrection.
¹⁹ And they took him along *and* brought *him* to the Ares Hill,* saying, 'May we know what *is* this new teaching which is being spoken by you? ²⁰ For you bring some startling things to our ears, so we want to know what you suppose these things to mean.'*
²¹ For all the Athenians and the inhabiting foreigners* spent their time in nothing else but telling or hearing about some latest matter.

²² Then Paul, standing at a central point of Mars Hill, said, 'Men of Athens, I perceive you are demon-fearing* in all things. ²³ For in *my* passing by and making observation of the objects of your worship,* I found also an altar on which had been inscribed "To an unknown God". The one, therefore, Whom you worship in ignorance, I declare Him to you.

²⁴ 'The God having created the world and all things in it, He being Lord of Heaven and Earth, does not inhabit shrines made with hands. ²⁵ Nor is He served by hands of men, as if needing something, He Himself giving life and breath to all things.* ²⁶ And He has made every nation of men out of one blood, to live over all the face of the Earth, marking out* in advance *the* times appointed,* and the boundaries of their residence,* ²⁷ to search out the Lord, if they might at least reach out for Him and find Him, even though being not far from each one of us. ²⁸ For by Him we live, and move, and have our being. As also some of your poets have said, "For we also* are His offspring".

²⁹ 'Being, then, the offspring of God, we ought not to reckon that which is* divine* to be* like gold, or silver, or stone, or an engraving* of art and the thought* of man. ³⁰ So God, having turned a blind eye to* the times of ignorance, now charges all men everywhere to submit, ³¹ because He has appointed a day* in which He is about to rule over* the habitable world in righteousness* through *the* man* whom He declared,* having given assurance to all, having raised him from *the* dead.'*

³² But on hearing of a resurrection of *the* dead, some were ridiculing, and others said, 'We will hear you again concerning this.'

³³ So Paul departed from their presence.

³⁴ But some men joining themselves to him believed, among whom *was* also Dionysius the Areopagite, as well as a woman, Damaris by name, and others with them.

Paul proclaims Jesus in the synagogue
in Corinth. Jews & Greeks believe.
Pronouncement by Paul of turning to the nations

18\1 After these things Paul departed from Athens, *and* he came into Corinth. ² And finding a certain Jew, Aquila by name, born in Pontus, having recently arrived from Italy with his wife Priscilla because Claudius had ordered all the Jews to get out of Rome, he attached *himself* to them.

³ And being* of the same trade, he was staying and working with them, for they were tent-makers in their craft. ⁴ And he reasoned in the synagogue Sabbath by Sabbath, and he was persuading Jews and Greeks.

⁵ Now when both Silas and Timothy came down from Macedonia, Paul was pressed by *the* Spirit,* giving solemn testimony* to the Jews *that* Jesus *is* the Christ.

⁶ But as they set themselves in opposition and blasphemed, he shook his garments *and* said to them, 'Your blood be on your heads! I am blameless. From now on, I will go to the other nations.'*

⁷ And he departed from there, *and* he went into the house of a certain Justus by name, who worshipped God, *and* whose house was adjoined to the synagogue. ⁸ But Crispus, the president of the synagogue, believed in the Lord, together with his whole household, and *when* many of the Corinthians heard they believed, and they were identified.

⁹ Then the Lord spoke to Paul through a vision* in *the* night: 'Do not be afraid, but speak out, and do not hold your silence. ¹⁰ For I am with you, and nobody will attack you to harm you, for there are many people for me in this town.'

¹¹ And he remained for a year and six months, teaching the oracle of God among them.

Paul accused before Gallio. Sosthenes beaten

¹² But *when* Gallio was proconsul of Achaia, the Jews rose up in one mind against Paul, and brought him before the judgement seat, ¹³ saying, 'This *man* persuades men to worship God, contrary to the law.'

¹⁴ But on Paul's being about to open *his* mouth, Gallio said to the Jews, 'If, then, you Jews, it was some injustice or nefarious criminality,* there would be a reason for me to bear hearing* you. ¹⁵ But if it's a question about a word and names, and a law among you, you see to it yourselves, for I do not intend to be* a judge of those things.'

¹⁶ And he dismissed them from the judgement seat. ¹⁷ Then all the Greeks seized Sosthenes, the president of the synagogue, *and* beat *him* in front of the judgement seat. But none of these things was of any concern to Gallio.

From town to town Paul
strengthens disciples
in the Ekklesia groups

[18] But Paul still stayed on for many days, *then* he took leave of the brothers *and* sailed away into Syria, also *taking* Priscilla and Aquila with him. He had shorn *his* head in Cenchreae because he had made a vow.

[19] And he came into Ephesus and left them there, but he himself went into the synagogue *and* conversed with the Jews.

[20] And *when* they asked *him* to stay for a longer time with them, he would not consent, [21] but left them, saying, 'I must without fail keep this coming Festival in Jerusalem, but I will bend back* *my steps* to you again, God being willing.'

He sailed away from Ephesus, [22] and, having landed at Caesarea and gone up and greeted the Ekklesia, he descended to Antioch. [23] After staying some time, he left, successively passing through the Galatian area and Phrygia, strengthening all the disciples.

Apollos instructed by
Aquila & Priscilla at Ephesus

[24] And a certain Jew named Apollos, Alexandrian by race, an eloquent man, mighty in the Scrolls, came into Ephesus. [25] This *man* was instructed in the way of the Lord, and, being fervent in spirit, he spoke and taught accurately the things concerning the Lord, knowing only the identification of John.

[26] And he began to speak boldly in the synagogue, and *when* they had heard him Aquila and Priscilla took him aside and expounded to him more accurately the way of God.

[27] And on his being minded to pass through into Achaia, the brothers urged *him** on and they wrote to the disciples to receive him who, *when* he arrived, had tremendously helped those who believed through merciful goodwill, [28] for he vigorously confuted* the Jews in public, demonstrating, through the Scrolls, Jesus to be* the Christ.*

Paul's work in the apostle-authorized
Ekklesia in Ephesus
(Eph. 1\1-2, Rev. 2\1-7).
About 12 men receive the divine spirit

19\1 **A**nd it so happened, in Apollos's* being* in Corinth, *that* Paul passed through the upper regions *and* came into Ephesus, and on finding certain disciples [2] he said to them, 'Have you received *the* divine spirit, having believed?'

And they said to him, 'No, we have not even heard if there is *any* divine spirit.'

[3] And he said to them, 'Into what, then, were you identified?'

And they said, 'Into the identification of John.'

[4] Then Paul said, 'John identified an identification of submission, speaking to the people that they should believe in him coming after him, that is, in the Christ, Jesus.'

[5] And *when* they had heard, they were identified into the name of the Lord Jesus. [6] And *when* Paul laid hands on them, *the* divine spirit came* on them, and they were speaking with foreign languages and prophesying. [7] And all the men were about twelve.

Paul proclaims Jesus
in the synagogue at Ephesus

[8] And he went into the synagogue, *and* he spoke boldly over three months, reasoning and persuading about the things concerning the Sovereign Rulership* of God. [9] But when some were hardened and unbelieving, speaking evil about the Way before the crowd, *he* departed from them *and* separated the disciples, reasoning daily in the lecture hall of a certain Tyrannus.

[10] And this happened over two years, so that all the inhabitants of Asia heard the oracle of the Lord Jesus, both Jews and Greeks.

Miracles through Paul.
Jewish exorcists beaten
by an evil spirit. Books burned

[11] And God was operating extraordinary miracles through the hands of Paul, [12] so that even sweat cloths or gowns from his skin were placed on the sick as well, and the diseases departed from them, and the evil spirits went out from them.

[13] Then some of the vagabond Jewish exorcists took it in hand to call the name of the Lord Jesus over those who had the evil spirits, saying, 'We adjure you through Jesus, whom Paul proclaims.'

[14] And there were certain *men*, seven sons of Sceva, a Jew, a chief priest, who were doing this.

[15] But in response, the evil spirit said, 'Jesus I know, and Paul I am acquainted with, but you,*

who are you?'
¹⁶ And the man in whom there was the evil spirit leaped on them and overpowered them, *and* he prevailed over them, so that they escaped out of that house unclothed and injured. ¹⁷ And this became known to all, both Jews and Greeks living in Ephesus, and fear came over them all, and the name of the Lord Jesus was magnified.
¹⁸ And many of those who believed came, pouring out and declaring their practices. ¹⁹ And a considerable number of those also who practiced magic arts collected their Scrolls* together *and* burned them up in the presence of everybody, and they reckoned up the price of them and found 50,000* *pieces* of silver. ²⁰ In this way the oracle of the Lord** increased with might and was strong.

Opposition to Paul from Demetrius
²¹ And as soon as these things were accomplished, Paul, having passed through Macedonia and Achaia, purposed in spirit to go into Jerusalem, saying, 'After my being* there, I must see Rome as well.'
²² So he sent by authority into Macedonia two of those who provided for him, Timothy and Erastus, but he stayed on *for* a time in Asia.
²³ And about that time a no small disturbance arose concerning the Way. ²⁴ For a certain Demetrius by name, a silversmith making silver shrines of Artemis,* brought no small income to the craftsmen, ²⁵ who, having gathered together with the workmen concerning such things, said, 'Men, you know that this prosperity is from our trade. ²⁶ And you see and hear that not only *those* of Ephesus but almost all of Asia this *man* Paul has persuaded, *and* he has led adrift* a large throng, saying that what are made by hands are no gods. ²⁷ Now not only is this dangerous to us, in case our craft should come into discredit, but the temple of the sacred* goddess Artemis might also be counted for nothing, and her magnificence also might be about to be taken down, whom all Asia and the habitable world worships.'*
²⁸ And having heard and become full of boiling anger, they were calling out, saying, 'Sacred *is* the Artemis of *the* Ephesians!'
²⁹ And the city was filled with confusion, and they rushed with one mind into the theatre,* keeping a firm grip on Gaius and Aristarchus, Macedonian fellow travellers of Paul.
³⁰ Paul was intending to go into the mob, but

the disciples would not let him. ³¹ Even some of the rulers of Asia as well, who were his friends, sent word to him exhorting *him* not to present himself in the theatre.* ³² So some were shouting out one thing, and some another, for the assembly* was confounded, and the majority did not realize for what reason they had come together.
³³ And they dragged Alexander* from among the people, the Jews thrusting him forward, and Alexander, indicating a signal with a hand, purposed to make a defence to the mob, ³⁴ but, on their finding out that he was a Jew, a unified* voice came out of everybody for about two hours screaming out, 'Sacred *is* Artemis of *the* Ephesians!'
³⁵ And *when* the recorder had calmed the crowd, he said, 'Men, Ephesians, what man is there who does not know the town of *the* Ephesians as being temple-keepers of the sacred goddess Artemis, and of the *image* fallen down from Zeus? ³⁶ These things, then, being indisputable, it is needful for you to be calmed and to do nothing reckless. ³⁷ For you have brought these men who are neither robbers of temples,* nor are they speaking evil of your goddess.
³⁸ 'If, then, Demetrius and the craftsmen who are with him have a case against anybody, courts are held, and there are proconsuls. Let them press charges against each other. ³⁹ If, though, you diligently search anything concerning other matters, it will be resolved in the legislative assembly.** ⁴⁰ For we also are in danger of being called into question concerning this day's insurrection, although there is no case about which we will not be able to give an account for this disorderly gathering.'
⁴¹ And *when* he had said these things, he dissolved the assembly.*

*Paul encourages disciples
in Macedonia & Greece*

20\1 **N**ow after the racket had ceased, Paul called the disciples and embraced *them, and* departed to go off into Macedonia.
² And *when* he had passed through those parts and exhorted them with many words, he came into Greece ³ and spent three months there.
On a plot by the Jews arising against him, at his being about to sail away to Syria, he became minded to return through Macedonia. ⁴ And Sopater, a Berean, was accompanying him as far

---

as Asia; and of the Thessalonians, *there were* Aristarchus and Secundus; and Gaius of Derbe, and Timothy; and of Asia, Tychicus and Trophimus. [5] Those going on ahead were waiting for us* in Troas.

[6] But after the days of Unleavened Bread, we sailed away from Philippi, and we came to them at Troas in five days, where we stayed *for* seven days.

At Troas, Eutychus falls through a window & is raised by Paul

[7] And on the First of Weeks,* the disciples were assembled together to break bread, *and* Paul reasoned with them, *and*, being about to depart in the morning, he was extending the discourse until midnight. [8] And there were many lamps in the upper room where we were assembled, [9] and a certain youth, Eutychus by name, was sitting by the window, *and* he was overpowered by a deep sleep (Paul having reasoned for longer still), *and*, being overborne from the sleep, he fell down from the third storey, and was taken up dead.

[10] And Paul went down and fell on him, and, embracing *him*, he said, 'Do not trouble yourselves, for his life is in him.'

[11] And he went up again and broke bread, and ate, and he conversed for a considerable time until the break of day, *and* then he departed. [12] And they brought the boy in alive, and were not a little comforted.

Paul journeys from Troas to Miletus

[13] And we* arrived and pressed ahead on the boat *and* sailed to Assos *as* we were about to receive Paul on board there, for that is what he had arranged, being himself about to go by foot. [14] And when he met with us at Assos, we took him in *and* came to Mitylene. [15] And we sailed away from there the next *day and* arrived *in waters* facing Chios. The next *day* we arrived in Samos, and after staying in Trogyllium the next *day* we came to Miletus. [16] For Paul had decided to sail past Ephesus, so that it might not fall on him to wear away time in Asia, for he was hurrying on, if it might be possible for him to arrive in Jerusalem for the Day of Pentecost.

Paul drawn to Jerusalem by the Angel of God (20\22). Paul instructs the apostle-authorized & God-authorized Ephesian leaders

that oppressive wolves will come (20\29)

[17] And from Miletus, after having sent word to Ephesus, he called for the leaders of the Ekklesia.

[18] And when they presented themselves to him, he said to them, 'You know how, from the first day on which I arrived in Asia, I have been with you all the time, [19] serving the Lord with all humility, and with many tears and trials* which befell me in the plots of the Jews, [20] *and* how I kept back nothing of the things profitable, as if to not declare* it to you, and to teach you publicly, and from house to house,* [21] testifying both to Jews and Greeks submission towards God, and faith towards our Lord Jesus.

[22] 'And now, look,* I go shackled by the Spirit* into Jerusalem, not knowing what things will befall me there,* [23] but only that the Holy Spirit* makes testimony in every town, saying that shackles and tribulations await me.

[24] 'But I make my life of no account, nor do I count *it* precious to myself, so as to finish with exuberance my course and the office which I received from the Lord Jesus, to give full testimony of the gospel of the merciful goodwill of God.

[25] 'And now, look, I know that all of you among whom I have gone about proclaiming the Sovereign Rulership* of God will no longer see my face. [26] Therefore, I solemnly affirm* to you this day that I am clear from the blood of everyone. [27] For I have not shrunk back from declaring to you all the counsel of God.* [28] Be watchful over yourselves, therefore, and to all the flock over* whom the Holy Spirit* has appointed you overseers, to shepherd the Ekklesia of the Lord and God which He has gained possession of by means of His own blood.*

[29] 'For I know this, that after my departure oppressive* wolves will come in among* you, not sparing the flock.* [30] And from among your own selves men will rise up speaking perverted things to draw away the disciples after themselves. [31] So watch, remembering that night and day for three years I did not cease admonishing each one with tears.

[32] 'And now, brothers, I commit you to God, and to the oracle of His merciful goodwill which is able to build you up, and to give you an inheritance among all those having been sanctified.* [33] I have desired silver, or gold, or fine clothing of nobody. [34] You yourselves

know that these hands provided for my necessities, and for those who were with me. ³⁵ I showed you all things, how, toiling in this way, you ought to support the weak, and to remember the oracle of the Lord Jesus, how he himself said, "It is more happy* to give than to receive." '

³⁶ And *when* he had said these things, *he* bowed his knees and prayed with them all. ³⁷And there was much weeping by everybody. And falling on Paul's neck, they ardently kissed him, ³⁸ grieving most of all* over the oracle which he had spoken that they were about to see his face no more. Then they accompanied him to the boat.

Paul not dissuaded from going to Jerusalem.
Prophecy concerning his fate there.
Willingness to die (before the offer to him
of the high calling of God, Phil. 3\14)

21\1 ᴀnd when it came to *the time* to sail away, *after* our having launched away from them, we came by a straight course to Cos, and the *day* following to Rhodes, and from there to Patara, ² and, finding a boat sailing over to Phoenicia, we embarked and launched off. ³ Then having come in sight of Cyprus, and going off from it on *the* left, we sailed into Syria and made a stop at Tyre, for the boat was discharging the cargo there. ⁴ And *when* we had found disciples, we* remained there for seven days, *and* they told Paul through the agency of* the Spirit* not to go up to Jerusalem. ⁵ But when it came about for us to complete the days *there*, we made our departure *and* set off on our way, everybody with wives and children bringing us on our way, as far as the outskirts of the city. And kneeling down on the shore, we prayed, ⁶ and when we had taken our leave of one another we boarded the ship, and they returned to their own *homes.* ⁷ And *when* we had finished the voyage from Tyre, we arrived at Ptolemais, and *after* greeting the brothers we stayed with them one day. ⁸ And the next *day* Paul and those around him departed *and* came to Caesarea, and we entered the house of Philip, the proclaimer of the gospel,* *who* was among the seven, *and* we stayed with him. ⁹ Now this *man* had four daughters, virgins, who prophesied. ¹⁰ Then during our staying over extra days, a certain prophet, Agabus by name, came down from Judea, ¹¹ and *when* he came to us *he* took

Paul's belt and shackled his own feet and hands, and he said, 'The Holy Spirit* says this: "Likewise will the Jews in Jerusalem bind the man who owns this belt, and they will give *him* into *the* hands of *the* nations." '

¹² And when we heard these things, both we* and the locals were begging him not to go up into Jerusalem.

¹³ Then Paul answered, 'What are you doing, weeping and crushing my heart? For I hold myself in readiness not only to be shackled, but to die as well in Jerusalem* for the name of the Lord Jesus.'

¹⁴ And *when* he would not be persuaded, we were silent, saying, 'The will of the Lord be accomplished.'

Paul in Jerusalem. Rejoicing
at his report concerning the nations.
Decision concerning Mosaic statutes

¹⁵ And after those days, we made our preparations* *and* went up into Jerusalem. ¹⁶ And *some* of the disciples from Caesarea accompanied us as well, bringing somebody with them whom we might lodge with, a certain Mnason, a Cypriot, an experienced disciple.

¹⁷ And when we arrived in Jerusalem, the brothers gladly received us. ¹⁸ And the following *day* Paul went in with us to Jacob, and all the leading men were assembled, ¹⁹ and *when* he had greeted them he related in detail what things God performed among the nations through his office.

²⁰ And *when* they heard, they were magnifying the Lord, and they said to him, 'You see, brother, how many tens of thousands* of Jews there are who have believed, and they are all zealous for the law. ²¹ And they were instructed concerning you that you teach all the Jews who are among the nations an apostasy* from Moses, telling them that they ought not to circumcise the children, nor to walk by the customs.*

²² 'What is this, then? The crowd are certainly bound to band together, for they will hear that you have come. ²³ So do this which we are saying to you. There are four men with us *who* have made a vow over themselves. ²⁴ Take these *men*, and be purified with them, and incur expenses for them, so that they will shave *their* heads, and everybody will know that those things of which they were told about you are nothing, but *that* you yourself walk well and you keep the law.

²⁵ 'But concerning the other nations who

believe, we have written *and* concluded that they observe no such thing, except only that they keep themselves from *things* offered to idols, and from blood, and from things strangled, and from fornication.'

²⁶ Then Paul took the men, and the next day, *after* being purified with them, they went into the Temple with them, declaring the fulfilment of the Days of the Purification, until the offering should be made for each one of them.

Paul arrested in the Temple

²⁷ But when the seven days were about to be completed, the Jews from Asia, having seen him in the Temple, excited all the crowd and gripped their hands on him, ²⁸ calling out, 'Men, Israelites, help! This is the man who teaches everyone everywhere against the people and the law and this place, and, in addition, he brought Greeks into the Temple, and he has defiled this holy place.'

²⁹ For they had noticed Trophimus the Ephesian with him in the town, whom, they concluded, Paul had brought into the Temple. ³⁰ And the whole town was stirred up, and there was a concourse of the people, and they seized Paul and dragged him outside the Temple, and the doors were shut immediately. ³¹ And as they were looking to murder him, a report came to the military commander of the cohort, so that all Jerusalem was in commotion, ³² who, immediately taking along soldiers and centurions, ran down to them, and on their seeing the military commander and the soldiers they left off beating Paul.

³³ Then the military commander drew near *and* took hold of him and ordered *him* to be shackled with two chains, and he enquired who he might be and what he had been doing. ³⁴ But some among the crowd were calling out one thing and some other things, and, not being able to ascertain the truth on account of the uproar, he ordered him to be brought into the barracks. ³⁵ And when he came onto the stairs, it came about that he was carried by the soldiers because of the violence of the people, ³⁶ since the mob of the people followed, calling out, 'Away with him!'

³⁷ But *as* Paul was about to be brought into the barracks, he said to the military commander, 'Is it permitted for me to speak to you?'

But he said, 'Do you know Greek? ³⁸ Are you not, then, the Egyptian who, before these days, stirred up a riot,* and led out into the

desert four thousand men of cut-throats?"*

³⁹ But Paul said, 'I am in fact a Jewish man, a Tarsean of Cilicia, a citizen* of a town not without distinction, and, I implore you, allow me to speak to the people.'

⁴⁰ And *when* he had given *him* licence, Paul, standing on the stairs, indicated to the people a signal with a hand, and when a long silence had fallen, he made an address in the Hebrew dialect, saying,

22\1 'Men, brothers, and fathers, now hear my defence to you."*

² And *when* they heard that he had addressed them in the Hebrew dialect, they showed more silence, and he said, ³ 'I am in fact a Jewish man, born in Tarsus of Cilicia, but brought up in this town at the feet of Gamaliel, having been instructed in keeping with exactness of the ancestral law, being a zealot towards God, just as you all are this day. ⁴ I persecuted this Way as far as death,* binding and delivering both men and women into jails. ⁵ As also the high priest bears me witness – and the whole council of the elders, from whom also I received letters to the brothers – I was going into Damascus to bring those who were also there shackled into Jerusalem, so that they could be punished.

⁶ 'And it came about for me, as I was making my journey and drawing near Damascus* around midday, *that* suddenly a bright light out of the sky flashed around me. ⁷ And I fell to the ground and heard a voice saying to me, "Saul, Saul, why do you persecute me?" ⁸ And I answered, "Who are you, Sir?"* And he said to me, "I am Jesus, the Nazarene** whom you persecute." ⁹ And those who were with me actually saw the light themselves, and they became alarmed, although they did not hear the voice of him speaking to me.

¹⁰ 'And I said, "What shall I do, Lord?" And the Lord said to me, "Rise up *and* go into Damascus, and there everything will be described to you concerning what has been appointed* *for* you to do." ¹¹ But as I was unable to see because of the dazzle of that light, I was led by the hand by those accompanying me, *and* I came into Damascus.

¹² 'And a certain Ananias, a devout man in respect of the law, having a good reputation* among all the resident Jews, ¹³ came to me and stood beside me *and* said, "Brother Saul, recover your sight." And in the same moment I recovered my sight, *I looked* at him, ¹⁴ and he

said, "The God of our fathers has appointed you to know His will and to see the Righteous One, and to hear a voice out of his *own* mouth, [15] for you will be a witness for him to all men of the things which you have seen and heard. [16] And now, why are you lingering? Rise up, *and* be identified, and wash away your violations, calling on the name of the Lord."

[17] 'And *when* I returned to Jerusalem, it came about for me, *while* I was praying in the Temple, to be* in an ecstasy* [18] and to see him saying to me, "Hurry, and go quickly out of Jerusalem, for they will not receive your testimony concerning me." [19] And I said, "Lord, they themselves know that from synagogue to synagogue I was imprisoning and lashing those who believed in you, [20] and when the blood of your witness Stephen was being poured out I myself was also standing by and consenting to his murder, while I was guarding the garments of those who murdered him." [21] And he said to me, "Go your way, for I will send you to nations far away." '

Paul's appeal to his Roman citizenship

[22] And they were listening to him until this oracle, and *then* they lifted up their voices, saying, 'Away from the Earth with such *a man*, for it's not fitting that he should live!'* [23] And as they were calling out, and tearing off outer garments, and tossing* dust into the air,* [24] the military commander ordered him to be brought into the barracks, *and* he issued an order for him to be interrogated by scourges,* so that he might discover why they were shouting at him like that.

[25] But as he stretched him out with straps, Paul said to the centurion who stood by, 'Is it lawful for you to scourge a Roman man, and uncondemned?'

[26] And *when* the centurion heard, he went *and* reported to the military commander, saying, 'Watch what you are about to do, for this man is a Roman.'

[27] Then the military commander came and said to him, 'Tell me, are you a Roman?'

And he said, 'Yes.'

[28] And the military commander answered, 'I bought this citizenship* with a vast price.'

Paul, though, said, 'But I was even born *a Roman.*'

[29] Then those being about to interrogate him at once stood away from him, and even the military commander was fearful, having

ascertained that he was a Roman, as well as for the fact that* he had shackled him.

Paul before the Sanhedrin

[30] And the next day, wanting to know the details of what matters he was accused of by the Jews, he loosed him from the shackles and ordered the senior priests and their whole Sanhedrin to come, and he brought Paul down and stood before them.

23\1 And Paul, looking intently at the Sanhedrin,* said, 'Men, brothers, I have expressed my character* in all good conscience to God until this day.'

[2] But the high priest Ananias ordered those standing by him to strike him on the mouth.

[3] Then Paul said to him, 'God is about to strike you, whitewashed wall! And do you sit judging me according to the law, and order me to be struck, acting against the law?'

[4] And those who stood by said, 'Do you revile the high priest of God?'

[5] And Paul said, 'I was not conscious, brothers, that he was a high priest, for it has been written: "You shall not speak evil of a ruler of your people." '*

[6] Now *when* Paul came to know that one section were Sadducees, and the other Pharisees, he called out in the Sanhedrin, 'Men, brothers, I am a Pharisee, son of a Pharisee. Concerning a hope and resurrection of *the* dead I am being called into question.'

[7] And when he had spoken this, a discord arose with the Pharisees,* and the crowd was divided. [8] For Sadducees allege there not in fact to be* a resurrection,* nor even angel nor spirit,* but Pharisees profess both.

[9] And a loud clamour* arose, and the scribes of the division of the Pharisees' rose up *and* were arguing vigorously, saying, 'We find nothing evil in this man, but if a spirit or an angel has spoken to him, we should not fight against God.'

[10] And on a serious discord having arisen, the military commander, fearing in case Paul might be torn in pieces by them, ordered the soldiers to go down *and* to take him by force out of their presence, and to bring *him* into the barracks.

[11] But the following night the Lord stood by him and said, 'Take courage, Paul, for just as you have given full testimony concerning me in Jerusalem, so must you bring witness in Rome

as well.'

*Over 40 Jews vow to taste nothing
until they murder Paul,
but get found out by Paul's nephew*

¹² And *when* it was day, some of the Jews made a conspiracy, *and* bound themselves under a curse,˙ declaring to neither eat˙ nor drink until they had murdered Paul.
¹³ Now there were more than forty making this conspiracy, ¹⁴ who, making an approach to the senior priests and leaders, said, 'With a curse˙ we have cursed ourselves˙ to taste nothing until we have killed Paul. ¹⁵ Now, therefore, you signify to the military commander with the Sanhedrin that he bring him down to you tomorrow as if being about to diagnoze more accurately the things about him. Then, before his approach, we are ready to kill him.'
¹⁶ But *when* the son of Paul's sister heard of their lying in wait, he came up and went into the barracks and reported *it* to Paul.
¹⁷ Then Paul called one of the centurions and said, 'Take this young man to the military commander, for he has something to report to him.'
¹⁸ So he took him *and* brought *him* to the military commander, and he said, 'The prisoner Paul˙ called me, *and* he asked me to lead to you this young man, having something to say to you.'
¹⁹ Then the military commander took him by the hand, and, drawing *him* aside privately, enquired, 'What is *it* that you have to report to me?'
²⁰ And he said, 'The Jews agreed to ask you that you would bring Paul down into the Sanhedrin tomorrow, as though you are about to enquire into something about him more accurately. ²¹ So do not be persuaded by them, for more than forty men among them lie in wait for him, who bound themselves under a curse˙ to neither eat˙ nor drink until they have murdered him, and now they are ready, waiting for the promise from you.'

Paul sent to the governor Felix in Caesarea
²² So the military commander sent the young man away, and ordered, 'You are to utter to nobody that you have reported these things to me.'
²³ And after calling for two of the centurions, he said, 'Prepare two hundred soldiers to go to

Caesarea, and seventy horsemen, and two hundred spearmen, from the third hour of the night, ²⁴ and to provide animals so that they could set Paul on *them and* bring *him* safely to the governor Felix.'
²⁵ *And* he wrote a letter having this form:

²⁶ 'Claudius Lysias, to the most excellent governor Felix, greetings. ²⁷ This man was seized by the Jews, and *on his* being on the point of being murdered by them I rescued him, having come up with the troop, and, having learned that he is a Roman, ²⁸ and, wanting to know the charge on account of which they were accusing him, I brought him down into their Sanhedrin. ²⁹ I found him to be accused of questions concerning their law, *though* having no accusation worthy of death or shackles. ³⁰ And when it was intimated to me about a plot against the man about to be carried out by the Jews, I sent him to you at once, having also charged the accusers to describe in your presence the things against him. Be prospered."

³¹ So the soldiers, in keeping with the orders given them, took Paul *and* brought *him* during the night to Antipatris. ³² And the next day they left the horsemen to go with him, *and* returned to the barracks, ³³ who, having come into Caesarea, gave up the letter to the governor, and they presented Paul to him.
³⁴ And *when* the governor had read *the letter*, he questioned what province he was from, and ascertaining that *he was* from Cilicia ³⁵ he said, 'I will hear you fully when your accusers have arrived as well.'
And he ordered him to be kept under guard in the judgement hall of Herod.

Paul's defence before Felix

24\1 **A**nd after five days the high priest Ananias came down with the leaders and with a certain orator, Tertullus, who made a representation to the governor against Paul.
² And *when* he was called forward, Tertullus began making accusations, saying, 'Obtaining much peace through you, and excellent reforms being achieved for this nation through your provident care, ³ both in every way and everywhere, we accept *this* gladly, most excellent Felix, with all thankfulness. ⁴ But so that I might not be any further hindrance to you, I ask you, in your forbearance, to hear us

briefly.*

5 'For we have found this man pestilent, and stirring up a sedition among all the Jews throughout the habitable world, and a ringleader of the sect of the Nazarenes, 6 who has attempted to pollute the Temple as well, and whom we seized,* 7 [*no verse 7 in RP Greek text*]* 8 from whom,* having made examination concerning all these things, you yourself will be able to know fully what things we accuse him of.'

9 And the Jews also joined in, affirming these things to hold up* so.

10 And the governor made a signal for him to speak, *and* Paul answered, 'In understanding of your having been for many years a judge over this nation, I the more cheerfully* make defence for the things concerning myself, 11 *because* you yourself can understand that it is no more than twelve days since I went up to Jerusalem to worship. 12 And they neither found me in the Temple arguing against anybody, nor raising up a seditious gathering, nor in the synagogues, nor throughout the town. 13 Nor are they able to incriminate me concerning what they now accuse me of. 14 But I profess this to you, that, in keeping with the Way which they call a sect, so do I serve the God of my fathers, believing all things written throughout the law by the prophets, 15 and having a hope in God, which they themselves also accept, *that* there will be a resurrection of the dead, both of righteous and unrighteous. 16 And in this I exercise myself to have at all times a conscience without offence towards God and men.

17 'Now after many years, I came bringing gifts and offerings to my nation, 18 during which they found me purified in the Temple, neither with a crowd, nor with an uproar. But *there are* certain Jews from Asia 19 who it is fitting to be present before you and to make accusation, if they have anything against me. 20 Or otherwise, let these *men* themselves say what evil-doing they found in me while I stood before the Sanhedrin, 21 unless it be concerning this one utterance which I called out as I stood among them: "Concerning a resurrection of *the* dead I am judged by you this day." '

Paul kept by Felix.
He proclaims Jesus to Felix & his wife

22 Now *when* Felix heard these things, having more accurate knowledge of the things concerning the Way, he put them off, saying,

'When Lysias, the military commander, comes down, I will investigate in detail the things about you.'*

23 And he ordered the centurion to keep Paul under guard and to have privileges, and not to forbid his own *people* to provide for or to visit him.

24 And after a few days, when Felix came with *his* wife Drusilla, who was a Jewess, he sent for Paul and he heard him concerning the faith in Christ.

25 And as he reasoned about righteousness, self-control, and the judgement to come, Felix, having become terrified, answered, 'Go your way for now, and when I find an opportunity I will call for you.'

26 And with it all he hoped that money would be given to him by Paul, so that he might release him, and so he sent for him more often, *and* held conversations with him.

Porcius Festus succeeded Felix.
A second plot to murder Paul.
False charges brought against him.
Paul's appeal to Caesar

27 But *when* two years had been fulfilled, Porcius Festus succeeded Felix, and Felix, wanting to lay up favours for himself with the Jews, left Paul shackled.

25\1 So when Festus came into the province,* after three days he went up to Jerusalem from Caesarea. 2 Then the high priest and the chief of the Jews made a representation to him against Paul, and they were pleading with him, 3 wanting a favour against *Paul* that he would summon him to Jerusalem, *then* form an ambush along the road to murder him. 4 So Festus responded *that* Paul should be kept in Caesarea, and *that* he himself was shortly going to set out.

5 'So let those who are of senior rank among you,' he said, 'go down too, and, if there is anything against this man, let them accuse him.'

6 And *when* he had spent more than ten days among them, he went down into Caesarea, and the next day, sitting on the judgement seat, he ordered Paul to be brought out. 7 And on his arrival, the Jews who travelled down from Jerusalem stood around bringing numerous and weighty charges against Paul which they were not able to prove.*

8 He said in defence, 'Neither against the law of the Jews, nor against the Temple, nor against

Caesar have I transgressed in anything.'

9 But Festus, purposing to win favour for himself with the Jews, answered Paul, *and* said, 'Are you willing to go up to Jerusalem, to be judged there concerning these things before me?'

10 But Paul said, 'I am standing before the judgement seat of Caesar, where I ought to be judged. The Jews I have wronged in nothing, as you also know thoroughly. 11 For if indeed I am doing wrong, or have committed anything worthy of death, I do not refuse to die.* But if there is nothing *in* what they accuse me of, nobody can hand me over to them. I appeal to Caesar.'

12 Then Festus, when he had conferred with the council, answered, 'You have appealed to Caesar: before Caesar you will go.'

Paul brought before Agrippa

13 Now *when* a few days had passed, Agrippa the king and Bernice came to Caesarea and greeted Festus.

14 And when he had been there *for* many days, Festus set out to the king the matters concerning Paul, saying, 'There is a certain man left by Felix *as* a prisoner, 15 concerning whom, on my being in Jerusalem, the senior priests and the leaders of the Jews made a representation, asking for judgement against him, 16 to whom I answered, "It is not a custom of the Romans to give up any man to destruction before he who is accused might have the accusers face-to-face, and he should receive an opportunity of defence concerning the accusation." 17 So *when* they had gathered together here, *and* no delay had been made, the next day I sat on the judgement seat, *and* ordered the man to be brought, 18 concerning whom, when the accusers stood up, they were bringing no charge of such things as I had supposed. 19 But they had certain questions against him concerning their own reverence for gods, and concerning a certain Jesus, who died, whom Paul was asserting to be alive. 20 And being at a loss as to the things concerning this enquiry, I asked if he would be willing to go to Jerusalem and be judged there concerning these things. 21 But on Paul's having appealed for himself to be guarded until the examination by Augustus, I ordered him to be guarded until I could send him to Caesar.'

22 And Agrippa said to Festus, 'I also was wanting to hear the man myself.'

He said, 'Tomorrow you shall hear him.'

23 So the next day, when Agrippa and Bernice had arrived with much pomp and gone into the auditorium with both the military commanders and men of eminence of the town, Paul was brought out at the order of Festus.

24 And Festus said, 'King Agrippa, and all men present with us, you see this *man* concerning whom the whole crowd of the Jews pleaded with me, both in Jerusalem and here, calling out that he ought to live no longer. 25 I, though, having perceived him to have committed nothing worthy of death, and he himself having appealed to Augustus, I decided to send him. 26 I do not have anything certain to write to the sovereign* concerning him, so I have brought him before you, and specifically* before you, King Agrippa, so that on the interrogation having taken place I might have something to write. 27 For it seems to me unreasonable sending a prisoner, and not to indicate the charges against him.'

Paul's defence & testimony.
Agrippa confronted.
The whole company pronounces Paul innocent

26\1 Then Agrippa said to Paul, 'It is permitted for you to speak on your own behalf.'

Then, stretching out *his* hands, Paul made a defence: 2 'Concerning all the things which I am accused of by Jews, King Agrippa, I consider myself fortunate* to be about to make a defence before you today, 3 especially* *with* your being expert in all customs and also questions in relation to the Jews, so I implore you to hear me patiently.

4 'My former manner of life from my youth, which from its commencement was among my own nation in Jerusalem, all the Jews know 5 – if those knowing me before, from the beginning, are willing to give testimony – that in keeping with the strictest sect of our form of worship* I lived as a Pharisee.

6 'And now, over the hope of the promise to the fathers made by God, 7 I stand being judged, to which our twelve tribes,* serving day and night in intensity, hope to attain, concerning which hope I am accused, King Agrippa, by Jews. 8 Why is it judged by you* *all* as not believable if God raises *the* dead?

9 'Indeed, I thought in myself that I must do many things against the name of Jesus the Nazarene,* 10 which I duly* carried out in

Jerusalem, and many of the holy people I shut up in jails, having received the authority from the senior priests, and I laid down a vote against those being put to death. ¹¹ And often punishing them throughout all the synagogues, I was compelling them to blaspheme, and, being exceedingly maddened against them, I persecuted *them* even to the extent of the outlying* cities.

¹² 'And during this, while I was also journeying to Damascus* with authority and a commission from the senior priests, ¹³ at midday, on the road, King, I saw a light from *the* sky,* above the brightness of the Sun, flashing around me and those travelling with me. ¹⁴ And all of us fell to the ground, *and* I heard a voice speaking to me and saying in the Hebrew dialect, "Saul, Saul, why do you persecute me? *It is* hard for you to offer vain resistance."*

¹⁵ 'And I said, "Who are you, Sir?" And he said, "I am* Jesus whom you persecute. ¹⁶ But rise up, and stand on your feet, for I was seen by you* for this purpose, to appoint you as a servant and a witness both of these things you have seen *and* in which I will be revealed* to you, ¹⁷ delivering you from the people* and the nations to whom I am authorizing you,* ¹⁸ to open their eyes to turn from darkness to light, and from the authority of Satan to God,* for them to receive forgiveness of violations, and an inheritance* among* those having been sanctified* by faith in me."

¹⁹ 'So, King Agrippa, I was not disobedient to the heavenly* vision,* ²⁰ but making the proclamation first to those in Damascus and Jerusalem, and throughout all the regions of Judea, and to the other nations to submit and turn to God, doing works appropriate for submission. ²¹ On account of these things, the Jews, having seized me in the Temple, were attempting* to murder *me*. ²² So having help from God up to this day, I have stood giving testimony to both *the* lowly and eminent, saying nothing other than those things which the prophets and Moses spoke should come, ²³ that the Christ is destined to suffer, *and* that, *the* first out of a resurrection of *the* dead, he should proclaim light to the people* and to the nations.'*

²⁴ And on his uttering these things in his defence, Festus said with a loud voice, 'You're beside yourself, Paul. Your vast learning is driving you out of your mind.'

²⁵ But he said, 'I am not mad, most noble Festus, but I speak in my defence words of truth and discretion. ²⁶ For the king, before whom I also speak out with boldness, is informed concerning these things, for I am persuaded that none of these things is hidden from him, for this thing has not been done in a corner. Do you, King Agrippa, believe the prophets? I know that you do believe.'

²⁸ Then Agrippa said to Paul, 'In brief,* you persuade me to become* a Christian!'*

²⁹ But Paul said, 'I could wish to God *that* not only you, but for all those also hearing me this day, both in little* and in much,* to become* such as I also am, apart from these shackles.'*

³⁰ And when he had spoken these things, the king rose up.

And the governor, and Bernice, and those who sat with them ³¹ turned aside *and* talked to one another, saying, 'This man does nothing worthy of death or of shackles.'

³² Then Agrippa said to Festus, 'This man could have been set at liberty if he had not appealed to Caesar.'

Paul's boat journey to Rome.
He predicts danger. A storm
& shipwreck at Malta. All are preserved

27\1 And as it was decided that we should sail into Italy, they were handing over Paul and some other prisoners to a centurion named Julius, of the cohort of Augustus. ² And we went on board a ship at Adramyttium, *and* we launched off, intending to sail along the coasts of Asia, *and* Aristarchus, a Macedonian of Thessalonica, was with us.

³ And the next *day* we landed at Sidon. And Julius treated Paul kindly and gave *him* liberty to go to *his* friends to receive care. ⁴ And when we had launched from there, we sailed below Cyprus because of the winds being* hostile. ⁵ And when we had sailed across the sea along Cilicia and Pamphylia, we came to Myra, *a town* of Lycia. ⁶ And the centurion there found a boat of Alexandria sailing into Italy, and he got us to embark on it.

⁷ And we sailed slowly along over many days, and *after* we arrived with difficulty off Cnidus, the wind preventing us from proceeding, we sailed below Crete, facing Salmone, ⁸ and, having sailed along it in difficulty, we came to a certain place called Fair Havens, near which was the town of Lasea.

⁹ Now when we had worn away much time,

and the voyage now being hazardous and the *time of* the fast now being about to pass,˙ Paul was admonishing, ¹⁰ saying to them, 'Men, I perceive that this voyage is about to end with a disaster and large loss, not only of the cargo and boat, but of our lives as well.'

¹¹ The centurion, though, was persuaded by the captain and the owner of the boat rather than by the things spoken by Paul, ¹² and, because the port was ill-adapted for wintering, the majority gave their decision to launch from there as well, if, by any means, *when* we reached Phoenix, they might be able to winter *at* a port of Crete looking down to *the* South-West wind and towards *the* North-West wind.˙

¹³   And a South wind blew softly, *and,* supposing to have achieved *their* objective, they loosed *anchor* close by *and* sailed close along Crete. ¹⁴ But not long after, a typhonic wind known as Euroclydon beat down, ¹⁵ and when the boat was caught up, and *we were* unable to look in the eye of the wind, we gave up *and* allowed ourselves to be driven along.˙

¹⁶   But *when* we ran under *shelter of* an island called Clauda, we hardly had the strength to come to˙ mastery of the skiff. ¹⁷ When they had hoisted it up, they used cables to undergird the boat. And fearing in case they should run aground into the quicksand, they lowered the gear, and so they were driven. ¹⁸ But being violently tossed about by a tempest, the next *day* they were conducting a throwing out *of some cargo.*

¹⁹   And on the third *day* we threw out with our own hands the boat's tackle. ²⁰ And neither Sun nor stars intervened favourably˙ for many days, and, *with* no small tempest pressing hard,˙ from that time all hope for us to be saved was lost.

²¹   But after much fasting, Paul stood up in their presence, and said, 'Men, you ought to have been obedient to me, and not set sail from Crete and run up this disaster and loss. ²² And now I encourage you to be cheerful, for there will not be any loss of a life among you, but only of the boat. ²³ For *the* Angel˙ of the God Whose I am, and Whom I serve, stood by me this night, ²⁴ saying, "Do not fear, Paul. You must stand before Caesar. And now look,˙ God has preserved for you all those who sail with you." ²⁵ Therefore, men, be of good cheer, for I believe God that it will happen in just the manner in which it was spoken to me. ²⁶ However, we must run aground on a certain island.'

²⁷   But when the fourteenth night had come, as we were driven up and down in the Adriatic, towards *the* middle of the night the sailors were supposing that some country was drawing near. ²⁸ And they took a sounding *and* found *it* twenty fathoms, and they went a little further, *and* again took a sounding and found *it* fifteen fathoms. ²⁹ Then fearing in case by chance we should have fallen on rocky places, *and* having dropped four anchors out of *the* stern, they were praying for day to come.

³⁰   And as the seamen were looking to flee out of the skiff, when they let the boat down into the sea with a pretence as though being about to throw anchors out of *the* prow, ³¹ Paul said to the centurion and to the soldiers, 'Unless these remain in the boat, you cannot be saved.'

³²   Then the soldiers cut away the ropes of the skiff, and let it fall off.

³³   And until the day was coming on, Paul was entreating everybody to partake of food, saying, 'Today *is* the fourteenth day when you have continued waiting without taking food, having taken nothing. ³⁴ Therefore I urge you to take food, for this is in the interest of your preservation, for not a hair will fall out of the head of any of you.'

³⁵   And *when* he had said these things and taken a loaf, he gave thanks to God in the presence of them all, and when he had broken *it* up he began to eat. ³⁶ Then they all became of good cheer, and they took food themselves as well. ³⁷ Now in all, there were two hundred and seventy-six of us in the boat.

³⁸   And having been satisfied with food, they lightened the boat *and* threw the wheat out into the sea. ³⁹ And when it was day, they did not recognize the land, but they discovered a certain bay˙ with a beach into which they planned, if possible, to run the boat. ⁴⁰ And when they had cut away the anchors, they left *them* in the sea, *and* at the same time loosened˙ the lashings of the rudders, and hoisted up the mainsail to the wind, *and* headed towards the beach.

⁴¹   But they were wrecked at a place with sea on two sides,˙ and they ran the boat aground, and the prow, being stuck fast, remained immoveable, but the stern began to break up with the pounding of the waves. ⁴² And the soldiers' counsel was that they should kill off the prisoners, in case anybody should swim out *and* make good his escape. ⁴³ But the centurion, purposing to save Paul, hindered them from

their purpose, and he ordered that those who were able to swim should jump overboard first, and get to land. ⁴⁴ And as for the rest, some *went* on planks, and others on *broken pieces* from the boat. And so it transpired for everybody to be saved onto the land.

The sojourn of Paul & his work in Malta

28\1 **A**nd having been saved, they then learned that the island was called Malta.* ² And the Barbarians* showed not ordinary kindness to us, for they kindled a fire *and* received all of us* because of the rain which had come on and because of the cold.
³ And when Paul had gathered a bundle of sticks and laid *them* on the fire, a viper came out of the heat and fastened on his hand.*
⁴ And when the Barbarians* saw the creature hanging from his hand, they said to one another, 'No doubt this man is a murderer, whom, being preserved out of the sea, justice has not allowed to live.'
⁵ Then he shook the creature off into the fire, *and* he suffered nothing injurious. ⁶ But they were watching in expectation for him to be about to become inflamed or to suddenly fall down* dead, but after they had waited for a long time *and* seen no harm having come to him they changed their minds and proclaimed him to be* a god.

⁷ Now, in the *parts* around that place there were lands *belonging* to the foremost man of the island, Publius by name, who welcomed us and hosted us in a friendly way *for* three days. ⁸ And it so happened that the father of Publius was lying down, taken with fevers and a dysentery, *and* Paul went to him and prayed, and laid hands on him and healed him. ⁹ So on this happening, the rest in the island who also had infirmities came and were cured, ¹⁰ *and* they also honoured us with many honours, and on our setting sail they supplied *us* with the things for our need.

Paul's journey to Rome

¹¹ And after three months, we sailed in an Alexandrian boat which had wintered in the island, with a figurehead of Castor and Pollux*.
¹² And being brought into Syracuse, we stayed for three days. ¹³ *And* from there we sailed around* *and* we arrived in Rhegium, and after one day a South wind blew, *and* on the second day we came to Puteoli, ¹⁴ where, on finding brothers, we were invited to remain seven days with them.

And so we came into Rome, ¹⁵ and from there, when the brothers heard the things concerning us, they came out to meet* us at the marketplace of Appius and Three Taverns, *and* when Paul saw them he thanked God and took courage.

Paul, in shackles, makes his first address to Jews in Rome

¹⁶ And when we came to Rome, the centurion handed over the prisoners to the captain of the guard, but Paul was permitted to live by himself with a soldier guarding him.
¹⁷ And it came about after three days that Paul called together the leaders of the Jews, and *when* they had come together he said to them, 'Men, brothers, even though I have committed nothing against the people or the ancestral customs, I was handed over from Jerusalem *as* a prisoner into the hands of the Romans, ¹⁸ who, when they had examined me, were wanting to let *me* go, because there was no charge against me for death. ¹⁹ But *when* the Jews started contradicting,* I was compelled to appeal to Caesar – not that I had anything to accuse my nation of. ²⁰ For this reason, therefore, I have called to see and to speak to you, because for the Hope of Israel* I have this chain around me.'*
²¹ And they said to him, 'We neither received letters from Judea concerning you, nor did any of the brothers who arrived report or state anything evil about you. ²² But we think it right to hear from you what you think, for indeed, concerning this sect, it is known to us that it is spoken against* everywhere.'*

Paul, from his lodgings in Rome, makes his second proclamation to Jews in Rome.
Final pronouncement of Isaiah's description of Israel's unbelief.*
Salvation authorized to the nations

²³ And when they had arranged* a day for him, many came to him in *his* lodging, to whom he gave exposition, thoroughly testifying the Sovereign Rulership* of God, persuading them of the things concerning Jesus, from both the law of Moses and the prophets, from morning until evening. ²⁴ And some were persuaded of the things being spoken, but some were

disbelieving.

²⁵ And *when* they disagreed with one another, they departed *after* Paul had spoken one oracle: 'Rightly did the Holy Spirit˙ speak to our fathers through the agency of the prophet Isaiah,˙ ²⁶ saying:

"Go to this people and say,
'In hearing you will hear
yet in no way will you understand,
and in seeing you will see
yet in no way will you perceive.
²⁷ For the heart of this people
has grown callous,˙
and with *their* ears they hardly hear
and they have closed their eyes,
in case at any time
they should see with the eyes,
and they should hear with the ears,
and they should understand with the heart,
and they would turn
and I would heal them.' "˙

²⁸ 'Let it be known to you, then, that the salvation-bringing *message*˙ of God has been authorized to the nations,˙ and they will hear.'
²⁹ And when he had said these things, the Jews departed, having˙ much˙ disputation˙ among˙ themselves.

Paul in Rome for two years
boldly proclaims the Sovereign Rulership of God
& the things concerning Jesus
³⁰ And Paul lived two whole years in his own rented house, and freely received everybody who came to him, ³¹ proclaiming the Sovereign Rulership˙ of God, and teaching the things concerning the Lord Jesus Christ, with all boldness, without hindrance.

~ ◆◆ ~

† The Letters of Paul* †

Romans

Apostleship of Paul. The gospel
was told in advance by prophets

1\1

Paul, a servant of Jesus Christ, a designated* apostle,* set apart for* *the* gospel of God, [2] which He had promised in advance through His prophets in *the* holy Scrolls, [3] concerning His Son who came out of a seed of David in relation to flesh, [4] declared* the Son of God with power, by the agency* of *the* Spirit of Holiness,** by resurrection of *the* dead, Jesus Christ our Lord,* [5] through whom we have received merciful goodwill, as well as apostleship, for obedience in faith among all the nations, on behalf of his name, [6] among whom you also are *the* called* of Jesus Christ.

[7] To all those being in Rome, richly loved of God, called holy people, merciful goodwill to you, and* peace, from God our Father, and* *from the* Lord* Jesus Christ.**

Prayer & desire
to visit Roman believers

[8] First of all, I thank my God through Jesus Christ for all of you, that your faith is spoken of throughout the whole world. [9] For God is my witness, Whom I serve in my spirit in the gospel of His Son, as to how without ceasing I make mention of you [10] always in my prayers* making request *that* if, by any means, sometime, at last, by the will of God, I might find a way to come to you.

[11] For I long to see you, in order that I might impart some spiritual gift to you for you to be established, [12] that is, to be encouraged together with you by the mutual faith of both you and me.

[13] Now I do not want you to be unaware, brothers, that many times I have proposed to come to you – but was hindered until* the present – in order that I might have some fruit among you also, in the same way as among* the remaining nations.

Work of Paul in the gospel. To the Jew
first, then to the Greek (1\16, 2\9-10).
The righteousness from God revealed.
Man without any excuse

[14] I am debtor both to Greeks and to Barbarians,* both to the wise and to the unwise. [15] So as far as *it lies in* me, I am eager to proclaim the gospel as well to you who *are* in Rome. [16] For I am not ashamed of the gospel of the Christ,* for it is the power of God for* salvation for everybody who believes, both to *the* Jew first,* then* to *the* Greek.*

[17] For in it *the* righteousness of God is revealed out of* faith, with a view to* faith,* just as* it has been written: 'But the righteous will live out of* faith." [18] For the indignation of God is revealed from Heaven against all ungodliness and unrighteousness of men who suppress* the truth in unrighteousness, [19] because that which might be known about God is clearly known among them, for God made the revelation* to them.

[20] For the invisible things of Him are perceived from* *the* creation of *the* world,* being realized* through the things created,* both* His perpetual* power and the nature of God,* for* them* to be* without excuse, [21] because having known God they did not magnify *Him* as God, nor were they thankful, but they became vain in their reasonings, and their foolish* heart was darkened. [22] Professing themselves to be wise, they became foolish, [23] and they changed the magnificence of the incorruptible* God into a likeness of an image of corruptible man, and of birds, and four-footed animals, and reptiles.*

[24] Because of this, God in turn* gave them over to uncleanness through the lusts of their own hearts, for their own bodies to be dishonoured among themselves, [25] since they exchanged the truth of God for* the* lie,* and they worshipped and served the created thing more than the Creator, Who is exalted* throughout* the Eons.** Amen.

[26] Because of this, God gave them over to* vile passions, for even the women exchanged the natural function for* one contrary to nature. [27] And likewise the males also, having forsaken the natural use of the female, were inflamed in their lust towards* each other, males committing with males a shameful thing, and receiving back on themselves the recompense which was fitting for their delusion.*

[28] And just as* they did not like to retain God in knowledge,* God gave them over to* a reprobate mind to do those things not right, [29] being filled with all unrighteousness, fornication, wickedness, fraud,* malice, full of jealousy, murder, strife, guile, evil disposition,

whisperers, [30] evil speakers, hateful to God, insolent, proud, boasters, devisers of evil things, disobedient to parents, [31] without understanding, covenant breakers, without natural affection, implacable, pitiless,˙ [32] who, having understood the righteous sentence of God that those committing such things are deserving of death, not only practise them, but are consenting also to those who practise them.

Man without excuse, faced with Eonian life
& honour & incorruption, or anger & tribulation
& destruction (Mat. 7\13-14, John 3\16,
Rev. 20\11-15). Paul's gospel (2\16, 14\24,
15\16, Eph. 1\3, 1\20, 2\6, 3\6, 2 Tim. 2\8)

2\1 Therefore you are without excuse, oh˙ man, everybody making judgement. For in whatever you judge˙ the other, you condemn yourself, for you who judge commit the same things. ² But we know that the judgement of God is in keeping with truth, against those committing such things.

³ And do you reckon this, oh˙ man, you judging those doing such things, even though committing them, that you will escape the judgement of God? ⁴ Or do you despise the riches of His kindness and forbearance and long-suffering, not knowing that the kindness of God leads you into submission?

⁵ But you, with your hardness and non-submitting heart, are treasuring up for yourself˙ indignation in *the* day of indignation˙ and revelation˙ and righteous judgement of God, ⁶ Who will recompense to each *man* in relation to his deeds:˙ ⁷ Eonian˙ life˙ for those *who*, in relation to patient endurance in good work, are searching for magnificence and honour and incorruption;˙ ⁸ but for those who, out of contention, disobey the truth but obey unrighteousness,˙ boiling anger and indignation, ⁹ tribulation and anguish on every mind˙ of a man who works evil, both for the Jew first, and for the Greek;˙ ¹⁰ but magnificence, honour, and peace for everybody who works good, both for the Jew first, and for the Greek.˙˙

¹¹ For there is no partiality with God. ¹² For as many who violated without law will perish also without law, and as many who violated in law will be judged by law. ¹³ For *it is* not the hearers of the law *who are* righteous before God, but the doers of the law *who* will be pronounced righteous. ¹⁴ For when *the* nations who do not have the law by nature carry out the things of

the law, these, not having law, are a law to themselves, ¹⁵ in that they demonstrate the work of the law written on their hearts, bearing witness with their conscience, and the thoughts between one another either accusing or else defending, ¹⁶ in a day when God will judge the hidden things of men through Jesus Christ in relation to my gospel.˙

The case of the Jew – circumcision is inward
¹⁷ Look now, you are called a Jew, and you rely on the law, and you make your boast in God, ¹⁸ and you know *His* will, and you look into the things which differ,˙ being instructed out of the law, ¹⁹ and having convinced yourself of being a guide for *the* blind, a light for those in darkness, ²⁰ an instructor of *the* foolish, a teacher of infants, having the external form of knowledge and of the truth in the law.

²¹ You, therefore, teaching another, will you not instruct yourself? You proclaiming not to steal, do you steal? ²² You saying not to commit adultery, do you commit adultery? You detesting idols, do you rob temples? ²³ You who make your boast in law, do you dishonour God through the transgression of the law? ²⁴ For, as it has been written,˙ 'the name of God is blasphemed among the nations through you.'˙ ²⁵ For circumcision profits if you carry out *the* law, but if you are a transgressor of *the* law your circumcision has become uncircumcision.

²⁶ Therefore, if the *man of* uncircumcision keeps the righteous requirements of the law, will his uncircumcision not be counted as circumcision? ²⁷ And will *the* uncircumcision, by nature fulfilling the law, *not* judge you a transgressor of *the* law, despite your Scrolls and circumcision?

²⁸ For he is not a Jew who is one in outward appearance. Nor *is* circumcision that which *is* in outward appearance in flesh. ²⁹ But he *is* a Jew *who is one* inwardly, and circumcision *is* of *the* heart,˙ in spirit,˙ not by letter, whose praise *is* not from men, but from God.

Advantage of the Jew.
Both Jews & nations under violation

3\1 What, then, is the advantage of the Jew? Or what *is* the profit of circumcision? ² Much from every standpoint.˙ Primarily, because they were entrusted with the oracles of God. ³ For what if some did not believe? Will their unbelief nullify the faithfulness of God? ⁴ May it not be!* Yes, let God be true, but every man a liar. As it has been written:

'so that You might be justified
in Your oracles,
and You might overcome
in Your being judged.'*

5 But if our unrighteousness establishes *the* righteousness of God, what shall we say? *Is* God Who inflicts vengeance unrighteous? I speak in the manner of men! 6 May it not be! For how, then, will God judge the world? 7 For if the truth of God abounded through my falsehood for* His preeminence,* why am I still also judged as a violator? 8 And *why* not *say*, as we are slanderously reported, and as some – the judgement* of whom is deserved – report us to say, 'Let us carry out the evil things so that the good things might come?'
9   What then? Do we have preeminence?* Undoubtedly not,* for we have previously convicted both Jews and Greeks to be under violation. 10 As it has been written:

'There is not a righteous *man*, not even one;
11 there is nobody who understands;
there is nobody who searches after God;
12 they all have turned away;
they are altogether worthless;
there is not one showing kindness;
there is not so much as one;
13 their throat *is* an opened tomb;
with their tongues they have deceived;
the poison of asps *is* under their lips;
14 their mouth *is* full of cursing and bitterness;
15 their feet *are* swift to shed blood;
16 destruction and distress *are* in their ways,
17 and they have not known a path of peace;
18 there is no reverence of God
before their eyes.'*

19 Now we know that whatever things the law says, it says to those under the law, in order that every mouth might be stopped, and all the world might be under judicial decision by God. 20 Consequently, no flesh* will be pronounced righteous before Him out of works of law, for through law *comes* the acknowledging of violation.
21 But at this present time the righteousness of God apart from law is brought to light* – having been testified to by the law and the prophets – 22 and the righteousness of God

through *the* faith of Jesus Christ,* towards all and on all those who believe, for there is no distinction.
23 For all have violated* and fall short of the magnificence of God, 24 being pronounced righteous* freely by His merciful goodwill through the redemption in Christ Jesus, 25 whom God preordained *as* a mercy seat* through faith in his blood, as a declaration of His righteousness by reason of the passing over of violations having previously occurred, in the forbearance of God,* 26 the declaration of His righteousness in the present time, for Him to be* righteous, and pronouncing as righteous him *who is* of *the* faith in Jesus.
27 Where, then, *is* boasting? It is excluded. Through what manner of law? Of works? No, but through a law of faith. 28 Consequently, we reckon a man to be pronounced righteous through faith, apart from works of law.
29 Or *is He* the God only of Jews, and not of other nations as well? Yes, of the other nations as well, 30 seeing, indeed, that God *is* one,* Who will pronounce righteous *the* circumcision out of faith, and *the* uncircumcision through faith. 31 Do we, then, make the law of no effect through faith? May it not be! Rather, we establish *the* law.

The faith of Abraham
reckoned for righteousness
not through circumcision
or law. Exaltation *

4\1 **W**hat, in that case, shall we say that our father Abraham discovered in relation to flesh? 2 For if Abraham was pronounced righteous out of works, he has a ground for boasting, but not before God. 3 For what does the Scroll say? 'And Abraham believed God, and it was reckoned to him for righteousness.'*
4   Now to him who performs works,* the reward is not reckoned in relation to goodwill, but as an obligation. 5 But to him who does not perform works,* but believes in Him Who pronounces righteous the ungodly, his faith is reckoned for righteousness, 6 just as David also says of the pronounced benefit* of the man to whom God reckons righteousness apart from works:*

7   'Exalted *are those* whose violations
of law are forgiven
and whose violations are covered over.

⁸ Exalted *is* the man to whom the Lord will in no way reckon violation."

⁹ Is this pronounced benefit,* then, on the circumcision, or on the uncircumcision as well? For we say that faith was reckoned to Abraham for righteousness.

¹⁰ How, then, was it reckoned? Being in circumcision, or in uncircumcision? Not in circumcision, but in uncircumcision. ¹¹ And he received *the* sign of circumcision, a seal of the righteousness of the faith in uncircumcision, for him to become* the father of all those who believe despite uncircumcision,* with a view to righteousness being reckoned to them also, ¹² and a father of circumcision to those not out of circumcision only, but to those also who walk in the footsteps of that faith of our father Abraham during *his* uncircumcision.

¹³ For not through law *was* the promise to Abraham and his seed for him to become* the heir of the world, but it was through *the* righteousness of faith. ¹⁴ For if they are heirs out of law, faith has been made void, and the promise made of no effect, ¹⁵ because the law engenders indignation, for where there is no law neither *is there* transgression.

¹⁶ On account of this, *it is* out of faith, so that *it might* be by merciful goodwill, for the promise to be* made secure* to all the seed, not only to those out of the law, but also to those who are out of the faith of Abraham, who is father of us all ¹⁷ – as it has been written: 'I have appointed you a father of many nations" – in the sight of Him Whom he believed, God, Who gives life to the dead and calls those things not in existence as if being in existence.

¹⁸ Against hope he believed in hope, for him to become* *the* father of many nations in relation to what had been spoken: 'So will your seed be."

¹⁹ And not being weak in faith, he did not consider his own body as already having been put to death,* being about a hundred years old, *nor* even the deadness of Sarah's womb. ²⁰ He did not stagger at the promise of God by unbelief, but was strengthened in faith, giving preeminence* to God, ²¹ and being fully persuaded that what He promised He was also able to carry out. ²² Consequently, in addition, it was accounted to him for righteousness.*

The resurrection of Jesus for our justification
²³ Now it was not written on account of

Abraham alone that it was reckoned to him, ²⁴ but on account of us also, to whom it is about to be accounted for those believing in Him Who raised up Jesus our Lord from *the* dead, ²⁵ who was given up for our offences, and was raised for our justification.

Pronounced righteous by faith; peace
towards God; enduring in tribulation.
The love of God through the new nature;
saved from indignation; exuberance in God

5\1 𝕎e, therefore, having been pronounced righteous out of faith, have peace towards* God* through our Lord Jesus Christ, ² through whom we have obtained access as well, through faith into this merciful goodwill in which we stand, and we exult in gladly-held expectation of the magnificence of God.

³ And not only *that*, but we exult as well in tribulations, knowing that afflictions work out patience; ⁴ and enduring *works out* tested character; and tested character *works out* gladly-held expectation; ⁵ and gladly-held expectation does not cause shame; because the love of God has been poured out in our hearts through* *the* divine spirit which* was given to us.

⁶ For *when* we were still without strength, in due season Christ died for *the* ungodly. ⁷ For scarcely will somebody die for a righteous man, yet perhaps on behalf of a good man somebody might even be bold to die.

⁸ God, though, commends His love towards us in that, we still being violators, Christ died for us. ⁹ How much more, then, being now pronounced righteous in his blood, will we be saved by him from indignation.* ¹⁰ For if, being enemies, we were reconciled to God through the death of His Son, so much more, having been reconciled, will we be saved by his life. ¹¹ And not only *that*, but we also exult in God through our Lord Jesus Christ, through whom we have now received the restoration.

Righteousness reckoned instead of violation.
Death through Adam; life through Christ;
justification of life for all men *
¹² On this account, just as violation entered into the world through one man, and by means of violation death *came*, so also death passed through* all mankind, all of whom violated.

¹³ For until law, violation was in *the* world. Violation, though, is not reckoned *where* there is no law. ¹⁴ Nevertheless, death reigned from

Adam until Moses,* including* over those who had not violated after the likeness of the transgression of Adam,* who is a figure* of the Coming One.* [15] But the free gift *is* not like the transgression. For if through the offence of the one the many died, so much more has the merciful goodwill of God, and the gift in merciful goodwill from the one man, Jesus Christ, abounded to the many.*

[16] And the free gift *is* not like what *came* through* the one having violated.* For *the* judgement *was* out of *the* one into condemnation,* but the free gift *is* out of* many transgressions into* justification. [17] For if, by the offence of the one, death reigned through that one, so much more will those receiving the abundance of merciful goodwill and the gift of righteousness reign in life through the one, Jesus Christ.

[18] So then, as through one act of transgression *judgement came,* resulting in condemnation* for all men, so also through one righteous act *did the free gift come,* resulting in justification of life for all men.* [19] For as through the disobedience of one man the many were declared violators, so also through the obedience of the one will the many* be declared righteous.*

[20] But the law came along,* in order that the offence might multiply.* But where violation abounded, merciful goodwill abounded much more, [21] so that, as violation reigned in death, so might merciful goodwill also* reign through righteousness into Eonian* life,* through* Jesus Christ our Lord.

*Identification with Christ into death
& being raised into new life (Gal. 3\27,
1 Cor. 12\13, Col. 2\12, Eph. 4\5)*

6\1 **W**hat shall we say, then? Do we persist in violation, in order that merciful goodwill might abound? [2] May it not be! How shall we, who died to violation, live in it any longer? [3] Or are you ignorant that as many who have been identified* into Christ Jesus have been identified* into his death?*

[4] Consequently, we were buried with him through identification* into death, so that just as Christ was raised* from *the* dead by the magnificent power* of the Father,* so also should we walk in newness of life. [5] For if we have become conjoined in the likeness of his death, so will we also be of *his* resurrection, [6] knowing this, that our old man was hanged* on

a stake with* *him*, in order that the body of violation might be annulled, for us to be subservient no longer to violation. [7] For he who died has been pronounced clear of violation.

[8] Now if we died together with Christ, we believe that we will live also with him, [9] knowing that Christ, having been raised from among *the* dead, dies no more. Death no more has dominion over* him. [10] For in that he died, he died to violation once. But in that he lives, he lives to God.

*Violation should no longer have dominion:
dead to law, alive to God*

[11] In the same way, reckon yourselves also to be dead to violation, but alive to God in Jesus Christ our Lord.

[12] So let violation not reign in your subject-to-death body, to obey it in its lusts. [13] Nor should you be yielding your members as weapons of unrighteousness to* violation. Present yourselves, though, to* God, as if alive from *the* dead, and your members *as* weapons* of righteousness to God. [14] For violation will not have dominion over you, for you are not under law, but under merciful goodwill.

[15] What, then? Shall we violate because we are not under law, but under merciful goodwill? May it not be! [16] Do you not know that to whomever you put yourselves at disposal as servants for obedience, you are servants to that one whom you obey, whether of violation leading to death, or of obedience leading to righteousness?

[17] Thanks to God, though, that you had been servants of violation, but out of *the* heart you have obeyed a form of teaching to which you were entrusted. [18] Having, then, been set free from violation, you were enslaved to righteousness.

[19] I speak after the manner of men on account of the failing of your flesh. For as you have presented your members in bondage to uncleanness and lawlessness leading into lawlessness, so now present your members in bondage to righteousness into sanctification. [20] For when you were servants of violation, you were freemen* with regard to righteousness.

[21] So what fruit did you have, then, in those things of which you are now ashamed? For the end of those things *is* death. [22] But now, having been set free from violation and having been enslaved to God, you have your fruit leading into sanctification, and the end, Eonian* life.

²³ For the wages* of violation *are* death, but the free gift of God *is* Eonian* life in Jesus Christ our Lord.

*Deliverance from law by the death
of Christ. Remarriage as a figure*

7\1 Do you not know, brothers – for I speak to those knowing *the* law – that the law lords it over the man for such time as he might live? ² For the married woman is bound by law to the living husband. But if the husband should die, she is released from the law of the husband. ³ So then, if, while the husband lives, she becomes married to another man, she will be called an adulteress. But if the husband should die, she becomes a freewoman* from the law,* not being an adulteress in becoming *wife* to another man. A wife is bound by law for such time as her husband lives.

⁴ Therefore, my brothers, you also were made dead to the law through Christ's body,* for you to become* *joined* to another, the one* having been raised from *the* dead, in order that we might produce fruit for God. ⁵ For when we were in the flesh,* the passions of the violations in the law operated* in our members in producing fruit resulting in death. ⁶ Now, though, we have been cleared from the law, and we have died *to* what we were being held in, for us to serve in newness of spirit, and not in oldness of *the* letter.

*Conflict of a new nature against an old.
Deliverance through Christ*

⁷ What shall we say, then? *Is* the law violation? May it not be! But I would not have recognized violation except through law. Indeed, I would not have known covetousness unless the law had said, 'You shall not covet.'*

⁸ But violation, having taken opportunity by the commandment, engendered in me every manner of lust.* For apart from law, violation *is* dead. ⁹ But I was alive once apart from law, and *when* the commandment came violation sprang into life, but I died. ¹⁰ And the commandment for life was itself found by me as leading to* death. ¹¹ For violation, having taken an occasion through the commandment, deceived me, and through it put me to death, ¹² so that* the law *is* indeed holy, and the commandment *is* holy, and righteous, and good.

¹³ Has, then, that which is good become death to me? May it not be! But violation, in order that it might be exposed as violation, was engendering death in me through that which is good, in order that violation, through the commandment, might become excessively full of violation.*

¹⁴ For we know that the law is spiritual, but I am flesh-natured, having been sold under violation. ¹⁵ For that which I bring about, I am not conscious of.* For that which I do not wish *to do*, this do I carry out. But that which I hate, this do I do. ¹⁶ But if I do that which I do not wish *to do*, I consent to the law that *it is* good.

¹⁷ But now *it is* no longer I bringing it about, but violation living in me. ¹⁸ For I know that in me – that is, in my flesh – no good thing is resident.* For to be inclined to pleasure has its presence with me.* But I do not discover *how* to bring about what *is* right. ¹⁹ For I do not do *the* good which I wish *to do*. But *the* evil which I do not wish *to do*, I carry that out.

²⁰ Now if I do that which I do not wish *to do*, *it is* no longer I bringing it about, but the violation living in me. ²¹ I find, then, the principle for me, willing to do the good, *is* that evil has its presence with me.

²² For I delight in the law of God from the inner* man.* ²³ But I see another law in my members,* making a battle against the law of my mind, and *looking* to make me captive to the law of violation which is in my members.

²⁴ Wretched man *that* I *am*!* Who will rescue me out of* this body of death? ²⁵ I thank God, through Jesus Christ our Lord. So then, with the mind I myself serve *the* law of God, but with the flesh *the* law of violation.*

*No condemnation for the man
of the new nature.
Not Christ's if not having his spirit*

8\1 There* *is*, then, no condemnation* now for those in Christ Jesus, walking* not in relation to flesh,* but in relation to spirit.* ² For the law of the spirit* of life in Christ Jesus has freed me from the law of violation and death.

³ For in whatever the law *was* powerless, in that it was impotent through the flesh, God *did* in sending His own Son in the likeness of violating flesh. And concerning violation, He condemned violation in the flesh, ⁴ in order that the requirement of the law might be fulfilled in us who walk* not after flesh but after spirit.* ⁵ For those being in relation to flesh direct their minds on the things of the flesh, but those in

relation to spirit* *on* the things of the spirit.*

6   For the mind of the flesh *is* death, but the mind of the spirit is life and peace, [7] because the mind of the flesh *is* hostile towards God, for it does not submit itself to the law of God, since neither, indeed, is it able to. [8] Those, however, who are in flesh are not able to please God.

9   You though, are not in flesh, but in spirit,* if, indeed, *the* spirit of God* inhabits* you. But if anybody does not have *the* spirit of Christ,** he is not* his.* [10] But if Christ *is* in you,* the body *is* dead because of violation, but the spirit* *is* life because of righteousness.

Resurrection assured. A spirit of sonship

11   But if the spirit* of the one* having raised up Jesus from *the* dead inhabits* you, He* having raised up the Christ from *the* dead will also give life to your mortal bodies,* through* His spirit which inhabits* you.*

12   So then, brothers, we are not debtors to the flesh, to live in relation to flesh. [13] For if you live in relation to flesh, you are going to perish.* But if through *the* spirit* you are putting to death the acts of the body, you will live. [14] For as many who are impelled* by *the* spirit* of God,* these are the Sons of God. [15] For you have not received a spirit of slavery bending back to fear, but you have received a spirit of sonship* by which we call out, 'Abba, Father.'

Inner witness to believers being Sons of God (Luke 6\35 etc.). The present suffering – then the revealing of the Sons of God

16   The spirit itself** gives witness with our spirit* that we are the Sons of God, [17] and if sons, also heirs, truly heirs of God, and joint heirs* with Christ,* if, indeed, we suffer together, in order that we might be magnified together* as well.*

18   For I reckon that the sufferings of the present time *are* not worthy *to be compared* to the radiance about to be revealed in us. [19] For the creation's anxious looking with a lifted head* assiduously waits it out for the revealing* of the Sons of God [20] – for the creation was made subject to futility,* not willingly, but by Him Who has subjected *it* – in gladly-held expectation, [21] because the creation itself also will be set free from the bondage of decay into the magnificent* freedom* of the Sons of God. [22] For we know that all the creation is groaning together and labouring together in pain until now.

Creation uniting in its groaning for the manifestation of the resurrection radiance. The spirit which inhabits believers states our case within us by inexpressible groans

23   And not only *that*, but even we ourselves, also having the firstfruit of the spirit,* groan within ourselves, assiduously waiting it out for adoption, the redemption of our body. [24] For we have been saved in gladly-held expectation. But gladly-held expectation *which* is seen is not hope. For what anybody sees, in what way does he hope for *it* as well? [25] But if we hope for what we do not see, we assiduously wait it out with patience.

26   Likewise the spirit* also jointly helps* *us in* our weaknesses, for we do not know what we should pray for as we ought, but the spirit itself** pleads our case* for us with inexpressible groans.** [27] But He Who* searches hearts knows what the mindset of the spirit* *is* because it intercedes* for *the* holy people in relation to God.

Already marked out now in advance (Eph. 1\4). Jesus our Lord & brother (8\29, Mat. 12\49-50, 25\40, 28\10, Gal. 3\16 & 3\29, Heb. 2\11 & 2\17), the First-honoured among many brothers. Security & no separation from God

28   But we know that for those who love God, all these things work together for good for those who are positioned in harmony with *His* purpose.* [29] Because whom He knows in advance, He marks out in advance* also *to be* conformed to the image of His Son, for himself to be* First-honoured* among many brothers. [30] But whom He marks out in advance,* these He appoints as well. And whom He appoints, these He also pronounces righteous. And whom He pronounces righteous, these He also magnifies.*

31   What, then, shall we say to these things? If God *is* for us, who *can be* against us? [32] He Who did not spare His own Son, but gave him up for us all, how shall He not together with him also freely give us all things?

33   Who can bring charges against *the* elect of God? God* *is* the one pronouncing *them* righteous. [34] Who *is* he condemning? Christ* *is* *the one* having died, but, rather, having also been raised, who is also at* *the* right hand* of God, and who also intercedes* for us.*

35   Who can separate us from the love of the

Christ? Tribulation, or distress, or persecution, or famine, or want of clothing, or peril, or sword? [36] As it has been written:

'For Your sake we are put to death
all day long;
we are considered as sheep of slaughter.'*

[37] But in all these things we are more than conquerors through him who loved us. [38] For I am persuaded that neither death, nor life, nor angels, nor rulers, nor forces of power, nor things present, nor things to come, [39] nor height, nor depth, nor any other created thing will be able to separate us from the love of God in Christ Jesus our Lord.

Paul's former vow against Christ.
The failure of Israel.
'God be exalted' (1\25, 2 Cor. 11\31)

9\1 I speak *the* truth by* Christ.* I am not lying, my conscience also bearing witness with me by* *the* divine spirit* [2] that for me there are immense sorrow and unceasing pains in my heart [3] – for I used to vow for* I myself* to be* a curse* from the Christ* – for the sake of my brothers, my countrymen in relation to flesh, [4] who are Israelites, whose *are* the adoption,* and the preeminence,* and the covenants,* and the giving of the law, and the service, and the promises, [5] whose *are* the fathers,* and from whom *is* the Christ in relation to flesh, he being over everything.
God be exalted* throughout* the Eons!*** Amen.*

Two Israels. The purposes of God
with Israel had relation only to a remnant

[6] *It is* not as though the oracle of God has taken no effect. For not all those of Israel *are* of Israel.* [7] Nor, because they are seed of Abraham, *are* all sons, but 'In Isaac a seed for you will be called.'* [8] That is, these Sons of God *are* not sons of the flesh, but sons of the promise, counted as seed. [9] For this *is* the oracle of promise: 'At this time I will come, and there will be a son for Sarah.'* [10] And not only *that*, but Rebecca also had *a seed* in *her* womb out of one man, our father Isaac. [11] For even in the sons not yet having been born nor having committed anything good or evil, in order that the purpose of God in

relation to election might remain – not out of works, but out of Him Who calls – [12] it was said to her, 'The elder will serve the younger.'* [13] As it has been written: 'Jacob I loved, but Esau I hated.'*

A remnant pronounced just

[14] What shall we say, then? *Is there* unrighteousness with God? May it not be! [15] For He says to Moses, 'I will pity whomever I will pity, and I will I will show mercy to whomever I will show mercy.'* [16] So then, *it is* not of him who is inclined to pleasure, nor of him who runs, but of God Who shows mercy. [17] For the Scroll says to Pharaoh, 'For this same thing I have raised you up, in order that in you I might display My power, and in order that My name might be declared in all the Earth.'* [18] So then, He shows mercy to whomever He wishes, and He hardens whomever He wishes. [19] You will say to me, then, 'Why does He still find fault, for who is withstanding* His purpose?' [20] But rather, oh* man, who are you who makes an answer against God? Shall the thing formed say to Him Who formed *it*, 'Why have You made me this way?'* [21] Does the potter not have power over the clay, to create out of the same lump one object for honour, and another for lack of honour? [22] But *what* if God, wanting to show indignation, and to make known His power, endured in much longsuffering *the* objects of indignation having been fitted for destruction, [23] and in order that He might make known the riches of His magnificence on the objects of mercy which He beforehand had prepared for magnificence,* [24] ourselves also whom He called, not only from among Jews, but also from among other nations? [25] As He says in Hosea as well:

'I will call them My people
who were not My people,
and *call* richly loved
she who was not richly loved.
[26] And it will come to pass
that in the place where it was said to them,
"You *are* not My people,"
there they will be called
Sons of *the* living God.'*

[27] But Isaiah cries out over Israel:

'Even if the number of the sons of Israel
were like the sand of the sea,
the remnant will be preserved.
²⁸ For He will conclude the matter
and cut *it* short in righteousness,
because the Lord will cause the matter
to be cut short on the Earth.'*

²⁹ And as Isaiah stated before:

'Unless *the* Lord of Hosts
had left us a seed,**
then* we would have been found*
like Sodom,
and we would have been made*
like Gomorrha.'*

Failure of Israel, despite the prophets.
Jesus 'the rock of offence' (Mat.16\18)
³⁰ What shall we say, then? That the other
nations, who do not follow after righteousness,
have obtained righteousness, but* a
righteousness out of faith. ³¹ Israel though,
following after a law of righteousness, did not
achieve a law of righteousness. ³² Why? Because
they did not *search for it* out of faith, but, as it
were, out of works of law. For they stumbled at
the stone of stumbling. ³³ As it has been
written:

'See now, I lay in Zion
a stone of stumbling
and a rock* of offence,
and whoever believes in Him
will not be put to shame.'*

Failure of Israel under law.
Jesus the end of the law

10\1 **B**rothers, the good pleasure of my own
heart and the prayer to God for Israel is for
salvation. ² For I bear them witness that they
have a zeal for God, but based not on
knowledge. ³ For being ignorant of the
righteousness of God, and endeavouring to
establish their own righteousness, they have not
submitted themselves to the righteousness of
God. ⁴ For Christ *is the* end of *the* law into*
righteousness for everyone believing. ⁵ For
Moses describes the righteousness which *is* out
of the law as 'The man having practised those
things will live by them.'*
⁶ But the righteousness out of faith speaks in
this way: Do not say in your heart, 'Who will

ascend into the Heaven?' – that is, to bring
Christ down – ⁷ nor, 'Who will descend into the
deep?'* – that is, to bring Christ up again from
the dead. ⁸ But what does it say? 'The
declaration is near you, in your mouth, and in
your heart.'* That is the declaration of the faith
which we proclaim, ⁹ so that if you profess with
your mouth *the* Lord Jesus, and if you believe in
your heart that God has raised him from* *the*
dead, you will be saved.
¹⁰ For with *the* heart is it believed into
righteousness, and with *the* mouth is profession
made into salvation. ¹¹ For the Scroll says,
'Everybody who believes in Him will not be
put to shame.'*
¹² For there is no difference between Jew and
Greek.* For the same Lord of all *is* rich to all
who call on Him. ¹³ For 'Everybody who calls
on the name of *the* Lord will be saved.'*
¹⁴ How, then, shall they call on *Him* in Whom
they have not believed? And how shall they
believe *Him* of Whom they have not heard?
And how shall they hear, apart from *somebody*
making proclamation? ¹⁵ And how shall they
proclaim, if they are not authorized?* As it has
been written:

'How beautiful are the feet
of those announcing the gospel of peace,
of those announcing the gospel
of excellent things!'*

¹⁶ But they have not all obeyed the gospel. For
Isaiah says:

'Lord, who has believed our report?'*

¹⁷ So then, faith *comes* out of hearing, and
hearing through a declaration* of God. ¹⁸ But, I
say, have they not heard? Yes, indeed:

'Their voice went out into all the Earth,
and their declarations to the ends
of the inhabited world.'*

¹⁹ But, I say, did Israel not know? First, Moses
says:

'I will provoke you to jealousy*
through *those who are* not a people;
through a people without understanding
I will provoke you to anger.'**

²⁰ Isaiah, though, is bold, and says:

'I have been found by those
not searching for Me;
I was brought to light to those
not enquiring after Me.'*

21 But to Israel he says:

'All day long I have stretched out My hands
to a disobeying and contradicting* people.'*

Purpose of God regarding the remnant

11\1 𝕴 say, then, did God throw aside His
people? May it not be!* For I also am an
Israelite, out of a seed of Abraham, of *the* tribe
of Benjamin.* ² God has not thrown aside His
people* whom He foreknew.*

Do you not know what the Scroll says about
Elijah, how he made intercession to God
against Israel, saying, ³ 'Lord, they murdered
Your prophets, and they dug down Your altars,
and I am left alone, and they are after my life'?*
⁴ But what does the divine response say to
him? 'I have reserved for Myself seven
thousand men who have not bowed a knee to
Baal.'*
⁵ Even so then, in this present time also there
has been a remnant in relation to an election of
favour. ⁶ If, however, through favour, then *it is*
no longer out of works. Otherwise, favour no
longer becomes favour. If, though, out of
works, it is no longer favour. Otherwise, work
is no longer work.
⁷ What then? Israel has not obtained what it
looks for. But the election obtained *it*, and the
rest were hardened, ⁸ just as* it has been
written:

'God gave them a spirit of stupor,
eyes not to see
and ears not to hear,*
until this day.'

⁹ And David says:

'Let their table become a snare
and a trap and a stumbling block
and a retribution for them.
¹⁰ Let their eyes be darkened
for them not to see,
and to perpetually bow down* their back.'*

*Rejection & divorce of Israel since the days
of Jeremiah (3\8) and Hosea (1\9)*

became a benefit to the world –
resurrection (11\15) through her restoration.
Israel provoked by the salvation of the nations
¹¹ I say, then,* did they not stumble in order
that they might fall? May it not be!* But through
their offence, salvation *has come* to the nations in
order to provoke them to jealousy.*
¹² Now if their offence *is the* wealth of *the*
world, and their decline *is the* wealth of *the*
nations, how much more *is* their fulness?
¹³ For I say to you, to the nations – since I am
indeed an apostle of *the* nations* – I make much
of my office, ¹⁴ if somehow I might perhaps
provoke to jealousy* my flesh,* and I might save
some from among them.
¹⁵ For if the rejection of them *is the* reconciling
of *the* world, what *will be* the receiving *of them* if
not life from *the* dead? ¹⁶ Now if the firstfruit *is*
holy, the lump also *is holy*. And if the root *is*
holy, the branches also *are holy*.
¹⁷ But if some of the branches were broken
off, and you, being a wild olive tree, were
grafted in among them, and became with them
a partaker of the root and of the fatness of the
olive tree, ¹⁸ do not boast against the branches.
But if you do boast against *them*, *know that* you
do not bear the root, but the root *bears* you.
¹⁹ You will say, then, 'Branches were broken
off, in order that I might be grafted in.' ²⁰ Well,
they were broken off because of unbelief, and
so you stand by faith.
Do not be arrogant, but be fearful. ²¹ For if
God did not spare the branches in relation to
nature, *watch out* in case He does not spare you
either. ²² See in this, consequently, *the* kindness
and severity of God: on those who fell, severity;
but towards you, kindness, if you continue in
kindness. Otherwise, you also will be cut off.
²³ And they also, if they do not persist in
unbelief, will be grafted in, for God is able to
graft them back in. ²⁴ For if you were cut out of
the olive tree, wild by natural order, and you
were grafted, contrary to natural order, into a
good olive tree, how much more can these who
are the *branches* by natural order be grafted into
their own olive tree? ²⁵ For I do not want you,
brothers, to be ignorant of this mystery – so
that you should not be wise in your own
estimation – that hardness in part* has happened
to Israel* until the fulness of the nations has
come in.
²⁶ And so all Israel will be preserved, as it has
been written:

'The Deliverer will come out of Zion,
and he will turn away ungodliness
from Jacob.
[27] And this *will be* the covenant
from Me to them,
when I will take out of the way
their violations.'*

[28] From the aspect of the gospel, *they are* enemies in respect of you. From the aspect of the election, though, *they are* the richly loved in respect of the patriarchs. [29] For the gifts and the calling of God *are* irrevocable.
[30] For as you also were at one time disobedient to God, but you have now obtained mercy through the unbelief of these, [31] so these also have now been disobedient, so that through your mercy they also might obtain mercy. [32] For God has classified them all together in unbelief, so that He might show mercy to them all.

[33] 'Oh *the* depth of *the* riches
both of *the* wisdom and knowledge of God!
How inscrutable His judgements
and His ways past finding out!
[34] For who has known *the* mind of *the* Lord,
or who has become His fellow counsellor?*
[35] Or who has first given to Him
but that* it will be recompensed to him?'*

[36] For out of* Him, and through* Him, and to* Him *are* all these. To Him *be* the preeminence* throughout* the Eons.* Amen.

One body in Christ (12\4-5; also 1 Cor. 10\17, 12\12-13, 12\20, 12\27, Eph. 1\23, 4\4, Col. 2\9, 3\15). Ekklesia gifts. Unfeigned love

12\1 I call on* you, therefore, brothers, moved by* the compassions of God, to present your bodies a living sacrifice, holy, well pleasing to God, your reasonable service, [2] and not to be fashioned in keeping with this Eon,* but to be transformed by the renewing of your mind,* for the testing* by you of what *is* the good and well pleasing and perfect will of God.*
[3] For through the merciful goodwill given to me, I say to everybody who is among you not to be high-minded above what is good to be minded, but to think to be sober-minded,* in relation to how for each one God has dealt a measure of faith .
[4] For as we have many members in one body,*

and all the members do not have the same function, [5] in the same way,* we, the many,* are one body* in Christ, and each one individually members of one another,* [6] having, though, differing gifts in relation to the merciful goodwill which is given to us: if prophecy, in relation to the proportion of the faith;* [7] if service, in serving; or if as a teacher, with teaching; [8] or if as one who exhorts, with exhortation; he who gives, *with* simplicity; he who takes the lead, with diligence; he who shows mercy, with cheerfulness.*
[9] *Let* love *be* unfeigned; abhorring the evil; clinging to the good; [10] being kindly disposed to one another in love for the brothers; in every honourable matter leading one another on; [11] in diligence not slothful; burning* in spirit; serving in season; [12] in the gladly-held expectation rejoicing; in tribulation enduring; in prayer continuing steadfastly;* [13] distributing to the needs of the holy people; pursuing kindness to strangers.*
[14] Speak good words to those who persecute you. Speak good words,* and do not curse.
[15] Rejoice with those rejoicing, and weep with those weeping, [16] having in mind the same things towards each other, not fixing the mind on high things, but going along with the lowly.
Do not become wise in yourselves.*
[17] Let nobody repay evil for evil. Have a predisposition for *what is* good in the sight of all men,* [18] if possible, as much as it lies in you, being at peace with all men. [19] Do not take revenge for yourselves, richly loved, but leave room for indignation, for it has been written:

' "Vengeance *is* Mine;
I will repay," says *the* Lord.
[20] If, then, your enemy is hungry, feed him;
if he is thirsty, give him a drink;
for doing this you will heap
on his head coals of fire."'*

[21] Do not be overpowered by evil, but overpower evil with good.

Supreme authority of apostles as agents appointed by God (Titus 3\1, Heb. 13\17), including tribute for their work (Luke 8\3, 1 Cor. 9\14, 1 Cor. 16\1, 2 Cor. 9\5, Gal. 6\6, Phil. 4\15-18)

13\1 Let every person* be subject to the supreme* authorities. For there is no authority unless from God, but the existing authorities˙ have been appointed˙ by God.˙ ² Whoever, in that case, withstands the authority, withstands the injunction˙ of God, and those who withstand will receive judgement˙ for themselves. ³ For the rulers are a terror not to good works, but to bad things.

Do you wish, then, to be unafraid of the authority?˙ Do good, and you will have praise for it. ⁴ For it is an agent of God to you for good. But if you commit evil, be fearful, for not in vain does it wear the sword. For it is an agent of God, an avenger for indignation on him committing evil. ⁵ *It is* necessary,˙ in that case, to be in subjection, not only on account of the indignation, but on account of conscience as well. ⁶ For on account of˙ this you pay tribute as well, for they are agents of God, persevering with this same thing. ⁷ Render to all, in that case, the debts: tribute to whom tribute, custom to whom custom, reverence to whom reverence, honour to whom honour.

⁸ Owe nothing to anybody, except to love one another, for he who loves another has fulfilled *the* law. ⁹ For in this – you shall not commit adultery; you shall not murder; you shall not steal; you shall not covet;˙ and if any other commandment – it is summed up in this oracle: 'You shall love your neighbour as yourself.'˙

¹⁰ Love does not operate evil towards the˙ neighbour. Love, consequently, *is the* fulness of *the* law.

¹¹ And *remember* this, knowing the time, that now *is* high time for us to be roused˙ out of sleep, for our salvation *is* now nearer than when we *first* believed. ¹² The night has far gone, and the day˙ has drawn near.˙ Let us, in that case, throw off˙ the works of the darkness, and let us put on the armour˙ of the light.˙

¹³ Let us walk decently, as in *the* day, not with orgies and in drunkenness, not in sexual immorality˙ and debauchery, not in strife and jealousy, ¹⁴ but put on the Lord Jesus Christ,˙ and make no provision for the lust of the flesh.

Sensitivity to the weak
in faith regarding eating

14\1 **B**ut receive him who is weak in the faith, not arbitrating in doubtful disputations. ² One has faith to eat all things. But another, being weak, eats vegetables.

³ Do not let him who eats despise him who does not eat. And do not let him who does not

eat judge him who does eat, for God has received him. ⁴ Who are you, judging the household servant of another man? To his own master he stands or falls. But he will be made to stand, for God is able to make him stand.

⁵ The one esteems a day above *another* day. Another esteems every day.˙ Let each be fully assured in his own mind. ⁶ He who observes the day, he observes *it* to *the* Lord. And he who does not observe the day, to *the* Lord he does not observe *it*. He who eats, eats to the Lord, for he gives thanks to God. And he who does not eat, to *the* Lord he does not eat, and he gives thanks to God.˙

⁷ For none of us lives for himself, and nobody dies for himself. ⁸ For if we should live, we should live for the Lord. And if we should die, we should die for the Lord. So then, whether we should live, or whether we should die, we are the Lord's. ⁹ Because for this Christ both died and rose and came alive, in order that he might rule over both *the* dead and *the* living.

¹⁰ But why do you pass judgement on your brother? And why do you despise your brother? For we will all stand before the judgement seat of the Christ.˙ ¹¹ For it has been written:

' "*As* I live," says *the* Lord,
"every knee will bow to Me,
and every tongue
will make admission to God." '˙

¹² So then, each of us will give to God an account concerning himself.˙ ¹³ We should, consequently, no longer pass judgement on one another, but, rather, make judgement in this: not to put an occasion of stumbling to a brother, nor a cause of offence.

¹⁴ I know, and I am persuaded by *the* Lord Jesus, that nothing in itself *is* profane. But to him who reckons anything to be profane, to him *it is* profane. ¹⁵ But if your brother is grieved on account of *your* food, you no longer walk in the way of love. Do not destroy, by your food, him for whom Christ died.

¹⁶ Do not, then, let evil be spoken of your advantage. ¹⁷ For the realm˙ of God is not eating and drinking,˙ but righteousness, and peace, and exuberance in *the* divine spirit.˙ ¹⁸ For he who serves the Christ in these things *is* well pleasing to God, and approved by men.

¹⁹ So then, we should pursue the things of peace, and the things for building one another up. ²⁰ For the matter of food does not destroy

the work of God. All things *are* clean, but *they are* evil for the man who eats with offence. [21] *It is* right not to eat flesh, nor drink wine, nor whatever your brother stumbles in, or is offended, or is weak.

[22] Do you possess faith? Possess *it* as your own in the sight of God. Exalted *is* he who does not judge himself in what he approves. [23] But he who doubts is condemned* if he eats, because *he does* not *eat* out of faith, and whatever *is* not out of faith is violation.

The revealing of Paul's gospel to the nations (2\16), once kept unvoiced & now made known (1 Cor. 2\7, Eph. 3\9-10, Col. 1\26-27, 2 Tim. 1\9, Titus 1\2)
[*verses 14\24-26 in other versions are at 16\25-27*]

[24] Now to the one being able* to establish you in relation to my gospel,* and the proclamation of Jesus Christ – in keeping with a revealing* of a mystery* kept in silence in Eonian* times,* [25] but now brought to light* through *the* prophetic Scrolls,* in harmony with a commandment of the Eonian* God, for an obedience of faith made known to all the nations,* [26] to *the* only wise God, through Jesus Christ – let there be magnificence* throughout the Eons.* Amen.*

Example of Christ, for the preeminence of God

15\1 And we who *are* strong* ought to bear the infirmities of the weak, and not please ourselves. [2] Let each one of us please *his* neighbour with a view to *what is* right for building up. [3] For even the Christ did not please himself, but, as it has been written:

'The revilings of those
who reviled You fell on me.'*

[4] For whatever things were written beforehand* for our teaching* were written beforehand* in order that through patient endurance, and through the encouragement of the Scrolls, we might have a gladly-held expectation.
[5] Now may the God of patient endurance and encouragement grant you to mind the same thing among yourselves, in keeping with Christ Jesus, [6] in order that with one accord, in one voice,* you might magnify God, that is,* the Father of our Lord Jesus Christ.*
[7] Therefore, receive one another, as the Christ also received you into *the* magnificence of God.

Jesus a servant of the circumcision.
Nations called to worship the God of Israel

[8] Now I proclaim Christ Jesus to have become* a servant* of the circumcision for *the* truth of God, for the confirming of the promises of the fathers, [9] and for the nations to magnify God for *His* mercy. As it has been written:

'For this cause, I will make declaration
among *the* nations,
and I will praise Your name.'*

[10] And additionally* it says:

'Rejoice, you nations, with His people.'*

[11] And further:*

'Give praise to the Lord, all nations,
and let all the peoples praise Him.'*

[12] And further,* Isaiah says:

'The root of Jesse and* the one raised up
to rule *the* nations will emerge,
and the nations will put their trust* in him.'*

Paul a servant of Jesus for the nations

[13] Now may the God of gladly-held expectation fill you with all exuberance and peace in believing, with a view to your abounding in gladly-held expectation, in *the* power of *the* divine spirit.* [14] And I myself am also persuaded concerning you, my brothers, that you also are full of goodness, being filled with all knowledge, being competent also to exhort one another.
[15] But, brothers, I wrote to you the more freely in some part,* as one reminding you – because of the merciful goodwill which was given to me by God – [16] for me to be* an agent of Christ Jesus for the nations, discharging like a priest* the gospel of God, in order that the offering up of the nations might be accepted, being sanctified in* *the* divine spirit.
[17] Therefore, I have exaltation in Christ Jesus in the things in relation to* God. [18] For I will not dare to speak of anything other than what Christ has operated through myself,* for obedience of the nations, by word and deed, [19] in *the* power of signs and wonders, by* *the* power of *the* Spirit of God,* for me to have fully proclaimed the gospel* of the Christ, from Jerusalem and in a circuit to Illyricum, [20] and

being so ambitious to proclaim the gospel, not where Christ was *already* named, in order that I should not build on the foundations of another, [21] but, as it has been written:

'*Those* to whom
it was not spoken
about Him will see,
and those who have not heard
will understand.'*

Desire & prayer to visit the Roman believers
[22] For that reason also, I have been hindered many times from coming to you. [23] But now, no longer having an opportunity in these regions, and having a longing for many years to come to you, [24] as soon as I take my journey into Spain I will come to you. For I hope to see you during my journey, and to be helped on my way there by you, if first I might enjoy your *company* for a while.
[25] Now, though, I am going to Jerusalem, attending to* the holy people. [26] For Macedonia and Achaia were pleased to make a certain contribution for the poor of the holy people in Jerusalem. [27] For they thought it good, and they are their debtors. For if the nations have been made partakers in their spiritual things, they ought to attend to them in material things as well. [28] So on having completed this, and having sealed this fruit to them, I will set off, by way of you, to Spain. [29] And I know that, in my coming to you, I will come in fulness of an invocation of favour* of the gospel of the Christ.
[30] Now I exhort you, brothers, through our Lord Jesus Christ, and through the love of *his* spirit, to strive together with me in prayers to God for me, [31] in order that I might be delivered from the unbelieving in Judea, and so that my service in Jerusalem might be acceptable to the holy people, [32] so that in exuberance I might come to you through *the* will of God, and I might be refreshed together with you.
[33] And the God of peace *be* with you all. Amen.

Salutations to friends of Paul

16\1 **N**ow I commend to you our sister Phoebe, she being a servant of the Ekklesia group at Cenchrea, [2] so that you receive her in *the* Lord in a manner worthy of the holy people,

and you might stand by her in whatever business she might have need of you, for she also has been a succourer of many, and of myself as well.
[3] Send greetings to Priscilla and Aquila, my fellow workers in Christ Jesus, [4] who have risked their own neck for my life, whom not only I but all the Ekklesia groups of the nations also thank. [5] *Greet* also their house-to-house* Ekklesia group. Greet my richly loved Epaenetus, who is a firstfruit of Achaia* for Christ.
[6] Greet Maria, who laboured hard on our behalf.
[7] Greet Andronicus and Junia, my relatives and my fellow prisoners, who are outstanding among the apostles,* who also were in Christ before me.
[8] Greet Amplias, my richly loved in *the* Lord.
[9] Greet Urbanus, our fellow worker in Christ, and Stachys, my richly loved.
[10] Greet Apelles, the approved *man* in Christ. Greet those of the *household* of Aristobulus.
[11] Greet Herodion, my relative.
Greet those of the *household* of Narcissus who are in *the* Lord.
[12] Greet Tryphena and Tryphosa, who laboured in *the* Lord.
Greet the richly loved Persis, who laboured hard in *the* Lord.
[13] Greet Rufus, eminent* in *the* Lord, and his mother and mine.
[14] Greet Asyncritus, Phlegon, Hermas, Patrobas, Hermes, and the brothers with them.
[15] Greet Philologus, and Julia, Nereus, and his sister, and Olympas, and all holy people with them.
[16] Greet each other with a holy kiss. The Ekklesia groups of Christ send you greetings.*

Avoid troublemakers. Victory over Satan
[17] Now I exhort you, brothers, to mark those who cause factions and stumbling blocks contrary to the teaching which you learned, and to turn away from them. [18] For these do not serve our Lord Jesus Christ, but their own belly, and by means of their smooth speech and fine discourses* they thoroughly deceive the hearts of the guileless. [19] For your obedience has reached everyone. I rejoice, therefore, concerning you. But yet I want you to be wise with respect to good, and harmless with respect to evil.
[20] And with speed the God of peace will crush

Satan in pieces under your feet.

The merciful goodwill of our Lord Jesus Christ *be* with you.

²¹ Timothy, my fellow worker, and Lucius, and Jason, and Sosipater, my relatives, send you greetings.

²² I, Tertius, the one writing *this* letter,* greet you in *the* Lord.

²³ Gaius, host of myself and of the whole Ekklesia, greets you.

Erastus, the treasurer of the city, greets you, and Quartus, the brother.

²⁴ The merciful goodwill of our Lord Jesus Christ *be* with you all. Amen.

*[verses 16\25-27 in other versions are at 14\24-26]**

† The Letters of Paul †

1 Corinthians

1\1

aul, a designated[*] apostle of Jesus Christ through *the* will of God, and the brother Sosthenes.

[2] To the Ekklesia group of God which is in Corinth, sanctified in Christ Jesus, designated as holy people,[*] with all those in every place appealing to the name of our Lord Jesus Christ, both theirs and ours, [3] merciful goodwill to you, and peace, from God our Father, and[*] *from the* Lord Jesus Christ.[**]

Thanksgiving & encouragements

[4] I thank my God always for you, for the merciful goodwill of God which was given to you in Christ Jesus, [5] so that in everything you were enriched in him,[*] in all speech, and all knowledge, [6] in keeping with the fact that[*] the testimony of the Christ was confirmed in you, [7] for you to be coming short in not a single gift, in waiting for the appearing[*] of our Lord Jesus Christ, [8] who will also keep you strong[*] until *the* end, blameless on the day of our Lord Jesus Christ.[*]

[9] God *is* faithful,[*] by Whom you were called to *the* partnership of His Son, Jesus Christ our Lord.

Rebuke for divisions, identifying with
& attaching to names of leaders rather than Christ.
Paul resists a party built around himself,
but identifies & designates
as trustworthy men Crispus & Gaius
& Stephanus' household (16\17, Acts 14\23)

[10] But I encourage you, brothers, in the name of our Lord Jesus Christ, that you all speak with one voice, and there should not be schisms among you, but you should be perfectly joined together in the same mind and in the same opinion. [11] For it has been shown to me concerning you, my brothers, by those *of the house* of Chloe, that there are strivings among you.[*]

[12] I mean, however, this: that each of you says, 'I am of Paul,'[*] and 'I of Apollos,' and 'I of Peter,' and 'I of Christ.' [13] Is the Christ divided? Was Paul hanged on a stake[*] on your behalf? Or were you identified into the name of Paul?[*]

[14] I thank God that I identified none of you, except Crispus and Gaius, [15] so that nobody should say that I made identifications into my own name. [16] And I identified the household of Stephanas as well. Other than that, I do not know if I identified any other.

Paul to proclaim the gospel,
not make identifications among men.
The message is 'the power of God'

[17] For Christ authorized me not to make identifications, but to proclaim the gospel, not in wisdom of language, so that the stake[*] of Christ should be made of no effect. [18] For the message of the stake[*] is foolishness; on the one hand, to those perishing, but, on the other hand, to us being saved[*] it is the power of God. [19] For it has been written:

'I will destroy the wisdom of the wise,
and I will set aside
the understanding of the intellectuals.'[*]

[20] Where *is the* wise *man*? Where *the* scribe? Where *the* disputer of this Eon?[*] Has God not made foolish the wisdom of this world? [21] For since, in the wisdom of God, the world did not know God through wisdom, God was pleased through the foolishness of what was proclaimed to save those who believe, [22] and because Jews ask for a sign[*] and Greeks search for wisdom. [23] But we proclaim Christ hanged on a stake:[*] to Jews a stumbling block, and to Greeks foolishness; [24] but to those designated,[*] both Jews and Greeks, *we proclaim* Christ, *the* power[*] of God, and wisdom[*] of God. [25] Because the foolish thing of God is wiser than men, and the weak thing of God is stronger than men.

[26] For look at your calling, brothers, how not many *are* wise in relation to flesh, not many mighty, not many high-born.[*] [27] But God chose the foolish things of the world in order that He might put to shame the wise;[*] and God has chosen the weak things of the world in order that He might put to shame the mighty; [28] and God has chosen the ignoble and the despised of the world and the things which are not in order that He might bring to nothing the things which are, [29] so that all flesh might have no cause to boast in God's presence.

[30] But from[*] Him you are in Christ Jesus, who became for us wisdom from God, both righteousness and holiness and redemption, [31] so that, as it has been written: 'He who boasts,

let him boast in *the* Lord."

Authorization of Paul

2\1 **A**nd brothers, *when* I came to you I did not come in the manner of superiority* of speech or wisdom in declaring to you the testimony of God. ² For I determined not to know anything among you except Jesus Christ and him having been hanged on a stake.*

³ And in weakness, and in fear, and in much trembling I myself was among you. ⁴ And my speech and my proclaiming *were* not in persuasive words of human wisdom, but in an exhibition* of spirit* and power,* ⁵ in order that your faith might not be by wisdom of men, but by *the* power of God.

Wisdom of God is in having the divine spirit which is 'from God' (2\12).
The mystery once 'kept hidden' (Rom. 14\24) now told 'in advance of the Eons' (2 Tim. 1\9).
Apostles 'have the mind of Christ'

⁶ But we* speak wisdom among those complete, yet not *the* wisdom of this Eon, nor of the rulers of this Eon* who are being brought to nothing. ⁷ But we speak *the* wisdom of God as a mystery which has been kept hidden, which God has marked out beforehand,* in advance of the Eons,** for our magnificence, ⁸ which none of the rulers of this Eon* has known, for if they had known they would not have hanged the Lord of radiance* on a stake.* ⁹ But as it has been written:

'Eye has not seen*
and ear has not heard,
and it has not entered
into *the* heart of man
the things which God has prepared
for those who love Him.'*

¹⁰ God, though, revealed *them* to us* through* His spirit.* For the spirit* searches all things – even* the deep things of God.* ¹¹ For who among men perceives* the things of man, except the spirit of the man which *is* in him?* So also, nobody perceives* the things of God except the spirit of God.

¹² But we received not the spirit of the world, but the spirit which *is* from God,* in order that we might perceive* the things freely given to us by God, ¹³ which things we also speak,* not in *the* taught subject matter of human wisdom, but

in *the* taught *subject matter* of *the* divine spirit,* making comparisons of spiritual *matters* with spiritual *matters.*

¹⁴ But a natural* man does not receive the things of *the* spirit of God,* for they are foolishness to him, and he cannot know *them*, because they are examined* spiritually. ¹⁵ The spiritual *man*, though, examines* all things,* yet he himself is examined* by nobody.

¹⁶ 'For who has known *the* mind of *the* Lord?
    Who can instruct* Him?'*

We,* however, have *the* mind* of Christ.*

Flesh-natured condition of the Corinthians

3\1 **A**nd, brothers, I was not able to speak to you as if to spiritual men, but *only* as if to flesh-natured *men*, as if to babies in Christ. ² I gave you milk to drink, and not* meat, for you were not yet able *to digest it*, but nor are you yet able to even now. ³ For you are still flesh-natured, for where among you *there is* envying, and strife, and divisions, are you not flesh-natured and walking according to man? ⁴ For whenever somebody might say, 'I am of Paul,' and another, 'I of Apollos,' are you not flesh-natured?

⁵ Well then, who is Paul, and who Apollos, but agents through whom you came to believe, and as the Lord has assigned to each?

⁶ I planted, Apollos watered, but God was causing it to grow. ⁷ So then, neither is he anything who plants, nor he who irrigates, but *it is* God Who gives increase. ⁸ Now he who plants and he who waters are one,* but each will receive his own reward in relation to his own labour.

Paul the wise architect.
All works to be judged.
The divine spirit is in those who believe

⁹ For we* are fellow workers* of God, a tilled field* of God. You are the building** of God.
¹⁰ In relation to the merciful goodwill of God which was given to me, I laid the foundation as a wise architect, and another builds on it. But let each *man* see to it how he builds, ¹¹ for nobody is able to lay another foundation* other than the one being laid up, which is Jesus Christ.

¹² But if anybody builds on this foundation *using* gold, silver, precious stones, wood, hay,

stubble, [13] the practise of each will be brought to light, for the day* will declare *it*, because it will be revealed in fire, and the fire will test the practise of each, of what sort it is.*

[14] If the work of anybody which he has built up remains, he will receive a reward. [15] If the work of anybody will be burned up, he will suffer loss, but he himself will be saved, but as if through fire.*

[16] Do you not know that you are a temple of God,* and the spirit of God* inhabits* you? [17] If any man should defile the temple of God, God will destroy him, for the temple of God is holy, which is *what* you are.*

Against wisdom of this world.
Believers are Christ's

[18] Let nobody deceive himself. If anybody supposes to be* wise in this Eon,* let him become a fool so that he might become wise. [19] For the wisdom of this world* is foolishness with God. For it has been written: 'He catches out the wise in their own craftiness.'* [20] And additionally:* '*The* Lord knows the reasonings of the wise, that they are vain.'*

[21] Consequently, let nobody among men boast. For all these things are yours. [22] Whether Paul, or Apollos, or Cephas, or *the* world, or life, or death, or things present, or things about to come, everything is yours,* [23] and you are Christ's, and Christ *is* God's.*

Authenticity & authority of apostles

4\1 Let a man consider us as the servants of Christ and house managers of mysteries of God. [2] But, in addition, it is looked for in the house managers that a person might be found faithful.

[3] But to me it is the smallest matter that I should be examined by you, or by *the* day of man.* Indeed, I do not even examine my own self. [4] For against myself I am conscious of nothing. Yet not in reference to that have I been pronounced righteous. Rather, he who examines me is *the* Lord.

[5] Therefore, do not judge anything before *the* season when the Lord should appear, who will both* shed light on the hidden things of darkness, as well as bring to light* the motives of hearts. And then there will be praise for each one from God.

[6] And* these things, brothers, I have figuratively transferred* to myself and Apollos on account of* you, so that in us you might learn

not to think* beyond* what* has been written,* so that none of you might be made puffed up,* on behalf of* one to the detriment of* somebody else.* [7] For who makes you differ?* And what do you have which you did not receive? Now if you did also receive *it*, why do you boast as if not having received *it*? [8] Already you have been filled. Already you are rich. You have reigned like kings* without us, and I wish you really did reign so that we also might reign together with* you.*

[9] For I think that God has put us apostles on display* last, as if appointed to death, for we have become a theatre* to the world, both* to angels* and to men.*

[10] We *are* fools on account of Christ; you, though, are wise in Christ. We are weak; you are strong. You are honourable; we are without honour.

[11] Even up to the present hour we have been hungry and thirsty; and we are poorly clothed and* have been beaten;* and we wander about homeless,* [12] and we labour, working with our own hands; being reviled, we speak good words;* being persecuted, we put up with *it*; [13] being spoken evil of, we encourage. We have until now become like filth of the world, wiped-off dirt of everything.*

[14] Not to put you to shame do I write these things, but as my richly loved sons I make admonishment. [15] For even if you might have ten thousand instructors in Christ, *you do* not, though, *have* many fathers, for in Christ Jesus I gave you birth* through the gospel.

[16] On account of this, I encourage you, become imitators* of me.* [17] On account of this, I have sent to you Timothy, who is my richly loved son and he *is* faithful in *the* Lord, *and* he will remind you of my ways in Christ, just as I teach everywhere in every Ekklesia group.

Corinthians disciplined by Paul

[18] Now some are puffed up,* as though I were not coming to you. [19] But I shall come to you soon, if the Lord wills, and I will get to know not the speech of those who are puffed up,* but the power. [20] For the Sovereign Rulership* of God *is established* not in talk, but in power.

[21] What do you prefer: I should come to you with a rod, or in love and a spirit of meekness?

Rebuke for fornication

5\1 It is commonly* heard *there is* fornication

among you, and such fornication which is not even named among the nations, for somebody to have *his* father's wife.[*] ² And you have been puffed up,[*] and did not rather mourn that he who did this deed might be taken away from your company.

³ For I, for my part, as if being absent in body, but being present in spirit, have already condemned him who committed[*] this deed, ⁴ in the name of our Lord Jesus Christ, yourselves and my spirit being brought together, with the power of our Lord Jesus Christ, ⁵ to hand such a man[*] over to Satan[*] for destruction[*] of the flesh,[*] so that the[*] spirit[*] can be saved[*] in the day of the Lord Jesus.[*]

Unleavened bread of sincerity & of truth
⁶ Your boasting *is* not good. Do you not know that a little leaven leavens the whole lump? ⁷ Purge out the old leaven, in order that you might become a new substance, since you are unleavened. For indeed, our Passover, Christ, has been sacrificed on our behalf.[*]

⁸ So then, we should keep the feast not with old leaven, nor with the leaven of malice and evil, but with unleavened[*] *bread* of sincerity and truth.

⁹ I wrote to you in the letter[*] not to mix closely together with fornicators, ¹⁰ not, *however, referring* altogether to the fornicators of this world, or to the fraudsters,[*] or swindlers, or idolaters, since in that case you would have to withdraw from the world. ¹¹ But now I have written to you not to mix[*] closely together if anybody designated a brother *is* either a fornicator, or a fraudster,[*] or an idolater, or an abusive speaker, or a drunkard, or a swindler, *and* not to eat with such a man. ¹² For what *is it* to me to judge also those outside? Do you not judge those inside? ¹³ But those outside God judges: 'You shall put away the evil *person* from among yourselves.'[*]

Rebuke for litigation
6\1 Does any of you, having a matter against another, dare to go to law before the unjust, and not before the holy people?

² Do you not know that the holy people will judge the world?[*] And if the world will be judged by you, you are unfit for[*] *the* least of *the* courts?[*] ³ Do you not know that we are going to judge angels?[*] – to say nothing of[*] the affairs of this life![*]

⁴ If, then, you have commonplace[*] court *cases,*[*]

you should appoint[*] as judges those who are counted as nothing[*] among the Ekklesia group. ⁵ I speak to your shame. Has it come to this, that there is not a wise *person* among you, no, not even one who will be able to make a decision over the brother in your company? ⁶ But brother goes to law with brother, and this in the sight of unbelievers!

⁷ Already, then, there is utter failure among you in that you have lawsuits among yourselves. Why not rather endure wrong? Why not rather be defrauded?[*] ⁸ Instead, you act unjustly and defraud – and these things to brothers.

List of those excluded from the Eon
(Gal. 5\19-21, Eph. 5\5, Rev. 21\8).
Others 'pronounced righteous' & 'joined to the Lord'
⁹ Do you not know that the unrighteous will not inherit the Sovereign Rulership of God? Do not be deceived. Neither fornicators, nor idolaters, nor adulterers, nor *the* effeminate,[*] nor homosexuals,[*] ¹⁰ nor fraudsters,[*] nor thieves, nor drunkards, nor abusive speakers, nor extortioners will inherit *the* Sovereign Rulership[*] of God.^{**}

¹¹ And some of you were those things. But you have had yourself washed,[*] but you have been sanctified, but you have been pronounced righteous in the name of the Lord Jesus and by means of the spirit of our God.[*]

¹² All things are lawful to me, but not all things are profitable. All things are lawful to me, but I will not be brought under power by[*] anything. ¹³ Foods for the belly, and the belly for foods – but God will bring both it and them to nothing. Now the body *is* not for fornication, but for the Lord, and the Lord for the body.

¹⁴ And God both raised up the Lord, and[*] He will raise up us by His own power.

¹⁵ Do you not know that your bodies are members of Christ? Having taken, then, the members of Christ, shall I make *them* members of a prostitute? May it not be![*]

¹⁶ Do you not know that he who is joined to a prostitute is one body? 'For the two,' He says, 'will become[*] one flesh.'[*] ¹⁷ But he who is joined to the Lord is one spirit.

¹⁸ Flee fornication. Whatever violation which a man might commit is outside the body, but he who commits fornication violates against[*] his own body.

¹⁹ Or do you not know that your body is a temple of *the* divine spirit[*] in you, which you have from God, and you are not your own? ²⁰

For you have been bought at a price. Magnify God, therefore, in your body, and in your spirit, which are God's.*

The married & unmarried

7\1 Now concerning what you wrote to me,* *it is* good for a man not to touch a woman. ² But on account of fornication, let each man have his own wife, and let each woman have her own husband.

³ Let the husband render to the wife due affection,* and likewise the wife also to the husband. ⁴ The wife does not have jurisdiction over her own body, but the husband *does*. And, likewise, the husband also does not have jurisdiction over* his own body, but the wife *does*.

⁵ Do not deprive each other,* except by consent for a time, so that you might be at leisure for fasting and for prayer, then you can come together again as one, so that Satan does not test you on account of your lack of self-control.

⁶ However, I speak this by way of permission,* not by way of a commandment. ⁷ For I wish all men to be even as I myself *am*, although each has his own gift from God, one in this matter, and another in that.

⁸ But to the unmarried and to the widows I say, it is good for them if they should remain even as I *am*.

⁹ If, though, they do not have self-control, let them marry, for it is better to marry than to burn.*

¹⁰ And to the married I command – not I, but the Lord – a wife is not to be separated from *her* husband. ¹¹ But even if she was made separate, let her remain unmarried, or be reconciled to the husband. And a husband is not to put away *his* wife.

Circumstances for remarriage

¹² But to the rest I myself speak, not the Lord.*

If any brother has an unbelieving wife and she consents to live with him, he must not put her away.

¹³ And *if* the woman who has an unbelieving husband and he consents to live with her, let her not leave him.

¹⁴ For the unbelieving husband is made holy by the wife, and the unbelieving wife is made holy* by the husband, since otherwise your children are unclean, but now they are holy.

¹⁵ But if the unbeliever does separate himself, let him* be separated. The brother or the sister has not been enslaved* in such *cases*, but God has called us in peace. ¹⁶ For how do you know, wife, if you will save the husband? Or how do you know, husband, if you will save the wife?

¹⁷ However, as God has imparted to each one as the Lord has called each one, let him walk in this manner. I also appoint this in all the Ekklesia groups.

Circumcision

¹⁸ Was anybody called having been circumcised? Let him not become uncircumcised. Was anybody called in uncircumcision? Let him not be circumcised. ¹⁹ Circumcision is nothing, and uncircumcision is nothing. Only keeping commandments of God *counts for anything.**

Service

²⁰ Let each one remain in the position in which he was called. ²¹ Were you called as a slave? Let it not be an anxiety to you. But even so, if you are able to become a freeman,* by all means use *it*. ²² For the one in *the* Lord having been called as a slave is a freeman* of *the* Lord. And, likewise, the one having been called as a freeman* is a slave of Christ. ²³ You were bought with a price. Do not be slaves of men. ²⁴ Brothers, into whatever he has been called, let each one remain in that with God.

Marriage & remarriage
not advisable in times of distress
& tribulation, but not a violation

²⁵ Now concerning virgins, I do not have a commandment from *the* Lord. Yet I give my opinion* as one having received mercy from *the* Lord to be* faithful.

²⁶ I reckon, therefore, this is good on account of the present distress,** that *it is* good for a man to remain the same. ²⁷ Have you been bound to a wife? Do not search to be released. Have you been broken* from a wife? Do not search for a wife. ²⁸ But even if you might have married, you have not violated. And if a virgin marries, she has not violated. Nevertheless, these will have tribulation in respect of the flesh. But I *say this* to spare you.

The time is short

²⁹ But I declare this, brothers: the time has been made short, so that from now on even

those having wives should be as if having none; [30] and those weeping as though not weeping; and those rejoicing as though not rejoicing; and those making purchases as though not possessing; [31] and those using this world as though not abusing *it*. For the system* of this world is passing away.*

[32] But I want you to be* free from anxiety. The unmarried man cares for the things of the Lord, how he will please the Lord. [33] But he who is married cares for the things of the world, how he will please the wife.

[34] There is also a difference between a wife and a virgin. The unmarried woman* cares for the things of the Lord, so that she might be set apart both in body and in spirit. But she who is married cares for the things of the world, how she will please the husband. [35] And I speak this for your own advantage, not so that I might tie a snare around you, but for the sake of what *is* appropriate, and a willing devotion to the Lord without distraction.

[36] If anybody, though, might think that he behaves himself in an unseemly manner towards his virgin,* if she is of the full flower of age, and *he thinks* it ought to be* so, let him do what he wishes. He does not violate. Let them marry.

[37] Nevertheless, he who stands firm in heart, not being in compulsion, but having power over his own will, and has so decided in his heart to keep his virgin *daughter at home*, he does well. [38] So then, both he who gives *her* in marriage does well, but he who does not give *her* in marriage does better.

[39] A wife is bound by law for such time as her husband lives.* But if her husband has fallen asleep, she is a freewoman* to be married to whomever she wishes, only in *the* Lord. [40] But she is happier* if she remains like this, according to my judgement,* and I think I also have *the* spirit of God.*

Sacrifices to idols. One God,
one Lord (Deut. 6\4, Eph. 4\5-6, etc.)

8\1 Now concerning things sacrificed to idols, we know – for we all have knowledge – that knowledge puffs up,* but love builds up. [2] But if anybody thinks he knows* anything, he has not yet come to knowledge of anything as he ought to know* *it*.

[3] But if anybody loves God, he is known* by Him.

[4] Concerning, then, the eating of the things

sacrificed to idols, we know* that an idol *is* nothing in *the* world,* and that *there is* no other God but *the* true one.* [5] For even if there are *those* known as gods, whether in Heaven or on Earth – as there are many gods, and many lords – [6] *there is* to us, though, one God,* the Father, from Whom *are* all these things, as well as ourselves for* Himself, and* one Lord, Jesus Christ, by means of whom *are* all these things,* as well as ourselves by means of* himself.

[7] But *this* knowledge *is* not in everybody, for until now some, being conscious of the idol, eat *it* as an idolatrous sacrifice, and their conscience, being weak, is polluted.* [8] But food does not commend us to God,* for we neither have advantage if we eat, nor do we fall short if we do not eat.

Liberty might cause
a weaker brother to stumble

[9] But look to it in case by any means this warrant* of yours should become a stumbling block to the weak. [10] For if anybody who has knowledge sees you taking a seat in a temple of an idol, would not the conscience of him being weak be indoctrinated* so as to eat the idolatrous sacrifice? [11] And over your knowledge, the weak brother, for whom Christ died, will wither. [12] But by violating in that way against the brothers, and striking their weak conscience, you violate against Christ. [13] That is why,* if food causes my brother to stumble, I would certainly not eat meat throughout the Eon,* so that I might not cause my brother to stumble.

Apostleship asserted

9\1 Am I not an apostle? Am I not a freeman?* Have I not seen Jesus Christ our Lord?* Are you not my work in *the* Lord?

[2] If I am not an apostle to others, yet at least I am to you, for you are the seal of my apostleship in *the* Lord.*

[3] My defence to those who examine me is this: [4] Do we not have authority to eat and to drink? [5] Do we not have authority to take along a wife *who is* a sister *in the Lord*, as *do* the rest of the apostles as well, and the brothers of the Lord and Peter? [6] Or *is it* only Barnabas and I *who* do not have a warrant for not working? [7] Who at any time serves as a soldier at his own expense? Who plants a vineyard and does not eat from its fruit? Or who shepherds a flock

and does not drink from the milk of the flock? [8] Do I just speak these things on a human level? Or does the law not say these things as well? [9] For it has been written in the law of Moses: 'You shall not muzzle an ox which threshes out corn.'* Is it oxen God is concerned about? [10] Or does He say *it* wholly because of us? Well, on our account it was written, in order that he who plows ought to plow in hope, and he who threshes corn ought, in hope, to be a partaker of his hope.
[11] If we have sown the spiritual things for you, *is it* an extraordinary thing if we reap your material things? [12] If others share in *this* authority over you, *should* we not *share in it* all the more? Nevertheless, we did not use this authority, but we put up with all things, in order that we should not give any hindrance to the gospel of the Christ.
[13] Do you not know that those labouring *in* consecrated things eat *from the income* of the Temple, *and* those officiating at the altar are partakers with the altar? [14] So did the Lord also make the command for those proclaiming the gospel to live out of the gospel. [15] But I have used none of these things, and I did not write these things in order that it should be so in my case. For *it would be* better, rather, for me to die than that anybody should make my exultation void. [16] For if I proclaim the gospel, there is no boasting for me, for necessity presses on me. But it would be woe to me if I did not proclaim the gospel! [17] For if I carry this out being willing, I have a reward. But if being unwilling, I have been entrusted with an oversight, [18] *so* what, then, would be my reward? That in announcing the gospel I should make the gospel of Christ without expense, not abusing my authority in the gospel.
[19] For being a freeman* from all things, I made myself a servant to all, so that I might gain the more. [20] And to the Jews I became as a Jew, so that I might gain the Jews; to those under law as under law, so that I might gain those under law; [21] to those without law as without law (being not without law to God, but under law to Christ), so that I might gain those without law; [22] to the weak I became as weak, so that I might gain the weak.* To all these I have become all things, so that I might by every means save some. [23] And I do this on account of the gospel, so that I might become a partaker with it.

Striving for reward of a crown

[24] Do you not know that those who run in a stadium* all run, but one receives the prize? Run in such a way that you might obtain *it*. [25] But everybody who strives for the mastery exercises self-control in all things. Now they *do it* in order that they might receive a corruptible crown; we, though, *to receive* an incorruptible* crown.
[26] I run, therefore, in this way, not uncertainly. I fight with the fists in this way, not beating* air.* [27] But I buffet my body, and reduce *it* into slavery, in case having proclaimed to others I myself might become disqualified.*

Mosaic dispensation as a type.
The rock of provision symbolized the Christ to come, he who is 'the rock' (Mat. 16\18, Rom. 9\33).
Ways out of trial

10\1 Now I do not want you to be ignorant, brothers, of how all our fathers were under the cloud, and all passed through the sea, [2] and they were all identified* into Moses in the cloud and in the sea, [3] and all ate the same spiritual food, [4] and all drank the same spiritual drink, for they drank out of a following spiritual rock, and the rock* symbolized* the Christ.* [5] But God was not pleased with the majority of them, for they became strewn around in the desert.* [6] But these things became our illustrative examples,* for* us not to be** cravers* of evil things, as they for their part lusted.
[7] Neither must you become idolaters, like some of them, as it has been written: 'The people sat down to eat and drink, and they rose up to play.'* [8] Nor should we commit sexual immorality, as some of them committed sexual immorality, and twenty-three thousand* fell in one day.* [9] Nor let us excessively put the Christ to the test,* as some of them put *God* to the test and they perished by the snakes,* [10] nor grumble, as some of them grumbled* and were destroyed by the destroyer.
[11] Now all these things happened to them as examples,* and they were written for our warning. On them have come* the ends of the Eons.** [12] So then, let he who thinks he stands firm look to it in case he might fall.
[13] No temptation has seized you except a human one. But God *is* faithful, Who will not allow you to be tested above what you are able, but with the temptation* He will also make a way out for you to be able to endure *it*.

¹⁴ Consequently, my richly loved, flee from idolatry.

All things lawful, not all things profitable. Sacrifices to demons

¹⁵ I speak as if to wise men. Judge what I say. ¹⁶ The cup of eulogy* which we lift up,* does it not represent* the partnership of the blood of the Christ? The bread which we break, does it not represent* the partnership of the body of the Christ? ¹⁷ Since there is one loaf, we, *being* the many, are one body,* for we all partake out of the one loaf.

¹⁸ Look at Israel concerning flesh. Are those eating the sacrifices not fellow partakers with the altar? ¹⁹ What do I say, then? That an idol is anything? Or that which is offered in sacrifice to an idol is anything? ²⁰ But what the nations sacrifice they sacrifice to demons, and not to God,* and I do not want you to be partakers with demons. ²¹ You cannot drink a cup of *the* Lord as well as a cup of demons. You cannot partake of a table of *the* Lord as well as of a table of demons. ²² Otherwise, do we provoke the Lord to jealousy?* Are we stronger than Him?

²³ All things are lawful for me, but not all things are profitable. All things are lawful for me, but not all things build up.

²⁴ Let nobody look to his own things, but each *to* the thing* of another. ²⁵ Eat everything which is sold in the market, questioning nothing on account of conscience. ²⁶ For 'The Earth *is* the Lord's, and the fulness of it." ²⁷ But if anybody among the unbelievers invites you, and you want to go, eat everything which is set before you, asking nothing on account of conscience.

²⁸ But if anybody says to you, 'This is offered in sacrifice to an idol,' do not eat *it*, on account of him who showed it, and of the conscience. For 'The Earth *is* the Lord's, and the fullness of it." ²⁹ And *by* the conscience, I mean not that of your own, but the other man's. For why is my freedom* judged by another's conscience? ³⁰ If by merciful goodwill I am a partaker, why am I spoken badly of because of that for which I give thanks?

³¹ Whether, therefore, you eat or you drink, or whatever you do, do all things for *the* preeminence of God. ³² Become without offence, neither to the Jews nor Greeks, nor to the Ekklesia groups of God, ³³ just as I please all in all things, not searching for that of my own profit, but that of the many in order that they might be saved.

11\1 Become imitators* of me, just as* I also *am* of Christ.

God, Christ & the man as fountainheads. Hair & head covering, as symbols of authority. Customs with public prayer. God 'the fountainhead of Christ' (John 6\57, 2 Cor. 13\4)

² Now I praise you, brothers, because you remember me in all things, and you hold fast the traditions as I delivered *them* to you. ³ But I want you to know that the fountainhead of every man is Christ,* but *the* fountainhead of *the* woman *is* the man, and the fountainhead of Christ *is* God.*

⁴ Every man praying or prophesying having nothing on *his* head puts his fountainhead* to disgrace. ⁵ But every woman praying or prophesying with the head unveiled puts her head to disgrace, for that is one and the same as having been shaved. ⁶ For if a woman is not covered, let her be shorn as well. But if *it is* dishonourable for a woman to be shorn or shaven, let her be covered. ⁷ For a man, being originally *the* image and magnificence of God, the head ought not to be covered. A woman, though, is *the* glory of man. ⁸ For man is not out of woman, but woman out of man.

⁹ And man was not created for the woman, but woman for* the man. ¹⁰ Because of this, the woman ought to have authority over *her* head, because of the angels.* ¹¹ Nevertheless, man *is* neither independent of woman, nor woman independent of man, in *the* Lord. ¹² For as the woman *is* out of the man, so also *is* the man through the woman. All this, though, *is* from God.

¹³ Judge in yourselves. Is it becoming for an uncovered woman to pray to God? ¹⁴ Or does not even nature itself teach you that if a man wears his hair long it is to his dishonour? ¹⁵ But if a woman wears her hair long it is to her honour, for long hair has been given instead of a head-dress. ¹⁶ But if anybody seems to be* fond of strife,* we have no such custom, neither *do* the Ekklesia groups of God.

Rebuke of selfish eating behaviours at suppers. Comparison of the selflessness of Jesus as demonstrated symbolically at his Passover supper

¹⁷ Now, in giving this instruction, I do not praise *you* that you come together not for the better, but for the worse. ¹⁸ For first of all, *when*

you come together among *the* Ekklesia group, I hear that there are schisms among you, and to some extent* I believe *that*. [19] For there must be* sects also among you, so that those approved might become brought to light among you.

[20] In coming together, therefore, into one place, *it is* not to eat a supper of *the* Lord. [21] For in eating each one takes his own supper first, and one goes hungry, and another gets drunk. [22] For is it that you do not have homes to eat and drink in? Or do you despise the Ekklesia of God,* and do you humiliate those who do not have *any*? What should I say to you? Shall I praise you in this? I do not praise *you*.

[23] For I received from the Lord* that which I handed down also to you: that the Lord Jesus, on the night in which he was betrayed, took bread, [24] and, having given thanks, he broke *it* and said, 'Take; eat. This represents* my body which is being broken on your behalf. Do this in remembrance of me.' [25] Likewise, after supper *he took* the cup as well, saying, 'This cup represents* the new covenant in my blood. Do this, as often as you drink *it*, in remembrance of me.' [26] For, until he comes,* as often as you eat this bread and drink this cup, you proclaim the death of the Lord.

[27] Therefore, whoever eats this bread and drinks the cup of the Lord unworthily of the Lord will be guilty in regard to the body and the blood of the Lord. [28] But let a man examine himself, and in that way let him eat from the bread and drink from the cup. [29] For he who eats and drinks unworthily eats and drinks judgement* for himself, not discerning the body of the Lord. [30] On account of this, many among you *are* weak and sick, and a number have fallen asleep.* [31] For if we were to judge ourselves, we should not be judged. [32] But when being judged, we are chastened by the Lord so that we should not be condemned with the world. [33] Therefore, my brothers, in coming together to eat, wait for each other. [34] But if anybody might be famished,* let him eat at home, in order that you do not come together for condemnation.

And I will set the other things in order when I come.

Spiritual gifts in one body

12\1 **N**ow concerning spiritual *matters*,* brothers, I do not want you to be ignorant.
[2] You know how, when you were inclined towards *the* nations,** you were being led away to voiceless idols, as you chanced somehow or other to be led astray.* [3] Therefore, I make known* to you that nobody speaking by* *the* spirit of God* says 'Jesus *is* anathema,'** and nobody is able to say 'Lord Jesus' except by* *the* divine spirit.**

[4] Now there are diversities of gifts, but the same spirit.* [5] And there are differences of services, but the same Lord. [6] And there are diversities of operations, but it is the same God,* the one* energizing* all these* among all. [7] But the manifestation of the spirit is given to each one* for benefit. [8] For to one an oracle of wisdom is given through* the spirit; and to another an oracle of knowledge by* the same spirit; [9] and to another faith by* the same spirit;* and to another gifts of healings* by* the same spirit;** [10] and to another operations of works of power;* and to another prophecy; and to another distinguishing of spirits;* and to another different kinds of languages; and to another the interpretation of languages.**

Gifts energized by means of the Spirit.
All identified into Jesus & the same spirit from God
(Rom. 6\3, Gal. 3\27, Eph. 4\5, Col. 2\12).
Human body as a figure of the one body
[11] But the one and the same Spirit* energizes* all these things, distributing individually* to each as he* wishes.*
[12] For as the body* is one, and has many parts – although all the parts of that one body, being many, are one body – so also *is* the Christ.*
[13] For in* one spirit* also* are we all identified* into one body,* whether Jews or Greeks,* whether servants or freemen.* And we were all made to drink* from one spirit.**
[14] For also, the body is not one part, but many. [15] If the foot should say, 'Because I am not a hand,* I am not of the body,' is it, on account of this,* not of the body? [16] And if the ear should say, 'Because I am not the eye, I am not of the body,' is it on account of this not of the body? [17] If the whole body *were* an eye, where *would* the hearing *be*? If *the* whole *were* hearing, where *would* the smelling *be*?* [18] But now God has arranged the parts, each one of them,* in the body, as He pleased.* [19] And if all these were one part, where *would* the body *be*? [20] But now *they are* many parts, but yet one body. [21] And the eye cannot say to the hand, 'I have no need of you.' Nor in addition* *can* the head* *say* to the feet, 'I have no need of you.' [22] But much rather,* those parts of the body which seem to

be weaker are indispensable. ²³ And those parts of the body which we think to be* more void of honour, *on* these we bestow more abundant honour, and the unpresentable *parts* of us have more abundant modesty. ²⁴ For our presentable *parts* need no special treatment, but God compounded* the body together, having given more abundant honour to that *part* which lacked* *it,* ²⁵ so that there might be no schism in the body, but the parts might have the same concern* on behalf of one another. ²⁶ And if one member should suffer, all the members suffer together.* If one member is magnified, all the members rejoice together.*

Believers as a body of Christ (Rom. 12\5, Eph. 4\4).
Offices among the apostle-authorized Ekklesias
²⁷ Now you stand for* Christ's body* and *are* members* each in their part.* ²⁸ And God has set some among the Ekklesia:* first apostles, second prophets, third teachers, after that workers of miracles, then gifts of healings, helps, governings, different kinds of languages. ²⁹ *Are* all apostles, all prophets, all teachers? *Do* all *have* works of miracles? ³⁰ Do all have gifts of healings? Do all speak with languages? Do all interpret?*
³¹ Be zealous, though, for the more excellent* gifts.*

Love more excellent than gifts which pass away
And yet I will show you a more excellent way.*
13\1 If I speak with the tongues of men and angels, but I do not have love, I have become sounding brass or a clanging cymbal. ² And although I have prophecy and I understand all mysteries, and all knowledge, and although I have all faith even to move mountains,* but I do not have love, I am nothing. ³ And even if I might give out all my belongings, and although I deliver up my body so that it might be burned, but I do not have love, I am profited nothing.
⁴ Love suffers long; is kind; love is not envious; love does not vaunt itself; is not puffed up;* ⁵ does not behave in an unseemly manner; does not strive after its own things;* is not roused to anger; does not reckon up the bad; ⁶ does not rejoice at unrighteousness, but rejoices with the truth; ⁷ is forbearing in all things; believes all things; hopes all things; endures all things. ⁸ Love never fails. But where *there are* prophecies, they will be brought to an end; where languages, they will cease; where knowledge, it will be

brought to an end.* ⁹ But we know in part, and we prophesy in part. ¹⁰ But when the culmination comes,* then what *is* in part will be brought to an end.*
¹¹ When I was a child, I spoke like a child; I thought like a child; I reasoned like a child. But when I became a man, I did away with the things of a child. ¹² For now we see through a mirror in an enigma,* but then face-to-face. Now I know in part, but then I will know fully, just as I also am known fully.
¹³ And now remain faith, hope, love, these three things. But the highest of these *is* love.

Prophecy better than languages.
Rebuke for seeming super-spiritual
by showing off different languages
14\1 Pursue love, and be zealous for spiritual things, but more so that you might prophesy.
² For he who speaks in a language* speaks not to men but to God,* for nobody understands, but he speaks mysteries in *his* spirit. ³ He, though, who prophesies speaks to men *for* building up, and for encouragement, and for comfort. ⁴ He who speaks in a language builds himself up,* but he who prophesies builds up the Ekklesia.
⁵ Now I would like you all to speak with languages. Rather, though, *I wish* that you prophesied. For he who prophesies *is* superior to he who speaks with languages, unless he interprets so that the Ekklesia might receive building up. ⁶ And now, brothers, if I come to you speaking with languages, in what way will I profit you unless I speak to you either in a revelation,* or in knowledge, or in prophesying, or in teaching?*
⁷ In the same way, if inanimate things giving out a sound, whether a pipe or a harp, give no distinction to the sounds, how will it be known what is being piped or harped? ⁸ For again, if the trumpet gives an uncertain sound, who is going to prepare himself for war? ⁹ So you also, if you do not give an intelligible word by the tongue, how will it be known what is being spoken, since you will be speaking into air?*
¹⁰ So as for all the many kinds of voices which there chance to be in *the* world, none is without a *distinct* sound.* ¹¹ If, therefore, I do not know the force of the sound, I will be a Barbarian to him who speaks, and he who speaks a Barbarian to me. ¹² So should you also, seeing that you are

zealots for spiritual things, look to it that you might excel towards* the edifying of the Ekklesia. [13] Therefore let him who speaks in a language pray that he might interpret. [14] For if I pray in a language, my spirit prays, but my understanding is unfruitful.

[15] What, then, is *the conclusion*? I will pray with the spirit, and I will also pray with the understanding. I will sing with the spirit, and I will also sing with the understanding.

[16] Otherwise, if you eulogize* with the spirit, how will he who occupies the room of the uninstructed say the amen at your giving of thanks, since he does not know what you say? [17] For you indeed give thanks well, but the other is not edified.

[18] I thank my God, speaking with languages more than all of you. [19] Yet in an Ekklesia I desire to speak five words with my understanding so that I might also instruct others, rather than ten thousand words in a language.

[20] Brothers, do not become children in understanding. However, regarding malice act as infants. In mentality, though, be full-grown. [21] In the law it has been written that:

'In other languages
and with lips of others
will I speak to this people,
yet not even for all that
will they listen to Me, says *the* Lord.'*

[22] Languages, in that case, are for a sign, not to those who believe, but to the unbelievers.* But prophecy *is* not for the unbelievers, but for those who believe. [23] If, therefore, the whole Ekklesia group should come together into one place, and all of you should speak with languages,* and the uninstructed* or unbelievers come in, will they not say that you are out of your mind? [24] But if all prophesy, and some unbeliever should come in, or *anybody* uninstructed, he is confronted* by all, he is challenged* by all,* [25] and so the secrets of his heart will become brought to light, and then falling down on *his* face he will worship God, declaring that God is truly among you.

Not showing off acquired gifts.
Order for prophecy & foreign languages
in an international audience

[26] How is it then, brothers, *that* when you come together each of you has a psalm, has a teaching,

has a language, has a revelation, has an interpretation?* Let all things be done for building up. [27] If anybody speaks in a language, *let it* be two at a time, or at the most three, and in turn, and let somebody interpret. [28] But if there is no interpreter, let him keep silence among an Ekklesia, and let him speak to himself, and to God.

[29] And let two or three prophets speak, and let the others discern. [30] But if there should be a revelation to another sitting nearby, let the first be silent. [31] For you can all prophesy, one after another, so that all might learn, and all might be encouraged. [32] And spiritual *gifts* of prophets are subject to prophets, [33] for God is not *a God* of commotion, but of peace, as among all the Ekklesia groups of the holy people.*   *means, not to disrupt, to be peaceful*

Women (1 Tim. 2\9-15)
[34] Let your women keep silence among the Ekklesia groups, for it is not permitted for them to speak, but to be in subjection, as the law also states. [35] But if they want to learn anything, let them ask their own husbands at home, for it is dishonourable for women to speak among an Ekklesia group.

[36] Or did the oracle of God go out from you? Or did it come to you only?* [37] If anybody supposes to be* a prophet or spiritual, let him fully understand that the things I write to you are commandments of the Lord.* [38] But if anybody is ignorant, let him stay ignorant.* [39] Therefore, brothers, be zealous to prophesy, and do not forbid speaking with languages. [40] Let all things be done decently and in an orderly way.

Apostleship asserted. Jesus' resurrection

15\1 Now, brothers, I make known to you the gospel which I proclaimed to you, which you also have received, in which you also stand, [2] through which you also are being saved,* if you keep secure what oracle I proclaimed to you – unless you believed to no purpose.

[3] For I handed down to you, among initial things, that which I also received: how Christ died for our violations in agreement with the Scrolls, [4] and that he was buried, and that he was raised *on* the third day in keeping with the Scrolls, [5] and that he was seen by Peter, then by the twelve. [6] After that, he was seen by over five hundred brothers at one time, out of whom the majority remain until now, although some

also* fell asleep.*

7   After that he was seen by Jacob, then by all the apostles. 8 And last of all, as if for one abnormally born, he was seen by me as well. 9 For I am the least of the apostles, and* I am not fit to be named as an apostle, seeing that I persecuted the Ekklesia of God. 10 But by *the* merciful goodwill of God I am what I am. And His merciful goodwill towards me did not turn out in vain, but I have toiled more abundantly than them all, yet not I, but the merciful goodwill of God with me.

11   Consequently, whether I or they, this *is* what we proclaim, and this *is* what you believed.

If no resurrection, then no hope
– only death. Order of resurrections

12   Now if it is proclaimed that Christ has been raised from *the* dead, how do some among you say that there is not a resurrection of *the* dead? 13 But if there is not a resurrection of *the* dead, not even Christ has been raised. 14 And if Christ has not been raised, then our proclamation *is* empty, and your faith also *is* empty.

15   In addition, we are also found false witnesses of God, because we have given testimony concerning God that He raised up the Christ whom He did not raise up, if it is so that *the* dead are not raised. 16 For if *the* dead are not raised, neither has Christ been raised. 17 And if Christ has not been raised, your faith *is* for no purpose: you are still in your violations. 18 Then those fallen asleep in Christ* have perished. 19 If only in this life are we having hope in Christ, we of all men are the most pitiable.

20   But as it is,* Christ has been raised from among *the* dead. He became* *the* firstfruit of those having fallen asleep. 21 For since death *came* through a man, resurrection of *the* dead* *came* also through a man.

22   For as in Adam all die, so also in the Christ will all* be made alive, 23 but each one in his own group:* Christ's* firstfruit;* afterwards those of Christ in* his magisterial presence;** 24 then the end, when he will have handed over the Sovereign Rulership* to Him Who *is* God and* Father,* when he will have brought down to nothing all rule and all authority and power.* 25 For he must reign until he will have subjected all enemies underneath his feet.

26   *The* last enemy to be brought to nothing is death.* 27 For he has subjected everything under his feet.* But when he might say that everything has been brought under subjection,* *it is* evident

that this *is* with the exception of Him Who subjects all these under Himself. 28 And whenever all these will have been brought into subjection underneath Him, then the Son himself also will be brought into subjection to Him Who brought all these into subjection under Himself, so that God might be everything in everybody.**

Identification towards certainty of resurrection,
not remaining only as corpses

29   Or* what are they doing* who are being identified? For the sake of *remaining* corpses? If *the* dead are not raised at all, why, indeed, are they being identified? For the sake of *remaining* corpses?* 30 And why are we also in peril every hour? 31 I affirm by the exaltation over you, which I have in Christ Jesus our Lord, *that* I die daily.

32   If, after the manner of men, I fought with beasts in Ephesus,* what is the profit for me if *the* dead are not raised? 'Let us eat and drink, for tomorrow we die.'* 33 Do not be deceived. Bad company corrupts good morals. 34 Return to sobriety of mind, as is right,* and do not commit violation, for some are ignorant of the knowledge of God. I speak to your shame.

The body, out of death, 'raised in power';
'star differs from star'

35   But somebody will say, 'How are the dead raised, and with what kind of body do they come?' 36 Fool! What you sow is not made alive unless it dies. 37 And of that which you sow, you are not sowing the body which is coming, but a naked grain, whether it might be of wheat or some of the rest. 38 But God gives it a body as He has purposed, and to each of the seeds its own body.

39   Not all flesh *is* the same flesh. But *there is* one of flesh of men, and another flesh of animals, and another of fish, and another of birds.

40   And *there are* celestial bodies, and terrestrial bodies, but the radiance of the celestial* body *is* certainly* different, and that of the terrestrial body *is* different:* 41 one radiance of *the* Sun, and another radiance of *the* Moon, and another radiance of stars, for star differs from star in radiance.*

42   So also *is* the resurrection of the dead:

It is sown in corruption:
it is raised in incorruption;*

⁴³ it is sown in dishonour:
it is raised in radiance;
it is sown in weakness:
it is raised in power;
⁴⁴ It is sown a natural˙ body:
it is raised a spiritual body.˙

Man, in the image of Adam,
to bear the image of the 'Most Exalted One'
(ἐπουράνιος, *epouranios;* 15\48-49)
and so to become among the 'most exalted men'
(ἐπουράνιος, *epouranios;* 15\48,
Eph. 1\3, 1\20, 2\6).
From dust to incorruption and exaltation
There is a natural˙ body, and there is a spiritual
body. ⁴⁵ As it has also been written: 'The first
man Adam became˙ a living being,˙' *so did* the
last Adam˙ *become* a life-giving spirit.˙ ⁴⁶ But the
spiritual˙ *was* not first, but the natural.˙ The
spiritual *came* afterwards.
⁴⁷ The first man *was* out of the Earth, created
from dust. The second man *is* the Lord from
Heaven. ⁴⁸ *As is* the one created of dust, so also
are those created from dust. And as *is* the Most
Exalted One, so also *are* the most exalted men.
⁴⁹ And as we have borne the image of the one
created from dust,˙ let us also wear˙ the image of
the Most Exalted One.˙
⁵⁰ Now I say this, brothers, that flesh and
blood˙ are not able to inherit *the* Sovereign
Rulership of God. Nor does corruption inherit
incorruption.
⁵¹ Hear now, I tell you a mystery: we will not
all be put into sleep,˙ but we will all be changed,
⁵² in an atom-like instant,˙ in a twinkling of an
eye,˙ at˙ the last trumpet. For a trumpet will
sound,˙ and the dead will be raised as
incorruptible,˙ and we will be changed. ⁵³ For
this corruption must put on incorruption,˙ and
this mortality put on immortality. ⁵⁴ So when this
corruption will have put on incorruption,˙ and
this mortality will have put on immortality, then
the oracle˙ which has been written will come
about:

'Death was swallowed up in victory.˙
⁵⁵ Where, oh death, *is* your sting?
Where, oh grave,˙ *is* your victory?'˙

⁵⁶ But the sting of death *is* violation, and the
power of violation *is* the law. ⁵⁷ But thanks to
God, Who gives us the victory through our Lord
Jesus Christ.
⁵⁸ So then, my richly loved brothers, be
steadfast, unmoveable, always abounding in the
work of the Lord, knowing that your labour in
the Lord is not in vain.

Collections at the apostle-authorized Ekklesias

16\1 **N**ow concerning the collection for the
holy people, just as I have directed the Ekklesia
groups of Galatia, you should do the same as
well. ² On the first *day* of every week,˙ let each
of you put *something* aside˙ himself, and
reserving˙ whatever he might be prospered in,
so that there might not be any collections when
I come.
³ And when I arrive, whomever you might
recommend, these I will send with letters, to
carry your generosity to Jerusalem. ⁴ And if it is
suitable for me to go as well, they will go with
me. ⁵ Now I will come to you when I pass
through Macedonia, for I am passing through
Macedonia. ⁶ And it might be that I will remain,
or even that I might spend the winter among
you, so that you might send me on my journey
wherever I go.
⁷ For I do not now wish in passing to see you,
but I hope to stay for some time among you, if
the Lord permits. ⁸ But I will stay in Ephesus
until Pentecost, ⁹ for an extremely effective
door has opened to me, as well as many
adversaries.˙

The work of Timothy, Apollos & Stephanas
¹⁰ Now if Timothy comes, see to it that he
might be among you without fear, for he is
carrying out the work of *the* Lord, just as I also
am. ¹¹ Nobody, therefore, should make light of
him, but send him on in peace so that he might
come to me, for I am expecting him along with
the brothers.
¹² Now concerning *our* brother Apollos, I
strongly urged him that he might come to you
with the brothers, but it was not wholly his will
that he could come at this time, but he will
come when he has opportunity.
¹³ Watch. Stand fast in the faith. Behave like
men. Be strong. ¹⁴ Let all your deeds be done in
love. ¹⁵ But I encourage you, brothers – you
know the house of Stephanas, that it is a
firstfruit of Achaia,˙ for they also have applied˙
themselves for service to the holy people – ¹⁶
that you also subject yourselves to such men,
and to everybody working and labouring with
us.
¹⁷ I rejoice, though, at the personal presence˙

of Stephanas and Fortunatus and Achaicus, for they filled up your deficiency, [18] for they gave rest to my spirit and to yours, so give recognition to those like that.

[19] The Ekklesia groups of Asia send you greetings. Aquila and Priscilla greet you enthusiastically* in *the* Lord, together with the Ekklesia group in their house. [20] All the brothers greet you. Greet one another with a holy kiss.
[21] The salutation of, Paul, with my own hand.*
[22] If anybody does not love the Lord Jesus Christ, let him be anathema.* Our Lord comes.**
[23] The merciful goodwill of our Lord Jesus Christ *be* with you. [24] My love *be* with you all in Christ Jesus. Amen.

~ ◆◆ ~

† The Letters of Paul †

2 Corinthians

From Paul & Timothy

1\1

aul, an apostle of Jesus Christ through the will of God, and Timothy,* the brother.
        To the Ekklesia group of God which is in Corinth, with all the holy people who are in all Achaia, [2] merciful goodwill to you, and peace, from God our Father, and *from the* Lord* Jesus Christ.*

Encouragement in the comfort of God
[3] Exalted* *be* the God and* Father of our Lord Jesus Christ,* the Father of mercies, and God of all comfort, [4] the one* comforting* us in all our tribulation, with a view to our being able to comfort those in every tribulation, by means of the comfort with which we ourselves are comforted by God.
[5] For as the sufferings of the Christ abound towards us, so through Christ our comfort* also abounds. [6] But if we are afflicted, *it is* for your comfort and salvation, being effective* in *the* enduring of the same sufferings which we suffer as well, and our gladly-held expectation for you *is* certain.** And if we are comforted, *it is* for your comfort and salvation, [7] knowing that as you are partakers of the sufferings, so *are you* also of the comfort.
[8] For we do not want you to be ignorant, brothers, of our trouble which came on us in Asia, so that we were excessively weighed down, beyond *our* strength,* so that we despaired even of surviving. [9] But we ourselves had the sentence of death in ourselves, so that we should have trust not in ourselves, but in God Who raises the dead,* [10] Who rescued us out of so terrible a death, and is rescuing* *us*, in Whom we have gladly-held expectation that He will still also deliver *us*, [11] *while* you also co-operate in prayer on our behalf, in order that the favour to us by many individuals might be the subject of thanksgiving through many on your behalf.*

The character of Paul's service. Proposed visit
[12] For our exultation is this: the testimony of

our conscience, that in guilelessness and sincerity of God – not in flesh-natured wisdom, but in *the* merciful goodwill of God – we have conducted ourselves in the world, and more abundantly towards you. [13] For we write no other things to you but what you read or acknowledge, and I hope you will acknowledge right to *the* end, [14] as you also in part have acknowledged us, that we are your ground for boasting, just as you indeed˙ *will be* ours in the day of the Lord Jesus.˙

[15] And with this confidence I wanted to come to you before, in order that you might have a second advantage, [16] and to travel by your way towards Macedonia, and to come back to you from Macedonia, and to be sent on my way by you into Judea.

[17] Purposing this, therefore, did I use fickleness at all?˙ Or the things I plan, do I plan in relation to the flesh, in order that with me there should be 'yes yes,' and 'no no'?[18] But *as* God *is* faithful, our oracle to you was not 'yes' and 'no'. [19] For the Son of God, Jesus Christ, who was proclaimed among you by us, by me, and by Silvanus and Timothy, was not 'yes' and 'no', but in him it was 'yes'. [20] For as many promises as there are of God, in Him *they are* 'yes', and in Him 'amen', to the magnificence of God through us. [21] Now He Who establishes˙ us with you in Christ, and anointed us, *is* God, [22] Who has also marked us with a seal, and given the deposit of the spirit in our hearts.˙

[23] In addition, I invoke God as a witness on my life that, to spare˙ you, I have not as yet come into Corinth, [24] not because we lord it over your faith, but *in that* we are fellow workers of your exuberance, for you stand by faith.

Restore the submissive man among you

2\1 **B**ut I decided this within myself: not to come to you again in sorrow. [2] For if I make you sorrowful, who is he who makes me glad but he who was made sorrowful by me?

[3] And I wrote this same *letter* to you in order that *when* I come I might not have sorrow from *those* over whom I ought to rejoice, having confidence in you all, so that my exuberance is of you all. [4] For I wrote to you out of much affliction and distress of heart, through many tears, not so that you might be grieved, but so that you might know the love which I have most profusely for you. [5] But if anybody has caused

grief, he has not grieved me except for a while,˙ so that I might not press heavily on you all. [6] This rebuke by the majority *is* sufficient for such a man, [7] for you, on the contrary,˙ rather to forgive and give comfort, in case somehow such a person should be swallowed up with overwhelming grief. [8] Therefore, I encourage you to confirm love towards him. [9] To this end I wrote as well, so that I might know your tested character, whether you are obedient in all things.

[10] But whomever you forgive anything, I *do* also. And indeed, if I have forgiven anything, whomever I forgave *it was* for your sakes in *the* face of Christ, [11] so that we should not be excessively weighed down by Satan, for we are not ignorant of his devices.˙

[12] Now, *when* I came to Troas for the purpose of the gospel of the Christ, and a door was opened to me in *the* Lord, [13] I did not have rest for my spirit at not finding my brother Titus, but having taken my leave of them I went on into Macedonia.

Triumph in Christ. Comparison
with those who corrupt the oracle of God

[14] Now thanks to God, Who always leads us˙ in triumph in the Christ, and brings to light˙ the savour of His knowledge through the agency of ourselves in every location.

[15] For we are to God a sweet savour of Christ among those being saved,˙ and among those who are perishing: [16] to the one the savour of death leading to death, but to the others the savour of life leading to˙ life.˙ And who *is* competent for˙ these things? [17] For we are not as the hoi polloi,˙ making money by corrupting˙ the oracle of God. But out of sincerity, but out of God, before God, we make our speech in Christ.

Assertion of apostleship

3\1 **A**re we beginning again to commend ourselves? Do we really need (like some), commendatory letters to you, or commendatory ones from you?

[2] You are our letter, written in our hearts, known and read by all men, [3] it being brought to light˙ that you are the letter of Christ, served by us, written not by ink, but by˙ *the* spirit of *the* living God,˙ not on stone tablets, but on fleshly writing-tablets of *the* heart.

Life-giving spirit of the new covenant

[4] And we have such confidence through the Christ towards God. [5] Not that we are competent from ourselves to reckon anything as if out of ourselves, but our competence *is* from God, [6] Who has made us competent as agents also of a new covenant,* not of *the* letter, but of *the* spirit. For the letter kills, but the spirit* gives life.

[7] But if the administration of death in letters engraved in stones was produced in radiance for the sons of Israel to be unable to look intently into the face of Moses on account of the radiance of his face* – which *radiance* is being done away with – [8] how shall the administration of the spirit* not rather be in radiance? [9] For if the administration of condemnation *is* radiance, so much more does the administration of righteousness abound in radiance. [10] For even that having been made radiant has not been made radiant compared to* this measure,* on account of its* surpassing radiance.* [11] For if that being done away with was with radiance, then how much more *will* that remaining *be* in radiance?

[12] Having, then, such gladly-held expectation, we use much bold outspokenness, [13] and not like Moses who put a covering over his face, with a view to the sons of Israel not gazing straight at the outcome* of what was being done away with. [14] But their thoughts were hardened,* for until today the same covering remains unlifted at the reading of the old covenant. This is being done away with in Christ. [15] But to this day when Moses is read, the covering lies over their heart, [16] but whenever it turns to *the* Lord, the veil is taken away.

[17] Now the Lord is the spirit,* and, wherever the spirit of *the* Lord* *might be*, there *there is* freedom.*

[18] But we all, with a face having been unveiled, reflecting the radiance of *the* Lord, are being transformed into the same image, from radiance to radiance,* just as* *comes* from* *the* spirit of *the* Lord.*

*Bearing afflictions for Christ contrasted
with false men who proclaim themselves*

4\1 On account of this, having this office, since we have received mercy we do not lose heart. [2] But we have renounced the hidden, shameful things, not walking about in craftiness, nor adulterating the oracle of God, but by

displaying the truth we commend ourselves to *the* conscience of every man in the sight of God. [3] But if, on the other hand, our gospel is hidden,* it is hidden among those who are perishing, [4] among whom the god of this Eon** has blinded the minds of those unbelieving,* so that* the brightness of the radiant gospel of the Christ, who is *the* image of God,* might not beam out* to them.

[5] For we proclaim as Lord not ourselves but Christ Jesus, and ourselves *as* your servants for the sake of Jesus. [6] For *it is* God Who commanded light to shine out of darkness, Who shone in our hearts, for *the* brightness of the knowledge of the radiance of God in *the* face of Jesus Christ.

[7] But we have this treasure in clay jars, so that the transcendency of the power might be from God, and not from ourselves. [8] For in everything *we are* afflicted, yet not distressed; perplexed, but not utterly at a loss; [9] persecuted, but not abandoned; struck down,* but not perishing; [10] always carrying about in the body the dying of the Lord Jesus, so that also* the life of Jesus might be brought to light in our body.*

[11] For we, the living, are continually handed over to death on account of* Jesus, in order that the life of Jesus might also* be brought to light* in our mortal flesh. [12] So then, death is at work* in us, but life in you.

[13] And having the same spirit of faith, in keeping with that having been written – 'I believed; therefore I spoke'* – we also believe, therefore we also speak, [14] knowing that the one having raised up the Lord Jesus will also raise us up through Jesus, and He will present *us* with you.*

[15] For all these things *are* for you, in order that the merciful goodwill abounding through* the majority* might cause thanksgiving to overflow for the magnificence of God.

[16] Therefore we do not faint. But even if our outward man is being brought to decay, still day by day* the inward *man* is being renewed. [17] For the momentary lightness of our affliction works out for us a transcendently transcendent* Eonian* weight of radiance, [18] while we fix our eyes not on the things seen, but *on* the things not seen. For the things seen *are* temporal, but the things not seen* *are* permanent.*

Expectation of a resurrection body
from God. Judgement seat of Christ

5\1 **F**or we know that if the earthly house of our tent˙ might be taken down, we have a house from˙ God, a house made not by hands, *but* Eonian,˙ *and* among the exalted.˙ [2] For indeed,˙ we groan in this *body*, so much longing˙ to be clothed with˙ our bodily habitation˙ which *is* from˙ the Heavenly One,˙˙ [3] if indeed,˙ also˙ being clothed, we will not be found naked.˙

[4] For indeed,˙ we who are in *this* tent groan, being weighed down, since we do not wish to be unclothed,˙ but to be clothed,˙ in order that what *is* mortal might be swallowed up by˙ life.˙

[5] Now the one having prepared˙ us for *this* same thing *is* God, Who˙ also gave˙ us the deposit of the spirit.˙ [6] In that case, being always of good courage, and knowing that being at home˙ in the body we are absent˙ from˙ the Lord [7] – for we walk by faith, not by˙ sight˙ – [8] we are of good courage and think it good rather to depart˙ out of˙ this body and to be at home˙ in relation to˙ the Lord. [9] Therefore, we are also ambitious, whether being at home˙ or being absent,˙ to be˙ pleasing to Him. [10] For all of us have to be made to appear in the presence of the judgement seat˙ of the Christ,˙ in order that each should receive the things *done* by means of the body, in relation to˙ what he has practised, whether good or bad.

[11] Knowing, therefore, the reverence of the Lord, we persuade men, but we have been made known to God, and I hope to have been made known˙ in your consciences as well. [12] For we will not commend ourselves to you again, but we are giving you an opportunity of taking pride in us, in order that you might have *it* against those taking pride in outward appearance but not in heart. [13] For if we are beside ourselves, *it is* for God; or *if* sound-minded, *it is* for you.

[14] For the love of the Christ constrains us, having judged this: that if one died for all, then all died. [15] And he died for all in order that the living should no longer live for themselves, but for him having died for them and having been raised.˙

[16] Therefore, from now on, we know nobody in relation to flesh. But even if we have known Christ in relation to flesh, yet from now on we no longer know *him in such a way*.

A new creation in Christ.
Ambassadors of reconciliation

[17] Therefore, if any man *is* in Christ, *he is* a new creation. The outworn things have passed away. See now, all things have become new.

[18] And all things *are* from God Who reconciled us to Himself through˙ Jesus Christ, and gave to us the office of reconciliation, [19] that is,˙ that God was in˙ Christ, reconciling *the* world to Himself, not reckoning their offences to them, and having put in us the oracle of reconciliation.˙ [20] We are, therefore, ambassadors for Christ, as though˙ God were encouraging *you* through us.

We implore *you* on behalf of Christ: be reconciled to God. [21] For He has made *him* who did not know violation *to be* violation for us, in order that we might become *the* righteousness of God in him.

Commendation of the apostles' suffering

6\1 **B**ut we, as fellow workers, encourage *you* also not to receive in vain the merciful goodwill of God. [2] For He says:

'In a time accepted
I have heard you with favour,
and in a day of salvation
I have succoured you.˙
Look, now *is the* well accepted time;
look, now *is the* day of salvation.'˙

[3] We give no offence in anything, so that the work is not blamed, [4] but in everything demonstrating ourselves as agents of God: in much endurance; in tribulations; in hardships;˙ in distresses; [5] in stripes; in imprisonments; in riots; in labours; in sleeplessness; in fastings; [6] in purity; in knowledge; in long-suffering; in kindness; in divine spirit; in unfeigned love; [7] in an oracle of truth; in power of God through the weapons˙ of righteousness˙ in the right hand and in *the* left hand; [8] through glory and shame; through defamation and good report; *regarded* as deceivers,˙ yet tellers of the truth;˙ [9] as being unknown, yet well known; as dying, yet, after all,˙ we live; as flogged, yet not put to death; [10] as grieved, yet always rejoicing; as poor, yet making many rich; as having nothing, yet possessing all things.˙

Being separate. Built into a sanctuary of God
for the New Jerusalem (6\16-18, Eph. 2\18-22).
Sons & Daughters of God (6\18, Luke 6\35)

[11] Corinthians, our mouth has been opened to you. Our heart has been enlarged. [12] You are

not restrained by us, yet you are being restrained in your affections.* [13] But so that you might recompense us* – I speak as to children – you also become open.**

[14] Do not become yoked unequally to unbelievers. For what partnership *do* righteousness and lawlessness *have*? And what association *does* light *have* among darkness? [15] And what concord *does* Christ *have* among a worthless person?* Or what part *has* a believer with an unbeliever? [16] And what agreement *has* a sanctuary of God with idols? For you are a sanctuary of the living God.* As God has said:

'I will make My habitation among them
and walk among *them,*
and I will be their God
and they will be My people.*
[17] Therefore, come out from among them*
and be separated, says *the* Lord,
and touch no unclean thing
and I will receive you,
[18] and I will be for a Father to you
and you will be My Sons and Daughters,*
says *the* Lord Almighty.'*

Encouragement to purity

7\1 Having, therefore, these promises, *my* richly loved, let us cleanse ourselves from all filthiness of flesh and spirit, perfecting holiness in reverence of God.

[2] Make room for us. We have wronged nobody; we have corrupted nobody; we have defrauded* nobody. [3] I do not speak for condemnation.* For I have said before that you are in our hearts, to die with *us* and to live with *us.* [4] I *have* much boldness of speech towards you, much boasting in respect of you. I have been filled with comfort. I overflow with exuberance at all our tribulation.*

No rest in flesh; comfort in God

[5] For indeed, *when* we came into Macedonia our flesh had no rest, but we were troubled in every *way* – conflicts outside, fears within.*

[6] Nevertheless, God, Who comforts those brought low, comforted us through the personal presence* of Titus, [7] and not only through his personal presence* but through the comfort also by which he was comforted over you in relating to us your earnest desire, your deep sorrow, your ardent concern on behalf of me, so that I rejoiced all the more.

Paul's former letter

[8] For although I also caused you sorrow by a letter, I do not regret *it,* even if I had regretted *it.* For I perceive that that letter did cause you sorrow, even if only for an hour.

[9] Now I rejoice, not that you were grieved, but in that you were grieved into submission, for you were grieved in line with* God, so that you were not caused harm through us in any respect.

[10] For the sorrow which is in line with* God engenders submission into salvation not to be regretted, but the sorrow of the world engenders death.

[11] For look at this same thing: how much diligence it worked out in you for you to be thrown into sorrow in a manner in line with* God; but what defence; but what indignation; but what reverence; but what longing; but what zeal; and* what vindication! In all things you have demonstrated yourselves to be* pure in the matter.* [12] So although I wrote to you, not on account of him who had done wrong, nor on account of him who had been wronged, but for our diligence on your behalf to be brought to light* to* you in the sight of God.

[13] Because of this, we were comforted. But we rejoiced all the more exuberantly* in your comfort, especially over the exuberance of Titus, because his spirit was refreshed by you all. [14] So if I have boasted anything to him about you, I was not put to shame. But as we spoke all things to you in truth, so also has our boasting before Titus been found as truth. [15] And his affections* are all the more exuberant* towards you, as he remembered the obedience of you all, how with fear and trembling you received him. [16] I rejoice that I have confidence in you in all things.

Example of Macedonians in trial & in generosity

8\1 In addition, we make known* to you, brothers, the merciful goodwill of God given among the Ekklesia groups of Macedonia, [2] in that, in a most severe trial of trouble, the overflowing of their exuberance and the extremity of their poverty abounded to the riches of their generosity. [3] For I give testimony that *they gave* willingly, according to means, and beyond *their* means,* [4] imploring us with much begging to receive the gift and the partnership for the holy people. [5] And not only as we expected, but they first gave themselves to the Lord, as well as to us, through *the* will of God [6] for us to call on Titus, so that, as he had begun earlier, so also should he complete this merciful goodwill in you as well.

[7] In addition, even as you abound in everything, *in* faith, and word, and knowledge, and all eagerness, and the love from you towards* us, *see to it* that* you might also abound in this merciful goodwill. [8] I do not speak in relation to any command, but moved by the diligence of others, and as one approving the genuineness of your love. [9] For you know the merciful goodwill of our Lord Jesus Christ, how, being rich, for your sakes he became poor, in order that you might be enriched through his poverty.

[10] And in this I give judgement, for this is profitable to you, not only to carry out but also to delight in what you previously began* since last year. [11] Now though, you must make completion to carry *it* out as well, so that just like the readiness to be willing, so also *might there be* to make completion from what you have.* [12] For if the willingness is present, *it is* well received in relation to whatever one might have, not in relation to what one does not have.*

[13] For *I mean* not that there should be ease for others, but affliction for you, [14] but, on the basis of an equality at the present time, your surplus *might be* for their deficiency, in order that their surplus also might be for your deficiency, so that there might be an equality.

[15] As it has been written: 'The one *gathering* much had nothing left over, and the one *gathering* little had no lack.'*

[16] But thanks to God, Who gives the same earnest care for you in the heart of Titus, [17] for he accepted the encouragement, but, being more diligent, he went to you out of* his own initiative.

[18] But we have sent with him the brother who *has* commendation in the gospel throughout all the Ekklesia groups, [19] and not only *that*, but *who* was also chosen by the Ekklesia groups as a travelling companion for us with this gift supplied by us towards* the magnificence of the Lord himself, and *to show*' your readiness of mind, [20] avoiding this: that nobody might blame us in this abundance supplied by us, [21] providing for honest things, not only in the sight of *the* Lord, but also in the sight of men.

[22] And we have sent with them our brother whom we have many times in many things proved zealous, yet *he is* now even more zealous

through much confidence in* you.

[23] Regarding Titus, *he is* my partner and fellow worker for you. Or regarding our brothers, *they are* messengers* of the Ekklesia groups, the magnificence of Christ. [24] Show them, therefore in *the* face of the Ekklesia groups, the proof of your love, and of our boasting for you.

Their zeal has provoked many

9\1 **F**or concerning the supplying* which *is* for the holy people, it is superfluous for me to write to you. [2] For I know your readiness of mind which I boast about on your behalf to the Macedonians, that Achaia has been prepared since last year, and your zeal stirred up* quite a few.* [3] Yet I sent the brothers so that our boasting on your behalf should not be made void* in this respect, so that, as I said, you might be prepared, [4] in case by any means the Macedonians should come with me and find you unprepared, so that we, not to mention you, should be ashamed in this boastful confidence.*

[5] Therefore I thought it necessary to encourage the brothers that they would go to you in advance, and should arrange ahead of time your donation* *which* was notified previously, so that it might be ready as a benefit,* and not *out of* covetousness.*

Sow bountifully & reap bountifully

[6] And *I say* this: he who sows sparingly will also reap sparingly; and he who sows generously will also reap generously,* [7] as each one purposes in *his* heart, not out of grudge, nor out of compulsion, for God loves a cheerful giver.* [8] And God is mighty to make every merciful goodwill abound* to* you, so that, always having all sufficiency in everything, you might abound* to every good work. [9] As it has been written:

'He scattered;
He gave to the poor;
His righteousness remains
throughout* the Eon.'*'

[10] Now may He Who supplies* seed to him who sows also supply bread for eating, and multiply your sowing, and increase the fruits of your righteousness, [11] in everything being enriched, progressing into every generosity, which through us works thanksgiving to God.

¹² For the administration of this service is not only completely filling up the deficiencies of the holy people, but is also overflowing through many expressions of thanks to God, ¹³ through the proof of this service magnifying God over the obedience of your profession of the gospel of the Christ, and for the bountifulness of *your* contribution towards them and towards everybody, ¹⁴ and by their prayer for you, whose heart goes out to you because of the transcendent merciful goodwill of God over you.

¹⁵ Now thanks to God for His indescribable free gift.

Spiritual might to pull down strongholds

10\1 **N**ow I, Paul myself, encourage you through the meekness and fairness of the Christ – I, who in outward appearance *am* lowly among you, although being absent am bold towards you. ² Though not being present, I want to be bold with the confidence with which I reckon to have dealt boldly towards some, those thinking of us as if we walk in the demands of flesh.

³ For walking about in flesh, we do not war in relation to the demands of flesh. ⁴ For the weapons* of our warfare *are* not flesh-natured, but powerful through God* towards *the* smashing down of strongholds, ⁵ smashing down arguments, and every high thing exalting against the knowledge of God, and bringing in captivity every thought into the obedience of the Christ, ⁶ and in having readiness to avenge all disobedience when your obedience is fulfilled.

Paul as mighty in word as in writing.
Irony concerning pseudo apostles

⁷ Do you look on things in relation to the outward appearance? If anybody is persuaded in himself to be Christ's, let him additionally* consider this from himself: that, as he *is* Christ's, so also *are* we Christ's. ⁸ For even if I should boast somewhat more concerning our authority which the Lord gave us for building up and not for overthrowing you, I will not be put to shame, ⁹ so that I might not seem to scare you by the letters.

¹⁰ For '*his* letters,' they say, 'are stern and forceful, but *his* personal presence* in body is weak, and *his* speech of little account.'* ¹¹ Let such a person think this: that what we are in word through letters in our being absent, so *will we* also *be* in deed in our being present.

¹² For we dare not to rank or to compare ourselves with some who commend themselves.* But they, self-measuring themselves among themselves, and comparing themselves with themselves, do not understand.* ¹³ We, though, will not boast excessively, but within the sphere of the jurisdiction* which God divided to us, a sphere to extend as far even as to you. ¹⁴ For we are not overstretching ourselves as if not extending to you, for we came even as far as you in the gospel of the Christ, ¹⁵ not boasting excessively in others' labours, but having a gladly-held expectation of your increasing faith, to be magnified into overflowing among you in line with our jurisdiction,* ¹⁶ to proclaim the gospel as far as the *regions* beyond you, not to boast in another's jurisdiction* in things accomplished.

¹⁷ 'But he who boasts
let him boast in the Lord.'*

¹⁸ For not he who commends himself is approved, but he whom the Lord commends.

Transformed agents of Satan
proclaim another Jesus,
a different spirit, & a different gospel

11\1 **I** wish you would put up with me in a little folly, but, indeed, you do put up with me. ² For I am jealous for you with a jealousy of God,* for I espoused you to one husband, to present* *you as* a chaste virgin to the Christ. ³ But I fear, in case by any opportunity, just as the Snake beguiled* Eve* in his craftiness, so might your thoughts be corrupted away from the simplicity in the Christ. ⁴ For if, indeed, he who comes proclaims another* Jesus* whom we did not proclaim, or if you receive a different spirit* which you did not receive *from us*, or a different* gospel* which you did not accept *from us*, you put up with* *him as* commendable.*

⁵ For in nothing do I reckon to have come behind the exceedingly superior apostles.* ⁶ But even if unskilled in speech, yet *I am* not in knowledge – but *we are* in every way being brought to light* to you in all things.

⁷ Or have I committed a violation *in* putting myself down so that you might be exalted, because I freely proclaimed to you the gospel of God? ⁸ I stripped other Ekklesia groups, having received wages for supply towards you.*

⁹ And in being present among you and being

put in deficiency, I was a burden to nobody. For the brothers having come from Macedonia fully made up for my lack, and in every way I have kept myself and I will keep *myself* not burdensome to you.
[10] The truth of Christ is in me that this boasting will not be restrained on my part in the regions of Achaia. [11] Why? Because I do not love you? God knows!˙ [12] But what I do I will also continue to do, so that I might cut off the opportunity of those wanting opportunity so that in what they boast about they might be found as we also *are*.
[13] For such men *are* pseudo apostles, deceitful workers, transforming˙ themselves into apostles of Christ. [14] And no wonder! For Satan himself transforms˙ himself into an angel of light. [15] Consequently, *it is* no big thing if his agents also transform˙ themselves into workers of righteousness,˙ whose end will be in line with the measure of˙ their works.˙
[16] I say again, nobody should think me to be˙ a fool. Yet if otherwise, receive me even as foolish, so that I might additionally boast a little.
[17] What I speak I speak not from *the* Lord's perspective,˙ but as if in folly, in this boastful confidence.
[18] Seeing that many boast after the flesh, I also will boast. [19] For you put up with fools gladly,˙ being wise. [20] For you put up with *it* if anybody enslaves you; if anybody exploits; if anybody takes advantage of you; if anybody pushes himself forward; if anybody beats you in the face. [21] I speak by way of shame that *it is* as if we had been weak. But in whatever anybody might dare – I speak in foolishness – I also dare.

Commendation of apostleship.
Ancestry of Paul & his sufferings for Christ
[22] Are they Hebrews? So *am* I. Are they Israelites? So *am* I. Are they the seed of Abraham? So *am* I. [23] Are they agents of Christ? I speak as if being beside myself! I *am* more: in labours more abundant; in stripes above measure; in imprisonments more frequently; in deaths many times; [24] five times I received forty *stripes* minus one from Jews; [25] three times I was beaten with rods; once I was stoned; three times I was shipwrecked; a night and a day I have spent in the deep; [26] journeying about often; in dangers of rivers; in dangers of bandits;˙ in dangers from *my* race; in dangers from *the* nations; in dangers in city; in dangers in *the* wilderness; in dangers at sea; in dangers among

pseudo brothers; [27] in weariness and toil; in sleeplessness many times; in hunger and thirst; in fastings many times; in cold and in want of clothing; [28] apart from those other matters, the crowding-in on me daily, the care concerning all the Ekklesia groups.
[29] Who is weak, and I am not weak? Who is offended, and I do not burn?˙ [30] If I must boast, I will boast of the things of my weakness. [31] The God and Father of the Lord Jesus Christ,˙ Who is exalted˙ throughout the Eons,˙˙ knows that I do not lie. [32] In Damascus, the governor under Aretas the king was guarding the city of the Damascenes, wanting to apprehend me, [33] and I was let down through a window in a basket alongside the wall, and I escaped his hands.

Extraordinary revelations, a vision of Paradise.
Struck by an angel of Satan. Strength in weakness

12\1 **I**t is not at all profitable for me to boast, for I will come on to visions˙ and revelations˙ of *the* Lord.
[2] I know a man in Christ – whether in *the* body I do not know, or out of the body I do not know; God knows – who, fourteen years ago, was caught away˙ up to *the* third heaven.˙
[3] And I know a man like this˙ – whether in body, or out of the body, I do not know; God knows – [4] how he was caught away˙ into the Paradise,˙ and heard inexpressible words which it is not permitted for a man to repeat.˙ [5] On behalf of a man like that˙ I will boast. Yet of myself˙ I will not boast, unless in my weaknesses. [6] For if I should desire to boast,˙ I will not be a fool, for I will speak truth. But I hold back, in case anybody should reckon me above what he sees me *to be*, or what he hears from me.
[7] And so that I might not be made arrogant by the super-abundance of the revelations,˙ a thorn in the flesh˙ was given to me, an angel˙ of Satan,˙ in order that he might strike˙ me, so that I might not be made arrogant. [8] About this, I asked the Lord three times that he might depart from me, [9] but he said to me, 'My merciful goodwill is sufficient for you, for my power is made perfect in weakness.'
Most gladly, in that case, will I rather boast in my weaknesses, in order that the power of the Christ might overshadow me. [10] Therefore, I take pleasure in weaknesses, in insults, in hardships, in persecutions, in difficulties for

Christ. For when I might be weak, then I am strong.

[11] I have become a fool *in* boasting. You have compelled me, for I ought to be commended by you. For I am behind those most superior apostles* in nothing, even if I am nothing.

Signs & wonders of the apostle
were performed among the Corinthians

[12] Truly the signs of the apostle were performed among you with all endurance, in signs and wonders, along with works of power. [13] For in what is it that you were inferior beyond the rest of the Ekklesia groups, except that I myself did not lazily burden you? Forgive me this injustice!*

A third visit promised

[14] Now then, a third time I hold myself in readiness to come to you, and I will not lazily burden you. For I search not after your things, but yourselves, for it is an obligation* not *for* the children to lay up treasure for the parents, but the parents for the children. [15] And I will most gladly incur expense and become exhausted by expending myself* for your lives,* even if the more abundantly I love you the less I am loved. [16] But let it be so. I did not weigh you down, but, being crafty, I caught you out with cunning.* [17] Indeed, did I take advantage of you through any of those whom I sent to you?* [18] I asked Titus, and sent the brother with *him*. Did Titus take advantage of you? *Did we* not *walk* by the same spirit? *Did we* not *walk* in the same steps?

[19] Again, do you think that we are defending ourselves to you? We speak in the sight of God in Christ. But all things, *my* richly loved, *we do* for your edifying. [20] For I fear, in case, in some way,* in coming I might not find you as I would like, and I might be found by you in a way that you do not like; in case, in any way,* *there are* contentions, jealousies, outbursts of boiling anger, rivalries, backbitings, gossip, puffings-up, acts of disorder.* [21] *When* I come to you again my God will not humble me, and I will* not have sorrow over many of those who have violated earlier, and have not unburdened themselves of the uncleanness and fornication and lasciviousness which they have committed.

13\1 This *is* the third *time* I am coming to you. In *the* mouth* of two or three witnesses every matter will stand.*

Weakness in the power of Jesus
who, as ourselves, 'lives by the power
of God' (John 6\57, 1 Cor. 11\3)

[2] I told you before, and I say beforehand, as in my being present on the second *occasion*, and being absent now – I write to those having previously violated, and to all others, so that if I do come again I will not spare *you*, [3] since you look for a proof of Christ speaking in me, who is not weak towards you but is mighty among you.*

[4] For in fact, although he was hanged on a stake* out of weakness, yet he lives by* *the* power of God.* And indeed, we also are weak in him, but we will live with him by* *the* power of God in us.*

Encouragement to self-examination

[5] Examine yourselves as to whether you are in the faith. Test yourselves. Or do you not yourselves perceive how Jesus Christ is among you,* if, indeed, you are not disqualified? [6] But I hope that you will know that we are not disqualified.

[7] Now I pray to God *that* you should not do anything evil, not so that we should be seen as approved, but so that you should do that which *is* honourable, even though we might seem as if disqualified. [8] For we have no power against the truth, but *only* on behalf of the truth. [9] For we rejoice when we are weak and you are strong. And this we pray for also: your strengthening.

[10] On account of this, I write these things being absent, in order that, being present, I might not use sharpness, in line with the authority which the Lord gave me for building up, and not for pulling down.

[11] Finally, brothers, rejoice.

Be perfected.

Be encouraged. Mind the same thing.

Be at peace, and the God of love and peace will be with you.

[12] Greet one another with a holy kiss. [13] All the holy people send you greetings.

[14] The merciful goodwill of the Lord Jesus Christ, and the love of God, and the partnership* of the Holy Spirit** *be* with you all. Amen.

~ ◆◆ ~

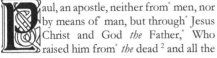

† The Letters of Paul †

Galatians

1\1

Paul, an apostle, neither from* men, nor by means of* man, but through* Jesus Christ and God *the* Father,* Who raised him from* *the* dead ² and all the brothers with me.

To the Ekklesia groups of Galatia, ³ merciful goodwill to you, and peace, from God *the* Father,* and *from* our Lord Jesus Christ,* ⁴ who gave himself for our violations, so that he might deliver us out of the present Eon* of evil,* in harmony with the will of our God and* Father,* ⁵ to Whom *be* the magnificence throughout* the durations of the Eons.* Amen.

*Rebel angels who proclaim
a different gospel (1\6, 1\9, 2 Cor. 11\4)*
⁶ I am astounded that you are so soon turned* away from* Him Who called* you in* *the* merciful goodwill of Christ into* a different* gospel,* ⁷ which is not another similar one.** But there are some who are troubling you and wanting to pervert the gospel of the Christ. ⁸ But even if we or an angel out of Heaven* were to proclaim to you a gospel contrary to the one we have proclaimed to you, let him be anathema.* ⁹ As we said before, and now I say again, if anybody proclaims to you a gospel contrary to* the one you received, let him be anathema.* ¹⁰ For am I now persuading men or God? Or am I looking to please men? For if I were still pleasing men, I would not be the servant of Christ.

*Paul's gospel a revelation from Jesus
(Rom. 2\16, 14\24, 2 Tim. 2\8)*
¹¹ But I make known* to you, brothers, that the gospel proclaimed by me is not from man.* ¹² For I neither received it from man, nor was I taught *it*, but *I received it* through a* revelation* from Jesus Christ.* ¹³ For you have heard of my previous manner of life* in the Jews' religion,* how with surpassing *zeal* I was persecuting the Ekklesia of God, and I was ravaging it, ¹⁴ and I was advancing in the Jews' religion* beyond many of my contemporaries in my own race, being more extremely zealous for traditions of

my fathers.
¹⁵ But when God, Who separated me from the womb of my mother and called *me* through His merciful goodwill, was pleased ¹⁶ to reveal His Son in me so that I might proclaim him among the nations, I did not immediately* confer with flesh and blood. ¹⁷ Nor did I go up to Jerusalem to those who were apostles before me, but I went into Arabia, and went back again to Damascus. ¹⁸ Then after three years I went up to Jerusalem to get to know Peter, and I stayed with him for fifteen days. ¹⁹ But I saw none of the other apostles, except Jacob, the brother of the Lord. ²⁰ Now with respect to what I am writing to you, you see, in the sight of God, I do not lie.
²¹ Then I came into the regions of Syria and Cilicia, ²² but I continued unknown by face to the Ekklesia groups of Judea in Christ. ²³ They, though, were hearing only that he who once persecuted us now proclaims the faith which once he ravaged. ²⁴ And because of me they were magnifying God.

*Recognition of Paul among other apostles.
Opposition from pseudo brothers*
2\1 Then after fourteen years, I again went up to Jerusalem with Barnabas, taking along Titus as well. ² And I went up *there* because of a revelation,* and I laid before them the gospel which I proclaim among the nations, although privately to those being of high reputation, in case I should somehow be running, or had run, in vain.
³ However, not even Titus who was with me, being a Greek, was compelled to be circumcised. ⁴ And on account of this, pseudo brothers* stole in to spy out our freedom* which we have in Christ Jesus, in order that they might enslave us to themselves. ⁵ We did not give way in subjection to them for even an hour, so that the truth of the gospel might hold its ground among you.
⁶ However, of those seeming to be* somebody, whatever they once were is nothing to me. God does not accept *the* face of man, for those seeming *to be somebody* imparted nothing to me.*
⁷ Rather, on the contrary,* having seen that I was entrusted with the gospel of the uncircumcision – just as *that* of the circumcision *was* to Peter, ⁸ for the one* working effectually by means of Peter for apostleship of the circumcision worked

effectually* in me also towards the nations – ⁹ Jacob, Cephas and John, those reputed to be* pillars, knowing the merciful goodwill given to me, gave me and Barnabas _the_ right hand of partnership,* that* we _should go_ to the nations,* and they to the circumcision,* ¹⁰ only _wishing_ that* we should remember the poor, the same thing I also was keen to do.

Correction of Peter's error
concerning eating with nations

¹¹ However, when Peter came to Antioch, I opposed him to _his_ face, because he was to be blamed. ¹² Because prior to some coming from Jacob, he was eating with the nations. But when they came, he began to withdraw and he was separating himself, being struck with the terror of those of _the_ circumcision. ¹³ And the rest of _the_ Jews also* played the hypocrite together with him, so that even* Barnabas was carried away by their hypocrisy.

¹⁴ But when I saw that they were not walking in line with the truth of the gospel, I said to Peter in front of everybody, 'If you, being a Jew, live in the custom of foreigners, and not as Jews, why do you compel _the_ nations to judaize?'**

Justification by faith alone, not works of law

¹⁵ We Jews by nature, and not violators from among _the_ nations – ¹⁶ knowing that a man is not pronounced righteous out of works of law, but through _the_ faith of Jesus Christ – also believed in Jesus Christ so that we might be pronounced righteous out of _the_ faith of Christ, and not out of works of law, for no flesh will be pronounced righteous out of works of law. ¹⁷ But if, looking to be pronounced righteous in Christ, we ourselves are in fact found as violators, _is_ Christ, in that case, an agent of violation? May it not be! ¹⁸ For if I build again the things which I destroyed, I confirm myself a transgressor.

¹⁹ For through law I died to law so that I might live to God. ²⁰ I have been hanged on a stake with* Christ. Nevertheless, I live, yet no longer I, but Christ lives in me,* and _the life_ which I now live in flesh I live by faith, that of the Son of God who loved me and gave himself up for me.

²¹ I am not setting aside the merciful goodwill of God, for if righteousness _comes_ through law, consequently Christ died for nothing.

The Galatians bewitched
into being judaized (2\14)

3\1 ☐h senseless Galatians! Who has spellbound* you into not obeying the truth, _you_ before whose eyes Jesus Christ was publicly exhibited* among you* as having been hanged on a stake?*

² Only this do I wish to learn from you: did you receive the spirit out of works of law, or out of hearing faith? ³ Are you so foolish? Having begun in spirit, do you finish off in flesh? ⁴ Have you suffered so many things in vain, if, that is, _it was_ in vain?

⁵ Does, therefore, He Who supplies* the spirit to you, and operates* works of power among you, _do it_ out of works of law, or out of _the_ hearing of faith?

Sons of Abraham.
Abraham an illustration
of justification by faith*

⁶ Just as* Abraham believed God, and it was accounted to him for righteousness,* ⁷ know, in that case, that those out of faith, these are sons of Abraham.*

⁸ And the Scroll, foreseeing that God would pronounce the nations* righteous by faith, proclaimed in advance the gospel to Abraham: 'In you all the nations will be benefitted,'** ⁹ so that those of faith are being benefitted* with believing Abraham.

¹⁰ For as many who are out of works of the law are under a curse. For it has been written: 'Cursed _is_ everyone who does not continue in practising all those things which have been written in the Scroll* of the law.'* ¹¹ But that nobody is pronounced righteous in law before God _is_ evident, because the righteous will live out of faith.* ¹² But the law is not out of faith.* Rather, he who does these things will live by them.*

¹³ Christ has redeemed us from the curse of the law, becoming a curse for us, for it has been written: 'Cursed _is_ everyone who hangs on a tree,'* ¹⁴ so that in Jesus Christ the benefit* of Abraham might come to the nations, so that we might receive the promise of the spirit through faith. ¹⁵ Brothers, I am speaking in the manner of man, like _the way_* nobody annuls or adds to a man's ratified covenant.

¹⁶ Now the promises* were spoken to Abraham and to his seed. It does not say 'and to seeds', as if concerning many, but as

concerning one, that is, 'to your seed', who' is Christ. [17] And I say this: the law, which took place four hundred and thirty years afterwards, does not make void' *the* covenant confirmed beforehand by God until' Christ,'' as if to make the promise of no effect. [18] For if the inheritance *is* out of the law, no more *is it* out of promise. God, though, has bestowed a gift to Abraham by a promise.

The law until Christ.
'God ... is one' (Deut. 6\4 etc.)

[19] What, then, about the law? It was added because of transgressions, until the seed should come to whom the promise was made, having been appointed by angels through the agency of a mediator.' [20] Now a mediator is not between one *side only*. God, though, is one.' [21] *Is* the law, then, contrary to the promises of God? May it not be! For if a law had been given which could have given life, righteousness really would have been out of law.

[22] The Scroll, though, has locked up everybody together under violation, so that the promise out of *the* faith of Jesus Christ might be given to those who believe, [23] whereas before the faith to come we were kept in custody under law, having been locked up until *the* faith being about to be revealed,' [24] so that the law became our pedagogue for Christ in order that we might be pronounced righteous out of faith. [25] But faith having come, no longer are we under a pedagogue.

Sons of God are the seed of Abraham, 'identified into Christ' (Rom. 6\3, 1 Cor. 12\13, Eph. 4\5, Col. 2\12). Illustration of child, servant, guardians. Jesus born of a woman. God as Father

[26] For you are all Sons of God' through faith in Christ Jesus. [27] For as many of you who were identified' into Christ have put on Christ.' [28] There is neither Jew nor Greek.' There is neither servant nor freeman.' There is neither male nor female.' For you are all one in Christ Jesus. [29] And if you are Christ's, then you are a seed of Abraham,' and heirs in keeping with a promise.

4\1 Now I say *that* for such a time while he is a child, the heir in no way differs from a servant, despite being owner of everything, [2] but he is under guardians and custodians until the time appointed by the father.

[3] So we also, when we were children, were held in bondage under the elementary principles of the world. [4] But when the fulness of the time came, God authorized His Son, born out of a woman,' born under law, [5] in order that He might redeem those under law, so that we might receive the sonship in full. [6] And in that you are Sons, God sent the spirit of His Son into your hearts, calling out, 'Abba, Father.' [7] Therefore, no longer are you a servant but a Son, and if a Son an heir also of God through Christ.

Bondage of service to man-made religion

[8] But not then knowing God, you were in bondage to those who by nature are not gods. [9] Now, though, knowing God, but especially being known by God, how do you turn back again to the weak and beggarly' elements' to which you desire to be in bondage all over again?' [10] You observe days, and months, and times, and years. [11] I am fearful for you, in case somehow I have laboured for you in vain.'

Commendation by Paul of his service

[12] Brothers, I implore you, become like me, for I *was* as you are. You have wronged me in nothing. [13] But you know how, on account of an infirmity of the flesh, I proclaimed the gospel to you before. [14] And my trial' in my flesh you did not disdain, nor did you spit *it* out with contempt, but you received me like *the* Angel' of God,' as if Christ Jesus. [15] What, then, was your pronounced benefit?' For I bear you witness that, if able, you would have given me your plucked-out eyes. [16] So have I become your enemy in dealing with you in truth? [17] They burn with zeal for' you, *but* not rightly. Rather, they want to shut you out so that you burn with zeal for' them. [18] *It is*, though, right to burn with zeal' in a good thing at all times, and not only in my being present among you, [19] my sons, for whom I am again in the pains of labour until Christ is formed in you. [20] And I desire' to come to' you now, and to alter my tone, because I am in perplexity about you.

Illustration of Sarah & Agar.
Jerusalem to come is 'mother of us all' (4\26, Eph. 2\18-22, Heb. 12\23, Rev. 21\2)

[21] Tell me, you who desire to be under law, do you not hear the law?' [22] For it has been written that Abraham had two sons, one out of a servant woman, and one out of a freewoman. [23] But the one out of the servant woman was

born by means of flesh, but the one out of* the freewoman* through the promise,* ²⁴ which things are being allegorized.* For these represent two covenants: one from Mount Sinai, giving birth to children* into bondage, which is Agar. ²⁵ For Agar represents* Mount Sinai in Arabia, and corresponds to* the Jerusalem now, and she performs her service together with her children. ²⁶ But the Jerusalem above,* which is freeborn,* is mother of us* all.* ²⁷ For it has been written:

'Rejoice, barren woman
not giving birth;
break out and cry aloud,
you not in labour pains;
because more *are* the children of the desolate
than of her having the husband.'*

²⁸ Now we, brothers, are, like Isaac, children of a promise.* ²⁹ But as *it was* then, so *is it* now also, *that* he who was born by means of flesh persecuted him *born* by means of spirit. ³⁰ Nevertheless, what does the Scroll say? 'Turn out the servant woman and her son, for in no way may the son of the servant woman share in the inheritance together with the son of the freewoman.'* ³¹ So then, brothers, we are not children of a servant woman, but of the freewoman.*

*Freedom from the old yoke
of bondage to man-made religion.
Not by circumcision, but righteousness by faith*

5\1 Stand fast, therefore, in the freedom* with which Christ made us free, and do not be entangled again with a yoke of bondage. ² Look, I, Paul, say to you that if you undergo circumcision, Christ will profit you nothing. ³ And I solemnly affirm* again to every man being circumcised that he is obligated to carry out the whole law. ⁴ Whoever *among you* are exhibited as justified* in law are disengaged from the Christ. You have fallen away from merciful goodwill. ⁵ For, through *the* spirit, we assiduously wait it out for gladly-held expectation of righteousness out of faith. ⁶ For in Christ Jesus neither circumcision is of any force, nor *is* uncircumcision, but faith energized* out of love *is of force.*

*Walk in fruits of the new spirit
which is against the lust of the flesh*

⁷ You were running well. Who undermined you to not obey* the truth? ⁸ That persuasion* *is* not out of Him Who calls you. ⁹ A little leaven leavens* the whole lump.
¹⁰ I have confidence in you in *the* Lord that you will be otherwise minded in nothing. The one throwing you into confusion, however, will bear the judgement, whoever he might be.
¹¹ And I, brothers, if I still proclaim circumcision, why am I still persecuted? In that case the offence of the stake* has been done away with. ¹² I wish those who are turning you upside-down* would even dismember themselves!* ¹³ For, brothers, you have been called on the basis of freedom. Only, *use* the freedom* not for an opportunity for flesh, but serve one another with love. ¹⁴ For the whole law is fulfilled in one oracle, in this:* 'You shall love your neighbour as yourself.'* ¹⁵ But if you bite and devour one another, watch out you are not consumed by one another.
¹⁶ I say, then, walk by *the* spirit,* and do not fulfil the lust of the flesh. ¹⁷ For the flesh militates lustfully against the spirit, and the spirit against the flesh, and these things are in opposition to each other, so that* whatever things you might not wish *to do*, these things you do. ¹⁸ If, though, you are impelled* by *the* spirit,* you are not under law.

*Exclusions from the Eon
(1 Cor. 6\9-10, Eph. 5\5, Rev. 21\8)*

¹⁹ Now the acts of the flesh are shown openly, *which* are things such as adultery,* sexual immorality, uncleanness, licentiousness, ²⁰ idolatry, sorcery, hatred, discord, jealousies, outbursts of boiling anger, selfish ambitions, divisions, heresies, ²¹ envyings, murders, drunkenness, orgies,* and things like these, of which I tell you beforehand, as I have said previously as well, that those who practise such things will not inherit the Sovereign Rulership* of God.*
²² On the other hand, the fruit of the spirit* is love, exuberance,* peace, long-suffering, kindness, goodness, faith,* ²³ meekness, self-control. Against such things there is no law.*
²⁴ And those who are of the Christ have hanged on a stake* the flesh with *its* passions and lusts. ²⁵ If we live by *the* spirit, let us also walk in line with *the* spirit.* ²⁶ Let us not become conceited, irritating each other, envying each

other.

Carry each other's burdens

6\1 **B**rothers, if a man is detected* in some fault, you *who are* spiritual ought to restore *a man* like that* in a spirit of meekness, making consideration about yourself in case you also are tempted.
2 Carry each other's burdens, and so fulfil the law of the Christ. 3 For if anybody thinks himself to be* something, being nothing, he deludes himself. 4 But let each one test his own actions, and then he will have pride in himself alone, and not in anybody else. 5 For each will bear his own load.

Sow to the new nature.
Boasting not in circumcision,
but in the stake of Christ
6 Let him getting taught in the oracle share in all good things with him who teaches.
7 Do not be led adrift. God is not mocked. For whatever a man sows, that also* will he reap. 8 For he who sows to his own flesh will reap corruption out of the flesh, but he who sows to the spirit will, out of the spirit, reap Eonian* life.
9 And we should not lose heart *in* well-doing, for we will reap a harvest in its proper season, not flagging. 10 Consequently then, as we have opportunity, we should work good towards everybody, and especially towards those of the household of the faith.
11 You see with what large* letters* I write* to you by my hand. 12 As many who desire to make a fair show in flesh, these are compelling you to be circumcised, only so that they might not suffer persecution for the stake* of the Christ. 13 For not even those who have been circumcised do themselves keep the law, yet they want you to be circumcised so that they can boast about your flesh.
14 But may it not be* for me to boast, except in the stake* of our Lord Jesus Christ, through whom the world to me has been hanged on a stake,* and I to the world. 15 For in Christ Jesus neither circumcision is of any force, nor *is* uncircumcision, but a new creation *is*. 16 And *to* as many who shall walk by this rule, peace on them, and mercy, and* on the Israel of God.*
17 From now on, let nobody give me aggravations,* for I bear in my body the brands* of the Lord Jesus.

18 Brothers, the merciful goodwill of our Lord Jesus Christ *be* with your spirit. Amen.

† **The Letters of Paul** †

Ephesians*

The apostle-authorized Ekklesia
in Ephesus (also in Acts 19 & 20, Rev. 2\1-7)

1\1

Paul, an apostle of Jesus Christ through the will of God.

To the holy people* who are in* Ephesus, namely,* to *the* believing in Christ Jesus, ² merciful goodwill to you, and* peace, from God our Father, and* *from the* Lord Jesus Christ.*

Revelation for the one body (Rom. 12\4-5 etc.)
of a new status in Jesus
who heads up all his 'most exalted'
(ἐπουράνιος, epouranios, Eph. 1\20, 2\6,
1 Cor. 15\48), who are marked out even now
(Luke 10\20, Rom. 8\29, Heb. 11\40).
Founding of God's coming world order
(John 17\5, 17\24, Acts 17\31).
Wisdom & understanding lavished on holy people
³ Exalted* be* the God and Father of our Lord Jesus Christ,** the one having exalted* us with* every* spiritual exaltation* *which is* among* the most exalted** *who are* in* Christ,** ⁴ in that,* in advance of* *the* foundation* of *the* world order,** He picks us out* *to be* in Himself, for us to be* holy and unblemished in His sight,* by means of *His* love,* ⁵ marking us out in advance* into sonship* to Himself through Jesus Christ, in harmony with the good pleasure of His will, ⁶ for the enthused praising of the magnificence of His merciful goodwill* through which He has made us objects of merciful goodwill* in the Richly Loved One,* ⁷ in whom we have redemption by means of his blood, the forgiveness of violations,* in harmony with the outflowing wealth of His merciful goodwill,* ⁸ which He has lavished towards us in all wisdom and understanding, ⁹ having made known to us the mystery* of His intention, in harmony with His good pleasure which He has purposed in him,* ¹⁰ for an administration* of the fulness of times, to head up* all these in the Christ,* the beings in the heavens** and the beings* on Earth, in him* ¹¹ in whom* also we have obtained an inheritance, being designated in advance,* and in harmony with *the* purpose of

the one energizing* all this,* after the counsel of His own will,* ¹² for us who first trusted in advance in the Christ to be* for the enthused praising of His magnificence, ¹³ in whom you also *hoped* after hearing the oracle of truth, the gospel of your salvation, in whom, believing also, you were marked with* a seal with the divine spirit* of promise, ¹⁴ which is the deposit* of our inheritance until the redemption of the special possession, for the enthused praising of His magnificence.*

Prayer for spirit of wisdom & revelation.
Change in the old world order.
Jesus now above all names. The body
(1\23, Rom. 7\4, 12\5, 1 Cor. 12\27)
¹⁵ On account of this, I also heard of the faith in the Lord Jesus among* you,* and *the* love *you* have for all the holy people. ¹⁶ I do not cease to give thanks for you, making mention of you in* my prayers ¹⁷ that the God of our Lord Jesus Christ,* the Father of magnificence, might give you the spirit of wisdom and revelation* in the realization of Him,* ¹⁸ the eyes of your heart* having been enlightened, for you to know* what is the expectation of His calling, and what *are* the riches of the magnificence of His inheritance among* the holy people, ¹⁹ and what *is* the transcendent immensity of His power towards us, the believing, in operation with the empowerment of the mightiness of His strength, ²⁰ which He energized* in the Christ, having raised him from the dead and seated *him* at* His right hand,* among the most exalted,* ²¹ over and above* all prime rulership, and forces of power,* and might,* and sovereignty, and every name having been named,* not only in this Eon,* but in the one coming* as well, ²² and He subordinated all things* under his feet,* and appoints him as fountainhead* over all these for the Ekklesia,* ²³ who are* his body,* the complement of him filling all these in all things.*

Dead to violations, 'alive ... with Christ'

2\1 **Y**ou* also were* dead* to the offences** and to the violations* ² in which you once walked in the manner of the Eon* of this world,* in keeping with the ruler of the influence* of the atmosphere,** of the spirit* which *is* now operating* among the sons* of disobedience,* ³ among whom we all also once had our mode of life,* in the lusts of our flesh,

fulfilling the cravings of the flesh and of the mind.*

And you were by nature the children of indignation,* just as the rest also *are*. [4] God, though, being rich in mercy, on account of His immense love with which He loved us [5] – we also being dead to the offences* – made *us* alive together with* the Christ.

By merciful goodwill are you saved.

Seated with Jesus in the New Jerusalem among the 'most exalted' (ἐπουράνιος; *1\3, 1\20*)

[6] He also raised *us* up together,* and seated *us* together,* among the most exalted* *who are* in Christ Jesus, [7] in order that in the coming Eons** He might show the transcendent wealth* of His merciful goodwill in kindness towards us in Christ Jesus. [8] For you are saved by merciful goodwill through faith. And this* is not out of yourselves, but *is* the gift of God. [9] Neither *is it* out of works, so that nobody at all might boast. [10] For we are His workmanship, created in Christ Jesus for good works which God prepared beforehand with the intent that we should walk in them.

[11] Consequently, remember that, you, in time past foreigners in flesh, *were* those known as foreskin by those known as the circumcision in flesh made by hands, [12] *and* that at that time you were without Christ, alienated from the citizenship* of Israel,* and strangers from the covenants of promise, having no gladly-held expectation, and without God in the world.

Joint access into the Temple for both nations & Israelites, until the New Jerusalem & a residence of God (2 Cor. 6\16, Heb. 3\6)

[13] But now in Christ Jesus, those once being far-off are made near* by the blood of the Christ. [14] For he is our peace, who has made both one. And he has broken down* the middle wall of partition,* [15] having annulled by his flesh the enmity, the law of commandments in decrees,* so that he might in himself transform* the two into one new man,* making peace, [16] and so that he might reconcile both to God in one body* by means of the stake,* having slain by it the enmity. [17] And he came *and* proclaimed peace to you, to those far-off and to those near.*

[18] For through him, by means of* one spirit,* we both* have access to the Father. [19] So then, you are no longer strangers and sojourners,* but fellow citizens* of* the holy people,** and the

household members* of God,* [20] built on the foundation* of the apostles and prophets,* Jesus Christ himself being *the* foundation cornerstone,* [21] in whom every building* being harmoniously framed together* is growing into* a holy sanctuary in *the* Lord,* [22] in whom you also are being built together into* a residence* of God** by means of* *the* Spirit.**

Revelation of the mystery of Christ of one body of Israelite & nation, without preference (Rom. 14\24-25)

3\1 𝔉or this reason,* I,* Paul, the shackled *man* of Christ Jesus, on behalf of you, the nations* – [2] if indeed you have heard of* the administration* of the merciful goodwill of God* given to me on your behalf [3] – *declare* that by revelation* He made known to me the mystery, as* I wrote previously* in a few words,* [4] in the light of which, in reading, you might realize my understanding in the mystery* of the Christ, [5] which to other generations* was not made known to the sons of men as it is now revealed to His holy apostles and prophets by means of* *the* Spirit,** [6] *for* the nations to be* joint heirs* and joint bodies,* and joint partakers** of His promise in the Christ through the gospel,* [7] of which I was made an agent,* in harmony with the gift of the merciful goodwill of God given to me in relation to the operation of the working of His power.

The mystery once hidden now made known (Rom. 14\24-25, Col. 1\24 etc.). Jesus, 'the Appointed One' (3\10, 3\21), to make known the wisdom of God to evil powers among the 'most eminent' (ἐπουράνιος; 3\10, 6\12)

[8] To myself, less than the least* of all holy people, this merciful goodwill is given so that I should proclaim among the nations* the good message of the unsearchable riches of the Christ, [9] and to enlighten everybody *in* what *is* the administration* of the mystery* which has been concealed from the Eons** by God, in having founded* all these things* through Jesus Christ, [10] in order that now* the manifold wisdom of God might be made known,* through the Appointed One,* to the prime rulers and the forces of power among the most eminent,* [11] in relation to *the* purpose of the Eons** which He accomplished* in Christ Jesus our Lord, [12] in whom we have boldness and

access in confidence through faith in him.*

¹³ I ask *you*, therefore, not to be dispirited at my tribulations on your behalf, which are your magnificence.* ¹⁴ For this reason,* I bow* my knees to the Father of our Lord Jesus Christ,* ¹⁵ out of Whom every progeny* in the heavens and Earth is named,* ¹⁶ that He would grant you, in harmony with the riches of His magnificence, to be strengthened with might in the inner man,* through* His spirit,* ¹⁷ for the Christ to inhabit your hearts* through faith, so that, having been rooted and founded in love, ¹⁸ you might be able to comprehend with all the holy people what *is* the breadth, and length, and depth, and height, ¹⁹ and to know the surpassing knowledge of the love of the Christ, in order that you might be filled to the extent of the entire complement of God.

²⁰ Now to Him being able, beyond all things, to perform superabundantly above what we might ask or think,* operating by the power working effectually* in us, ²¹ to Him *be* magnificence in* the Appointed One,* Christ Jesus, throughout* all the generations of the duration of the Eons.* Amen.

One body of Christ (Rom. 12\4-5 etc.).
One Lord, one God (1 Cor. 8\6, Deut. 6\4 etc.),
'one identification into Christ'
(Rom. 6\3, Gal. 3\27, Col. 2\12 etc.)

4\1 **I**, therefore, the shackled *man* in the Lord, admonish you that you walk in a manner worthy of the position* in which you have been placed, ² with all lowliness and meekness, with longsuffering, bearing with one another in love, ³ making an effort* to safeguard the unity of the spirit* in the binding* of peace.

⁴ There *is* one body,* and one spirit,* in the same way that* you are called for your part* in one gladly-held expectation of your calling, ⁵ one Lord, one faith, one identification,* ⁶ one God* and* Father of all, Who *is* above all, and through all, and among us all.*

Jesus 'descended' in burial (Mat. 12\40, Rom. 10\7)
& in resurrection taken up (Mark 16\19 etc.)
Gifts to the body, from Jesus the fountainhead

⁷ But merciful goodwill was given to each one of us* in relation to the measure of the gift of the Christ. ⁸ For this reason, He says:

'He ascended into the height;
he led captivity captive

and gave gifts to men.'*

⁹ Now that* 'He ascended', what does it imply* but that he first descended also into the lower parts of the ground?'* ¹⁰ He who descended is the same who ascended* also way beyond* all the heavens,* in order that he might fill all things.

¹¹ And some he appointed* as apostles, and some prophets, and some proclaimers of the gospel,* and some shepherds* and* teachers,* ¹² towards* the proper equipping* of the holy people, for* *the* carrying out of the work,* into* *the* building up* of the body of the Christ,* ¹³ to the end that we should all come into* the unity of the faith, and of the knowledge of the Son of God, into a full-grown man,* into* *the* measure of *the* stature of the full complement of the Christ, ¹⁴ so that no longer may we be infants, tossed here and there, and carried about with every wind of teaching,* in the roguery* of men, intent on craftiness,* intent on the systematizing* of deception,* ¹⁵ but rather we, holding the truth in love, might grow up into all things in him who is the fountainhead,* the Christ, ¹⁶ out of whom the entire body, being joined closely together,* and compacted together* by every contact* of supply, in line with the effectual working in the measure of every single part, is making for the growth of the body for the building up* of itself in love.

The new nature; rejuvenation
of the mind; 'the truth is in Jesus'

¹⁷ I am saying this, therefore, and I am solemnly affirming* in *the* Lord, that from now on you should no longer walk as* other nations also walk, in the vanity of their mind, ¹⁸ having been darkened in intellect, being alienated from the life of God on account of the ignorance which is in them because of the callousness of their heart,* ¹⁹ who, having thrown off feeling,* have given themselves over to lasciviousness, for the working* of all uncleanness with craving.*

²⁰ You, however, have not learned the Christ in this manner* ²¹ if, indeed, you heard him and have been taught in keeping with* him, as* *the* truth is in Jesus, ²² for you* to have pushed aside* the previous* conduct* in the way of* the old man,* being corrupted* in line with seductive lusts, ²³ and to be rejuvenated* by* the spirit of your mind,* ²⁴ and to put on* the new man* which is being created in line with God, in

righteousness and true holiness.

²⁵ For this reason, having driven aside˙ the˙ lie,˙ let every man be speaking truth with his neighbour,˙ because we are members of each other.

²⁶ Stand in awe,˙ but do not violate.

Do not let the Sun go down on your anger, ²⁷ nor give an opportunity to the Devil.

²⁸ Let the one stealing steal no more. But, rather, let him labour, working with the hands what *is* good, so that he might have *something* to give to him who has need.

²⁹ Let no filthy˙ remark proceed out of your mouth, but only whatever might be good for the use of building up,˙ so that it might be giving merciful goodwill to the hearers.

³⁰ And do not grieve the divine spirit of God,˙ by˙ which you are marked with a seal for˙ *the* day of redemption.˙

³¹ Let all bitterness, and boiling anger, and indignation,˙ and uproar,˙ and evil speaking˙ be rooted out from you, together with all malice. ³² And be kind to each other, tender hearted, dealing graciously among yourselves, in the same way that˙ for His part˙ God, in Christ, deals graciously with˙ you.˙

Imitators of God

5\1 **I**n view of this, be imitators˙ of God, as richly loved children. ² And walk in love, in the same way that˙ the Christ also loved us, and gave himself for us as an offering and a sacrifice to God, for a sweet-smelling savour.

Spiritual health

³ But *regarding*˙ fornication, and all uncleanness, and fraud,˙ let them not once be named among you, as˙ is becoming to holy people, ⁴ nor filthiness, nor stupid talking, nor coarse jesting, which are not becoming, but, rather, *let there be* a giving of thanks.

Exclusions from the Eon
(1 Cor. 6\9-10, Gal. 5\19-21, Rev. 21\8)

⁵ For this you know, that no fornicator, nor unclean person, nor a fraudster˙ who is an idolater, has any inheritance˙ in the Sovereign Rulership˙ of the Christ and God.˙˙

Walking in light

⁶ Let nobody deceive you with empty words, for because of these things the indignation of God comes against the sons of disobedience.˙ ⁷

Do not, therefore, be partners˙ of these things.˙ ⁸ For once you were darkness, but now a light in *the* Lord. Walk as sons of light,˙ ⁹ for the fruit of the spirit˙ *is* in all goodness and righteousness and truth.

¹⁰ Find out what is pleasing to the Lord.˙

¹¹ In addition, have no partnership˙ with the unfruitful works of darkness, but, rather, particularly˙ rebuke˙ *them*. ¹² For it is dishonourable even˙ to speak of those things˙ going on˙ through them in secret. ¹³ But all things being rebuked˙ are brought to light by the light, for everything which is brought to light˙ is light. ¹⁴ Therefore, He says:

'Wake up,˙ sleeper,
and stand up from˙ the dead,
and the Christ will present you in light.'˙

¹⁵ Watch out,˙ then, that˙ you walk circumspectly,˙ not as unwise,˙ but as wise, ¹⁶ redeeming˙ the time, because the days are evil. ¹⁷ On account of this,˙ do not be foolish,˙ but *be* understanding in what *is* the will of the Lord.˙

Not drunk; filled with the spirit of Christ

¹⁸ In addition, do not be drunk with wine, in which there is debauchery,˙ but be filled with˙ *the* spirit, ¹⁹ making voice to yourselves˙ in psalms and praise songs and spiritual songs,˙ singing and making melody˙ in˙ your heart to the Lord,˙ ²⁰ giving thanks at all times˙ for all things, in *the* name of our Lord Jesus Christ, to Him Who˙ *is* God and Father, ²¹ being subject to one another in reverence˙ of Christ.˙

The new Ekklesia 'in Christ' (1\2-3, 2\6) 'his body' (1\22-23, 5\30) & a 'new man' (2\15), & is the bridegroom with Jesus as a model for righteous marriage

²² Wives, subject yourselves to your own husbands as to the Lord, ²³ because a husband is a fountainhead of supply˙ for the wife, in the same way that the Christ also is fountainhead of supply˙ for the Ekklesia, and he is Saviour˙ of the body. ²⁴ But˙ in the same way that˙ the Ekklesia is subject to the Christ, *let* the wives also˙ in the same *act* way towards their own husbands in everything.

²⁵ Husbands, love your own˙ wives in the same way that˙ the Christ also loved the Ekklesia, and gave himself for it, ²⁶ so that he might sanctify it, having cleansed˙ *it* by the washing utensil˙ of water,˙ by˙ an oracle, ²⁷ so that he might present

it to himself *as* the˙ glorious Ekklesia,˙ not having stain, or wrinkle, or any such thing,˙ but so that it might be˙ holy and without blemish. [28] So ought men to love their own wives˙ as their own˙ bodies.˙ He who loves his wife loves himself. [29] For nobody˙ at any time˙ hated his own flesh, but he nourishes and cherishes it, in the same way that˙ the Lord for his part˙ *does* the Ekklesia, [30] seeing that we are members of his body,˙ out of his flesh, and out of˙ his bones. [31] For this reason,˙ a man will leave his father and mother, and he will be joined to˙ his wife, and the two will become˙ one flesh.˙

[32] This mystery is immense.˙ However, I speak concerning Christ and concerning˙ the Ekklesia. [33] But still,˙ let each˙ one of you individually so much˙ love his wife˙ in the same way that *he does* himself, but *let* the wife *see* that˙ she might revere˙ the husband.

Children & parents

6\1 **C**hildren,˙ listen submissively˙ to your parents in the Lord, for this is righteous.˙ [2] Honour your father and mother,˙ which is *the* first commandment in connection with a promise, [3] so that it might go well with you, and you might be˙ a long time˙ on the Earth.

[4] And, you fathers,˙˙ do not provoke your children into anger,˙ but bring them up in *the* education˙ and admonishing of the Lord.˙

Employers & employees

[5] Servants,˙ obey submissively *your* masters according to flesh with fear and trembling, in singleness of your heart, as if to the Christ, [6] not in the manner of eye-slavery, as pleasers of men, but as servants˙ of the Christ, doing the will of God˙ out of˙ *the* heart,˙ [7] performing service with goodwill as if to the Lord˙ and not to men, [8] knowing that whatever good˙ any man might have done˙ he will receive the same˙ back from the Lord, whether a servant˙ or a freeman.˙˙

[9] And you, masters, do the same things to them, refraining from˙ threatening, knowing that your Master for his part˙ is in *the* heavens.˙ And˙ there is no˙ partiality with him.

Instructions regarding 'the day of evil'
at the end of the 490 years (Daniel 9\24;
the revolt also seen in 2 Thess. 2\3-4)
against the evil powers who are among
the 'most eminent' (ἐπουράνιος; 6\12, 3\10)

[10] Finally,˙ my brothers, be empowered˙ in the Lord, and in the might˙ of his strength.˙ [11] Put on the complete armour˙ of God, for˙ you to be able˙ to hold your ground against˙ the stratagems˙ of the Devil, [12] because the combat˙ for us˙ is˙ not against blood and flesh,˙˙ but against the prime rulers,˙ against the forces of power,˙ against the world rulers˙ of this Eon˙ of darkness, against the spiritual forces˙ of evil among the most eminent.˙

[13] Because of this,˙ take up the complete armour˙ of God˙ so that you might be able to withstand in the day of evil,˙ and, having worked out the whole thing, to hold your ground.

[14] Hold your ground,˙ in that case, having belted up˙ your waist in˙ truth, and having put on the breastplate of righteousness, [15] and having booted up your feet with the readiness of the gospel of peace,˙ [16] *and* above all, having lifted up the shield of faith, by which you will be able to extinguish all the set-aflame˙ ballistics˙ of the Evil One˙ [17] and to receive˙ the helmet˙ of the salvation-bringing *gospel,*˙˙ that is, the sword of the spirit,˙ which is the oracle of God, [18] praying on every occasion˙ with all prayer and supplication˙ in *the* spirit,˙ and watching wakefully to this same thing,˙ with all perseverance and supplication for all the˙ holy people, [19] and on my behalf that utterance˙ may be given˙ to me in *the* opening up of my mouth in boldness, to make known the mystery of the gospel, [20] for which I act as ambassador in a manacle, so that I might speak boldly in it, as it is fitting for me to speak.

[21] And so that you also might know my affairs *and* what I am doing, Tychicus, a richly loved brother and faithful agent˙ in the Lord,˙ will make all things known to you. [22] I sent˙ him to you for the same purpose, so that you might get to know the things concerning us, and *so that* he might encourage˙ your hearts.

[23] Peace to the brothers, and love with faith, from God *the* Father, and˙ *the* Lord Jesus Christ. [24] May merciful goodwill *be* with all those who love our Lord Jesus Christ in incorruptibility. Amen.

† The Letters of Paul †

Philippians*

1 \ 1

aul and Timothy, servants of Jesus Christ.
To all the holy people in Christ Jesus who are in Philippi, with overseers and attendants, [2] merciful goodwill to you, and peace, from God our Father, and *from the* Lord Jesus Christ.*

[3] I thank my God at every mention of you, [4] always in every petition of mine, making petition for you all with exuberance, [5] for your partnership* in the gospel from the first day until now, [6] being persuaded of this same thing, that He Who began a good work among you will be carrying *it* on through to completion* until *the* day of Christ Jesus,** [7] just as* it is right* for me to think this of all of you, because, having you in my heart,* both in my shackles as well as in the defence and confirmation of the gospel, you are all fellow sharers* of my merciful goodwill.* [8] For God is my witness how I long after you all in compassion of Jesus Christ.

[9] And this I pray,* that your love might abound yet more and more in knowledge and all intelligent judgement, [10] in* your looking into the things which differ,* so that you might be sincere and without offence in* *the* day of Christ,* [11] having been filled with fruits of righteousness, through Jesus Christ, to* *the* magnificence and praise of God.

Jesus proclaimed by the broadcast of the imprisonment of Paul
[12] But I want you to understand, brothers, that the things against me have turned out rather for *the* progress* of the gospel, [13] for my shackles in Christ to appear as* open-view* among all the judgement hall *guard,* and to all the rest, [14] and for the majority of the brothers in *the* Lord, having become confident by my shackles to dare more boldly than ever* to speak the oracle fearlessly.
[15] Some, indeed, proclaim Christ even through envy and wrangling, some also, though, through goodwill. [16] Those *former* actually* proclaim Christ out of rivalry, not out of a pure motive,

supposing to add tribulation to my shackles, [17] those *others,* however, out of love, being conscious that I am appointed for the defence of the gospel.

Dilemma for Paul between
remaining to proclaim Christ,
or death for others' gain,
or being taken up to Christ
in 'the high calling' (3\14) as Enoch & Elijah
were (Paul later taking the latter choice:
2 Tim. 4\6-8, 4\18)
[18] For what? Nevertheless,* in every way, whether in falsehood or in truth, Christ is proclaimed. And in this I rejoice; not only that, but I will rejoice, [19] for I am aware* that this will turn out for me* into deliverance through your prayer and supply of the spirit of Jesus Christ, [20] because of my anxious looking with a lifted head,* and gladly-held expectation that in nothing will I be ashamed, but in all boldness, as always and now, Christ will be magnified in my body, whether by life, or by death.
[21] For to me, to be living *is gain for* Christ, and to be dying *is* gain *for Christ.* [22] But if *I am* to go on living in flesh, this for me *will be the* fruit of *my* labour.
Yet what I will choose I cannot tell.* [23] But* I am pressed* out of* the two,* having *instead* the* longing* for the departure* and to be* with Christ, *which is* so much* better.* [24] Nevertheless, to remain in the flesh *is* more needful for your sake.*
[25] And being convinced* of this, I know that I will remain and continue with you all for your progress* and exuberance of the faith, [26] so that your rejoicing might abound in Christ Jesus because of me, through my personal presence* with you once more.

Example of Christ.
Unity & suffering
[27] Only* express your conduct* worthily of the gospel of Christ, so that whether I come and see you, or whether I am absent, I might hear of the things concerning you, that you are standing fast in one spirit, with one mind,* striving together for the faith of the gospel, [28] and being alarmed* in nothing by those who oppose, which is a demonstration to them of destruction,* but to you of salvation, and that from God.
[29] For it was granted to you on behalf of Christ not only to believe in him, but also to

suffer for his sake, [30] having the same conflict which you saw in me, and you now hear of in myself.

2\1 **I**f *there is*, then, any encouragement in Christ, if any comfort of love, if any partnership* of spirit,* if any tender compassions and mercies, [2] make complete my exuberance by being of this same mind, having the same love, joined in mind, being mindful of the one thing.** [3] *Let* nothing *be done* for rivalry or groundless self-esteem, but by humility of mind esteem one another as surpassing yourselves.

Jesus, although in the likeness of men,
also in the form & image of God
once lost in Adam (Gen. 1\26, 5\3),
who was the first human Son of God (Luke 3\38).
That image now recovered in Jesus (2\6)
who has become so much more (Heb. 1\3)
with the highest name,
so that we might become Sons of God (2\15).
The Son called equal with God
because God is his Father (John 5\18).
Jesus given a new name (Mat. 28\19)
[4] Do not look individually to the interests of yourselves, but to the interests of others as well. [5] For this mind must be directed* in you which *was* also in Christ Jesus, [6] who, subsisting* in *the* form* of God, considered it not an act of robbery to become* equal to God.** [7] He had, though, made himself nothing, choosing* *the* form* of a servant, having come* in likeness of man. [8] And being found* in appearance* as a man, he abased himself, becoming obedient to the point of death, that is, the death *by* a stake.* [9] Because of this, God also highly exalted him, and He gave him a name above every name, so that:

[10] at the name of Jesus every knee might bow,
knees of heavenly beings,*
and of beings on Earth,
and of beings underneath the Earth,
[11] and every tongue
should make admission
that Jesus Christ *is* Lord,
to *the* magnificence of God *the* Father.*

[12] Therefore, my richly loved, just as you have always obeyed – not as in my personal presence* only, but now much more in my absence – work out your own salvation with fear and trembling. [13] For it is God operating* in you, both to will and to work effectually* for the realization of *His* good pleasure.

Blameless in a crooked generation.
Paul's life poured out like an offering
[14] Do all things without murmurings and disputings, [15] in order that you might become blameless and unspoiled,* Sons of God,* without rebuke, in *the* thick of a crooked and perverse generation, among whom you shine as luminaries in *the* world, [16] holding out an oracle of life, for my rejoicing on the day of Christ,* in that I have neither run in vain, nor laboured in vain.
[17] Yes, even if I am poured out* on the sacrifice and service of your faith, I rejoice and I will jointly rejoice with you all. [18] And for the same reason do you also rejoice, and you rejoice with me.

Example of Timothy
[19] But I hope in *the* Lord Jesus to send Timothy to you soon, so that I also might be of good comfort, having got to know the matters concerning you. [20] For I have nobody of a comparable mind who will genuinely care for your condition. [21] For all are searching their own things, not the things of Christ Jesus. [22] But you should get to know* the tested character of him, how, like a son with a father, he served with me for the gospel. [23] I hope, therefore, to send him straightaway, just as soon as I might have seen to* the affairs concerning myself. [24] But I have trusted in *the* Lord that I myself will also come shortly.

Example of Epaphroditus
[25] Yet I supposed it necessary to send to you Epaphroditus, my brother and companion in labour, and fellow soldier, but your messenger,* and provider of my need. [26] For he was longing after you all, and was full of heaviness, because you heard that he had been sick. [27] For indeed, he was sick to the point of death, but God had mercy on him,* and not on him only, but on me also, so that I might not have sorrow added to sorrow.
[28] So I sent him the more diligently so that in seeing him again you ought to be cheered, and I should be somewhat relieved* from sorrow. [29] Receive him, therefore, in *the* Lord, with all gladness, and hold such men as these in honour, [30] because for the work of the Christ

he drew near to death, having disregarded life, so that he might fill up your deficiency of service towards me.

Example of Paul.
Circumcision in spirit

3\1 **F**inally, my brothers, rejoice in *the* Lord. *It is* not irksome for me to write the same things to you, but for you *this is* a safeguard. ² Beware of dogs. Beware of evil workers. Beware of the mutilation *party.* ³ For we are the circumcision, serving by *the* spirit of God,* and rejoicing in Christ Jesus, and not putting trust in flesh.

⁴ I myself, though, might also have confidence in the flesh. If anybody else supposes to have confidence in flesh, I the more so: ⁵ in circumcision on *the* eighth day; out of *the* people of Israel; of *the* tribe of Benjamin; a Hebrew out of *the* Hebrews; concerning the law a Pharisee; ⁶ zealously persecuting the Ekklesia groups; but being blameless concerning righteousness in *the* law.

Desire for perfection expressed as
the power of Christ's resurrection
& as attaining to the 'out-resurrection'
(ἐξανάστασις, exanastasis),
a metaphor here for fulness of perfection

⁷ However, whatever things were gain to me, those I esteemed loss on account of the Christ ⁸ – yes, without doubt – and I count all these to be loss for the superiority of the knowledge of Christ Jesus, my Lord for whom I have suffered the loss of all things, and I count to be* dung in order that I might gain Christ ⁹ and be found in him, not having any righteousness of my own out of law, but that which is through Christ's faith, the righteousness from God based on faith, ¹⁰ to know him, and the power of his resurrection,* and the partnership of his sufferings,* being made conformable to his death, ¹¹ if, by any means, I might attain to* the out-resurrection* of the dead* – ¹² not that I already have taken hold of* *that*, or have already been brought to perfection, but I am pressing on, in order that I might lay hold also of that which I have been taken possession of for my part by Christ Jesus.

Parenthesis concerning himself.
Paul pressing on for his prize
of 'the high calling of God'

which Enoch & Elijah had
¹³ Brothers, I do not count myself to have taken possession. But *this* one thing *I do*: forgetting those things which are behind, and reaching forward to those things ahead, ¹⁴ I press on* towards the mark for the prize of the high calling of God in Christ Jesus.

A frame of mind conformed to Jesus (also 2\5).
Example of Paul.
Waiting for Jesus to appear (1 Thes. 1\10).
A body conformed to his
¹⁵ As, then, for the many mature, we might be of this frame of mind,* and if you are otherwise minded *in* anything God will reveal this to you as well. ¹⁶ Nevertheless, to that which* we have attained, let us walk by the same rule,* to be of the same frame of mind.*
¹⁷ Brothers, become fellow imitators of me, and mark those walking like this, just as you have us *as* an example.* ¹⁸ For many are walking – *of* whom I have told you often, and now tell you even weeping – as the enemies of the stake* of the Christ, ¹⁹ whose end *is* destruction, whose god *is their* innermost part,* and *whose* glory *is* in their shame, those directing their minds on earthly things.
²⁰ For our acquired character* is inherent* in *the* exalted,* out of which* *character* we are also assiduously waiting it out for* a Saviour, the Lord Jesus Christ, ²¹ who will change the form of* the body of our humiliation, for it to become* conformed to the body of his magnificence, by* the working of his power, and* to put all things in subjection* to himself.

4\1 **I**n that case, my brothers, richly loved and longed-for, my joy and crown, in this manner* stand fast in *the* Lord, *my* richly loved.

The divine secret of contentment
² I encourage Euodias, and I encourage Syntyche, to be of the same mind in *the* Lord. ³ Yes, and I ask you also, true yoke-fellow, help these *women*, since they laboured together with me in the gospel, with Clement as well, and the rest of my fellow labourers whose names *are* in the Scroll* of Life.
⁴ Rejoice in *the* Lord always. Again I say, rejoice.
⁵ Make your reasonableness known to all men.
The Lord *is* near.*
⁶ Be anxious about nothing, but in all things*

by prayer and supplication,* with thanksgivings, let your requests be made known to God, [7] and the peace of God, which transcends every understanding, will garrison* your hearts and thoughts in Christ Jesus.

[8] Finally, brothers, whatever things are true, whatever things _are_ honourable, whatever things _are_ just, whatever things _are_ pure, whatever things _are_ lovely, whatever things _are_ of good report, if _there is_ any virtue, if any praise, reckon inwardly on* these things.*

[9] What you both learned and received and you heard and saw in me, put those things into practice, and the God of peace will be with you.

[10] But I rejoiced tremendously in _the_ Lord that now at last you have revived your concern for me, in which, although you had indeed been mindful, you were lacking opportunity. [11] Not that I speak in respect of want, for I have learned, in whatever _state_ I am, to be* contented.

[12] And I experience _what it is_ to be brought low, and I experience _what it is_* to abound. In every place and among all, I have been taught the secret of being fed and going hungry,* and of having more than enough and of suffering.*

[13] I am strong for* all these things through* Christ who empowers me.

Commendation for generosity
in 'the beginning of the gospel' (John 1\1)

[14] Yet you have done well in having been a joint partaker in* my affliction. [15] Now you Philippians are aware also that in the beginning of the gospel,* when I departed from Macedonia, not any Ekklesia group contributed to me in settlement of* giving and receiving except you only, [16] because even in Thessalonica you more than once sent me something towards my need. [17] Not that I look for a gift, but I look for the fruit which might abound to your account. [18] I have received everything in full, and I have surplus.* I have been amply supplied, having received from Epaphroditus the things from you, an odour of sweet fragrance, an acceptable sacrifice, well pleasing to God.

[19] But my God will supply all your need, in keeping with His riches in _the_ magnificence in Christ Jesus.

[20] Now* magnificence to our God and* Father throughout* the durations of the Eons.* Amen.

[21] Greet every holy person in Christ Jesus. The brothers who are with me greet you.

[22] All the holy people send you greetings, especially those who are of the household of Caesar.

[23] The merciful goodwill of the Lord Jesus Christ _be_ with you all. Amen.

† The Letters of Paul †

Colossians

1\1

Paul, an apostle of Jesus Christ through the will of God, and Timothy *our* brother. [2] To the holy people in Colosse, and* the faithful brothers in Christ, merciful goodwill to you, and peace, from God our Father, and *from* the Lord Jesus Christ.*

Apostles' work fulfilled, to proclaim
the gospel in all the known world

[3] We give thanks to *the* God and* Father of our Lord Jesus Christ,* praying always for you,* [4] having heard of your faith in Christ Jesus, and of the love for all the holy people, [5] on account of the gladly-held expectation stored away for you in the heavens,** which you have heard of before in the oracle of the truth of the gospel,* [6] coming to you as also in all the world, and is producing fruit, and is increasing, as among you also from the day you heard of *it* and knew the merciful goodwill of God in truth, [7] as you learned also from Epaphras, our richly loved fellow servant, who is for you a faithful agent of the Christ, [8] who also signified to us your love in *the* spirit.*

Prayer for spiritual understanding

[9] On account of this, we too, from the day we heard, do not cease praying* for you,* and asking* that you might be filled* with the knowledge of His will* in all wisdom and spiritual understanding, [10] *for* you* to walk* worthily of the Lord with a view to being pleasing in all things, being fruit-bearing in every good work, and growing in acknowledgment of God, [11] being empowered with all might, in accordance with His glorious power, with a view to all endurance* and long-suffering, together with exuberance,* [12] giving thanks to the Father, Who made us fit for the share of the inheritance of the holy people in the light, [13] Who rescued us from the power of darkness, and translated *us* into the Sovereign Rulership* of the Son of His love, [14] in whom we have redemption,* the forgiveness of violations,* [15] who is *the* representation of the invisible God, *the* First-honoured* of every creation.*

Everything now 'is founded' in Jesus (John 1\10),
who as 'the last Adam' (1 Cor. 15\45)
is 'the Beginning' of a new race
of reconciled & holy people, they being a new order
founded under Jesus in his supreme status
after his entry into Heaven (Phil. 2\9, Heb. 1\3)

[16] For everything* is founded* in him:* the beings in the heavens, and the beings on the Earth, the visible and the invisible. Whether seats of government* or sovereignties, whether prime rulers or forces of power,* everything* has been founded* through him* and for him, [17] and he is over* all these things, and everything holds together* in* him.* [18] And he himself is the fountainhead* of the body* of the Ekklesia, who is *the* Beginning,* *the* First-honoured* from among the dead, so that among all he might be holding the preeminence.* [19] For the entire complement is pleased to settle** in him, [20] he having also made peace through the blood of his stake,* to reconcile through him all beings to himself, by him, whether beings on the Earth, or beings* in the heavens.* [21] And you, once being alienated* and hostile* in mind by wicked works, he has now reconciled [22] in the body of his flesh through death, to present you holy and without blemish and unaccused in his sight, [23] if, indeed, you remain in the faith, having been founded, and stable, and not being moved away from the gladly-held expectation of the gospel which you heard, *and* was proclaimed among all the creation which is under Heaven,* of which I, Paul, became an agent.

The mystery once hidden now made known
among nations (1 Tim. 3\16, Rom. 14\24-25)

[24] Now I am rejoicing in sufferings for you, and I fill up that which is lacking of* the tribulations of the Christ in my flesh on behalf of his body,* which is the Ekklesia, [25] of whom I became an agent as regards* the management of God which was given to me for you, to complete the oracle of God,* [26] the mystery* having been hidden from the Eons* and from the generations, but it has now been brought to light* for* His holy people, [27] to whom God wished* to make known* what *are* the riches of the magnificence* of this mystery among* the

nations,˙ which˙ is Christ among˙ you,˙ the gladly-held expectation of magnificence,˙ ²⁸ whom we announce,˙ admonishing every man, and teaching every man in all wisdom, so that we might present every man perfect˙ in Christ Jesus, ²⁹ towards which I labour also, striving in accordance with his working, operating effectually˙ in me with power.

Established in faith
& the mystery of God & Christ

2\1 **F**or I wish that you knew how much of a struggle˙ I have for you and those in Laodicea,˙ and *for* as many who have not seen my face in flesh,˙ ² in order that their hearts might be encouraged, being joined together˙ in love and into all richness of the most certain confidence of understanding, leading on to knowledge of the mystery of God and of *the* Father, and˙ of Christ, ³ in Whom are hidden all the treasures of wisdom and knowledge.˙

⁴ And I say this in order that nobody should beguile you with persuasive arguments.˙ ⁵ For even if I am absent in flesh, yet I am with you in spirit, rejoicing, and observing your orderly character, and the steadfastness of your faith in Christ. ⁶ Therefore, just as you have received Christ Jesus the Lord, walk in him, ⁷ having been rooted and built up in him, and being established in the faith, as you were taught, abounding in it with thanksgiving.

The emptiness & deceit of men's ideas & traditions.
Completeness (2 Tim. 3\17) in Christ
as 'the fountainhead' (also Col. 1\18),
through true circumcision (as a figure),
& the true 'one identification into Christ'
(Gal. 3\27, Eph. 4\5). All rituals scrapped.
The consequent vain uselessness
of man-made religious tradition

⁸ See to it in case there might be anybody who makes a prey of you through philosophy and empty deceit, after the tradition of men, after the elementary principles of the world, and not after Christ, ⁹ because in him the entire complement of God's headship˙ resides as a body,˙ ¹⁰ and having been made complete˙ you are in him˙ who is the fountainhead˙ of all prime rulership and power.˙

¹¹ In him you were circumcised also with the circumcision not made by hands, in putting off the body of the violations of the flesh˙ in the circumcision of the Christ, ¹² having been buried together in the identification˙ with him in whom you also were jointly raised up,˙ through the belief of the operation of God,˙ Who raised him from the dead.

¹³ And you, being dead in your violations and the uncircumcision of your flesh, he has made alive together˙ with him, having graciously forgiven us all our offences, ¹⁴ having blotted out˙ the handwriting of the decrees˙ which was against us, which was in opposition to us, and he has removed˙ it out of the way, having nailed it to the stake,˙ ¹⁵ *and*, having stripped˙ the prime rulers and the authorities,˙ he made an exhibition publicly, triumphing over them in it.

¹⁶ Let nobody, therefore, judge you in eating, or in drinking, or in respect of a festival, or of a New Moon, or of Sabbaths, ¹⁷ which are a shadow of things coming.˙ But the reality˙ *is* of the Christ.

¹⁸ Let nobody defraud you of the prize by means of˙ a voluntary humility and worship˙ of angels,˙ pushing into˙ things which he has not seen,˙ vainly puffed up˙ by the mind of his flesh,˙ ¹⁹ and not taking hold of the fountainhead,˙ from where˙ all the entire body˙ – by means of the contacts˙ and connections˙ being supplied˙ and being compacted together˙ – increases with the growth of God.˙

²⁰ If you died with the Christ from the elementary rules of the world, why, as though living in *the* world, do you subject yourselves to decrees: ²¹ you may not touch; you may not taste; you may not handle;˙ ²² which are all destined for decay by collapsing into disuse,˙ after the injunctions and teachings of men? ²³ That order of things˙ is indeed having a reputation of wisdom in self-imposed religion˙ and humility and unsparing abuse˙ of *the* body, without any due value with respect to the satisfying˙ of the flesh.

Risen with Jesus. Jesus will be 'brought to light'
in the heavens (3\4, Is. 40\5, John 1\51,
1 Tim. 6\14, 2 Tim. 4\1, 4\8, Titus 2\13,
1 Peter 4\13, 5\4, 1 John 32),
which will be his ἐπιφάνεια *(epiphaneia),*
'favourable intervention';
and believers will see him as he is & be changed
in order to live 'throughout the Eon'
(John 11\26, 1 Cor. 15\42-54, 1 John 3\2)

3\1 **I**f, then, you were raised up together˙ with the Christ, search for those things above,˙ where the Christ is sitting at˙ *the* right hand˙ of

God.

² Set your mind on things above,* not on things on the Earth. ³ For you died, and your life is hidden with the Christ in God.

⁴ When the Christ, our life, might be brought to light,* then you also will be brought to light* with him* in a glorified state.*

A new nature

⁵ In view of that, put to death your members on the Earth: fornication, uncleanness, lust, evil craving* and covetousness which is idolatry. ⁶ On account of such things the indignation of God comes against the sons of disobedience,* ⁷ among whom you also once walked when you were living it out in these things.

⁸ Now though, in addition, shed off* all these:* indignation, boiling anger, malice, detracting speech, obscene language out of your mouth.*

⁹ Do not lie to each other, having stripped off* the old man with his practices, ¹⁰ and having put on the new *man,* renewed in knowledge in harmony with *the* image of the one transforming him, ¹¹ where there is neither Greek nor Jew,* circumcision nor uncircumcision, Barbarian, Scythian, servant, freeman.* Christ, though, is everything in everybody.*

¹² Therefore, as an elect of God, holy and richly loved, clothe yourselves in compassionate feelings,* kindness, humility of mind, meekness, long-suffering, ¹³ bearing with one another, and dealing graciously among* yourselves if anybody should be having a grievance against anybody. Just as the Christ also deals graciously with* you, you should *do* the same as well.*

¹⁴ And, above all these things, *add* love, which is *the* binding* of perfection. ¹⁵ And let the peace of God preside in your hearts, to which you were called also in one body.* In addition, be thankful.

¹⁶ Let the oracle of the Christ* inhabit you with richness in all wisdom – teaching and admonishing yourselves in psalms and praise songs and spiritual songs, singing to the Lord with merciful goodwill in your hearts.*

¹⁷ And everything, whatever you do in word or in deed, *do* all things in *the* name of *the* Lord Jesus, giving thanks to God and* *the* Father* through him.

Family relationships

¹⁸ Wives, put yourselves in subjection to your own husbands, as is becoming in *the* Lord.

¹⁹ Husbands, love *your* wives, and do not be harsh towards them.

²⁰ Children, obey *your* parents in respect of all things, for this is well pleasing with *the* Lord.

²¹ Fathers,* do not provoke* your children, so that they might not have their spirit broken.*

Employers & employees

²² Servants, obey masters in all things as far as it goes regarding flesh, not with eye-service, as men-pleasers, but in singleness of heart, revering God. ²³ And whatever you do, carry *it* out from *the* inner being,* as if to the Lord, and not to men, ²⁴ knowing that you will receive from *the* Lord the recompense of the inheritance, for you serve the Lord Christ.

²⁵ He who does wrong, however, will be repaid for the wrong which he committed, and there is no partiality.

4\1 **M**asters, give fairness and equality to* servants, knowing that you also have a Lord in *the* heavens.*

Prayer, wisdom & speech.
Friends of Paul

² Persevere in prayer, being watchful in it, adding thanksgiving,* ³ at the same time praying for us also that God might open to us a door of utterance, to speak the mystery of the Christ, on account of which I have been shackled as well, ⁴ so that I may bring it to light* in the way I ought to speak.

⁵ Walk in wisdom with respect to those outside, redeeming the time.*

⁶ *Let* your speech *be* always with favourable goodwill, seasoned with salt, to know how you ought to answer everybody.*

⁷ Tychicus, the richly loved brother and faithful worker and fellow servant in *the* Lord, will make known* to you all* the affairs* about* me. ⁸ I am sending him on to you for* the same purpose, so that he might know the affairs* about* you, and he might encourage your hearts, ⁹ together with Onesimus, the faithful and richly loved brother, who is *one* of* you. They will make everything here known to you.

¹⁰ My fellow prisoner Aristarchus greets you. And if Mark, the cousin of Barnabas, concerning* whom you received instructions, comes to you, receive him, ¹¹ as well as Jesus, known as Justus, who are out of *the* circumcision. These *are the* only fellow workers for the Sovereign Rulership* of God who have been found* a comfort to me.*

¹² Epaphras, who is of your own, a servant of Christ, sends you greetings, struggling always for you in prayers that you might stand mature and having been filled* in all *the* will of God. ¹³ For I bear witness to him that he has much zeal for you, as well as those in Laodicea and those in Hierapolis.

¹⁴ Luke, the richly loved physician, greets you, as does Demas.* ¹⁵ Greet the brothers in Laodicea, and Nymphas, and the Ekklesia group in his house.
¹⁶ And when this letter is read among you, arrange* that it is read among the Ekklesia group of Laodiceans as well, and that you yourselves likewise read the *letter* from Laodicea.*
¹⁷ And tell* Archippus, 'See to* the office which you received in *the* Lord, that you fulfil it.'
¹⁸ The salutation of Paul in my own handwriting.* Remember my shackles. Merciful goodwill *be* with you. Amen.

~ ◆◆ ~

1\1

Paul, and Silvanus, and Timothy.
To the Ekklesia group of Thessalonians, in God *the* Father* and* in *the* Lord Jesus Christ, merciful goodwill to you, and peace, from our God and Father, and* *from the* Lord Jesus Christ.*

Thanksgiving & prayer.
Thessalonians proclaiming the oracle
of God & Christ are examples to all
² We give thanks to God constantly* concerning you all, making mention of you in our prayers, ³ ceaselessly remembering your work proceeding from faith, and labour proceeding from love, and endurance of gladly-held expectation of our Lord Jesus Christ, in the sight of our God and* Father, ⁴ knowing, brothers loved by God, your election.
⁵ For our gospel came to you not in oracle only, but in power also, and in *the* divine spirit, and in a most certain confidence, as you know what we became* among you for your sake. ⁶ And you became* imitators* of us and of the Lord, having received the oracle in much affliction, with exuberance of *the* divine spirit, ⁷ for you to become* illustrative examples to all those in Macedonia and Achaia who believe.
⁸ For from you the oracle of the Lord sounded out* not only in Macedonia and in Achaia, but your faith towards God has gone out in every place as well, so that *there is* no need for us to speak anything. ⁹ For they themselves report back about us what kind of approach we took with you, and how you turned to God from idols to serve a living and true God, ¹⁰ and to wait for His Son from the heavens,* whom He raised from *the* dead, Jesus, who rescues us from the coming indignation.

Speaking to please God.
The gospel of God not a burden

2\1 **F**or you yourselves, brothers, know our approach with you, that it has not arisen* in vain. ² But even after having suffered previously, and having been insulted, as you know, in Philippi, we were bold in our God to

speak to you the gospel of God amid much contest.
³ For our encouragement *did* not *come* out of deceit, nor out of uncleanness, nor by guile. ⁴ But just as we have been approved by God to be entrusted with the gospel, so, consequently,˙ do we speak, not as pleasing men, but God, Who tests our hearts. ⁵ For not at any time˙ did we come with any expression of flattery, as you know, nor in any pretence of covetousness – God *is our* witness – ⁶ nor searching for glory˙ from men, neither from you, nor from others, able as apostles of Christ to come˙ in heaviness.˙˙ ⁷ But we were gentle among you, in the way a nursing mother would cherish her own children. ⁸ So, yearning over you, we were delighted to impart to you not only the gospel of God, but our own selves˙ as well, because you have become richly loved to us.
⁹ For you remember, brothers, our labour and toil. For we laboured night and day, in order not to put a burden on any of you, when we proclaimed to you the gospel of God. ¹⁰ You *are* witnesses, and God *is*, of how purely˙ and justly and blamelessly we were found˙ towards you, the believers, ¹¹ as you know, *and* how, like a father with his own children,˙ *we were* encouraging and comforting you, every one of you, ¹² and testifying for you to walk worthily of God, Who called you to His own Sovereign Rulership˙ and magnificence.˙

Thessalonians receive the apostles
as speaking the oracle of God.
Murderous opposition
¹³ On account of this,˙ we also ceaselessly give thanks to God, how, having received from us the reported oracle of God, you received *it* not *as* a word of men, but just as˙ it truly is, the oracle of God,˙ Who works effectually˙ also in you who believe.
¹⁴ For you, brothers, became imitators˙ of the Ekklesia group˙ of God who are in Judea, in Christ Jesus,˙ for you also suffered similar things from *your* own countrymen, just as˙ they also˙ *do* from the Jews,˙ ¹⁵ those˙ killing˙ even the Lord Jesus˙ and their own prophets, and having driven us out,˙ and not pleasing˙ God, and opposed to all men – ¹⁶ preventing us from speaking to the nations˙ so that they might be saved – so as˙ to constantly˙ fill up˙ their violations,˙ for˙ anger has come against them to˙ *the* utmost.˙˙

Paul's desire to visit
hindered by Satan. Timothy sent
¹⁷ But we, brothers, being taken away from you for a short time˙ – in face, not in heart – endeavoured more eagerly, with much longing,˙ to see your face, ¹⁸ which is why we wanted to come to you, truly, I, Paul, time and again, but Satan hindered us.¹⁹ For what *is* our gladly-held expectation, or exuberance, or crown of rejoicing? *Is it* anything but you, in the sight of our Lord Jesus in his magisterial presence?˙ ²⁰ For you are our magnificence˙ and exuberance.

3\1 Therefore, no longer bearing *it*, we were pleased to be left alone in Athens, ² and we sent Timothy, our brother and an agent of God, and our fellow labourer in the gospel of the Christ, to establish you, and to encourage you concerning your faith, ³ so that nobody should be disturbed by these afflictions, for you yourselves know that we are appointed to this.
⁴ For indeed, when we were among you we told you in advance that we were about to be afflicted, just as˙ it turned out as well, as you know. ⁵ Because of this, I also, bearing it no longer, sent word to know of your faith, as to whether the Tempter˙ has somehow tempted you, and our labour would be in vain.
⁶ But now with Timothy having come from you to us, and his bringing us good news about your faith and love, and that you always˙ have good recollection of us, *and* you long to see us, as we also *long to see* you, ⁷ because of this, brothers, in all our affliction and distress we were encouraged about you by your faith. ⁸ For now we are among the living, if you make a stand in *the* Lord.

Rejoicing for Thessalonians
& desire to visit them.
Increase of love & blameless hearts.
Walk to please God
⁹ For what thanks can we return to God concerning you for all the exuberance with which we rejoice on account of you before our God, ¹⁰ night and day praying strenuously with a view to seeing your face, and to rectify the things deficient in your faith? ¹¹ Now may our God and Father Himself, and˙ our Lord Jesus Christ, direct our way to you.
¹² And may the Lord make you increase and overflow in love towards one another, and towards everybody, just as we also˙ *do* towards you,¹³ in order to establish your hearts as

blameless in holiness before God and* our Father, in* the magisterial presence* of our Lord Jesus Christ with all* his holy ones.*

4\1 **F**inally then, we beseech and encourage *you*, brothers, in *the* Lord Jesus, how, as you have received from us, you ought to walk and to please God, so that you should abound all the more. ² For you know what instructions we gave you through the Lord Jesus. ³ For this is *the* will of God: your sanctification;* for you to abstain from fornication; ⁴ each one of you to know how to control his own stuff** in sanctification and honour; ⁵ not in *the* passion of lust* in the manner of the nations also who do not know God; ⁶ not to take advantage of or defraud his brother in business. For the Lord *is* the avenger concerning all these, as, indeed, we have warned and fully given testimony to you. ⁷ For God called us not with a view to uncleanness, but to sanctification. ⁸ Consequently, he who rejects this rejects not man, but God, Who has also given you His divine spirit. ⁹ But concerning brotherly love, you do not need *for me* to write to you, for you yourselves are taught by God to love each other. ¹⁰ For indeed, you do this towards all the brothers in the whole of Macedonia. But we encourage you, brothers, to abound all the more, ¹¹ and to study to be quiet, and to attend to your own affairs,* and to work with your own hands,* as we commanded you, ¹² in order that you should walk in an appropriate manner towards those outside, and you might have a lack of nothing.

Sleep as the divine view of believers' death.
Jesus' return & presence
at the end of the 490 year Eon
¹³ But we do not want you to be ignorant, brothers, concerning those fallen asleep,* so that you should not be grieved, and like others who have no gladly-held expectation. ¹⁴ For if we believe that Jesus died and rose, so also* will God through* Jesus bring* with himself those having been put to sleep.* ¹⁵ For we say this to you by an oracle of *the* Lord, that we, the living left remaining* until* the magisterial presence* of the Lord, will certainly not precede* those put to sleep.** ¹⁶ For the Lord himself will come down from Heaven with an oracle of command,* with *the* voice of *the* Archangel,* and with *the* trumpet of

God,* and the dead in Christ will be raised first.* ¹⁷ After that, we, the living left remaining,* will be caught away* together with them in clouds to meet the Lord in* *the* air,* and so will we always* be with *the* Lord. ¹⁸ So then, comfort one another with these oracles.

Peace and safety, sudden destruction

5\1 **B**ut of the times and the seasons, brothers, you have no need for yourselves to be written to. ² For you yourselves know perfectly that the day of *the* Lord* comes like a thief in *the* night. ³ For when they say, 'Peace and safety,' then sudden destruction comes on them, like birth pains to her *who is* in labour, and they will certainly not escape. ⁴ But you, brothers, are not in darkness, that* that day should overtake you like a thief.* ⁵ You are all the sons of light, and the sons of day.* We are not of night, nor of darkness. ⁶ So then, we should sleep not as the rest also *do*, but we should watch and be sober. ⁷ For those sleeping take sleep at night, and those getting themselves drunk get drunk at night. ⁸ But we existing of *the* day* ought to be sober, having put on a breastplate of faith and love, and, for a helmet, the gladly-held expectation of salvation.* ⁹ For God did not appoint us for anger, but for obtaining* salvation* through our Lord Jesus Christ, ¹⁰ having died for us, so that whether we might watch* or we might sleep, we might live together with him. ¹¹ So encourage one another, and build one another up, just as indeed you are doing. ¹² And we ask you, brothers, to recognize those labouring among you and being your guardians in *the* Lord, and exhorting you, ¹³ and to esteem them beyond measure in love on account of their work.

Be at peace among yourselves.
¹⁴ Now we encourage you, brothers: admonish the unruly; console the faint-hearted; sustain the weak; be patient towards all.
¹⁵ See that nobody renders evil for evil to anybody, but always* pursue the good, both towards each other and towards everybody.
¹⁶ Rejoice always.*
¹⁷ Pray without ceasing.*
¹⁸ In everything give thanks, for this *is the* will of God* in Christ Jesus for you.
¹⁹ Do not quench the spirit.*

²⁰ Do not despise prophecies. ²¹ But test all things. Hold fast that which is good.
²² Keep back from every form* of evil.

Sanctification & blamelessness
²³ Now may the God of peace Himself sanctify you wholly, and may your spirit and inner being* and body be preserved entire *and* blameless in* the magisterial presence of* our Lord Jesus Christ. ²⁴ He Who calls you *is* faithful, and He will do *it.*

²⁵ Brothers, pray for us.
²⁶ Give greetings to all the brothers with a holy kiss.
²⁷ I adjure you by *the* Lord for this letter to be read by all the holy brothers. ²⁸ The merciful goodwill of our Lord Jesus Christ *be* with you. Amen.

~ ◆◆ ~

† **The Letters of Paul** †

2 Thessalonians*

1\1

aul, and Silvanus, and Timothy.
To the Ekklesia group of the Thessalonians, in God our Father and* *the* Lord Jesus Christ, ² merciful goodwill to you, and peace, from God our Father, and *from the* Lord Jesus Christ.*

Vengeance on persecutors & all adversaries at Jesus' coming (Rom. 2\8-9)
³ We are compelled always to give thanks* to God concerning you, brothers, as is fitting, because your faith is growing beyond measure, and the love of each one of all of you abounds* towards one another, ⁴ so much for ourselves to rejoice about you among the Ekklesia groups of God for your patience and faith* in all your persecutions and tribulations which you endure, ⁵ a clear token of the righteous judgement of God, for you to be counted worthy of the Sovereign Rulership of God, for which you do indeed undergo suffering, ⁶ since *it is* a righteous thing with God to pay back tribulation to those oppressing you,* ⁷ and, to those of you being oppressed, relief with us,* at* the revealing* of the Lord Jesus from Heaven with his mighty angels,* ⁸ awarding vengeance* by flaming fire on those being ignorant of God, and those not being obedient to the gospel of our Lord Jesus,* ⁹ who will suffer the penalty: Eonian* destruction* from *the* face of the Lord, and from the magnificence of his power, ¹⁰ in the time he comes to be magnified* among his holy people, and to be wondered at* in that day** among all those believing, because our testimony to you was believed.
¹¹ And towards this we pray constantly for you* that our God might make you worthy of the calling, and He might fulfil every resolve* of goodness and work of faith with power, ¹² so that the name of our Lord Jesus might be magnified* in you, and you in him, in harmony with the merciful goodwill of our God and of *the* Lord Jesus Christ.*

The angelic being called the Man of Violation
released out of the abyss
which now holds him secure
(also at Rev. 11\7, 17\8, with 9\1-2).
Lying signs & wonders

2\1 Now we ask you, brothers, concerning the magisterial presence* of our Lord Jesus Christ, and by our gathering together to him,* [2] not to be quickly shaken* from mind, nor to be disturbed, neither through a spirit,* nor through a word, nor through a letter as if from us, as if the day of the Christ* has come in sight. [3] Nobody should deceive you in any way, because *that gathering will not come* unless the revolt* comes first, and the Man of Violation will have been made known, the Son of Destruction,* [4] the one opposing and exalting himself above everything which is called God or any object of veneration, so as to sit as if God in the Temple of God,* displaying* himself that he is God. [5] Do you not remember that, while still being among you, I told you these things? [6] And now you know the thing holding *him* secure, for him to be made known in his own time [7] – for the mystery of lawlessness already works actively* – that thing alone holding *him* secure* at present until he should appear out of *the* middle *of the Earth,* [8] and then the Lawless One* will be made known, whom the Lord will consume with the breath of his mouth and he will bring to nothing by the favourable intervention* of his magisterial presence,* [9] whose presence* is after the working of Satan with every power, and signs and false wonders,** [10] and in every unjust deceit of those on the road to perishing, because they did not receive the love of the truth for them to be saved. [11] And because of this, God will send them a working of delusion,* for them to believe the lie,* [12] in order that all those who have not believed the truth, but were satisfied in unrighteousness,* might be condemned.*

Chosen for salvation
& belief of the truth.
Eonian comfort in the hope of the gospel

[13] But we are compelled at all times to give thanks* to God concerning you, brothers, loved by *the* Lord, because God from *the* beginning* chose you for salvation by sanctification of *the* spirit and belief of *the* truth, [14] to which He called you by our gospel,* for obtainment of *the*

magnificence of our Lord Jesus Christ. [15] So then, brothers, stand fast, and hold fixed the traditions which you were taught, whether by word, or by our letter. [16] But may our Lord Jesus Christ himself and* our God and* Father, Who loved us and gave Eonian* comfort* and good hope through merciful goodwill, [17] encourage your hearts, and establish you in every good word and work.

Withdraw from the disorderly.
Apostles as examples

3\1 Finally, brothers, pray for us that the oracle of the Lord might have free course and be magnified, just as it is for you as well,* [2] and that we might be delivered from perverse and wicked men,* for not all have the faith. [3] But the Lord is faithful, Who will establish and guard you from the Evil One.* [4] And we have confidence in *the* Lord concerning you that you are both doing and will do the things which we charge you with. [5] And may the Lord direct your hearts into the love of God, and into endurance of the Christ. [6] Now we charge you, brothers, in *the* name of our Lord Jesus Christ, to draw yourselves back from every brother walking in a disorderly way and not in line with the way handed on* which they received* from us. [7] For you yourselves know how you ought to imitate us, for we have not behaved ourselves in a disorderly way among you, [8] nor did we eat bread from anybody without payment, but we worked night and day in labour and toil, with a view to our not being burdensome to any of you. [9] Not that we do not have authority, but *it is* so that we might give ourselves as a model for you to imitate us. [10] For even when we were among you, we charged you this: that if anybody is not willing to work, do not let him eat.* [11] For we hear of some among you walking in a disorderly way, not working at all, but bustling about uselessly.* [12] Now those like that we charge and encourage by our Lord Jesus Christ, that working with quietness they might eat their own bread. [13] But you, brothers, do not lose heart in doing good. [14] But if anybody does not obey our oracle through this letter, mark that man, and do not associate with him, so that he might be put to shame. [15] Yet reckon *him* not as an enemy, but admonish *him* as a brother.

[16] Now may the Lord of peace* Himself give

you peace through everything in every way. The Lord *be* with you all.

[17] The greeting of Paul with my hand, which is a sign* which I write in every letter.

[18] The merciful goodwill of our Lord Jesus Christ *be* with you all. Amen.

~ ◆◆ ~

† **The Letters of Paul** †

1 Timothy

1 \ 1

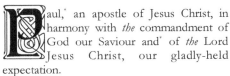

aul,* an apostle of Jesus Christ, in harmony with *the* commandment of God our Saviour and* of *the* Lord Jesus Christ, our gladly-held expectation.

[2] To Timothy, a true son in *the* faith, goodwill, mercy,* *and* peace, from God our Father, and Christ Jesus* our Lord.*

Confront false teaching.
Commandment of love,
& what springs out of it

[3] Just as I made appeal to you on my going into Macedonia, *I appeal to you now* to remain in Ephesus* in order that you might charge some not to teach different doctrines,* [4] nor to give attention to fables and interminable* genealogies which serve up questions, rather than nurture* in relation to God* in faith.

[5] Now the end of the commandment is love out of a pure heart, and a good conscience, and unfeigned faith, [6] from which some, missing the mark, turned aside to vain jangling, [7] wanting to be* teachers of the law, understanding neither what they say, nor concerning what they assert.

[8] But we know that the law *is* good if anybody uses it lawfully, [9] knowing this: that the law was not appointed for a righteous *person*, but for *the* lawless and unruly, for *the* ungodly and violating, for *the* unholy and profane, for murderers of fathers and murderers of mothers, for manslayers, [10] for fornicators, for homosexuals,* for kidnappers, for liars, for perjurers,* and if anything else is opposed to sound teaching* [11] in harmony with the gospel of the magnificence of the Exalted God, with which I was entrusted.

Paul, chief of violators, the example
[12] And I have gratitude for the one empowering me, Christ Jesus our Lord, that he counted me faithful, appointing into service [13] one who was previously a blasphemer, and a persecutor, and an insulter. But I was shown mercy because, being ignorant, I did it in unbelief. [14] And the

merciful goodwill of our Lord overflowed with faith and love in Christ Jesus.
¹⁵ *The* oracle *is* faithful and worthy of all acceptance, that Christ Jesus came into the world to save violators, of whom I am chief.
¹⁶ But I was shown mercy on account of this: that in me first Jesus Christ might demonstrate all long-suffering, for an example to those who will believe˙ in him for˙ Eonian˙ life.
¹⁷ Now to the King of the Eons,˙˙ incorruptible,˙ invisible, *the* only wise God,˙ honour and magnificence throughout˙ the durations of the Eons.˙ Amen.
¹⁸ I commit this charge to you, *my* son Timothy, in keeping with the prophecies made previously over you, so that by them you might fight the good fight, ¹⁹ holding on to faith and a good conscience, of which some, having driven *it* away in respect of the faith, have suffered shipwreck, ²⁰ among whom are Hymenaeus and Alexander whom I handed over to Satan,˙ in order that they might be disciplined not to blaspheme.

Prayer for all men,˙ for rulers.
The 'man Christ Jesus', the only mediator
between God & men. 'God is one' (Deut. 6\4 etc.)

2\1 𝕴 encourage, therefore, first of all, *that* supplications, prayers, intercessions *and* giving of thanks be made for all men, ² for rulers, and all who are in a high position, in order that we might lead a quiet and peaceable existence in all holiness and gravity.˙˙ ³ For this *is* good and acceptable in the sight of God our Saviour, ⁴ Who wishes˙ all men˙ to be saved, and to come to knowledge of *the* truth.
⁵ For God *is* one,˙ and *there is* one mediator˙ between God and men, *the* man˙ Christ Jesus,˙ ⁶ the one having given himself as a redemption price for all,˙ the testimony *to be given* in its own time, ⁷ for which I was appointed a herald and an apostle – I speak *the* truth in Christ; I do not lie – a teacher of *the* nations in faith and truth.
⁸ I want the men, therefore, to pray in every place, lifting up holy hands, without indignation and disputing.

Women˙ (1 Cor. 14\34-35)
⁹ Likewise also, let the women adorn themselves in discreet clothing, with modesty˙ and soberness,˙ not with braided hair, nor gold, nor pearls, nor costly clothing, ¹⁰ but with good works, which is becoming to women professing

reverence of God.
¹¹ Let a woman learn in quietness, in all subjection. ¹² But I do not permit a woman to teach, nor to usurp authority over *her* husband,˙ but to be˙ in quietness. ¹³ For Adam was formed first, then Eve. ¹⁴ And Adam was not deceived, but the woman, having been deceived, came to be in transgression.˙
¹⁵ Nevertheless,˙ she will be preserved˙ throughout˙ childbearing˙˙ – if they˙ continue˙ in faith and love and sanctification˙ with soberness.˙

Overseers in apostle-authorized Ekklesias

3\1 𝕿his *is* a faithful oracle: if anybody is ambitious for the office of an overseer, he desires a good work.˙ ² For it does the overseer˙ well to be irreproachable, husband of one wife, sober, discreet, of good behaviour, given to hospitality, able to teach, ³ not given to wine, not violent, not greedy for base gain,˙ but patient, not contentious, not money-loving, ⁴ ruling his own house well, having *his* children in subjection with all gravity.˙ ⁵ But if a man does not know how to rule his own house, how will he take care of an Ekklesia group of God? ⁶ *And he must* not *be* newly planted,˙ in case, smoking up with pride,˙ he might fall into the condemnation of the Devil. ⁷ He must have, though, a good testimony also from˙ those outside, in case he might fall into reproach and a snare of the Devil.˙

Attendants in apostle-authorized Ekklesias
⁸ Likewise, the attendants *must be* grave, not double-tongued, not given to much wine, not greedy for base gain, ⁹ holding the mystery of the faith in a clean conscience. ¹⁰ And let these also be tested first, then let them serve, being *found* blameless. ¹¹ Wives, likewise, *must be* grave, not evil speakers, sober, faithful in all things. ¹² The attendants must be husbands of one wife, ruling *their* children and their own households well. ¹³ For those having served well acquire for themselves a good standing, and much boldness in *the* faith in Christ Jesus.

Conduct among believers
in apostle-authorized Ekklesias
¹⁴ I write these things to you – hoping to come to you shortly, ¹⁵ although I might delay – in order that you might know how you ought to conduct yourself among *the* household of God,

which is *the* Ekklesia of *the* living God.

The mystery of godliness (Col. 1\27)
and events concerning Jesus after his resurrection:
appearances when 'brought to light [ἐφανερώθη,
ephanerothee; Mark 16\12, 16\14, John 21\14,
1 John 1\2] in flesh' to his disciples;
'declared righteous' (Heb. 9\14); 'seen by angels'
(Mat. 28\2, John 20\12, Acts 1\10),
'proclaimed among nations' (Rom. 14\25,
Col. 1\27-28), 'believed' (Acts 2\41, Rom. 1\8),
'taken up' (Mark 16\19, Luke 24\51)
A pillar˙ and foundation of the truth˙ ¹⁶ and˙
tremendous˙ beyond question is the mystery of
godliness:˙

He˙ was brought to light˙ in˙ flesh;˙˙
he was declared righteous˙ in spirit;˙
he was seen by angels;
he was proclaimed among nations;
he was believed in *the* world;
he was taken up in magnificence.˙˙

The Angel of God's revelations to Paul:
the great rebellion to come
in latter times (1 Tim. 4\3-4),
deceiving spirits, teachings of demons, & asceticism

4\1 **N**ow the Spirit˙ speaks in persuasive
oracles that in latter times˙ some will apostatize
from˙ the faith,˙ adhering to deceiving˙ spirits
and teachings of demons,˙ ² in hypocrisy of
liars,˙ having been branded in their conscience
with a branding iron,˙ ³ forbidding to marry, *and*
saying to abstain from foods which God created
for taking with thanksgiving by believers and
those fully knowing the truth.˙

Antidotes to asceticism.
God the Saviour of all men
⁴ For every creature of God *is* good and
nothing *is* to be refused, having been received
with thanksgiving,˙ ⁵ for it is sanctified by *the*
oracle of God and prayer.
⁶ In proposing these things to the brothers,
you will be a good agent for Jesus Christ, being
nourished up in the oracles of *the* faith, and of
good teaching˙ which you have closely
followed.
⁷ Reject, though, the profane and old
womanish fables, but, rather, exercise yourself
towards holiness. ⁸ For bodily exercise is
profitable towards a little, but holiness is
profitable towards everything, having the

promise of the life now and the one coming. ⁹
This *is* a faithful saying and worthy of all
acceptance. ¹⁰ For towards this we both labour
and are reviled, because we set hope in the
living God Who is Saviour of all men,
especially˙ of believers.˙
¹¹ Command and teach these things.
¹² Nobody must despise your youth.˙ But
become an example for the believers, in word,
in conduct,˙ in love, in spirit, in faith, in purity.
¹³ Until I come, fix attention to reading, to
encouragement, to teaching.˙
¹⁴ Do not be neglectful of the gift in you
which was given to you through prophecy, with
the laying on of the hands of the leading men.
¹⁵ Attend carefully to these things. Be wholly
occupied in them, so that your advancement
might be plain among all. ¹⁶ Keep watch on
yourself, and *on* the teaching.˙ Be relentless in
them, for in doing this you will preserve both
yourself and those listening to you.

Instruction & discipline regarding
older men, older women, widows,
& younger women not marrying outside the faith

5\1 **Y**ou ought not to rebuke an older man,
but exhort *him* as a father, the younger men as
brothers, ² the older women as mothers,
younger women as sisters, with all purity.
³ Widows who truly *are* so, honour as widows.
⁴ But if any widow has children or descendants,˙
they must first learn to be dutiful *in* their own
home, and to render reward to forbears,˙˙ for
this is acceptable in the sight of God. ⁵ Now
she having been left alone as a true widow has
hope in God, and she continues in requests and
prayers night and day. ⁶ In contrast, she living a
voluptuous life has died *while* still living.
⁷ And these things prescribe, so that they
might be irreproachable.
⁸ But if anybody does not provide for his own,
and especially for those of the household,˙ he
has denied the faith and is worse than an
unbeliever.
⁹ A widow under sixty years old must not be
enrolled into the number, *but* have been the
wife of one man,˙ ¹⁰ being of a good reputation˙
in good works, if she has brought up children,
if she has been hospitable, if she has washed *the*
feet of the holy people,˙ if she has imparted
relief to the oppressed, if she has diligently
engaged in every good work.
¹¹ Younger widows, though, refuse, for when

they grow impulses of lust *and turn* against˙ the Christ they hanker to marry, [12] having condemnation,˙ because they have thrown off the initial faith. [13] And with all that, they learn *to be* lazy as well, wandering about from house to house, and not only idle, but tattlers as well, and busybodies, prattling improper things.

[14] I want, therefore, younger women to marry, to bear children, to run the home, to give on account of reproach no opportunity to the one opposing. [15] For some already have turned aside, after Satan.

[16] If any believing man or believing woman has widows, he should impart relief to them, and do not let the Ekklesia be burdened, so that it might impart relief to those really *being* widows.

Apostle-authorized leaders

[17] The leading men ruling should be counted worthy of double honour, especially those labouring in *the* oracle and teaching.˙ [18] For the Scroll says, 'You shall not muzzle an ox treading down grain,'˙ and, 'The labourer *is* worthy of his wages.'˙

[19] Do not receive an accusation against a leader, unless˙ before two or three witnesses. [20] Those violating rebuke˙ in the presence of all, so that the rest might also have fear.

[21] I solemnly charge *you* before God, and *the* Lord Jesus Christ, and the elect angels,˙ that you should guard these things without prejudice, doing nothing by partiality.

Laying on of hands.
Wine for Timothy's weaknesses of health

[22] Lay hands hastily on nobody.
Nor take part in the violations of others.
Keep yourself pure.

[23] No longer drink *only* water, but use a little wine on account of your stomach and your frequent failings of health.˙˙

Comparing violators to believers

[24] The violations of some men are shown openly, going on ahead into judgement, but *the* violations of some *men* trail behind *them* as well.

[25] And similarly, the good works are known to all, and those being˙ otherwise cannot be hidden.

Servants

6\1 Let as many servants who are under the

yoke esteem their own masters worthy of all honour, so that the name of God and the teaching might not be spoken against.

[2] And let those who have believing masters not despise *them*, because they are brothers. But, rather, let *them* serve *them*, because those receiving in return the good service are believers and richly loved.

Teach and encourage these things.

Nature of pseudo teachers

[3] If anybody teaches another doctrine,˙ and does not consent to wholesome words, those of our Lord Jesus Christ, and to doctrine˙ in relation to godliness [4] – *but is* smoked up with pride, understanding nothing, but diseased about questions and arguments over words, out of which arise˙ envy, strife, evil speakings, evil surmisings, [5] useless wranglings˙ of men of corrupted mind and defrauded of the truth, supposing reverence to be˙ a source of gain – from such withdraw yourself.

Love of riches as a root of all evil

[6] But reverence with contentment is an immense acquisition.˙ [7] For we have brought along nothing into the world, *and it is* plain that neither are we able to carry anything out. [8] And, having nourishment and covering, with these let us be content.

[9] But those wanting to be rich fall into a temptation˙ and a snare, and many foolish and harmful lusts, which cause men to sink into destruction and perdition.˙ [10] For the love of money is a root˙ of all the evils˙ by which some, in their coveting, were seduced away from the faith, and they pierced themselves through with many sorrows.

[11] But you, oh˙ man of God,˙ flee these things, and follow after righteousness, godliness, faith, love, endurance, meekness.

'Eonian life' & the coming
'favourable intervention' of Jesus,
which is his ἐπιφάνεια *(epiphaneia)*

[12] Fight the good fight of the faith.
Seize hold of Eonian˙ life, to which you were called, having also proclaimed the good declaration in the sight of many witnesses.

[13] I charge you in the sight of God – the one˙ giving life to˙ all things˙ – and˙ of Christ Jesus, the one˙ having witnessed before˙ Pontius Pilate the good declaration, [14] to keep *this*˙ commandment without spot, beyond rebuke,

until the favourable intervention˙ of our Lord Jesus Christ, [15] which *God* is going to bring to light in His own times,˙ the Exalted and only Potentate,˙ the King of those reigning, and Lord of those ruling,˙ [16] the one alone having deathlessness,˙ inhabiting unapproachable light, whom nobody among men has seen, nor is able to see,˙ *and* to whom *be* honour and Eonian˙ might. Amen.

[17] Charge those rich in the present Eon˙ not to be haughty, nor to set their hope on an uncertainty of riches, but in the living God, the one richly providing us with all things for enjoyment,˙ [18] to do good, to be rich in good works, to be˙ liberal in distributing, ready to share, [19] treasuring up in store for themselves a good foundation for the coming *Eon*,˙˙ so that they might seize hold of Eonian˙ life.

Guarding against falsehood

[20] Oh˙ Timothy, guard the entrusted deposit, having turned from profane *and* empty babblings,˙ and opposing theories of falsely-named science,˙ [21] which some, professing, have missed the mark concerning the faith.

Merciful goodwill *be* with you. Amen.

~ ◆◆ ~

† The Letters of Paul †

2 Timothy

1\1

Paul, an apostle of Jesus Christ through *the* will of God, in relation to the promise of life in Christ Jesus. [2] To Timothy, richly loved son, goodwill, mercy, *and* peace, from God *the* Father, and *from* Christ Jesus our Lord.˙

Desire to visit Timothy

[3] I have gratitude to God – Whom I serve in a clean conscience, following on from *my* forefathers – when I unceasingly have remembrance of you in my prayers night and day,˙ [4] longing to see you, being reminded of your tears, so that I might be filled with exuberance [5] in recalling the unfeigned faith in you, which first inhabited your grandmother Lois and your mother Eunice, and I am persuaded that *is* in you as well.

The flame of God's gift & a sound mind.
A promise previously 'kept hidden'
(Rom. 14\24-25, 1 Cor. 2\7),
but now 'given' and 'brought to light'
'in advance of Eonian times'
which are the coming Eons (Titus 1\2)

[6] On account of this, I remind you to kindle up into flame the gift of God which is in you through the laying on of my hands. [7] For God did not give us a spirit of cowardice, but of power, and of love, and of a sound mind.˙

[8] So you should not be ashamed of the testimony of our Lord, nor of me, his prisoner. You are, though, going to have to suffer afflictions along with the gospel of *the* power of God, [9] the one having saved us, and having called *us* in a holy calling, not in keeping with our works, but in keeping with His own purpose and merciful goodwill given to us in Christ Jesus in advance of Eonian˙ times,˙ [10] and now brought to light˙ by the favourable intervention˙ of our Saviour Jesus Christ, in his having nullified death, and having brought to light life˙ and incorruption˙ through the gospel,˙ [11] of which I have been appointed a herald, and an apostle, and a teacher of nations, [12] for which cause I also suffer these things.

Nevertheless, I am not ashamed, for I know whom I have believed, and I am persuaded that he is able to keep guard of my entrusted deposit until that day.˙
[13] Hold *the* pattern of sound words which you have heard from me, in faith and love in Christ Jesus. [14] Safeguard the good deposit entrusted through *the* divine spirit˙ inhabiting˙ us.

All in Asia turned from Paul

[15] You know this, that all those in Asia turned away from me,˙ among whom are Phygellus and Hermogenes.

Onesiphorus in Ephesus

[16] May the Lord show mercy to the household of Onesiphorus, because often he refreshed me, and he was not ashamed of my handcuff,˙ [17] but when he came to Rome he searched me out most diligently and found *me*.
[18] May the Lord grant *it* to him to find mercy from *the* Lord in that day,˙ and how much he served˙ in Ephesus you know well.

Commit the truth to other faithful men

2\1 You, therefore, my son, be strengthened in the merciful goodwill which *is* in Christ Jesus. [2] And the things which you have heard from me by means of˙ many witnesses, set these down before faithful men who also will be competent to teach others.˙

Enduring evil. Examples
of soldier, athlete & farmer

[3] You, therefore, endure evil, as a good soldier of Jesus Christ. [4] Nobody serving as a soldier tangles himself up with the affairs of life, in order that he can please him who enrolled him as a soldier.
[5] And if anybody competes as an athlete˙ also, he is not crowned if he does not compete˙ lawfully.˙
[6] The hard-working farmer must be first partaker of the crops.
[7] Reflect on the things I am saying, and may the Lord give you understanding in all these things.

Example of Christ,
in death & resurrection,
if we endure, we will reign

[8] Remember that Jesus Christ, out of a seed of David, was raised from *the* dead, in harmony with my gospel,˙ [9] on account of which I suffer affliction as if a criminal, even to the extent of captivity. The oracle of God, though, has not been fastened down with shackles. [10] On account of this, I endure all things for the sake of the elect,˙ in order that they also might obtain salvation in Christ Jesus, together with Eonian˙ magnificence.
[11] *This is* a trustworthy saying:

For if we died together with *him*,
we will live together with *him* as well;˙
[12] if we endure,˙
we will reign together with˙ *him* as well;
if we deny *him*,
he will deny us.˙

[13] If we are unbelieving, he stays fixed as faithful. He cannot deny himself.

Overthrow of faith.
Rightly dividing the oracle of truth.
Effect of false teaching
about the coming resurrection

[14] Put *them* in remembrance of these things, earnestly giving testimony before the Lord not to wrangle about words in nothing profitable, to the overthrow˙ of those listening.
[15] Be diligent to present yourself as approved to God, a workman not ashamed,˙ rightly dividing˙ the oracle of truth.˙
[16] But stand aloof from profane *and* empty babblings,˙ for they will advance to even more irreverence, [17] and their word will consume like gangrene, of whom are Hymenaeus and Philetus, [18] for concerning the truth they missed the mark, asserting the resurrection to have already taken place,˙ and they overturn˙ the faith of some.˙
[19] Nevertheless, God's firm foundation stands sure, having this seal: 'The Lord knows those who are His;'˙ and: 'Everybody who calls on the name of *the* Lord must depart from unrighteousness.'˙

Honour & dishonour.
Youthful lusts. Be competent to teach

[20] But in a large house˙ there are not only vases of gold and of silver, but wooden also, and of clay, and some for honour, and others for dishonour.
[21] If, therefore, one thoroughly purges himself from these, he will be a vase for honour, sanctified, and profitable for the master's use,

prepared for every good work.
²² But flee youthful lusts. Instead, follow righteousness, faith, love, peace, along with those calling on the Lord out of a clean heart.
²³   But reject foolish and uninstructed questions, knowing that they generate* contentions.
²⁴ And a servant of the Lord must not be aggressively contentious, but be* gentle towards all, competent to teach, patient, ²⁵ in mildness correcting those antagonizing, if perhaps God should grant them submission into full knowledge of truth, ²⁶ and they might sober up again, out of the snare of the Devil,* having been captured by him to do his will.*

Bad character, including magic, in the last days (Gen. 49\1 etc.) of the 490 year Eon

3\1 **B**ut realize this: that in *the* last days* dangerous* times* will come. ² For men will be intent on their own interests, lovers of money, boasters, proud, blasphemers, disobedient to parents, unthankful, virulently malignant,* ³ without natural affection, implacable,* evil speakers,* unrestrained, savage, despisers of good, ⁴ traitors, headstrong, smoked up with pride, lovers of pleasures more than lovers of God, ⁵ having an outward form of godliness,* but denying the power of it. And from these turn away.
⁶   For among them are those worming their way into homes and leading captive gullible women, heaped up with violations, led adrift by various lusts,* ⁷ always* learning, and never being able to come into full knowledge* of *the* truth. ⁸ Now in the way Jannes and Jambres opposed Moses, so do these also oppose the truth, men corrupted in mind, worthless concerning the faith. ⁹ They will not advance further,* though. For their lack of understanding* will be plain to all, as theirs also became.*

Sufferings & persecutions for the gospel
¹⁰   You, however, closely followed my teaching,* manner of life, purpose, faith, long-suffering, love, endurance,* ¹¹ persecutions *and* afflictions which happened* to me in Antioch, in Iconium, in Lystra, what persecutions I endured, and the Lord delivered me out of* all these things.*
¹² Yes, and indeed all wanting to live ruled by reverence in Christ Jesus will be persecuted.*

In the thick of evil deceivers persevere in the Scrolls.
Completeness through the Scrolls (Col. 2\10)
¹³   But evil men and cheats will progress from bad to worse, deceiving, and being deceived.
¹⁴ You, though, continue in the things you learned and were assured of, knowing from whom you learned *them,* ¹⁵ and that from a child you have known the holy Scrolls,** which *are* able to make you wise for* salvation through belief in Christ Jesus.
¹⁶ Every passage* *is* given by inspiration of God, and *is* profitable* for teaching, for conviction, for correction, for discipline in righteousness,* ¹⁷ in order that the man* of God* can be complete, equipped* for every good work.

In the assessments at 'the favourable intervention' of Jesus which is his ἐπιφάνεια *(epiphaneia) at the founding of the new Eon's order, the names of the believing are written in the Scroll of Life (Rev. 13\8, 17\8). Charge to proclaim the oracle. Bad character in the last days restated (1 Tim. 4\1). Against natural religion*

4\1 **I** solemnly charge, consequently – in the sight of God and* of *the* Lord Jesus Christ, the one* about* to fully assess* *the* living and *the* dead** at* his favourable intervention,* that is,* his Sovereign Rulership* ² – proclaim the oracle.* Keep at it,* in season, out of season. Make the facts known,* rebuke,* encourage* with all long-suffering, and with teaching.*
³ For there will be a season when they are not going to bear hearing* the sound teaching,* but after their own lusts they will heap up for themselves teachers itching in regard to hearing, ⁴ and they will turn the hearing away from the truth, and they will be turned aside to fables.
⁵   You, though, in all things be sober.
Endure evil.
Do *the* work of a proclaimer of the gospel.*
Fully accomplish your duty.

Paul, about to be taken up for 'the prize of the high calling' (Phil. 3\14) of Enoch & Elijah, anticipates his reward of 'the crown of righteousness' (Jacob 1\12, Rev. 2\10) for himself & those who love the coming favourable intervention of Jesus which is his ἐπιφάνεια *(epiphaneia)*
⁶   For already I am being poured out,* and the

time of my departure* has arrived. ⁷ I have fought the good fight. I have finished the course. I have kept the faith. ⁸ Finally, the crown of righteousness* is reserved for me, which the Lord, the Righteous Judge, will recompense me in that day,* and not to me only, but also to all those loving his favourable intervention.*

Paul left with only Luke.
Various opponents & helpers

⁹ Exert yourself to come to me speedily. ¹⁰ For Demas deserted me, loving this present Eon,* and he departed into Thessalonica, Crescens into Galatia, Titus into Dalmatia. ¹¹ Only Luke is with me.*

Take Mark on the way,* *and* bring him with you, for he is profitable to me for *the* work. ¹² And Tychicus I sent to Ephesus.

¹³ *When* you come* bring along the cloak which I left in Troas with Carpus, and the Scrolls,* especially the parchments.

¹⁴ Alexander the coppersmith did many evil things against me. May the Lord render to him in return for his works, ¹⁵ whom you also must guard against, as he heavily opposed* our words.

¹⁶ In my first defence nobody stood with me, but they all deserted me. May it not be held against them. ¹⁷ The Lord, though, stood with me and made me strong, so that through me the proclamation might be accomplished, and all the nations might hear.

Again, Paul's immediate anticipation (4\6-8,
Phil. 1\18-25) of 'the high calling' (Phil. 3\14)
And I was delivered out of *the* mouth of *the* lion.

¹⁸ And the Lord will deliver me from every evil work,* and He will bring me safe into* His heavenly* realm,* to Whom *be* magnificence throughout* the durations of the Eons.* Amen.

¹⁹ Give greetings to Prisca and Aquila, and the household of Onesiphorus.

²⁰ Erastus remained in Corinth, but Trophimus I have left sick in Miletum.*

²¹ Be diligent to come before winter. Eubulus greets you, and Pudens, and Linus, and Claudia,* and all the brothers.

²² The Lord Jesus Christ *be* with your spirit. Merciful goodwill *be* with you. Amen.

~ ◆◆ ~

† The Letters of Paul †

Titus

*A promise made now 'in advance
of Eonian times' (2 Tim. 1\9, Rom. 14\24-25)
God brought to light His oracle
(John 1\1) of Eonian life. Paul chosen*

1\1

aul, a servant of God, and an apostle of Jesus Christ, for *the* faith of the elect of God, and the full knowledge of truth in relation to holiness, ² in gladly-held expectation of Eonian* life, which the never-lying God promised in advance of Eonian* times,** ³ but in His own times brought to light* His oracle in a proclamation which I was entrusted with in relation to *the* command of God our Saviour.* ⁴ To Titus, a true son with a common faith, goodwill, mercy, *and* peace, from God *the* Father, and *from the* Lord Jesus Christ our Saviour.**

*Apostle-authorized appointments
through Titus of Ekklesia rulers*
⁵ For this reason, I left you in Crete, so that you might arrange the things left undone, and city by city you might appoint leading men,* as I instructed you, ⁶ if anyone is blameless, a husband of one wife, having believing children not in any accusation of wild living or unwilling to be corrected.
⁷ For it does the overseer well to be* unimpeachable as a house manager of God, not self-willed, not easily angered, not given to wine, not violent, not greedy of base gain, ⁸ but hospitable, a lover of good, right-minded, just, pure,* temperate, ⁹ holding fast to the faithful oracle in agreement with the teaching, so that in sound teaching* he may be able both to exhort and to convict* the* contradictors.*

Pseudo teachers
¹⁰ For there are many unruly and empty talkers and mind-deluders,* especially those of *the* circumcision,* ¹¹ whose mouths you ought to bring to silence,* who overthrow* entire households,* teaching things *they* should not, for the sake of shameful profit.
¹² One of them, a prophet of their own, said,

'Cretans *are* always liars, evil wild beasts, lazy* bellies.'* ¹³ This testimony is true. On account of this, rebuke* them sharply, in order that they might become sound in the faith, ¹⁴ not giving an ear to Jewish myths and commandments of men, making perversions away from* the truth. ¹⁵ To the pure all things *are* pure. But to those defiled and unbelieving nothing *is* pure, but even their understanding and conscience are defiled. ¹⁶ They profess to know God, but by the works they make denial, being abominable, and disobedient, and disqualified in relation to every good work.

*Titus to be a model in works & teaching.
Women. Younger men. Servants*
2\1 ou, though, speak the things which are fitting for sound teaching:* ² the aged men to be* sober, grave, discreet, sound in the faith, in love, in endurance; ³ aged women, similarly, *to be* in deportment what becomes holy women, not false accusers, not enslaved to much wine, teachers of what is right, ⁴ so that they might school the young women to be* lovers of *their* husbands,* lovers of *their* children, ⁵ discreet, chaste, keepers at home, good, subject to their own husbands, so that the oracle of God might not be blasphemed.
⁶ The younger men, in the same way, encourage to be sober-minded, ⁷ concerning all things showing yourself a model of good works, in integrity in teaching,* gravity,* incorruptibility, ⁸ *and in* sound speech without condemnation, so that whoever *is* antagonistic* might be put to shame, having nothing bad to say about us.
⁹ *Encourage* servants to be obedient to their own masters, and to be* well pleasing in everything, not contradicting,* ¹⁰ not pilfering, but showing all good faith,* in order that they might adorn the teaching of God our Saviour* in everything.

*Anticipating the coming 'favourable intervention'
of Jesus which is his ἐπιφάνεια (epiphaneia)*
¹¹ For the salvation-bringing* merciful goodwill of God has been made to intervene favourably* for all men,* ¹² instructing us that, having abnegated* ungodliness and worldly* cravings,* we should live discreetly, righteously, and ruled by reverence in the present Eon,* ¹³ anticipating* the exalted* gladly-held expectation, and* the favourable intervention*

of the magnificence* of the Mighty God, and* of our Saviour* Jesus Christ,* [14] who gave himself on our behalf* in order that he might redeem us from all lawlessness, and purify for himself as an acquisition* a people zealous for good works.

[15] Speak these things, and encourage and rebuke* with all authority. Let nobody condemn you.

Subjection to the spiritual leaders
appointed by God (Rom. 13\1, Heb. 13\17).
As witness of Christ.
Expectation of being heirs of Eonian life

3\1 But them in mind to be subject to rulers and authorities, to be obedient, to be* ready for every good work, [2] to speak evil of nobody, to be* not quarrelsome, gentle, showing mildness of disposition to all men. [3] For we ourselves also were at one time foolish, disobedient, led adrift, serving various lusts* and pleasures, living in malice and envy, hateful, hating each other.*

[4] But when the kindness and love of God our Saviour towards man was made to intervene favourably* [5] − not out of works of righteousness which we practised but in relation to His mercy − He saved us, through *the* regenerative washing utensil* and renewing of *the* divine spirit,* [6] which He poured on us richly through Jesus Christ our Saviour, [7] in order that, having been pronounced righteous through His merciful goodwill, we might become heirs in relation to a gladly-held expectation of Eonian* life.

Good works. Admonish
the divisive. Helpers

[8] The oracle *is* faithful, and I want you to stress constantly about these things, so that those who have believed God might take thought to keep up good works. These things are good and profitable for men. [9] But stand aloof from foolish questions, and genealogies, and contentions, and quarrels about law, for they are unprofitable and vain.

[10] After a first and second admonition, reject a divisive man, [11] knowing that such a person is subverted, and he commits violation, being self-condemned.

[12] When I send Artemas or Tychicus to you, be diligent to come to me at Nicopolis, for I have determined to winter there. [13] Be diligent

to set forward Zenas the lawyer and Apollos on their way, so that nothing might be lacking for them. [14] And let our own *people* also learn to give priority to good works for pressing needs, so that they might not be unfruitful.

[15] All those with me send you greetings. Give greetings to those who love us in faith.

Merciful goodwill *be* with all of you. Amen.

† The Letters of Paul †

Philemon

1\1

Paul, a prisoner of Christ Jesus, and Timothy the brother.

To Philemon, our richly loved* and fellow worker, ² and to Apphia the richly loved,* and to Archippus our fellow soldier, and to the Ekklesia* in your house, ³ merciful goodwill to you, and peace, from God our Father, and *from the* Lord Jesus Christ.*

The faith & love of Philemon
⁴ I thank my God, always* making mention of you in my prayers,* ⁵ hearing of your love and the faith which you have towards the Lord Jesus, and towards all the holy people, ⁶ so that the communicating of your faith may become effective in full knowledge of every good thing among us for* Christ Jesus. ⁷ For we have much thankfulness and encouragement from your love, because the heart* of the holy people has been refreshed by you, brother.

Restore Onesimus
⁸ So, having much boldness in Christ to command you *in* what *is* fitting, ⁹ for the sake of love, I rather encourage *you*, I being such a man as I am, Paul, an aged man, and now also a prisoner of Jesus Christ.
¹⁰ I encourage you on behalf of my son Onesimus to* whom I was a father in my shackles, ¹¹ in time past not useful to you, but now profitable to you and to me. ¹² I sent him back, but you should receive him who is as my own heart,* ¹³ whom I was minded to hold back with me, in order that he, instead of you, might provide for me in the shackles of the gospel.*
¹⁴ But without your consent I was willing to do nothing, so that your benefit might not be as if out of compulsion, but out of willingness. ¹⁵ For he was, perhaps, because of this, separated from you for a time, in order that you might receive him back permanently,* ¹⁶ no longer as a servant, but above a servant, a richly loved* brother, especially to me, but so much the more to you, both in flesh and in *the* Lord. ¹⁷ If you, therefore, count me a partaker, receive him as if myself. ¹⁸ But if he has wronged or owes you

anything, put that on my account. ¹⁹ I, Paul, have written with my hand:* I will repay, so that I might not say to you how you also owe me even your own self. ²⁰ Yes, brother, let me have profit from you in *the* Lord. Refresh my heart* in *the* Lord.

Paul's intended visit
²¹ Being persuaded of your obedience, I wrote to you knowing that you will do even above what I might say. ²² But, meanwhile, prepare a lodging for me as well, for I hope that through your prayers I will be restored to you.
²³ Epaphras, my fellow prisoner in Christ Jesus, ²⁴ Marcus, Aristarchus, Demas, Lucas, my fellow labourers, greet you.
²⁵ The merciful goodwill of our Lord Jesus Christ *be* with your spirit. Amen.

~ ◆◆ ~

† The Letters of Paul* †

Hebrews

God speaking through prophets
& now through the Son of God.
God designed the coming Eons (1\2, 9\26,
11\3, Acts 17\26, 1 Cor. 10\11).
The Son appointed heir
& being the exact expression of God.
A new order under the Son
who became superior to angels

1\1

In many stages,* and in many ways,* in time past,** God, having spoken* to the fathers by means of the prophets, [2] at* *the* end* of these* days* spoke* to us by means of *His* Son* whom He appointed* heir of all things,* through* whom also He designed* the Eons,* ³ who, being *the* radiance* of *His* magnificence, and *the* exact expression* of His essence,* and bringing in* all things by* his powerful oracle,* having provided* through* himself purification** of our violations, sat down at* *the* right hand* of the Majesty on* high, ⁴ by having become so much more superior than the angels, in that he has inherited a more excellent name than theirs.**

⁵ For to whom of the angels did He at any time* say:

'You are My son;
this day I have generated* you,'*

and additionally:*

'I will be a Father to him
and he will be a son to Me'?*

⁶ But when He again brings the first-honoured* into* the inhabited world, He says:

'And let all *the* angels of God worship Him.'*

⁷ And to the angels He says:

'He makes His angels spirits,
and His envoys a fiery flame.'*

The Father cites the Psalm to the Son,
including its interlude addressed to God (Ps. 45\6)
⁸ But to the Son He cites this:

'Your seat of government, oh* God,*
is throughout the duration of the Eon;**
the sceptre of your Sovereign Rulership*
is a sceptre of righteousness.*
⁹ You loved righteousness
and hated lawlessness;
because of this, God, your God,
has anointed you with the oil of extreme joy,
alongside your companions.'**

¹⁰ And:

'You Yourself, Lord, at *the* beginning,*
founded* the Earth,
and the heavens are the works
of Your hands.
¹¹ They will vanish away, but You remain,
and they will all wax old like a garment,
¹² and You will roll them up like a covering
and they will be changed;*
You, though, are the same,
and Your years will not fail.'**

¹³ But to which of the angels did He at any time* say:

'Sit at* My right hand*
until I place your enemies
as a stool for your feet'?*

¹⁴ Are they not all attending spirits, being authorized for helping those being about to* inherit salvation?

A wonderful salvation

2\1

On account of this, it is more abundantly fitting for us to pay attention to the things heard, *so that* we should not ever* drift away.** ² For if the oracle spoken through angels became inviolable,** and every transgression and disobedience received a judicious recompense,* ³ how shall we escape if we neglect such a wonderful salvation, which, having received a commencement to be spoken by the Lord, was confirmed to us by those having heard, ⁴ God also adding testimony by* signs and* wonders, and by* many acts of power, and by* distributions of *the* divine spirit,* in accordance with His will?

Man made lower than angels.
Job 7\17-18 & Psalm 8\4-6
citations applied to Jesus

[5] For not to angels has He put under subjection the coming inhabited world* of which we speak. [6] Somebody, though, in a certain place gave testimony, saying:

'What is mortal man
that You are mindful of him,
or a son of a man
that You watch over him?
[7] You made him for a little while*
lower than angels;*
with preeminence and honour
You crowned him.*
[8] You have put everything
in subjection under his feet.'*

For in putting everything in subjection to him, He left nothing not put in subjection to him. Not yet, though, do we see everything put in subjection to him.

His fitness for dominion
by suffering & death.
Jesus like his brothers –
& not ashamed to call them brothers
(2\11, 2\17, Mat. 12\49-50,
28\10, Rom. 8\29). His fitness to help others

[9] We do see, though, him who was made a little lower than angels, Jesus, through* suffering death, crowned with preeminence and honour, so that by *the* merciful goodwill of God he might taste death on behalf of everybody. [10] For it was fitting for Him – because of Whom *are* all things, and through* Whom *are* all things – in bringing many sons into preeminence, to bring to perfection, through sufferings, the author of their salvation. [11] For both he who sanctifies and those sanctified *are* all out of *the* one, and for this reason he is not ashamed to call them brothers, [12] saying:

'I will declare Your name to my brothers;
in *the* presence of *the* Ekklesia*
I will sing praise to You;'*

[13] and additionally:*

'I will be putting my trust in Him;'*

and additionally:*

'Here am I,
and the sons whom God gave me.'*

[14] Since, then, as the sons* are sharers of* flesh and blood, he himself also in a similar way partook of the same things, so that through death he might destroy him who has the power of death, that is,* the Devil, [15] and he might release those who in fear of death were all through their lifetime subjected to enslavement. [16] For certainly he does not take on *the likeness of* angels, but he takes on* *the* seed of Abraham. [17] Therefore in all things he had to be made like *his* brothers, in order that he might become a merciful and faithful high priest *of* things in relation to God, to make reconciliation for the violations of the people. [18] For, tested in what he has suffered, he is able to run to the cry of those being tempted.

God's act of creating Jesus (Mat. 1\18,
Luke 1\30), 'created' being ποιέω *(poyeo),*
as at Mat. 19\4, Mark 10\6, Acts 4\24,
14\15, 17\24, Rom. 1\20, Heb. 12\27,
Rev. 14\7 etc., equivalent of the Hebrew
ברא *(bara), 'created', at Genesis 1\1.*
Jesus of more eminence than Moses.
Hardness of heart & unbelief

3\1 Consequently, holy brothers, partakers of a most exalted* position,* consider the apostle and high priest of our declaration, Jesus Christ,* [2] faithful to Him Who created* him, as Moses also *was* in all his house. [3] For he has been counted worthy of more eminence than Moses, since the one having constructed it has more honour than the house. [4] For every house is built by somebody, but He Who built all things *is* God. [5] And Moses *was* indeed faithful in all his house as a servant, for a testimony of those things going to be spoken* afterwards. [6] Christ, though, *is faithful* as a son over his house, whose house we are,* if we hold fixed the firm* confidence and the rejoicing of the hope until *the* end.* [7] Therefore, just as* the Holy Spirit* says:

'Today, if you hear His voice,
[8] do not harden your hearts
as in the rebellion,
as on the day of tempting* in the wilderness,
[9] when your fathers provoked Me,
putting Me to the test,
and they saw My works *for* forty years.

¹⁰ So I was angry with that generation,
and I said, "They always go astray in heart,
and they have not known My ways."
¹¹ So I swore in My indignation,
"They shall certainly not* enter
into My rest." *

¹² Watch, brothers, in case there is among anyone of yourselves an evil heart of unbelief so as to fall away from *the* living God. ¹³ But encourage one another daily, as long as it is called today, so that none of you might be hardened* through the deceitfulness of violation.

Partakers of Jesus
¹⁴ For we have become partakers* of the Christ if we hold fixed the source of our confidence,* certain* until *the* end,* ¹⁵ with this to be said:

'Today, if you hear His voice,
do not harden your hearts
as in the rebellion.'*

¹⁶ For some, having heard, rebelled, although not all those having come out of Egypt by Moses. ¹⁷ But with whom was He indignant *for* forty years, if not with those who violated, whose corpses fell in the desert? ¹⁸ And to whom did He swear they should not enter into His rest if not to those who disobeyed? ¹⁹ And we see that they were not able to enter in on account of unbelief.

Rest for God's people
4\1 We should, therefore, be fearful, in case perhaps, being left a promise to enter into His rest, any of you might seem to have fallen short. ² For we are indeed those who have had the gospel proclaimed, as they also *did*. The oracle which was heard, though, did not profit them, not being mixed with faith in those having heard.
³ For we *who* have believed are entering into that rest, as He has said:

'As I have sworn in my indignation,
"They shall certainly not* enter
into My rest," '*

– even though the works were completed since* *the* foundation* of *the* world.* ⁴ For in a certain

place He has spoken this concerning the seventh *day*: 'And God rested on the seventh day from all His works.'*
⁵ And in this *passage* additionally:*

'They shall certainly not* enter into My rest.'*

⁶ Seeing that it therefore remains for some to enter into it, and those who first heard the gospel did not enter in because of disobedience, ⁷ He again designates* a certain day as today, speaking through David, after so long a time. As it has been said:

'Today, if you hear His voice,
do not harden your hearts.'*

⁸ For if Joshua* had caused them to rest, He* would not after these things have spoken about another day. ⁹ Consequently, a rest day* remains for the people of God. ¹⁰ For he who has entered into His rest has also rested from his works, as God *has* from His own. ¹¹ We should, therefore, be diligent to enter into that rest, in case anybody might fall into the same example of unbelief.

The spiritual powers of God-authorized oracles. Jesus 'without violation' (also at 9\28)
¹² For the oracle of God *is* living, and powerful, and sharper than any two-edged sword, piercing even to division of natural being* and spirit, of both joints and marrow, and a discerner of thoughts and intentions of *the* heart.
¹³ And there is not a created thing not in His sight, but all things *are* uncovered and laid open to the eyes of Him to* Whom *there will be* an account* for us* *to give*. ¹⁴ Having, then, an eminent high priest having passed through the heavens, Jesus, the Son of God, we should hold fixed the declaration. ¹⁵ For we do not have a high priest not being able to sympathize with our weaknesses, but *one* having been tempted* in all things in the same way as ourselves – *yet was* without* violation.*

Encouragement to approach God with boldness, in time of need
¹⁶ We should, in that case, with confidence draw near to the throne of merciful goodwill, so that we might receive mercy, and find merciful goodwill for help in time of need.

The high priest. Jesus made high priest.
Rescued out of death before the time
(5\7, Luke 4\13, 22\44)

5\1 For every high priest chosen˙ from among men is appointed for men *in* things *in* relation to God, so that he can offer both gifts and sacrifices for violations, ² being able to exercise moderation towards those being ignorant and being led astray, since he himself also is subject to weakness. ³ And on account of this, he ought – just as concerning the people, so also for himself – to make offering for violations. ⁴ And nobody takes the honour to himself, unless called by God, as Aaron indeed *was*.
⁵ So Christ also did not magnify himself to be made˙ high priest, but *it was by* the one having said to him:

'You are My Son;
today I have generated˙ you.'"

⁶ As He says in another *place* as well,

'You *are* a priest throughout the Eon,˙
after the order of Melchizedek'"

⁷ He who,˙ in the days of his flesh, offered up prayers and˙ requests with strong crying˙ and tears to Him being able to rescue him out of death, was also heard˙ because of his reverence.
⁸ Although being a son, he learned obedience from the things which he suffered, ⁹ and, having come to perfection, he became *the* source of Eonian˙ salvation for all those who obey him, ¹⁰ having been designated by God as high priest after the order of Melchizedek, ¹¹ concerning whom˙ *we have* much discourse,˙ difficult to interpret, since you have become dull in hearing.

The 'rudiments of … the oracles of God'.
Moving from milk to strong food by 'constant use'

¹² For, in fact, being due to be˙ teachers by this time,˙ you have need of somebody to teach you again the rudiments of the beginning˙ of the oracles of God, and you have become in need of having milk and not solid food. ¹³ For everybody who partakes of milk *is* inexperienced in *the* oracle of righteousness, for he is an infant. ¹⁴ Solid food, though, is for *the* mature, who through constant use have had their faculties trained for discerning both good

and evil.

The 'beginning of the Christ'.
The deep peril of apostasy.
Hope coming out of the heavens

6\1 Having, therefore, left the discussion of the beginning˙ of the Christ,˙ we should be borne along to full growth, not laying down˙ again a foundation˙ of unburdening ourselves from dead works, and of faith in God, ² the teaching of washings,˙ and laying on of hands, and resurrection of *the* dead, and of Eonian˙ judgement.˙ ³ And this we would do,˙ if God at all permits.
⁴ For *it is* impossible for those who have once been enlightened, and have tasted˙ the most exalted˙ gift, and become partakers˙ of *the* Holy Spirit,˙˙ ⁵ and tasted *the* good oracle of God, and works of power of *the* coming Eon˙ ⁶ and *who* fall away,˙ to renew *them* again˙ into submission,˙ hanging on a stake all over again˙ for themselves the Son of God, and putting *him* to open shame.˙
⁷ For the ground which drinks in rain often falling on it, and produces plants fit for those by whom it is farmed as well, has a share in favour˙ from God.˙
⁸ That which produces thorns and briers, however, *is* rejected and near to a curse, whose end *is* for burning.˙
⁹ But concerning you, richly loved, we have been persuaded of better things˙ connected with salvation, even though we speak in this way. ¹⁰ For God *is* not unrighteous to be forgetful of your work and the labour of love which you exhibited towards His name, having provided for the holy people, and you still are providing.
¹¹ But we are wanting each of you to show the same eagerness towards the full assurance of the hope until *the* end,˙ ¹² so that you should not become slothful, but imitators˙ of those who through faith and long-suffering are inheritors of the promises.˙ ¹³ For God, having made the promise to Abraham, since He had nobody more eminent to swear by, swore by Himself, ¹⁴ saying, 'I will surely richly favour˙ you, and I will richly multiply˙ you.' ¹⁵ And so, having had much patience, he obtained the promise.
¹⁶ For men swear truly by someone more eminent, and such oath for confirmation *is* to them an end of all contradiction.
¹⁷ In this way, God, wishing more abundantly

to show to the heirs of the promise the unchangeableness of His counsel, intervened with an oath, [18] so that, by two unchangeable things, in which *it is* impossible *for* God to lie, we who have fled for refuge to lay hold of the gladly-held expectation set before *us* can have strong* encouragement, [19] which we have as an anchor of life, firm and* secure,* and making entrance into the inner area of the veil,* [20] where a forerunner has entered for us, Jesus, having become high priest throughout the Eon,* in line with the order of Melchizedek.

A priesthood after the order
of the angel Melchizedek,
an order superior to that of the Levites

7\1 For this Melchizedek – King of Salem, priest of the Most High God, meeting Abraham returning from the defeat of the kings, also invoking favour on* him, [2] to whom in fact Abraham divided a tenth part of all, first, being by translation, King of Righteousness, and after that also King of Salem, which is King of Peace, [3] without father, without mother, without genealogy, having neither beginning of days nor an end of life,* but having been made like the Son of God* – remains a priest throughout the course.**

[4] Now consider how distinguished *was* this* *angel,* to whom even the patriarch Abraham gave a tenth out of the best produce. [5] And indeed, those from among the sons of Levi, receiving the office of the priesthood, have a commandment to take tithes from the people in agreement with the law, that is, their brothers, even though they came out of the loins of Abraham. [6] But he who reckons no descent out of them received tithes from Abraham, and invoked favour on** the one holding the promises. [7] And without all contradiction, the inferior has favour invoked* by the superior.

[8] And in such a circumstance mortal men receive tithes. In this case, though, it is witnessed that he is living. [9] And, so to speak, Levi also, who received tithes, has been tithed through Abraham. [10] For he was still in the loins of *his* father when Melchizedek met him.*

[11] If indeed, then, perfection were through the Levitical priesthood – for, on the basis of* it, the people had been placed under law – what further need *was there for* another priest to have arisen after the order of Melchizedek, and not be called after the order of Aaron?

[12] For on the priesthood being changed, out of compulsion a change of the law also arises.* [13] For he about whom these things are spoken belongs to a different tribe, from whom nobody has attended at the altar. [14] For *it is* openly evident that our Lord has arisen out of Judah,* regarding which tribe Moses spoke nothing concerning priesthood, [15] and it is yet far more abundantly evident if, after the likeness of Melchizedek, another priest appears, [16] who has arisen* not in line with a law of a flesh-natured commandment, but in line with *the* power of a life unable to be destroyed.* [17] For He gives testimony:

'You *are* a priest throughout the Eon,*
after the order of Melchizedek.'*

[18] For there indeed comes to be* a disannulling of the preceding commandment, because of its *being* destitute of power and its unprofitableness. [19] For the law perfected nothing, but *the* bringing in of a better hope *has done*, through which we draw near to God. [20] And since *it was* not without swearing of an oath – for, indeed, those became priests without swearing of an oath – [21] but by swearing of an oath by Him Who said to him:

'*The* Lord has sworn
and He will not make revocation:
"You *are* a priest throughout the Eon,*
after the order of Melchizedek," '*

[22] *then* Jesus has become guarantee by a much better covenant. [23] And indeed, there were many priests, on account of their being prevented by death to continue.

His fitness as high priest & Saviour
[24] But since he is to continue throughout the Eon,* he has the non-transferable priestly office. [25] He is, then, also able to save to the uttermost those who approach God through him, he perpetually* living in order to make intercession for them.* [26] For such a high priest was fitting for us, holy, harmless, undefiled, separate from violators, and having become* higher than the exalted men,* [27] who does not have day-by-day compulsion, like the high priests, to offer up sacrifices, first for his own violations, then for the people's, for he did this once, when he offered up himself.
[28] For the law appoints as high priests men

having infirmity, but the word of the swearing of the oath after the law *appoints* throughout˙ the Eon˙ a Son having been perfected.

Efficacy of Jesus' priesthood.
A more excellent service

8\1 Now in summary over the things being spoken: we have such a high priest who sat down at˙ *the* right hand˙ of the governmental seat of the Majesty in the heavens,˙ 2 a servant of the Most Holy Place,˙ and of the true Tent which the Lord pitched, and not man.
3 For every high priest is appointed to offer gifts and sacrifices, from which it is needful for this high priest˙ also to have something which he can offer. 4 For indeed, if he were on Earth, he would not even be a priest, there already being the priests who offer the gifts in accordance with law, 5 who serve a representation and shadow of heavenly things,˙ as Moses was divinely instructed *when* being about to construct the Tabernacle, for, he said, 'Make everything in agreement with the pattern shown to you on the mountain.'˙
6 But now that *Jesus* has obtained a more excellent service, much more so is he also mediator of a better covenant, which has been enacted on the basis of better promises. 7 For if that first had been faultless, no place would have been searched for a second.
8 For, finding fault, *God* said to them:˙

'Mark well that days are coming,
says the Lord,
when I will ratify a new covenant
over the house of Israel
and over the house of Judah,
9 not in accordance with the covenant
which I made with their fathers
in *the* day of my taking hold of their hand
to lead them out of *the* land of Egypt,
since they did not continue in My covenant,
and I disdained˙ them, says *the* Lord.
10 For this *is* the covenant which I will make
with the house of Israel
after those days, says *the* Lord,
giving My laws into their mind,
and I will inscribe them on their hearts,
and I will be God to them
and they will be a people for Me.
11 And no longer should everyone teach
their fellow citizen,
nor everybody˙ their brother,

saying, "Know the Lord,"
because they will all know Me,
from their least to their eminent.
12 For I will be merciful
towards their unrighteousness
and towards their violations,
and I will no more remember
their lawless acts.'˙

13 In saying 'new', He has made the first obsolete, but the thing being made obsolete and waxing old *is* near to vanishing.˙

The earthly Sanctuary
a copy of the heavenly pattern

9\1 Then even the first *Tabernacle*˙ did indeed have judicial requirements of divine service˙ and the Holy Place, an earthly˙ one.˙ 2 For *the* first Tabernacle was constructed, in which *were* both the lampstand˙ and the table, and the setting out of the loaves, which is called *the* Most Holy Place.˙
3 And after the second veil *came* a Tabernacle called *the* Most Holy Place,˙ 4 having the golden censer, and the Ark of the Covenant overlaid in every part with gold, in which *there was* a golden pot holding the manna, and the rod of Aaron which budded, and the tablets of the covenant, 5 and above˙ it the keruvim˙ of glory overshadowing the Mercy Seat, concerning whom˙ it is not now *the time* to speak in detail.˙

The blood of Jesus, not of animals,
nor flesh-natured observances

6 Now with these things having been prepared in this way, the priests at all times enter into the first Tabernacle, carrying out the services. 7 But the high priest *goes* into the second *tabernacle* alone once in the year, not without blood which he offers for himself and the violations of ignorance˙ of the people 8 – the Holy Spirit˙ signifying this – the way *into* the Most Holy Place˙ not yet to have been brought to light˙ *while* the first Tabernacle was still having a standing, 9 which *was* a figure pointing to the present time, in which gifts and˙ sacrifices were offered, not being able to make the worshipper˙ perfect in regard to conscience, 10 *consisting* only of foods and drinks, and various washing rituals, and flesh-natured requirements, imposed until *the* time of reform.

Jesus offered without spot
by the Eonian Spirit (1 Tim. 3\16)

[11] Christ, though, having become high priest of the good things coming, by the superior and more perfect Tabernacle made not by hand, that is, not of this creation, [12] nor by blood of goats and calves, but by his own blood, entered once and for all into the Most Holy Place, having obtained Eonian redemption.

[13] For if the blood of bulls and of goats and ashes of a heifer sprinkling whatever *is* unclean make sanctification towards the purifying of the flesh, [14] how much more will the blood of the Christ, who through *the* Eonian Spirit offered himself without spot to God, purge your conscience from dead works into the serving of *the* living God?

A better covenant

[15] And on account of this, he is the mediator of a new covenant, so that, on a death having taken place as a redemption price for transgressions under the first covenant, those having been called might receive the promised Eonian inheritance.

[16] For where *there is* a testament, it has to be announced *at the* death of the testator. [17] For a testament *is* confirmed on the basis of the deceased, since it is of no force while the testator is alive, [18] on which grounds not even the first was inaugurated without blood. [19] For on every commandment according to the law spoken by Moses to all the people, he took blood of calves and goats, with water, and scarlet wool, and hyssop, *and* he sprinkled both the Scroll itself and all the people, [20] saying, 'This *is* the blood of the covenant which God commanded to you.'

[21] In addition, he likewise sprinkled with blood both the Tabernacle and all the equipment of the service. [22] And, in agreement with the law, almost everything has to be purified by blood, and without shedding of blood there is to be no forgiveness. [23] *It was* necessary, then, for the representations of the things in the heavens to be cleansed by these, but the heavenly things themselves by better sacrifices than these.

[24] For Christ did not enter into the Most Holy Place made by hands, antitypes of the true things, but into Heaven itself, now to appear on our behalf in the presence of God. [25] Nor *was it* so that he should offer himself repeatedly, in the way the high priest enters into the Most Holy Place year by year by the blood of another, [26] since it would have been necessary for him to have suffered repeatedly since the foundation of *the* world, but now, once, towards the completion of the Eons, he has been revealed for *the* putting away of violation through the sacrifice of himself.

[27] And just as it is destined for men to die once, and after this *the* judgement, [28] so also Christ, having been offered once to bear *the* violations of many, will be brought to light a second time without violation, to those assiduously waiting it out for him for salvation.

The law a shadow of good things coming.
Yearly sacrifices ineffectual.
Jesus, having sat down,
made his sacrifice effectual once & for all

10\1 For the law, having a shadow of the good things coming, *but* not itself *being* the real representation of the things, is never able with the same sacrifices which they offer throughout the course *of the priesthood* year by year to perfect those approaching. [2] Otherwise, would they not then have ceased being offered, since the worshippers would no longer have any conscience of violations? [3] But in those *sacrifices* a year by year reminder *is made* of violations. [4] For *it is* not possible for the blood of bulls and goats to take away violations. [5] For that reason, coming into the world, he says:

'You did not want sacrifice and offering,
but You prepared a body *for* me.
[6] You took no pleasure
in whole burned offerings
and *sacrifices* for violations.
[7] Then I said, "See, I come
to do Your will, oh God;
in *the* volume of *the* Scroll
it has been written about me;" '

[8] saying above *that*:

'You did not want sacrifice
and offering and whole burned offerings
and *sacrifices* for violations,
nor did You take pleasure *in them*'

– of such a nature that they are offered in accordance with the law. [9] He then said:

'See, I come to do Your will, oh God.'

He sets aside the first in order that he might establish the second. [10] By this will we are sanctified once for all through the offering of the body of Jesus Christ.
[11]   And every priest stands daily, serving and offering continually the same sacrifices which are never able to take away violations.* [12] But he, having offered one sacrifice for violations, sat down in perpetuity* at* *the* right hand* of God, [13] from then on waiting until his enemies are made a stool for his feet. [14] For by one offering he has perfected in perpetuity* those being sanctified.
[15]   The Holy Spirit* also bears witness to us, for, after having previously said, [16] 'This *is* the covenant which I will covenant to them after those days, says *the* Lord, giving My laws on their hearts and I will inscribe them on their minds, [17] and I will not at all* remember their violations and lawlessness,'* [18] now, where *there is* forgiveness of these, *there is* no longer an offering for violation.

Draw near to God
[19]   Having in that case, brothers, boldness for entry into the Most Holy Place* through the blood of Jesus [20] – a way newly made and living, which he has dedicated for us through the curtain, that is to say, his flesh, [21] and an eminent* priest over the House of God – [22] we should approach with a true heart in a most certain confidence of faith, the hearts having been sprinkled from a wicked conscience, and the body having been washed in pure water.
[23]   Let us hold fast the profession of the gladly-held expectation** without wavering, for He Who promised *is* faithful.
[24]   And we should keep in mind stirring each other up to love and good works, [25] not forsaking the assembling together of ourselves,** as is a custom with some, but being encouraging, and so much the more as you see the day* drawing near.
[26]   For if we violate wilfully after receiving the knowledge of the truth, there no longer remains a sacrifice for violations, [27] but a certain fearful expectation of judgement and a fire of zeal about to devour the adversaries.*

Death without mercy under law
[28]   Anybody who disregards the law of Moses, on the basis of two or three witnesses, dies without mercy. [29] Of how much worse punishment, do you suppose, will he be considered deserving who has trampled underfoot the Son of God, and esteems as profane the blood of the covenant in which he was sanctified, and has insulted the spirit* of merciful goodwill?
[30]   For we know Him Who said:

" 'Vengeance *belongs* to Me;
I will recompense," says *the* Lord,'

and additionally:*

'*The* Lord will judge His people."*

[31]   *It is* a fearful thing to fall into the hands of *the* living God!

Confidence & perseverance
even under extreme persecution
[32]   Always keep in mind, though,* the former days in which, having been illuminated, you stood your ground in much struggling of sufferings,* [33] at times being made a gazing-stock* by insults and* persecutions, and at other times having become partners of those living that way.
[34]   For you indeed sympathized with my shackles, and you took with exuberance the plundering of your possessions,* understanding to have for* yourselves a better and an enduring possession* in *the* heavens.*
[35]   Do not, in that case, throw off your confidence which has rich recompense. [36] For you have need of patience, so that, having done the will of God, you might receive the promise:

[37]   'For in just a little while yet
the Coming One* will be present
and he will not delay.
[38]   Now the righteous man will live by faith,
but if he draws back
I Myself will have no pleasure in him."*

[39]   But we are not those who withdraw, leading into destruction,* but of faith leading to* preservation of life.*

The Eons (αἰών, aion)
framed by God (11\3, 1\2,
Acts 17\26, 1 Cor. 10\11)
& the world (κόσμος, kosmos)
condemned by Noah (11\7).
Impressive men & women of faith seeing ahead,
such as Enoch taken

in 'the prize of the high calling' (Phil. 3\14)

11\1 Now faith* is *the* substance* of things being hoped for, conviction of things not being seen. ² For in* this the eldermen* were of good reputation.*

³ By faith we understand the Eons* to have been framed* by an oracle of God,* for* the things being seen not to have come about* out of things being visible.**

⁴ By faith Abel offered to God a more excellent sacrifice than Cain,* by which he was attested to be* righteous, God Himself giving testimony to his gifts. And through it, having died, he still speaks.

⁵ By faith Enoch was taken away so that he did not see death, and he was not found because God had taken him away, for before his being taken he was commended as having pleased God.

⁶ But without faith *it is* impossible to please *Him*, for he who comes to God must believe that He exists, and He is a rewarder to those who diligently search Him out.

⁷ By faith Noah, having been divinely instructed concerning things not yet seen, was moved with reverence, *and* he prepared an ark for preservation of his household, by which he condemned the world and he became* an heir of righteousness through faith.

⁸ By faith Abraham, being called to go out into the place which he was about to receive for an inheritance, obeyed, and he went out not understanding where he was going. ⁹ By faith he was a tenant in a land of the promise as if a stranger,* living in tents with Isaac and Jacob, the joint heirs* of the same promise, ¹⁰ for he was waiting for the city having foundations whose builder and constructor *is* God.*

¹¹ By faith Sarah herself also* received strength for* laying down* of a sperm, and she gave birth beyond seasonable age, because she esteemed as faithful Him Who had made a promise. ¹² And so from one man were generated* – and these out of one destroyed of strength* – as many as the stars of the sky* in multitude, and as innumerable as sand by the shore of the sea.*

*They looked for the Holy City
in the New Earth (12\22,
Eph. 2\19-22, Rev. 21 & 22)*

¹³ These all died in faith, not having received the promises, but having seen them from afar, and they embraced *them*, and professed that they were foreigners and sojourners on the Earth.*

¹⁴ For those who say such things declare plainly that they are searching for a fatherland. ¹⁵ And if, indeed, they had kept on remembering* where they came from, they might have had opportunity to return. ¹⁶ But as a matter of fact, they* press forward to a better *homeland*, that is,* a most exalted one,* so then God is not ashamed of them to be called their God, for He has prepared a city for them.*

¹⁷ By faith Abraham, being tested, offered up* Isaac, and he who had received the promises was offering up* *his* favoured* *son*, ¹⁸ to* whom it was said, 'Your seed will be reckoned in Isaac,'* ¹⁹ having supposed that God *was* able to raise *him* up, even from *the* dead, from where, in a figure, he did in fact* receive him back.*

²⁰ By faith Isaac invoked favour on* Jacob and Esau concerning things to come.

²¹ By faith Jacob, in dying, invoked favour on* each of the sons of Joseph, and he worshipped, *leaning* on the top of his staff.*

²² By faith Joseph, coming to his end, made mention of the exodus of the sons of Israel, and gave instructions concerning his bones.

²³ By faith Moses, after being born,* was hidden *for* three months by his parents, because they saw the little child was good looking, and they had no fear of the king's injunction.

²⁴ By faith Moses, having become eminent, refused to be called a son of Pharaoh's daughter, ²⁵ choosing* rather to suffer affliction with the people of God than to have the temporary indulgence of violation, ²⁶ esteeming the reproach of the Christ superior riches to the treasures of Egypt, for he always looked ahead towards the recompense.* ²⁷ By faith he forsook Egypt, not fearing the boiling anger of the king, for he persevered as if seeing the invisible *King*.

²⁸ By faith he kept the Passover and the sprinkling of blood, so that the destroyer of the first-honoured* might not touch them.

²⁹ By faith they passed through the Red Sea as if through dry land, which the Egyptians in attempting got swallowed.

³⁰ By faith the walls of Jericho fell down, having been surrounded for seven days.

³¹ By faith the prostitute Rahab did not perish with those who were disobedient, having received the spies with peace.

*Prophets who overcame kingdoms
& made the armies of foreigners fall.*

God foresaw something better involving us
& which is not complete without us (11\40)
who also are among
the exalted (Eph. 1\3, 2\6)

³² And what more could I say? For time would fail in narrating about Gideon, Barak and* Samson and Jephthah, and David and Samuel and the prophets,* ³³ who through faith overcame kingdoms, practised righteousness, obtained promises, stopped mouths of lions, ³⁴ snuffed out *the* power of fire, escaped edges of a sword, out of weakness acquired strength, grew mighty in war, made the armies of foreigners fall back. ³⁵ Women received back their dead out of resurrection, and others were tortured,* not having accepted deliverance* so that they might attain to a better resurrection.* ³⁶ And others received a trial of mockings and floggings,* yes, in addition, of shackles and jail. ³⁷ They were stoned; they were sawn up; they were put to the test; they died by murder of a sword; they wandered about in sheepskins, in goatskins, being destitute, oppressed, ill-treated ³⁸ – of whom the world was not worthy, wandering around in deserts, and in mountains, and in caves, and in holes in the ground. ³⁹ And all these, being well proven* through faith, did not receive the promise, ⁴⁰ God having foreseen something better involving us, so that they should not be complete without us.

Purity & enduring chastisement
by the Father of spirits
(Num. 16\22, 27\16),
in view of the vast cloud of witnesses

12\1 Consequently, we too, having so vast a cloud* of witnesses surrounding us, throwing aside* every weight, and the easily-surrounding violation, should by patient endurance run the race lying ahead of us, ² turning our sight to the originator and perfecter of the faith, Jesus, who, in view of the exuberance lying ahead of him, endured a stake,* having scorned shame, and he has sat down at* *the* right hand* of the governmental seat of God. ³ For consider him who endured against himself such a contradiction by violators, so that you are not wearied, fainting in your minds.* ⁴ You have not yet resisted to the point of blood, wrestling against violation. ⁵ And you have forgotten the encouragement by which He speaks to you as to sons:*

'My son, do not despise
the discipline of *the* Lord,
nor faint at being rebuked* by Him,
⁶ for he whom He loves *the* Lord disciplines,
and He scourges every son
whom He receives.'*

⁷ Be patient in being disciplined when God is dealing with you as with sons.* For who is *the* son whom a father does not discipline? ⁸ But if you were without chastening, of which all have become sharers, then you are illegitimate children and not sons.* ⁹ Furthermore, we indeed had fathers of our flesh *as* correctors, and we respected *them.* Shall we not much rather be in subjection to the Father of spirits* and live? ¹⁰ For they indeed, for a few days, chastened *us* in line with what to them seemed *beneficial,* but He *chastens us for* the profit of sharing in His holiness. ¹¹ Now no chastening at the time seems to be *a thing* of joy, but of grief. Afterwards, though, it renders a peaceable fruit of righteousness for those having been exercised by it.

Counsels & encouragements

¹² Straighten up, therefore, the hanging-down hands and the paralyzed knees,* ¹³ and make straight tracks for your feet, so that *what is* lame might not be turned aside, but, rather, might be healed.

¹⁴ Pursue peace with everybody, and sanctification, without which nobody will see the Lord, ¹⁵ watching diligently in case anybody should fall short from the merciful goodwill of God, in case any root of bitterness germinating up should cause trouble, and many should be defiled by this, ¹⁶ in case *there might be* any fornicator, or profane person, like Esau, who for the sake of one piece of food sold his birthright. ¹⁷ For you know how later on, also wanting to inherit the invocation of favour,* he was rejected, for he found no place of comfort, despite having searched for it earnestly with tears.

Promise of the New Jerusalem
coming out of Heaven
(12\22-23, Gal. 4\26, Rev. 21\1)

¹⁸ For you have not drawn near to a mountain being touched, and having been kindled with fire, and to a thick cloud, and to darkness, and a tempest, ¹⁹ and ringing in the ears* of a trumpet, and a sound of words which those

having heard begged for not a word to be addressed* to them, [20] for they could not bear what was commanded: 'If so much as an animal touches the mountain it shall be stoned.'**

[21] And so terrible was the spectacle *that* Moses said, 'I am trembling with fear.'*

[22] You have, though, drawn near to Mount Zion; and to *the* city of *the* living God, *the* heavenly* Jerusalem;* and to myriads* of angels;* [23] to *the* universal gathering and to *the* Ekklesia of *the* first-honoured,** enrolled in *the* heavens;* and to God, judge of all; and to *the* spirits of *the* righteous having been perfected;* [24] and to Jesus, mediator of the fresh covenant; and to *the* blood of sprinkling which speaks of better things than *that of* Abel.

Encouragement to not neglect* such a wonderful salvation

[25] Watch out you do not refuse the one speaking. For if these did not escape, having refused the one divinely instructing on the Earth, how much more ourselves in turning away from the one from *the* heavens, [26] Whose voice then shook the Earth? But now He has promised, saying, 'Yet once more I shake not only the Earth, but the heaven as well.'* [27] Now that 'Yet once more' signifies the removal of those things being shaken, as* things having been created, so that those* not being shaken might remain.

[28] In that case, receiving an unshakeable kingdom, we should have merciful goodwill, by which we serve God acceptably, with reverence* and godly fear. [29] For our God *is* indeed a consuming fire.*

Love & righteous living

13\1 Let brotherly love continue.

[2] Do not forget to entertain strangers, for by this some have unknowingly entertained angels.*

[3] Remember those in shackles as if shackled with *them, and* those being ill-treated as if you yourselves were in *their* body.*

[4] Marriage *should be* honourable in everything, and the bed undefiled. God, however, will judge fornicators and adulterers.

[5] *Let your* manner of life *be* without love of money, satisfied with present circumstances, for He Himself has said, 'I will most certainly not fail to uphold you,* nor will I by any means forsake you,'* [6] so that we might boldly say:

'*The* Lord *is* a helper for me and I will not fear what man might do to me.'*

[7] Remember your leaders who spoke the oracle of God to you, whose faith imitate, considering the outflowing of *their* conduct.

[8] Jesus Christ yesterday and today *is* the same, and throughout the Eons.** [9] Do not be carried away with various and foreign teachings.* For *it is* a good thing *for* the heart to be established by merciful goodwill, not with foods by which those occupied in *them* were not profited. [10] We have an altar from which those who serve the Tabernacle system do not have authority to eat. [11] For the bodies of those animals, whose blood is brought by the high priest into the Most Holy Place* concerning violation, are burned outside the camp. [12] Consequently Jesus also, so that he might sanctify the people by his own blood, suffered outside the gate. [13] Let us, then, go to him outside the camp, bearing his disgrace. [14] For we do not here have a permanent city, but we are searching for the one coming.

[15] Through him, then, let us offer up the sacrifice of praise to God through all things, that is,* the fruit of lips giving thanks to His name.

[16] But do not be forgetful of doing good, and of fellowship, for with such sacrifices God is well pleased.

Obedience to God-authorized authorities (Rom. 13\1-3, Titus 3\1)

[17] Obey your leaders* and be submissive – for they watch wakefully on behalf of your lives,* as if about to give account* – in order that they might do this with exuberance, and not groaning, for this *would be* unprofitable for you.

[18] Pray for us, for we are persuaded that we have a good conscience in all things, willing to conduct ourselves honestly. [19] And all the more do I urge *you* to do this so that I might be restored to you more quickly.

[20] Now may the God of peace, Who brought up from *the* dead our Lord Jesus, the awesome Shepherd of the sheep, under the terms of blood of *the* Eonian* covenant, [21] perfect* you in every good work to do His will, working in you what *is* pleasing in His sight, through Jesus Christ, to whom *be* magnificence throughout the durations of the Eons.* Amen.

[22] And I encourage you, brothers, bear with the word of encouragement, for, in fact, I have

written to you in few words.

²³ You should know' brother Timothy has been released, with whom, if he comes sooner, I am going to see you.

²⁴ Send greetings to all your leaders, and all the holy people. Those from Italy greet you.

²⁵ Merciful goodwill *be* with you all. Amen.

~ ◆◆ ~

† **The Letters of the Other Apostles** †

Jacob (James)*

1\1

acob, a servant of God, and* of *the* Lord Jesus Christ. To the twelve tribes among the dispersion, greetings.

Patience developed by trials, wisdom by prayer

² Count it all exuberance, my brothers, when you fall into various trials,* ³ knowing that the proving of your faith develops endurance. ⁴ But let endurance have *its* perfect work, so that you might be mature and complete, being left behind in nothing.

⁵ If, though, any of you should lack wisdom, let him ask from God Who gives generously to all, and not begrudgingly, and it will be given to him. ⁶ But let him ask in faith, not at all doubting. As the case stands,* he who doubts is like a wave of *the* sea being driven and tossed around by the wind. ⁷ For that man must not suppose that he will receive anything from the Lord. ⁸ *Such* a man *is* double-minded,* undependable in all his ways.

The low exalted, the rich made low

⁹ But the brother of low degree ought to rejoice in his high position, ¹⁰ the rich man, though, in his low position, because like *the* flower of grass* he will pass away.

¹¹ For the Sun rose with the scorching wind,
and it withered the grass,
and its flower fell,
and the beauty of its face perished.
So will the rich man
also fade away in his ways.

Endure against the temptations of lust
for the crown of life (2 Tim. 4\8, Rev. 2\10)

¹² Exalted *is the* man who endures a trial,* because, having been tempted, he will receive the crown of life which the Lord has promised to those who love Him.
¹³ Let nobody say, when he is being tempted, that 'I am being tempted* by God.' For God is not tempted by evils, and He Himself does not tempt* anybody. ¹⁴ Everybody, though, is tempted* *when* he is drawn away and allured by

his own lust. ¹⁵ Then lust, having conceived, gives birth to violation, and violation, being full-grown, engenders death. ¹⁶ Do not be deceived, my richly loved brothers.

Gifts from above.
God's oracle & its effects

¹⁷ Every act of giving and every perfect gift is from above, coming down from the Father of lights, with Whom there is no variableness nor shadow of turning.
¹⁸ Having willed *it*, He generated us through an oracle of truth, for us to be* a kind of* firstfruit of His created beings. ¹⁹ Therefore, my richly loved brothers, let every man be swift to hear, slow to speak, slow to anger, ²⁰ for the anger of man does not engender the righteousness of God.*
²¹ So, having pushed aside* all filthiness and residue of wickedness, receive in meekness* the implanted oracle, which *has* the power to save your lives.*
²² But become doers of *the* oracle, and not only hearers, beguiling yourselves. ²³ Because if anybody is a hearer of the oracle but not a doer, he is like a man looking at his natural face* in a mirror, ²⁴ for he looks at himself, and goes off on his way, and at once forgets what he is* like.
²⁵ But looking into the perfect law of freedom,* and continuing, such a person becomes* not a forgetful hearer, but a practiser of work. Such a person will be exalted in his action.
²⁶ If anybody among you thinks himself to be* observant, but does not bridle his tongue, he deceives his heart. The observance* of this *man* is worthless.
²⁷ Pure and undefiled observance* before God and *the* Father is this: to visit orphans* and widows in their affliction, *and* to keep oneself unspotted from the world.

Faith is without partiality

2\1 My brothers, you should not hold the faith of our Lord Jesus Christ of magnificence with partiality. ² For if a man goes into your synagogue with gold rings on his fingers *and* in splendid clothing, and a poor man in shabby clothing also goes in, ³ and you have shown special attention to him who wears impressive clothing, and you say to him, 'You sit here comfortably,' and you say to the poor man, 'You stand there, or sit here, beneath my footstool,' ⁴ were you not also* biased among* yourselves,

and having become judges of evil reasonings? [5] Listen, my richly loved brothers, did God not choose the poor of this world, rich in faith and heirs of the kingdom which He promised to those who love Him? [6] You, though, dishonoured the poor man. Do rich men not exercise harsh control over you and they themselves drag you to judgement seats? [7] Do they not speak injuriously of the noble name conferred on you?*

One offence breaks the royal law
of love. The law of freedom
[8] If you really fulfil the royal law in harmony with the text 'You shall love your neighbour as yourself,'* you do well. [9] But if you show partiality, you commit a violation, being convicted* by the law as lawbreakers. [10] For whoever keeps the whole law, yet stumbles in one *point*, has become guilty of *it* all. [11] For He Who said, 'Do not commit adultery,' also* said, 'Do not commit murder.'* Now if you do not commit adultery, yet you murder, you have become a transgressor of *the* law. [12] As you speak, so should you act, as if being about to be judged by *the* law of freedom.* [13] For judgement *will be* without mercy to him who has not exercised mercy. Mercy triumphs over judgement.

Faith dead without works.
'God is one' (Deut. 6\4, 1 Cor. 8\4-6 etc.)
[14] What *is* the profit, my brothers, if anybody should claim to have faith, yet he does not have works? Is faith able to save him? [15] And if a brother or a sister should go unclothed, and might be destitute of daily food, [16] and anybody among you should say to them, 'Depart in peace, warm yourselves, and satisfy yourselves with food,' but you do not give them those things needful for the body, what *is* the profit? [17] So faith also, if it does not have works, is dead by itself. [18] But somebody will say, 'You have faith, and I have works.' Show me your faith out of your works, and out of my works I will show you my faith.* [19] You acknowledge that God is one.* You do well. Even the demons acknowledge* *that*, yet shudder! [20] But are you willing to know, oh* empty man, that faith without works is dead?* [21] Was our father Abraham not pronounced righteous by works, having offered his son Isaac on the altar?* [22] Do you see how faith was working together with his works, and faith was made perfect by works? [23] And the text was fulfilled saying, 'Now Abraham believed God, and it was reckoned to him as righteousness,'* and he was called a friend of God.* [24] You see, then, how that by works a man is pronounced righteous, and not by faith alone.
[25] In the same way, though, was the prostitute Rahab not also pronounced righteous out of works, having given lodgings to the messengers, and having sent *them* out on a different route? [26] For just as the body without breath is dead, so also dead is faith without works.

Man's word & its effects.
The tongue a fire, like Jerusalem's
perpetually burning rubbish tip
in the Valley of Hinnom
(Joshua 15\8, Mat. 23\15 etc.)
3\1 My brothers, do not let many be teachers, knowing that we will receive a more severe judgement. [2] For we all stumble often. If anybody does not stumble in word, he *is* a perfect man, able to bridle the whole body as well. [3] See now, we put bits in the mouths of horses for them to obey us, and we turn their whole body around. [4] And look at* the ships, being so large, and driven by hard winds, *yet* turned about* by *the* smallest rudder, wherever the impulse of the helmsman directs.
[5] So also is the tongue a small part, and it boasts grandiloquent things. Behold how small a fire sets alight so huge a forest fire! [6] The tongue also *is* a fire, a world of iniquity. So is the tongue constituted among our members as the defiler *of* the whole body, and setting on fire the course of nature,* and being set on fire by the Valley of Hinnom.* [7] For every kind of wild animal, and* of birds, and of snakes, and of things in the sea, can be tamed, and has been tamed* by human nature, [8] but nobody is able to tame the tongue of men, an unrestrainable evil, full of death-dealing venom.* [9] With it we eulogize* *our* God* and Father, and with it we curse men who are made after *the* likeness of God.*
[10] Out of the same mouth pour eulogy* and cursing. My brothers, it is not good* *for* these things to arise.* [11] Does a fountain gush* sweet as well as bitter *water* out of the same source? [12] Can the fig tree, my brothers, possibly* produce olive berries, or a vine figs? In the same way, no

fountain* *is able* to produce salt and sweet water.

The wisdom 'from above'
(ἄνωθεν, *anothen*, John 3\3)

¹³ Who *is* wise and intelligent among you? Let him, out of *his* good conduct,* show his works in meekness of wisdom. ¹⁴ But if you have bitter jealousy and contention in your hearts, do not boast injuriously and lie against the truth. ¹⁵ Such wisdom is not coming down from above, but *is* earthly, natural, demonic. ¹⁶ For where jealousy and contention *are*, there commotion and every foul act *arise.*

¹⁷ But the wisdom from above is first pure, then peaceable, gentle, yielding, full of mercy and good fruits, without partiality, and unfeigned. ¹⁸ And *the* fruit of righteousness is sown in peace by those making peace.

Desires of the flesh

4\1 **W**here do battles and fightings *come* from among you? *Are they* not from this: out of* your pleasures which wage war in your body parts? ² You desire, but you do not obtain.* You kill and you are jealous, *yet* you are not able to obtain. You fight and you wage war, yet you do not obtain because of your not asking.* ³ You ask, and you do not receive, because you ask with a wrong motive, so that you might go squandering on your pleasures.

⁴ Adulterers and adulteresses! Do you not know that friendship with the world is hostility to God? Whoever, in that case, is minded to be* a friend of the world is an enemy of God. ⁵ Or do you think that the Scroll speaks in vain *that* the spirit which is naturally resident in us yearns towards* envy?*

The proud resisted: the humble exalted

⁶ But He gives more abundant merciful goodwill. So He says:

'God sets Himself against *the* arrogant,
but He gives merciful goodwill to *the* lowly.'*

⁷ Submit yourselves, therefore, to God, and resist the Devil,* and he will flee from you. ⁸ Draw near to God, and He will draw near to you.

Cleanse your hands, violators, and purify *your* hearts, *you* double-minded.*

⁹ Be afflicted, and mourn, and weep. Let your laughter be turned into mourning, and the exuberance into gloom.

¹⁰ Make yourselves abased in the sight of the Lord, and He will exalt you.

Life like a vapour

¹¹ Do not speak ill against each other, brothers. He who speaks ill against a brother and judges his brother speaks against *the* law and judges *the* law. But if you judge *the* law, you are not a doer of *the* law, but a judge. ¹² There is one lawgiver Who is able to save and to destroy. Who are you who judges another?

¹³ Come now, you who say, 'Today and tomorrow let us go into such-and-such a city, and spend a year there, and traffic business, and make a profit.' ¹⁴ You who do not know of tomorrow, what kind of life do you have, then? Well, it is a vapour which appears for a little time, and then it vanishes away. ¹⁵ Instead of saying, 'If the Lord should will, let us live, and we might do this or that,' ¹⁶ you, though, now rejoice in your arrogance. All such rejoicings are evil. ¹⁷ To someone, then, who knows *what* good to do but does not do *it*, to him it is a violation.

The rich man

5\1 **C**ome now, you rich men, weep, howling aloud over your coming miseries. ² Your riches have rotted, and your garments have become moth-eaten. ³ Your gold and silver have been eaten away with rust, and their rust will be a testimony against you, and it will eat your flesh like fire. You have heaped up treasure together in *the* last days.*

⁴ Look now, the pay of the labourers who harvested your fields, which has been fraudulently kept back by you, cries out, and the cries of those who reaped have entered into the ears of *the* Lord of Sabaoth. ⁵ You have lived in indulgence on the Earth, and you have lived in self-gratification. You have nourished your hearts, as if in a day of slaughter. ⁶ You have condemned; you have murdered the righteous man; he does not resist you.**

Patience for the magisterial presence of Jesus

⁷ Be patient then, brothers, for the magisterial presence* of the Lord. See how the farmer waits for the precious fruit of the ground, being patient for it, until it receives an early and a latter rain. ⁸ You also must be long-suffering. Strengthen your hearts, because the magisterial presence* of the Lord has drawn near.*

⁹ Do not groan against each other, brothers, so that you might not be judged. Look now, the Judge is standing at the doors.*
¹⁰ My brothers, take as an example of suffering evils and of long-suffering the prophets who spoke in the name of *the* Lord. ¹¹ Consider, we count as favoured* those who endure. You heard of the endurance of Job. Understand,* then,* the outcome of *the* Lord, that He is full of tender pity and compassion.
¹² But before* all things, my brothers, do not swear, neither by Heaven, nor by the Earth, nor by any other oath. Rather, let your yes be yes, and *your* no *be* no, so that you might not fall into hypocrisy.

Effectiveness of prayer
¹³ Does anybody suffer hardships among you? He should pray. Is anybody cheerful? He should sing psalms. ¹⁴ Is anybody among you sick? He should summon the leading men of the Ekklesia group, and they should pray over him, having anointed him with oil in* the name of the Lord, ¹⁵ and the prayer of faith will save the one being ill, and the Lord will raise him up, and if he has committed violations it* will be forgiven him.
¹⁶ Admit *your* offences, and pray for each other that you might be healed.* An energized* petition* of a righteous *man* is powerful* for many things.**
¹⁷ Elijah was a man of the same feelings as ourselves, and he prayed with requests for it not to rain, and it did not rain on the land *for* three years and six months. ¹⁸ And he prayed again, and the sky gave rain, and the soil caused its fruit to sprout.

Encouraging others
¹⁹ Brothers, if anybody among you should err away from the truth and somebody brings him back, ²⁰ let him know that he who brings back a violator from *the* error of his way will save a person* out of death,* and he will cover over a multitude of violations.

~ ◆◆ ~

1 Peter

1\1

eter, an apostle of Jesus Christ.
To elect sojourners* of the dispersion of Pontus, of Galatia, of Cappadocia, of Asia, and Bithynia,* ² in alignment with foreknowledge* of God *the* Father,* in making holy *the* spirit,* leading to *the* obedience and sprinkling of *the* blood of Jesus Christ, merciful goodwill to you, and peace be multiplied.

An incorruptible inheritance from God
³ Exalted* *be* the God and Father of our Lord Jesus Christ,** Who, in harmony with His abundant mercy, has regenerated us into a vigorous hope through *the* resurrection of Jesus Christ from *the* dead, ⁴ into an inheritance incorruptible* and undefiled and unfading,* reserved in *the* heavens* for you,* ⁵ who, by *the* power of God, are being garrisoned through faith into a salvation ready to be revealed in *the* latter time, ⁶ in which* you rejoice tremendously, although for a little while yet it is needful, in your having been thrown into sorrow by various trials,* ⁷ that the testing of your faith – far more precious than perishable gold – although being tested with fire, might be found as praise and honour and magnificence in* *the* revealing* of Jesus Christ, ⁸ whom, although not knowing, you love; in whom, although not seeing, you believe; but *whom* you exult with inexpressible and magnificent exuberance, ⁹ obtaining the end of your faith, salvation of *your* lives.**

Authority of the oracles
of apostles & prophets.
Prophecy came from the Angel of God
who is the Spirit of Christ
& the Holy Spirit (1\11, 1\12, 2 Peter 1\21)
¹⁰ The prophets who prophesied of the merciful goodwill *towards* you enquired about this salvation, and they searched diligently, ¹¹ searching into what time and* under what circumstances the Spirit of Christ* by means of them* was signifying, giving testimony beforehand of the sufferings of Christ, and of the glories after that. ¹² To them it was revealed**

by means of *the* Holy Spirit˙ sent from Heaven,˙˙ that, not to themselves, but to you they were supplying the same things which have now been announced to you through those having proclaimed the gospel to you, which things the angels long to stoop down to see.˙

Encouragement to sobriety
¹³ Therefore, having tightened up the loins of your mind, being sober, have perfect hope in the merciful goodwill being conveyed to you in˙ revelation˙ of Jesus Christ, ¹⁴ as sons of obedience,˙ not fashioning yourselves in keeping with the former lusts in your ignorance. ¹⁵ Just as, though, He Who called you *is* holy, you yourselves also ought to make yourselves holy in all behaviour,˙ ¹⁶ because it has been written: 'You be holy, for I am holy.'˙
¹⁷ And if you call on *the* Father – Who, without partiality of character, judges in keeping with the work of each one – you should conduct in fear the time of your strange sojourning,˙ ¹⁸ knowing that, not by corruptible things, by silver and gold, were you redeemed from your vain manner of life˙ handed down from fathers, ¹⁹ but by precious blood of Christ, as of a lamb˙ unblemished and without spot, ²⁰ having been known beforehand, in advance of˙ *the* foundation˙ of *the* world order,˙ but brought to light˙ in *these* last times for you ²¹ who through him believe in God, the one having raised him up from *the* dead and having given him magnificence, for your faith and hope to be˙ in God.
²² Having purified your inner selves˙ in obedience to the truth through *the* spirit towards non-hypocritical brotherly love, love one another fervently out of a pure heart, ²³ having been brought to birth again, not out of a corruptible seed, but of incorruptible,˙ through the living oracle of God which continues throughout˙ the Eon.˙

²⁴ 'For all flesh *is* like grass,˙
and all *the* glory of man
like a flower of the grass;˙
the grass withered and its flower fell away,
²⁵ but the oracle of *the* Lord
continues throughout˙ the Eon.'˙˙

And this is the oracle which was proclaimed to you.

Jesus 'the rock' of the 'spiritual house' (Mat. 16\18)
2\1 **S**o having pushed aside˙ all malice, and all guile, and hypocrisies, and envyings, and all evil speaking, ² long, like newborn babies, after the pure milk of the oracle, so that you might grow by it,˙ ³ if, indeed, you have tasted that the Lord *is* gracious, ⁴ to whom, drawing near – a living stone,˙ having been rejected by men, but being chosen in the sight of God *as* precious – ⁵ you also, as living˙ stones, are being built into a spiritual house,˙ a holy priesthood,˙ to offer up spiritual sacrifices, acceptable to God through˙ Jesus Christ. ⁶ It is, then, also contained in the Scroll:

'See now, I place in Zion
a stone,˙ a foundation cornerstone,˙
chosen, precious,
and the one believing in˙ him
will in no way be put to shame.'˙

⁷ To you, then, who believe, *it is*˙ of precious value. To those disobeying, though, *it says*:

'*The* stone˙ which the builders rejected,
this is made *the* head˙ of *the* corner,
⁸ and a stone˙ of stumbling
and a rock˙ of offence.'˙

Those being disobedient stumble at the oracle to which they also were appointed.
⁹ You, though, *are* a chosen race, a royal priesthood, a holy nation,˙ a people destined to be a special possession, in order that you might proclaim the virtues of Him Who has called you out of darkness into His wonderful light, ¹⁰ who at one time *were* not a people, but now a people of God,˙ who had not obtained mercy, but now have obtained mercy.

Abstaining from lusts
¹¹ *My* richly loved, I encourage *you* as strangers and foreigners: abstain from fleshly lusts which war against the inner self,˙ ¹² having your manner of life˙ among the other nations *as* honourable˙, so that, in whatever˙ they assert against you as evildoers, they might, out of˙ witnessing˙ *your* good˙ works, magnify˙ God in *the* day of visitation.˙

Secular human institutions (Mat. 22\21),
(compare Mat. 23\3, Acts 5\29, Rom. 13\1,
Titus 3\1, Heb. 13\17). Example of Jesus

[13] Be in subjection, therefore, to every human institution˙ on account of the Lord, whether to a king as supreme, [14] or to rulers as those sent by Him for vengeance on evildoers˙ and praise for those who act profitably.˙ [15] For this is the will of God:˙ acting correctly˙ to muzzle the ignorance of senseless men, [16] as freemen,˙ and not having freedom˙ as a cloak of malice, but as servants of God.

[17] Show honour to all *men.* Love the band of brothers. Revere God. Honour the king.˙

[18] House servants, be subject in all reverence to masters, not only to the good and gentle, but to the villainous˙ as well. [19] For this *is* a commendation:˙ if on account of conscience towards God anybody endures griefs, suffering unjustly. [20] For what good report *is it* if, violating and being knocked about, you take it patiently? But if in doing good and suffering you take it patiently, this *is* a commendation˙ with God. [21] For to this you were called, seeing that Christ also suffered on our behalf, leaving you a model so that you should diligently follow *the* steps of him

[22] 'who committed no violation,
    nor was guile found in his mouth;'˙

[23] who, being reviled, did not revile in return;˙ when suffering, did not threaten, but committed *himself* to Him Who judges righteously; [24] who himself took the burden of our violations˙ in his body on the tree,˙˙ so that, dying to violations, we might live to righteousness, he

'by whose fatal wound˙ you were healed,˙
[25] for you were like wandering sheep.'˙

Now though, you are turned around to the Shepherd and Overseer of your lives.˙

Sarah a pattern for wives.
Husbands to honour wives

3\1 **E**qually, you˙ wives, in your submitting yourselves to your own husbands, they will, where˙ even if any disobey the oracle, without a word be won over through the manner of life˙ of their wives, [2] having witnessed˙ your chaste behaviour˙ *conducted* in fear, [3] of whom it should not be the exterior˙ braiding of hair-styles, and putting on of gold things, nor the adornment˙ of clothing, [4] but, rather, the hidden person of the heart, in the incorruptibility of a gentle and quiet spirit which is of vast price in the sight of God. [5] For in the old time, the holy women also, those having hope in God, used to adorn themselves like this,˙ being in subjection to their own husbands, [6] just as Sarah obeyed Abraham, calling lord him whose daughters you have become, doing good, and not fearing any terror. [7] Equally, you˙ husbands, live with *them* with understanding, dispensing honour to the female partner as weaker, as being also heirs together˙ of *the* merciful goodwill of life, for your prayers not to be cut off.˙

Unity through compassion & love.
Suffering for righteousness

[8] Finally, *be* all of one mind, sympathizing, loving as brothers, tender hearted, friendly, [9] not rendering evil for evil, nor insult for insult, but, on the contrary,˙ invoking favour,˙ knowing that you were called to this in order that you might inherit an invocation of favour.˙

[10] 'For he who wants to love life
    and to see good days,
    let him cause his tongue to cease from evil
    and his lips not speak guile;
[11] let him turn aside from evil and do good;
    let him search for peace and follow after it,
[12] for the eyes of *the* Lord
    are on *the* righteous,
    and His ears *are inclined* to their prayers,˙
    but *the* face of *the* Lord
    is against those committing evil things.'˙

[13] And who is he doing you harm if you become imitators˙ of what *is* good? [14] But even if you do suffer on account of righteousness, *then you are* exalted. You should not, though, be afraid of their terror, nor be troubled. [15] But set apart the Lord God in your hearts.˙ And always *be* ready to make a defence to everybody who demands of you an account concerning the gladly-held expectation in you, with meekness and reverence, [16] having a good conscience, so that those who falsely accuse your good manner of life˙ in Christ might be ashamed in what they speak against you as evildoers.

Jesus raised by the 'Spirit' (the Angel of God).
The Angel proclaimed God's message
in the time of Noah to those people in captivity
of disobedience (Gen. 6\3-5, 2 Peter 2\5).
Suffering of Jesus & God proven fruitful.
The Flood a figure of baptism into Christ

[17] For *it is* better, if the will of God might wish *it*, to suffer for doing good than *for* doing evil. [18] For Christ also suffered once concerning violations, *the* righteous for *the* unrighteous, in order that he might bring you to God. Having been put to death in flesh, he was, though, made alive by* *the* Spirit,* [19] by whose agency* he also* went to the spirits in prison,* *and* he made the announcement* [20] to those who disobeyed then, at the time the long-suffering of God was waiting it out in *the* days of Noah, an ark having being prepared, in which a few, that is,* eight lives,* were saved through water. [21] This prefigure now saves us as well, by identification,* not a removal of *the* filth of *the* flesh, but a searching of a good conscience towards God, through *the* resurrection of Jesus Christ, [22] who is at* *the* right hand* of God, having gone into Heaven, angels and authorities and powers having been put in subjection to him.

New life in Christ. The gospel to those dead
in their violations (Mat. 8\22, Luke 9\60)

4\1 Since Christ has suffered for us in flesh, you in turn* put on as armour the same mind.

For he who has suffered in flesh has been released* from violation, [2] for him no longer *to be* in *the* cravings of men, but to spend *his* remaining time in flesh in *the* will of God. [3] For the time of the life having perished away *was* enough for us to have carried out the inclination of the other nations, having gone on in lasciviousness, lusts, excess of wine, revellings, banquetings, and unlawful idolatries, [4] in which they think strange your not running into the same overflow* of debauchery,** blaspheming, [5] those who will give an account to him who* is ready to judge *the* living and *the* dead. [6] For to this end the gospel was also proclaimed to *the* dead,* in order that they might indeed be judged as men in flesh, but might live in line with* God in spirit.*

Fiery trial of persecution.

Judgement & the household of God
[7] But the end of all these things has drawn near.* On account of this, be sober minded, and be watchful in prayers.* [8] But before* all these things, have fervent love towards each other, for love will cover over a multitude of violations.* [9] Be hospitable to each other, without grudgings, [10] as each one has received a gift, supplying it to* each other, as good house managers of *the* manifold merciful goodwill of God. [11] If anybody speaks, *let him speak* in harmony with *the* oracles of God.* If anybody serves out of such strength which God gives, *let it be* so that God might be magnified in all things – through Jesus Christ – to Whom is the magnificence and the dominion throughout* the durations of the Eons.* Amen.

[12] Richly loved, think not strange the fire of persecution happening among you as a trial* to you, as if a strange thing is going on with you. [13] But since you have a share in the sufferings of the Christ, rejoice, so that you in turn might rejoice tremendously in* the revealing* of his radiance. [14] If you are reproached *in the* name of Christ, *you are* exalted, for the spirit of magnificence and of God rests on you. From their perspective he is reviled,* but from your perspective* he is magnified. [15] For do not let any one of you suffer as a murderer, or a thief, or an evildoer, or as an interferer in the matters of other people;* [16] but if as a Christian, he ought not to be ashamed, but to magnify God in this respect. [17] For the time *has come* for the judgement to begin from the household of God.* But if first from* us, what *will be* the end of those disobeying the gospel of God?*

[18] 'And if with difficulty
the righteous *man* is saved,
where will the ungodly
and violator appear?'*

[19] In that case, those indeed suffering in alignment with the will of God, let them commit their lives* to a faithful Creator in well-doing.

Encouragement to leading men.
The crown of radiance

5\1 The leading men* among you – I, a fellow leading man, and a witness of the sufferings of the Christ, and a partaker of the radiance about to be revealed – I exhort: [2] shepherd the flock of God among you, exercising oversight not by compulsion, but willingly; nor for filthy gain, but out of a ready mind; [3] nor as exercising lordship over those entrusted to you, but becoming examples to the flock. [4] Then at the bringing to light of the Chief Shepherd,* you will receive the crown of unfading radiance.*

Younger men to submit to older men.
The roaming Devil (Job 1\6-7, 2\1-2)
[5]   In the same way, you younger men, be subject to older men, and everyone being in subjection to each other, be clothed with humility, for:

> 'God sets Himself against *the* proud,
> but gives merciful goodwill
> to *the* lowly in attitude.'**

[6]   Submit yourselves,* therefore, under the mighty hand of God, so that in due time He might exalt you, [7] you having laid down all your anxiety on Him, because it matters to Him about you.*
[8]   Be sober. Be vigilant. Your adversary *the* Devil roams around like a roaring lion, searching for whomever he can swallow up. [9] Resist him, immovable in the faith, knowing the same sufferings are being afflicted among your brothers in *the* world.

Prayer for completeness in God *
[10]   But may the God of all merciful goodwill, Him calling you to His Eonian* magnificence in Christ Jesus, *after* your having suffered a short while, make you perfect, *and* He will establish, strengthen, *and* ground *you.*
[11]   To Him *be* the magnificence and the might throughout the durations of the Eons.* Amen.

[12]   Through Silvanus, whom I regard as a faithful brother to you, I have written in a few *words*, encouraging earnestly and testifying this to be* *the* true merciful goodwill of God in which you stand.
[13]   She* in Babylon, elected together with *you*, sends you greetings, and *so does* my son Mark. [14] Greet one another with a kiss of love.
      Peace to you, all those in Christ Jesus. Amen.

~ ◆◆ ~

1 \ 1

Simon Peter, a servant and an apostle of Jesus Christ.
      To those having obtained the same precious faith with us through *the* righteousness of our God, and* of *the* Saviour Jesus Christ,* [2] merciful goodwill to you and peace be multiplied in* full knowledge of God, and of Jesus our Lord,* [3] as His divine power has been given to us for all things concerning life and holiness, through* the knowledge of Him having called us through* magnificence and virtue, [4] by which He has given us precious and most magnificent* promises, in order that by means of* these you might become partakers of divine* nature,* having escaped the corruption in *the* world through lust.

Entrance into 'the Eonian
Sovereign Rulership' of Jesus
[5]   And also, bringing in all diligence alongside this same thing, liberally add* virtue to knowledge; [6] and to knowledge, self-control; and to self-control, endurance; and to endurance, holiness; [7] and to holiness, brotherly affection; and to brotherly affection, love.
[8]   For these things, existing in you and increasing, constitute *you* as neither idle nor unfruitful in *the* knowledge of our Lord Jesus Christ. [9] For he with whom these things are not present is short-sighted, having taken hold of* forgetfulness* of the cleansing* of his violations of old.*
[10]   Rather, therefore, brothers, be diligent to confirm your designation and your calling as certain,* for doing these things you will not at all* stumble at any time.** [11] For such an entrance into the Eonian* Sovereign Rulership* of our Lord and* Saviour Jesus Christ will be richly supplied* to you.
[12]   In view of this, I will not be negligent to put you always* in remembrance concerning these things, even though knowing *them* and having been established in the present truth.
[13]   And I esteem it right, for as long as I am in this tent, to stir you up in a reminder, [14] knowing that soon* is the putting off of *this* tent of mine,

as our Lord Jesus Christ has also signified to me.* ¹⁵ But I will also be diligent to cause you to at all times* have memory of these things after my departure.

Authority of the oracles of apostles & prophets.
Prophecy came by directions of the Angel of God,
the Holy Spirit (1\21, 1 Peter 1\11, 1\12)
¹⁶ For we have not followed cleverly imagined fables. We made known to you the power and magisterial presence* of our Lord Jesus Christ. We, though, became* eyewitnesses of his majesty. ¹⁷ For he received honour and magnificence alongside God *the* Father, a voice having been conveyed to him from the Most Excellent Magnificence: 'This is My Son, the Richly Loved One,* in whom I have found delight.' ¹⁸ And we heard this voice being conveyed out of Heaven when we were with him on the holy mountain.*
¹⁹ We have also the more certain* prophetic oracle, in which you do well in guarding in your hearts – as if to a light which shines in a murky place, until the day* dawns and *the* daystar* rises* – ²⁰ knowing this first, that every prophecy of *the* Scroll* comes into being not of its own issuing,* ²¹ for prophecy was not brought about at any time* by any will of man, but, being directed* by* *the* Holy Spirit,* the holy men of God* spoke.*

Pseudo prophets & pseudo teachers
whom Jesus & Peter foretold would come *
2\1 **B**ut pseudo prophets* also rose up among the people, just as* there will also* be pseudo teachers among you, who will bring in secretly heresies of destruction, also* denying the Sovereign Lord Who bought them,* bringing in swift destruction* on themselves. ² And many will follow their lusts, because of whom the way of truth will be blasphemed. ³ And prompted by greed, they will make merchandise of you with fabricated words, for whom the judgement from of old* is not idle, and their destruction* will not slumber.

Judgement of violating messengers
Korah & Dathan & Abiram
(Num. 16\30-34, Jude 5, 6, 11),
who were 'swallowed underground'
(ταρταρόω, tartaroo), now held down
in captivity of death's dark chains;
& judgement of the ancient world
& Sodom & Gomorrah
(Gen. 6\2-4, 1 Peter 3\19-20, Jude 6);
rescue of Noah & Lot & all living righteously

⁴ For if* God did not spare violating messengers but, holding *them* by chains of darkness, swallowed underground, reserved for judgement, ⁵ and He did not spare *the* ancient world, but preserved Noah, one of eight, a messenger of righteousness, bringing in a flood on *the* world of *the* ungodly, ⁶ and, having reduced *the* cities of Sodom and Gomorrah into ashes, He condemned *them* with a catastrophe,* establishing* an example for those intending to live it out in an ungodly manner, ⁷ and He rescued righteous Lot, worn down among* *the* lasciviousness* of *the* behaviour** of the lawless ⁸ – for that righteous *man*, in seeing, and hearing, *and* living among them, tormented* *his* righteous mind* from day to day with unlawful works ⁹ – then *the* Lord knows *how* to deliver out of a trial* those ruled by devotion,* but to reserve the unrighteous for *the* day of judgement* to be punished,* ¹⁰ but most of all those taking themselves off in pursuit of flesh* in lust of defilement and despising sovereignty.*

Daring, self-willed, they do not tremor at speaking evil about majestic beings, ¹¹ whereas *the* angels, being superior* in strength and power, do not bring against them in the presence of *the* Lord any slandering accusation.
¹² But these, as brute animals, destitute of reason,* having been born* for capture and corruption,* speaking evil things in which they are ignorant, will perish utterly in their corruption, ¹³ being about to receive wages of unrighteousness, esteeming dissolute living in the daytime a pleasure, stains and blemishes, revelling in their own deceivings, feasting along with you,* ¹⁴ having eyes full of an adulteress, and not ceasing from violation, beguiling unstable people,* having a heart exercised in fraud,* sons of curse.
¹⁵ Having abandoned *the* right way, they went astray, following in the way of Balaam, *son of* Beor,* who loved *the* wages of unrighteousness, ¹⁶ but had rebuke for his own wickedness *in that* a dumb donkey speaking in a voice of a man restrained the madness of the prophet.
¹⁷ These are fountains* without water, clouds driven along by a storm, for whom is reserved* the gloom of darkness throughout* *the* Eon.* ¹⁸ For, speaking swollen *words* of vanity,* they allure by lusts of flesh *and* unbridled cravings those escaping clean from those going about in delusion, ¹⁹ promising them freedom,* themselves being servants of corruption. For anybody by whom he has been subdued, he is

enslaved by him as well.

²⁰ For if, having escaped the defilements of the world through knowledge of the Lord and Saviour Jesus Christ, but having again been entangled by them, they are overcome, the final *state* has become˙ worse for them than the original.˙ ²¹ For it would have been better for them˙ not to have known the way of righteousness˙ than having known *and* to have turned back from the sacred commandment delivered to them. ²² But to them has come the *word* of the˙ true proverb: 'A dog turned back to its own vomit,˙ and a washed sow to her rolling-place in mud.'˙

Mockers against the return of Jesus
in the last days. Day of judgement certain
& 'destruction of ungodly men' (John 3\16)

3\1 This second *of my* letters I write to you now, *my* richly loved,˙ in which I stir up your sincere mind in putting *you* in remembrance ² to remember the oracles spoken by the holy prophets, and of your commandment of the apostles of the Lord and Saviour, ³ knowing this first, that mockers will come in the last days,˙˙ walking after their own lusts, ⁴ and saying, 'Where is the promise of his magisterial presence?'˙ For since the fathers fell asleep, all things continue as from *the* beginning of creation.'˙

⁵ For this is hidden from them by their own will, that the heavens were in existence from of old,˙˙ and *the* Earth, standing out of water and in the water, by the oracle of God,˙ ⁶ by which means˙ the world order at that time,˙ being overflowed with water, perished. ⁷ But the skies and the Earth now˙ are stored up by His oracle, being reserved for fire until *the* day of judgement˙ and destruction˙ of ungodly men.

⁸ But, *my* richly loved, do not let this one thing be hidden from you, that one day with *the* Lord *is* like a thousand years, and a thousand years *are* like one day.˙ ⁹ The Lord will not delay His promise, as some consider delay, but He is long-suffering towards us, not willing for any to perish, but for all to come to submission.

The 'day of the Lord',
the heavens & Earth destroyed;
then 'the day of God'
& new heavens & a new Earth

¹⁰ But the day of *the* Lord˙ will come like a thief in *the* night, in which *the* heavens will pass

away with a rushing noise, and *the* elements will be dissolved, being burnt up, and *the* Earth and the works in it will be burned up.˙

¹¹ Since these things, then, are going to be dissolved, of what manner ought you to have in holy behaviour˙ and godliness, ¹² expecting and hastening the coming˙ of the day of God,˙ by means of which *the* heavens, being on fire, will be dissolved, and *the* elements will melt with burning heat?

¹³ Nevertheless, in line with His promise, we expect new heavens˙ and a new Earth˙ in which righteousness is resident.

Watchfulness. Destruction for perverting
Paul's letters & 'other Writings' (Rev. 22\18-19)

¹⁴ Therefore, *my* richly loved, expecting these things, be diligent to be found by Him without spot, and blameless, in peace. ¹⁵ And reckon the long-suffering of our Lord as salvation, just as our richly loved brother Paul also, with the wisdom given to him, wrote to you,˙ ¹⁶ as also in all *his* letters, speaking in them about these things, among which there are some things hard to be understood which the untaught and unstable make perversions of, as *they do* also to the other Writings,˙ to their own destruction.

Against being deceived.
Grow in merciful goodwill.
The 'day of the Eon'

¹⁷ You, therefore, *my* richly loved, having knowledge in advance, keep guard, so that, having been likewise led adrift with the delusion of the wicked, you should not˙ fall from your own firm standing. ¹⁸ But grow in merciful goodwill, and *in* the knowledge of our Lord and Saviour Jesus Christ.

To him *be* magnificence, both now and throughout *the* day of *the* Eon.˙ Amen.

~ ◆◆ ~

† The Letters of Other Apostles †

1 John

The beginning of the gospel (Mark 1\1,
Luke 1\2, Phil. 4\15, John 1\1 etc.),
& 'the oracle of life ... in relation to the Father'
(1\1-2, John 1\1-2 etc.)
The true Christ. The apostles' authority

1\1

That which was from *the* beginning,* that which we heard, that which we saw with our eyes, that which we gazed on, and our hands touched concerning the oracle* of life* 2 – for the life also was brought to light – and *that which* we have seen and given witness to, and proclaim to you, the Eonian* life which was in relation to* the Father, and was brought to light* to us, 3 that which we have seen and heard, we proclaim to you in order that you also might have partnership with* us, and truly our partnership *is* with* the Father, and* with His Son, Jesus Christ.*

4 And we write these things to you in order that our exuberance might be fulfilled. 5 And this is the message which we have heard from him and proclaim to you: that God is light, and in Him there is not any darkness at all, nothing whatever.*

True partnership with God

6 If we should say that we have partnership with Him but walk in darkness, we lie and do not practise the truth. 7 But if we should walk in the light, as He is in the light, we have partnership with each other, and the blood of Jesus Christ His Son cleanses us from every violation.

Cleansing from violation (cp. 3\6)

8 If we should say that we do not have violation, we deceive ourselves and the truth is not in us. 9 If we should admit our violations, He is faithful and righteous, so that He might forgive us the violations, and cleanse us from all unrighteousness.

10 If we should say that we have not committed violation, we make Him a liar, and His oracle is not in us.

Jesus as a counsellor in relation
to the Father (Isaiah 9\6) – compare
the Angel of God as 'another Counsellor'
(John 14\16, 14\26, 15\26, 16\7).
The love of God is in those
who keep the commandments of Jesus

2\1

My little children,* I write these things to you in order that you might not violate. But should anybody commit a violation, we have a counsellor* in relation to* the Father, Jesus Christ *the* Righteous One. 2 And he is *the* atoning sacrifice for our violations, and not only concerning* ours, but concerning* *those of* all the world* as well.

3 And in this we know that we have known him: if we keep his commandments. 4 He who says, 'I have come to know him', but is not keeping his commandments, is a liar, and the truth is not in him.

5 But whoever might keep his oracle, the love of God has been truly perfected in him. By this we know that we are in him.

6 He who says he remains in him ought also to walk just as he walked.

A new commandment, with apostolic authority,
from John. Test of being in the light

7 Brothers, I do not write a new commandment to you, but an old commandment which you had from *the* beginning.* The old commandment is the oracle which you heard from *the* beginning.*

8 On the other hand,* I am writing a new commandment to you, that which is true in him and in you, because the darkness is passing away, and the true light is already shining.

9 He claiming to be* in the light yet hating his brother is still in the darkness. 10 He who loves his brother* remains in the light, and there is no cause of stumbling in him. 11 But he who hates his brother is in the darkness, and he walks around in the darkness and does not know where he goes, because that darkness has blinded his eyes.

Reasons for writing: overcoming violation,
overcoming Satan, & having known Jesus
from the beginning of the gospel (2\7, 2\13,
2\14, 2\24, 3\11, John 1\1, 2 John 5-6);
remaining throughout the Eon (2\17, John 11\26)

12 I am writing to you, little children,* because *your* violations have been forgiven you on account of his name.*

13 I am writing to you, fathers, because you

have known him˙ from *the* beginning.˙

I am writing to you, young men, because you have overcome the Evil One.˙

I am writing to you, little children,˙ because you have known the Father.

[14] I have written to you, fathers, because you have known him˙ from *the* beginning.˙

I have written to you, young men, because you are strong, and the oracle of God remains in you, and you have overcome the Evil One.˙

Emptiness without hope of life in the Eon

[15] Do not love the world, nor the things in the world. If anybody should love the world, the love of the Father is not in him. [16] For everything which *is* in the world – the lust of the flesh, and the lust of the eyes, and the empty assurance˙ of life – is not out of the Father, but is out of the world. [17] And the world with its lust is passing away, but he who does the will of God remains throughout the Eon.˙

The Antichrist. Opposition of antichrists by infiltration

[18] Little children, it is *the* last hour,˙ and just as you have heard that the Antichrist˙ is coming, so now many antichrists˙˙ have arisen, by which we know that it is a last hour. [19] They went out from us, but they were not from us – for if they had been from among us they would have continued with us – but with the result that they might be exposed˙ that they are not all from us.

[20] And you have an anointing from the Holy One, and you know all these things. [21] I have written to you not because you do not know the truth, but because you do know it, and that no lie is out of the truth.

[22] Who is the liar but he who denies that Jesus is the Christ? He is an antichrist˙ who denies the Father and the Son.˙ [23] Whoever denies the Son does not have the Father.˙

Remaining in the Son & the Father

[24] What, then, you heard from *the* beginning˙ let it remain in you. If what you heard from *the* beginning˙ does remain in you, then˙ you will remain in the Son and in the Father. [25] And this is the promise which he promised you: Eonian˙ life.

John draws on Jeremiah & the future covenant

concerning being taught (*cp. 2\20, 2\27 & Jer. 31\33-34*)

[26] I have written these things to you concerning those who lead you adrift. [27] But the anointing which you received from him remains in you, and you do not have need that anybody should teach you.˙ But as the same anointing teaches you concerning all things, and is true, and is not a lie, so,˙ just as it has taught you, you will remain in him.

[28] And now, little children,˙ remain in him so that when he might be brought to light˙ we might have boldness, and not be put to shame before him˙ in his magisterial presence.˙ [29] If you know that he is righteous, you know that everybody who practises righteousness has been generated out of him.

The Father's immense love that they should be called Sons of God (Luke 6\35, John 1\12, Rom. 8\16, 2 Cor. 6\18 etc.); seeing Jesus at his ἐπιφάνεια (epiphaneia) & becoming like him for life 'throughout the Eon' (1 Cor. 15\42-54 , John 11\26 etc.)

3\1 Consider what immense˙ love the Father has given us in that we should be called Sons of God.˙˙ On account of this, because the world˙ does not know Him, it does not know you.˙

[2] *My* richly loved, we are now Sons of God, and it is not yet brought to light what we will be. We do know, however, that when he is brought to light˙ we will be like him, for we will see him as he is.

[3] And everybody who has this gladly-held expectation fixed in him purifies himself, just as˙ he is pure. [4] Everybody who practises violation also practises lawlessness, for violation is lawlessness. [5] And you know that he was brought to light˙˙ in order that he might take away our violations,˙ and there is in him no violation.

Future state of being without violation when the new covenant comes (*cp. 3\6, 3\9 & Jer. 31\34*). The Devil violated from the beginning (John 8\44, Gen. 1-3)

[6] Everybody who remains in him does not violate.˙ Everybody who violates has neither seen him nor has he known him.

[7] Little children, let nobody lead you adrift. He who practises righteousness is righteous, just as he is righteous.

[8] He who practises violation is out of˙ the

Devil, for from *the* beginning* the Devil commits violation. For this the Son of God was brought to light:** that he might destroy the works of the Devil.

9 Everybody who has been generated out of God does not practise violation, because His seed* remains in him, and he is unable to violate* because he has been generated* out of* God. 10 In this the Sons of God are brought to light, and *so are* the sons of the Devil.*

They had heard from beginning of the gospel.
Cain, a murderer, born seed of Satan (Gen. 3\15)
Everybody who does not practise righteousness is not out of* God, nor *is* he who does not love his brother. 11 For this is the message which you heard from *the* beginning:* that we should love one another, 12 unlike Cain *who* was out of* the Evil One** and murdered his brother. And why did he murder him? Because his works were evil, while those of his brother *were* righteous.*

13 Do not marvel, my brothers, if the world* hates you. 14 We know that, since we love the brothers, we have passed from death into life. The one not loving *his* brother remains in death. 15 Everyone hating his brother is a murderer, and you know that no murderer has Eonian* life remaining in him.

Love in action & truth.
The spirit of the new nature
16 By this we perceive love:* in that he laid down his life for us, and we ought to lay down *our* lives for the brothers.

17 But whoever might have the means of life of the world and sees his brother having need, but shuts up his pity from him, how could the love of God live in him? 18 My little children, let us not love by word, nor by tongue, but by action and by truth. 19 And in this we know that we are out of the truth, and before Him we will persuade our hearts, 20 that, if our heart should condemn us, God is bigger than our heart, and He knows all things. 21 *My* richly loved, if our heart does not condemn us, we have known boldness towards God.

22 And whatever we ask, we receive from Him, because we keep His commandments, and we practise the things which are pleasing in His sight.

23 And this is His commandment: that we should believe in the name of His Son Jesus Christ and love one another, as He gave commandment. 24 And he who keeps His commandments remains in Him, and He in him. And by this we know that He remains in us: by the spirit which He has given us.*

Testing spirit beings who are going
to make appearances, by asking them
about Jesus Christ having come in flesh.
The Antichrist already 'in the world',
now locked under the Earth (2 Thess. 2\7)

4\1 𝕸y* richly loved, do not believe every spirit,* but put the spirits to the test, whether they are from God, because many pseudo prophets* have gone out into the world.

2 By this the spirit of God* is recognized: every spirit who* professes* Jesus Christ having come in flesh* is from God. 3 And every spirit who* does not profess* Jesus Christ having come in flesh* is not from God – and this is that *teaching* of the Antichrist* which* you have heard that is coming, and is already now* in the world.*

4 You are from God, little children,* and you have overcome them, because He Who *is* in you is mightier than he who *is* in* the world.*

5 Those are out of the world. Because of this they speak out of the world, and the world* hears them.

6 We are from God. The one knowing God hears us. He who is not from God does not hear us. By this we recognize the spirit of the truth,* and the spirit of delusion.

Love is from God.
Jesus the 'Saviour of the world'
(John 4\42, Rom. 5\15, 1 Tim. 2\4-6)

7 *My* richly loved, let us love one another, for love is from God, and everybody who loves has been generated out of God and knows God. 8 He who does not love does not know God, because God is love.

9 In this the love of God was brought to light* among us: in that God authorized* His only* Son into the world in order that we might live through him. 10 In this is love: not that we loved God, but that He loved us, and authorized* His Son as appeasement concerning* our violations.

11 *My* richly loved, if God so much loved us, we in turn ought to love one another.

12 Nobody has seen God at any time.** If we love one another, God remains in us, and His love is made perfect in us. 13 In this we know that we remain in Him, and He in us: in that He has given to us out of His spirit. 14 And we have seen and we bear witness that the Father

authorized˙ the Son as Saviour of the world.˙˙
¹⁵ Whoever professes that Jesus is the Son of God, God remains in him, and he in God. ¹⁶ And we have known and we have believed the love which God has among us. God is love, and he who remains in love remains in God, and God remains in him. ¹⁷ In this, love has been perfected˙ with us, in order that we might have confidence in the day of judgement,˙˙ because, as He is, so also are we in this world.
¹⁸ There is no fear in love, but perfect love drives out fear, because fear involves punishment.˙ He who fears has not been perfected in love. ¹⁹ We love Him because He first loved us.
²⁰ If anybody should say, 'I love God,' but hates his brother, he is a liar. For how can he who does not love his brother whom he has seen, love God Whom he has not seen? ²¹ And we have this commandment from Him: that he who loves God should also love his brother.

Confidence in the love of God.
'God is one' (Deut. 6\4 etc.)

5\1 **E**veryone believing that Jesus is the Christ has been generated˙ out of God. And everybody loving the one generating˙ should also love the one generated˙ out of Him.
² In this we know that we love the Sons of God:˙ when we love God and keep His commandments. ³ For this is the love of God: that˙ we should keep His commandments, and His commandments are not burdensome. ⁴ Because everybody having been generated out of God overcomes the world.
And this is the victory overcoming the world: our faith. ⁵ Who is the one overcoming the world if not the one believing that Jesus is the Son of God?
⁶ This is the one coming through water and blood,˙ Jesus Christ, not in˙ the water only, but in˙ the water as well as the blood.˙ And the Spirit is the one giving witness,˙ because the Spirit is the truth.˙
⁷ For there are three giving witness:˙ ⁸ the Spirit,˙ and the water, and the blood,˙ and the˙ three are˙ *pointers* to the one.˙ ⁹ If we receive the witness of men, the witness of God is superior, for this is the witness of God which He has testified concerning His Son.
¹⁰ The one believing in the Son of God has the witness in him. The one not believing God has made Him a liar, because he has not believed in

the witness which God has given concerning His Son.
¹¹ And this is the witness: that God has given us Eonian˙ life, and this life is in His Son. ¹² The one having the Son has that life. The one not having the Son of God does not have that life.˙
¹³ I wrote these things to you, those believing in the name of the Son of God, so that you might know that you have Eonian˙ life, and so that you might believe in the name of the Son of God.
¹⁴ And this is the confidence which we have towards Him: that if we ask anything in harmony with His will,˙ He hears us. ¹⁵ And if we know that He hears us, whatever we might ask, we know that we have the requests which we have asked from Him.
¹⁶ If anybody should see his brother committing a violation not in relation to˙ death, he can ask and He will give life˙ to those not violating in relation to˙ death. There is violation resulting in˙ death.˙ I do not say that he should pray concerning that. ¹⁷ Every unrighteousness is violation – and there is violation *which is* not in relation to˙ death.

Being guarded from the god of this Eon.
To know 'Him Who is true'
& 'the only true God' is to have 'Eonian life'
(John 17\3). Against idols
¹⁸ We know that everyone having been born˙ out of God does not violate,˙ but the one generated˙ out of God keeps a guard on himself, and the Evil One˙ does not touch him. ¹⁹ We know that we are out of God, and the whole world lies in the sway of the Evil One.˙
²⁰ And we know that the Son of God has come, and he has given us an understanding in order that we might get to know˙ Him Who *is* true, and *that* we are in Him Who *is* true, in His Son, Jesus Christ.
This is the true God,˙ and Eonian˙ life.
²¹ Little children,˙ garrison yourselves from idols. Amen.

~ ◆◆ ~

† The Letters of the Other Apostles †

2 John

1\1

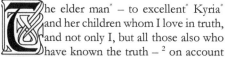

he elder man* – to excellent* Kyria* and her children whom I love in truth, and not only I, but all those also who have known the truth – ² on account of the truth remaining in us and *which* will be with us throughout* the Eon.* ³ Let goodwill, mercy, *and* peace be with us* from God *the* Father,* and from *the* Lord Jesus Christ, the Son of the Father,** in truth and love.*

Walking in agreement with the Father's commandment heard 'from the beginning' (John 1\1, 1 John 1\1, 2\13 etc.)

⁴ I rejoiced tremendously that I found* some of your children walking in truth, since we received commandment from the Father. ⁵ And now I ask you, Kyria* – not as though I wrote a new commandment to you,* but only that which we had from *the* beginning* – that we love one another. ⁶ And this is love: that we walk after His commandments. This is the commandment, as you *all* heard* from *the* beginning,* that you* *all* should walk in it.

Warning against deceivers

⁷ For many deceivers have entered into the world, those not professing Jesus Christ coming in flesh.* This is the deceiver* and the Antichrist.*
⁸ Watch yourselves, so that we might not lose the things which we have worked, but we should receive a full reward.

Transgressors rejecting the teaching of Christ. Not welcoming those with false teachings

⁹ Everybody transgressing and not continuing in the teaching of Christ does not have God. The one continuing in the teaching of the Christ has both the Father and the Son. ¹⁰ If anybody comes to you* and does not convey this teaching,* do not receive him into any house, and do not speak to make a welcome to him. ¹¹ For anyone speaking to welcome him partakes in his evil works.

Concluding salutation

¹² Having many things to write to you all,* I do not intend *to speak to you* by paper and ink, but I am hoping to come to you* and to speak face-to-face, so that our exuberance might be fulfilled.

Personal closure

¹³ The children of your elect sister send you greetings.* Amen.

~ ◆◆ ~

† The Letters of the Other Apostles †

3 John

1 \ 1

The elder man, to the richly loved Gaius, whom I love in truth. ² *My* richly loved, I pray for you to be prospered and to be in health˙ concerning˙ all things, just as˙ your inner being˙ prospers.

Witnesses who walk in truth.
Love to strangers
³ For I rejoiced tremendously in brothers coming and giving testimony to your truthfulness, just as˙ you walk in truth. ⁴ I have no more abundant exuberance than these things: that I might hear of my children walking in the truth.
⁵ *My* richly loved, you are acting faithfully in whatever you undertake for the benefit of the brothers and for the benefit of˙ strangers, ⁶ who bear witness of your love in the presence of the Ekklesia, *concerning* whom you will do well in sending on their way˙ in a manner worthy of God. ⁷ For they went out for the good of the name,˙ taking nothing from the other nations. ⁸ We ought, therefore, to welcome such men, so that we might become fellow workers for the truth.

The malice of Diotrephes
⁹ I wrote to the Ekklesia group, but Diotrephes, loving to be preeminent over them, does not receive us. ¹⁰ For this reason, if I come I will bring to remembrance his deeds which he carries out, rattling on against us with malicious words. And not being satisfied with these things, he does not receive the brothers either, and he prevents those so-minded, and he throws *them* out of the Ekklesia.

Encouragement to follow good
¹¹ *My* richly loved, do not imitate the bad, but the good. The one carrying out good is of God, but the one carrying out evil has not perceived God.

Witness of Demetrius
¹² Good report has been given˙ for Demetrius by everybody, and by the truth itself.
And we also give good report,˙ and you *all* know˙ that our testimony is true.

Personal closure
¹³ I had many things to write, but I do not want to write to you˙ with ink and pen, ¹⁴ but I am hoping to see you˙ shortly, and we will speak face-to-face.
Peace to you.˙ The friends send you greetings.˙ Give greetings˙ to the friends by name.

~ ◆◆ ~

† The Letters of the Other Apostles †

Jude

1\1

Jude, a servant of Jesus Christ, and brother of Jacob.

To those sanctified in God *the* Father,˙ and˙ preserved in Jesus Christ, *and* positioned,˙ ² mercy to you, and peace, and love be multiplied.

Contending for the faith
against deceptions by pseudo prophets
³ *My* richly loved, using all diligence to write to you concerning the common salvation, I had the need to write to you encouraging *you* to contend strongly for the faith once˙ delivered˙ to the holy people.
⁴ For certain men crept in secretly,˙ those from of old˙ marked out˙ for˙ this judgement, ungodly, perverting the merciful goodwill of our God into unbridled licentiousness, and denying God, the only Sovereign Lord,˙ and˙ denying our Lord Jesus Christ.˙

Reminder of divine judgement
on disobedient Israelites, rebel angels,
& Sodom & Gomorrah
⁵ But I want to put you in remembrance – you at one time knowing this – how the Lord, having rescued a people out of *the* land of Egypt, at the second time destroyed˙ those not believing.˙
⁶ And angels who did not keep to their own original state, but deserted their own bodily habitation,˙ He keeps in perpetual˙ chains, under darkness˙ until *the* judgement of *the* terrible day,˙ ⁷ in the same way that Sodom and Gomorrah, and the cities around them in similar manner to these, giving themselves over to self-satiating perversion, and having gone after other˙ flesh, stand as an example, undergoing the penalty of Eonian˙ fire.˙ ⁸ Yet similarly, these also in their dreamings˙ defile flesh, and despise sovereignty,˙ and speak evil of magnificent beings.˙
⁹ But the Archangel˙ Michael,˙ when contending with the Devil argued about the legislative body of Moses,˙ did not dare bring a judgement of slandering accusation against *him*,

but said, '*The* Lord rebuke you!'
¹⁰ But these *men*˙ speak evil of things they do not have knowledge in. But whatever things they do understand by nature, like animals, destitute of reason,˙ they are corrupted in those same things.

Divine judgement on Cain, Balaam,
and Korah. Pseudo prophets' corruption
by means of infiltration. Enoch prophesied
about them long ago. God's vengeance
¹¹ Woe to them! For they went off in the way of Cain,˙ and gushed themselves out after the delusion of Balaam's recompense, and they have suffered destruction by the rebellion of Korah.
¹² These are hidden rocky reefs in your love feasts, feasting together with *you*,˙ fearlessly˙ feeding themselves, clouds without water, being driven off course by winds, trees in autumnal decay, without fruit, twice dying, plucked up by the roots, ¹³ wild waves of *the* sea, foaming up their own shame, wandering stars˙ for whom the gloom of darkness has been reserved˙ throughout˙ *the* Eon.˙
¹⁴ And Enoch, seventh from Adam, prophesied also about these men,˙ saying, 'See now, *the* Lord has come˙ among myriads˙ of his holy *angels*,˙ ¹⁵ to execute judgement against all, and to convict all the ungodly among them concerning all their deeds of ungodliness which they committed in an ungodly manner, and concerning all their hard things which ungodly violators spoke against him.'˙ ¹⁶ These are grumblers, complainers,˙ walking by their lusts, and their mouth speaks grandiloquent swelling things, holding in admiration outward appearances, for the purpose of their own advantage.˙

Mockers in the last time
¹⁷ But you, *my* richly loved, remember the words spoken before by the apostles of our Lord Jesus Christ, ¹⁸ how they said to you that there will be mockers in a latter time,˙˙ walking after their own lusts in line with their ungodliness. ¹⁹ These are those causing disjoint, animal-like, not having *the* spirit.˙
²⁰ But you, *my* richly loved, building yourselves up in your most holy faith, praying by *the* divine spirit,˙ ²¹ garrison yourselves in *the* love of God, looking for the mercy of our Lord Jesus Christ resulting in˙ Eonian˙ life.˙
²² And on some have compassion, making a distinction, ²³ but others save with fear, snatching *them* out of fire, hating even the

garment stained from the flesh.

²⁴ Now to Him being able to care for them without stumbling, and to make *them* stand blameless in the presence of His magnificence, in extreme joy, ²⁵ to *the* only wise God our Saviour, *be* magnificence and majesty, might and authority, both now and throughout* all* the Eons.* Amen.

~ ◆◆ ~

† The Revelation* of Jesus Christ* †

John

A revelation given by God to Jesus through John
by means of the Angel of God (1\10, 22\8),
concerning events at the end of the coming
490 year Eon (Daniel 9\24, Mat. 18\22).
The 1,000 years (ch. 20). The new Earth (21-22)

1\1

A revelation* of Jesus Christ* which God gave to him to show His servants things which must be soon* to arise,** and *which* He signified by sending through the agency of His Angel* to His servant John, ² who gave testimony to the oracle of God* and the testimony* of Jesus, of everything that* he saw.*

Exaltation for believing this prophecy
(also 22\7; cp. 22\18-19, 2 Peter 3\16)
³ Exalted *is* the one reading, and those hearing the oracles of the prophecy, and those keeping the things written in it,* for the time *is* near.*

John's salutation to the 7 Ekklesia groups.
Prophecy of Jesus' return with clouds of angels
(19\14, Mat. 24\30, Acts 1\9-11)
⁴ John, to the seven Ekklesia groups in Asia.

Merciful goodwill to you, and peace, from God* Who is, and Who was, and Who *is* to come,* and from the seven spirits** before His governmental seat, ⁵ and* from Jesus Christ, the Faithful Witness, the First-honoured* of* the dead, and the Ruler of the kings of the Earth.*

To him loving* us, and having washed us from our violations by his own blood, ⁶ and having made us a kingdom,* priests to God and* his Father – to him *be* the preeminence and the dominion throughout* the durations of the Eons.* Amen.

⁷ Be watchful. He comes with the clouds,* and every eye will see him, and* those who pierced him* and all the tribes of the Earth will wail over him.* Yes, amen.

⁸ 'I am the Alpha and the Omega,'** says the Lord God,* Who is, and Who was, and Who *is* to come,* the Almighty.*

John taken to Patmos by the Angel of God,
as also at 4\2, 21\10, in the manner Philip

was taken to Ashdod (Acts 8\39-40).
Jesus' appearance to John, & John given
a vision of the coming 'day of the Lord'
(Isaiah 2\12, 13\6), & his appointment
to write to the Ekklesia groups
⁹ I, John, your brother and fellow-partaker in the tribulation,* and in *the* Sovereign Rulership and endurance of Christ Jesus, arrived* in the island called Patmos, for the oracle of God and for the testimony of Jesus Christ.

¹⁰ I arrived* by the agency of* *the* Spirit** in the day of *the* Lord,* and I heard a voice behind me, loud like a trumpet, ¹¹ saying,* 'What you see have written* in* a Scroll,* and have *it* sent* to the seven Ekklesia groups, to Ephesus, and to Smyrna, and to Pergamos,* and to Thyatira, and to Sardis, and to Philadelphia, and to Laodicea.'

¹² And I turned around there* to discern the voice which was speaking with me, and on turning I saw seven golden lampstands, ¹³ and in *the* centre of the seven lampstands *there was* one like *the* Son of Man,* robed down to *his* feet, and dressed* at* the chest with a golden sash.*

¹⁴ And his head and hair *were* white like wool, as white as snow, and his eyes like a flame of fire, ¹⁵ and his feet like refined brass as if glowing in a furnace, and his voice like the sound of many waters, ¹⁶ and holding in his right hand seven stars,* and a sharp two-edged sword proceeding out of his mouth,* and his countenance like the Sun shining in its strength.*

¹⁷ And when I saw him, I fell at his feet as if dead, but he laid his right *hand* on me, saying, 'Do not fear. I am the First and the Last,* ¹⁸ and the Living One,* and I became dead, and, see now, I live* throughout* the durations of the Eons.* Amen. And I have the keys of death and of the grave.*

¹⁹ 'Now write down the things which you saw, and the things which are, and the things which are going to take place after these things ²⁰ – the secret symbol of the seven stars which you saw in my right hand, and the seven golden lampstands.

'The seven stars* signify angels of the seven Ekklesia groups, and the seven lampstands* signify seven Ekklesia groups.

7 letters to the 7 angels of the 7 Ekklesia groups* *
& who will each have an overseeing angel.
To the angel of the Ekklesia group in Ephesus
(Acts 19 & 20, Eph. 1\1). Paradise & 'the Tree

of Life' (2\27, 22\2, 22\14, Luke 23\43)

2\1 'To the angel of the Ekklesia group* in Ephesus write:

'He who holds the seven stars* in his right hand, who walks in *the* centre of the seven golden lampstands,* says these things:
² 'I know your works, and your toils, and your endurance, and how you cannot tolerate the wicked, and you tested those pretending to be* apostles but are not, and you found them liars, ³ and you have endurance and have lasted it out on account of my name, and you have not wearied.*
⁴ Nevertheless, I have it against you that you forsook your first love. ⁵ Remember, in that case, where you have fallen from, and submit, and put into practice the first works. If not though, I am coming to you quickly,* and I will move your lampstand* out of its place, unless you submit. ⁶ But you do have this: that you hate the works of the Nicolaitans, which I also hate.
⁷ 'He who has an ear, let him hear what the spirit* is saying to the Ekklesia groups.

'To him who overcomes I will give him the right to eat from the Tree* of Life,* which is in the Paradise of God.*

To the angel of the Ekklesia group in Smyrna
⁸ 'And to the angel of the Ekklesia group* in Smyrna write:

'The First and the Last,* who became dead yet lived, says these things:
⁹ 'I know your works, and tribulation, and poverty – even though you are rich – and the evil speaking from those who declare themselves to be* Jews* and are not, but *are* a synagogue of Satan. ¹⁰ Do not at all fear those things which you are about to suffer. As you will see, the Devil will certainly throw some of you into jail*so that you might be tested, and you will have affliction *over* ten days. Become faithful to the point of death, and I will give you the crown of life.
¹¹ 'He who has an ear, let him hear what the spirit* says to the Ekklesia groups.

'He who overcomes will not be injured by the second death.*

To the angel of the Ekklesia group in Pergamos
¹² 'And to the angel of the Ekklesia group* in Pergamos write:

'He who has the sharp two-edged sword says

these things:
¹³ 'I know your works and where you live, the location of the throne of Satan, and you hold fast to my name, and you did not deny my faith* in those days in which my faithful witness Antipas* was around *and* was murdered nearby you, where Satan lives.* ¹⁴ But I have a few things against you, because you have there those holding the teaching of Balaam, who instructed Balak to throw a snare in front of the sons of Israel, and to eat things sacrificed to idols, and to commit sexual immorality. ¹⁵ So do you also have those holding to the teaching of the Nicolaitans.* ¹⁶ So submit. Otherwise, if you do not, I am coming to you quickly,* and I will make war against them with the sword of my mouth.
¹⁷ 'He who has an ear, let him hear what the spirit* says to the Ekklesia groups.

'To him who overcomes I will give him the right to eat hidden manna, and I will give him a white pebble, and on the pebble a new name is written which nobody will know except he who receives *it*.

To the angel of the Ekklesia group in Thyatira
¹⁸ 'And to the angel of the Ekklesia group* in Thyatira write:

'The Son of God who has* eyes like a flame of fire, and his feet like refined bronze, says these things:
¹⁹ 'I know your works, and love, and faith, and service, and your endurance, and your works, and your last works exceed the first.
²⁰ 'All the same, I have against you how you condone your* woman Jezebel,* who calls herself a prophetess, and teaches and seduces my servants to commit sexual immorality, and to eat idol sacrifices. ²¹ And I gave her time to unburden herself, but she refuses to unburden herself of her sexual immorality. ²² Watch out! I myself will throw her into a bed, and those committing adultery with her into terrible tribulation if they do not unburden themselves out of her deeds.
²³ 'And I will strike her children with a death-blow, and all the Ekklesia groups will know that I am he who searches kidneys and hearts, and I will give to each of you what is appropriate for your deeds.
²⁴ 'But I say to you others in Thyatira – as many who do not have this teaching, who have not known the deep things of Satan, as they say – I am not imposing on you any other burden.

[25] But what you have, hold fast until I come. [26] 'And to him who overcomes and keeps my works until *the* end,* I will give him authority over the nations.

[27] 'And he will shepherd* them
with a spectre* of iron;*
like* the bowl* of potters*
they will be shattered into shivers'**

– 'just as* I also have received *authority* alongside my Father – [28] and I will give him the Morning Star.*
[29] 'He who has an ear, let him hear what the spirit* says to the Ekklesia groups.

To the angel of the Ekklesia group in Sardis

3\1 'And to the angel of the Ekklesia group* in Sardis write:

'He who has the seven spirits* of God* and* the seven stars,** says these things:

'I know your works, *and* that you have a reputation that you are alive, although you are dead. [2] Become watchful, and strengthen the remaining things which you were about to abandon,* for I have not found your works as fulfilled before my God. [3] Remember, therefore, how you received and heard them – and keep to *them* and submit. If, then, you are not watchful, I will come against you like a thief, and you will in no way know what hour I will come against you. [4] But you* have a few names* in Sardis who have not defiled their garments, and they will walk with me in white, because they are worthy.

[5] 'He who overcomes will be clothed in white garments, and I will in no way blot his name out* of the Scroll* of Life, and I will vouch for his name before my Father, and before His angels.

[6] 'He who has an ear, let him hear what the spirit* says to the Ekklesia groups.

To the angel of the Ekklesia group in Philadelphia. God's new name (3\12, Mat. 28\19) & the new name of Jesus (3\12, 19\12, Mat. 28\19.)

[7] 'And to the angel of the Ekklesia* group in Philadelphia write:

'The True and Holy One, he who has the key of David, he who when he opens nobody can shut except he who opens, nor is anybody able to open, says these things:

[8] 'I know your works. See now, I have given you in your sight an opened door, and nobody is able to shut it, because you have a little strength, and you kept my oracle, and you did not deny my name.

[9] 'As you will see, I will cause those from the synagogue of Satan, those declaring themselves to be* Jews* and are not, but they lie, as you will see, I will cause it that they should come and bow down* before your feet, and know that I have loved you. [10] Because you have kept the oracle of my endurance, I for my part will keep you from the hour of testing* which is about to come over the whole inhabited world, to test those who live on the Earth.* [11] I am coming quickly.* Hold fast what you have in order that nobody might take away your crown.

[12] 'I will make him who overcomes a pillar in the Sanctuary* of my God, and he will go out no more, and I will write on him the name of my God, and the name of the city of my God, the New Jerusalem, which comes down out of Heaven* from my God,* and my new name.

[13] 'He who has an ear, let him hear what the spirit* says to the Ekklesia groups.

To the angel of the Ekklesia group in Laodicea

[14] 'And to the angel of the Ekklesia group* in Laodicea* write:

'The Amen, the faithful and true Witness, the Ruler* of the creation of God, says these things:

[15] 'I know your works, that you are neither cold nor hot. I wish you were cold or hot. [16] So then, because you are lukewarm, and neither hot nor cold,* I am about to spit you out of my mouth.

[17] 'Because you say, "I am rich, and I have increased with goods, and have need of nothing," and you do not know that you are wretched, and most pitiable, and poor, and blind, and naked, [18] I counsel you to buy from me gold purified out of fire in order that you might become rich, and white garments in order that you might clothe yourself and the shame of your nakedness might not be revealed,* and eye salve to apply to your eyes in order that you can see. [19] As many as I love I convict* and discipline. Be zealous, then, and submit.

[20] 'See now, I have taken my station at the door, and I knock. If anybody hears my voice and opens the door, I will come to him and I will eat with him, and he with me.

21 'To him who overcomes I will grant it to him to sit with me on my throne, as I for my part overcame and sat down with my Father in His throne.

22 'He who has an ear, let him hear what the spirit˙ says to the Ekklesia groups.'

Visions of events to come
at the end of the 490 year Eon.
The 1st vision in Heaven (Chapters 4 – 5).
The throne, eldermen, & zoa

4\1 **A**fter these things I looked, and just then˙ a door opened in Heaven, and the first voice which I heard *was* like a trumpet speaking with me, saying, 'Come up here,˙ and I will show you what things have to come to pass˙ after these things.'*

2   And immediately I arrived *there* by the agency of *the* Spirit,** and a throne was laid down in Heaven, and one was seated˙ on the throne˙ 3 like a jasper stone˙ and a sardius stone in appearance, and an iridescent sheen˙ encircled the throne, like the appearance of emeralds.˙

4   And around the throne *were* twenty-four thrones, and twenty-four eldermen sitting on the thrones, clothed in white garments and golden crowns on their heads.˙ 5 And from the throne proceed flashes of lightning and voices and thunderclaps, and in front of his throne seven lamps of fire *are* blazing, which represent˙ seven spirits of God.

6   And in front of the throne *was* a sea *of* glass like crystal, and in proximity˙ of the throne and around the throne *were* four living creatures˙ full of eyes in the front and at the back.

7   And the first living creature *was* like a lion, and the second living creature like a calf, and the third living creature had the face of a man, and the fourth living creature *was* like a flying eagle. 8 And the four living creatures had, respectively, six wings around *them*, and inside they are full of eyes, and day and night they have no ceasing in saying:

'Holy, holy, holy,
Lord God the Almighty,˙
Who was, and Who is, and Who *is* to come.'*

9   And when the living creatures give preeminence and honour and thanksgiving to Him sitting on the throne,˙ Who lives throughout˙ the durations of the Eons,˙ 10 the

twenty-four eldermen fall down before Him sitting on the throne, and they worship Him Who lives throughout˙ the durations of the Eons,˙ and they place their crowns before the throne, saying:

11 'You are worthy,
Lord and our holy God,˙
to receive preeminence
and honour and power,
because You created all things,
and for Your enjoyment
they had existence and were created.'

The Lion of the tribe of Judah.
The Scroll sealed with 7 seals
which the Lion of Judah opens.
The lamb symbolizing Christ

5\1 **A**nd I saw in the right hand of Him sitting on the throne a Scroll,˙ written on the inside and outside, sealed up with seven seals.˙

2   And I saw a strong angel proclaiming with a loud voice, 'Who is worthy to open the Scroll, and to break its seals?'

3   And nobody in Heaven above, nor on the Earth, nor under the Earth, was able to open the Scroll, nor to look in it. 4 And I was weeping and weeping,˙ because nobody was found worthy to open the Scroll, nor to look in it.

5   And one of the eldermen said to me, 'Do not weep. See now, the Lion who is out of the tribe of Judah,˙ the Root of David, has come off victorious, he who is opening the Scroll'* and its seven seals.'

6   And I saw among the throne and the four living creatures and among the eldermen a Lamb˙ standing˙ as if having been killed, having seven horns and seven eyes, which are˙ the seven spirits of God sent out into all the Earth.˙ 7 And it˙ came and took *it* ˙ out of the right hand of Him Who sits on the throne.

New song of the zoa & eldermen
8   And when it˙ took the Scroll, the four living creatures and twenty-four eldermen fell down before the˙ Lamb,˙ each having a harp,˙ and golden bowls full of incenses, which symbolize˙ the prayers of the holy people.˙

9   And they sung a new song, saying:

'You are worthy to take the Scroll˙
and to open its seals,

for you were murdered
and you purchased us for God
by your blood,
out of every tribe and language
and people and nation,
¹⁰ and you made them kings
and priests to our God,
and they will reign over the Earth.'*

¹¹ And I looked, and I heard a sound of many angels around the throne, and of the living creatures and of the eldermen, and the number of them was myriads of myriads,* and thousands of thousands, ¹² saying with a loud voice:

'Worthy is the Lamb*
who was murdered
to receive the power and riches,
and wisdom and strength and honour,
and preeminence and eulogy.'*

¹³ And every created being* in Heaven, and on the Earth, and under the Earth, and those who are in the sea, and all the things in them, I heard saying:

'Eulogy* and honour
and preeminence and power
to Him Who sits on the throne,
and* to the Lamb,*
throughout* the durations of the Eons.*
Amen.'

¹⁴ And the four living creatures were saying, 'Amen,' *and* the eldermen* fell down and they were worshipping* God.*

The 1st vision on the Earth* (6\1 – 7\8).
The 1st punishments,
the 1st 6 seals opened. The 4 horses*

6\1 And I saw that the Lamb* had opened one of the seven seals.*
And I heard one of the four living creatures saying, like a voice of thunder, 'Come and see.'*
² And there was a white horse, and the one sitting on it had a bow, and a crown was given to him, and he rode out conquering, and so that he might conquer.
³ And when *the Lamb* opened the second seal, I heard the second living creature saying, 'Come.'
⁴ And another horse went out, fiery-red, and

the one sitting on it was authorized to take the peace from the Earth, so that they might kill one another, and a large sword was given to him.
⁵ And when *the Lamb* opened the third seal, I heard the third living creature saying, 'Come and see.'
And there was a black horse, and the one sitting on it had in his hand a pair of balances.
⁶ And I heard a voice in *the* centre of the four living creatures say, 'A measure* of wheat for a denarion,* and three measures of barley for a denarion, and do not ruin the oil and the wine!'*
⁷ And when *the Lamb* opened the fourth seal, I heard the fourth living creature say, 'Come and see.'
⁸ And then there was* a pale horse, and the name of the one sitting on it *was* Death. And the grave* followed him, and authority was given to him over a quarter of the Earth to kill by sword, and by famine, and by death, and by the wild animals of the Earth.
⁹ And when *the Lamb* opened the fifth seal, I saw underneath the altar the corpses* of those murdered on account of the oracle* of God, and on account of* the testimony which they held concerning the Lamb.
¹⁰ And they were calling out with a loud voice, saying, 'How long, Sovereign Lord, the Holy and the True One? Do You not judge and avenge our blood on those living on the Earth?'
¹¹ And to each of them a white robe was given, and it was said to them that they should rest a while longer, until their fellow servants, and their brothers, and those about to be murdered as they also *were murdered*, should bring in the full measure.
¹² And I watched while *the Lamb* opened the sixth seal, and there came to be* a mighty earthquake, and the Sun turned* black like a sackcloth of hair, and the entire Moon turned* like blood. ¹³ And the stars* of the sky fell to the Earth, like* a fig tree shaken* by a strong wind shedding its untimely figs. ¹⁴ And the sky was parted, rolled up* like a scroll* rolling itself up, and every mountain and island were moved out of their places.
¹⁵ And the kings of the Earth, and the high-ranking, and the military commanders, and the rich, and the mighty men,* and every servant and freeman* hid themselves inside the caves and inside the rocks of the mountains, ¹⁶ and they said to the mountains and to the rocks, 'Fall on us,* and hide us from *the* face of Him

sitting on the throne, and* from the anger of the Lamb,* ¹⁷ because the terrible day of his anger* has come, and who is able to stand?'

Answer to 'who is able to stand?'

7\1 𝐀nd after this* I saw four angels standing on the four corners of the Earth, holding fast the four winds of the Earth, so that no wind could blow on the Earth, nor on the sea, nor on any tree.
² And I saw another angel ascending from *the* rising of *the* Sun, having a seal of *the* living God, and he called out with a loud voice to the four angels to whom it was given to injure the Earth and the sea, ³ saying, 'Do not injure the land, or the sea, or the trees, until we have sealed the servants of our God on their foreheads.'
⁴ And I heard the number of the sealed, 144,000* sealed out of every tribe of *the* sons of Israel.*

⁵ Out of *the* tribe of Judah, 12,000 sealed;*
   out of *the* tribe of Reuben, 12,000;
   out of *the* tribe of Gad, 12,000;
⁶ out of *the* tribe of Asher, 12,000;
   out of *the* tribe of Nephthalim, 12,000;
   out of *the* tribe of Manasseh, 12,000;
⁷ out of *the* tribe of Simeon, 12,000;
   out of *the* tribe of Levi, 12,000;
   out of *the* tribe of Issachar, 12,000;
⁸ out of *the* tribe of Zebulon, 12,000;
   out of *the* tribe of Joseph, 12,000;
   out of *the* tribe of Benjamin, 12,000 sealed.*

The 2nd vision in Heaven * (7\9 – 8\6).
Multitudes of every nation and tribe
⁹ And after I saw these things there was a large multitude whom nobody was able to count, out of* every nation, and tribe, and peoples, and languages, standing before the throne and before the Lamb,* clothed with white robes, and palms in their hands, ¹⁰ and they were calling out with a loud voice, saying:

'Salvation to our God
sitting on the throne,
and* to the Lamb.'*

¹¹ And all the angels, and the eldermen, and the four living creatures were standing around the throne, and they fell down before the throne on their faces and worshipped God, ¹² saying:

'Amen! The eulogy*
and the preeminence and the wisdom,
and the thanksgiving and the honour,
and the power and the strength
be to our God,
throughout* the durations of the Eons.*
Amen!'

¹³ And one of the eldermen asked, saying to me, 'Who are these clothed in white robes? Who are they, and where have they come from?'
¹⁴ And I said to him, 'My lord, you know.'
And he said to me, 'These are those who came out of the mighty tribulation, and they washed their robes, and made their robes white* by virtue of the blood of the Lamb.'* ¹⁵ On account of this they are before the throne of God, and they serve Him day and night in His Sanctuary,* and He Who sits on the throne will spread His tent over* them.
¹⁶ 'They will not hunger any longer, nor will they thirst any longer, nor will the Sun fall on them at all, nor any scorching heat. ¹⁷ For the Lamb* in *the* proximity of the throne is a shepherd to them, and he leads* them to living fountains* of waters, and God will wipe away* every tear from their eyes.'*

The 7th seal. The 7 trumpets

8\1 𝐀nd when *the Lamb** opened the seventh seal, silence arose in Heaven for about half an hour.
² And I saw the seven angels who stand before God, and they were given seven trumpets.
³ And another angel came and stood on the altar, having a golden censer, and he was given many incenses so that he might offer *them* with the prayers of all the holy people on the altar of gold in front of the throne.
⁴ And the smoke of the incenses with the prayers of the holy people ascended before God out of a hand of the angel. ⁵ And the angel took the censer and he filled *it* from the fire of the altar, and he threw *it* into the Earth, and thunderings broke out,* and rumblings, and lightnings, and an earthquake.
⁶ And the seven angels having the seven trumpets prepared themselves so that they might sound the trumpets.

The 2nd vision on the Earth
(8\7 – 11\14). The 1st trumpet

[7] And the first *angel* sounded the trumpet, and there was hail and fire mixed with blood, and it was hurled into the Earth, and a third of the Earth was burned up, and a third of the trees were burned up, and all green grass was burned up.

The 2nd trumpet

[8] And the second angel sounded the trumpet, and something like a mighty mountain burning with fire was hurled into the sea, and a third of the sea turned to* blood, [9] and a third of the creatures having life in the sea died, and a third of the ships were wrecked.

The 3rd trumpet

[10] And the third angel sounded the trumpet, and an immense star burning like a lamp fell out of the sky, and it fell on a third of the rivers and on the fountains* of waters. [11] And the name of the star is called Wormwood, and a third of the water became* wormwood, and many men died from the waters because they had been made bitter.

The 4th trumpet

[12] And the fourth angel sounded the trumpet, and a third of the Sun, and a third of the Moon, and a third of the stars were struck so that a third of them should be darkened, and for a third of the day *it* should not have light, and the same with the night.*

[13] And I looked, and I heard an eagle* flying at a high point in the sky, calling with a loud voice, 'Woe, woe, woe to those living on the Earth, from the remaining sounds of the trumpet of the three angels about to sound the trumpet!'

The 5th trumpet (the 1st woe).
1st release: locusts from the abyss
where the Wild Beast comes from (11\7)

9\1 **A**nd the fifth angel sounded the trumpet, and I saw a star fallen out of the sky into the Earth, and the key of the pit of the abyss was given to him.* [2] And he opened the pit of the abyss, and smoke went up out of the pit, like smoke of a blazing furnace, and the Sun was darkened, and the air,* by the smoke of the pit.*

[3] And out of the smoke locusts* came into the Earth, and power was given to them in the way that the scorpions of the Earth have power. [4] And it was spoken to them that they should not injure the grass of the ground, nor any green thing, nor any tree, but only the men who do not have the seal of God on their foreheads. [5] And it was not permitted for them that they could kill them, but rather that they should be tormented for five months, and their torment *was* like a torment of a scorpion when it stings a man. [6] And in those days men will search for death but they will not find it, and they will want to die and death will flee from them.

[7] And the appearances of the locusts *were* like horses prepared for war, with crowns of gold on their heads, and their faces *were* like faces of men. [8] And they had hair like the hair of women, and their teeth were like lions' teeth. [9] And they had breastplates like breastplates of iron, and the sound of their wings *was* like the sound of chariots of many horses running into battle. [10] And they have tails and stings the same as scorpions. And in their tails they have power to injure men for five months.

[11] They have a king over them, *the* angel of the abyss,* whose name in Hebrew *is* Abaddon, and in the Greek he has *the* name Apollyon.

[12] The first woe is past. Watch now! Still two more woes come after these things.

The 6th trumpet (the 2nd woe).
2nd release: four angels from the abyss

[13] And the sixth angel sounded the trumpet, and I heard one voice out of the four horns of the golden altar which *is* before God, [14] saying to the sixth angel who had the trumpet, 'Release the four angels chained at the great river Euphrates.'

[15] And the four angels kept ready for the hour, and for the day, and month, and year, were released so that they might kill a third of men. [16] And the number of the armies of the horsemen *was* a hundred million.* I heard* the number of them. [17] And in this way I saw the horses in the vision, and those sitting on them having breastplates, fire-coloured and dusky red and like brimstone, and the heads of the horses *were* like heads of lions, and out of their mouths issue fire and smoke and brimstone.

[18] One third of men were killed by these three plagues,* by the fire, and by the smoke and the brimstone which issue out of their mouths. [19] For the power of the horses is in their mouth and in their tails, for their tails *are* like snakes, having heads, and they cause injury with them.

²⁰ And the rest of the men who were not killed by these plagues did not even unburden themselves from the works of their hands so that they should not worship the demons, or the golden and silver idols, or the brass and the stone and the wooden idols, which are able neither to see, nor to hear, nor to walk. ²¹ And they did not unburden themselves out of their murders, nor out of their sorceries,˙ nor out of their fornication, nor out of their thefts.

The mighty angel who is the 7th angel & his descent to Earth with the open Scroll. The 7 thunders

10\1 **A**nd I saw a mighty angel˙ coming down out of the sky, clothed with a cloud and an iridescent sheen over his head, and his face *was* like the Sun, and his legs˙ like pillars of fire. ² And he had open in his hand a Scroll,˙˙ and he placed his right foot on the sea, and *his* left *foot* on the Earth, ³ and he called out with a loud voice like when a lion roars,˙ and when he called out the seven thunders uttered their sounds.

⁴ And when the seven thunders had spoken I was about to write, but I heard a voice out of the sky saying, 'Seal up the matters the seven thunders uttered, and do not write them.'

⁵ And the angel whom I saw standing on the sea and on the Earth lifted up his right hand into the sky, ⁶ and he swore by Him Who lives throughout the durations of the Eons,˙ He Who created Heaven and the things in it, and the Earth and the things in it, and the sea and the things in it, that there will no longer be any delay. ⁷ But in the days of the voice of the seventh angel, when he is about to sound,˙ then˙ the mystery of God is brought to a close,˙ as He has declared to His servants the prophets.˙

John's consuming the Scrolls & his order to prophesy to the nations

⁸ And the voice which I heard out of the sky was again speaking with me, and saying, 'Go *and* take the little Scroll˙ opened in the hand of the angel standing on the sea and on the Earth.'

⁹ And I went off to the angel, asking him to give me the little Scroll, and he said to me, 'Take *it*, and eat it up, and it will make your belly bitter, but in your mouth it will be as sweet as honey.'

¹⁰ And I took the Scroll out of the hand of the angel, and I ate it up, and in my mouth it was as sweet as honey, and as soon as I had eaten it my stomach was made bitter.

¹¹ And he˙ said to me, 'You must prophesy again concerning many peoples, and nations, and languages, and kings.'˙

The rebuilt Sanctuary & Jerusalem trampled (Luke 21\24), & the two witnesses

11\1 **A**nd a reed like a sceptre was given to me,˙ *and* he said, 'Rise up, and measure the Sanctuary˙ of God, and the altar, and those worshipping in it. ² But exclude the court outside the Sanctuary,˙ and do not measure it, because it was given up to the nations, and they will trample the Holy City underfoot for 42 months.˙ ³ And I will give authority˙ to my˙ two witnesses, and they will prophesy for 1,260 days, clothed in sackcloth.'

⁴ These are the two olive trees and two lampstands˙ which stand before the Lord of the Earth. ⁵ And if anybody should wish to injure them, fire will proceed out of their mouth˙ and devour their enemies. And if anybody should wish to bring harm to them, he must be killed in this manner. ⁶ These have authority to shut the sky so that no rain might fall in the duration of their prophecy, and they have authority over the waters to turn them into blood, and to strike the Earth with every plague as often as they might wish.

The Wild Beast from the abyss (11\7, 17\8, 2 Thes. 2\6-8). Murder of the two witnesses & their resurrection

⁷ And when they finish their testimony, the Wild Beast coming up out of the abyss˙ will make war against them, and he will overcome them and kill them. ⁸ And their corpses *will lie* on the plaza of the mighty city,˙ which spiritually is called Sodom and Egypt,˙ where also their Lord was hanged on a stake.˙ ⁹ And those of the peoples and tribes and languages and nations will see their corpses for three *and* a half days, and they will not allow their corpses to be put in a tomb.

¹⁰ And those living on the Earth˙ will gloat over them, and they will celebrate and give gifts to each other, because these two prophets tormented˙ those living on the Earth.

¹¹ And after the three and a half days *the* spirit of life from God entered into them, and they stood up on their feet, and dreadful terror fell

on those gazing attentively on them.
[12] And I heard a loud voice out of Heaven saying to them, 'Come up here.'*

And they ascended into the sky in the cloud, and their enemies saw them.* [13] Then on that day* a terrible earthquake broke out,* and a tenth of the city collapsed, and in the earthquake 7,000 names of men* were killed, and the rest became afraid and gave preeminence to the God of Heaven.
[14] The second woe passed away. Be watchful!* The third woe is coming quickly.*

The 3rd vision in Heaven (11\15-19).
The 7th trumpet (the 3rd woe)

[15] And the seventh angel sounded the trumpet,* and loud voices rose up* in Heaven saying, 'The government of this world has become* our Lord's and* His Christ's, and he will reign throughout* the durations of the Eons.'**
[16] And the twenty-four eldermen sitting on their thrones before the throne of God fell on their faces and worshipped God, [17] saying:

'We give You thanks,
Lord God the Almighty,*
Who is, and Who was,*
because You have taken up
Your mighty power
and You have exerted government.*
[18] And the nations were made angry,*
and Your indignation arose
and the time of the dead to be judged,
and to give the reward
to Your servants the prophets,
and to the holy people,
and to those fearing Your name,
to the lowly* and the eminent,*
and to bring destruction
to those destroying the Earth.'

[19] And the Sanctuary of God was opened in Heaven, and the Ark of the Lord's Covenant was seen in His Sanctuary.*

The 3rd vision on the Earth

And lightning flashes, and rumblings, and thunderclaps broke out,* and an earthquake, and a heavy hailstorm.

The 4th vision in Heaven (12\1-12).
Satan the terrible Dragon,
the woman, & the child.
The Dragon drags

fellow rebel angels to Earth.
The woman flees into the wilderness

12\1 And a tremendous sign* was seen in Heaven,* a woman* clothed with the Sun, and the Moon underneath her feet, and on her head a crown of twelve stars, [2] *and* having *a child* in her womb, and she cried out, being in the pains of childbirth and in distress to give birth.
[3] And another sign was seen in Heaven,* and there was* a terrible fiery-red Dragon, having seven heads and ten horns, and seven diadems on his heads. [4] And his tail* dragged the third of the Stars of Heaven,** and he flung them onto the Earth. And the Dragon stood before the woman about to give birth, so that when she gives birth he might devour her child.
[5] And she gave birth to a son,* a male, who was going to shepherd* all the nations with an iron rod, and her child was caught away* to God and His throne. [6] And the woman fled into the wilderness, where she has a place made ready by God, to nourish her there for 1,260 days.

War by Michael
& his angels against Satan.
Satan & his angels hurled to Earth

[7] And war broke out* in Heaven,* Michael* and his angels fighting* against the Dragon.* And the Dragon and his angels fought, [8] but he did not have the strength, nor was a place for him found any longer in the sky. [9] And the terrible Dragon was hurled out, the ancient Snake called the Devil and Satan, the one deceiving the whole inhabited world. He was hurled onto the Earth,* and his angels were hurled down with him.*
[10] And I heard a loud voice in Heaven saying, 'Now the salvation and power have come, and the government of our God, and* the authority of His Christ, because the accuser of our brothers is hurled down,* the one accusing them before our God day and night.* [11] And they overcame him through the blood of the Lamb,* and through the oracle of their testimony, and they did not love their life* to the extent of death.*
[12] Rejoice on account of this,* you heavens,* and you inhabiting them.* Woe to the Earth** and the sea! For the Devil has come down to you, having terrible boiling anger, knowing that he has a short time.'*

The 4th vision on the Earth.
Satan's persecution
of the woman (12\13 – 13\18)

¹³ And when the Dragon saw that he was hurled down onto the Earth, he pursued˙ the woman who had given birth to the male child. ¹⁴ And two wings of the large eagle were given to the woman, so that she might fly into the wilderness, into her place where she should be nourished there for a time, and times, and half a time, away from *the* face of the Snake.

¹⁵ And the Snake spewed out of his mouth water like a river, in pursuit of the woman, so that he might cause˙ her *to be* swept away by a river.˙ ¹⁶ And the ground helped the woman, and the ground opened its mouth and swallowed up the river which the Dragon spewed out of his mouth. ¹⁷ And the Dragon was enraged with the woman, and he went off to make war with the remnant of her seed, those holding to the commandments of God, and having the testimony of Jesus.

An individual emerges (11\7, 17\8,
2 Thes. 2\6-8) & is enthroned by Satan,
& who is the Wild Beast out of the sea of people,
being a composite kingdom having 7 heads
& 10 horns (Daniel 2\41-43, 7\7-8, 7\19-20,
8\9-14, 8\23-25, 11\29–45)

13\1 **A**nd I stood on the sand of the sea, and I saw a Wild Beast˙ rising up out of the sea,˙ having ten horns and seven heads, and on its horns ten diadems, and on its heads blasphemous names. ² And the Wild Beast whom I saw was like a leopard, and his feet were like a bear's, and his mouth like a mouth of a lion, and the Dragon gave him his authority, and his throne, and immense power. ³ And one of his heads˙ *was* as if struck to death, but his death-stroke was healed, and all the Earth marvelled at the Wild Beast.˙

⁴ And they worshipped the Dragon who had given the authority to the Wild Beast, and they worshipped the Wild Beast, saying, 'Who *is* like the Wild Beast? And who is able to make war with him?'

⁵ And a mouth was given to him, speaking grandiloquent things and blasphemy, and authority was given to him to make war for 42 months.

The Wild Beast's war with the holy people.
All but the names written in the Scroll of Life

at the founding of the new Eon's order of things
will worship him (17\8, 2 Tim. 4\1)

⁶ And he opened his mouth in blasphemy towards God,˙ to blaspheme His name and His Tabernacle, those tabernacling in Heaven.˙ ⁷ And it was given to him to make war against the holy people, and to overcome them, and authority was given to him over every tribe, and people, and language, and nation. ⁸ And they will worship him, all those living on the Earth, everybody whose name, since˙ *the* foundation˙ of *the* world order,˙˙ has not been written in the Scroll˙ of Life˙ of the slain Lamb.˙˙

⁹ If anybody has an ear, let him hear.

¹⁰ If anybody lives in captivity, he will go free. If anybody murders with a sword, he must be put to death by a sword. This is the patience and the faith of the holy people.

The Wild Beast who is out of the Earth.
Evil signs deceiving idolaters.
An idolatrous image
& the tattoo of the Wild Beast (666)

¹¹ And I saw another Wild Beast rising up out of the Earth,˙ and he had two horns like a lamb,˙ and he spoke like a dragon.˙ ¹² And he exercises all the power of the first Wild Beast in his sight,˙ and he causes the Earth and those living in it that they should worship the first Wild Beast whose deadly wound was healed. ¹³ And he performs extraordinary signs so that he should cause fire to come down out of the sky˙ to the Earth in full view of men, ¹⁴ and he leads astray those of mine˙ living on the Earth through those signs which were given to him to perform in the sight of the Wild Beast, telling those living on the Earth to make an image to the Wild Beast who has the wound yet came alive again after the strike of the sword.˙

¹⁵ And it was given to him to give breath to the image of the Wild Beast, so that the image of the Wild Beast should also speak, and to cause as many who would not worship the image of the Wild Beast that they should be put to death.˙ ¹⁶ And he forced everybody, the lowly and the eminent, and the rich and the poor, and the freeman˙ and the servants, that he might give them tattoos˙ on their right *hand,* or on their forehead, ¹⁷ and that nobody should be able to buy or to sell unless having the tattoo,˙ the name˙ of the Wild Beast, or the number of his name.

¹⁸ Here is wisdom:˙ let him who has understanding˙ calculate the number of the

Wild Beast, for it is a number of a man, and his number *is* 666.*

The 5th vision in Heaven (14\1-5).
The Lamb on Mount Zion and the 144,000

14\1 ▉nd I looked, and there was* the Lamb,* standing on Mount Zion, and with him 144,000 in number, having his own name, and the name of his Father* written on their foreheads.*
² And I heard a voice out of Heaven,* like a sound of many waters, and like a sound of loud thunder. And the sound which I heard was like harpists strumming on their harps, ³ and they sang a new kind of song in the sight of* the governmental seat and in the sight of the four living creatures and the eldermen, and nobody was able to learn the song except the 144,000,* those redeemed from the Earth. ⁴ These are those who were not defiled with women because they are virgins. These are those who follow the Lamb wherever he goes. These were redeemed by Jesus from among men, firstfruits to God, and* to the Lamb.* ⁵ And no falsehood was found in their mouth, for they are blameless.*

The 5th vision on the Earth (14\6-20).
The 1st angel proclaims the Eonian gospel
⁶ And I saw an angel flying at a high point in the sky, having *the* Eonian* gospel to announce to those living on the Earth, and to every nation, and tribe, and language, and people, ⁷ saying in a loud voice, 'Revere the Lord, and give preeminence to Him, for the hour of His judgement has come. And worship Him Who created* Heaven and the Earth, and the sea, and springs* of waters.'

The 2nd angel: his prophecy of Babylon
⁸ And another, a second angel followed, saying, 'Babylon* the Mighty* has fallen.* She made all the nations drink from the wine of the boiling anger of her fornication.'

The 3rd angel: his warning of judgement
stated in prophetic hyperbole (14\11,
Isaiah 66\24, Mark 9\44, 9\46, 9\48)
concerning those with the tattoo of the Wild Beast.
The harvest with a sharp sickle
⁹ And another angel, a third, followed them, saying with a loud voice, 'If anybody worships the Wild Beast and his image, and receives a

tattoo* in his forehead, or on his hand, ¹⁰ then he will drink from the wine of the boiling anger* of God, which *is* poured undiluted into the cup of His indignation,* and he will be tormented with interrogation* in fire and brimstone, in the sight of the holy angels, and in the sight* of the Lamb,* ¹¹ and the smoke of their torture* will ascend throughout* *the* durations of *the* Eons.'*

And those worshipping the Wild Beast and his image, or if anybody should receive the tattoo* of his name, they have no rest day and night.'* ¹² This is the endurance of the holy people, those keeping the commandments of God, and the faith of Jesus.
¹³ And I heard a voice out of Heaven saying, 'Write: Exalted *are* the dead, those dying in *the* Lord from now. The Spirit* says, "Yes, let them rest from their toilsome labours, and their works proceed with* them." '

The 4th angel: the command to reap
¹⁴ And I looked, and there was* a white cloud, and one like a son of man* sitting on the cloud, having on his head a golden crown, and in his hand a sharp sickle.
¹⁵ And another angel came out of the Sanctuary,* calling out with a loud voice to the one sitting on the cloud, 'Swing in* your sickle and reap, for the hour for reaping has come, for the harvest of the Earth has dried up.'*
¹⁶ And the one sitting on the cloud swung* his sickle over* the Earth, and the Earth was harvested.

The 5th angel, having a sharp sickle.
The 6th angel's command to reap
¹⁷ And another angel came out of the Sanctuary* which *is* in Heaven, he also having a sharp sickle.
¹⁸ And another angel came out from the altar, having authority over* the fire, and he called with a loud shout* to him having the sharp sickle, saying, 'Swing in* your sharp sickle, and harvest the grapes of the vine of the Earth, because its grapes have become fully ripened.'
¹⁹ And the angel swung* his sickle into the Earth, and he gathered the vineyard of the Earth, and he threw *it* into* the vast winepress of the boiling anger of God. ²⁰ And the winepress was trampled outside the city, and blood oozed out of the winepress, as high as* the bridle of horses, from* the distance of 1,600 stadium lengths.*

The 6th vision in Heaven (15\1-8).
7 angels with 7 plagues.
Song of Moses & the Lamb

15\1 **A**nd I saw another sign in Heaven, tremendous and wonderful: seven angels having the seven last plagues, for in them the boiling anger of God was filled up.
² And I saw as it were a sea of glass mixed with fire, and those emerging victorious from* the Wild Beast, and from* his image,* and from* the number of his name, standing on the sea of glass, holding harps of God.
³ And they sang the song of Moses,* the servant of God, and the song of the Lamb,* saying:

'Tremendous and wonderful
are Your works,
Lord God the Almighty;*
righteous and true *are* Your ways,*
the King of the nations.*
⁴ Who cannot fear You, Lord,
and magnify Your name?
For *You* alone *are* holy,
for all the nations will come
and worship before You,
for Your righteous sentences
have been brought to light.'**

⁵ And after these things I looked, and the Sanctuary* of the Tabernacle of the Testimony in Heaven was opened. ⁶ And the seven angels having the seven plagues came out of the Sanctuary,* *and* they were clothed in pure bright white linen, and dressed* around* the chest with golden sashes.*
⁷ And one of the four living creatures gave to the seven angels seven golden bowls full of the boiling anger of God, the one living throughout* the durations of the Eons.* ⁸ And the Sanctuary was filled with smoke from the magnificence of God and from His power, and nobody was able to enter into the Sanctuary* until the seven plagues of the seven angels should be fulfilled.

The 6th vision on the Earth
(16\1 – 18\24). The 1st plague

16\1 **A**nd I heard a loud voice out of the Sanctuary* saying to the seven angels, 'Go your ways, and pour out onto the Earth the seven bowls of the boiling anger of God.'

² And the first *angel* went off, and he poured out his bowl on the Earth, and a foul and painful ulcer* came out* on the men having the tattoo* of the Wild Beast, and those worshipping his image.

The 2nd plague
³ And the second angel poured out his bowl into the sea, and it became* like the blood of a dead *man*, and every creature* living in the sea died.

The 3rd plague
⁴ And the third *angel* poured out his bowl into the rivers and into the fountains* of waters, and it turned to* blood.
⁵ And I heard the angel of the waters saying:

'You are righteous, Lord,
You Who are, and Who were,
You Who are holy,*
because You have exercised judgement
in these things.
⁶ For they poured out blood
of holy people and of prophets,
and You have given them blood to drink,
for they are deserving.'

⁷ And I heard *a voice* from the altar saying:

'Yes,* Lord God the Almighty,*
true and righteous *are* Your judgements.'

The 4th plague
⁸ And the fourth angel poured out his bowl on the Sun, and it was authorized for him to scorch men in fire. ⁹ And men were scorched with intense heat, and the men blasphemed the name of God holding authority over these plagues, and they did not submit so as to give Him preeminence.

The 5th plague
¹⁰ And the fifth *angel* poured out his bowl over the throne of the Wild Beast, and his kingdom became* darkened, and they gnawed their tongues out of distress, ¹¹ and they blasphemed the God of Heaven because of their distresses, and because of* their sores, and they did not unburden themselves out of their deeds.

The 6th plague:
the gathering at Armageddon
¹² And the *sixth* angel poured out his bowl on

the great river Euphrates, and its water was dried up, so that the road of the kings from the rising of *the* Sun might be prepared.

[13] And out of the mouth of the Dragon, and out of the mouth of the Wild Beast, and out of the mouth of the Pseudo Prophet, I saw three unclean spirits like frogs, [14] for they symbolize spirits of demons,* performing signs which go out to the kings of the whole inhabited world,* to assemble them for the battle of the terrible day of God the Almighty.**

[15] Watch out! I come like a thief. Exalted *is* the one watching and keeping his garments, so that he might not walk naked and they would see his shame.*

[16] And he gathered them together into the place which in the Hebrew language is called Armageddon.**

The 7th plague.
Jerusalem divided into three

[17] And the seventh *angel* poured out his bowl into the air,* and a loud voice came from the Sanctuary* of Heaven, from the throne, saying, 'It has come.'*

[18] And flashes of lightning and thunderclaps, and rumblings* broke out,* and a mighty earthquake,* such a severe, so mighty an earthquake whose likeness has not arisen* since men have been* on the Earth. [19] And the mighty city* came to be* in three parts, and the cities of the nations collapsed, and Babylon the Mighty came into remembrance before God, to give to her the cup of the wine of the boiling anger of His indignation. [20] And every island fled away, and no mountains were found. [21] And a mighty hailstorm, like a hundred pound weight,* dropped down out of the sky, and men blasphemed God because of the plague of the hail, because its plague was extremely severe.

The judgement of the Great Whore,
Babylon (Isaiah 47, Jer. 50-51)

17\1 **A**nd one of the seven angels of those having the seven bowls came and spoke with me, saying,* 'Come here, *and* I will show you the judgement of the Great Whore sitting on the many waters, [2] with whom the kings of the Earth committed sexual immorality, and those living on the Earth were made drunk from the wine of her fornication.'

[3] And he transported me by the agency of* *the* Spirit* into a desert, and I saw a woman siting

on a scarlet Wild Beast, full of names of blasphemy, having seven heads and ten horns. [4] And the woman was clothed in purple and scarlet, *and* gilded with gold and precious gemstones* and pearls, holding a golden cup in her hand, filled with abominations and the filthy things of her fornication, [5] and a name written on her forehead:

'Mystery, Babylon the Mighty,*
the Mother of the Whores
and of the Abominations of the Earth.'*

[6] And I saw the woman drunk from the blood of the holy people, *and* from the blood of the witnesses of Jesus.* And having seen her, I marvelled with tremendous amazement.

Those not in the Scroll of Life will be enthralled by the Wild Beast (13\8, 2 Tim. 4\1), who comes out of the abyss (Rev. 11\7, 17\8, 2 Thes. 2\6-8). Interpretation of the Great Whore & the Wild Beast out of the sea

[7] And the angel said to me, 'Why were you amazed? I will tell you the mystery of the woman and the Wild Beast sustaining her *and* having the seven heads and the ten horns. [8] The Wild Beast whom you saw was, and is not, and is about to come up out of the abyss* and to go into destruction.* And those living on the Earth, whose names have not been written in the Scroll* of Life since* *the* foundation* of *the* world order,** will marvel in seeing that the Wild Beast was, and is not, and will be present.*

[9] 'Here *is* the mind which has wisdom: The seven heads represent* seven mountains where the woman sits on them, [10] and they are seven kings: five fell; one is;* the other has not yet come, and when he comes he must remain for a short *time.*

[11] 'And the Wild Beast who was, and is not, is also himself an eighth, yet is out of the seven, and he goes into destruction.*

[12] 'And the ten horns which you saw are ten kings who have not yet received a kingdom, but they receive authority as kings *for* one hour along with the Wild Beast. [13] These have one mind, and they will give up the power and the authority of themselves to the Wild Beast. [14] These will make war with the Lamb, and the Lamb* will overcome them, because he is Lord of lords and King of kings, and those with him *are* designated, and chosen,* and faithful.'

[15] And he said to me, 'The waters which you

saw, where the Whore sits, are peoples, and multitudes, and nations, and languages.* ¹⁶ And the ten horns which you saw, and* the Wild Beast, these will hate the Whore, and they will make her be reduced to nothing, and naked, and they will eat her flesh, and they will burn her down with fire. ¹⁷ For God has given *it* into their hearts to carry out His purpose,* and to create one mind,** and to give their sovereignty to the Wild Beast, until the oracles of God should be fulfilled. ¹⁸ And the woman whom you saw is the* mighty city* which has sovereignty** over the kings of the Earth.'

Judgement of Babylon the Mighty

18\1 **A**nd after these things I saw another angel coming down out of the sky, having immense power, and the Earth was illuminated from his brightness.
² And he called out with a strong voice, saying:

> 'Babylon the Mighty has fallen,
> and it has become* a residence* of demons,*
> and a prison of every unclean spirit
> and a prison of every unclean
> and detested bird.'

³ 'For all the nations have fallen because of the wine of the boiling anger of her fornication, and the kings of the Earth committed fornication with her, and the merchants of the Earth have become rich out of the capacity of her excessive luxury.'

⁴ And I heard another voice from Heaven, saying:

> 'Get out of her, My people,*
> so that you might have no partnership
> with* her violations,
> and so that you might not receive
> *anything* from her plagues.
⁵ For her violations have been piled
> up to Heaven,*
> and God has remembered
> her unrighteous acts.
⁶ Give back to her
> as she in turn gave back to you,
> and repay her double
> in proportion to her works;
> in the cup which she mixed
> mix double for her.
⁷ As much as she magnified herself

and lived luxuriously,
give her the equivalent torment and sorrow,
for she says in her heart,
"I sit as queen, and I am not a widow,
and I will in no way see sorrow."
⁸ On account of this, her plagues
will come in one day,
death and mourning and famine,
and she will be burned up with fire,
for the Lord God
Who has judged her* *is* powerful.
⁹ And the kings of the Earth,
those having committed fornication
with her, and having lived luxuriously,
will weep and lament over her
when they see the smoke of her burning,
¹⁰ *while* they stand from afar
on account of the fear of her torment,
saying, "Woe, woe, the mighty city,
Babylon, the strong city!*
For in one hour your judgement has come."
¹¹ And the merchants of the Earth
will wail and mourn over her,
because nobody buys
their cargo any longer,
¹² cargo of gold and silver
and precious gemstones and pearls
and of fine linen and purple
and of silk and scarlet
and all citron wood
and every object of ivory
and every object of the most precious wood
and of copper and iron and marble,
¹³ and cinnamon and incenses
and scented ointment and frankincense
and wine and oil
and fine flour and wheat
and sheep and cattle
and horses and carriages
and of bodies and lives* of men,*
¹⁴ and the ripe fruits
of the craving* of your life*
have become deprived from you,
and all the luxurious and splendid things
have become lost to you,
and you will in no way find them any more.
¹⁵ The merchants of these things,
those enriched from her,
will stand at a distance
because of the fear of her torment,
weeping and wailing,
¹⁶ and saying, "Woe, woe, the mighty city
clothed in fine linen
and purple and scarlet

and ornamented with gold
and precious gemstones* and pearls!
¹⁷ For in one hour
such immense wealth was laid waste."
And every captain of a ship
and all the passenger company on the ships
and sailors
and as many who trade by the sea
stood at a distance,
¹⁸ and on turning their gaze
over the smoke of her burning
they were saying,
"What *is* comparable to the mighty city!"
¹⁹ And they threw dust on their heads
and called out, weeping and wailing,
and saying, "Alas, alas! That mighty city,
in which all having boats on the sea
were enriched from her wealth!
For in one hour she was brought to ruin."
²⁰ Rejoice over her, Heaven,*
and you holy people,*
and you apostles and you prophets,
because God exercised judgement
against her in your favour.'

²¹ And one strong angel took up a boulder like
a large millstone, and he threw *it* into the sea,
saying:

'With such violence
will Babylon, the mighty city,
be thrown down,
then it might be found no more.
²² And the sound of harpers and musicians
and of flute players and trumpeters
will not be heard in you any more,
and every craftsman of every craft
will not be found in you any more,
and a sound of a millstone
will not be heard in you any more,
²³ and a light of a lamp
will not shine in you any more,
and a voice of a bridegroom and bride
will not be heard in you any more,
for your merchants were
the magnates of the Earth,
for by your sorcery*
all the nations were deceived,
²⁴ and in her was found blood
of prophets and of holy people
and of all those murdered on the Earth."

The 7th vision in Heaven (19\1-16).
Rejoicing over judgement of the Great Whore.
Marriage to Israel the covenanted bride
(Jer. 31\31, Mat. 26\29)

19\1 **A**nd after these things I heard a loud
sound like a vast multitude in Heaven, saying:

'Alleluyah! The salvation and the power
and the preeminence of our God!
² For true and righteous *are* His judgements,
for He judged the Great Whore
who brought the Earth into ruin
with her fornication;
He has avenged the blood of His servants
shed by her hand.'*

³ And a second time they said, 'Alleluyah! And
her smoke ascends throughout the durations of
the Eons."**
⁴ And the twenty-four eldermen and the four
living creatures fell down and worshipped God,
the one sitting on the throne, saying, 'Amen.
Alleluyah!'
⁵ And a voice came from the throne, saying:

'Praise our God,
all you His servants
and those fearing Him,
the lowly and the eminent.'

⁶ And I heard a voice as if of a vast multitude,
and like a sound of many waters, and like a
sound of mighty thunderings, saying:

'Alleluyah! For *the* Lord our God,
the Almighty,* has exerted government.*
⁷ Let us rejoice and be exceedingly glad,
and give the preeminence to Him,
for the marriage* of the Lamb* has come,
and his wife has made herself ready.
⁸ And it was given to her
that she should be clothed
in resplendent and pure fine linen,
for fine linen stands for*
the righteous acts of the holy people.'

The Angel of God refuses worship (22\9)
⁹ And he said to me, 'Write: Exalted *are* those
called to the banquet of the marriage of the
Lamb.'*
And he said to me, 'These are the true oracles
of God.'
¹⁰ And I fell before his feet to worship him,

but he said to me, 'See not *to do that*!' I am a fellow servant of yours and of your brothers having the testimony of Jesus. Give worship to God, for the testimony of Jesus is the spirit of prophecy.'

The return & personal presence
(παρουσία, *parousia*) *of Jesus*
at the closure of the 490 year Eon.
His new name then, 'the Oracle of God'.
Preparation for the battle at Armageddon

[11] And I saw Heaven opened, and there was a white horse, and one sitting on it called Faithful and True, and in righteousness he judges and makes war. [12] And his eyes *were* like a flame of fire, and on his head *were* many diadems, having names written, and a name which nobody knows but himself, [13] and clothed with a garment dyed with blood, and his name is called the Oracle of God. [14] And the armies in Heaven followed him on white horses, clothed in fine linen, white and pure. [15] And out of his mouth goes a sharp double-edged sword so that he can strike the nations with it. And he himself will shepherd them with an iron sceptre, and he himself treads the winepress of the wine of the boiling anger of the indignation of God the Almighty. [16] And on *his* garment and on his thigh he has a name written, King of kings and Lord of lords.

The 7th vision on the Earth (19\17 – 20\15).
Destruction of the Wild Beast & Pseudo Prophet

[17] And I saw an angel standing on the Sun, and he called out with a loud voice, saying to all the birds flying at a high point of the sky:

'Come and gather yourselves together
    for the feast of the mighty God,
[18]   so that you can eat flesh of kings
    and flesh of commanders of a thousand
    and flesh of the mighty men
    and flesh of horses
    and of those who sit on them
    and flesh of all *men*,
    both freemen and servants,
    and both lowly and eminent.'

[19] And I saw the Wild Beast, and the kings of the Earth, and their armies, gathered together to make war with the one sitting on the horse and with his army. [20] And the Wild Beast was captured, and with him the Pseudo Prophet performing the signs in his presence, by which he deluded those having received the tattoo of the Wild Beast, and those worshipping his image. These two were hurled alive into the lake of fire burning with brimstone. [21] And the rest were killed with the sword having projected out of the mouth of the one sitting on the horse, and all the birds were filled with their flesh.

The imprisonment of Satan
at the opening of the 1,000 year Eon.
Overcomers reign with Jesus for the 1,000 years

20\1 And I saw an angel coming down out of Heaven, having the key of the abyss and a large chain in his hand. [2] And he took hold of the Dragon, the Snake of old, who is *the* Devil and Satan, and he shackled him up for a thousand years, [3] and he threw him into the abyss, and shut and sealed it over him, so that he no longer deceives the nations until the thousand years should be fulfilled. And after that he has to be loosed a short time.

[4] And I saw thrones, and *people* took their seats on them, and judgement was given to them. And *I saw* the corpses of those having been beheaded with an axe on account of the testimony of Jesus, and on account of the oracle of God, and whoever did not worship the Wild Beast or his image, and did not receive the tattoo on the foreheads and on their hand, and they lived again and reigned with Christ for the thousand years.

[5]   But the rest of the dead did not live until the thousand years would be finished.

This *is* the former resurrection. [6] Exalted and holy *is* he having part in the former resurrection. The second death has no power over these, but they will be priests of God and of the Christ, and they will reign with him for a thousand years.

Final judgement of Satan
at the end of the 1,000 year Eon

[7]   And when the thousand years have been completed, Satan will be loosed out of his prison, [8] and he will go out to delude the nations, those in the four quarters of the Earth, Gog and Magog, to gather them together for the war, whose number *is* like the sand of the seashore. [9] And they went through the breadth of the land, and encircled the camp of the holy people and the Loved City, and fire came down out of Heaven from God and devoured them,

[10] and the Devil deluding them was hurled into the lake of fire and brimstone* where the Wild Beast and the Pseudo Prophet also *had been hurled*, and they will be* tormented* day and night, throughout* the durations of the Eons.**

Judgements before the white throne
from the Scrolls & the Scroll of Life.
The 'destruction of ungodly men'
(2 Peter 3\7, Mat. 7\13-14, John 3\16)
[11]   And I saw a tremendous white throne,* and Him sitting on it, from Whose face the Earth and the sky* fled away, and no place was found for them. [12] And I saw the dead, the eminent and the lowly,** standing before the throne, and the Scrolls were opened, and another Scroll was opened which is *the Scroll* of Life, and the dead were judged out of the things written in the Scrolls,* in relation to their works. [13] And the sea gave up the dead in it, and death and the grave* gave up the dead in them, and they were judged, each in relation to their works. [14] And death and the grave* were hurled into the lake of fire.*

This* is the second death,* the lake of fire.
[15]   And if anybody* was found not written* in the Scroll* of Life,* he was hurled into the lake of fire.*

The 'day of God' (2 Peter 3\12).
The new heaven & the new Earth.
Believers seated in the New Jerusalem (21\3,
2 Cor. 6\16, Gal. 4\26, Eph. 1\3, 2\6,
2\18-22, Heb. 12\22-23).
Other kings & people on the new Earth (21\24).
Exclusions (21\8, 1 Cor. 6\9-10, etc.)

21\1   **A**nd I saw a new heaven and a new Earth, for the former heaven* and the former* Earth had come to an end,* and there is no longer any sea.*
[2]   And I saw the Holy City, New Jerusalem,* coming down out of Heaven* from God, and prepared like a bride adorned for her husband.
[3]   And I heard a loud voice out of Heaven saying:

'See this now:
the Tabernacle of God *is* with men,
and He will tabernacle with them*
and they will be His peoples
and God Himself will be with them.
[4]   And He will wipe away*
every tear from their eyes,*

and no longer will there be death,
nor sorrow, nor wailing,*
nor will there be any more distress,
for the former things
have come to an end.'*

[5]   And the one sitting on the throne said, 'See now, I make all things new.'*

And He said to me, 'Write *it* down, for these oracles are true and faithful.'*
[6] And He said to me, 'It has come!' I am* the Alpha and the Omega,* the Beginning and the End.* To him who is thirsty I will freely give *drink* out of the fountain* of the water of life. [7] The one overcoming will inherit these things, and I will be God to him, and he will be a son to Me.* [8] But for *the* cowardly,* and those against the faith, and violators, and *the* detested, and murderers, and sexually filthy,* and sorcerers,* and idolaters, and all the pseudos,* their part *is* in the lake burning with fire and brimstone, which is the second death.'*

John taken by one of the angels
& shown the New Jerusalem
[9]   And one of the seven angels holding the seven bowls, being full* of the seven last plagues, came and spoke with me, saying, 'Come,* *and* I will show you the wife, the bride of the Lamb.'**
[10]   And he transported me by the agency of *the* Spirit* to a vast and high mountain, and he showed me the mighty city, the holy Jerusalem, descending out of Heaven* from God,* [11] having the magnificence of God, its brilliant light *sparkling* like an especially precious gemstone, like a jasper gem, shining with crystalline brilliance, [12] having a vast and high wall, having twelve gates, and twelve angels at the gates, and names inscribed which are names of the twelve tribes of the sons of Israel: [13] from* *the* East three gates, and from *the* North three gates, and from *the* South three gates, and from *the* West three gates, [14] and the wall of the city has twelve foundations, and names on them* of the twelve apostles of the Lamb.*
[15]   And the one speaking with me had a golden reed so that he could measure the city, and its gates, and its wall. [16] And the city lies as a quadrangle, and its length *is* the same as the breadth, and he measured the city with the reed *as* 12,012* stadium lengths.* The length and the breadth and the height of it are equal.
[17]   And he measured its wall as 144 forearm

lengths,* by a man's measurement, which is the angel's.* ¹⁸ And the structure* of its wall was *of* jasper, and the city *was* pure gold, like clear glass.

¹⁹ The foundations of the wall of the city were adorned with every precious stone. The first foundation *was* jasper, the second sapphire, the third chalcedony, the fourth emerald, ²⁰ the fifth sardonyx, the sixth sardius, the seventh chrysolyte, the eighth beryl, the ninth topaz, the tenth chrysoprasus, the eleventh jacinth, the twelfth amethyst.

²¹ And the twelve gates *were* twelve pearls. Each one of the gates respectively* was from one pearl, and the street of the city pure gold, like transparent glass.

²² And I saw no Sanctuary in it, for the Lord God the Almighty* is* its Sanctuary,* the Lamb also. ²³ And the city has no need of the Sun or of the Moon that they should shine in* it, for the radiance of God illuminated it, and* the Lamb* *is* its light.*

Kings of the Earth
bring tribute to the New Jerusalem

²⁴ And the nations* will walk by its light, and the kings of the Earth bring into it for him* *the* glory and honour* of the nations.* ²⁵ And its gates will not be closed at all by day, for there will be no night there, ²⁶ and they will bring into it the glory and honour of the nations.

²⁷ And nothing profane will in any way enter into it, nor those committing an abomination and a lie,* but only those written in the Scroll* of Life of the Lamb.*

The river of life & the Tree of Life
in the Paradise of God (2\7, Luke 23\43)
for healing the nations

22\1 **A**nd he showed me a pure river of water of life, as bright as crystal, proceeding out of the throne of God and* of the Lamb.* ² In the middle of its street, and on each side of the river, *was* the Tree* of Life,* producing twelve types of fruits every month, each yielding its fruit, and the leaves of the Tree* *are* for the healing* of the nations.

The thrones of the Father and the Son
will be in the New Jerusalem

³ And every curse will be no more,* and the throne of God and* of the Lamb* will be in it. And His servants will serve Him, ⁴ and they will

see His face, and His name *will be* on their foreheads. ⁵ And there will be no night there, and they will have no need of a lamp or light of *the* Sun, for *the* Lord God will give them light, and they will reign throughout* the durations of the Eons.*

Jesus speaks to John. Exaltation
repeated for believing this prophecy (1\3)

⁶ And he said to me, 'These oracles *are* faithful and true, and *the* Lord God of the spirits of the prophets* authorized His Angel* to show His servants the things which must be soon* to arise.* ⁷ And see now,* I am coming quickly.* Exalted *is* the one keeping the oracles of the prophecy of this Scroll.'*

The Angel of God
again refuses worship (19\10)

⁸ And I, John,* *am* the one hearing and seeing* these things. And when I heard and saw, I fell down to worship at the feet of the Angel* showing me these things.

⁹ And he said to me, 'See not *to do that*' I am a fellow servant of you, and of your brothers the prophets, and of those who keep the oracles of this Scroll.* Give worship to God.'*

¹⁰ And he said to me, 'You should not seal the oracles of the prophecy of this Scroll,* for the time is near.* ¹¹ The one acting wickedly let him act more wickedly still; and the one defiled in filth let him be more defiled in filth still; and the one righteous let him exert more righteousness still; and the one who *is* holy let him be made more holy still.'*

Jesus addresses John concerning his return

¹² 'And, as you will see,* I am coming quickly,* and my reward *is* with me, to give to each individually, whatever his work will be.

¹³ 'I *am* the Alpha and the Omega,* the First and the Last,* the Beginning and the End.*

¹⁴ 'Exalted *are* those carrying out His commandments, so that their authority will be over the Tree* of Life,* and they can enter by the gates into the city. ¹⁵ Outside *are* the dogs, and the sorcerers,* and the sexually filthy,* and the murderers, and the idolaters, and everybody loving and fashioning a lie.*

¹⁶ 'I, Jesus, sent my Angel* to testify to you these things concerning* the Ekklesia groups. I am the Root and the Lineage of David, the Bright and Morning Star.'*

[17] And the Spirit* and the bride say, 'Come.'*

And let him hearing confirm, 'Come.'*

And him thirsting let him come,* *and* him being resolved let him gather* freely *the* water of life.*

Plagues & destruction for adding to or taking from this prophecy (cp. 1\3, 22\7; & 2 Peter 3\16)

[18] I myself make the testimony to everybody hearing the oracles of the prophecy of this Scroll: If anybody should add to them, God will add* to him the plagues written in this Scroll.* [19] And if anybody should take away from the oracles of the Scroll* of this prophecy, may God take away his share from the Tree of Life,* and from the Holy City *and* the things written in this Scroll.**

[20] The one testifying to these things says, 'Yes, I am coming quickly.'*

Amen. Yes,* come,* Lord Jesus.

[21] The merciful goodwill of the Lord Jesus Christ *be* with all the holy people.* Amen.

~ *the end of the Revelation of Jesus Christ* ~
~ *& the end of the God-authorized Greek Books* ~
~ *& the end of all the body*
of God-authorized Hebrew & Greek Writings ~
~ *& the end of all spoken*
& written revelation in all languages
until the favourable intervention,
which is the ἐπιφάνεια *(epiphaneia) of Jesus.* ~
Amen.

~ ◆◆ ~

Eonian Document 3

**The Development of the God-authorized Books
translated into English
from the Hebrew Masoretic Text
and
the Greek Byzantine Majority Texts**

✦

The Anglo-Saxons began the first English translations, made only in parts. John Wycliffe (1320-1384) and William Tyndale (?-1536) made complete translations, and were murdered for their work. Since Wycliffe's first complete English translation, 635 years ago, there have been over 150 English versions. *The Concordant Version*, by AE Knoch (1926), commendably has 'eonian life' and 'ecclesia'; it understood Romans 9\3; it had a fair go at John 1\1; it almost got John 11\26 right; but it is based on deplete manuscripts; has traditional errors; its John 17\5 is ungrammatical; it is archaic; mixes tenses; and has many curiosities ('log of life'; 'flying creatures') and numerous other problems. One million copies of the *Revised Standard Version* (based on a non-Byzantine text) are said to have been sold on the first day of its publication on the 30th of September 1952. Since that version, over 90 English versions have been made, most of them no more than paraphrases based on deplete manuscripts.

The Law and Prophets and Psalms, Genesis to 2 Chronicles,
written in Hebrew
by the God-authorized prophets and scribes,
starting with Moses (probably about 1400 BC),
probably completed by about 500 BC;
preserved in Hebrew Masoretic Scrolls
∎
∎
The Gospel Accounts and the Letters and Revelation
written in Greek
by the God-authorized apostles,
probably completed by about 68 AD;
preserved in Greek Majority (Byzantine) texts

∎
∎ [← Latin Vulgate, principally Jerome,
c. 390 AD]
∎
∎
Early English (Anglo-Saxon) versions:
Caedmon's Paraphrase (7th century);
Aldhelm, Abbot of Malmesbury, translation of Psalms (8th century);
Egbert (?-766), translation of Gospels (8th century);
Bede, an Abbot, translation of Gospel of John (735);
King Alfred the Great's Psalms (9th century);
Aldred, The Lindisfarne Gospels (10th century);
Aelfric, sections of the Hebrew Books (10th century)
The Wessex Gospels, also known as West Saxon Gospels (c990)
∎

■

Wycliffe Bible (John Wycliffe, 1380, revised & completed 1384, 1388-90);
translated from the Latin Vulgate,
the first full *hand-written* English manuscripts;
Wycliffe was declared a 'heretic' and his writings banned;
died of a stroke 1384; in 1428 Pope Martin V commanded Wycliffe's body
to be exhumed and burned and his ashes to be scattered in the River Swift;
'You say it is heresy to speak of the Holy Scriptures in English.
You call me a heretic because I have translated the Bible into the common tongue
of the people. Do you know whom you blaspheme?'

■

■

William Tyndale's New Testament (1526, 1534);
first translation into English
directly from the Greek manuscripts;
first New Testament *printed* in English;
murdered by strangling and burning in 1536:
'If God spare my life, I will see to it that the boy who drives the plowshare
knows more of the scripture than you, Sir';
described as 'the architect of the English language'

■

Coverdale Bible (1535);
sourced from Tyndale, Latin and Luther's German versions;
first *complete printed* English Bible

■

John Rogers, pseudonym Thomas Matthew (1537, 1549);
first version translated wholly from the Hebrew and Greek,
composite of own work and Tyndale's and Coverdale's;
second complete Bible printed in English;
Rogers burned in 1555

■

Taverner Bible (Richard Taverner, 1539);
mostly revision of Matthews Bible;
first Bible allowed for public use

■

Great Bible (Miles Coverdale, 1539, revised 1541);
worked mostly from Tyndale, Apocrypha,
Latin Vulgate, and German versions

■

Geneva Bible (1560);
Calvinist; first Bible with verse numbers

■

Bishops' Bible (1568);
mostly work of English bishops

■

Rheims New Testament (1582);
Roman Catholic version, from the Latin Vulgate

■

■

Douai Old Testament (1609);
Roman Catholic version, from the Latin Vulgate

■

King James Version (1611);
also known as the Authorised Version;
ordered by King James 1 in 1604, the work of about 54 men;
revised 1629, 1638, 1762, 1769

■

Rheims-Douai Bible OT and NT (1633);
first complete Roman Catholic version

■

Robert Aitken (1734-1802);
first English Bible printed in America

■

Noah Webster (1833);
mainly revision of KJV; sometimes called The Common Version

■

Young's Literal Translation (Robert Young, 1862)

■

The Englishman's Greek New Testament Interlinear (Samuel Bagster, 1877)

■

■ [← new form of attack launched by
Westcott and Hort, from deplete Greek
manuscripts, The Revised Version, 1881]

■

Interlinear Greek-English New Testament (GR Berry, 1897)

■

The Holy Scriptures (JN Darby, 1890)

■

The Book of Job (EW Bullinger, c1910?)

■

The Companion Bible (EW Bullinger, 1921)
a King James Version, a pioneering work with countless corrections,
enhancements, and 198 appendices

■

The Interlinear Bible: Greek-English (Jay P Green, Sr., 1980);
and Hebrew-Greek-English (Jay P Green, Sr., 1986)

■

Revised Authorized Version, New King James Version (1979, 1982)

■

The Resultant Version: a translation of Ephesians
with notes (Otis Q Sellers, c1980)

■

The 21st Century New King James Version (1994)

■

Analytical-Literal Translation (Gary Zeolla, 1999-2001)[1]

■

English Majority Text Version (Paul Esposito, 2010?)[2]

■

Far Above All, New Testament (Graham Thomason, 2011)[3]

■

The Eonian Books: Matthew to Revelation (Christopher Sparkes, 2015)[4]
The Eonian Books: Genesis to 2 Chronicles (Christopher Sparkes, in preparation)

1, 2, 3, 4. All these are based on the Robinson-Pierpont Textform.

Eonian Document 4
The Proper Order of the Books

English translations have the Hebrew Books in the wrong order, creating an annoying mess of the divine structure. We know from the words of Christ what the order is: 'all things must be fulfilled which have been written in **the Law of Moses, and the Prophets, and the Psalms** concerning me' (Luke 24\44). Christ spoke of 'the blood of the righteous **Abel** to the blood of **Zechariah**' (Matthew 23\35); that is, from the time of Abel in Genesis 4\2 to the time of Zechariah in 2 Chronicles 35\8, the last Hebrew book). So 2 Chronicles marks the end of the Hebrew Books. This order which Christ described can be ascertained from any Hebrew Bible. (Exceptionally, though, the *Hebrew-English Interlinear* of JP Green Sr. unfortunately follows the errant order, although Green did know the proper order.) There is, therefore, an internal divinely-established order of the Hebrew Books. The correct order makes finding Books in the Hebrew Writings easy because it is in three logical sections, whereas the current order in English translations is illogical, wrong, and unhelpful.

There is no internal passage giving a divinely-established order of the Greek Books. In the Robinson-Pierpont text, the individual Books follow the familiar *groupings*; however, the *order* within the groupings in their text is not the same: the four Gospels, Acts, other apostles' letters (Jacob (James), 1 Peter, 2 Peter, 1 John, 2 John, 3 John, Jude), Paul's letters (in this order: Romans, 1 Corinthians, 2 Corinthians, Galatians, Ephesians, Philippians, Colossians, 1 Thessalonians, 2 Thessalonians, Hebrews, 1 Timothy, 2 Timothy, Titus, Philemon), and Revelation. The position of Hebrews, standing between 2 Thessalonians and 1 Timothy, intentionally separates Paul's local Ekklesia letters from those written to individuals. Robinson and Pierpont comment on this ordering: 'Individual manuscripts present the New Testament books in various arrangements; nevertheless, a particular Greek "canonical order" seems to have been popular during early transmissional history. This order is partially evidenced within various early papyri and manuscripts, and occurs in the fourth-century Festal Letter of Athanasius (AD 367) and the list of canonical books attributed to the Laodicean Council (AD 360/363) ... The individual books within each category follow the familiar order ... [William HP] Hatch shows that this order is found among early and geographically diverse Greek manuscripts, fathers, and versions, and was retained among some manuscripts over many centuries' (Robinson and Pierpont, pp. xvi-xvii, and footnote).

The *internally divine-set order* of Hebrew Books is this:

'The Law of Moses'
- Genesis
- Exodus
- Leviticus
- Numbers
- Deuteronomy

'The Prophets'
- Joshua
- Judges
- 1 & 2 Samuel
- 1 & 2 Kings
- Isaiah
- Jeremiah
- Ezekiel
- Hosea
- Joel
- Amos
- Obadiah
- Jonah
- Micah
- Nahum
- Habakkuk
- Zephaniah
- Haggai
- Zechariah
- Malachi

'The Psalms'
- The Book of Psalms
- Proverbs
- Job
- Song of Songs
- Ruth
- Lamentations
- Ecclesiastes
- Esther
- Daniel
- Ezra
- Nehemiah
- 1 and 2 Chronicles

Eonian Document 6: Coins and Measures and Occurrences
✦

CURRENCY

assarion: ασσάριον (= *assarion*). A Roman copper coin, equivalent to 1/10th of a drachma, 1/16th of a denarion. KJV has 'farthing'. Matthew 10\29, Luke 12\6.

denarion: δηνάριον (= *deenarion*). A Roman silver coin, about a day's wages (Matthew 22\10). It originally consisted of ten (hence its name) and later (from BC 217) sixteen asses (Thayer). KJV has 'pence', 'penny', 'pennyworth'. Matthew 18\28, 20\2, 20\9, 20\10, 20\13, 22\19, Mark 6\37, 12\15, 14\5, Luke 7\41, 10\35, 20\24, John 6\7, 12\5, Revelation 6\6 (twice).

double-drachma: δίδραχμον (= *didrachmon*). A two drachma coin. Thayer: 'silver coin equivalent to two Attic drachmas or one Alexandrian, or half a shekel.' KJV has 'tribute'. Only occurs at Matthew 17\24 (twice).

drachma: δραχμή (= *drachmee*). A Greek silver coin, about a day's wages. Thayer: 'prop. a grip, a handful ... a silver coin of [nearly] the same weight as the Roman *denarius*.' KJV has 'pieces of silver', 'piece'. Luke 15\8 (twice) and 15\9, in the parable of the lost coin.

kodrantes: κοδράντης (= *kodrantees*). Greek form of a Latin word for Roman coin *quadrans*. Low value coin, equivalent to 2 leptons (see Mark 12\42), ¼ of an assarion. KJV has 'farthing'. Matthew 5\26, Mark 12\42.

lepton: λεπτός (= *leptos*). Small Greek brass coins of the lowest value, ½ value of a kodrantes, 1/8th of an assarion. Thayer: 'λέπω to strip off the bark, to peel ... *thin, small ... a very small brass coin*, equiv. to the eighth part of an [assarion]'. KJV has 'mite'. Mark 12\42, Luke 12\59, 21\2.

silver coin: στατήρ (= *stateer*). A silver coin (see Matthew 17\24, 17\27). Thayer: 'fr. ἵστημι, to place in the scales, weigh out ... equiv. to four Attic or two Alexandrian drachmas, a Jewish shekel.' KJV has 'piece of money'. Only occurs at Matthew 17\27.

talent: τάλαντον (= *talanton*). A currency weight, at some time equal to 6,000 drachmas, probably in Jesus' time about a quarter of that. Matthew 18\24, 25\15-28. There is also ταλαντιαῖος (= *talantiaios*) at Revelation 16\21, meaning 'talent-sized', which *The Companion Bible* gives as 'About 114 lb.'. I translate this loosely as 'about a hundred pound weight'.

MEASURES

forearm's length: πῆχυς (= *peekus*). Thayer: 'a measure of length equal to the distance from the joint of the elbow to the tip of the middle finger'. This measurement of a forearm is the same for a man as it is for an angel's (Revelation 21\17). KJV has 'cubit'. Matthew 6\27, Luke 12\25, John 21\8, Revelation 21\17.

litra: λίτρα (= *litra*). A litra was about 12 ounces, ¾ of a pound. Thayer: 'a weight of twelve ounces'. KJV has 'pound'. John 12\3, 19\39.

mina: μνᾶ (= *mna*). 1.25 pounds weight, equivalent to 50 shekels. Thayer: 'in the O.T. a weight, and an imaginary coin or money of account, equal to one hundred shekels ... In Attic a weight and a sum of money equal to one hundred drachmae.' KJV has 'pound'. Only in the narrative in Luke: 19\13, 19\16 (twice), 19\18 (twice), 19\20, 19\24 (twice), 19\25.

shekel: שֶׁקֶל (= *shekel*). Israeli measurement. About 4 day's wages in money, and about 11.4 grams in weight. The shekel is 20 gerahs (see Leviticus 27\25). Does not occur in the God-authorized Greek Writings.

stadium length: στάδιον (= *stadion*). Same word for 'stadium' at 1 Corinthians 9\24, so presumably the length of a stadium. According to Thayer, 600 Greek feet, 625 Roman feet, 125 Roman paces, 1/8th Roman mile. KJV has 'furlong', 'race' (1 Corinthians 9\24). Luke 24\13, John 6\19, 11\18, 1 Corinthians 9\24, Revelation 14\20, 21\16.

Eonian Document 11

Companion Eonian Notes to Daniel 9\20-27:
Concerning the Future 490 Years

✦

THE TEXT OF DANIEL 9\20-27
(notes are indicated by a superscripted asterisk on that word or phrase)

The angel Gabriel gives Daniel
understanding about the vision & his people Israel
²⁰ And while I was speaking, and praying, and declaring my violation and the violation of my people Israel, and presenting my request before Yahweh my Elohim, for the holy mountain of my Elohim, ²¹ yes, while I was speaking in prayer, the man Gabriel,* whom I had seen in the vision at the beginning, then touched me during *my* severe exhaustion at about the time of the evening sacrifice.
²² And he enlightened *me*, and he talked with me and said, 'Daniel, I have now come to teach you skill and understanding. ²³ At the beginning of your requests the oracle went out, and I have come to make a revelation to *you*, for you are deeply loved. Therefore understand the oracle,* and consider the vision:*

Gabriel tells Daniel of the future 70 sevens
(490 years; also at Mat. 18\22),
a time for the six awesome purposes of righteousness
& purity in Israel to endure for the Eons
²⁴ 'Seventy sevens** are determined* for your people* and for your holy city, to put an end to the transgression, and to make an end of violations, and to make atonement for iniquity,* and to bring in the righteousness of the Eons,* and to seal up the vision and prophecy, and to anoint *the* Most Holy Place.**

Cyrus to restore the damaged Jerusalem over 49 years.
434 years to follow, under the anointed man David
²⁵ 'Know therefore, and understand, *that* from the issuing of the command to restore and to build Jerusalem,* until *the time of* the anointed *man*,* the prince,* *there will be* 7 sevens,** and 62 sevens.** The plaza* will be built again, and the narrow street,* during times of affliction.**

Before the final 7 of the 490 years,
David cut off by a despot;
the Temple given over to abominations
²⁶ 'And after the 62 sevens** the anointed *man** will be cut off,** but *with* no sign of anything for himself.* And a people of the coming ruler* will destroy the city and the Holy Place. But his own end *will come* with a flood, and until the full end of the war desolate places are determined.
²⁷ And he will make a firm covenant with the many for 1 seven, and in the middle of that seven* he will cause the sacrifice and the offering to cease, and in its place *he will arrange* for the overspreading of the abomination which causes desolation* until* the consummation, and that *which is* determined will come pouring out on the causes of desolation.'

✱

9\21 *the man Gabriel.* Most angels (though not all; eg Isaiah 6\2, Ezekiel 28\12-13), appear in the form of men, not as Christmas card images.

9\23 *oracle ... oracle:* רבד (= *dabar*). KJV renders this word differently in this verse, having 'commandment' and 'matter'.

9\23 *the vision:* It is important to recognize that the angel and Daniel himself refer to the 'seventy sevens' as 'the vision'. The 'vision' which the angel gives to Daniel – and is described in chapters 10, 11 and 12 – concerns Daniel's 'people' (9\24) 'in the latter days' and in '*many* days yet' (10\14). Even today, not one micro-second of the vision of the 'seventy sevens' has been fulfilled.

9\24 *sevens:* שבוע (= *shabua*). Seven, often signifying weeks. KJV has 'weeks' and always renders as 'week' except at Ezekiel 45\21. When this word means 'week', or when it means the cardinal number 'seven', is determined by context.

9\24 *Seventy sevens:* שבעים שבעים (= *shabueem shebueem*). So 490 years. This 490 year Eon is the same as the coming Eon (Mark 10\30, Luke 18\30) and 'the Sovereign Rule of the heavens' (Matthew 3\2). Peter speaks of 'the Eonian Sovereign Rulership of our Lord and Saviour Jesus Christ' (2 Peter 1\11).

These 'seventy sevens' are not the same period as the 'seventy years' referred to earlier in Daniel 9\2. Nor are they the same as the 'day for a year' principles at Numbers 14\34 and Ezekiel 4\6.

Christ hinted at this time of the 490 years when he spoke of having forgiveness 'seventy times seven' times (Matthew 18\22), that is, 490 times, and in his next sentence he spoke of 'the Sovereign Rule of the heavens'. That Christ should speak of 'seventy times 7' in this way shows that the 490 years were still unfulfilled in his time, still very much FUTURE – and still are FUTURE.

The 'Eonian life' and 'the Sovereign Rule of the heavens' spoken of time and again by Christ meant life throughout the 490 years. Jesus told Martha that whoever believes in him 'will most certainly not die throughout the Eon' (John 11\26).

Daniel too spoke of this 'Eonian life', saying: 'And many from among them who sleep in the dust of the ground will awake, some to Eonian life, and some to reproaches and Eonian abhorrence. And those who are wise will shine like the brightness of the firmament, and those who turn many to righteousness like the stars throughout the Eon and its duration' (Daniel 12\2-3).

9\24 *determined:* התך (= *hathak*). KJV has the same. Only occurs here. Gesenius (see Bibliography) says: 'properly TO CUT, TO DIVIDE ... hence *to decree, to determine*'. The *Companion Bible* (TCB) says: 'cut off: i.e. divided off from all other years'. These years, then, are not like other years. TCB continues: 'The verb is in the singular to indicate the unity of the whole period.' The continuous and uninterrupted 490 years are measured by Gabriel in this way:

7 sevens =	49 years of rebuilding and restoring;
62 sevens =	434 years;
1 seven =	7 years of rebellion and the Wild Beast

Total: 70 x 7 = 490 years

That these 'seventy sevens' each represent seven year periods is shown in the corresponding parallel passages in Daniel and Revelation. They describe the final 7 years being divided in 'years' and 'months' and 'days'.

The 70th 'seven' – the last 7 years of the 490 years – is described in two halves, one half being 'a time and times and the dividing of time' and '3½ years' and '42 months' and '1,260 days' (Daniel 7\25, 8\14, also see 12\11-12, and Revelation 11\2-3, 12\6, 13\5). This last 7 years will be the time of the Wild Beast and the Pseudo Prophet.

The word of tradition spoke falsely and made pretence that the 490 years suffer a long interruption between the 69 sevens (483 years) and the final 1 seven (7 years). Those mistaken theologians said that the 49 and 434 years (= 483) already occurred between the time of Daniel and the time of Christ. And they claimed that only the 70th, the final 7 years, remain – so, nearly a 2,000 year hiatus so far by their scheme (actually, 2,500 years, since none of it has even started). But that reasoning is no good. If interruptions should be made between the periods, why, then, did those errant theologians make a wild interruption between the 483 years and the 7 years, but make no interruption between the first period, the 7 sevens (49 years) and the 62 sevens (434 years)? But the fact is, there is no interruption at all in any of the 490 year period. If there were, Gabriel would have said so. The 490 years are a continuous, uninterrupted period which will commence with a resurrection and the rebuilding of a destroyed Jerusalem.

All the tension disappears when we project the whole of this 490 years into the FUTURE, as we must do. All the moral and social conditions and the standing before God demonstrate that this is unfulfilled: 'to finish the transgression ... to make an end of violations ... to make reconciliation for iniquity ... to bring in the righteousness of the Eons ... to seal up the vision and prophecy ... to anoint the Most Holy Place' (9\24). It could not be more obvious that not a single one of these conditions has ever been fulfilled anywhere at any time.

The conditions in Israel between the time of Daniel and the time of Christ were the *opposite* conditions of these listed in Daniel 9\24.

On top of it all, Israel was not even under covenant with God in that period between Daniel and Jesus, Jeremiah having already written of the divorce by God from Israel, Hosea having made declaration that Israel was not God's people.

9\24 *seventy sevens are determined for your people*: That is, as shown:

       '7 sevens' of rebuilding;

       '62 sevens';

       '1 seven' of desolation.

This period, 'for your people', is for Daniel's people – Israel and Judah. There must be a resurrection, therefore, before the 490 years to enable this to happen. It is, presumably, the dramatic resurrection described in Ezekiel 37. For how can they enjoy the 490 years if they are not raised? If they are not raised, then it is not a time for Daniel's people. Also, Christ spoke of having forgiveness 'seventy times seven' times (Matthew 18\22), that is, 490 times: that demands their being alive for each

year of the 490 years. There has to be a resurrection first.

The old floggers of the word of tradition went to endless efforts to squeeze 483 of the 490 years into historical events which they randomly selected from the time of Daniel. The argument is false, because the 490 years are a time, Gabriel says here, for Daniel's 'people Israel' (Daniel 9\20, 9\24). When Gabriel spoke those words to Daniel, Israel was 'not My people' (Hosea 1\9), and was already divorced from God (Jeremiah 3\8). The designation shown by Gabriel is of 490 years of bringing in righteousness and of divine exaltation, not 490 years of Israel being divorced from God because of her iniquity. So how can the time between Daniel and Christ be thought of as a time for Daniel's people when those people were already cut off and divorced from God because of their iniquity and spiritual adultery? During the time between Daniel and Christ, Israel continued in iniquity, so much so that the leaders of Israel murdered Jesus. How could such a time of transgression and violation and iniquity also be a time of divine exaltation and making an end of transgression and violation and iniquity? How could a time of unrighteousness also be a time of establishing 'the righteousness of the Eons' (Daniel 9\24; with עוֹלָם = *olam*, in the plural, 'Eons')? How could a time being 'not' God's people also be a time for 'My people Israel'?

What a wide and wild chasm between detailed examination of the prophets and the cursory traditions of theology!

Because Israel was divorced from God, Christ had to speak of a time of a new covenant. The old marriage covenant had been annulled. So the idea that 483 of the 490 years were fulfilled in Christ's day implies that a time when Israel was divorced from God and 'not My people' is the same as a time of righteousness 'for your people'. That is a hopeless idea. Israel's divorce from God was because of her transgression, violation and iniquity. If that period did establish 'righteousness of the Eons', why did Israel's rulers reject and murder Jesus?

Those who do not believe in Christ will not inherit this coming 490 year period – nor the 1,000 years after it – and they will be resurrected at the end of the 1,000 years. Those who do believe in the true Jesus will be resurrected at the opening of the Eon (or will be already alive), and they will share in the inheritance of the fullness of the length of this Eonian life. Otherwise the constant phrase 'throughout the Eon' (John 11\26 et cetera) has no sense or meaning. This inheritance is 'Eonian life'. Daniel himself spoke of a coming 'Eonian life' (Daniel 12\2). And this is the same 'Eonian life' which Christ spoke of: 'For God so much loved the world that He gave His only Son, in order that everybody believing in him might not suffer destruction, but might have Eonian life' (John 3\16). Believers then will have life throughout the 490 years, and throughout the 1,000 years: 1,490 years of living throughout the dramatic events of Christ's rule, so by the end their wisdom will be vastly superior to the so-called wisdom of the ancients.

These 490 years are, Gabriel says, a time of establishing 'the righteousness of the Eons' ('establishing' because it will take time to progress), of putting 'an end to the transgression', to 'make an end of violations', and 'to make atonement for iniquity'. Israel, then, in this 490 years, will at last receive the divine exaltations looked forward to by the patriarchs and the prophets and the apostles.

For those who can receive the oracle of Christ and the prophets and apostles, the next major event is the favourable intervention, that is, the ἐπιφάνεια (= epiphaneia) of Christ, then will follow these 490 years. The apostle Paul tells us that we ought to 'live discreetly, righteously, and ruled by reverence in the present Eon, anticipating the exalted gladly-held expectation, and the favourable intervention of the magnificence of the Mighty God, and of our Saviour Jesus Christ' (Titus 2\12-13). For those, though, who want to stumble at the word of tradition and say that only 7 years of the 490 remain to be fulfilled, the next major event is the rise of the Wild Beast. Wild Beast next, or Jesus' rule next? It's Jesus, of course. We await 'the favourable intervention of the magnificence of the Mighty God, and of our Saviour Jesus Christ'.

9\24 *iniquity*. The rejection by Israel of God's commandments and His prophets (see Daniel 9\5-6).

9\24 *of the Eons*. עלמים (= olamim). Plural from

the noun עולם (= olam), 'Eon'. KJV has the errant 'everlasting', an adjective wrongly put for a plural noun, a grammatical violation masking the truth.

9\24 *the Most Holy Place*. Literally, 'the Holy of Holies'. Compare 'the Holy Place' at 9\26. KJV has just 'the most Holy'. TCB has 'a Holy of Holies', and it comments: 'Never used of a person. This answers to the cleansing of the sanctuary (8.14) which immediately precedes the end.'

9\24 *to put an end to the transgression ... to make an end of violations ... to make atonement for iniquity ... to bring in the righteousness of the Eons ... to seal up the vision and prophecy ... to anoint the Most Holy Place*. These six awesome purposes, determined for Israel in the duration of the seventy sevens, remain unfulfilled in Jerusalem. These are the delights Jerusalem has to look forward to in the coming Eons:

> to put an end to the transgression;
> to make an end of violations;
> to make atonement for iniquity;
> to bring in the righteousness of the Eons;
> to seal up the vision and prophecy;
> to anoint the Most Holy Place.

The single phrase 'the righteousness of the Eons' shows that the whole of the 490 years is FUTURE. No 'atonement for iniquity' could be made before Jesus, so the 490 years could not have begun in Daniel's day. It's impossible to say that those six purposes were fulfilled by the time of Christ's birth. The very *opposite* conditions were manifest in Israel between the time of Daniel and the time of Christ. For example, far from 'the Most Holy Place' being anointed at the time of Christ, Christ said of it, 'The scribes and the Pharisees have taken their place on [that is, stolen] the seat of Moses' (Matthew 23\2), then he proclaimed eight woes against those thieves. Within four decades, the Temple was destroyed.

These six purposes determined for Israel will take 490 years to fulfill. Isaiah 40\1-2 speaks prophetically of the fulfilment of God's awesome purposes:

[1] 'Comfort, comfort My people',
says your Elohim;

² 'Speak affectionately to Jerusalem,
and proclaim to her
that her hard service
is accomplished,
that her iniquity is pardoned,
for she has received in full
from the hand of Yahweh
for all her violations.' ~ Isaiah 40\1-2

9\25 *the command to restore and to build Jerusalem.*
The need to do this suggests that Jerusalem is going to be devastated. The 490 years will open with a resurrection and the time of rebuilding Jerusalem, and they will conclude with Christ's return to the Earth, as described in Matthew 24, 1 Thessalonians 4\13-18 and Revelation 19.

The issuing of 'the command to restore and to build Jerusalem' will one day in the FUTURE come from a resurrected Cyrus:

²⁸ '[He] says of Cyrus, "*He is* My shepherd
and he will perform all My pleasure",
and he will say to Jerusalem,
"You will be built",
and to the Temple,
"Your foundation will be laid."
¹ 'Yahweh says this to His anointed *man,*
to Cyrus, whose right hand I have held
to subdue nations before him
and I will weaken the loins of kings,
to open before him the two-leaved gates
so that the gates will not be shut:
² "I will go ahead of you
and make the crooked places level;
I will tear apart the gates of bronze
and cut apart the bars of iron."
~ Isaiah 44\28 – 45\1

This 'command' by Cyrus remains unfulfilled, therefore FUTURE. This FUTURE command for Cyrus cannot be anything to do with Artaxerxes' HISTORICAL letters of permission to Nehemiah, concerning restoration work which took just **52 days** (Nehemiah 2\7-9, 2\17, 6\15), and was the work of Nehemiah, not Cyrus. Nor can this FUTURE command by Cyrus be anything to do with his HISTORICAL command to build **the Temple** (Ezra 1\2-4), which is quite a different matter from both building the city of **Jerusalem** *and* laying the foundations of **the Temple** (Isaiah 44\28).

In the Isaiah passage cited above, Isaiah shows that Cyrus will in the FUTURE 'build'

Jerusalem and 'lay the foundations' of **the Temple** (Isaiah 44\28). Like Isaiah, Gabriel too speaks of restoring and building '**Jerusalem**' and Gabriel implies the building of a **Temple** with the words 'Most Holy Place' (Daniel 9\24) and 'Holy Place' (Daniel 9\26). So then, these FUTURE restorations are not the same as Cyrus's HISTORICAL command which was only for 'building [God] a **House** in Jerusalem' (Ezra 1\2, 1\3).

As a parenthesis, we should note that one of the accomplishments of the 490 years is 'to anoint the Most Holy Place' (Daniel 9\24; that cannot come until Christ's descent). After the end of the '62 sevens', the 'city and the Holy Place' will be destroyed (Daniel 9\26). These demand, then, that Cyrus's command to lay the foundations of **the Temple** (Isaiah 44\28) will have had fulfilment.

It might – *might* – indeed be correct that the time for carrying out Cyrus's command in Ezra 1\2-4 took from 454-405 BC (according to TCB, Appendix 50, p. 60), which is 49 years, if, that is, those dates can be relied on. It is also true that Herod's Temple took 46 years (John 2\20). Nevertheless, neither of those can be said to fulfill the FUTURE 'command to restore and to build **Jerusalem**' spoken of by Gabriel, nor can they be said to fulfill Cyrus's FUTURE command to build **Jerusalem** and lay the foundations of **the Temple** spoken of by Isaiah.

The opening of the book of Ezra says:

¹ ... Cyrus, king of Persia, ... made a proclamation throughout all his kingdom, and he *put it* in writing as well, saying: ² 'Cyrus, king of Persia, says this: Yahweh Elohim of the heavens has given me all the kingdoms of the Earth, and He has charged me with building Him a House in Jerusalem, which *is* in Judah. ³ Who *is there* among you, of all His people? May his Elohim be with him, and let him go up to Jerusalem, which *is* in Judah, and rebuild the House of Yahweh Elohim of Israel – He *is* the *true* Elohim – which *is* in Jerusalem.'
~ Ezra 1\1-3

Cyrus built a **HOUSE**, not the **city** of Jerusalem. In the FUTURE, Cyrus *will* build **JERUSALEM** *and* 'lay the foundations' of **THE TEMPLE**, which is '**THE HOUSE**'.

If anybody of an untidy mind should object to the differences between 'Jerusalem' and

'Temple', would he rather have his city wrecked, or a single building? One building restored, or the whole city? Pay architects for designing a city, or one building?

As a child I saw the bomb-wrecked Guildhall of Portsmouth under restoration, and I remember walking to school through a bomb-site somewhere near Palmerston Road. We can now say that the city has been rebuilt, but we would not say of Portsmouth that only the Guildhall has been rebuilt. The city includes the Guildhall, but the Guildhall does not include the city. Likewise, Cyrus's FUTURE command to restore **Jerusalem** *includes* laying 'the foundations' of **the Temple**, but Ezra's HISTORICAL command *did not include* the city, for 'Yahweh Elohim of the heavens' charged him only with 'building Him **a House** in Jerusalem' (Ezra 1\2).

On top of it all, Daniel's vision, according to TCB, was in 426 BC, and is all expressed in the FUTURE tense, whereas Cyrus's HISTORICAL command – expressed in the past tense – to build the Temple recorded in Ezra 1\2-4 was somewhere around 454 BC, 28 years *before* Daniel's vision. There is no justification for backdating the commencement of the 'seventy sevens'. On the contrary: Daniel was told that the vision the angel gave him after this one 'refers to *many* days yet' (Daniel 10\14); that applies to this 490 years vision as well. It cannot all be back-dated to 454 BC!

It seems that the restoring of Jerusalem will take 49 years ('7 sevens') during 'troublesome times'.

9\25 *anointed man*: מָשִׁיחַ (= *mashiach*). KJV has 'Messiah'. This 'anointed *man*' would seem to signify David. David refers to himself as 'the anointed of the Elohim of Jacob' (2 Samuel 23\1) and 'the anointed of Elohim' (2 Samuel 22\51), because he had been anointed as king of Israel: 'they anointed David king over Israel' (2 Samuel 5\3); and God promised him that 'your house and your kingdom will be established throughout the duration of the Eon before you. Your throne will be established throughout the duration of the Eon' (2 Samuel 7\16). David uses the word 'anointed' of himself in Psalms 18\50, 20\6, 28\8, 84\9, 89\38, 89\51, 105\15, 132\10, 132\17. At Psalm 18\43 he says, 'You have made me the head of the nations'. Psalm 89\27 calls David

the 'first-honoured, lord over the kings of the Earth'. Once Jerusalem has been restored, fit for a king, David will take up his position as anointed prince and ruler. At Isaiah 45\1 'the anointed *man*' is used of Cyrus. Christ is indeed the Messiah (μεσσίας – John 1\41, 4\25) and the anointed one (χριστός) but that מָשִׁיחַ (= *mashiach*) here in Daniel 9\25 does not refer to Christ (nor at Psalm 2\2 either), but to David.

9\25 *prince*: נָגִיד (= *nahgeed*). Here 'prince', in a positive sense, because David is the son of the King. KJV has 'ruler'. Also at 9\26 and 11\22 as 'ruler', in a negative sense.

9\25 *sevens*: שָׁבוּעַ (= *shabua*). KJV has 'weeks'.

9\25 *7 sevens*: It will take at least this long, 49 years, to rebuild Jerusalem after its coming desolation. Herod's Temple, Jesus said, 'was 46 years in being built' (John 2\20).

9\25 *sevens*: שָׁבוּעַ (= *shabua*). KJV has 'weeks'.

9\25 *62 sevens*: That is, with David as the anointed ruler (2 Samuel 7\16), in 'the Sovereign Rulership of the heavens' (Matthew 3\2). Nothing like that has been seen, but it will be seen.

9\25 *plaza*: רְחוֹב (= *r'chob*). TCB has 'the broadway or open space', KJV 'street'. First occurrence at Genesis 19\2 as 'street'.

9\25 *narrow street*: חָרוּץ (= *charuz*). KJV has 'wall'. TCB comments: 'Whatever it may mean, it cannot be "wall", for that is *homah* (that which surrounds).'

9\25 *in times of affliction*: This is nothing to do with the opposition to Nehemiah's work, which was only during the time he took of '52 days' (Nehemiah 6\15).

9\25 *to restore and to build Jerusalem ... the plaza ... the narrow street ... in times of affliction*: This implied devastation of Jerusalem is as yet unfulfilled. This, as already discussed, is nothing to do with the decree in Ezra, because that concerned a decree to build 'the **House** of Yahweh Elohim ... in Jerusalem' (Ezra 1\3), 'the **House** of Yahweh' (Ezra 1\5, 1\7 et cetera), but it did not concern the city of **Jerusalem** and its streets. Here is the comparison:

Daniel 9\25:
  'restore and ... build **JERUSALEM** ...
  the plaza ... and the narrow street';
Ezra 1\2:
  'building Him a **HOUSE** in Jerusalem'.

Those are not the same event and they are not the same conditions. We cannot pretend that **JERUSALEM** and **HOUSE** refer to the same thing. **The Temple** is God's **HOUSE**. **The Temple** and **the city** are not the same thing. The crippling reasoning that they *are* the same is perhaps derived from some unacknowledged fear that one's eschatology has been mangled – hence one's imagined (and false) hope for the future is exposed.

9\26 *sevens:* שבוע (= *shabua*). As 9\24. KJV has 'weeks'.

9\26 *And after the 62 sevens:* When the '62 sevens' (434 years) are finished, the '1 seven' (7 years) will commence, the days of the rebellion and the Wild Beast. There is no justification for inserting any gap of time between the 69th and 70th 'seven' as tradition has recklessly done. Not any single hint is given anywhere that we should do that. Somebody made it up.

Such false reasoning of inserting a gap is assisted by the wrong notion which many have taught that Israel was divorced at the time of Acts 28\28. That, however, is deep error, contradicting Jeremiah and Hosea and Jesus.

First, Paul could not have announced Israel's divorce because Israel was *already* divorced from God. She could not be divorced twice! Centuries earlier the prophet Jeremiah had announced Israel's divorce, saying, 'for all the causes by which rebellious Israel committed adultery, I had put her away, and I gave her a bill of divorce' (Jeremiah 3\8).

Second, this divorce was confirmed by the prophet Hosea who declared Israel to be 'lo-ammi', that is, 'not My people' (Hosea 1\9).

Third, in Paul's statement at Acts 28\28, he does not utter a single word about Israel being cut off. Where is that in the passage? What Paul actually said was, 'Let it be known to you, then, that the salvation-bringing *message* of God has been authorized to the nations, and they will

hear' – not a word about Israel's divorce.

What happened at the end of Acts concerned only the proclamation of the gospel: Paul would no longer proclaim 'to the Jew first' (Romans 1\16) – that is all that Acts 28\28 signifies. You cannot make Paul say anew what Jeremiah and Hosea had already pronounced centuries before, otherwise you can do anything you like with prophecy. Paul has nothing to say in Acts 28 concerning the divorce and cutting off of Israel; that was done centuries before him. To say that the apostle Paul pronounced the divorce and 'lo-ammi' which were, in undeniable fact, actually pronounced by the prophets Jeremiah and Hosea is like trying to say that Shakespeare wrote Chaucer's *Canterbury Tales*. You cannot legally forward-date a divorce certificate.

9\26 *anointed man:* משיח (= *mashiach*). David. KJV has 'Messiah', which is wrong. See note on this word at 9\25.

9\26 *will be cut off:* כרת (= *karath*). This shows that 'the anointed *man*' is not Jesus, as is claimed by the errant HISTORICAL view of the 490 years. Jesus was not 'cut off'! This is not the language ever used about Jesus. Nowhere in all the prophets and apostles is it suggested that Jesus was 'cut off'. On the contrary. He was raised out of death and ascended to the right hand of God: 'cut off' has absolutely no application whatever to any events concerning Jesus Christ.

9\26 *the anointed man will be cut off:* So that 'the day of the Lord' may begin, which is at the end of the 490 years.

9\26 *but with no sign of anything for himself:* After TCB. KJV has 'but not for himself'.

9\26 *ruler:* נגיד (= *nahgeed*). Here 'ruler', in a negative sense because this one is an enemy of God. KJV has 'ruler'. Also at 9\25 as 'prince', in a positive sense, and at 11\22 as 'ruler' in the negative sense.

9\27 *seven ... seven:* שבוע (= *shabua*). As the 'sevens' at 9\24, meaning 7 years. KJV has 'weeks'.

9\27 *the abomination which causes desolation:* Also

at 11\31, 12\11, and cited by Christ at Matthew 24\15.

9\27 *until.* עַד (= *ad*).

Conclusion
The building programmes
Passages concerning building programmes in Jerusalem can be summarized this way:

Past programmes
1. Cyrus, Ezra 1, the Temple, (time not stated) – *past.*
2. Nehemiah, Nehemiah 2–6, the city, 52 days – *past.*
3. Herod, John 2\20, the Temple, 46 years – *past.*

The future programme
4. Cyrus, Isaiah 44\28 – 45\1, (time not stated), the city and the Temple – *future.*
5. A command (Cyrus), Daniel 9\25, the city and the Temple, 490 years – *future.*

The building programme described by the prophets Isaiah and Daniel is still future. It will be taken up at the commencement of the 490 years which Daniel describes.

The six awesome purposes
We can conclude this prospect of the six awesome purposes of Daniel 9\24, which are determined for Israel in the duration of the 70 sevens, with this table, holding in the front of our minds that we must stick hard to Daniel's text in that these concern Daniel's people, Israel, and every defence of tradition's error has got to be utterly blocked out and crushed:–

to put an end to the transgression;	in Israel, for Daniel's people; hasn't happened;
to make an end of violations;	in Israel, for Daniel's people; hasn't happened;
to make atonement for iniquity;	in Israel, for Daniel's people; the atonement was made by Jesus and offered to Israel, but it was not accepted by the rulers of Israel; it went to the nations instead; Israel is still divorced from God and in iniquity; hasn't happened;
to bring in the righteousness of the Eons;	in Israel, for Daniel's people; Israel is still divorced from God; the Eons have not begun; there is a righteousness now, but it is a status granted mercifully by God, and it is abused by our violations; by contrast, in the coming Eons the Sons and Daughters of the Almighty will have complete righteousness that is from a mind able to overcome every violation, like their Lord and brother Jesus, and a resurrection body like his; the change now through conversion is only part complete; hasn't happened;
to seal up the vision and prophecy;	in Israel, for Daniel's people; vision and prophecy went on long after Jesus; hasn't happened;
to anoint the Most Holy Place.	in the Holy City; Temple destroyed AD 70; hasn't happened.

The word of tradition vainly wants us to believe that 483 of Daniel's 490 years – which are all future – were completed some time before and during Jesus' life. Those errant theologians attempted in vain to slyly spiritualize away the

490 years by speaking cloudily about righteousness in Jesus, as if that somehow unlocks the whole historical key of the 490 years in Israel. We are not confused by their error and pretence: Israel, divorced from God ever since the days of Jeremiah and Hosea, and *still* divorced from God, has not yet had her 490 year Eon of purity and righteousness, nor has her Most Holy Place been anointed.

The six beautiful conditions of those future 490 years are, Daniel says: 'to put an end to the transgression, and to make an end of violations, and to make atonement for iniquity, and to bring in the righteousness of the Eons, and to seal up the vision and prophecy, and to anoint *the* Most Holy Place' (Daniel 9\24). So then – far from light and righteousness – what do we find in Jesus' day?

Jesus came to an Israel already divorced from God. How, then, could she have been enjoying 'the righteousness of the Eons' (Daniel 9\24)? How can she have 'the righteousness of the Eons' when those 'Eons' have not even yet begun, not even now?

So: we find that Israel was long divorced from God; Joseph and Maria had to be warned to 'flee into Egypt' (Matthew 2\13); an evil child-killer was king of Israel (Matthew 2\16); 'the people ... were sitting in darkness' (Matthew 4\16); Israel was overrun with a 'progeny of snakes' (Matthew 3\7); the house of Israel were 'lost sheep' (Matthew 109\6); homicides, apostates and bad men were sitting in Moses' seat, hypocrites who had mangled the law with legalisms, imported Hellenistic Mysticism, and who could not 'escape from the judgement of the Valley of Hinnom' (Matthew 23\1-3, 23\33); Jesus was hunted, betrayed, and assassinated; the apostles were persecuted and put in jail; John the Identifier was assassinated; Jacob (James), brother of John, was assassinated; there was a plot to assassinate Paul. Some end of transgression, some end of violation, some atonement, some righteousness, some anointing of the Temple! Some beginning of the Eons! And 'vision and prophecy' were anything but sealed up: there were yet to come many prophecies and visions from Jesus, from John, from Peter, from Jude and from Paul. Far from 'righteousness of the Eons', this now is 'the Eon of darkness' and 'of evil' (Ephesians 6\12, Galatians 1\4), and 'the day of man' (1 Corinthians 4\3).

Tradition clings hard to its idle and fantastical notion that the 483 years were completed some time between the days of Daniel and the days of Jesus.

The truth, though, is that this present 'Eon of darkness' and 'of evil', 'the day of man', will soon come to an end. There will be a resurrection in Israel (Ezekiel 37), and a resurrection of all those who have believed in Jesus. Enoch and Elijah (Matthew 17\10-11), and Paul and all the prophets and apostles will appear (Deuteronomy 11\21, Psalm 89\29, Ephesians 1\3, 2\6, 2 Timothy 2\11-12, 4\1). Jerusalem will be rebuilt under the command of Cyrus. The Angel of God will guide the apostles with counsel from God (John 14\16-17, 14\26, 15\26, 16\7-11, Matthew 28\20) so that it truly will be a Sovereign Rulership from the heavens. The apostles will travel the world explaining the teachings about Jesus (Matthew 28\19-20). Israel will be purified and cleansed and she will be the head nation (Deuteronomy 28\13). Everything of the six awesome purposes in Daniel 9\24 will be accomplished. Believers will have indestructible bodies, not subject to death, and minds which cannot violate against God. They will live right throughout the 490 years, and then throughout the 1,000 years. Then they will be with God and Jesus as a ruling body in the New Jerusalem.

✳

Eonian Document 12A
Bibliography

✦

Alford, Henry, *The Greek Testament*, Vols. I-IV, Deighton, Bell, And Co., 3rd Edition (1866)

Bagster, Samuel, *The Analytical Greek Lexicon*, Samuel Bagster & Sons Limited, London W1 (1973, originally published 1870)

Bagster, Samuel *The Englishman's Greek New Testament*, Samuel Bagster & Sons Limited, London W1 (1896, originally published 1877)

Bagster, Samuel, *The Interlinear Greek-English New Testament*, Samuel Bagster & Sons Limited, London W1 (1958)

Berry, George Ricker, *Interlinear Greek-English New Testament*, Baker Book House, Michigan (1991, originally published 1897)

Bullinger, EW, *A Critical Lexicon and Concordance of the English and Greek New Testament*, Zondervan Publishing House, Grand Rapids, Michigan 49530 (1975, originally published 1887)

Bullinger, EW, *Also: A Biblical Study of the Usage of This Word in the Gospels and New Testament*, American Christian Press, New Knoxville, Ohio 45871 (no date)

Bullinger, EW, *Commentary on Revelation*, Kregel Publications, Grand Rapids, Michigan 4950 (1984, originally published 1902)

Bullinger, EW, *Figures of Speech Used in the Bible Explained and Illustrated*, Baker Book House, Grand Rapids, Michigan (1968, originally published 1898)

Bullinger, EW, *How to Enjoy the Bible*, Kregel Publications, Grand Rapids, Michigan 49501 (1990, originally published 1907)

Bullinger, EW, *The Book of Job*, Kregel Publications, Grand Rapids, Michigan 49501 (1990, originally published ?)

Bullinger, EW, *The Companion Bible*, Kregel Publications, Grand Rapids, Michigan 49501 (1990, 1st part 1909, complete volume 1922)

Bullinger, EW, *The Divine Names and Titles*, Truth for Today Bible Fellowship, P.O. Box 6358, Lafayette, IN 47903 (1983, originally published ?)

Bullinger, EW, *The Rich Man and Lazarus: the intermediate state*, The Open Bible Trust (1992, originally published 1902)

Bullinger, EW, *The Spirits in Prison*, The Open Bible Trust (2000, originally published ?)

Bullinger, EW, *Word Studies on the Holy Spirit*, Kregel Publications, Grand Rapids, Michigan 49501 (1979, originally published 1905)

Burgon, John, *The Revision Revised: a Refutation of Westcott and Hort's False Greek Text and Theory*, distributed by Penfold Book & Bible House, Bicester, Oxon, OX6 8PB (no date, originally published 1883)

Burgon, John, *The Last Twelve Verses of the Gospel According to Mark*, The Sovereign Grace Book Club, Michigan (1959, originally published 1871)

Cohen, A (ed.), *The Psalms*, The Soncino Press (1945)

Campbell, William, *The Book of the Revelation of Jesus Christ*, The Open Bible Trust (2000, originally published 1934, revised 1939)

Daniell, David (ed.), *William Tyndale's New Testament*, ©1995 by Yale University. Originally published by Yale University Press

Daniell, David (ed.), *Tyndale's Old Testament: A modern-spelling edition*, ©1992 by Yale University. Originally published by Yale University Press

Darby, JN, *The Holy Scriptures: a New Translation from the Original Languages*, Word of Truth, PO Box 1126 Kaduna (1988, originally published 1890)

Davidson, Benjamin, *The Analytical Hebrew and Chaldee Lexicon*, Hendrickson Publishers, Peabody, Michigan, 01961-3473 (1981, originally published 1848)

Gesenius, HWF, *Hebrew and Chaldee Lexicon to the Old Testament Scriptures*, Baker Books, Grand Rapids, Michigan 49516 (1996, originally published 1847)

Green, Jay P Sr., *Interlinear Bible: Greek-English*, Baker Books, Grand Rapids, Michigan 49516, 4th edition (1996, first published 1980)

Green, Jay P Sr., *Interlinear Bible: Hebrew-Greek-English*, Sovereign Grace Publishers, Lafayette, Indiana (1986)

Hills, Edward F, *The King James Version Defended*, distributed by Penfold Book and Bible House, Bicester, UK (no date)

Hislop, Alexander, *The Two Babylons*, SW Partridge & Co, London (1916)

John-Charles, Dr Peter, *When Was Christ's Death & Resurrection?* Open Bible Trust (2001)

Josephus, *The Works of Flavius Josephus*, translated by William Whiston, Nimmo, Hay, & Mitchell, Edinburgh (no date)

Keller, Werner *The Bible as History (Revised): Archaeology confirms the Book of Books*, Hodder and Stoughton (1980)

Knoch, AE, *The Concordant Version*, Concordant Publishing Concern, 15570 Knochaven Road, Santa Clarita, CA 91387 (first published 1926)

La Sainte Bible, Trinitarian Bible Society, London (1995)

Liddell and Scott, *An Intermediate Greek-English Lexicon*, Oxford (1889)

Marshall, Alfred, *The Interlinear Greek-English New Testament: the Nestle Greek Text*, Samuel Bagster and Sons Ltd, Second Edition (1966)

Meyer the Levi, תורה נביאים וכתובים (= *Torah, Nevi'im, ve Kethuvim*, The Law, The Prophets, and The Psalms), a Hebrew text, Berlin (1674, reprinted 1914)

Nicolson, Adam, *Power and Glory: Jacobean England and the Making of the King James Bible*, HarperCollins (2003)

Pember, GH, *Earth's Earliest Ages*, Kregel Publications (1995, originally published in 1876)

Ribbens, John C, *On the Right Hand of God*, The Word of Truth Ministry (1996)

Robinson, Maurice A, and Pierpont, William G, *The New Testament in the Original Greek, Byzantine Textform 2005*, Chilton Book Publishing, MA 01772-0606 (2005) ISBN 0-7598-0077-4 (2005) (and available online at http://www.byztxt.com/GreekNT/RP2005.htm)

Robinson, MA, and Pierpont, WG, *Byzantine Parsed Text*, 2000, http://www.byztxt.com/download

Rogers, John, *New Testament (1537) Tindale's Triumph, John Rogers' Monument: The Newe Testament of the Matthew's Bible*, The Martyrs Bible Series, John Wesley Sawyer, PO Box 12964, Houston, 77217-2964 (1989)

Scrivener, FH, *Novum Testamentum (New Testament in Greek)*, Cambridge (1877)

Sellers, Otis Q, *Seed & Bread, Volumes 1 & 2*, The Word of Truth Ministry, Los Angeles (c1980)

Sellers, Otis Q, *The Challenge Stands*, The Word of Truth Ministry (1960)

Sellers, Otis Q, *The Earth, not Heaven, is the Future Home of God's Redeemed*, The Word of Truth Ministry (1955)

Sellers, Otis Q, *The Foundation of the World*, The Word of Truth Ministry (c1958)

Skeat, WW, *The Cambridge Companion to the Bible*, Cambridge (no date)

Streets, Ernest, *Think on These Things*, The Open Bible Trust (1993)

Sweet, Colin, *Hell & Judgement in the Book of Revelation*, The Open Bible Trust (1992)

Tanakh: The Holy Scriptures, The Jewish Publication Society, Philadelphia (1985)

Thayer, Joseph H, *Thayer's Greek-English Lexicon of the New Testament*, Baker Book House, Grand Rapids, Michigan (1977, originally published 1901)

The New Bible Commentary Revised, ed. D. Guthrie et al, Inter-Varsity Press (1970)

The New King James Version, Thomas Nelson Publishers, Nashville (1985)

The Revised Version, Oxford University Press, Oxford (1895)

Thomason, Graham, *Far Above All Translation of the New Testament*, www.FarAboveAll.com

Thomason, Graham, *Greek Prepositions and Conjunctions*, www.FarAboveAll.com

Thomason, Graham, *Scripture, Authentic and Fabricated*, www.FarAboveAll.com

Thomason, Graham, *Translation Issues in the New Testament*, www.FarAboveAll.com

Vine, WE, *Expository Dictionary of Bible Words*, Marshall Morgan & Scott, London (1981)

Vulgate – Novum Testamentum Latine, Simon Wallberg 1889, reprinted by Simon Wallberg Press (2007)

Westcott, BF, *The Bible in the Church*, Macmillan and Co (1866)

Westcott, BF, *The Gospel of John*, John Murray, London (1882)

Wheadon, Denis A, *In the Beginning*, The Open Bible Trust (2001)

Wigram, George V, *The Englishman's Greek Concordance of the New Testament*, Hendrickson Publishers, Inc., PO Box 3473, Peabody, Massachusetts 01961-3473 (1999, originally published 1839)

Wigram, George V, *The Englishman's Hebrew Concordance of the Old Testament*, Hendrickson Publishers, Inc., PO Box 3473, Peabody, Massachusetts 01961-3473 (1999, originally published 1874)

Williams, George, *The Student's Commentary On The Holy Scriptures*, Chas. J. Thynne & Jarvis, Ltd., 2nd ed. (no date)

Woodrow, Ralph Edward, *Babylon Mystery Religion*, Ralph Woodrow Evangelistic Association, Inc. (1966)

Young, Robert, *Analytical Concordance To The Holy Bible*, Lutterworth Press (1879)

Young, Robert, *Young's Literal Translation*, Greater Truth Publishers, PO Box 4332, Lafayette, IN 47903 (2005, originally published 1862)

Eonian Document 19

The Eons and Jesus' Personal Promise

✦

We know that divisions in time of various 'Eons' have been designed and framed by God, marked out by prophetic events: 'By faith we understand the Eons to have been framed by an oracle of God' (Hebrews 11\3, 1\2); God has marked out 'in advance *the* times appointed' (Acts 17\26). Knowledge of these Eons gives us a proper framework for history, the present, and the future: where we have come from, where we are now, and where we are going.

The 'Eons past' and 'the coming Eons' can be understood in these ways:

'the Eons past' (Isaiah 63\16, Psalm 93\2); 'Eonian times' (Rom. 14\24); these would include: Adam to Noah, the patriarchs, Moses and the prophets (law);

'the present Eon' (1 Tim. 6\17, Titus 2\12): '*the* day of man' (1 Cor. 4\3); 'the present Eon of evil' (Gal. 1\4); 'this Eon of darkness' (Eph. 6\12); 'this present Eon' (2 Tim. 4\10); this is from the time of the end of the Book of Acts period until the next Eon commences;

'the coming Eons' (Eph. 2\7): 'Eonian times' (2 Tim. 1\9, Titus 1\2); 'the Eons' (Daniel 9\24 et cetera); these are the coming 490 years, the 1,000 years, then 'the day of God';

'the Eon' (Gen. 3\22, Ex. 3\15, Psalm 133\3, et cetera): 'seventy sevens' (Dan. 9\24, Mat. 18\22); 'that day' (Mat. 7\22, John 14\20, 2 Tim. 1\12, 1\18, 4\8); '*the* coming Eon' (Heb. 6\5); 'the day' (1 Cor. 3\13, Heb. 10\25, 2 Peter 1\19); '*the* day of Christ' (Phil. 1\10, 2\16, 2 Thes. 2\2); '*the* day of Christ Jesus' (Phil. 1\6); 'the day of our Lord Jesus Christ' (1 Cor. 1\8); '*the* day of redemption' (Eph. 4\30); '*the* day of *the* Eon' (2 Peter 3\18); 'the day of the Lord Jesus' (1 Cor. 5\5, 2 Cor. 1\14); '*the* day of visitation' (1 Peter 2\12); 'the end' (1 Cor. 15\24); 'the Eonian Sovereign Rulership of our Lord and Saviour Jesus Christ' (2 Peter

1\11); 'the Eon which is coming' (Mark 10\30, Luke 18\30, Eph. 1\21); 'the favourable intervention' (2 Thes. 2\8 etc.); 'the last day' (John 6\39, 6\40, 6\44, 6\54, 11\24, 12\48); 'the resurrection of the righteous' (Luke 14\14); 'the Sovereign Rulership' (Mat. 4\23, Luke 23\42); 'the Sovereign Rulership of God' (Mat. 6\33); 'the Sovereign Rulership of our father David' (Mark 11\10); 'the Sovereign Rulership of the heavens' (Mat. 3\2 etc.); '*the* times of restoration of all things' (Acts 3\21); this is the coming 490 years.

'the day of the Lord' (Isaiah 2\12, 13\6, 13\9, 2 Peter 3\10, Acts 2\20, 1 Thes. 5\2, Rev. 1\10): 'a latter time' (Jude 18); 'that day' (Luke 21\34, 1 Thes. 5\4, 2 Thes. 1\10); 'the day of evil' (Eph. 6\13, Psalm 27\5, 41\1, Prov. 16\4, Jer. 17\18, 51\2); 'the days of vengeance' (Luke 21\22); 'the last days' (Acts 2\17, 2 Tim. 3\1, 2 Peter 3\3); 'the terrible day of God the Almighty' (Rev. 16\14); 'the terrible day of his anger' (Rev. 6\17); 'the time of the end' (Dan. 12\4, 12\9); 'the times of *the* nations' (Luke 21\24); this is the end of the 490 year Eon;

'the 1,000 years' (Rev. 20\2, 20\3, 20\4, 20\5, 20\6, 20\7): '*the* day of indignation and revelation and righteous judgement of God' (Rom. 2\5); 'the day of judgement' (Mat. 1\22, 10\15, 11\24, 12\36, Mark 6\11); '*the* day of judgement and destruction of ungodly men' (2 Peter 3\7, 2\9, Mat. 12\36, 1 John 4\17); '*the* judgement of *the* terrible day' (Jude 6); 'the making new of all things' (Mat.19\28); 'the magisterial presence' (Mat. 24\3 etc.); Jesus will be on Earth and the judgement comes at the end of the 1,000 years;

'the day of God' (2 Peter 3\12): 'the new Earth', 'the Holy City, New Jerusalem' (Gal. 4\26, Rev. 21\1-2).

The personal promise to you
In this evil Eon we all are subject to death. It all goes back to Eden when Adam and Eve gave in to Satan – and God began His redemption plan by providing them with 'coats of skin' (Genesis 3\21).

The fact is, we are all infested with a violating nature against the one true holy God, and 'the wages of violation *are* death, but the free gift of God *is* Eonian life in Jesus Christ our Lord' (Romans 6\23). And 'all have violated and fall short of the magnificence of God' (Romans 3\23). Committing acts and thoughts we know are displeasing to our Creator, we are 'without excuse' (Romans 1\20, 2\1).

For those unrighteous who reject God and Christ, that means remaining in the grave with no life until the day of judgement at the end of the 1,000 years. At that time, rebels against God and Christ, the unrighteous, will face the prospect of the severest judgement. Peter speaks of the day of judgement and the 'destruction of ungodly men' (2 Peter 3\7). Jesus speaks of 'the road that leads off into destruction' (Matthew 7\13), and suffering 'destruction' (John 3\16). But these warnings are in contrast to 'the road leading into life' (Matthew 7\14) and 'Eonian life' (John 3\16) and not dying 'throughout the Eon' (John 11\26). Paul speaks of those who, 'out of contention, disobey the truth but obey unrighteousness', treasuring up for themselves 'boiling anger' in the day of judgement, but 'Eonian life' for those who search for 'honour and incorruption' (Romans 2\5-10). 'God is love' (1 John 4\7), but those who reject the love and kindness of their Creator, and who are not found 'written in the Scroll of Life', will be thrown into the lake of fire and destroyed, burnt to nothing, by their own choice to reject the ultimate love (Revelation 20\11-15).

However, boiling anger and destruction are not the case for those who believe Jesus and accept forgiveness for their violating acts and nature. Jesus is 'Saviour of the world' (John 4\42, 1 John 4\14, 1 Timothy 4\10). The mercy of God goes out to 'all men', and He wishes 'all men to be saved, and to come to knowledge of *the* truth' (Titus 2\11, 1 Timothy 2\4). God is kind, swift to forgive. His sacrifice of His Son, a wholly innocent man going to a violent and agonizing death at Golgotha, and being raised after three days, pays off the penalty we deserve. We accept that that penalty is paid for us, and we are freely forgiven, and we become Sons and Daughters of God. We are raised into new life.

Those who believe and put into practise the declarations and commands of God and Christ will be resurrected at the end of this Eon. They – and any believers living – will live throughout the coming Eons and beyond, no longer subject to violation and mortality. The coming Eons are the 490 years, the 1,000 years, and 'the day of God' in the new Earth. This is the free gift of Eonian life.

In speaking of the believers' resurrection, Paul wrote: 'For this corruption must put on incorruption, and this mortality put on immortality. So when this *body of* corruption will have put on incorruption, and this *body of* mortality will have put on immortality, then the oracle which has been written will come about: Death was swallowed up in victory' (1 Corinthians 15\53-54).

Jesus made a declaration to Nicodemus that everybody who believes in him will receive 'Eonian life'. Jesus made a similar declaration to Martha that everyone believing in him will not be subject to death throughout the entire long period of the coming Eon. The word 'everyone' means that Jesus' promise is personal to you also, as if spoken to you by a friend, even if you were the last person on Earth. Jesus wants you to enjoy every fulness and exuberant exaltation of his promise.

We have the oracles of his promises: 'we have ... by means of his blood, the forgiveness of violations' (Ephesians 1\7); 'he gave himself for our violations, so that he might deliver us out of the present Eon of evil' (Galatians 1\4).

In an incorruptible mind and body you can enjoy life throughout 'the coming Eons' (Ephesians 2\7), not subject to violation, never again subject to death.

This is the true gospel.

★

THE EONS PAST, THE PRESENT EON, & THE EONS COMING (*not proportionate time-scales*)

1. The 'Eons past' (Isaiah 63\16, Psalm 93\2, Romans 14\24); and 'the present Eon' (Galatians 1\4)

Original creation of Earth — Restoration of Earth — 2015

- Adam and Eve
- Flood — Noah
- Patriarchs — Abraham, Isaac, Jacob, Joseph
- Exodus Red Sea — Moses & the prophets: law, covenant with Israel
- Jesus Christ 'Son of Man' — John the Identifier & the Apostles, then Acts period & Paul's ending
- God's divorce from Israel (Jer. 3\8, Hos. 1\9-10, Heb. 8\9)
- the Israelite privilege to hear the gospel first (Acts 28\25-28, Rom. 11\16); Paul apostle to the nations
- present Eon of evil & Eon of darkness (Gal. 1\4, Eph. 6\12), the day of man (1 Cor. 4\3)
- the God-authorized Writings of the prophets and apostles obscured — 2015
- Church Fathers & global system

2. The 'Eons coming' (Ephesians 2\7)

2015 ?

the favourable intervention of God and Jesus ($\dot{\epsilon}\pi\iota\varphi\acute{\alpha}\nu\epsilon\iota\alpha$ = *epiphaneia*)

Jesus' return and magisterial presence on Earth ($\pi\alpha\rho\text{ου}\sigma\acute{\iota}\alpha$ = *parousia*)

general resurrection and judgement — the paradise of God (Rev. 2\27, Luke 23\43)

- Jerusalem destroyed (Daniel 9\25); resurrection of righteous; appearance of Elijah
- 490 year Eon — Sovereign Rulership of the heavens; the coming Eon; the day of Christ (Phil. 1\6)
- the day of the Lord (Rev. 1\10, Is. 13\6) days of vengeance
- new covenant with Israel (Jer. 31\31-34, Heb. 9\15, 10\16, Rev. 19\7-9)
- the 1,000 years (Rev. 20)
- present Earth burned up (2 Peter 3\10)
- the day of God (2 Peter 3\12) — New Earth & heavens (Rev. 21\1, Gal. 4\26, Eph. 2, Heb. 12\22); New Jerusalem the Holy City
- believers to rule with Jesus over the nations (2 Tim. 2\12, Rev. 2\26)

Pre-Adamite → Adam → Noah → Moses → John; Jesus; the apostles; → Paul apostle to the nations → Jesus' favourable intervention (the $\dot{\epsilon}\pi\iota\varphi\acute{\alpha}\nu\epsilon\iota\alpha$ = *epiphaneia*); the 490 years; the day of the Lord → Jesus' return and magisterial presence (his $\pi\alpha\rho\text{ου}\sigma\acute{\iota}\alpha$ = *parousia*) on the Earth; the 1,000 years → the general resurrection and judgement; the New Earth → the day of God. Whereas we cannot be dogmatic about the designations of 'the Eons past', other than that the prophets described them so, we can be certain about 'the Eons coming' because we have the numbers of their years. Those who are in Christ will live throughout both the 490 year and 1,000 year Eons with an incorruptible resurrection mind and body, and so will see 1,490 years of life (the 490 + the 1,000) before the final judgment and the New Earth. They will then be with God and Christ in the Holy City, the New Jerusalem, which 'is mother of us all' (Galatians 4\26), and 'the paradise of God' (Revelation 2\27, Luke 23\43).

Eonian Document 69

The True Meanings of *aion* and *aionios*

✦

'Where *is the* disputer of this Eon?'
~1 Corinthians 1\20

There's an old English word 'aeon'. Contemporary spelling prefers 'eon'. An 'eon' is a long period of time, in Geology a major division of time, subdivided into eras. In such secular measurements its boundaries are vague. In the divine measurement, though, the boundaries of an eon are distinct, having a known beginning and a known end, marked by events and by the pronouncements of prophets and apostles of God.

The Greek word αἰών (= *aion*) means 'Eon'

Our English word 'eon' is derived from the Greek word αἰών (= *aion*). This is one of the most important words for everybody in the world to understand. It occurs 126 times (in the RP text; 128 in the TR text, with two extra occurrences at Revelation 5\14), the first at Matthew 6\13. This Greek word αἰών is a simple word to translate. It means 'Eon' (which I capitalize because of its importance), defining, just as it does in English, a time dimension. In 100 of its 126 occurrences it is translated in *The Eonian Books* as 'Eon' or, plural, 'Eons'.

Only the rendering 'Eon' is good enough. Other words, such as 'age', will not do, as that's a shorter time, as in 'the age of Dostoyevsky', and is ambiguous ('a good age'??); 'era' is too short; 'epoch' is too short and does not have the same connotation. It has to be 'Eon': that is the derivation, the meaning and the right translation of αἰών. For example, Jesus spoke of 'the Eon which is coming' (Mark 10\30, Luke 18\30). So did Paul (Hebrews 6\5, Ephesians 1\21). Paul spoke of 'the present Eon of evil' (Galatians 1\4) and 'this Eon of darkness' (Ephesians 6\12), which is our present time. Paul spoke also of 'the coming Eons' (Ephesians 2\7), which are the coming 490 years, then the 1,000 years, then 'the day of God' in the new Earth.

Thayer comments: 'probable is the conjecture ... that αἰών is so connected with ἄημι *to breathe, blow*, as to denote properly *that which*

causes life, vital force; ... *age* (Lat. *Aevum*, which is αἰών with the Aeolic digamma), *a human lifetime* (in Hom., Hdt., Pind., Tragic poets), *life itself* (pp. 18-19). Otis Q Sellers gives a fine analysis of αἰών in his Seed & Bread 128, '*What Does* Aion *Mean?*'

What this *abstract noun* αἰών (= *aion*) does not mean is 'ever' or 'for ever': it is not an *adverb*, and αἰών does not mean a concept of eternity. Nor is it 'for ever and ever', nor 'evermore'. Nor does the *abstract noun* αἰών mean the *concrete noun* 'world'.

The apostle Paul would not have spoken of 'the present Eon' (Galatians 1\4, 2 Timothy 4\10) if there were not another Eon to come. In fact, there are 'Eons' to come: Paul also spoke of 'the coming Eons' (Ephesians 2\7).

The KJV

The translators of the *King James Version* (KJV), 1611 – concealing Jesus' gospel promise of 'Eonian life' – translated αἰών in 8 different ways: 'ages' (twice); 'course' (once); 'end' (once); 'eternal' (twice); 'ever' (51 times); 'evermore' (3 times); 'never' (7 times); 'world' or 'worlds' (39 times). And 22 times they totally ignored it. Not once did they translate it correctly as 'Eon'.

39 times the KJV has αἰών as 'world' or 'worlds', which is a concrete *space* dimension, but αἰών is an abstract *time* dimension. Not one single time does αἰών mean 'world'. The Greek for 'world' is κόσμος (= *kosmos*), not αἰών. The word αἰών is an *abstract noun* – and nothing could be more abstract than a long measurement of time. κόσμος is a *concrete noun* – and nothing could be more concrete, could it, than the mass of the world?

The KJV also sloppily translates αἰών as 'ever' or 'evermore' or 'never' ('ever' with a negative) 61 times. But again, αἰών is an *abstract noun*, not an *adverb* of time. It also twice has the noun αἰών as an *adjective*, 'eternal', and once as the *noun* 'end' – badly wrong in both.

Just three of the KJV's renderings αἰών are acceptable: twice as 'ages' (Ephesians 2\7, Colossians 1\26), and once idiomatically as 'course' (Ephesians 2\2).

By the KJV's slovenly blunders, both God's arrangement of the Eons and His precious gospel promise of 'Eonian life' have been masked. These absurd renderings – perpetuated in version after version – have held the world back, prolonging suffering. It is my conviction that without the pronouncement of the Eon there will be no event of the Eon. Eon-marking events of God have been signalled in advance by the prophets. The prophet Amos wrote that 'Adonai Yahweh does nothing unless He reveals His secret counsel to His servants the prophets. The lion has roared – who will not fear? Adonai Yahweh has spoken – who can but prophesy?' (Amos 3\7).

At Matthew 13\38-39 we see Jesus say of his parable of the tares that 'the field represents the world [κόσμος]' and '*the* harvest represents *the* completion of the Eon [αἰών]'. We could not wish for a sharper distinction between these two Greek words. The KJV, though, puts both words as 'world', spoiling Jesus' explanation: both the field *and* the harvest cannot represent the world.

At John 11\26-27 we have both words αἰών, 'Eon', and κόσμος, 'world': Jesus spoke of life throughout the *timespan* of the Eon (αἰών), and Martha spoke of his having come into the *concrete* world (κόσμος), showing the difference of the words, but the KJV men failed to see it.

At Acts 3\21, the Greek text has the phrase ἀπ' αἰῶνος (= *ap aionos*), which is 'from of old', using αἰών (= *aion*) idiomatically, and referring to God speaking through His holy prophets 'from of old'. The KJV, though, has that Greek phrase as 'since the world began', but no words with any of those meanings are in the Greek; and it wrongly renders αἰών as 'world'; and, further, the KJV's words are wrong in their contexts here as well because there have not been 'holy prophets' since the world began. The first prophet was Enoch, who was the 'seventh from Adam' (Jude 14, Genesis 5\18-23).

At Acts 15\18, the Greek text again has the phrase ἀπ' αἰῶνός (= *ap aionos*), which, again, is idiomatic and is 'from of old'. But the KJV wrongly has it as 'the beginning of the world', yet no words with any of those meanings match any of the Greek words.

At 1 Corinthians 2\7, Paul speaks of the wisdom which God has marked out beforehand, 'in advance of the Eons'. The KJV, though, only managed that as 'before the world', so that αἰών is wrongly put as 'world', a plural is put as a singular, and the future Eons are strangely put into the past. Furthermore, the KJV by that error suggests some sort of predestination.

At 1 Corinthians 3\18-19 there are the two

clauses 'If anybody among you thinks *himself* to be wise in this Eon [αἰών]' and 'the wisdom of this world [κόσμος] is foolishness with God'. So we have 'this Eon' followed by 'this world'. Nevertheless, the KJV translators did not drop their refusal to translate αἰών as 'Eon', and they stuck to their rendering of 'world'. Both phrases they put as 'this world'. If Paul had meant 'world' in both places he would have written κόσμος in both places.

At 1 Corinthians 10\11, Paul says of idolaters, 'on them have come the ends of the Eons', meaning the last judgement, at the end of the 1,000 years (Revelation 20\11-15). But the KJV men were only able to manage that as 'upon whom the ends of the world are come'. So they translated αἰώνων, 'Eons', plural, as 'world', singular, and their insistence on αἰών as 'world' found them out, since they could not sensibly write 'the end of the worlds'. There are not 'worlds', plural. So they pulled off a dodge and wrote it as singular.

At Ephesians 3\9, the Greek has the phrase ἀπὸ τῶν αἰώνων (= *apo ton aionon*), which is 'from the Eons'. The KJV has that as 'from the beginning of the world', but that does not in the slightest measure reflect the Greek since the only one of those KJV words which in the Greek is 'the' (!), and the word αἰώνων is 'Eons', *plural*, not 'world', *singular*.

Ephesians 3\11 has '*the* purpose of the Eons', αἰών being in the genitive plural, αἰώνων, but the KJV conjures 'Eons' plural into an *adjective*, 'eternal', entirely wiping out Paul's point.

Ephesians 3\21 is particularly interesting. The Greek has the phrase τοῦ αἰῶνος τῶν αἰώνων (= *tou aionos ton aionon*), meaning literally 'the Eon of the Eons', but better rendered, in my view, as 'the duration of the Eons'. The KJV translators, though, put that as 'world without end', but there is no Greek word there for 'world', no Greek word for 'without', and no Greek word for 'end'. That KJV translating is made even worse in that it has contradictory phrases such as 'the end of the world' at Matthew 13\39 and elsewhere (14 times altogether). So, the KJV has two contradictory phrases: 'world without end' and 'at the end of the world'. And both are wrong anyway.

Colossians 1\26 has the phrase 'the mystery having been hidden from the Eons'. Imagine trying to make the plural of αἰών in that phrase mean 'world' or 'ever': 'the mystery which has been hidden from the evers' (grammatical nonsense), or 'from the worlds' (What 'worlds' would those be, then? There's only one world). At least the KJV has 'ages' there.

At 1 Timothy 1\17 Paul describes God with the majestic title 'the King of the Eons', the noun αἰών being plural (that is, αἰώνων = *aionon*). The KJV has that as 'the King eternal', twisting a plural *noun* into an *adjective*. Without an understanding of the coming Eons, our vision of the future and our inheritance in Christ is nullified, smeared out.

Hebrews 1\2 and 11\3 state clearly that God 'designed the Eons' (αἰώνας, plural), meaning that He has framed all the past and present and coming Eons, divisions of time marked by His different ways of speaking to and dealing with mankind. However, in these two verses the KJV translators put 'he made the worlds' and 'the worlds were framed', but there is only one world. Also, when speaking of the creation of the heavens and the Earth, or the Earth in relation to the heavens, the Greek usually uses γῆ (= *gee*, 'Earth'; see Matthew 5\18, 11\25, Acts 4\24, 14\15, 17\24, 1 Corinthians 8\5, Ephesians 1\10, 3\15, Colossians 1\16, 1\20, Hebrews 1\10, 2 Peter 3\7, 3\13, Revelation 6\13, 14\7, 20\11, 21\1). Just twice it uses κόσμος in relation to creation (Acts 17\24, Romans 1\20). Furthermore, γῆ and κόσμος, in such contexts, appear in the singular: one Earth, one world. There are, though, several Eons. Hebrews 1\2 and 11\3 concern *arranging* – not *creating* – the arranging and framing of the Eons, not the creating of the world. αἰών most certainly does not mean 'worlds'.

In addition, if even more fixed certainty were wanted that αἰών does not mean 'world', then Ephesians 2\2 and Hebrews 9\26 most happily provide that certainty. For in both those verses both words occur, αἰών, 'Eon', and κόσμος, 'world'. Ephesians 2\2 has both words in the same phrase, 'the Eon of this world', so the KJV men were forced to make a distinction – even *they* would not write 'the world of this world' – and so they wrote 'the course of this world'.

Hebrews 9\26 has the two phrases '*the* foundation of *the* world [κόσμος]', 'world' singular, and '*the* completion of the Eons [αἰών]', 'Eons' plural. Hence it's absurd to want both κόσμος and αἰών as 'world' singular; yet that is exactly what the KJV does have, having 'the foundation of the world' and 'the end of the world' – wrong in number, and as if, absurdly, Jesus' death was at the end of the world.

At Hebrews 11\3 and 11\7 we yet again see the clear distinctions: 'the Eons [αἰών] ... have been framed by ... God' and 'Noah ... condemned the world [κόσμος]'. Noah did not condemn what God designed and framed!

Hebrews 13\8 says 'Jesus Christ yesterday and today *is* the same, and throughout the Eons'. For that last phrase, though, all the KJV could manage was 'for ever'. To represent a *plural noun* with an *adverb* 'ever' is curious mischief indeed. How can a plural *abstract noun* become an *adverb*? What happened to the Eons God designed?

All these are subjects of simple and straightforward grammar and logic. There are many more such blunders in the KJV with the word αἰών. There is one good way which the KJV men refused to translate αἰών – and that is 'Eon', the one way it ought to be translated.

The Hebrew word עוֹלָם (= *olam*), and the Chaldee word עָלַם (= *alam*) both mean 'Eon' and are the equivalents of the Greek word αἰών

The word αἰών is the Greek equivalent of the Hebrew word עוֹלָם (= *olam*) and of the Chaldee word עָלַם (= *alam*), which also both mean 'Eon'. The noun עוֹלָם occurs 438 times in the Hebrew Books, first at Genesis 3\22; not even once does the KJV manage to translate it as 'Eon'. The Chaldee noun עָלַם occurs 19 times (in Daniel and Ezra), first at Daniel 2\4; not even once does the KJV manage to translate it as 'Eon'.

In Exodus and Leviticus the KJV makes reference to statutes as being 'everlasting' and 'for ever' (עוֹלָם). But they are not 'for ever', since they will have completion and be forgotten in the New Jerusalem on the New Earth.

At Isaiah 45\17, the Hebrew word עוֹלָם is in the plural, עוֹלָמִים (= *olamim*), and means 'for the Eons'. The KJV, however, translates it as 'everlasting', an *adjective* clumsily put for Isaiah's *adverbial phrase*.

Also in Isaiah 45\17 there is the phrase עַד עֲד־עוֹלְמֵי (= *ad oleme ad*), 'throughout the Eon and its duration'. The KJV has it as 'world without end', which is wrong linguistically,

wrong contextually, and wrong thematically–
not a word of the Hebrew there means either
'world' or 'without' or 'end'. This is the same
blunder the KJV has in Ephesians 3\21 where
it also has 'world without end', creating a
clumsy contradiction of its own phrase 'end of
the world' in other places.

At Isaiah 64\4, the Hebrew has the phrase
לְמֵעוֹלָם (= leme olam), which is well rendered as
'from of old', using עוֹלָם ('Eon') idiomatically.
But the KJV translates the phrase as 'since the
beginning of the world', but that reflects not a
word of the Hebrew, and is wrong contextually.

Ecclesiastes 3\11 has '[God] has set the Eon
in their heart' – signifying that we all long for a
golden age. But the KJV, by its refusal to put
עוֹלָם as 'Eon', has that clause as a curiosity, 'he
hath set the world in their heart', which is
without meaning.

The Greek word αἰώνιος
(= aionios) means 'Eonian'

Our beautiful English word 'eonian' is the
adjective form of 'eon'. (There is also an old
adjective, 'eval'. Think of 'medieval', from Latin
medius middle + aevum age.) The Greek αἰών,
too, has an adjective form, αἰώνιος (= aionios),
and it means 'Eonian', that is, relating to an
Eon. It occurs 71 times. Not even once does
the KJV have αἰώνιος correctly as 'Eonian'.

Mark 10\30 and Luke 18\30 have the
phrases 'in the Eon [αἰών] which is coming,
Eonian [αἰώνιος] life'. But the KJV has these
as 'in the world to come life everlasting'. So the
noun αἰών ('Eon') they twisted to 'world', and
the adjective αἰώνιος ('Eonian') they twisted to
'everlasting'. This twisting thieves from the
believer the knowledge of the true inheritance
in Jesus, life in the coming Eon. No wonder the
phrase of the real gospel promise of 'Eonian
life' is alien to the ears of so many. The lying
notion of eternal undying man comes not from
the prophets and apostles of God, but was
stolen out of ancient paganism, as is seen in the
rebellious writings of the so-called 'fathers'.

If anything could mean the opposite of
'everlasting' it is the adjective αἰώνιος. This
adjective αἰώνιος describes a time with limits, a
beginning and an end, marked by prophetic
announcements. But 'eternal' describes a time
without limits, time without beginning or end. If
the KJV men wanted αἰών as 'world', then they

should have been consistent and had its
adjective form αἰώνιος as 'worldly', and
translated the gospel phrase as 'worldly life', and
so at Mark 10\30 and Luke 18\30 they should
have written 'in the world which is coming,
worldly life'.

The phrase χρόνοις αἰωνίοις (= kronois
aioniois), meaning 'Eonian times', magnificently
illustrates and demands that αἰώνιος has to
mean 'Eonian', not 'eternal'. It occurs at
Romans 14\24 (RP text), 2 Timothy 1\9 and
Titus 1\2, where the adjective αἰώνιος is
linked to the plural noun 'times', χρόνοις. It
would be utterly senseless to translate χρόνοις
αἰωνίοις as 'eternal times', since eternity can
have no pluralities, and 'eternal times' would be
a curiosity without sense, yet one version does
exactly that.

In Romans 14\24 (RP text) the phrase
χρόνοις αἰωνίοις speaks of the 'Eonian times'
when the gospel to the nations was kept in
silence – so looking back to Eons past. In 2
Timothy 1\9 and Titus 1\2 the phrase χρόνοις
αἰωνίοις concerns the gospel being promised
'in advance of Eonian times' – so looking ahead
to Eons coming. There are no times before
eternity, and there are no times after eternity: it
has no pluralities. Even the KJV men
recognized the senselessness of writing 'eternal
times'. But instead of 'Eonian times' they
invented something else and wrote 'since the
world began'. Not one of those KJV's words
vaguely represents a single word of the Greek (I
thought the idea was to translate the Greek), all
of them wrong linguistically, thematically, and
contextually; nor are they what the writer Paul
was saying; nor are they true to the facts; and at
2 Timothy 1\9 and Titus 1\2 the KJV's ragged
phrase 'since the world began' puts into the past
what is meant as future. And if this promise of
life were, as the KJV has it in Titus 1\2,
'promised before the world began', to whom,
then, was it promised if the world was not even
made? Again, in one place, Romans 16\25, the
KJV says that the gospel was 'kept secret since
the world began', but then in 2 Timothy and
Titus the KJV says, in contradiction of itself,
that the gospel was given and promised 'before
the world began'. In contrast, having χρόνοις
αἰωνίοις correctly as 'Eonian times' makes
perfect sense in its occurrences; fits its contexts;
is what Paul meant; is true to the facts.

I translate αἰώνιος as 'Eonian' in all but
three of its 71 occurrences where in those three

occurrences its usage seems idiomatic. At Luke 16\9 I translate it as 'permanent' in the phrase 'permanent habitations', which seems preferable there, I think, to 'Eonian habitations' (the KJV's 'everlasting habitations' makes no sense: no house is 'everlasting'). At 2 Corinthians 4\18 I translate αἰώνιος as 'permanent' because it's set in apposition to 'temporal'. At Philemon 15 I translate it as 'permanently' because, unusually, Paul uses it adverbially.

The KJV has αἰώνιος as 'eternal' 42 times, 'everlasting' 25 times, 'for ever' 1 time, and 'world' 3 times – all of those wrong and, what is injurious, concealing the fact of the coming Eons on Earth, and consequently masking the truth of the gospel promise, 'Eonian life'.

The Greek phrase ζωὴ αἰώνιος (= *zoe aionios*) means 'Eonian life'

The phrase ζωὴ αἰώνιος occurs 44 times in the God-authorized Greek Books, the first at Matthew 19\16. 'Eonian life' is exactly how ζωὴ αἰώνιος (= *zoe aionios*) should be translated.

The famous gospel promise at John 3\15-16 is 'everyone believing in [Jesus] ... might have Eonian life', that is, life right throughout the whole of 'the Eon which is coming' (Mark 10\30, Luke 28\30). That is the gospel which Jesus and Paul and the other apostles proclaimed.

The KJV for this phrase ζωὴ αἰώνιος (= *zoe aionios*) alternates randomly between 'eternal life' and 'everlasting life', unable to make up its mind. Both are wrong: in fact, αἰώνιος could hardly more strongly mean the opposite of eternity, which is a time *without limits*, without beginning and without end. While it is true that believers in God and Jesus will – after resurrection – have life without end, throughout the Eons, and in 'the day of God' in the New Earth (2 Peter 3\12), that was not the point being made. The point being made in the gospel promise is that those in Jesus have the promise of 'Eonian life', living throughout the entire course of the coming Eons, whereas those who have lived against God and Jesus will not have any life at all in those Eons. This is the true gospel.

There is the same gospel promise of 'life throughout the duration of the Eon' spoken by David (Psalm 133\3). And it is the same gospel promise of 'Eonian life' spoken by Daniel (Daniel 12\2), 'Eonian life' represented by עוֹלָם לְחַיֵּי (= *le chaye olam*), the Hebrew's equivalent of the Greek ζωὴ αἰώνιος.

It is the greatest reward and privilege of all to receive life throughout the coming Messianic Eon, and those against Jesus reject that privilege and they will not have any life during that time but will be resurrected at the end of the 1,000 years in the last judgement (Revelation 20\12-14, 22\2). Those surviving the judgement will live on the New Earth but have no part in the privilege and ruling position of the Holy City.

The words ζωὴ αἰώνιος (= *zoe aionios*), meaning 'Eonian life', ought to be constantly on the lips of every exuberant believer in the true God and Jesus Christ.

The Greek phrase εἰς τὸν αἰῶνα (= *eis ton aiona*) means 'throughout the Eon'

The Greek phrase εἰς τὸν αἰῶνα (= *eis ton aiona*), meaning 'throughout the Eon', has its Hebrew equivalent in לְעוֹלָם (= *le olam*), which first appears at Genesis 3\22 and appears 162 times in all. The Greek phrase εἰς τὸν αἰῶνα (= *eis ton aiona*), 'throughout the Eon', appears 27 times.

This promise of life 'throughout the Eon' is shown exactly or implied in the words of Jesus at John 4\14, 6\51, 6\58, 8\35 (twice), 8\51, 8\52 (reported speech), 10\28, 11\26, 12\34, 14\16, 1 John 2\17. At John 11\26, Jesus said to Martha, 'everyone living and believing in me will most certainly not die throughout the Eon. Do you believe this?' Yes, I do believe that. The KJV, however, most unfortunately has Jesus promising Martha that whoever believes in him 'shall never die. Believest thou this?' As a matter of fact, no, I do not believe that at all. It is not true. Even Jesus himself died for three days and three nights. And everybody since has died and gone into the grave, and they await resurrection, whether believer or not (there's an exceptional case involving Paul who was taken up like Enoch). The words of the KJV are not true. They make Jesus' promise a lie.

In John 11\26 (and 10\28) the two phrases meaning 'most certainly not' and 'throughout the Eon' represent five Greek words, οὐ μὴ ... εἰς τὸν αἰῶνα (= *ou me ... eis ton aiona*). But the KJV only translated those five Greek words as one word, 'never'. One word for five words leaves four words untranslated. Words out of their meaning; a wrong word; words left untranslated; internal disharmony: that is not the way to go about translating the great oracles of the Son of God. There is a Greek word for 'never', οὐδέποτε (= *oudepote*) – see Matthew 7\23, 1 Corinthians 13\8 et cetera – but it does not appear in John 11\26. When Jesus meant 'never' he said 'never': for example, 'Have you never [οὐδέποτε] read ...?' (Matthew 21\16, 21\42).

In John 11\26 Jesus did not say 'never' and he did not mean 'never' because it would have made his statement untrue. The Greek way to say 'never' is not by the two phrases οὐ μὴ and εἰς τὸν αἰῶνα (which often appear independently, meaning 'most certainly not' and 'throughout the Eon'). The KJV's 'never' is a blunder, a poisoning at the root of the promise of Jesus, shipwrecking at every point the resurrection and his gospel promise. The KJV's having Jesus say that men 'will never die' is the same lie Satan told Eve in Eden (Genesis 3\4): 'You will not surely die'. So the KJV puts the lie of Satan into the mouth of Jesus.

Where in John 11\26 the KJV wants the *abstract noun* αἰών as the *adverb* 'ever', it constructs nonsense. Furthermore, in the phrase εἰς τὸν αἰῶνα the KJV is omitting to translate the definite article τὸν. It is also omitting to translate the preposition εἰς (which it manages to have correctly as 'throughout' at Ephesians 3\21). And, if it wants αἰῶνα as 'ever', then it should have 'throughout the ever', grammatical nonsense. So too if it wants αἰών as world here: 'will ... not die throughout the world' is semantic nonsense.

This is the truth, though: Jesus said, 'I give them Eonian life, and they will most certainly not suffer destruction throughout the Eon' (John 10\28).

And as Jesus had to correct the traditions of the scribes who mangled the law, so have we to say today: You have heard it said that whoever believes in Jesus 'will never die'. But truly I tell you, whoever believes in Jesus will be resurrected, Sons and Daughters of Almighty God, and then he or she will most certainly not die throughout the coming Messianic Eon.

The phrase εἰς τὸν αἰῶνα could be well translated idiomatically as 'permanently' at 1 Corinthians 8\13, so reading 'I would certainly not eat flesh permanently [εἰς τὸν αἰῶνα]', but I prefer to let the hyperbole of 'throughout the Eon' remain. The phrase also might be

idiomatic (but maybe not?) as at John 13\8, concerning the washing of Peter's feet, but, once again, I prefer to let the hyperbole remain.

αἰών can sometimes be translated as 'duration'
In the opening of his letter to the Galatians, Paul has the phrase 'throughout the durations of the Eons' (Galatians 1\5). The Greek of that is εἰς τοὺς αἰῶνας τῶν αἰώνων (= *eis tous aionas ton aionon*). This could be rendered literally as 'throughout the Eons of the Eons', but is more meaningful as 'throughout the durations of the Eons'.

The same phrase – with minor variations – also appears at Ephesians 3\21 ('the duration of the Eons'), Philippians 4\20, 1 Timothy 1\17, 2 Timothy 4\18, Hebrews 1\8 ('the duration of the Eon'), 13\21, 1 Peter 4\11, 5\11, Revelation 1\6, 1\18, 4\9, 4\10, 5\13, 5\14 (in TR text, not RP text), 7\12, 10\6, 11\15, 14\11, 15\7, 19\3, 20\10, 22\5.

In the Hebrews 1\8 occurrence of the phrase Paul is citing Psalm 45\6-7, so his Greek reflects the Hebrew, which is לְעֹלָם וָעֶד = (*le olam va ed*), a phrase first occurring at Exodus 15\18. Two different Hebrew words are used in that, עֹלָם (= *olam*) and עַד (= *ad*), so 'duration' and 'Eon' seem the sensible renderings, strengthening the case for 'duration of the Eons' in Paul's writings – hence they are reflected in *The Eonian Books* rendering of the Greek phrase (and its two variants) εἰς τοὺς αἰῶνας τῶν αἰώνων (= *eis tous aionas ton aionon*).

The true gospel promise
The promise of the coming Eon is also expressed in 'proclaiming the gospel, the Sovereign Rulership [or 'kingdom'] of God' (Luke 4\43), or as 'the Sovereign Rulership of the heavens' (Matthew 3\2). Resurrection and life throughout the coming Eon are the true hope of the 'members of the resurrection' (Luke 20\36), the Sons and Daughters of God.

As Jesus said, 'Labour ... for the food enduring into Eonian life, which the Son of Man will give you' (John 6\27).

A new Eon is on its way – hear the hoofbeats – as the prophets and apostles declare, and we are hurtling towards it. Daniel and Jesus tell us that it will be an Eon of 490 years, which time is also 'the Sovereign Rulership of God', and 'the kingdom of God'. Then Jesus returns to the Earth, and after that, as John tells us six times, there will come the 1,000 years (Revelation 20\2-7), and then 'the day of God' (2 Peter 3\12) which is the New Earth and New Jerusalem (Revelation 21 and 22).

*

Concordance of how I've translated the 126 occurrences of αἰών

as '**Eon**' (60 times) or 'Eons' (40 times) (total: = 100 times): Matthew 6\13, 12\32, 13\22, 13\39, 13\40, 13\49, 21\19, 24\3, 28\20, Mark 3\29, 4\19, 10\30, 11\14, Luke 1\33, Luke 1\55, 16\8, 18\30, 20\34, 20\35, John 4\14, 6\51, 6\58, 8\35 (twice), 8\51, 8\52, 10\28, 11\26, 12\34, 13\8, 14\16, Romans 1\25, 9\5, 11\36, 12\2, 14\26, 1 Corinthians 1\20, 2\6 (twice), 2\7, 2\8, 3\18, 8\13, 10\11, 2 Corinthians 4\4, 9\9, 11\31, Galatians 1\4, 1\5, Ephesians 1\21, 2\2, 2\7, 3\9, 3\11, 3\21, 6\12, Philippians 4\20, Colossians 1\26, 1 Timothy 1\17 (twice), 6\17, 2 Timothy 4\10, 4\18, Titus 2\12, Hebrews 1\2, 1\8, 5\6, 6\5, 6\20, 7\17, 7\21, 7\24, 7\28, 9\26, 11\3, 13\8, 13\21, 1 Peter 1\23, 1\25, 4\11, 5\11, 2 Peter 2\17, 3\18, 1 John 2\17, 2 John 1\2, Jude 1\13, 1\25, Revelation 1\6, 1\18, 4\9, 4\10, 5\13, (twice in TR text at 5\14, but not in RP text so not included), 7\12, 10\6, 11\15, 14\11, 15\7, 19\3, 20\10, 22\5;

as '**of old**' (4 times): Luke 1\70, John 9\32, Acts 3\21, 15\18;

as '**duration**' (2 times): Ephesians 3\21, Hebrews 1\8;

as '**durations**' (20 times): Galatians 1\5, Philippians 4\20, 1 Timothy 1\17, 2 Timothy 4\18, Hebrews 13\21, 1 Peter 4\11, 5\11, Revelation 1\6, 1\18, 4\9, 4\10, 5\13 (not in RP text at 5\14), 7\12, 10\6, 11\15, 14\11, 15\7, 19\3, 20\10, 22\5.

The 45 occurrences of 'Eonian life'

Daniel 12\2, Matthew 19\16, 19\29, 25\46, Mark 10\17, 10\30, Luke 10\25, Luke 18\18, 18\30, John 3\15, John 3\16, John 3\36, 4\14, 4\36, 5\24, 5\39, 6\27, 6\40, 6\47, 6\54, 6\68, 10\28, 12\25, 12\50, 17\2, 17\3, Acts 13\46, 13\48, Romans 2\7, 5\21, 6\22, 6\23, Galatians 6\8, 1 Timothy 1\16, 6\12, 6\19, Titus 1\2, 3\7, 1 John 1\2, 2\25, 3\15, 5\11, 5\13, 5\20, Jude 21.

Honours and Acknowledgments

No work such as this can be undertaken without its author benefitting ten thousand-fold from the multitude of the golden-rich fruits of others' labours. I am indescribably indebted to the following scholars whose works have been a guide and inspiration, whose majestic lexical works have not been surpassed, and without whom this work would be impoverished and would have taken twice as long:

John Wycliffe, and William Tyndale (assassinated 1536), who both worked outside the city gates to make the God-authorized Books available in English;
George V Wigram, for his Hebrew and Greek concordances;
HWF Gesenius, for his Hebrew and Chaldee lexicon;
Benjamin Davidson, for his Analytical Hebrew and Chaldee lexicon;
Samuel Bagster, for his analytical Greek lexicon, and his Greek interlinear;
Robert Young, for his Analytical Concordance;
Dr Henry Alford, for the depth of his commentary, and initiating the emphasis on philology;
John Burgon, for his *Revision Revised*, and his other textual masterpieces, and who defended the Majority Greek texts from illogical and ill-founded attack;
Dr Ethelbert William Bullinger for his *Companion Bible* and other works, and who began the superior enhancements to translation and understanding, and who worked outside the city gate;
James Strong, for his Concordance, and for his inspired numbering system, a magnificent moment in Biblical history;
George Ricker Berry, for his Greek interlinear;
Joseph H Thayer, for his Greek-English lexicon, which is the most impressive book I've ever seen;
Otis Q Sellers, for his 200 *Seed & Bread* studies, and other works, and who furthered the quest for superior enhancements to translation and understanding, and who worked outside the city gate;
Jay P Green Sr., for his Hebrew and Greek interlinears, the most important books of the twentieth century;
Errol Palmer, whose conversations in the summer of 1997 in Berwick-on-Tweed helped to get this work started;
Maurice A Robinson and William G Pierpont, for their Byzantine Textform 2005, to date the most important book of the twenty-first century, representing probably the closest we have to the writings of the apostles;
Dr Graham Thomason, for his outstanding textual work, translation work, and countless advices;
Paul Ferdinand, for proofreading and editing, for his own deep studies and labours, and for insights and questions beyond price
Paul Ferdinand, for proofreading and editing, for his own deep studies and labours, and for insights and questions beyond price;
Professor David Daniell, for his brilliant and inspiring work on William Tyndale.

TO COME FROM EONIAN BOOKS

How and Why *The Eonian Books* Translation Was Made (2013-14)

How the KJV Conceals the True Jesus and his Salvation; and *The Latin Vulgate*, a Triumph of Poison (2013)

Rebel Angels and Their Seed (1999)

Secrets of the Beginning of History (1997)

The Companion Notes to the God-authorized Greek Writings (ongoing)

The Companion Notes to the God-authorized Hebrew Writings (ongoing)

The Earth-Shaking Truth: How and Why *The Eonian Books* Translation Was Made (2015)

The Eonian Books: Genesis to 2 Chronicles: The God-authorized Hebrew Writings (in preparation)

The Eon in the God-authorized Hebrew and Greek Books: Concerning the Future of the World, examining nine Hebrew words, one Chaldee word, and eight Greek words, in their every occurrence, totalling 884 words, in every phrase, in every context, in relation to the Eons (2013)

The Man Christ Jesus: The Hoax of Polytheism Exposed (2014)

What Happens When You Die (2000)

Who Is the Counsellor and the Holy Spirit?: The Hoax of Polytheism Exposed (2012)

100 + Eonian Documents (ongoing)

From time to time the Angel of Elohim delivered messages from Heaven to men of a single spirit. The Scrolls of the men of a single spirit, whose messages were a speech of fire, came to be collected in one Book, their purpose to reconcile men to the one true God and Creator, Who is the King of the Eons, and to be of one mind, with a view to spiritually-activated, inexpressible exuberance.

After a time, men of a different spirit arose, jangling the keys of another kingdom, in another realm. They burned strange fire and brewed a hybrid religion with mystifying creeds, so that the messages of the men of a single spirit were subverted. The copied manuscripts of the messages fell into the wrong hands, devilish minds. A twisted and fabled translation of the one Book was made in a strange tongue to make a smokescreen agreement with the creeds and to keep the millions shrouded in darkness.

This was the era of the Great Rebellion, the Unholy Backlash. Rather than adjusting their character, the men with the counterfeit keys, satisfied with unrighteousness and its empty assurance of life, connived to adjust the message to their own advantage, and they became as those who cannot perceive themselves cast in a drama of the occulted guilt of an ignoble king. Believing in false deities, they sabotaged the message and the salvation promises. They buried the key of knowledge. By a reverse process, the messages of angels were alchemized into the messages of men. By the mystifying creeds and the twisted translation, they created a strong delusion: a Mythology of multiple deities, a cloudy heaven, fiery underground hells, gods in the fat of men's bellies, flying souls of the dead as they were depicted in the tombs of Egypt; a delusion stuffed fat with Idolatry, Angel Worship, Mysticism, Apostasy, elements as gods, Predestination, futures turned into pasts, a false saviour, a false message, and heavy with Institutionalism. The pillars of antiquity, meanwhile, were allowed to crumble in order to obfuscate the delusions.

Armies stampeded across the world with the poison rivers of the twisted translation and the strange creeds. It was the greatest political and religious upheaval ever come on the world. Empires were founded and Constitutions written in the name of the new idolatry, haunted by unworthy obeisance to the creeds, duped hypnotically by the twisted translation, the whole order and its systems founded on lies and violence.

So potent was the delusion that even the new translations by the best of men were strangled on its burning ropes. Every translation was overshadowed by the twisted translation and the creeds. The God-authorized Hebrew and Greek Writings were clamped in obscurity. The bewildering creeds and the fabled translation were upheld in order to serve the hybrid religion: nouns and adjectives, pronouns, verbs and adverbs, and prepositions were falsified; punctuation fidgeted; capitalizations wrongly inserted; words and passages taken out; words added; words changed; words left untranslated; Scrolls shuffled haphazardly. The twisted translations were not the works of righteousness. They put the mind and words of Satan spoken in the Garden of Eden into the mouth of the Messiah.

Accordingly, the world boiled with wars and rebellion and hunger and every crime and debauchery. Men suffered misery, sadness and melancholy in place of energized love and joy. Children perished under mind-controls and evil revolutions which swept the Earth like a destroying angel with an iron broom. The fangs of the misty delusion sank into the world. Men staggered about with airy nothings in their heads, images of cold edifices, migrating souls, and gods in incensed heavens. All these came about because of the men of the hybrid religion with positions of cruel power and their creeds and twisted translations and their keys of the wrong kingdom. They held the world up. The true message was smothered so that the coming Eon could not be proclaimed. Billions of the false translations spread across the continents. It was the greatest mind conspiracy and psycho warfare ever conducted, and the greatest literary scandal of all time. Several wrote corrections but the corrections were not put into a translation of the one Book. If those hybrid creeds had never been written, and the first twisted translation had been a pure translation, the Earth would be a different place, safer, happier, more peaceable.

Because of the strong delusion of the Great Rebellion and the Unholy Backlash, the collected Scrolls of the men of a single spirit remained for centuries untranslated in purity and truth, trapped in prejudice, orthodoxy, Institutionalism. The true oracle lay like a smashed star, yet still blinking out prisms of light. The history of man is a war for truth. Now, after nearly two millennia, out of the impregnable foundations of the Science of Deep Grammar, Transcendent Logic, Internal Harmony, and Diamond-Mining Research, a true translation of the one Book has been made from the languages of the men of a single spirit, and having no allegiances to the false creeds and the idolatrous and fusty translation. Everything advantageous to the truth has conspired together, converged in these days. New translations will be needed for the languages of the world, new lexicons, new concordances. The chains and barbed wire have been unpicked.

In an exhausted and self-congratulatory world, centuries gone beyond any expectation of messianic intervention, the divine invitation is announced to all mankind. This is an invitation to leave the broad road of destruction and enter through the narrow gate which leads to Eonian life. The gates of the new Eon are swinging open. 'Lift up your heads, you gates; yes, lift them up, you Eonian entrances' (Psalm 24\9).

The new translation changes everything. It hoists the world the right way up. The secrets are made known. The torrents of impurity have been exposed and put to shame. The delusion at last is over. The evil creeds are struck a death-blow. They are condemned in the Eonian courts of justice. The priests of old Canaan banged their drums to silence the screams of their victims, the priests of Babylon chanted their Mysteries, but the dragnet will be cast, and the good fish kept, the useless thrown away.

And what is left for the adversary of God, transmogrifiers caught red-handed, in retaliation against the force of truth? Incensed men of stubborn hearts, boiling with rage, unable to beat back the angelic message, diseased with contradictions, stumble and repeat their errors and gossip false things about the messengers, even assassinate them, as Satan's Cain, whose works were evil, out of jealousy murdered his righteous half-brother. They are not clean because the oracle of God is not in them. Exalted are the prophets and apostles, and manifold is their reward on Earth.

The new translation is a death certificate and a howl of doom to the evil kingdoms of this dark Eon, a breaking of the seal to open the new civilization. The Earth is illuminated with a light like lightning. The light of the recovered treasures of God busts up the cracked foundations of the empires of men. Minds are refreshed with images of resurrections, epiphanies of Christ, apostles travelling the world, and a new legislative body. Minds of men and women are changed; hearts are healed; strongholds and arguments demolished; histories and epochs rewritten; corruptions knocked over; a new Eon is announced; new civilizations are built – under the government of God and Christ.

The holy and gentle and understanding, those with a noble name and heart, are exalted with the highest exaltation a man or woman can ever achieve, Sons and Daughters of Almighty God. The divinely-activated and inexpressible exuberance is released among multitudes, an exuberance which overcomes the world.

The vision of the men of a single spirit – the prophets and apostles, and the Messiah – is of a resurrection out of the ground for the righteous; those resurrected righteous being made incorruptible in mind and indestructible in body; the reappearances of Enoch and Elijah and Paul; divine rulership and government under God's resurrected prophets and apostles; a rebuilt Jerusalem; a purified and righteous Israel as the head nation; the apostles travelling the world to instruct men about the divine government, which is the Sovereign Rulership of God and Christ. Instead though, we have imperial global powers of evil; global religion not consanguineous with the Holy Scrolls of Elohim; men bent down under the yoke of the oppressive and deluding spells of the creeds and Vulgate; and, with all the grave works of their bedevilments, the twisted translations created as much harm as they did good. There has never been a day like this day: everything has had to be unlocked and untangled so the Eonian gates can be exhibited. These are the times the messenger of the nations called the Eon of darkness and evil, and how great grows that darkness and that evil.

This is the vision of the prophets restored. This is a message as strong as Noah's. Earth's greatest secrets are brought to light. The bell is beating ... The Sun is setting on this civilization of brooding and ominous villainy. A bright new Eon is coming ... times of global renewal and conquering death.

The translator was born in Birmingham, and lives in Hampshire with his family. After lecturing in Higher and Further Education, he is now a free-lance educator. He runs writing groups, manages a trout fishery and runs a folk and poetry club. As well as being co-author of textbooks on writing and grammar, he has published poetry, short fiction, academic essays, reviews and artwork. His other interests are trout fishing, cricket, cycling, oil painting, birdwatching, and playing the guitar and harmonica.

Lightning Source UK Ltd.
Milton Keynes UK
UKOW06f0234200116

266733UK00001B/53/P

9 781910 819166